THE
CRICKETERS'
WHO'S WHO
1995

THE CRICKETERS' WHO'S WHO 1995

Introduction by
ALAN FORDHAM

Statistics by
RICHARD LOCKWOOD

Portraits photographed or researched by
BILL SMITH

Queen Anne Press

QUEEN ANNE PRESS
a division of Lennard Associates Limited
Mackerye End, Harpenden, Herts AL5 5DR

Published in association with
The Cricketers' Who's Who Limited

First published in Great Britain 1995

© The Cricketers' Who's Who Limited

British Library Cataloguing in Publication is available

ISBN 1 85291 565 X

Typeset in Times and Univers Condensed
Editorial Assistants William Hodge and Jacky Cleaver
Cover design by Paul Cooper

Printed and bound by
Butler and Tanner Limited, Frome and London

PICTURE ACKNOWLEDGEMENTS

Cover photographs by Allsport
(*front, clockwise from top left*) Daryll Cullinan, Michael Bevan,
Dion Nash, Hansie Cronje, Javagal Srinath
(*background photograph*) Anil Kumble

The publishers would also like to thank the following for their help
in providing portraits of several players who had not previously
been photographed in a county photocall:
Allsport, *Bristol Evening Post*, *Derby Evening Telegraph*,
Evening Sentinel (Stoke), Sportsline Photographic
and a number of players who provided their own photos

CONTENTS

THE QUIZ

Throughout this book there are 100 quiz questions

The answers can be found on page 672

INTRODUCTION

There would, I hope, be few professional cricketers in the country who have taken any delight in England's recent tour of Australia. Indeed, the disappointment that the nation felt is markedly more acute in the minds of the county players. For clearly, as the media keep reminding us, the national side's failures are a sad indictment of the quality of the county game. Rightly so. It would be wrong to lay blame solely at the feet of those men who went to Australia. They were the best we had and I don't recall too much moaning when the squad was announced last September. It is that phrase 'the quality of the county game', which requires analysis and examination. It embodies a huge array of subjects, ideas and arguments and it is where we as players and as the Professional Cricketers's Association have a vital role.

1994 was the most significant year in the history of the PCA since its formation in 1967. For the first time a full-time salaried General Secretary was appointed in David Graveney who had previously been the Assocation's Treasurer for 15 years. A respected man of undoubted experience, he now has the time to do the vital work which county cricket couldn't afford him. We are honoured to have as our President Jack Bannister whose involvement with the Association over the years, together with his vast knowledge of the game and the journalistic world, make him an invaluable asset. Tim Curtis continues as Chairman while Matthew Fleming becomes his deputy (a new position) and I have been appointed Treasurer. A new look, if you like, to the PCA. All of us are committed to what I see as the Assocation's two fundamental aims: to maintain and improve the standard of English cricket and to maintain and improve the package offered to the cricketer himself. We wish to achieve this without discarding the traditions that give English cricket its character and we also want to work with the Test and County Cricket

Board and the county clubs towards common goals.

There can be no argument that the main factor affecting the quality of the cricket that we play in England (and for that matter the quality of cricket anywhere in the world) is the surface that we play on. In the comparatively short time that I have played first-team cricket, the majority of clubs have been producing 'result' pitches – pitches of a nature that will suit the strengths of their own sides and thus increase the chance of a home victory. The TCCB have introduced, at various times, criteria that a pitch should meet, for example that they should be 'dry' or 'straw-coloured'. Good intentions to eradicate this pitch-doctoring I'm sure, but soil science doesn't work like that. What will produce the best cricket pitch at Hove won't necessarily do the same at Hartlepool. And again, when a county needs a win groundsmen will come under pressure from captains, managers and committees to begin bending the rules once more. In the view of the PCA there is only one solution; the TCCB must employ the groundsmen themselves and so have direct control over the pitches produced. As long as clubs are the employers, groundsmen will for ever be trying to serve two masters. Australian pitches encourage quality cricket. A bowler whether a seamer, swinger or spinner must be good at his art for the pitch will be unforgiving; and the batsmen must be good enough to cope with a more testing examination. In England, pitches flatter the bowlers and discourage good, correct batting; a situation which is horribly exposed when we play Test matches on good pitches both here and abroad. The TCCB , the groundsmen and the cricketers all want the game played on the best possible surfaces. The PCA are sure of two things; one, that good pitches will kick-start an improvement in English cricket and two, that the central employment of groundsmen by the TCCB is the best way to achieve that aim.

A county championship of four-day matches is now two years old and although there may be some reservations in the commercial offices around the counties, approval is widespread through the playing ranks. However, one area in which the four-day programme has failed to live up to its expectations is in providing opportunities for extra practice. With the Benson and Hedges Cup returning to a zonal format this season, we have only seven more days free for practice, which over the course of a season is not a lot. Practice makes perfect is only a half truth, rather perfect practice is more likely to make perfect; but for perfect practice we need time and facilities. It is generally recognised that in many centres around the country practice facilities are not what they should be and the PCA are delighted that a proportion of the extra revenue from television rights will be going towards the improvement of these facilities. We must now have time to use them and, given that in the summer time is short, it has been notioned that increasing the length of a cricketer's contract from six to nine months would satisfy the individual's desire to improve his cricket skills along with his physical and mental fitness. At present, a three-week pre-season preparation is not proving to be adequate. Lengthening the contract would obviously have other implications, not least regarding salaries, but for the good of English cricket it is a path the PCA believes we should go down.

So far, I've been discussing more immediate ideas but we as an Assocation must not ignore the longer term. Again, with television rights providing extra income for the game, we strongly advocate the spending of some of this on what has been commonly termed 'grass roots' cricket. Since I left school twelve years ago, I have noticed that there was a reduction in the quality of cricket and coaching in schools in general. Maybe teachers are preferring to play their own cricket or, more likely, there simply hasn't been the money available for what is, in comparison to many other sports, an expensive game. Today's school-children are cricket's stars of twelve years hence and we mustn't neglect that. I'm pleased to say that in many places, not least in my own county, new initiatives are firmly in place to coach, nurture, and bring out the best in the next generation. This grass-roots development must continue to evolve and can at the same time provide more opportunities for the members of our profession to be employed during the winter. It is absolutely criminal that the majority of coaching undertaken by our own professional cricketers is done abroad. These skills should be used primarily for the development of the English game and it is to that end that the PCA aims to make it compulsory for its members to have, or be

9

prepared to take, the appropriate coaching certificates.

So much for the welfare of our game. What about the welfare of the individual? A cricket career is a short career and financial considerations are therefore all the more pertinent. The Association believes that there are many aspects in need of an overhaul, such as salaries, pensions, insurances, and post-career employment opportunities. We need to create a package which will attract the school leaver who may have professional football as an option, or be a viable alternative to the graduate for whom a career in merchant banking may also beckon. At the moment this is not always the case and it is cricket that is losing out. Now that English cricket is on a healthy financial footing, we believe it is time to address these issues.

Having stated our case, I am delighted to report that we are moving forward. The PCA has representation on various committees of the TCCB, such as cricket, registration and discipline, and we are working hard with the Board on many of the financial considerations mentioned above. On all these points we have established that it is our aim to work with the TCCB and its member counties, not against them, in the development of a healthy future for cricketers and for the game itself. It is time to recognise that English cricket has stood still while the Australian game has leapt forward. The PCA, with motivated members who have a deep-rooted concern for English and England cricket, aim to play a big part in moving our game back to where it belongs. The media will, I am sure, let us know how we're doing.

ALAN FORDHAM
March 1995

THE PLAYERS

Editor's Notes

The cricketers listed in this volume include all those who played for a first-class county at least once last season, in any form of cricket, and all those registered (at the time of going to press) to play for the 18 first-class counties in 1995, even those who have yet to make a first-team appearance. All statistics are complete to the end of the last English season. Figures about 1000 runs and 50 wickets in a season refer to matches in England only. All first-class figures include figures for Test matches which are also extracted and listed separately. One-day 100s and one-day five wickets in an innings are for the English domestic competitions and all one-day Internationals, home and abroad. Career records include 'rebel' tours to South Africa.

The following abbreviations apply: * means not out; All First – all first-class matches; 1-day Int – one-day Internationals; Sunday – Sunday League; NatWest – NatWest Trophy; B&H – Benson & Hedges Cup. The figures for batting and bowling averages refer to the full first-class English list for 1994, followed in brackets by the 1993 figures. Inclusion in the batting averages depends on a minimum of six completed innings, and an average of at least 10 runs; a bowler has to have taken at least 10 wickets. The same qualification has been used for compiling the bowlers' strike rate.

Readers will notice occasional differences in the way the same kind of information is presented. This is because it is has been decided to follow the way in which the cricketers themselves have provided the relevant information.

Each year in *The Cricketers' Who's Who,* in addition to those cricketers who are playing during the current season, we also include the biographical and career details of those who played in the previous season but retired at the end of it. The purpose of this is to have, on the record, the full and final cricketing achievements of every player when his career has ended.

A book of this complexity and detail has to be prepared several months in advance of the cricket season, and occasionally there are recent changes in a player's circumstances which cannot be included in time. Many examples of facts and statistics which can quickly become outdated in the period between the actual compilation of the book and its publication, months later, will spring to the reader's mind, and I ask him or her to make the necessary commonsense allowance and adjustments.

Richard Lockwood, March 1995

ADAMS, C. J.   Derbyshire

Name: Christopher John Adams
Role: Right-hand bat, right-arm medium bowler, slip fielder
Born: 6 May 1970, Whitwell, Derbyshire
Height: 6ft **Weight:** 13st 7lbs
Nickname: Grizzly
County debut: 1988
County cap: 1992
1000 runs in season: 1
1st-Class 50s: 23
1st-Class 100s: 10
1st-Class catches: 104
One-Day 100s: 3
Place in batting averages: 105th av. 33.41 (1993 125th av. 28.10)
Strike rate: (career 80.33)
Parents: John and Eluned (Lyn)
Wife and date of marriage: Samantha Claire, 26 September 1992
Children: Georgia Louise, 4 October 1993
Family links with cricket: Brother David played 2nd XI cricket for Derbyshire and Gloucestershire. Father played for Yorkshire Schools and uncle played for Essex 2nd XI
Education: Tapton House School; Chesterfield Boys Grammar School; Repton School
Qualifications: 6 O-levels, NCA coaching awards
Off-season: Working for the club sponsors, coaching and playing for Stumps in the National Indoor Cricket League
Overseas tours: Repton School to Barbados 1987; England NCA North to N Ireland 1987
Overseas teams played for: Takapuna, New Zealand 1987-88; Te Puke, New Zealand 1989-90; Primrose, Cape Town, South Africa 1991-92
Cricketers particularly admired: Ian Botham, Geoff Palmer, Adrian Kuiper
Other sports followed: Football, golf, rally driving and Formula 1
Relaxations: Mountain biking, golf and squash. 'My daughter, Georgia, is very interesting but definitely not relaxing.'
Extras: Beat Richard Hutton's 25-year-old record for most runs scored in a season at Repton. Represented English Schools U15 and U19, MCC Schools U19 and, in 1989, England YC. Took two catches as 12th man for England v India at Old Trafford in 1990. Holds county records for the fastest century by a Derbyshire batsman (57 mins) and the highest score in the Sunday League (141*). Whittingdale Young Player Award 1992
Opinions on cricket: 'I love it.'
Best batting: 175 Derbyshire v Nottinghamshire, Trent Bridge 1993
Best bowling: 4-29 Derbyshire v Lancashire, Derby 1991

1994 Season

	M	Inns	NO	Runs	HS	Avge	100s	50s	Ct	St	O	M	Runs	Wkts	Avge	Best	5wI	10wM
Test																		
All First	18	32	3	969	109 *	33.41	1	5	17	-	30	3	114	3	38.00	2-16	-	-
1-day Int																		
NatWest	3	3	0	81	52	27.00	-	1	2	-								
B & H	2	2	0	43	34	21.50	-	-	-	-								
Sunday	14	13	3	485	119 *	48.50	1	2	9	-	4	0	46	0	-		-	-

Career Performances

	M	Inns	NO	Runs	HS	Avge	100s	50s	Ct	St	Balls	Runs	Wkts	Avge	Best	5wI	10wM
Test																	
All First	105	165	16	4826	175	32.38	10	23	104	-	1446	981	18	54.50	4-29	-	-
1-day Int																	
NatWest	9	8	1	323	106 *	46.14	1	2	6	-	18	15	1	15.00	1-15	-	
B & H	19	17	3	293	58	20.92	-	2	8	-	24	21	0	-	-	-	
Sunday	80	74	15	2308	141 *	39.11	2	17	41	-	178	181	2	90.50	2-15	-	

ADAMS, J. C.　　　　　　Nottinghamshire

Name: James Clive Adams
Role: Left-hand bat, slow left-arm bowler and wicket-keeper
Born: 9 January 1968, Kingston, Jamaica
Test debut: 1992
Tests: 9
One-Day Internationals: 28
1st-Class 50s: 21
1st-Class 100s: 10
1st-Class catches: 81
Place in batting averages: 90th av. 35.18
Place in bowling averages: 73rd av. 31.30
Strike rate: 88.91 (career 88.71)
Parents: Newton and Carolyn
Marital status: Single
Education: Port Maria Primary; Jamaica College
Off-season: Touring India, New Zealand and home series with Australia
Overseas tours: West Indies YC to Australia 1988; West Indies B to Zimbabwe 1986 and 1989; West Indies to Australia and South Africa 1992-93, to Sharjah, India (Hero Cup) and Sri Lanka 1993-94, to India and New Zealand 1994-95

Overseas teams played for: Kingston, Jamaica
Cricketers particularly admired: Richie Richardson and Viv Richards
Other sports followed: Football and tennis
Relaxations: Reading and playing football
Extras: Played three Tests for West Indies YC against England YC in the West Indies in 1985. Expected to tour England with the West Indies in 1995 so not signed for Nottinghamshire
Opinions on cricket: 'Cricketers at all levels are underpaid.'
Best batting: 144* Nottinghamshire v Somerset, Taunton 1994
Best bowling: 4-43 West Indies v South Africa, Bridgetown 1991-92

1994 Season

	M	Inns	NO	Runs	HS	Avge	100s	50s	Ct	St	O	M	Runs	Wkts	Avge	Best	5wI	10wM
Test																		
All First	18	32	5	950	144 *	35.18	3	2	17	-	340.5	125	720	23	31.30	4-63	-	-
1-day Int																		
NatWest	2	2	0	12	11	6.00	-	-	-	-								
B & H	3	3	0	133	86	44.33	-	1	2	-	3	0	21	0	-	-	-	-
Sunday	15	15	4	674	93 *	61.27	-	7	5	-	49.2	2	199	6	33.16	2-26	-	

Career Performances

	M	Inns	NO	Runs	HS	Avge	100s	50s	Ct	St	Balls	Runs	Wkts	Avge	Best	5wI	10wM
Test	9	13	3	612	137	61.20	1	4	12	-	621	335	9	37.22	4-43	-	-
All First	82	136	22	4461	144 *	39.13	10	21	81	-	3992	1655	45	36.77	4-43	-	-
1-day Int	28	18	8	425	81 *	42.50	-	3	11	2	42	35	1	35.00	1-2	-	
NatWest	2	2	0	12	11	6.00	-	-	-	-							
B & H	3	3	0	133	86	44.33	-	1	2	-	18	21	0	-	-	-	
Sunday	15	15	4	674	93 *	61.27	-	7	5	-	296	199	6	33.16	2-26	-	

Name: John Andrew Afford
Role: Slow left-arm 'high' bowler, right-hand bat and 'hopeless fielder'
Born: 12 May 1964, Crowland, Peterborough
Height: 6ft 2in **Weight:** 13st 7lbs
Nickname: Aff, Des
County debut: 1984
County cap: 1990
50 wickets in a season: 4
1st-Class 5 w. in innings: 14
1st-Class 10 w. in match: 2
1st-Class catches: 47
Place in bowling averages: 92nd av. 34.40 (1993 63rd av. 29.10)
Strike rate: 81.22 (career 72.06)
Parents: Jill
Wife and date of marriage: Lynn, 1 October 1988
Children: Lily Meagan, 1 June 1991; Daisy Tallulah, 12 October 1993
Education: Spalding Grammar School; Stamford College for Further Education
Qualifications: 5 O-levels, NCA coaching certificate
Off-season: Working at Trent Bridge
Overseas tours: England A to Kenya and Zimbabwe 1989-90; Nottinghamshire to Cape Town 1992-93
Overseas teams played for: Upper Hutt, Taita and Petone, all in Wellington, New Zealand between 1984 and 1991
Cricketers particularly admired: Everyone who bowls a lot. In recent times – John Childs, 'he is everything people see as being nice'
Other sports followed: Football (Peterborough United)
Extras: Hat-trick against Leics 2nd XI in 1989, also took 100 wickets in that season, 47 in 2nd XI and 53 in 1st XI. 'I think I beat Chris Cairns for player of the month once!'
Opinions on cricket: 'Elvis is alive and batting and bowling for Notts. National Anthem should be played before international cricket matches.'
Best batting: 22* Nottinghamshire v Leicestershire, Trent Bridge 1989
Best bowling: 6-68 Nottinghamshire v Sussex, Trent Bridge 1992

---

1. Which former Surrey player is now the county's Director of Cricket?

1994 Season

	M	Inns	NO	Runs	HS	Avge	100s	50s	Ct	St	O	M	Runs	Wkts	Avge	Best	5wI	10wM
Test																		
All First	15	17	6	36	10	3.27	-	-	5	-	541.3	164	1376	40	34.40	5-48	2	-
1-day Int																		
NatWest																		
B & H	3	0	0	0	0	-	-	-	-	-	32.4	2	120	4	30.00	3-34	-	
Sunday																		

Career Performances

	M	Inns	NO	Runs	HS	Avge	100s	50s	Ct	St	Balls	Runs	Wkts	Avge	Best	5wI	10wM
Test																	
All First	144	133	55	294	22 *	3.76	-	-	47	-	28322	12935	393	32.91	6-68	14	2
1-day Int																	
NatWest	7	4	3	3	2 *	3.00	-	-	-	-	486	218	6	36.33	3-32	-	
B & H	15	1	1	1	1 *	-	-	-	2	-	958	634	17	37.29	4-38	-	
Sunday	19	5	3	1	1	0.50	-	-	7	-	690	576	15	38.40	3-33	-	

AFZAAL, U.   Nottinghamshire

Name: Usman Afzaal
Role: Left-hand bat, slow left-arm bowler
Born: 9 June 1977, Rawalpindi, Pakistan
Height: 6ft **Weight:** 11st 7lbs
Nickname: Gulfraz
County debut: No first team appearance
Parents: Mohammed and Firdous
Marital satus: Single
Family links with cricket: Brother played for Nottinghamshire U9
Education: Manvers Pierrepont School
Qualifications: NCA coaching certificate
Off-season: Playing for England U19
Overseas tours: England U19 to West Indies 1994-95
Cricketers particularly admired: Paul Johnson, Phil Tufnell, Mick Newell
Other sports followed: 'Cricket and cricket'
Relaxations: Watching movies and listening to music
Extras: Played for England U15 against South Africa and, in 1994, for England U17 against India. Was leading wicket-taker in the Texaco U16 County Championship

ALDRED, P. Derbyshire

Name: Paul Aldred
Role: Right-hand bat, right-arm medium bowler
Born: 4 February 1969, Chellaston, Derby
Height: 5ft 11in **Weight:** 12st
Nickname: Aldo
County debut: No first-team appearance
Parents: Harry and Lynette
Marital status: Single
Family links with cricket: 'My dad was a pretty good local player.'
Education: Chellaston Primary School; Lady Manners, Bakenall, Derbyshire
Qualifications: 'Not many – showed more interest on the sports field.'
Career outside cricket: Building trade – self-employed
Off-season: 'Would like to go to South Africa, because I have been told what a beautiful country it is.'
Cricketers particularly admired: Ian Botham for pure determination to win in any situation and Alan Border – a gritty player
Other sports followed: 'Any sport – apart from horse racing: it bores me to death.'
Relaxations: Any sport and then relax with a pint in the local pub with friends
Extras: 'Had the great opportunity to play against New Zealand with the England NCA team in 1994 which was a great day.' Represented Derbyshire U18 and U21 hockey team at the age of 15
Opinions on cricket: 'I think a lot of injuries picked up are due to the amount of cricket played in England. You just don't have time to recover to full fitness. I think the cricket schedule could be lightened a little, at first-class level at least.'

ALLEYNE, M. W. Gloucestershire

Name: Mark Wayne Alleyne
Role: Right-hand bat, right-arm medium bowler, cover fielder, occasional wicket-keeper
Born: 23 May 1968, Tottenham
Height: 5ft 11in **Weight:** 13st 7lbs
Nickname: Boo-Boo
County debut: 1986

18

County cap: 1990
1000 runs in a season: 3
1st-Class 50s: 36
1st-Class 100s: 10
1st-Class 200s: 1
1st-Class catches: 131
1st-Class stumpings: 2
One-Day 100s: 2
One-Day 5 w. in innings: 2
Place in batting averages: 107th av. 32.88 (1993 108th av. 31.06)
Place in bowling averages: 37th av. 26.90 (1993 89th 27.19)
Strike rate: 51.43 (career 59.62)
Parents: Euclid Clevis and Hyacinth Cordeilla
Marital status: Single
Family links with cricket: Brother played for Gloucestershire 2nd XI and Middlesex YCs. Father played club cricket in Barbados and England
Education: Harrison College, Barbados; Cardinal Pole School, E London
Qualifications: 6 O-levels, NCA Senior Coaching Award, volleyball coaching certificate
Overseas tours: England YC to Sri Lanka 1986-87 and Australia 1987-88
Cricketers particularly admired: Gordon Greenidge, Viv Richards
Other sports followed: Football, volleyball, athletics
Relaxations: Watching films and sport; listening to music
Extras: Youngest player to score a century for Gloucestershire. In 1990 also became the youngest to score a double hundred for the county. Graduate of Haringey Cricket College. Cricket Select Sunday League Player of the Year 1992. Highest Sunday League score for Gloucestershire
Opinions on cricket: 'Happy with the full introduction of four-day cricket. Registration rules should be relaxed once a player is out of contract.'
Best batting: 256 Gloucestershire v Northamptonshire, Northampton 1990
Best bowling: 5-78 Gloucestershire v Kent, Cheltenham 1994

1994 Season

	M	Inns	NO	Runs	HS	Avge	100s	50s	Ct	St	O	M	Runs	Wkts	Avge	Best	5wI	10wM
Test																		
All First	20	37	1	1184	109	32.88	2	6	16	-	351.3	68	1103	41	26.90	5-78	1	-
1-day Int																		
NatWest	1	1	0	24	24	24.00	-	-	-	-	11.2	0	59	1	59.00	1-59	-	
B & H	1	1	0	18	18	18.00	-	-	-	-	11	1	63	0	-	-	-	
Sunday	16	16	3	588	102 *	45.23	1	2	14	-	86.4	1	497	11	45.18	2-25	-	

Career Performances

	M	Inns	NO	Runs	HS	Avge	100s	50s	Ct	St	Balls	Runs	Wkts	Avge	Best	5wI	10wM
Test																	
All First	163	267	28	7286	256	30.48	10	36	131	2	7691	4315	129	33.44	5-78	1	-
1-day Int																	
NatWest	20	16	4	265	73	22.08	-	1	9	-	608	418	14	29.85	5-30	1	
B & H	27	21	4	279	36	16.41	-	-	7	-	961	702	22	31.90	5-27	1	
Sunday	130	115	29	2754	134 *	32.02	2	10	47	-	3848	3248	106	30.64	4-35	-	

ALTREE, D. A.   Warwickshire

Name: Darren Anthony Altree
Role: Right-hand bat, left-arm fast bowler
Born: 30 September 1974, Rugby
Height: 5ft 11in
Weight: 11st 7lbs
County debut: No first-team appearance
Parents: Tony and Margaret
Marital status: Single
Education: Ashlawn School, Rugby
Overseas tours: Warwickshire U19 to
Cape Town 1992-93
Cricketers particularly admired:
Dennis Lillee, Dennis Amiss, Jeff Thomson
Injuries: Knee problems
Relaxations: Watching television

AMBROSE, C. E. L.   Northamptonshire

Name: Curtly Elconn Lynwall Ambrose
Role: Left-hand bat, right-arm fast bowler; 'like the gully area'
Born: 21 September 1963, Antigua
Height: 6ft 7in **Weight:** 14st
Nickname: Ambie
County debut: 1989
County cap: 1990
Test debut: 1987-88

Tests: 48
One-Day Internationals: 104
50 wickets in a season: 7
1st-Class 50s: 4
1st-Class 5 w. in innings: 32
1st-Class 10 w. in match: 7
1st-Class catches: 51
One-Day 5 w. in innings: 4
Place in batting averages: 214th av. 18.35
(1993 227th av. 15.15)
Place in bowling averages: 2nd av. 14.45
(1993 7th av. 20.45)
Strike rate: 42.07 (career 51.19)
Parents: Jasper (deceased) and Hillie
Wife and date of marriage: Bridgette, 6
September 1991
Children: Tanya, May 1990
Family links with cricket: Brother used to
play club cricket and had trials for Antigua.
Cousin Rolston Otto plays for Antigua and Leeward Islands
Education: Swetes Primary School; All Saints Secondary School
Qualifications: 3 O-levels, 3 A-levels, qualified carpenter
Career outside cricket: 'Hoping to become a professional musician (bass guitar)'
Off-season: Playing for West Indies
Overseas tours: West Indies to England 1988, to Australia 1988-89, to India for Nehru
Cup 1989-90, to Pakistan 1990-91, to England 1991, to Pakistan 1991-92, to Australia for
Benson & Hedges World Series and World Cup 1991-92, to Australia and South Africa
1992-93, to Sharjah, India (Hero Cup) and Sri Lanka 1993-94, to New Zealand 1994-95
Overseas teams played for: Leeward Islands
Cricketers particularly admired: David Gower, Richard Hadlee, Robin Smith and all
West Indies Test cricketers
Other sports followed: NBA (American) basketball and tennis
Relaxations: Going to the movies, relaxing on the beach, listening to and playing music
(bass guitar)
Extras: A basketball player who only began playing cricket seriously at age 17. Took a
wicket with his first ball on Championship debut for Northamptonshire against Glamorgan
in 1989. Played in two NatWest finals in three years with Northants. Figures of 8 for 45
are the best in Tests for W Indies v England. One of *Wisden*'s Five Cricketers of the Year
1992
Opinions on cricket: 'Too much cricket played. It's almost impossible to play cricket
every day for five months and still play international cricket. It could shorten your career.
You get tired and when you are tired it affects your game.'
Best batting: 78 Northamptonshire v Somerset, Taunton 1994
Best bowling: 8-45 West Indies v England, Bridgetown 1989-90

1994 Season

	M	Inns	NO	Runs	HS	Avge	100s	50s	Ct	St	O	M	Runs	Wkts	Avge	Best	5wI	10wM
Test																		
All First	14	16	2	257	78	18.35	-	1	16	-	540	159	1113	77	14.45	7-44	6	2
1-day Int																		
NatWest	3	1	0	7	7	7.00	-	-	2	-	36	12	59	7	8.42	3-16	-	
B & H																		
Sunday	11	7	1	92	37	15.33	-	-	4	-	78.1	13	264	13	20.30	4-20	-	

Career Performances

	M	Inns	NO	Runs	HS	Avge	100s	50s	Ct	St	Balls	Runs	Wkts	Avge	Best	5wI	10wM
Test	48	70	13	680	53	11.92	-	1	10	-	11808	4616	219	21.07	8-45	11	2
All First	157	199	45	2301	78	14.94	-	4	51	-	33329	13278	651	20.39	8-45	32	7
1-day Int	104	53	24	371	26 *	12.79	-	-	29	-	5579	3247	151	21.50	5-17	4	
NatWest	19	7	1	89	48	14.83	-	-	6	-	1265	474	29	16.34	4-7	-	
B & H	10	7	4	71	17 *	23.66	-	-	5	-	619	302	20	15.10	4-31	-	
Sunday	45	23	8	201	37	13.40	-	-	8	-	1979	1211	41	29.53	4-20	-	

ANDREW, S. J. W.   Essex

Name: Stephen Jon Walter Andrew
Role: Right-hand bat, right-arm
fast-medium bowler
Born: 27 January 1966, London
Height: 6ft 3in **Weight:** 14st
Nickname: Rip, Chinny, His Chinness,
Le Grand Chien, G.O.S.
County debut: 1984 (Hampshire),
1990 (Essex)
1st-Class 5 w. in innings: 7
1st-Class catches: 24
One-Day 5 w. in innings: 1
Place in bowling averages:
(1993 96th av. 33.35)
Strike rate: (career 59.45)
Parents: Jon and Victoria
Marital status: Single
Education: Hordle House Prep School;
Milton Abbey School
Qualifications: 3 O-levels
Overseas tours: England YC to West Indies 1984-85
Overseas teams played for: Pirates, Durban 1983-84; SAP, Durban 1984-86; Manly,

Sydney 1987-88; Pinetown, Durban 1988-89; Taita, Wellington 1990-91; Parnell, Auckland, 1991-92

Cricketers particularly admired: Dennis Lillee ('god')

Other sports followed: Interested in most sports

Relaxations: Music, videos, films, books, playing golf, sleeping, drinking

Best batting: 35 Essex v Northamptonshire, Chelmsford 1990

Best bowling: 7-47 Essex v Lancashire, Old Trafford 1993

1994 Season

	M	Inns	NO	Runs	HS	Avge	100s	50s	Ct	St	O	M	Runs	Wkts	Avge	Best	5wl	10wM
Test																		
All First	6	8	1	37	11	5.28	-	-	-	-	150.3	33	425	9	47.22	2-28	-	-
1-day Int																		
NatWest																		
B & H																		
Sunday	1	1	0	4	4	4.00	-	-	-	-	3	1	23	0	-	-	-	-

Career Performances

	M	Inns	NO	Runs	HS	Avge	100s	50s	Ct	St	Balls	Runs	Wkts	Avge	Best	5wl	10wM
Test																	
All First	117	91	36	404	35	7.34	-	-	24	-	17659	9708	297	32.68	7-47	7	1
1-day Int																	
NatWest	8	2	2	1	1 *	-	-	-	2	-	426	256	9	28.44	2-34	-	
B & H	11	3	3	5	4 *	-	-	-	1	-	654	363	20	18.15	5-24	1	
Sunday	40	11	4	56	14	8.00	-	-	2	-	1590	1362	31	43.93	4-50	-	

Name: Graeme Francis Archer
Role: Right-hand bat
Born: 26 September 1970, Carlisle, Cumbria
Height: 6ft 1in **Weight:** 13st
Nickname: Archie Bunka, Astro Chimp and Florence
County debut: 1992
1st-Class 50s: 9
1st-Class 100s: 3
1st-Class catches: 28
Place in batting averages: 103rd av. 33.76 (1993 114th av. 29.71)
Parents: Christopher William and Jean Elizabeth
Marital status: Single
Family links with cricket: Father played for Carlisle in N Lancashire League; brother Neil plays in the S Cheshire Alliance League
Education: King Edward VI High School; Stafford College
Qualifications: 3 O-levels, City & Guilds and BTEC National Diploma in Leisure Management, NCA Senior Coaching Award
Career outside cricket: 'Not decided yet'
Off-season: Playing and coaching in Christchurch, New Zealand
Overseas teams played for: Hutt Districts, New Zealand 1991-92; also played for Hutt Valley representative side
Cricketers particularly admired: Graeme Hick, Ian Botham, Derek Randall, Chris Cairns and Jimmy Adams
Other sports followed: Football (Carlisle United) and rugby
Relaxations: Music and concerts, 'the odd round of golf', photography, spending time with friends
Extras: Scored 200* in a 15 (8-ball) over match for Walsall U18s. Awarded the A.A.Thompson Fielding Prize by The Cricket Society in 1990. Made 2nd XI debut for Notts in 1987 aged 15. Played for Staffordshire in 1990-91. Rapid Cricketline Player of the Month April/May 1994
Opinions on cricket: 'Andy Afford is alive and playing at Gracelands.'
Best batting: 168 Nottinghamshire v Glamorgan, Worksop 1994

1994 Season

	M	Inns	NO	Runs	HS	Avge	100s	50s	Ct	St	O	M	Runs	Wkts	Avge	Best	5wI	10wM
Test																		
All First	16	26	0	878	168	33.76	2	4	17	-								
1-day Int																		
NatWest																		
B & H	1	1	0	9	9	9.00	-	-	-	-								
Sunday	8	8	1	114	49	16.28	-	-	1	-								

Career Performances

	M	Inns	NO	Runs	HS	Avge	100s	50s	Ct	St	Balls	Runs	Wkts	Avge	Best	5wI	10wM
Test																	
All First	29	48	5	1561	168	36.30	3	9	28	-	39	72	0	-	-	-	-
1-day Int																	
NatWest	1	1	0	39	39	39.00	-	-	-	-							
B & H	1	1	0	9	9	9.00	-	-	-	-							
Sunday	16	13	1	169	49	14.08	-	-	3	-							

ASIF DIN, M.   Warwickshire

Name: Mohamed Asif Din
Role: Right-hand bat, leg-spin bowler
Born: 21 September 1960, Kampala, Uganda
Height: 5ft 9in **Weight:** 10st 7lbs
Nickname: Gunga 'and many others'
County debut: 1981
County cap: 1987
Benefit: 1994
1000 runs in a season: 2
1st-Class 50s: 42
1st-Class 100s: 9
1st-Class 200s: 1
1st-Class 5 w. in innings: 2
1st-Class catches: 114
One-Day 100s: 7
One-Day 5 w. in innings: 1
Place in batting averages:
(1993 98th av. 32.33)
Strike rate: (career 83.20)
Parents: Jamiz and Mumtaz
Wife and date of marriage: Ahmerin, 27 September 1987
Children: Zahra, 18 October 1990; Sarah, 14 December 1991

Family links with cricket: Brothers Khalid and Abid play in Birmingham League
Education: Ladywood Comprehensive School, Birmingham
Qualifications: CSEs and O-levels and qualified coach
Off-season: Playing indoor cricket for Stumps
Overseas tours: Warwickshire to Zimbabwe April 1994
Cricketers particularly admired: Zaheer Abbas, Majid Khan
Injuries: Left shoulder, missed last month of season
Other sports followed: American football, basketball
Relaxations: Fishing and shooting
Extras: Man of the Match in NatWest final 1993, Man of the Match in NatWest semi-final 1989
Best batting: 217 Warwickshire v Mashonaland XI, Harare 1993-94
Best bowling: 5-61 Warwickshire v Boland, Brackenfell 1992-93

1994 Season

	M	Inns	NO	Runs	HS	Avge	100s	50s	Ct	St	O	M	Runs	Wkts	Avge	Best	5wI	10wM
Test																		
All First	3	4	1	107	42 *	35.66	-	-	1	-	2	0	9	0	-	-	-	-
1-day Int																		
NatWest	2	2	0	42	24	21.00	-	-	-	-	5	0	11	0	-	-	-	
B & H	2	2	0	34	19	17.00	-	-	-	-								
Sunday	12	12	3	265	86 *	29.44	-	2	2	-	3	0	22	0	-	-	-	

Career Performances

	M	Inns	NO	Runs	HS	Avge	100s	50s	Ct	St	Balls	Runs	Wkts	Avge	Best	5wI	10wM
Test																	
All First	210	341	45	9058	217	30.60	9	42	114	-	6573	4393	79	55.60	5-61	2	-
1-day Int																	
NatWest	30	27	7	806	104	40.30	1	3	6	-	169	99	7	14.14	5-40	1	
B & H	43	40	5	1211	137	34.60	2	5	5	-	126	102	1	102.00	1-26	-	
Sunday	169	154	27	3788	132 *	29.82	4	16	31	-	230	261	4	65.25	1-11	-	

ATHERTON, M. A.   Lancashire

Name: Michael Andrew Atherton
Role: Right-hand bat, leg-break bowler, county vice-captain
Born: 23 March 1968, Manchester
Height: 6ft **Weight:** 12st 7lbs
Nickname: Athers, Dread
County debut: 1987
County cap: 1989
Test debut: 1989

Tests: 40
One-Day Internationals: 18
1000 runs in a season: 6
1st-Class 50s: 52
1st-Class 100s: 34
1st-Class 5 w. in innings: 3
1st-Class catches: 145
One-Day 100s: 5
Place in batting averages: 87th av. 35.96
(1993 31st av. 44.00)
Strike rate: (career 83.03)
Parents: Alan and Wendy
Marital status: Single
Family links with cricket: Father and brother
both play league cricket
Education: Briscoe Lane Primary;
Manchester GS; Downing College,
Cambridge
Qualifications: 10 O-levels, 3 A-levels; BA (Hons) (Cantab)
Off-season: In Australia with England
Overseas tours: England YC to Sri Lanka 1986-87, to Australia 1987-88; England A to
Zimbabwe 1989-90; England to Australia and New Zealand 1990-91, to India and Sri
Lanka 1992-93, to West Indies 1993-94, to Australia 1994-95
Cricketers particularly admired: Graham Gooch
Other sports followed: Golf, squash, football
Relaxations: 'Decent novels (Heller, Kundera, etc.), good movies, food and wine,
travelling, most sports, music'
Extras: In 1987 was first player to score 1000 runs in his debut season since Paul Parker
in 1976. Youngest Lancastrian to score a Test century (151 v NZ at Trent Bridge in 1990);
second Lancastrian to score a Test century at Old Trafford (138 v India in 1990). First
captained England U19 aged 16. Selected for England tour to New Zealand and also
England A tour to Bermuda and West Indies in 1991-92 but ruled out of both through
injury. Appointed England captain in 1993. Cornhill England Player of the Year 1994
Best batting: 199 Lancashire v Durham, Gateshead Fell 1992
Best bowling: 6-78 Lancashire v Nottinghamshire, Trent Bridge 1990

1994 Season

	M	Inns	NO	Runs	HS	Avge	100s	50s	Ct	St	O	M	Runs	Wkts	Avge	Best	5wI	10wM
Test	6	10	0	480	111	48.00	2	2	3	-								
All First	16	27	2	899	111	35.96	2	4	14	-	7	2	10	0	-	-	-	-
I-day Int	3	3	0	149	81	49.66	-	1	-	-								
NatWest	2	2	0	60	50	30.00	-	1	1	-								
B & H	1	1	0	100	100	100.00	1	-	2	-								
Sunday	10	10	1	264	101 *	29.33	1	-	5	-								

27

Career Performances

	M	Inns	NO	Runs	HS	Avge	100s	50s	Ct	St	Balls	Runs	Wkts	Avge	Best	5wl	10wM
Test	40	74	1	2917	151	39.95	7	19	30	-	366	282	1	282.00	1-60	-	-
All First	170	292	30	11644	199	44.44	34	52	145	-	8885	4684	107	43.77	6-78	3	-
1-day Int	18	18	2	727	86	45.43	-	6	4	-							
NatWest	12	12	2	443	109 *	44.30	1	2	5	-	188	154	6	25.66	2-15	-	
B & H	34	34	2	1178	100	36.81	1	9	15	-	252	228	7	32.57	4-42	-	
Sunday	56	55	3	1790	111	34.42	3	9	19	-	216	248	7	35.42	3-33	-	

ATHEY, C. W. J.   Sussex

Name: Charles William Jeffrey Athey
Role: Right-hand bat, right-arm medium bowler
Born: 27 September 1957, Middlesbrough
Height: 5ft 10in **Weight:** 12st 7lbs
Nickname: Bumper, Wingnut, Ath
County debut: 1976 (Yorkshire),
1984 (Gloucestershire), 1993 (Sussex)
County cap: 1980 (Yorkshire),
1985 (Gloucestershire), 1993 (Sussex)
Benefit: 1990
Test debut: 1980
Tests: 23
One-Day Internationals: 31
1000 runs in a season: 12
1st-Class 50s: 111
1st-Class 100s: 49
1st-Class catches: 399
1st-Class stumpings: 2
One-Day 100s: 10
One-Day 5 w. in innings: 1
Place in batting averages: 122nd av. 30.96 (1993 6th av. 64.00)
Strike rate: (career 98.87)
Parents: Peter and Maree
Wife and date of marriage: Janet Linda, 9 October 1982
Family links with cricket: 'Father played league cricket in North Yorkshire and South Durham League for 29 years, 25 of them with Middlesbrough, and has been President of Middlesbrough CC since 1975. Brother-in-law Colin Cook played for Middlesex, other brother-in-law (Martin) plays in Thames Valley League. Father-in-law deeply involved in Middlesex Youth cricket'

Education: Linthorpe Junior School; Stainsby Secondary School; Acklam Hall High School
Qualifications: 4 O-levels, some CSEs, NCA coaching certificate
Off-season: Coaching. Playing football. Short tour to Australia
Overseas tours: England YC to West Indies 1975-76; England to West Indies 1980-81, to Australia 1986-87, to Pakistan, Australia and New Zealand 1987-88; England B to Sri Lanka 1985-86; unofficial English XI to South Africa 1989-90; MCC to Bahrain 1994-95
Cricketers particularly admired: 'Too many to mention.'
Other sports followed: Most sports
Injuries: Left elbow, did not miss any cricket
Relaxations: Gardening, music, good films, good food
Extras: Played for Teesside County Schools U16 at age 12. Played for Yorkshire Colts 1974. Played football for Middlesbrough Schools U16 and Junior XI. Offered but declined apprenticeship terms with Middlesbrough FC. Captain of Gloucestershire in 1989. Suspension for playing in South Africa in 1990 was remitted in 1992.
Opinions on cricket: 'Must play county cricket on better wickets.'
Best batting: 184 England B v Sri Lanka XI, Galle 1985-86
Best bowling: 3-3 Gloucestershire v Hampshire, Bristol 1985

1994 Season

	M	Inns	NO	Runs	HS	Avge	100s	50s	Ct	St	O	M	Runs	Wkts	Avge	Best	5wI	10wM
Test																		
All First	18	34	1	1022	169 *	30.96	2	3	14	-	18	1	78	1	78.00	1-1	-	-
1-day Int																		
NatWest	1	1	0	20	20	20.00	-	-	-	-								
B & H	2	2	0	55	32	27.50	-	-	1	-								
Sunday	10	10	1	183	58 *	20.33	-	1	3	-	16.2	0	89	3	29.66	2-27	-	

Career Performances

	M	Inns	NO	Runs	HS	Avge	100s	50s	Ct	St	Balls	Runs	Wkts	Avge	Best	5wI	10wM
Test	23	41	1	919	123	22.97	1	4	13	-							
All First	422	703	68	22751	184	35.82	49	111	399	2	4726	2617	48	54.52	3-3	-	-
1-day Int	31	30	3	848	142 *	31.40	2	4	16	-	6	10	0	-	-	-	-
NatWest	45	44	8	1616	115	44.88	2	12	21	-	187	156	1	156.00	1-18	-	
B & H	71	67	11	2037	95	36.37	-	17	33	-	478	364	16	22.75	4-48	-	
Sunday	246	236	20	6935	121 *	32.10	6	44	95	-	913	857	30	28.56	5-35	1	

AUSTIN, I. D.   Lancashire

Name: Ian David Austin
Role: Left-hand bat,
right-arm medium bowler
Born: 30 May 1966, Haslingden, Lancs
Height: 5ft 10in **Weight:** 14st 7lbs
Nickname: Oscar, Bully
County debut: 1986
County cap: 1990
1st-Class 100s: 2
1st-Class 50s: 6
1st-Class 5 w. in innings: 4
1st-Class 10 w. in match: 1
1st-Class catches: 12
One-Day 5 w. in innings: 1
Place in batting averages: 156th av. 25.73
Place in bowling averages: 5th av. 20.06
Strike rate: 45.78 (career 70.02)
Parents: Jack and Ursula

Wife and date of marriage:
Alexandra, 27 February 1993
Family links with cricket: Father opened batting for Haslingden CC
Education: Haslingden High School
Qualifications: 4 O-levels, NCA coaching certificate
Career outside cricket: 'Trying to qualify as a wine taster'
Off-season: Working for local bed firm
Overseas tours: NAYC to Bermuda 1985; Lancashire to Jamaica 1986-87, 1987-88, to Zimbabwe 1988-89, to Tasmania and Western Australia 1989-90, 1990-91
Overseas teams played for: Maroochydore, Queensland 1987-88, 1991-92; Randwick, Sydney 1990-91
Cricketers particularly admired: Ian Botham, Hartley Alleyne
Other sports followed: Football (Burnley), golf
Relaxations: Golf, and listening to music
Extras: Holds amateur Lancashire League record for highest individual score (147*). Broke Lancashire CCC record for most wickets in the Sunday League in 1991. Scored quickest first-class century in 1991 off authentic bowling (64 balls)
Best batting: 115* Lancashire v Derbyshire, Blackpool 1992
Best bowling: 5-23 Lancashire v Middlesex, Old Trafford 1994

1994 Season

	M	Inns	NO	Runs	HS	Avge	100s	50s	Ct	St	O	M	Runs	Wkts	Avge	Best	5wI	10wM
Test																		
All First	11	16	1	386	50	25.73	-	1	5	-	251.5	72	662	33	20.06	5-23	3	1
1-day Int																		
NatWest	2	2	1	62	57	62.00	-	1	-	-	24	2	97	2	48.50	2-29	-	
B & H	2	1	1	3	3 *	-	-	-	-	-	22	1	112	1	112.00	1-65	-	
Sunday	16	10	2	120	27	15.00	-	-	3	-	104.3	1	488	15	32.53	4-34	-	

Career Performances

	M	Inns	NO	Runs	HS	Avge	100s	50s	Ct	St	Balls	Runs	Wkts	Avge	Best	5wI	10wM
Test																	
All First	64	85	18	1666	115 *	24.86	2	6	12	-	7843	3714	112	33.16	5-23	4	1
1-day Int																	
NatWest	13	8	5	161	57	53.66	-	1	1	-	857	578	12	48.16	3-36	-	
B & H	29	17	6	285	80	25.90	-	2	5	-	1713	1155	27	42.77	4-25	-	
Sunday	110	63	23	693	48	17.32	-	-	21	-	4457	3489	120	29.07	5-56	1	

AVERIS, J. M. M.   Gloucestershire

Name: James Max Michael Averis
Role: Right-hand bat, right-arm medium bowler
Born: 28 May 1974, Bristol
Height: 5ft 11in **Weight:** 12st 7lb
Nickname: Fish
County debut: 1994 (one-day)
Parents: Michael and Carol
Marital status: Single
Family links with cricket: Grandfather played club cricket for Gloucester Gypsies
Education: Bristol Cathedral School, Portsmouth University
Qualifications: 10 GCSEs, 3 A-levels
Career outside cricket: Studying Geography at Portsmouth University
Overseas tours: Bristol Schools to Australia 1990-91
Other sports followed: Rugby and football
Extras: Played for Gloucestershire from U16 to U19 and ESCA U19. On Bristol RFC U21 tour to South Africa in Spring 1995

1994 Season

	M	Inns	NO	Runs	HS	Avge	100s	50s	Ct	St	O	M	Runs	Wkts	Avge	Best	5wI	10wM
Test																		
All First																		
1-day Int																		
NatWest																		
B & H																		
Sunday	1	1	1	2	2*	-	-	-	1	-	6	0	44	0	-	-	-	

Career Performances

	M	Inns	NO	Runs	HS	Avge	100s	50s	Ct	St	Balls	Runs	Wkts	Avge	Best	5wI	10wM
Test																	
All First																	
1-day Int																	
NatWest																	
B & H																	
Sunday	1	1	1	2	2*	-	-	-	1	-	36	44	0	-	-	-	

AYMES, A. N. Hampshire

Name: Adrian Nigel Aymes
Role: Right-hand bat, wicket-keeper
Born: 4 June 1964, Southampton
Height: 6ft **Weight:** 13st
Nickname: Aymser, Adi
County debut: 1987
County cap: 1991
1st-Class 50s: 15
1st-Class 100s: 1
1st-Class catches: 191
1st-Class stumpings: 18
Place in batting averages: 173rd av. 24.03
(1993 53rd av. 39.38)
Parents: Michael and Barbara
Wife and date of marriage: Marie,
12 November 1992
Family links with cricket: 'Father once
walked into a Holt and Haskell Sports Shop'
Education: Shirley Middle; Bellemoor
Secondary; Hill College
Qualifications: 4 O-levels, 1 A-level, NCA coaching award
Career outside cricket: Selling cricket equipment

Cricketers particularly admired: Gordon Greenidge, Martyn Moxon – 'honest batter.'
Other sports followed: Most sports
Relaxations: Watching videos, DIY at home
Extras: Half century on debut v Surrey; equalled club record of 6 catches in an innings and 10 in a match. Hampshire Exiles Young Player of the Year 1990.
Opinions on cricket: 'Great game.'
Best batting: 107* Hampshire v Sussex, Portsmouth 1993
Best bowling: 1-75 Hampshire v Sussex, Southampton 1992

1994 Season

	M	Inns	NO	Runs	HS	Avge	100s	50s	Ct	St	O	M	Runs	Wkts	Avge	Best	5wI	10wM
Test																		
All First	19	32	3	697	76	24.03	-	2	36	4								
1-day Int																		
NatWest	2	1	0	34	34	34.00	-	-	4	-								
B & H	3	1	1	4	4 *	-	-	-	2	-								
Sunday	17	13	7	289	54	48.16	-	1	21	5								

Career Performances

	M	Inns	NO	Runs	HS	Avge	100s	50s	Ct	St	Balls	Runs	Wkts	Avge	Best	5wI	10wM
Test																	
All First	88	124	31	2808	107 *	30.19	1	15	191	18	42	75	1	75.00	1-75	-	-
1-day Int																	
NatWest	9	2	0	36	34	18.00	-	-	10	2							
B & H	17	6	3	51	23 *	17.00	-	-	14	7							
Sunday	61	39	20	651	54	34.26	-	1	54	12							

2. Who in 1993-94 made the highest score by an Englishman abroad since Mike Brearley's 312* in 1966-67, how many did he score, who was he playing for and against whom?

AYRES, D. W.   Essex

Name: Duncan Wallace Ayres
Role: Right-hand bat, right-arm
medium bowler
Born: 8 October 1976, Basildon
Height: 5ft 11in **Weight:** 12st 7lbs
County debut: No first-team appearance
Parents: Andrew and Betty
Marital status: Single
Family links with cricket: Father plays
club cricket for Eton Manor and is a qualified
coach
Education: Falmouth Comprehensive;
Millfield School
Career outside cricket: Car sales
Off-season: Coaching and playing in Sydney
Overseas tours: West of England U11 to
Holland 1988; West of England U15 to
West Indies 1990-91, 1991-92

Overseas teams played for: St Gluvias
Cricketers particularly admired: Eldine Baptiste, Allan Donald
Other sports followed: Football (Manchester United), rugby (Cornwall), golf
Injuries: Shoulder dislocation, missed half of 1993 season
Relaxations: Round of golf, listening to music
Extras: Has played soccer for Wimbledon and minor county cricket for Cornwall

AZHARUDDIN, M.   Derbyshire

Name: Mohammad Azharuddin
Role: Right-hand bat, leg-break bowler
Born: 8 January 1963, Hyderabad, India
Height: 5ft 11in
Nickname: Azzy
County debut: 1991
County cap: 1991
Test debut: 1984-85
Tests: 62
One-Day Internationals: 174
1000 runs in a season: 1
1st-Class 50s: 50

1st-Class 100s: 36
1st-Class catches: 138
One-Day 100s: 4
Place in batting averages: 35th av. 44.50
Education: Nizam College; Osmania University
Off-season: Captaining India
Overseas tours: Young India to Zimbabwe 1984; India to Sri Lanka 1985-86, England 1986, West Indies 1988-89, Pakistan 1989-90, New Zealand 1989-90, England 1990, Australia 1991-92, South Africa 1992-93, Zimbabwe 1992-93, Sri Lanka 1993-94
Overseas teams played for: Hyderabad 1981-95 and South Zone
Extras: First appointed captain of India for the tour to New Zealand 1989-90. Scored a century in each of his first three Tests (against

England 1984-85). One of *Wisden*'s Five Cricketers of the Year 1990. Broke the record for the fastest century in limited-over internationals in December 1988, reaching three figures in 62 deliveries against New Zealand at Baroda. Stepped in as overseas player for Derbyshire in 1994 when Ian Bishop was ruled out through injury. Not signed for 1995
Best batting: 226 South Zone v East Zone, Jamadoba 1983-84
Best bowling: 2-33 Hyderabad v Adhra, Hyderabad 1987-88

1994 Season

	M	Inns	NO	Runs	HS	Avge	100s	50s	Ct	St	O	M	Runs	Wkts	Avge	Best	5wl	10wM
Test																		
All First	9	17	1	712	205	44.50	2	1	5	-	8	0	46	0	-	-	-	-
1-day Int																		
NatWest	3	3	1	88	74 *	44.00	-	1	-	-								
B & H	2	2	0	9	5	4.50	-	-	-	-								
Sunday	10	7	4	436	111 *	145.33	1	4	1	-								

Career Performances

	M	Inns	NO	Runs	HS	Avge	100s	50s	Ct	St	Balls	Runs	Wkts	Avge	Best	5wl	10wM
Test	62	88	3	4020	199	47.29	14	13	61	-	7	12	0	-	-	-	-
All First	161	243	27	11420	226	52.87	39	50	151	-	1028	593	7	84.71	2-33	-	-
1-day Int	174	161	31	4661	108 *	35.85	3	26	68		540	460	12	39.00	3-19	-	
NatWest	3	3	1	88	74 *	44.00	-	1	-	-							
B & H	6	6	1	134	44 *	26.80	-	-	4	-	96	58	1	58.00	1-17	-	
Sunday	25	21	6	807	111 *	53.80	1	6	7	-	5	5	0	-	-	-	

BABINGTON, A. M.   Gloucestershire

Name: Andrew Mark Babington
Role: Left-hand bat, right-arm fast-medium
bowler
Born: 22 July 1963, London
Height: 6ft 2in **Weight:** 13st 5lbs
Nickname: Gypsy, Vinny Jones, Oscar
County debut: 1986 (Sussex);
1991 (Gloucestershire)
1st-Class 50s: 1
1st-Class 5 w. in innings: 3
1st-Class catches: 32
Place in bowling averages:
(1993 135th av. 48.76)
Strike rate: (career 69.52)
Parents: Roy and Maureen
Marital status: Single
Family links with cricket: Father and
brother played club cricket
Education: Reigate Grammar School;
Borough Road College of Education
Qualifications: 5 O-levels, 2 A-levels, NCA coaching certificate, Member of Institute of
Legal Executives, holds LAUTRO and consumer credit licence towork in financial
services
Career outside cricket:
Developing own business
Overseas tours:
Surrey YC to Australia 1980; Gloucestershire to Kenya 1991, to Sri Lanka 1993
Overseas teams played for:
Gosnalls, Perth 1991-92
Cricketers particularly admired:
John Snow, Michael Holding, David Smith, Courtney Walsh
Other sports followed: Rallying, motor sports, golf, boxing
Injuries: Rib muscle; missed two weeks
Relaxations: 'Rally driving, all motor sports, playing golf, spending time with Charlotta,
visiting Sweden'
Extras: Took hat-trick (3rd, 4th & 5th Championship wickets) v Gloucestershire in 1986
and another v Durham in Tetley Trophy 1993 at Scarborough. Scored maiden 1st-class 50
off 30 balls (5 sixes) v Sussex at Cheltenham 1991. Released by Gloucestershire at end of
1994 season
Opinions on cricket: 'It is a batter's game. People's futures and livelihoods should be
taken more seriously by respective committees and selection panels. Let umpires decide
on bouncers and remove one-per-over rule.'

Best batting: 58 Gloucestershire v Sussex, Cheltenham 1991
Best bowling: 8-107 Gloucestershire v Kent, Bristol 1992

1994 Season

	M	Inns	NO	Runs	HS	Avge	100s	50s	Ct	St	O	M	Runs	Wkts	Avge	Best	5wl	10wM
Test																		
All First	1	0	0	0	0	-	-	-	-	-	23.5	7	42	1	42.00	1-27	-	-
1-day Int																		
NatWest																		
B & H																		
Sunday	6	2	1	4	4 *	4.00	-	-	1	-	41	3	232	7	33.14	3-9	-	

Career Performances

	M	Inns	NO	Runs	HS	Avge	100s	50s	Ct	St	Balls	Runs	Wkts	Avge	Best	5wl	10wM
Test																	
All First	95	101	40	515	58	8.44	-	1	32	-	14461	7587	208	36.47	8-107	3	-
1-day Int																	
NatWest	12	4	4	6	4 *	-	-	-	4	-	642	416	16	26.00	3-8	-	
B & H	20	9	4	63	27	12.60	-	-	3	-	1166	694	28	24.78	4-29	-	
Sunday	91	28	8	74	11	3.70	-	-	21	-	3593	2710	82	33.04	4-21	-	

BAILEY, R. J.   Northamptonshire

Name: Robert John Bailey
Role: Right-hand bat, off-spin bowler,
county vice-captain
Born: 28 October 1963, Biddulph,
Stoke-on-Trent
Height: 6ft 3in **Weight:** 14st 7lbs
Nickname: Bailers, Nose Bag ('I eat a lot!')
County debut: 1982
County cap: 1985
Benefit: 1993
Test debut: 1988
Tests: 4
One-Day Internationals: 4
1000 runs in a season: 11
1st-Class 50s: 89
1st-Class 100s: 34
1st-Class 200s: 4
1st-Class 5 w. in innings: 2
1st-Class catches: 193

One-Day 100s: 7
Place in batting averages: 42nd av. 43.35 (1993 18th av. 51.28)
Place in bowling averages: 143rd av. 51.63 (1993 99th av. 34.00)
Strike rate: 90.63 (career 79.70)
Parents: Marie, father deceased
Wife and date of marriage: Rachel, 11 April 1987
Children: Harry John, 7 March 1991; Alexandra, 13 November 1993
Family links with cricket: Father played in North Staffordshire League for 30 years for Knypersley and Minor Counties cricket for Staffordshire as wicket-keeper. Brother Simon now plays for Knypersley in the North Staffs/South Cheshire League
Education: Biddulph High School
Qualifications: 6 CSEs, 1 O-level, NCA advanced cricket coach
Off-season: 'Working for John Liddington, drinks suppliers to the licensed trade, as a rep.'
Overseas tours: England to Sharjah 1984-85 and 1986-87, to West Indies 1989-90; Northants to Durban 1991-92, to Cape Town 1992-93; Singapore Sixes October 1994
Overseas teams played for: Rhodes University, South Africa 1982-83; Uitenhage, Melbourne 1983-84, 1984-85; Fitzroy, Melbourne, 1985-86; Crosnells, Perth 1987-88.
Cricketers particularly admired: Dennis Lillee, David Steele
Other sports followed: Football (Stoke City)
Relaxations: Walking and drinking at the local village pub
Extras: Played for Young England v Young Australia 1983. Selected for cancelled tour of India 1988-89. Youngest Northamptonshire player to score 10,000 runs
Best batting: 224* Northamptonshire v Glamorgan, Swansea 1986
Best bowling: 5-54 Northamptonshire v Nottinghamshire, Northampton 1993

1994 Season

	M	Inns	NO	Runs	HS	Avge	100s	50s	Ct	St	O	M	Runs	Wkts	Avge	Best	5wI	10wM
Test																		
All First	18	33	5	1214	129 *	43.35	3	7	12	-	166.1	33	568	11	51.63	5-59	1	-
1-day Int																		
NatWest	3	3	0	84	52	28.00	-	1	2	-	18	4	47	2	23.50	1-20	-	
B & H	1	1	0	19	19	19.00	-	-	-	-	6	0	25	0	-	-	-	-
Sunday	15	15	3	421	94 *	35.08	-	2	6	-	55.1	1	295	11	26.81	3-33	-	

Career Performances

	M	Inns	NO	Runs	HS	Avge	100s	50s	Ct	St	Balls	Runs	Wkts	Avge	Best	5wI	10wM
Test	4	8	0	119	43	14.87	-	-	-	-							
All First	269	453	70	16221	224 *	42.35	34	89	193	-	6695	3541	84	42.15	5-54	2	-
1-day Int	4	4	2	137	43 *	68.50	-	-	1	-	36	25	0	-	-	-	-
NatWest	37	37	10	1240	145	45.92	1	8	9	-	402	236	10	23.60	3-47	-	
B & H	47	44	4	1667	134	41.67	2	12	10	-	204	130	1	130.00	1-22	-	
Sunday	167	159	22	4958	125 *	36.18	4	30	40	-	808	731	23	31.78	3-23	-	

BAINBRIDGE, M. R. Surrey

Name: Mark Robert Bainbridge
Role: Right-hand bat, left-arm bowler
Born: 11 May 1973, Isleworth, Middlesex
Height: 5ft 9in **Weight:** 11st
Nickname: Baino
County debut: No first-team appearance
Parents: Robert and Susan
Marital status: Single
Family links with cricket: Brother Paul plays
for Surrey YC
Education: Teddington School;
Richmond-upon-Thames College
Qualifications: 8 GCSEs, BTEC
in Business Studies
Career outside cricket: 'Something in
the leisure industry'
Overseas tours: England U18 to Canada 1991

(International Youth Tournament); England
YC to Barbados 1991; England U19 to Pakistan 1991-92
Overseas teams played for: Durbanville, Cape Town 1993-95
Cricketers particularly admired: Joey Benjamin, Phil Tufnell, Graham Thorpe
Other sports followed: Rugby union, football, golf
Relaxations: Going out with friends, watching Harlequins play rugby and playing golf
Opinions on cricket: 'There is too much cricket played in short spaces of time. Some
weeks you can play 14 days on the trot, have a break for a day or two and then a further 14
days solid cricket. It should be spread out so that players can have one or two days off each
week when they can practise or rest.'

---

3. Who was the batsman at the non-striker's end when Brian Lara made
his record 501* against Durham in 1994, and what was his score?

BAINBRIDGE, P. Durham

Name: Philip Bainbridge
Role: Right-hand bat, right-arm medium bowler
Born: 16 April 1958, Stoke-on-Trent
Height: 5ft 10in **Weight:** 12st 7lbs
Nickname: Bains, Robbo, Red
County debut: 1977 (Gloucestershire), 1992 (Durham)
County cap: 1981
Benefit: 1989
1000 runs in a season: 9
1st-Class 50s: 89
1st-Class 100s: 24
1st-Class 5 w. in innings: 10
1st-Class catches: 125
One-Day 100s: 1
One-Day 5 w. in innings: 1
Place in batting averages: 188th 22.00 (1993 61st av. 38.33)
Place in bowling averages: 147th av. 77.28 (1993 33rd av. 25.52)
Strike rate: 135.28 (career 73.06)
Parents: Leonard George and Lilian Rose
Wife and date of marriage: Barbara, 22 September 1979
Children: Neil, 11 January 1984; Laura, 15 January 1985
Family links with cricket: Cousin, Stephen Wilkinson, played for Somerset
Education: Hanley High School; Stoke-on-Trent Sixth Form College; Borough Road College of Education
Qualifications: 9 O-levels, 2 A-levels, BEd
Career outside cricket: Runs own corporate hospitality company and sports tour operators – Rhodes Leisure, Bristol. Specialise in sports tours to South Africa
Off-season: 'Working in my office at Rhodes Leisure'
Overseas tours: British Colleges to West Indies 1978; English Counties XI to Zimbabwe 1984-85; plus other tours to West Indies, Sri Lanka, Holland, South Africa, Pakistan and Zimbabwe
Overseas teams played for: Alberton, Johannesburg 1980-81, 1982-83
Cricketers particularly admired: Mike Procter
Other sports followed: Rugby union, soccer, golf, American football, boxing
Relaxations: 'Sport, my business, music, watching my son's mini-rugby team and watching my daughter compete on her pony'
Extras: Played for four 2nd XIs in 1976 – Gloucestershire, Derbyshire, Northamptonshire and Warwickshire. Played for Young England v Australia 1977. Scored first century for

Stoke-on-Trent aged 14. One of *Wisden*'s Five Cricketers of the Year 1985. Joined Durham for their first season in first-class cricket after 14 seasons with Gloucestershire. Played for Leyland CC as professional in 1991 – they won the Northern League. Player of the Year for Durham 1993. Appointed captain of Durham for 1994

Opinions on cricket: 'I think the four-day format has worked very well.'
Best batting: 169 Gloucestershire v Yorkshire, Cheltenham 1988
Best bowling: 8-53 Gloucestershire v Somerset, Bristol 1986

1994 Season

	M	Inns	NO	Runs	HS	Avge	100s	50s	Ct	St	O	M	Runs	Wkts	Avge	Best	5wI	10wM
Test																		
All First	18	31	1	660	68	22.00	-	5	13	-	315.4	67	1082	14	77.28	4-72	-	-
1-day Int																		
NatWest	2	2	1	102	85	102.00	-	1	1	-	21	2	67	2	33.50	1-23	-	
B & H	1	1	0	28	28	28.00	-	-	-	-	8	0	49	0	-	-	-	
Sunday	14	10	1	196	32	21.77	-	-	3	-	92.2	3	493	14	35.21	4-32	-	

Career Performances

	M	Inns	NO	Runs	HS	Avge	100s	50s	Ct	St	Balls	Runs	Wkts	Avge	Best	5wI	10wM
Test																	
All First	311	517	72	15086	169	33.90	24	89	138	-	24915	12657	341	37.11	8-53	10	-
1-day Int																	
NatWest	31	27	4	837	89	36.39	-	8	5	-	1789	1037	32	32.40	3-49	-	
B & H	53	49	9	1104	96	27.60	-	6	17	-	2524	1539	47	32.74	4-38	-	
Sunday	200	174	29	3274	106 *	22.57	1	13	46	-	7201	6030	203	29.70	5-22	1	

4. Who was England's top-scorer during their innings of 46 against the West Indies at Port of Spain in 1994, how many did he score?

BALL, M. C. J.   Gloucestershire

Name: Martyn Charles John Ball
Role: Right-hand bat, off-spin bowler,
slip fielder
Born: 26 April 1970, Bristol
Height: 5ft 9in **Weight:** 12st 2lbs
Nickname: Benny
County debut: 1988
1st-Class 50s: 3
1st-Class 5 w. in innings: 5
1st-Class 10 w. in match: 1
1st-Class catches: 67
Place in batting averages: 211th av. 18.72
(1993 234th av. 14.12)
Place in bowling averages: 135th av. 45.47
(1993 26th av. 24.38)
Strike rate: 93.00 (career 68.59)
Parents: Kenneth Charles and Pamela Wendy
Wife and date of marriage: Mona,
28 September 1991
Children: Kristina, 9 May 1990; Alexandra, 2 August 1993
Education: King Edmund Secondary School, Yate; Bath College of Further Education
Qualifications: 6 O-levels, 3 AO-levels
Off-season: 'Working for father's security fencing company. Playing football for Horton
FC and following Manchester City FC'
Overseas tours: Gloucestershire to Namibia 1991, to Kenya 1992, Sri Lanka 1993
Overseas teams played for: North Melbourne, Australia 1988-89; Old Hararians,
Zimbabwe 1990-91
Cricketers most admired: Ian Botham, John Emburey, Martin Gerrard and Andrew
Brown
Other sports followed: All sports except show-jumping
Injuries: Broken left hand, missed 3-4 weeks
Relaxations: 'Following Manchester City FC. A few pints with the boys during the winter
after another famous Horton FC victory.'
Extras: Played for Young England against New Zealand in 1989. Produced best bowling
figures in a match for the Britannic County Championship 1993 season – 14-169 against
Somerset
Opinions on cricket: 'With all the money coming into the game (i.e. Television revenue),
cricketers should start having 12-month contracts with adequate wages!'
Best batting: 71 Gloucestershire v Nottinghamshire, Bristol 1993
Best bowling: 8-46 Gloucestershire v Somerset, Taunton 1993

1994 Season

	M	Inns	NO	Runs	HS	Avge	100s	50s	Ct	St	O	M	Runs	Wkts	Avge	Best	5wI	10wM
Test																		
All First	17	28	3	468	45	18.72	-	-	31	-	325.3	78	955	21	45.47	5-69	1	-
1-day Int																		
NatWest																		
B & H	1	1	1	20	20 *	-	-	-	-	-	11	1	32	2	16.00	2-32	-	
Sunday	11	9	4	81	28 *	16.20	-	-	3	-	63.3	0	368	7	52.57	2-26	-	

Career Performances

	M	Inns	NO	Runs	HS	Avge	100s	50s	Ct	St	Balls	Runs	Wkts	Avge	Best	5wI	10wM
Test																	
All First	54	82	12	991	71	14.15	-	3	67	-	7614	3946	111	35.54	8-46	5	-
1-day Int																	
NatWest	3	1	1	16	16 *	-	-	-	1	-	120	75	4	18.75	3-42	-	
B & H	9	4	1	45	20 *	15.00	-	-	4	-	438	307	5	61.40	2-32	-	
Sunday	40	26	11	166	28 *	11.06	-	-	11	-	1250	1050	20	52.50	3-24	-	

BANTON, C.   Nottinghamshire

Name: Colin Banton
Role: Right-hand bat
Born: 15 September 1969, Fishhoek, Cape Town
Height: 5ft 9in **Weight:** 12st
Nickname: Bants, Bobby
County debut: No first team appearance
Parents: Frank and Coralie Patricia
Marital status: Engaged
Education: Fishhoek High School
Qualifications: Matriculation
Career outside cricket: Qualifying as an accountant
Off-season: Working in accountancy
Overseas teams played for: Fishhoek, Cape Town; Western Province Defence Force
Cricketers particularly admired:
Peter Kirsten, Ken McEwan
Other sports followed: Hockey
Injuries: Missed three weeks with torn ankle ligaments
Relaxations: Eating out and working out
Extras: Plays hockey for Slough in the National League and played hockey for Western Province in South Africa

BARNETT, A. A. Lancashire

Name: Alex Anthony Barnett
Role: Right-hand bat, slow left-arm bowler
Born: 11 September 1970, Malaga, Spain
Height: 6ft **Weight:** 11st 7lbs
Nickname: Bung, AB, George, Barnstormer
County debut: 1991 (Middlesex),
1992 (Lancashire)
1st-Class 5 w. in innings: 5
1st-Class catches: 14
Place in bowling averages: 145th av. 62.70
(1993 124th av. 42.66)
Strike rate: 115.00 (career 86.79)
Parents: Michael and Patricia
Marital status: Single
Family links with cricket: Great uncle, Charlie J. Barnett, was opening batsman for Gloucester and England. Father founded LCCA (London County Cricket Association) and is chairman of the London Cricket College
Education: Primrose Hill Primary; William Ellis Secondary
Qualifications: 'Not many Os, no As, no degrees, but have got scuba diving novice certificate and moped driving licence in New Zealand'
Career outside cricket: 'Professional out-of-work cricketer'
Off-season: Working in London helping my father in letting agency
Overseas tours: England YC to Australia 1989-90
Overseas teams played for: Parnell CC, Auckland 1988-89; Avondale CC, Cape Town, 1992-93; North Sydney CC, Sydney 1993-94
Cricketers particularly admired: Don Wilson, Clive Radley, Mike Gatting, Wasim Akram
Other sports followed: Golf, boxing
Relaxations: Trying new restaurants with girlfriend Kate, playing golf, watching films, playing chess
Extras: First-class debut aged 17. Hit first first-class ball for four (between 1st and 2nd slip). Joined Lancashire from Middlesex at the end of the 1991 season
Opinions on cricket: 'LBW law regarding ball pitching outside leg stump is unfair to left-arm spinners and seamers and an advantage to left-handed batsmen. Getting rid of overseas players would be a great loss to county cricket for the spectators and for the fact that we learn so much from these players.'
Best batting: 38 Lancashire v Durham, Old Trafford 1993
Best bowling: 5-36 Lancashire v Durham, Old Trafford 1993

1994 Season

	M	Inns	NO	Runs	HS	Avge	100s	50s	Ct	St	O	M	Runs	Wkts	Avge	Best	5wI	10wM
Test																		
All First	6	5	1	14	10	3.50	-	-	3	-	191.4	39	627	10	62.70	2-35	-	-
1-day Int																		
NatWest																		
B & H																		
Sunday																		

Career Performances

	M	Inns	NO	Runs	HS	Avge	100s	50s	Ct	St	Balls	Runs	Wkts	Avge	Best	5wI	10wM
Test																	
All First	50	48	20	263	38	9.39	-	-	14	-	9808	5191	113	45.93	5-36	5	-
1-day Int																	
NatWest	1	0	0	0	0	-	-	-	-	-	72	29	2	14.50	2-29	-	
B & H	5	0	0	0	0	-	-	-	-	-	264	182	3	60.66	3-43	-	
Sunday	10	3	2	21	11 *	21.00	-	-	3	-	383	327	9	36.33	3-15	-	

BARNETT, K. J.   Derbyshire

Name: Kim John Barnett
Role: Right-hand bat, leg-break bowler, county captain
Born: 17 July 1960, Stoke-on-Trent
Height: 6ft **Weight:** 13st 7lbs
Nickname: Skippo, Barn
County debut: 1979
County cap: 1982
Benefit: 1993 (£37,056)
Test debut: 1988
Tests: 4
One-Day Internationals: 1
1000 runs in a season: 11
1st-Class 50s: 110
1st-Class 100s: 44
1st-Class 200s: 2
1st-Class 5 w. in innings: 3
1st-Class catches: 229
One-Day 100s: 10
One-Day 5 w. in innings: 1
Place in batting averages: 65th av. 38.50 (1993 5th av. 64.36)
Place in bowling averages: 1st av. 13.30

Strike rate: 25.07 (career 74.18)
Parents: Derek and Doreen
Marital status: Engaged to Janet
Children: Michael Nicholas, 24 April 1990
Education: Leek High School, Staffs
Qualifications: 7 O-levels
Career outside cricket: Bank clerk
Overseas tours: English Schools to India 1977-78; England YC to Australia 1978-79; England B to Sri Lanka 1985-86 (vice-captain); unofficial English XI to South Africa 1989-90
Overseas teams played for: Boland 1980-81, 1982-83
Cricketers particularly admired: Gordon Greenidge, Malcolm Marshall
Other sports followed: Horse racing, most sports
Relaxations: Eating and sleeping
Extras: Played for Northamptonshire 2nd XI when aged 15, Staffordshire and Warwickshire 2nd XI. Became youngest captain of a first-class county when appointed in 1983. One of *Wisden*'s Five Cricketers of the Year 1989. Banned from Test cricket after joining tour to South Africa, suspension remitted in 1992
Opinions on cricket: 'Forget all the trivia about pitches, how the game should be in length of time, covering etc. Let's get on with playing attractive, entertaining cricket.'
Best batting: 239* Derbyshire v Leicestershire, Leicester 1988
Best bowling: 6-28 Derbyshire v Glamorgan, Chesterfield 1991

1994 Season

	M	Inns	NO	Runs	HS	Avge	100s	50s	Ct	St	O	M	Runs	Wkts	Avge	Best	5wI	10wM
Test																		
All First	15	24	2	847	148	38.50	1	7	7	-	54.2	5	173	13	13.30	5-31	1	-
1-day Int																		
NatWest	3	3	1	117	113 *	58.50	1	-	2	-								
B & H																		
Sunday	13	12	4	379	56 *	47.37	-	2	6	-	6	0	50	1	50.00	1-13	-	

Career Performances

	M	Inns	NO	Runs	HS	Avge	100s	50s	Ct	St	Balls	Runs	Wkts	Avge	Best	5wI	10wM
Test	4	7	0	207	80	29.57	-	2	1	-	36	32	0	-	-	-	-
All First	364	581	54	20565	239 *	39.02	44	110	229	-	11276	5575	152	36.67	6-28	3	-
1-day Int	1	1	0	84	84	84.00	-	1	-	-							
NatWest	30	30	3	976	113 *	36.14	1	7	13	-	226	137	11	12.45	6-24	1	
B & H	68	59	3	2075	115	37.05	3	15	27	-	306	198	6	33.00	1-10	-	
Sunday	223	213	34	6130	131 *	34.24	6	31	80	-	761	687	21	32.71	3-39	-	

BARTLE, S.   Leicestershire

Name: Steven Bartle
Role: Left-hand bat, right-arm medium bowler
Born: 5 September 1971, Shipley, Yorkshire
Height: 6ft 4in **Weight:** 15st
Nickname: Barts
County debut: No first-team appearance
Parents: John and Judith
Marital status: Single
Family links with cricket: Father played for Windhill in the Bradford League
Education: Wood End Middle School; Beckfoot GS; Windhill College of Education; Calderdale College
Qualifications: 7 GCSEs, coaching qualifications
Overseas tours: England U19 to New Zealand 1990-91
Overseas teams played for: Mossman, Sydney 1993-94
Cricketers particularly admired: David Gower, Curtly Ambrose, Robin Smith
Other sports followed: Football, tennis, golf, snooker, squash, badminton
Relaxations: Astronomy and weight-lifting
Extras: Was on the Yorkshire staff in 1993, joined Leicestershire for 1995 season
Opinions on cricket: 'More one-day cricket. Coloured clothing is a good idea, it brings out the crowds.'

5. Which English player passed 40,000 first-class runs in September 1994?

BARWICK, S. R.   Glamorgan

Name: Stephen Royston Barwick
Role: Right-hand bat, right-arm
medium bowler
Born: 6 September 1960, Neath
Height: 6ft 2in **Weight:** 13st
Nickname: Bas
County debut: 1981
County cap: 1987
Benefit: 1995
50 wickets in a season: 2
1st-Class 5 w. in innings: 10
1st-Class 10 w. in match: 1
1st-Class catches: 43
One-Day 5 w. in innings: 3
Place in bowling averages: 76th av. 31.41
(1993 133rd av. 48.38)
Strike rate: 106.38 (career 78.57)
Parents: Margaret and Roy
Wife and date of marriage: Margaret, 12 December 1987
Children: Michael Warren, 25 September 1990; Katheryn Elizabeth, 17 February 1993;
Jessica Margaret, 30 July 1994
Family links with cricket: 'My Uncle David played for Glamorgan 2nd XI'
Education: Cwrt Sart Comprehensive; Dwr-y-Felin Comprehensive
Qualifications: 'Commerce, human biology, mathematics, English'
Career outside cricket: Ex-steelworker
Off-season: Working on benefit for 1995
Overseas teams played for: Benoni, South Africa
Cricketers particularly admired: Ian Botham, Richard Hadlee
Other sports followed: Football and rugby
Relaxations: 'Spending time with my little boy, sea fishing and the odd pint or two'
Best batting: 30 Glamorgan v Hampshire, Bournemouth 1988
Best bowling: 8-42 Glamorgan v Worcestershire, Worcester 1983

1994 Season

	M	Inns	NO	Runs	HS	Avge	100s	50s	Ct	St	O	M	Runs	Wkts	Avge	Best	5wI	10wM
Test																		
All First	12	16	6	35	8	3.50	-	-	3	-	549.4	208	1131	36	31.41	5-44	1	-
1-day Int																		
NatWest	3	1	1	0	0 *	-	-	-	1	-	34	5	97	4	24.25	2-30	-	
B & H	1	0	0	0	0	-	-	-	-	-	9	1	24	0	-	-	-	
Sunday	17	6	3	17	8 *	5.66	-	-	2	-	120	3	483	21	23.00	5-36	1	

Career Performances

	M	Inns	NO	Runs	HS	Avge	100s	50s	Ct	St	Balls	Runs	Wkts	Avge	Best	5wl	10wM
Test																	
All First	197	189	71	819	30	6.94	-	-	43	-	34182	15078	435	34.66	8-42	10	1
1-day Int																	
NatWest	26	10	5	22	6	4.40	-	-	4	-	1494	798	39	20.46	5-26	1	
B & H	43	24	12	87	18	7.25	-	-	9	-	2377	1469	54	27.20	4-11	-	
Sunday	152	49	28	210	48*	10.00	-	-	22	-	6011	4497	156	28.82	6-28	2	

BASE, S. J.   Derbyshire

Name: Simon John Base
Role: Right-hand bat, right-arm
fast-medium bowler
Born: 2 January 1960, Maidstone
Height: 6ft 3in **Weight:** 14st 7lbs
Nickname: Basey, Moose Man
County debut: 1986 (Glamorgan),
1988 (Derbyshire)
County cap: 1990
50 wickets in a season: 1
1st-Class 50s: 2
1st-Class 5 w. in innings: 16
1st-Class 10 w. in match: 1
1st-Class catches: 60
Place in batting averages: 243rd av. 14.54
Place in bowling averages: 90th av. 34.00
(1993 68th av. 30.00)
Strike rate: 51.91 (career 53.98)
Parents: Christine and Peter (deceased)
Wife and date of marriage: Louise Ann, 23 September 1989
Children: Christopher Peter Elliott, 15 December 1991
Family links with cricket: Grandfather played, 'brother-in-law pretends he can!'
Education: Fish Hoek Primary School; Fish Hoek High School, Cape Town, South Africa
Qualifications: High School, School Certificate Matriculation, refrigeration and air
conditioning technician
Career outside cricket: Hall-Thermotank in South Africa as a technician, GSPK
Electronics, Rhodes Fabrics
Off season: 'Spending time with my family and having a holiday in South Africa.'
Overseas tours: England XI to Holland 1989
Overseas teams played for: Western Province B 1982-83; Boland 1986-89; Border
1989-94 (all South Africa)

Cricketers particularly admired: Graham Gooch, Graeme Pollock, Mike Procter, Richard Hadlee, Malcolm Marshall
Other sports followed: Most other sports
Relaxations: Spending time with family, swimming, windsurfing, 'braaing'
Extras: Suspended from first-class cricket for ten weeks during 1988 season for a supposed breach of contract, joining Derbyshire when he was still said to be contracted to Glamorgan. The TCCB fined Derbyshire £2000. Retired from county cricket at end of 1993 season to play as a non-overseas player for Border, South Africa
Opinions on cricket: 'Happy with four-day cricket and coloured clothing in Sunday League cricket.'
Best batting: 58 Derbyshire v Yorkshire, Chesterfield 1990
Best bowling: 7-60 Derbyshire v Yorkshire, Chesterfield 1989

1994 Season

	M	Inns	NO	Runs	HS	Avge	100s	50s	Ct	St	O	M	Runs	Wkts	Avge	Best	5wI	10wM
Test																		
All First	8	12	1	160	33	14.54	-	-	6	-	199	30	782	23	34.00	5-92	1	-
1-day Int																		
NatWest	1	0	0	0	0	-	-	-	-	-	11	0	63	1	63.00	1-63	-	
B & H																		
Sunday	10	1	0	3	3	3.00	-	-	1	-	72	3	274	14	19.57	3-20	-	

Career Performances

	M	Inns	NO	Runs	HS	Avge	100s	50s	Ct	St	Balls	Runs	Wkts	Avge	Best	5wI	10wM
Test																	
All First	131	167	34	1508	58	11.33	-	2	60	-	20837	11159	386	28.90	7-60	16	1
1-day Int																	
NatWest	3	2	0	6	4	3.00	-	-	1	-	156	124	3	41.33	2-49	-	
B & H	15	9	3	53	15 *	8.83	-	-	-	-	870	629	15	41.93	3-33	-	
Sunday	87	35	8	179	31	6.62	-	-	24	-	3735	2710	110	24.63	4-14	-	

BASTIEN, S.   Glamorgan

Name: Steven Bastien
Role: Right-hand bat, right-arm fast-medium bowler, outfielder
Born: 13 March 1963, Stepney, London
Height: 6ft 1in **Weight:** 13st
Nickname: Bassie
County debut: 1988
1st-Class 5 w. in innings: 7
1st-Class 10 w. in match: 1
1st-Class catches: 7

Place in bowling averages:
(1993 70th av. 30.15)
Strike rate: (career 72.30)
Parents: Anthony and Francisca
Marital status: Single
Children: Linden Kieron,
20 December 1990
Family links with cricket: Brother Roger
plays in the Essex League
Education: St Mary's Academy School,
Dominica; St Bonaventure School, London
Qualifications: 3 CSEs, NCA coaching
certificate, carpentry and CCPR course
Career outside cricket:
Carpenter, labourer, salesman
Off-season: Helping out at London
Cricket College
Cricketers particularly admired:
Viv Richards, Robin Smith, Malcolm Marshall, Carl Hooper, Curtly Ambrose
Other sports followed: Football, boxing, basketball, athletics, rugby
Relaxations: Listening to reggae, soul and calypso music
Extras: Took five wickets on first-class debut in 1988. Took career best innings figures
of 6-52 and personal best match figures of 12-105 in the same match, against Essex, in
1993. Released by Glamorgan at end of 1994 season
Best batting: 36* Glamorgan v Warwickshire, Edgbaston 1988
Best bowling: 6-52 Glamorgan v Essex, Cardiff 1993

1994 Season

	M	Inns	NO	Runs	HS	Avge	100s	50s	Ct	St	O	M	Runs	Wkts	Avge	Best	5wI	10wM
Test																		
All First	5	3	0	7	6	2.33	-	-	2	-	138.3	40	384	8	48.00	2-47	-	-
1-day Int																		
NatWest																		
B & H																		
Sunday																		

Career Performances

	M	Inns	NO	Runs	HS	Avge	100s	50s	Ct	St	Balls	Runs	Wkts	Avge	Best	5wI	10wM
Test																	
All First	54	41	18	182	36 *	7.91			7	-	8894	4672	123	37.98	6-52	7	1
1 day Int																	
NatWest	2	1	1	7	7 *	-	-	-	-	-	114	98	1	98.00	1-42	-
B & H	4	2	1	10	7	10.00	-	-	-	-	198	137	1	137.00	1-29	-
Sunday	12	2	1	1	1	1.00	-	-	1	-	414	298	6	49.66	2-42	-

BATES, J. J. Sussex

Name: Justin J. Bates
Role: Right-hand bat, off-spin bowler
Born: 9 April 1976, Farnborough, Hants
Height: 6ft **Weight:** 12st 7lbs
County debut: No first-team appearance
Parents: Barry and Sandra
Marital status: Single
Family links with cricket: Father played cricket for Staplefield and Crawley; brother plays for Three Bridges and used to play for Sussex Young Cricketers; Alan Igglesden (Kent and England) is second cousin
Education: St Mark's Primary School; Warden Park Secondary School; Hurstpierpoint College
Qualifications: 8 GCSEs, 3 A-levels, NCA coaching award
Career outside cricket: Freelance computer graphic designer
Off-season: Touring with Sussex YC and coaching
Overseas tours: Sussex YC to India 1990-91, to Barbados 1992-93, to Sri Lanka 1994-95
Cricketers particularly admired: Robin Smith, Tim May, Mark Newell, Stan Berry
Other sports followed: Golf and rugby
Relaxations: Computing, reading
Opinions on cricket: 'Within the past few years cricket, along with most sports, is becoming more competitive, raising the standard of the game. If the level of English cricket is to compare to other countries we must become tougher and more dedicated in our training and during the game.'

BATES, R. T. Nottinghamshire

Name: Richard Terry Bates
Role: Right-hand bat, off-spin bowler, slip fielder
Born: 17 June 1972, Stamford, Lincs
Height: 6ft 1in **Weight:** 14st
Nickname: Blast, Batesy, Beaver
County debut: 1993
1st-Class catches: 3
Parents: Terry and Sue
Marital status: Engaged

Family links with cricket: Father is NCA Development and Administration Manager
Education: Bourne Grammar School; Stamford College for Further Education
Qualifications: 8 GCSEs, BTEC in Business and Finance, NCA Advanced Coach
Career outside cricket: Employed by Notts CCC to coach during the winter
Off-season: Coaching, keeping fit, nets
Overseas tours: Lincolnshire Colts (U19) to Australia 1989-90
Overseas teams played for: Redwood, New Zealand 1991-92
Cricketers particularly admired:
Ian Botham, Derek Randall, Viv Richards, Paul Johnson, James Hindson, David Pennett
Other sports followed: Football
Injuries: Fractured finger, missed three weeks
Relaxations: Socialising, films, Chinese and Indian food, 'visiting the Black Orchid (nightclub) occasionally'

Opinions on cricket: 'More second team fixtures on first-class grounds. Better prospects for winter employment, i.e. coaching jobs.'
Best batting: 33* Nottinghamshire v Oxford University, The Parks 1993
Best bowling: 2-43 Nottinghamshire v Sussex, Eastbourne 1993

1994 Season

	M	Inns	NO	Runs	HS	Avge	100s	50s	Ct	St	O	M	Runs	Wkts	Avge	Best	5wI	10wM
Test																		
All First	2	4	1	15	8	5.00	-	-	1	-	47	8	147	2	73.50	1-52	-	-
1-day Int																		
NatWest																		
B & H																		
Sunday	3	1	0	16	16	16.00	-	-	-	-	21	2	96	3	32.00	2-34	-	

Career Performances

	M	Inns	NO	Runs	HS	Avge	100s	50s	Ct	St	Balls	Runs	Wkts	Avge	Best	5wI	10wM
Test																	
All First	7	9	4	85	33 *	17.00	-	-	3	-	960	425	8	53.12	2-43	-	-
1-day Int																	
NatWest																	
B & H																	
Sunday	9	4	1	18	16	6.00	-	-	2	-	365	333	10	33.30	3-43	-	

BATTY, J. D.   Somerset

Name: Jeremy David Batty
Role: Right-hand bat, off-spin bowler,
cover fielder
Born: 15 May 1971, Bradford
Height: 6ft 1in **Weight:** 11st 10lbs
Nickname: Bullfrog, Sniper, Nora
County debut: 1989 (Yorkshire)
1st-Class 50s: 2
1st-Class 5 w. in innings: 3
1st-Class catches: 22
Place in batting averages:
(1993 244th av. 13.00)
Place in bowling averages:
(1993 100th av. 34.35)
Strike rate: (career 71.82)
Parents: David and Rosemary
Marital status: Single
Family links with cricket: Father took
over 1000 wickets in the Bradford League
Education: Parkside Middle School; Bingley Grammar School; Horsforth College
Qualifications: 5 O-levels, BTEC Diploma in Leisure Studies, coaching certificate
Overseas tours: England YC to Australia 1989-90
Overseas teams played for: Sunrise 1989-90, Country Districts 1990-91 (both Zimbabwe)
Cricketers particularly admired: Phil Carrick, John Emburey, Ian Botham, Mike
Gatting
Other sports followed: Rugby league, rugby union, football
Relaxations: Drink, food, music and movies
Extras: Took five wickets on first-class debut v Lancashire in 1989. Moved to Somerset
for the 1995 season
Best batting: 51 Yorkshire v Sri Lanka, Headingley 1991
Best bowling: 6-48 Yorkshire v Nottinghamshire, Worksop 1991

1994 Season

	M	Inns	NO	Runs	HS	Avge	100s	50s	Ct	St	O	M	Runs	Wkts	Avge	Best	5wI	10wM
Test																		
All First	3	6	5	78	26 *	78.00	-	-	3	-	77.4	18	259	6	43.16	2-57	-	-
1-day Int																		
NatWest																		
B & H																		
Sunday																		

Career Performances

	M	Inns	NO	Runs	HS	Avge	100s	50s	Ct	St	Balls	Runs	Wkts	Avge	Best	5wl	10wM
Test																	
All First	64	67	20	703	51	14.95	-	2	25	-	10055	5286	140	37.75	6-48	3	-
1-day Int																	
NatWest	3	2	0	7	4	3.50	-	-	1	-	126	97	1	97.00	1-17	-	
B & H	4	1	1	2	2*	-	-	-	1	-	174	109	1	109.00	1-34	-	
Sunday	31	13	6	41	13*	5.85	-	-	16	-	1392	1091	40	27.27	4-33	-	

BELL, M. A. V. Warwickshire

Name: Michael Anthony Vincent Bell
Role: Right-hand bat, left-arm
fast-medium bowler
Born: 19 December 1967, Birmingham
Height: 6ft 2in **Weight:** 13st 2lbs
Nickname: Belly, Nelly, Breezer
County debut: 1992
1st-Class 5 w. in innings: 3
1st-Class catches: 5
One-Day 5 w. in innings: 2
Place in bowling averages:
(1993 36th av. 25.96)
Strike rate: (career 52.69)
Parents: Vincent and Adelheid
Marital status: Single
Family links with cricket: Father played
cricket mainly for Mitchells & Butler in
the Birmingham League. An uncle played
a few games for Jamaica
Education: Bishop Milner Comprehensive; Dudley Technical College
Qualifications: 5 O-levels, City and Guilds in Recreation and Leisure Parts 1 & 2
Career outside cricket: Casino croupier, worked with the PE staff at Earls High School
and also worked in the corporate hospitality department at EMP plc for two years
Overseas tours: BWIA to Barbados and Trinidad & Tobago 1989; John Morris's Madcap
CC to Australia 1992
Overseas teams played for: Swanbourne, Perth 1986-87; Norwood, Melbourne 1989-90;
Phoenix, Perth 1992-93; Sunshine Heights 1993-94
Cricketers particularly admired: Dennis Lillee, Viv Richards, Michael Holding, Imran
Khan, Wasim Akram, Shane Warne
Other sports followed: Any sport played by the best in that particular field

Injuries: Lower back problem, out for most of the season

Relaxations: 'Golf (although I'm no Calvin Peete), good movies and going to a hot country before winter sets in.'

Opinions on cricket: 'When are the batsmen going to be prevented from taking the initiative over the bowlers and get limited to, for instance, one extra-cover drive – on the up – per over ... and when will a cow jump over the moon!'

Best batting: 22* Warwickshire v Gloucestershire, Edgbaston 1993

Best bowling: 7-48 Warwickshire v Gloucestershire, Edgbaston 1993

1994 Season

	M	Inns	NO	Runs	HS	Avge	100s	50s	Ct	St	O	M	Runs	Wkts	Avge	Best	5wl	10wM
Test																		
All First	1	1	1	4	4 *	-	-	-	1	-	31	5	108	3	36.00	3-89	-	-
1-day Int																		
NatWest																		
B & H	1	0	0	0	0	-	-	-	1	-	11	1	34	2	17.00	2-34	-	
Sunday	1	0	0	0	0	-	-	-	-	-	8	0	19	5	3.80	5-19	1	

Career Performances

	M	Inns	NO	Runs	HS	Avge	100s	50s	Ct	St	Balls	Runs	Wkts	Avge	Best	5wl	10wM
Test																	
All First	14	20	9	79	22 *	7.18	-	-	5	-	2055	1068	39	27.38	7-48	3	-
1-day Int																	
NatWest																	
B & H	1	0	0	0	0	-	-	-	1	-	66	34	2	17.00	2-34	-	
Sunday	6	4	1	19	6 *	6.33	-	-	-	-	288	205	12	17.08	5-19	2	

BENJAMIN, J. E. Surrey

Name: Joseph Emmanuel Benjamin

Role: Right-hand bat, right-arm fast-medium bowler

Born: 2 February 1961, Christchurch, St Kitts, West Indies

Height: 6ft 2in **Weight:** 12st 7lbs

Nickname: Boggy, Moon Man

County debut: 1988 (Warwickshire), 1992 (Surrey)

County cap: 1993 (Surrey)

Test debut: 1994

Tests: 1

50 wickets in a season: 2

1st-Class 5 w. in innings: 13

1st-Class 10 w. in match: 1

1st-Class catches: 20

Place in bowling averages: 7th av. 20.72
(1993 53rd av. 27.85)
Strike rate: 44.35 (career 58.27)
Parents: Henry and Judith
Marital status: Single
Education: Cayon High School, St Kitts;
Mount Pleasant, Highgate, Birmingham
Qualifications: 4 O-levels
Career outside cricket: Landscape gardener,
store manager
Off-season: Touring with England
Overseas teams played for:
Prahran, Melbourne 1992-93
Overseas tours:
England to Australia 1994-95
Cricketers particularly admired:
Imran Khan, Viv Richards, Malcolm Marshall
Other sports followed: Rugby, squash,
football

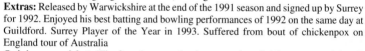

Relaxations: Music, going to the cinema, reading
Extras: Released by Warwickshire at the end of the 1991 season and signed up by Surrey
for 1992. Enjoyed his best batting and bowling performances of 1992 on the same day at
Guildford. Surrey Player of the Year in 1993. Suffered from bout of chickenpox on
England tour of Australia
Opinions on cricket: 'The four-day game has been very beneficial to county cricket. It
helps batters and bowlers to achieve individual milestones and gives players more time to
recover after the game.'
Best batting: 42 Surrey v Kent, Guildford 1992
Best bowling: 6-19 Surrey v Nottinghamshire, The Oval 1993

1994 Season

	M	Inns	NO	Runs	HS	Avge	100s	50s	Ct	St	O	M	Runs	Wkts	Avge	Best	5wI	10wM
Test	1	1	0	0	0	0.00	-	-	-	-	28	3	80	4	20.00	4-42	-	-
All First	16	17	1	148	33 *	9.25	-	-	5	-	591.2	130	1658	80	20.72	6-27	5	1
1-day Int																		
NatWest	4	1	0	25	25	25.00	-	-	-	-	44.3	7	156	5	31.20	3-26	-	
B & H	4	0	0	0	0	-	-	-	-	-	43	5	191	5	38.20	3-52	-	
Sunday	8	3	1	11	7	5.50	-	-	1	-	60	5	283	5	56.60	3-40	-	

6. Who won the Player of the Tournament award in the 1994 Hong
Kong Sixes?

Career Performances

	M	Inns	NO	Runs	HS	Avge	100s	50s	Ct	St	Balls	Runs	Wkts	Avge	Best	5wI	10wM
Test	1	1	0	0	0	0.00	-	-	-	-	168	80	4	20.00	4-42	-	-
All First	76	83	24	617	42	10.45	-	-	20	-	14743	7241	253	28.62	6-19	13	1
1-day Int																	
NatWest	12	6	3	53	25	17.66	-	-	2	-	693	426	9	47.33	3-26	-	
B & H	14	3	2	24	20	24.00	-	-	5	-	864	561	16	35.06	3-52	-	
Sunday	58	26	12	153	24	10.92	-	-	12	-	2583	1924	56	34.35	4-44	-	

BENJAMIN, W. K. M.   Hampshire

Name: Winston Keithroy Matthew Benjamin
Role: Right-hand bat, right-arm fast bowler
Born: 31 December 1964, St John's, Antigua
Height: 6ft 3in
County debut: 1986 (Leicestershire),
1994 (Hampshire)
County cap: 1989 (Leicestershire)
Test debut: 1987-88
Tests: 16
One-Day Internationals: 75
50 wickets in a season: 1
1st-Class 50s: 19
1st-Class 100s: 1
1st-Class 5 w. in innings: 23
1st-Class 10 w. in match: 2
1st-Class catches: 87
One-Day 5 w. in innings: 4
Place in batting averages: 220th av. 17.76
(1993 177th av. 22.61)
Place in bowling averages: 18th av. 24.37 (1993 11th av. 21.93)
Strike rate: 70.25 (career 55.44)
Education: All Saints School, Antigua
Overseas teams played for: Leeward Islands 1985-93
Overseas tours: West Indies to Australia 1986-87, to Pakistan 1986-87, to India 1987-88, to Sharjah 1988, to England 1988, to Australia 1988-89, to Sharjah 1991, to Australia and New Zealand 1992-93, to Sharjah, India (Hero Cup) and Sri Lanka 1993-94
Extras: Signed for Hampshire in 1994 after seven years at Leicestershire. During net practice in 1994 he smashed a ball through the rear window of a Hampshire committee member's Porsche! Expected to be in West Indies party to tour England in 1995, so unlikely to be available to Hampshire

Best batting: 101* Leicestershire v Derbyshire, Leicester 1992
Best bowling: 7-54 Leicestershire v Australia, Leicester 1992

1994 Season

	M	Inns	NO	Runs	HS	Avge	100s	50s	Ct	St	O	M	Runs	Wkts	Avge	Best	5wI	10wM
Test																		
All First	9	14	1	231	54	17.76	-	2	4	-	281	97	585	24	24.37	6-46	2	-
1-day Int																		
NatWest	2	1	0	5	5	5.00	-	-	1	-	22	3	53	2	26.50	2-24	-	
B & H	3	1	0	18	18	18.00	-	-	-	-	25.4	2	101	2	50.50	1-26	-	
Sunday	7	3	0	39	35	13.00	-	-	3	-	55.1	4	227	12	18.91	3-19	-	

Career Performances

	M	Inns	NO	Runs	HS	Avge	100s	50s	Ct	St	Balls	Runs	Wkts	Avge	Best	5wI	10wM
Test	16	19	1	276	44	15.33	-	-	8	-	2882	1251	51	24.52	4-46	-	-
All First	161	200	36	3640	101 *	22.19	1	19	87	-	25450	11687	459	25.46	7-54	23	2
1-day Int	75	47	12	245	31	7.00	-	-	13	-	3933	2713	86	31.54	5-22	1	
NatWest	16	12	2	76	24 *	7.60	-	-	4	-	1011	528	22	24.00	5-32	1	
B & H	19	13	3	188	45	18.80	-	-	3	-	1115	645	31	20.80	5-17	2	
Sunday	58	42	8	385	55	11.32	-	1	9	-	2532	1753	66	26.56	4-19	-	

BENSON, M. R.   Kent

Name: Mark Richard Benson
Role: Left-hand bat, off-spin bowler, county captain
Born: 6 July 1958, Shoreham, Sussex
Height: 5ft 10in **Weight:** 12st 7lbs
Nickname: Benny
County debut: 1980
County cap: 1981
Benefit: 1991 (£174,619)
Test debut: 1986
Tests: 1
One-Day Internationals: 1
1000 runs in a season: 11
1st-Class 50s: 98
1st-Class 100s: 46
1st-Class 200s: 1
1st-Class catches: 136
One-Day 100s: 4

Place in batting averages: 144th av. 27.29 (1993 35th av. 43.47)
Parents: Frank and Judy
Wife and date of marriage: Sarah, 20 September 1986
Children: Laurence Mark Edward, 16 October 1987; Edward 23 June 1990
Family links with cricket: Father played for Ghana; sister Tina is marketing manager for Kent CCC
Education: Sutton Valence School
Qualifications: O and A-levels and 1 S-level, qualified tennis coach
Career outside cricket: Marketing assistant with Shell Oil UK; financial adviser
Cricketers particularly admired: Malcolm Marshall, Jimmy Cook, Chris Tavaré
Other sports followed: Baseball, golf, horse racing, athletics
Relaxations: Horse racing, cards, 'playing with my children'
Extras: Scored 1000 runs in first full season. Record for most runs in career and season at Sutton Valence School. Appointed Kent captain at end of 1990 season. Captained England in two one-day matches against Holland in 1993
Best batting: 257 Kent v Hampshire, Southampton 1991
Best bowling: 2-55 Kent v Surrey, Dartford 1986

1994 Season

	M	Inns	NO	Runs	HS	Avge	100s	50s	Ct	St	O	M	Runs	Wkts	Avge	Best	5wl	10wM
Test																		
All First	16	28	1	737	159	27.29	1	4	10	-								
1-day Int																		
NatWest	4	4	0	60	44	15.00	-	-	1	-								
B & H	1	1	0	47	47	47.00	-	-	1	-								
Sunday	8	8	0	256	74	32.00	-	1	3	-								

Career Performances

	M	Inns	NO	Runs	HS	Avge	100s	50s	Ct	St	Balls	Runs	Wkts	Avge	Best	5wl	10wM
Test	1	2	0	51	30	25.50	-	-	-	-							
All First	279	470	34	17685	257	40.56	46	98	136	-	467	493	5	98.60	2-55	-	-
1-day Int	1	1	0	24	24	24.00	-	-	-	-							
NatWest	35	35	1	1136	113 *	33.41	1	8	11	-							
B & H	59	58	6	2049	118	39.40	3	14	9	-							
Sunday	155	145	2	3959	97	27.68	-	26	43	-							

BERRY, P. J.   Durham

Name: Philip John Berry
Role: Right-hand bat, off-spin bowler
Born: 28 December 1966, Saltburn
Height: 6ft **Weight:** 12st

Nickname: Chuck
County debut: 1986 (Yorkshire), 1992 (Durham)
1st-Class 50s: 1
1st-Class 5 w. in innings: 1
1st-Class 10 w. in match: 1
1st-Class catches: 10
Place in batting averages: (1993 164th av. 23.20)
Place in bowling averages: (1993 126th av. 43.20)
Strike rate: (career 81.46)
Parents: John and Beryl
Wife: Judith
Children: Jack Thomas, 23 March 1993
Family links with cricket: Brother used to play league cricket for Saltburn
Education: Saltscar Comprehensive School; Longlands College of FE
Qualifications: 1 O-level, City & Guilds passes in Public and Recreational Services
Overseas tours: NCA to Bermuda for U19 (International Youth Tournament) 1985
Cricketers particularly admired: John Emburey, David Gower
Other sports followed: Horse racing, rugby union, Middlesbrough FC, anything except motor racing
Relaxations: Reading, crosswords, horse racing, eating and drinking
Extras: Enjoyed best batting and bowling performances in the same game against Middlesex at Lord's. Released by Durham at end of 1994 season
Opinions on cricket: 'Not enough done for players once the season ends. No effort to find winter employment.'
Best batting: 76 Durham v Middlesex, Lord's 1992
Best bowling: 7-113 Durham v Middlesex, Lord's 1992

1994 Season

	M	Inns	NO	Runs	HS	Avge	100s	50s	Ct	St	O	M	Runs	Wkts	Avge	Best	5wI	10wM
Test																		
All First	1	2	0	3	3	1.50	-	-	1	-	15	2	58	0	-	-	-	-
1-day Int																		
NatWest																		
B & H																		
Sunday																		

Career Performances

	M	Inns	NO	Runs	HS	Avge	100s	50s	Ct	St	Balls	Runs	Wkts	Avge	Best	5wI	10wM
Test																	
All First	26	38	13	516	76	20.64	-	1	10	-	3177	1756	39	45.02	7-113	1	-
1-day Int																	
NatWest	2	1	0	9	9	9.00	-	-	-	-	108	83	2	41.50	2-35	-	
B & H	2	0	0	0	0	-	-	-	-	-	96	77	0	-	-	-	-
Sunday	3	2	0	12	6	6.00	-	-	1	-	150	109	1	109.00	1-35	-	

BETTS, M. M.   Durham

Name: Melvyn Morris Betts
Role: Right-hand bat,
right-arm medium-fast bowler
Born: 26 March 1975, Durham
Height: 5ft 11in **Weight:** 10st 12lbs
Nickname: Alpha
County debut: 1993
Parents: Melvyn and Shirley
Marital status: Engaged
Family links with cricket: Father and uncle
played for local club, Salmiston
Education: Fyndoune Comprehensive
Qualifications: 9 GCSEs, plus qualifications
in engineering and sports and recreational
studies
Career outside cricket: Football
Overseas tours: England U19 to Sri Lanka
1993-94
Cricketers particularly admired:
Graham Gooch, David Gower
Other sports followed: Football
Injuries: Double stress fracture, missed nine months
Relaxations: Football
Extras: Played for England U19 in home series against India in 1994
Opinions on cricket: 'I think that it is getting harder for bowlers due to the reduction in
the seam on the cricket ball and now the one-bouncer-per-over rule.'
Best batting: 4 Durham v Somerset, Hartlepool 1993
Best bowling: 1-19 Durham v Somerset, Hartlepool 1993

Career Performances

	M	Inns	NO	Runs	HS	Avge	100s	50s	Ct	St	Balls	Runs	Wkts	Avge	Best	5wI	10wM
Test																	
All First	1	2	1	4	4	4.00	-	-	-	-	36	19	1	19.00	1-19	-	-
1-day Int																	
NatWest																	
B & H																	
Sunday																	

BEVAN, M. G. Yorkshire

Name: Michael Gwyl Bevan
Role: Left-hand bat, slow left-arm bowler
Born: 8 May 1970, Canberra, Australia
County debut: No first team appearance
1st-Class 50s: 19
1st-Class 100s: 15
1st-Class 200s: 1
1st-Class catches: 28
Strike rate: (career 155.00)
Marital status: Single
Education: Australian Cricket Academy
Off-season: Playing for New South Wales and Australia
Overseas teams played for: South Australia 1989-90, New South Wales 1990-95
Overseas tours: Australia to Sharjah 1994, to Pakistan 1994-95
Extras: In 1990-91 he became the first player to score a century in five successive Sheffield Shield matches. Made 82 on his Test debut against Pakistan in Karachi, 1994-95. Played for Rawtenstall in the Lancashire League in 1993 and 1994
Best batting: 203* New South Wales v Western Australia, Sydney 1993-94
Best bowling: 3-6 New South Wales v Wellington, North Sydney 1990-91

1994 Season (did not make any first-class or one-day appearance)

Career Performances

	M	Inns	NO	Runs	HS	Avge	100s	50s	Ct	St	Balls	Runs	Wkts	Avge	Best	5wI	10wM
Test																	
All First	54	91	16	4041	203 *	53.88	15	19	28	-	1395	762	9	84.66	3-6	-	-
1-day Int	3	2	1	64	39 *	64.00	-	-	2	-							
NatWest																	
B & H																	
Sunday																	

BICKNELL, D. J.   Surrey

Name: Darren John Bicknell
Role: Left-hand opening bat,
left-arm medium bowler, gully fielder
Born: 24 June 1967, Guildford
Height: 6ft 5in **Weight:** 13st 7lbs
Nickname: Denzil
County debut: 1987
County cap: 1990
1000 runs in a season: 6
1st-Class 50s: 51
1st-Class 100s: 24
1st-Class 200s: 1
1st-Class catches: 60
One-Day 100s: 6
Place in batting averages: 15th av. 52.07
(1993 38th av. 42.97)
Parents: Vic and Valerie
Wife and date of marriage: Rebecca,
26 September 1992
Children: Lauren, 21 October 1993
Family links with cricket: Brother Martin plays for Surrey; younger brother Stuart is assistant groundsman at Guildford; father is a qualified umpire
Education: Robert Haining County Secondary; Guildford County College of Technology
Qualifications: 2 O-levels, 7 CSEs, City & Guilds qualification in Recreation Administration and Sports Studies, coaching award
Career outside cricket: Coach
Off-season: 'Working as a coach in the Ken Barrington Centre (Oval indoor school)'
Overseas tours: Surrey to Sharjah 1988, 1989, to Dubai 1990; England A to Zimbabwe and Kenya 1989-90, to Pakistan 1990-91, to Bermuda and West Indies 1991-92
Overseas teams played for: Coburg, Melbourne 1986-87

Cricketers particularly admired: Waqar Younis, Graham Gooch, Carl Hooper, Mark Waugh and Tony Murphy

Other sports followed: Football ('follow the fortunes of West Ham, used to follow Aldershot'), golf

Relaxations: Eating out and participating in many sports including golf and snooker

Extras: Shared county record third-wicket stand of 413 with David Ward v Kent at Canterbury in 1990 – both made career bests

Opinions on cricket: 'Players should be treated as individuals and not as school children. More should be done to help players during the winter months.'

Best batting: 235* Surrey v Nottinghamshire, Trent Bridge 1994

Best bowling: 2-62 Surrey v Northamptonshire, Northampton 1991

1994 Season

	M	Inns	NO	Runs	HS	Avge	100s	50s	Ct	St	O	M	Runs	Wkts	Avge	Best	5wI	10wM
Test																		
All First	18	30	4	1354	235 *	52.07	3	7	4	-	1	0	1	0	-	-	-	-
1-day Int																		
NatWest	4	4	1	186	89	62.00	-	2	-	-								
B & H	4	4	0	246	109	61.50	1	1	-	-								
Sunday	12	12	3	459	95 *	51.00	-	4	3	-								

Career Performances

	M	Inns	NO	Runs	HS	Avge	100s	50s	Ct	St	Balls	Runs	Wkts	Avge	Best	5wI	10wM
Test																	
All First	159	278	28	10136	235 *	40.54	24	51	60	-	267	287	3	95.66	2-62	-	-
1-day Int																	
NatWest	16	16	3	596	135 *	45.84	1	3	1	-							
B & H	24	24	1	1028	119	44.69	2	8	6	-							
Sunday	67	64	8	2011	125	35.91	3	11	13	-							

BICKNELL, M. P.   Surrey

Name: Martin Paul Bicknell
Role: Right-hand bat, right-arm
fast-medium bowler
Born: 14 January 1969, Guildford
Height: 6ft 4in **Weight:** 15st
Nickname: Bickers
County debut: 1986
County cap: 1989
Test debut: 1993
Tests: 2
One-Day Internationals: 7
50 wickets in a season: 5
1st-Class 50s: 6
1st-Class 5 w. in innings: 20
1st-Class 10 w. in match: 2
1st-Class catches: 52
Place in batting averages: 235th av. 15.55
(1993 162nd av. 23.41)
Place in bowling averages: 88th av. 33.68 (1993 6th av. 20.01)
Strike rate: 66.13 (career 56.27)
Parents: Vic and Valerie
Marital status: Engaged
Family links with cricket: All play to varying standards, brother Darren plays for Surrey, younger brother Stuart is assistant groundsman at Guildford, father umpires
Education: Robert Haining County Secondary
Qualifications: 2 O-levels, 5 CSEs, NCA coach
Off-season: Working – getting fit
Overseas tours: England YC to Sri Lanka 1986-87, to Australia 1987-88; England A to Zimbabwe and Kenya 1989-90, to Bermuda and West Indies 1991-92, to South Africa 1993-94; England to Australia 1990-91
Cricketers particularly admired: Richard Hadlee, Dennis Lillee, Ian Botham
Other sports followed: 'Leeds United, and generally most sports'
Injuries: Stress fracture of right foot. Dislocated shoulder. Missed three months in middle of season
Relaxations: Playing golf
Extras: Youngest player to play for Surrey since David Smith. His figures of 9 for 45 were the best for the county for 30 years. One of four players on stand-by as reserves for England's World Cup squad 1991-92. Supporters' Player of the Year 1993. Had to return home early from England A tour to South Africa through injury
Opinions on cricket: 'It's still a batsman's game.'
Best batting: 88 Surrey v Hampshire, Southampton 1992
Best bowling: 9-45 Surrey v Cambridge University, Fenner's 1988

1994 Season

	M	Inns	NO	Runs	HS	Avge	100s	50s	Ct	St	O	M	Runs	Wkts	Avge	Best	5wl	10wM
Test																		
All First	9	11	2	140	41	15.55	-	-	5	-	319.4	75	977	29	33.68	5-44	1	-
1-day Int																		
NatWest	2	2	0	9	7	4.50	-	-	1	-	22	2	110	1	110.00	1-48	-	
B & H	3	1	1	2	2 *	-	-	-	-	-	32.2	4	117	6	19.50	4-49	-	
Sunday	10	4	0	22	9	5.50	-	-	4	-	75	6	358	15	23.86	5-12	1	

Career Performances

	M	Inns	NO	Runs	HS	Avge	100s	50s	Ct	St	Balls	Runs	Wkts	Avge	Best	5wl	10wM
Test	2	4	0	26	14	6.50	-	-	-	-	522	263	4	65.75	3-99	-	-
All First	141	165	45	2128	88	17.73	-	6	52	-	26956	12620	479	26.34	9-45	20	2
1-day Int	7	6	2	96	31 *	24.00	-	-	2	-	413	347	13	26.69	3-55	-	
NatWest	23	12	5	102	66 *	14.57	-	1	10	-	1455	816	31	26.32	4-35	-	
B & H	28	17	3	117	27 *	8.35	-	-	8	-	1692	1075	45	23.88	4-49	-	
Sunday	96	38	18	245	20 *	12.25	-	-	26	-	4183	2927	118	24.80	5-12	1	

BIRBECK, S. D   Durham

Name: Shaun Birbeck
Role: Left-hand bat, right-arm medium bowler
Born: 22 July 1972, Sunderland
Height: 5ft 11in **Weight:** 14st
County debut: 1994
1st-Class catches: 1
Parents: James and Joyce
Marital status: Single
Family links with cricket:
Brother Tony played Minor Counties cricket for Durham
Education: Hetton Comprehensive
Qualifications: GCSEs
Off-season: Playing in Western Australia
Overseas teams played for: Scarborough, Perth, Western Australia 1992-94
Cricketers particularly admired:
Jimmy Adams
Other sports followed: Football (Sunderland),golf, tennis, 'any sport'
Relaxations: Reading and listening to music
Extras: Captained Durham U19 1992

Best batting: 6 Durham v Oxford University, The Parks 1994

1994 Season

	M	Inns	NO	Runs	HS	Avge	100s	50s	Ct	St	O	M	Runs	Wkts	Avge	Best	5wI	10wM
Test																		
All First	1	1	0	6	6	6.00	-	-	1	-	7	2	13	2	6.50	2-13	-	-
1-day Int																		
NatWest																			
B & H																			
Sunday	5	2	0	9	9	4.50	-	-	1	-	26	0	166	1	166.00	1-47	-	

Career Performances

	M	Inns	NO	Runs	HS	Avge	100s	50s	Ct	St	Balls	Runs	Wkts	Avge	Best	5wI	10wM
Test																	
All First	1	1	0	6	6	6.00	-	-	1	-	42	13	2	6.50	2-13	-	-
1-day Int																	
NatWest																		
B & H																		
Sunday	5	2	0	9	9	4.50	-	-	1	-	156	166	1	166.00	1-47	-	

BIRD, P. J.   Somerset

Name: Paul James Bird
Role: Right-hand bat,
right-arm fast-medium bowler
Born: 7 May 1971, Bristol
Height: 6ft 3in **Weight:** 14st
Nickname: Harold, Kerby, Brian
County debut: 1994
Parents: Garry and Elizabeth
Marital status: Single
Family links with cricket: Father is
Vice-Chairman of Claverham Cricket Club
Education: Backwell Comprehensive, Bristol
Qualifications: 8 O-levels
Off-season: Playing in Melbourne
Overseas teams played for: McKinnon CC,
Melbourne 1993-95
Cricketers particularly admired:
Andrew 'Goochie' Payne, Richard Hadlee,
Viv Richards, Richard Cook
Other sports followed: Football (Bristol City), tennis, boxing

Injuries: Side injury, missed 3 weeks
Relaxations: Socialising with friends, spending time in St Ives, Cornwall. Eating out and keeping fit
Extras: Played in winning Optimists side at Lord's 1992 in National Cricket Association Knockout competition
Opinions on cricket: 'More 2nd XI games should be played on first-class grounds.'
Best batting: 7 Somerset v Nottinghamshire, Taunton 1994

1994 Season

	M	Inns	NO	Runs	HS	Avge	100s	50s	Ct	St	O	M	Runs	Wkts	Avge	Best	5wI	10wM
Test																		
All First	2	3	1	12	7	6.00	-	-	-	-	44.5	9	166	0	-		-	-
1-day Int																		
NatWest																		
B & H																		
Sunday	5	1	0	4	4	4.00	-	-	2	-	28	1	129	3	43.00	1-18	-	

Career Performances

	M	Inns	NO	Runs	HS	Avge	100s	50s	Ct	St	Balls	Runs	Wkts	Avge	Best	5wI	10wM
Test																	
All First	2	3	1	12	7	6.00	-	-	-	-	269	166	0	-		-	-
1-day Int																	
NatWest																	
B & H																	
Sunday	5	1	0	4	4	4.00	-	-	2	-	168	129	3	43.00	1-18	-	

7. Which Australian opening batsman and former Test player retired from first-class cricket in 1994 at the age of 35?

BLAKEY, R. J.   Yorkshire

Name: Richard John Blakey
Role: Right-hand bat, wicket-keeper
Born: 15 January 1967, Huddersfield
Height: 5ft 10in **Weight:** 11st 4lbs
Nickname: Dick
County debut: 1985
County cap: 1987
Test debut: 1992-93
Tests: 2
One-Day Internationals: 3
1000 runs in a season: 4
1st-Class 50s: 55
1st-Class 100s: 9
1st-Class 200s: 2
1st-Class catches: 361
1st-Class stumpings: 34
One-Day 100s: 3
Place in batting averages: 32nd av. 45.77
(1993 118th av. 28.63)

Parents: Brian and Pauline
Wife and date of marriage: Michelle, 28 September 1991
Children: Harrison Brad, 22 September 1993
Family links with cricket: Father played local cricket
Education: Woodhouse Primary; Rastrick Grammar School
Qualifications: 4 O-levels, Senior NCA Coach
Career outside cricket: Started own leisure company
Off season: Working on business. Coaching in primary schools. Spending time at home
Overseas tours: England YC to West Indies 1984-85; Yorkshire to Barbados 1986-87, to Cape Town 1990-91; England A to Zimbabwe and Kenya 1989-90, to Pakistan 1990-91; England to India and Sri Lanka 1992-93
Overseas teams played for: Waverley, Sydney 1985-87; Mt Waverley, Sydney 1987-88; Bionics, Zimbabwe 1989-90
Cricketers particularly admired: Martyn Moxon, Dermot Reeve, Ian Botham, Alan Knott
Other sports followed: All
Relaxations: All sports, particularly golf and squash, eating out, drawing, photography
Extras: Established himself in Huddersfield League. Made record 2nd XI score – 273* v Northamptonshire 1986. Yorkshire's Young Player of the Year 1989. Made Test debut in second Test against India at Madras, February 1993
Opinions on cricket: 'Four-day game is much more enjoyable and the best team wins. Back to 40 overs on Sundays – better for players and spectators alike. National anthem should be played before the start of every international, like football.'

Best batting: 221 England A v Zimbabwe, Bulawayo 1989-90
Best bowling: 1-68 Yorkshire v Nottinghamshire, Sheffield 1986

1994 Season

	M	Inns	NO	Runs	HS	Avge	100s	50s	Ct	St	O	M	Runs	Wkts	Avge	Best	5wI	10wM
Test																		
All First	20	36	9	1236	94 *	45.77	-	11	65	4								
1-day Int																		
NatWest	2	2	0	31	18	15.50	-	-	2	-								
B & H	1	1	0	40	40	40.00	-	-	2	-								
Sunday	16	15	2	314	55 *	24.15	-	1	15	2								

Career Performances

	M	Inns	NO	Runs	HS	Avge	100s	50s	Ct	St	Balls	Runs	Wkts	Avge	Best	5wI	10wM
Test	2	4	0	7	6	1.75	-	-	2	-							
All First	199	327	47	9407	221	33.59	9	55	361	34	63	68	1	68.00	1-68	-	-
1-day Int	3	2	0	25	25	12.50	-	-	2	1							
NatWest	17	13	2	276	75	25.09	-	2	20	1							
B & H	30	27	3	695	79	28.95	-	5	26	-							
Sunday	100	96	16	3255	130 *	40.68	3	20	75	13							

BLENKIRON, D. A.   Durham

Name: Darren Andrew Blenkiron
Role: Left-hand bat, right-arm
medium bowler
Born: 4 February 1974, Solihull
Height: 5ft 10in **Weight:** 12st 7lbs
County debut: 1991 (one-day),
1994 (first-class)
Parents: William and Margaret
Marital status: Single
Family links with cricket: Father played
for Warwickshire and MCC
Education: Bishop Barrington
Comprehensive School
Qualifications: 4 O-Levels
Career outside cricket: Helping in father's
sports shop
Off-season: Hopes to play cricket abroad
Overseas tours:
England U19 to Pakistan 1991-92

Cricketers particularly admired: Ian Botham, Graeme Hick, David Gower
Other sports followed: Football, golf
Relaxations: Music, socialising
Opinions on cricket: 'I agree with four-day cricket.'

1994 Season

	M	Inns	NO	Runs	HS	Avge	100s	50s	Ct	St	O	M	Runs	Wkts	Avge	Best	5wl	10wM
Test																		
All First	1	0	0	0	0	-	-	-	-	-								
1-day Int																		
NatWest																		
B & H																		
Sunday	1	1	1	39	39 *	-	-	-	-	-	3	0	25	0	-		-	-

Career Performances

	M	Inns	NO	Runs	HS	Avge	100s	50s	Ct	St	Balls	Runs	Wkts	Avge	Best	5wl	10wM
Test																	
All First	1	0	0	0	0	-	-	-	-	-							
1-day Int																	
NatWest	1	1	0	56	56	56.00	-	1	-	-							
B & H																	
Sunday	2	1	1	39	39 *	-	-	-	-	-	18	25	0	-		-	-

8. Which former England Test captain will succeed Prince Edward as President of the Lord's Taverners?

BODEN, D. J. P.   Gloucestershire

Name: David Jonathan Peter Boden
Role: Right-hand bat, right-arm fast bowler
Born: 26 November 1970, Eccleshall, Staffs
Height: 6ft 3in **Weight:** 14st 7lbs
Nickname: Horse
County debut: 1989 (Middlesex),
1992 (Essex)
1st-Class catches: 2
Parents: Peter and Mary
Marital status: Single
Family links with cricket: 'Dad is an avid
follower of the game and ferried me
everywhere when I was younger'
Education: Stone Alleynes High School;
Stafford College of Further Education
Qualifications: 3 CSEs, 6 O-levels, BTEC
National Diploma in Business
Studies, NCA coaching certificate,
Senior NCA Coach

Off-season: Playing cricket in Australia for Waverley CC, Sydney
Overseas teams played for: Waverley, Sydney 1990-93
Cricketers particularly admired: Ian Botham, Don Topley
Other sports followed: Tiddlywinks, rugby, golf
Relaxations: Playing golf, sunbathing and talking to women on Bondi Beach. Listening
to Replacements, Pink Floyd and Cold Chisel. Reading any of Les Norton's books
Extras: Staffordshire Wellington Boot Throwing Champion. Signed by Gloucestershire
for 1995 season after spells with both Middlesex and Essex
Best batting: 5 Essex v Cambridge University, Fenner's 1992. 5 Essex v Middlesex,
Colchester 1993
Best bowling: 4-11 Middlesex v Oxford University, The Parks 1989

1994 Season (did not make any first-class or one-day appearance)

Career Performances

	M	Inns	NO	Runs	HS	Avge	100s	50s	Ct	St	Balls	Runs	Wkts	Avge	Best	5wl	10wM
Test																	
All First	4	3	0	10	5	3.33	-	-	2	-	425	284	7	40.57	4-11	-	-
1-day Int																	
NatWest																	
B & H																	
Sunday	4	2	0	4	2	2.00	-	-	2	-	204	162	4	40.50	2-48	-	

BOILING, J.   Durham

Name: James Boiling
Role: Right-hand bat, right-arm off-spin
bowler, dependable nightwatchman
Born: 8 April 1968, New Delhi
Height: 6ft 2in **Weight:** 13st
Nickname: Charlie 'from the Alec Guinness
character in *Kind Hearts and Coronets*'
County debut: 1988 (Surrey)
1st-Class 5 w. in innings: 2
1st-Class 10 w. in match: 1
1st-Class catches: 38
One-Day 5 w. in innings: 1
Place in batting averages:
(1993 247th av. 12.50)
Place in bowling averages:
(1993 147th av. 60.81)
Strike rate: (career 91.77)
Parents: Graham and Geraldine
Marital status: Engaged

Family links with cricket: 'Father once sat opposite Tony Lewis on a train. Younger
brother a willing and able back-garden bowler'
Education: Rutlish School, Merton; Durham University (College of St. Hild and Bede)
Qualifications: 10 O-levels, 3 A-levels, BA (Hons) in History, NCA Senior Coaching
Award. Currently studying Fabric and Textile Design at night school
Career outside cricket: 'I intend eventually to have my own label of designer cricket
clothing – JB Sports ©.'
Off-season: 'Working for Lloyd's Bank Treasury Division in an advisory capacity
and helping out at weekends on my Uncle Sam's fruit and veg stall.'
Overseas tours: Surrey Schools to Australia 1985-86; England YC to Australia (Youth
World Cup) 1987-88; England A to Australia 1992-93
Overseas teams played for: Bionics, Harare 1991-92; St Augustine, Cape Town 1992-93
Cricketers particularly admired: Carl Hooper, Tim May, Graham Thorpe, Neil Smith,
Tony 'the bionic man' Pigott
Other sports followed: Rugby league and union, baseball, swimming, diving (especially
men's 3m board), Gladiators
Injuries: Broken thumb 'courtesy of Waim Akram', missed four weeks
Relaxations: 'Anything that takes my mind off cricket. At the moment I am learning to
play bridge and my fiancée and I enjoy many pleasant evenings around the card table.'
Extras: Believed to be the only player to win a Gold Award against his own county,
returning 8-3-9-3 analysis for Combined Universities against Surrey in 1989. Late call-up
for England A tour to Australia when Ian Salisbury stayed in India. Moved to Durham for
1995 season

Opinions on cricket: 'The English game is in need of a radical overhaul: 1) There are too many professionals trying to have their cake and eat it. Each county should have a playing staff of 12 with a colts or U19 team to provide the back up, alternatively, there should be no more than eight teams. To achieve this, two counties could be amalgamated, e.g. Surrey and Middlesex, Lancashire and Yorkshire, Warwickshire and Worcestershire. This would lead to a manageable number of paid county cricketers and would ensure a better salary for all without reducing levels of interest in the county game. 2) Groundsmen should be employed by the TCCB and not the counties. This would alleviate the pressure on them to produce "result" pitches and would surely lead to the abolition of the ludicrous 25-point penalty system. I am sure that groundsmen would feel happier knowing that they were working for a caring employer. 3) Scrap the Sunday League and have benefit matches instead on Sundays. This would improve the standard of Sunday play. 4) Introduce a new one-day competition – a six-a-side knockout competition to be played during September. This would provide counties with something extra to play for when the season is traditionally dead. Prize money to come from over-rate fines during the season. 5) Encourage sponsors to get more involved in the running of county clubs. Most counties' administrative and bureaucratic infrastructures are primitive compared to the large multinationals. Consultants should be hired on 6-month winter contracts to improve the state of the game's finances. 6) Spectators should be allowed in free – gate receipts are infinitesimal compared to revenue from corporate hospitality. 7) Players should be on 12-month contracts, or should be amateurs with jobs outside cricket – perhaps in a promotional capacity for a large company. 8) Umpires should be enlisted to help select the Test team. 9) The season should start in May and finish in August to sustain interest. 10) Humorous banter between players should be allowed. 11) Geoff Boycott should be appointed supremo of English cricket with Ian Botham as his second-in-command.'

Best batting: 34* Surrey v Durham, Darlington 1994
Best bowling: 6-84 Surrey v Gloucestershire, Bristol 1992

1994 Season

	M	Inns	NO	Runs	HS	Avge	100s	50s	Ct	St	O	M	Runs	Wkts	Avge	Best	5wI	10wM
Test																		
All First	6	6	2	75	34 *	18.75	-	-	7	-	107	33	237	6	39.50	2-38	-	-
1-day Int																		
NatWest	4	2	1	29	24	29.00	-	-	1	-	29	1	109	1	109.00	1-23	-	
B & H	2	1	1	9	9 *	-	-	-	-	-	22	1	79	1	79.00	1-42	-	
Sunday	14	6	3	52	16 *	17.33	-	-	7	-	89	2	482	15	32.13	3-27	-	

Career Performances

	M	Inns	NO	Runs	HS	Avge	100s	50s	Ct	St	Balls	Runs	Wkts	Avge	Best	5wI	10wM
Test																	
All First	45	56	23	434	34 *	13.15	-	-	38	-	7617	3424	83	41.25	6-84	2	1
1-day Int																	
NatWest	12	5	1	60	24	15.00	-	-	6	-	750	389	9	43.22	2-22	-	
B & H	25	15	10	58	9 *	11.60	-	-	12	-	1432	983	22	44.68	3-9	-	
Sunday	57	24	11	127	23 *	9.76	-	-	18	-	2434	1880	66	28.48	5-24	1	

BOON, T. J. Leicestershire

Name: Timothy James Boon
Role: Right-hand bat, right-arm medium bowler
Born: 1 November 1961, Doncaster
Height: 6ft **Weight:** 12st 7lbs
Nickname: Boony, Ted
County debut: 1980
County cap: 1986
1000 runs in a season: 7
1st-Class 50s: 68
1st-Class 100s: 14
1st-Class catches: 119
One-Day 100s: 3
Place in batting averages: 176th av. 23.30
(1993 95th av. 32.89)
Parents: Jeffrey and Elizabeth
Marital status: Single
Family links with cricket: Father played
club cricket

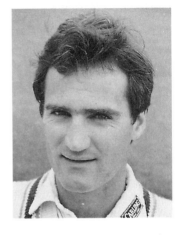

Education: Mill Lane Primary; Edlington Comprehensive; three months at Doncaster Art School; Peter Van School of Business
Qualifications: 6 O-levels, 1 A-level, advanced coach
Career outside cricket: Selling, owning a fitness studio, renovating property
Overseas tours: England YC to West Indies 1980-81;
Leicestershire to Zimbabwe 1980-81
Overseas teams played for: Old Hararians, Zimbabwe 1980;
Pirates, Pinetown, Natal 1990-91
Cricketers particularly admired: 'All those who have made it into international cricket, all those who have given me assistance (such as Chris Balderstone, Ken Higgs, Bob Simpson, Jackie Birkenshaw and many more)'
Other sports followed: Leicester Tigers (rugby union) and Leicester City FC
Relaxations: Keeping fit at the University, following local sport, 'producing zany ideas'
Extras: Captain England YC v West Indies 1980 and v India 1981; missed 1985 season due to broken leg sustained in a car crash in South Africa the previous winter. 'Would dearly love to play in a Leicestershire Championship-winning side'
Opinions on cricket: 'More direction should be given to young cricketers off-season by providing assistance with winter/future employment.'
Best batting: 144 Leicestershire v Gloucestershire, Leicester 1984
Best bowling: 3-40 Leicestershire v Yorkshire, Leicester 1986

1994 Season

	M	Inns	NO	Runs	HS	Avge	100s	50s	Ct	St	O	M	Runs	Wkts	Avge	Best	5wI	10wM
Test																		
All First	16	28	2	606	74	23.30	-	4	5	-								
1-day Int																		
NatWest	1	1	0	55	55	55.00	-	1	-	-								
B & H	1	1	1	19	19 *	-	-	-	-	-								
Sunday	1	0	0	0	0	-	-	-	-	-								

Career Performances

	M	Inns	NO	Runs	HS	Avge	100s	50s	Ct	St	Balls	Runs	Wkts	Avge	Best	5wI	10wM
Test																	
All First	242	407	42	11644	144	31.90	14	68	119	-	667	563	11	51.18	3-40	-	-
1-day Int																	
NatWest	19	17	4	498	117	38.30	1	2	8	-	6	2	0	-	-	-	-
B & H	33	30	7	812	103	35.30	1	5	9	-							
Sunday	115	102	11	2175	135 *	23.90	1	9	25	-	42	55	1	55.00	1-23	-	

BOSWELL, S. A. J.　　　　Northamptonshire

Name: Scott Antony John Boswell
Role: Right-hand bat, right-hand fast-medium bowler
Born: 11 September 1974, York
Height: 6ft 4in **Weight:** 14st 2lbs
Nickname: Joey, Bogan
County debut: No first-team appearance
Parents: Tony and Judy
Marital status: Single
Education: Pocklington School
Qualifications: 9 GCSEs, 3 A-levels
Career outside cricket: Hopefully going to study Sport Studies at Wolverhampton University
Off-season: Touring New Zealand on a scholarship from Northants for six months
Overseas teams played for: Hutt Valley, New Zealand 1994-95
Cricketers particularly admired: Dennis Lillee and Richard Hadlee
Other sports followed: Football, rugby union
Injuries: Shin splints, missed three weeks

Relaxations: Listening to music, socialising and spending time with girlfriend and family
Opinions on cricket: 'Overseas players should be allowed in the county championship because they are essential for younger players like myself, to learn from and to play with and against. Also for the crowds to be able to watch top international players perform.'

BOTHAM, L. J.   Hampshire

Name: Liam James Botham
Role: Right-hand bat, right-arm fast bowler
Born: 26 August 1977, Doncaster
Height: 6ft
Nickname: Limo
County debut: No first-team appearance
Parents: Ian and Kathy
Marital status: Single
Family links with cricket: 'Father played a bit!'
Education: Cundall Manor Prep School; Rossall School
Off-season: School doing A-levels
Overseas tours: Rossall School to Australia 1994-95
Others sports followed: Rugby
Relaxations: Fishing, shooting, rugby
Extras: Played for England U17 v India U17 in 1994. Plays rugby for Lancashire U18.
Appeared on *Beadle's About*, as the victim of a practical joke set up by his father

---

BOVILL, J. N. B.   Hampshire

Name: James Noel Bruce Bovill
Role: Right-hand bat, r ight-arm fast-medium bowler
Born: 2 June 1971, High Wycombe
Height: 6ft **Weight:** 12st 8lbs
Nickname: Jimmer, Ned, Chopsy
County debut: 1993
1st-Class 5 w. in innings: 1
1st-Class catches: 1
Place in bowling averages: 60th av. 30.07
Strike rate: 51.28 (career 49.29)
Parents: Mike and Anne

Marital status: Single
Family links with cricket: Father played for Dorset and captained Basingstoke
Education: Sandroyd Preparatory School; Charterhouse; Durham University
Qualifications: 8 O-levels, 3 A-levels, BA (Hons) in Combined Social Sciences
Off-season: Playing and coaching in Cape Town, South Africa
Overseas tours: Hampshire Maniacs to Guernsey and Jersey 1989; Bucks to Zimbabwe 1991-92; Durham University to South Africa 1991-92
Overseas teams played for: Western Province, South Africa 1989-90
Cricketers particularly admired:
Wayne Larkins, Allan Donald, Rupert Cox, Martin Jean-Jaques, Reg Peacock
Other sports followed: Rugby, soccer, kabaddi

Injuries: Stress fracture of left foot, missed July and August
Relaxations: 'Watching Gregor Macmillan bat. Stitching up Giles "Chalky" White, yachting'
Extras: Member of the Durham University team that won the indoor six-a-side club championship at Lord's, March 1993. Organised University tour to South Africa 1991-92. Played for Buckinghamshire 1990-92 and for Combined Universities in the B&H Cup in 1992. Holds school U14 javelin record
Opinions on cricket: 'A Combined Universities side should replace Oxford/Cambridge in first-class cricket.'
Best batting: 10 Hampshire v Glamorgan, Southampton 1994
Best bowling: 5-108 Hampshire v Leicestershire, Leicester 1994

1994 Season

	M	Inns	NO	Runs	HS	Avge	100s	50s	Ct	St	O	M	Runs	Wkts	Avge	Best	5wI	10wM
Test																		
All First	6	9	5	35	10	8.75	-	-	1	-	119.4	23	421	14	30.07	5-108	1	-
1-day Int																		
NatWest																		
B & H	1	0	0	0	0	-	-	-	-	-	11	1	21	2	10.50	2-21	-	
Sunday	4	1	0	1	1	1.00	-	-	-	-	27.3	2	117	2	58.50	2-25	-	

Career Performances

	M	Inns	NO	Runs	HS	Avge	100s	50s	Ct	St	Balls	Runs	Wkts	Avge	Best	5wl	10wM
Test																	
All First	7	11	7	38	10	9.50	-	-	1	-	838	469	17	27.58	5-108	1	-
1-day Int																	
NatWest																	
B & H	5	1	1	14	14 *	-	-	-	1	-	276	162	4	40.50	2-21	-	
Sunday	6	3	1	8	7 *	4.00	-	-	-	-	267	212	5	42.40	3-40	-	

BOWEN, M. N.   Northamptonshire

Name: Mark Nicholas Bowen
Role: Right-hand bat, right-arm medium bowler
Born: 6 December 1967, Redcar
Height: 6ft 1in **Weight:** 13st
Nickname: Jim ('or anything relating to Jim Bowen's *Bullseye*')
County debut: 1991-92
1st-Class catches: 3
Place in bowling averages: (1993 31st av. 25.18)
Strike rate: (career 65.80)
Parents: Keith
Marital status: Single
Family links with cricket: Father has always played club cricket
Education: Sacred Heart Secondary School, Redcar; St Mary's Sixth Form College, Middlesbrough; Teesside Polytechnic
Qualifications: 8 O-levels, 3 A-levels, BSc (Hons) in Chemical Engineering
Career outside cricket: Technical support engineer and commissioning engineer in nuclear industry
Off-season: Christians in Sport tour to Zimbabwe. Working at Sellafield as a technical support engineer for British Nuclear Fuels
Overseas tours: Northamptonshire to Durban 1992, to Cape Town 1993; Christians in Sport to Zimbabwe 1994-95
Cricketers particularly admired: Richard Hadlee, Dennis Lillee, Ian Botham
Other sports followed: Rugby union, football (Middlesbrough FC)
Relaxations: Keeping fit, playing golf, and good ale
Extras: Made debut for Northants first team in Natal on 1991-92 tour to South Africa before playing in the 2nd XI

Opinions on cricket: 'Four-day cricket is producing good contests, testing the strength in depth of teams and squads. The balance between bat and ball, however, still needs to be struck as far as pitches are concerned. Surfaces used for 2nd XI fixtures should be closer to those used in first-class games.'

Best batting: 23* Northamptonshire v Durham, Northampton 1993
Best bowling: 4-124 Northamptonshire v Kent, Canterbury 1993

1994 Season

	M	Inns	NO	Runs	HS	Avge	100s	50s	Ct	St	O	M	Runs	Wkts	Avge	Best	5wI	10wM
Test																		
All First	5	5	0	18	13	3.60	-	-	2	-	113.1	21	395	6	65.83	2-90	-	-
1-day Int																		
NatWest																		
B & H	1	1	0	0	0	0.00	-	-	-	-	10	1	39	1	39.00	1-39	-	
Sunday	8	5	4	49	27 *	49.00	-	-	-	-	43	0	256	3	85.33	1-28	-	

Career Performances

	M	Inns	NO	Runs	HS	Avge	100s	50s	Ct	St	Balls	Runs	Wkts	Avge	Best	5wI	10wM
Test																	
All First	13	14	4	116	23 *	11.60	-	-	3	-	1974	1196	30	39.86	4-124	-	-
1-day Int																	
NatWest																	
B & H	1	1	0	0	0	0.00	-	-	-	-	60	39	1	39.00	1-39	-	
Sunday	16	8	4	79	27 *	19.75	-	-	-	-	612	500	11	45.45	3-35	-	

BOWLER, P. D.   Somerset

Name: Peter Duncan Bowler
Role: Right-hand opening bat,
occasional off-spin bowler, wicket-keeper
Born: 30 July 1963, Plymouth
Height: 6ft 1in **Weight:** 13st
Nickname: Croc
County debut: 1986 (Leicestershire),
1988 (Derbyshire)
County cap: 1989 (Derbyshire)
1000 runs in a season: 6
1st-Class 50s: 58
1st-Class 100s: 20
1st-Class 200s: 2
1st-Class catches: 106
1st-Class stumpings: 1
One-Day 100s: 5
Place in batting averages: 174th av. 23.73
(1993 36th av. 43.19)
Parents: Peter and Etta
Wife and date of marriage: Joanne, 10 October 1992
Children: Peter Robert, 21 September 1993
Education: Daramalan College, Canberra, Australia
Qualifications: Australian Year 12 certificate
Career outside cricket: Has worked for BBC Radio as a sports journalist on occasions
Cricketers particularly admired: Gus Valence, Rob Jeffery
Other sports followed: Rugby union, football
Relaxations: Spending time with the family, reading, gardening, decorating
Extras: First Leicestershire player to score a first-class century on debut (100* v Hampshire 1986). Moved to Derbyshire at end of 1987 season and scored a hundred on his debut v Cambridge University in 1988. First batsman to 2000 runs in 1992, finishing equal leading run-scorer (2044) with Mike Roseberry of Middlesex. Derbyshire Player of the Year 1992. Signed a five-year contract with Somerset starting in 1995
Opinions on cricket: 'Traditional attire for all competitions please!'
Best batting: 241* Derbyshire v Hampshire, Portsmouth 1992
Best bowling: 3-41 Derbyshire v Leicestershire, Leicester 1991

---

9. How were Pakistan's winning runs scored in their one-wicket win over Australia in the First Test at Karachi in October 1994?

1994 Season

	M	Inns	NO	Runs	HS	Avge	100s	50s	Ct	St	O	M	Runs	Wkts	Avge	Best	5wI	10wM
Test																		
All First	13	23	0	546	88	23.73	-	2	11	-	1	0	17	0	-	-	-	-
1-day Int																		
NatWest	1	1	0	9	9	9.00	-	-	1	-								
B & H	2	2	0	15	15	7.50	-	-	-	-								
Sunday	12	11	1	354	67	35.40	-	4	2	-								

Career Performances

	M	Inns	NO	Runs	HS	Avge	100s	50s	Ct	St	Balls	Runs	Wkts	Avge	Best	5wI	10wM
Test																	
All First	158	275	25	9925	241 *	39.70	20	58	106	1	2409	1511	20	75.55	3-41	-	-
1-day Int																	
NatWest	12	12	0	286	111	23.83	1	1	6	-	36	26	0	-	-	-
B & H	30	29	1	962	109	34.35	2	7	16	1	246	125	4	31.25	1-15	-
Sunday	115	111	14	3501	138 *	36.09	2	28	47	1	242	237	7	33.85	3-31	-

BRIERS, N. E. Leicestershire

Name: Nigel Edwin Briers
Role: Right-hand opening bat, right-arm
medium bowler, county captain
Born: 15 January 1955, Leicester
Height: 6ft **Weight:** 13st
Nickname: Kudu
County debut: 1971
County cap: 1981
Benefit: 1990
1000 runs in a season: 10
1st-Class 50s: 92
1st-Class 100s: 28
1st-Class 200s: 1
1st-Class catches: 151
One-Day 100s: 5
Place in batting averages:
69th av. 38.00 (1993 144th av. 27.05)
Parents: Leonard Arthur Roger and Eveline
Wife and date of marriage:
Suzanne Mary Tudor, 3 September 1977
Children: Michael Edward Tudor, 25 March 1983; Andrew James Tudor, 30 June 1986
Family links with cricket: Father was captain and wicket-keeper of Narborough and

83

Littlethorpe in the South Leicestershire League for 15 years and mother was scorer. Father was also captain of South Leicestershire Representative XI and played for the Royal Marines in the same team as Trevor Bailey. Cousin, Norman Briers, played once for Leicestershire in 1967

Education: Lutterworth Grammar School; Borough Road College of Education
Qualifications: Qualified teacher (Cert Ed), BEd (Hons), MCC advanced cricket coach
Career outside cricket: Teaching at Ludgrove School
Off-season: Teaching PE and History at Ludgrove School
Overseas tours: Derrick Robbins tour to South America 1978-79; MCC to the Far East 1980-81; Leicestershire to Zimbabwe, Holland, Jersey and Guernsey; MCC to the Virgin and Leeward Islands 1991-92
Cricketers particularly admired: Ray Illingworth, Richard Hadlee, Geoff Boycott, Barry Richards, Viv Richards
Other sports followed: Rugby (Leicester Tigers) and football (Leicester City)
Extras: Youngest player ever to appear for Leicestershire (aged 16 years 104 days). Shares county record with Roger Tolchard for highest fifth wicket stand of 233 v Somerset, 1979. Appointed county captain in 1990. Captained MCC on 1991-92 tour of the Virgin and Leeward Islands. Wombwell Cricket Lovers' Society Captain of the Year 1992. One of *Wisden*'s Five Cricketers of the Year 1993.
Best batting: 201* Leicestershire v Warwickshire, Edgbaston 1983
Best bowling: 4-29 Leicestershire v Derbyshire, Leicester 1985

1994 Season

	M	Inns	NO	Runs	HS		Avge	100s	50s	Ct	St	O	M	Runs	Wkts	Avge	Best	5wI	10wM
Test																			
All First	19	35	3	1216	154		38.00	2	5	5	-								
1-day Int																			
NatWest	2	2	0	27	25		13.50	-	-	3	-								
B & H	2	2	1	109	70	*	109.00	-	1	1	-								
Sunday	8	7	0	171	105		24.42	1	-	4	-								

Career Performances

	M	Inns	NO	Runs	HS		Avge	100s	50s	Ct	St	Balls	Runs	Wkts	Avge	Best	5wI	10wM
Test																		
All First	366	601	59	17680	201	*	32.61	28	92	151	-	2047	988	32	30.87	4-29	-	-
1-day Int																		
NatWest	37	37	2	714	88		20.40	-	2	9	-	84	75	6	12.50	2-6	-	
B & H	59	54	5	1271	102		25.93	1	7	20	-	330	266	3	88.66	1-26	-	
Sunday	218	214	24	5650	119	*	29.73	4	29	60	-	482	384	10	38.40	3-29	-	

BRIMSON, M. T.   Leicestershire

Name: Matthew Thomas Brimson
Role: Right-hand bat, slow left-arm bowler
Born: 1 December 1970, Plumstead, London
Height: 6ft **Weight:** 11st 6lbs
Nickname: Brimmo, Doogie
County debut: 1993
Parents: David and Jennifer
Wife and date of marriage:
Lyn, 29 December 1993
Family links with cricket: Brother plays club
cricket with Beckenham
Education: St Joseph's Preparatory School,
Blackheath; Chislehurst and Sidcup
Grammar School, Sidcup; Durham University
Qualifications: 8 O-levels, 3 A-levels,
BA (Hons) degree in Geography
Off-season: Working in Leicester
Overseas tours: Kent Schools U17 to
Singapore and New Zealand 1987-88;
Leicestershire to South Africa 1994

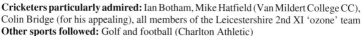

Cricketers particularly admired: Ian Botham, Mike Hatfield (Van Mildert College CC),
Colin Bridge (for his appealing), all members of the Leicestershire 2nd XI 'ozone' team
Other sports followed: Golf and football (Charlton Athletic)
Injuries: Pulled left thigh muscle, missed three weeks
Relaxations: Playing golf and tennis. Going out and relaxing with Lyn. Living in new
house. Beating Alamgir Sheriyar at snooker
Extras: Was on the Kent staff in 1991
Opinions on cricket: 'Clubs should do more to find their players winter employment
given the number of contracts they have. Every journalist in the national press appears to
be anti-Leicestershire.'
Best batting: 17* Leicestershire v Oxford University, The Parks 1994
Best bowling: 2-66 Leicestershire v Glamorgan, Leicester 1993

1994 Season

	M	Inns	NO	Runs	HS	Avge	100s	50s	Ct	St	O	M	Runs	Wkts	Avge	Best	5wI	10wM
Test																		
All First	5	9	3	45	17 *	7.50	-	-	-	-	121.1	31	347	5	69.40	1-25	-	-
1-day Int																		
NatWest																		
B & H																		
Sunday																		

Career Performances

	M	Inns	NO	Runs	HS	Avge	100s	50s	Ct	St	Balls	Runs	Wkts	Avge	Best	5wl	10wM
Test																	
All First	7	10	3	45	17 *	6.42	-	-	-	-	847	413	7	59.00	2-66	-	-
1-day Int																	
NatWest																	
B & H																	
Sunday	1	0	0	0	0	-	-	-	-	-	60	28	1	28.00	1-28	-	

BRINKLEY, J. E. Worcestershire

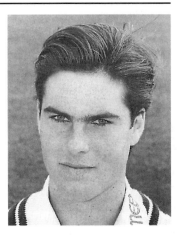

Name: James Edward Brinkley
Role: Right-hand bat, right-arm
fast-medium bowler
Born: 13 March 1974,
Helensburgh, Scotland
Height: 6ft 3in **Weight:** 13st 6lbs
Nickname: JB
County debut: 1993-94
1st-Class catches: 3
1st-Class 5 w. in innings: 1
Place in bowling averages: 130th av. 43.27
Strike rate: 77.66 (career 66.29)
Parents: Tom and Sharon
Marital status: Single
Family links with cricket: Father played
service cricket in the Royal Navy, mother
coaches junior teams in Western Australia
Education: Marist College, Canberra;
Trinity College, Perth
Qualifications: West Australian Tertiary Entrance Examinations
Career outside cricket: Advertising
Off-season: Playing A Grade cricket in Perth, Australia
Overseas teams played for: Scarborough, Perth 1990-93; Western Australian U19 1993
Cricketers particularly admired: Michael Holding, Viv Richards, Ian Botham, David
Gower
Other sports followed: Rugby union and golf
Relaxations: Golf, fitness training, music, reading, cricket
Extras: Taken a hat-trick in both the 2nd XI Championship and the Bain Clarkson Trophy,
against Surrey and Somerset respectively
Opinions on cricket: 'Wickets in 2nd XI cricket need to be quicker. Low, slow pitches are
of benefit to no one! Sunday League coloured clothing has been a success.'

Best batting: 10* Worcestershire v Invitation XI, Bulawayo 1993-94
Best bowling: 6-98 Worcestershire v Surrey, The Oval 1994

1994 Season

	M	Inns	NO	Runs	HS	Avge	100s	50s	Ct	St	O	M	Runs	Wkts	Avge	Best	5wl	10wM
Test																		
All First	10	10	2	16	5	2.00	-	-	3	-	233	40	779	18	43.27	6-98	1	-
1-day Int																		
NatWest																		
B & H																		
Sunday																		

Career Performances

	M	Inns	NO	Runs	HS	Avge	100s	50s	Ct	St	Balls	Runs	Wkts	Avge	Best	5wl	10wM
Test																	
All First	11	11	3	26	10 *	3.25	-	-	3	-	1591	858	24	35.75	6-98	1	-
1-day Int																	
NatWest																	
B & H																	
Sunday																	

BROAD, B. C.   Gloucestershire

Name: Brian Christopher Broad
Role: Left-hand bat,
right-arm medium bowler
Born: 29 September 1957, Bristol
Height: 6ft 4in **Weight:** 14st 7lbs
Nickname: Walter, Broadie
County debut: 1979 (Gloucestershire),
1984 (Nottinghamshire)
County cap: 1981 (Gloucs), 1984 (Notts)
Test debut: 1984
Tests: 25
One-Day Internationals: 34
1000 runs in a season: 11
1st-Class 50s: 105
1st-Class 100s: 50
1st-Class 200s: 1
1st-Class catches: 189
One-Day 100s: 11
Place in batting averages: 164th av. 24.80 (1993 86th av. 34.14)

Parents: Nancy and Kenneth

Marital status: Divorced

Children: Gemma Joanne, 14 January 1984; Stuart Christopher John, 24 June 1986

Family links with cricket: Father and grandfather both played local cricket. Father member of Gloucestershire committee until retired

Education: Colston's School, Bristol; St Paul's College, Cheltenham

Qualifications: 5 O-levels, NCA advanced coach

Career outside cricket: Runs his own furniture import business

Off-season: At home pursuing interests outside the game

Overseas tours: English Counties to Zimbabwe 1984-85; England to Australia 1986-87, to Pakistan, Australia and New Zealand 1987-88; unofficial English team to South Africa 1989-90

Overseas teams played for: Orange Free State 1985-86 (captain)

Cricketers particularly admired: Graham Gooch, Richard Hadlee, Clive Rice

Other sports followed: Rugby

Relaxations: 'Playing any sport, spending time with my family'

Extras: Struck down by osteomyelitis at age 15. First played adult cricket for Downend, where W.G. Grace learnt to play; played with Allan Border in Gloucestershire 2nd XI. Published autobiography *Home Thoughts from Abroad* in 1987 after he had hit three centuries in a row in Test series v Australia, 1986-87. Banned from Test cricket for five years for joining tour to South Africa. Passed 2000 runs in a season for the first time and made his first double hundred in 1990. Released by Notts before the end of the 1992 season and decided to return to Gloucestershire

Opinions on cricket: 'Cricket is a game played by professionals but run by amateurs. This needs to be changed for the game to go forward into the 21st century.'

Best batting: 227* Nottinghamshire v Kent, Tunbridge Wells 1990

Best bowling: 2-14 Gloucestershire v West Indians, Bristol 1980

1994 Season

	M	Inns	NO	Runs	HS	Avge	100s	50s	Ct	St	O	M	Runs	Wkts	Avge	Best	5wI	10wM
Test																		
All First	10	20	0	496	128	24.80	1	2	9	-								
1-day Int																		
NatWest	1	1	0	44	44	44.00	-	-	-	-								
B & H	1	1	0	1	1	1.00	-	-	-	-								
Sunday																		

Career Performances

	M	Inns	NO	Runs	HS	Avge	100s	50s	Ct	St	Balls	Runs	Wkts	Avge	Best	5wI	10wM
Test	25	44	2	1661	162	39.54	6	6	10	-	6	4	0	-	-	-	
All First	340	613	38	21892	227 *	38.07	50	105	189	-	1631	1037	16	64.81	2-14	-	-
1-day Int	34	34	0	1361	106	40.02	1	11	10	-	6	6	0	-	-	-	
NatWest	35	35	1	1350	115	39.70	2	11	8	-							
B & H	63	62	3	1933	122	32.76	3	11	14	-	348	308	6	51.33	2-73	-	
Sunday	173	169	11	5411	108	34.24	5	34	45	-	669	602	19	31.68	3-46	-	

BROADHURST, M.   Nottinghamshire

Name: Mark Broadhurst
Role: Right-hand (lower order) bat, right-arm
fast-medium bowler
Born: 20 June 1974, Barnsley
Height: 6ft **Weight:** 11st 5lbs
Nickname: Broady, Stanley, Ditherer, Gibby
County debut: 1991 (Yorkshire)
Parents: Robert and Pamela
Marital status: Single
Family links with cricket: Father played
local league cricket for Ward Green
Education: Worsborough Common Junior
School; Kingstone Comprehensive
Qualifications: 8 GCSEs, City and Guilds
qualification in Leisure and Recreation
Overseas tours: England U19 to New
Zealand 1990-91, to India 1992-93; NCA
YC to Canada 1991
Cricketers particularly admired: Dennis
Lillee, Richard Hadlee, Michael Holding, Malcolm Marshall, Arnie Sidebottom, Steve
Oldham
Other sports followed: Football, golf, athletics
Relaxations: 'I enjoy watching cricket videos, listening to music and reading'
Extras: Selected for England U19 squad aged 16. Made first-class debut for Yorks at age
16, becoming the third youngest in Yorkshire history. Contributor to Wombwell
Cricket Society's *Twelfth Man* magazine. Played for England U19 v Australia 1991.
Selected for England U19 tour to Pakistan 1991-92 but forced to drop out through back
injury. Signed by Nottinghamshire for 1995 season
Opinions on cricket: 'Not enough cricket played in comprehensive schools.'
Best batting: 1 Yorkshire v Sri Lanka, Headingley 1991
Best bowling: 3-61 Yorkshire v Oxford University, The Parks 1991

1994 Season

	M	Inns	NO	Runs	HS	Avge	100s	50s	Ct	St	O	M	Runs	Wkts	Avge	Best	5wI	10wM
Test																		
All First	1	1	0	6	6	6.00	-	-	-	-	11	0	52	1	52.00	1-45	-	-
1-day Int																		
NatWest																		
B & H																		
Sunday																		

	M	Inns	NO	Runs	HS	Avge	100s	50s	Ct	St	Balls	Runs	Wkts	Avge	Best	5wI	10wM
Test																	
All First	5	3	0	7	6	2.33	-	-	-	-	415	231	7	33.00	3-61	-	-
1-day Int																	
NatWest																		
B & H																		
Sunday	1	0	0	0	0	-	-	-	-	-	48	27	0	-		-	-

BROOKE, M. P.   Worcestershire

Name: Matthew Peter Brooke
Role: Right-hand bat,
right-arm fast-medium bowler
Born: 14 April 1972, Morley
Height: 6ft 2in   **Weight:** 13st
County debut: No first-team appearance
Parents: Michael and Joan
Marital status: Single
Education: Peel Street Junior School;
Bruncliffe High School
Off-season: Working
Cricketers particularly admired:
Ian Botham
Other sports followed: Football
Injuries: Back, missed previous four seasons
Relaxations: Weight training
Extras: Released by Worcestershire at end of
1994 season

Opinions on cricket: 'The fun and
excitement seem to be lacking in today's cricket games, although after the matches the
social side is very good.'

BROWN, A. D.   Surrey

Name: Alistair Duncan Brown
Role: Right-hand bat, occasional leg-break
bowler, occasional wicket-keeper
Born: 11 February 1970, Beckenham
Height: 5ft 10in **Weight:** 12st
Nickname: Lordy
County debut: 1992
1000 runs in a season: 2
1st-Class 50s: 13
1st-Class 100s: 8
1st-Class catches: 40
One-Day 100s: 5
Place in batting averages: 25th av. 47.68
(1993 28th av. 44.58)
Parents: Robert and Ann
Marital status: Single
Family links with cricket: Father played for

Surrey Young Amateurs
Education: Cumnor House School;
Caterham School
Qualifications: 5 O-levels, NCA Senior Coach
Career outside cricket: Cricket coach, insurance administrator, amateur golfer
Overseas tours: England 6-a-side to Singapore 1993
Overseas teams played for: North Perth, Australia 1990-91
Cricketers particularly admired: Ian Botham, Viv Richards, David Gower
Other sports followed: Horse racing, tennis, football, golf, greyhound racing
Relaxations: Tennis and golf
Extras: Scored three of the eight fastest centuries of the 1992 season (71, 78 & 79 balls)
Opinions on cricket: 'Four-day cricket has proved very successful. 40 overs is right for
Sundays with coloured clothing and white balls.'
Best batting: 175 Surrey v Durham, Durham University 1992

1994 Season

	M	Inns	NO	Runs	HS	Avge	100s	50s	Ct	St	O	M	Runs	Wkts	Avge	Best	5wI	10wM
Test																		
All First	17	24	2	1049	172	47.68	2	6	16	-	15	1	47	0	-	-	-	-
1-day Int																		
NatWest	4	3	0	92	52	30.66	-	1	2	-								
B & H	4	4	2	91	38	45.50	-	-	1	-								
Sunday	17	16	1	688	142 *	45.86	2	3	1	-								

Career Performances

	M	Inns	NO	Runs	HS	Avge	100s	50s	Ct	St	Balls	Runs	Wkts	Avge	Best	5wl	10wM
Test																	
All First	47	74	6	3171	175	46.63	8	13	40	-	192	131	0	-	-	-	-
1-day Int																	
NatWest	7	5	1	132	52	33.00	-	1	2	-							
B & H	13	13	4	299	41	33.22	-	-	2	-							
Sunday	62	58	2	1928	142 *	34.42	5	9	15	-							

BROWN, C. Lancashire

Name: Christopher Brown
Role: Right-hand bat, off-spin bowler
Born: 16 August 1974, Oldham
Height: 6ft 2in **Weight:** 12st
Nickname: Browney, Browneye, Tnuc, Skick
County debut: No first-team appearance
Parents: Paul and Anne
Marital status: Single
Family links with cricket: Uncle played for Middletown in the Central Lancashire League
Education: Failsworth High School; Tameside College of Technology
Qualifications: 5 GCSEs, City and Guilds qualification in Recreation and Leisure
Off-season: Playing for Cape Town CC, South Africa
Overseas teams played for: Cape Town, South Africa 1992-95
Cricketers particularly admired: Phil Tufnell, Tim May, Greg Matthews, Steve O'Shaughnessy, Peter Such, Peter Seal
Other sports followed: Football (Manchester United), horse racing
Relaxations: 'Listening to good music, following Man Utd Drinking good beer, socialising, and listening to P. Seal's views on dodging nets.'
Extras: Equalled Gary Yates's 32 wickets in a season in 1993 with Lancashire Cricket Federation. Represented Lancashire Schools U19 1991-92, Lancashire Cricket Federation 1992-93, Lancashire Cricket Federation Player of the Year 1992, 1993. Member of the Lancashire Cricket Federation side which won the the NAYC Cambridge/Oxford Festival 1993. Played for NAYC 1993 and Werneth CC in Central Lancashire League.
Opinions on cricket: 'League cricket across the country should be extended from 40 or

50-over "slogs" to two-day cricket. This would produce better players as in South Africa and abroad. Far too much cricket is being played on the county circuit – results in average performances – quality not quantity.'

BROWN, D. R.　　　　　　Warwickshire

Name: Douglas Robert Brown
Role: Right-hand bat, right-arm fast-medium bowler
Born: 29 October 1969, Stirling
Height: 6ft 2in **Weight:** 13st 4lbs
Nickname: 'Anything which sounds remotely Scottish'
County debut: 1992
1st-Class 50s: 1
1st-Class catches: 2
Parents: Alastair and Janette
Wife and date of marriage:
Brenda, 2 October 1993
Family links with cricket: Both grandfathers played club cricket
Education: Alloa Academy;
West London Institute of Higher Education (Borough Road College)
Qualifications: 9 O-Grades, 5 Higher Grades;
BEd (Hons) Physical Education; qualified coach football, cricket, basketball, trampolining and rugby league
Career outside cricket: PE teacher
Off-season: Supply teacher in Birmingham. Coaching with Warwickshire
Overseas tours: Scotland XI to Pakistan 1988-89
Overseas teams played for: Primrose, Cape Town 1992-93; Uredenburg Salohana, Cape Town 1994
Cricketers particularly admired: Tim Munton, Richard Hadlee, Brian Lara
Other sports followed: 'Everything'
Relaxations: 'Spending time with Brenda, eating out, listening to music, playing golf and watching sport'
Extras: Played football at Hampden Park for Scotland U18. Played first-class and B & H cricket for Scotland in 1989, and played again for Scotland against Ireland in 1992
Opinions on cricket: 'What a great game!'
Best batting: 54 Warwickshire v Surrey, Guildford 1994
Best bowling: 4-25 Warwickshire v Essex, Edgbaston 1994

1994 Season

	M	Inns	NO	Runs	HS	Avge	100s	50s	Ct	St	O	M	Runs	Wkts	Avge	Best	5wI	10wM
Test																		
All First	3	6	2	113	54	28.25	-	1	-	-	35	5	118	5	23.60	4-25	-	-
1-day Int																		
NatWest																		
B & H																		
Sunday	1	1	0	1	1	1.00	-	-	-	-								

Career Performances

	M	Inns	NO	Runs	HS	Avge	100s	50s	Ct	St	Balls	Runs	Wkts	Avge	Best	5wI	10wM
Test																	
All First	6	9	4	167	54	33.40	-	1	2	-	655	322	13	24.76	4-25	-	-
1-day Int																	
NatWest																	
B & H	3	3	0	57	24	19.00	-	-	1	-	183	140	3	46.66	3-50	-
Sunday	8	4	1	29	14	9.66	-	-	-	-	300	190	6	31.66	3-21	-

BROWN, J. F.   Northamptonshire

Name: Jason F. Brown
Role: Right-hand bat, off-spin bowler
Born: 10 October 1974, Stoke-on-Trent
Height: 6ft 1in **Weight:** 12st
Nickname: Macey
County debut: No first-team appearance
Parents: Peter and Cynthia
Marital status: Single
Education: St Margaret Ward RC School
Qualifications: 8 O-levels
Off-season: 'Look for a part-time job and have a holiday.'
Overseas tours: Kidsgrove League U18 to Australia 1991
Cricketers particularly admired: John Emburey
Other sports followed: Football, golf
Relaxations: Watching videos and listening to music. Playing and watching all sports
Extras: Represented Staffordshire at all junior levels and Staffordshire's Minor Counties
Opinions on cricket: 'I would like to see the game a fairer contest between bat and ball, as the majority of wickets favour the batsmen.'

BROWN, K. R.   Middlesex

Name: Keith Robert Brown
Role: Right-hand bat, wicket-keeper
Born: 18 March 1963, Edmonton
Height: 5ft 11in **Weight:** 13st 7lbs
Nickname: Browny, Scarface, Stally
County debut: 1984
County cap: 1990
1000 runs in a season: 2
1st-Class 50s: 37
1st-Class 100s: 11
1st-Class 200s: 1
1st-Class catches: 273
1st-Class stumpings: 18
One-Day 100s: 2
Place in batting averages:
55th av. 39.93 (1993 47th av. 40.27)
Parents: Kenneth William and Margaret
Sonia
Wife and date of marriage:
Marie, 3 November 1984
Children: Zachary, 24 February 1987; Rosanna, 18 December 1989;
Alex, 29 December 1992
Family links with cricket: Brother Gary was on Middlesex staff for three years and then
played for Durham. Father is a qualified umpire
Education: Chace Comprehensive School, Enfield
Qualifications: French O-level; NCA Senior Coaching Award; qualified plasterer
Career outside cricket: Plasterer, PE instructor, coach
Off-season: Coaching. Spending time with family and redecorating
Overseas tours: NCA Youth tour to Denmark; Middlesex pre-season tours to La Manga
1985, 1986 and Portugal 1991, 1992, 1993
Overseas teams played for: Sydney University, Australia 1988-89; Motueka Cricket
Association, Nelson, New Zealand 1991-92
Cricketers particularly admired: Clive Radley and Derek Randall
Other sports followed: Most sports apart from motor racing
Relaxations: 'Long country walks with family and pet greyhound, finishing with a couple
of pints in local.'
Extras: Had promising boxing career but gave it up in order to concentrate on cricket.
Picked to play rugby for Essex
Opinions on cricket: '110 overs in a day is too many.'
Best batting: 200* Middlesex v Nottinghamshire, Lord's 1990
Best bowling: 2-7 Middlesex v Gloucestershire, Bristol 1987

1994 Season

	M	Inns	NO	Runs	HS	Avge	100s	50s	Ct	St	O	M	Runs	Wkts	Avge	Best	5wI	10wM
Test																		
All First	20	25	9	639	102 *	39.93	1	1	55	1								
1-day Int																		
NatWest	2	1	0	34	34	34.00	-	-	5	1								
B & H	2	2	1	39	24	39.00	-	-	-	-								
Sunday	17	15	7	355	52 *	44.37	-	1	11	4								

Career Performances

	M	Inns	NO	Runs	HS	Avge	100s	50s	Ct	St	Balls	Runs	Wkts	Avge	Best	5wI	10wM
Test																	
All First	174	261	51	7423	200 *	35.34	11	37	273	18	231	162	5	32.40	2-7	-	-
1-day Int																	
NatWest	16	13	3	359	103 *	35.90	1	-	10	1	6	8	0	-		-	-
B & H	24	22	4	430	56	23.88	-	1	11	5	6	0	0	-		-	-
Sunday	118	97	30	2072	102	30.92	1	8	62	17	28	29	0	-		-	-

BROWN, S. J. E. Durham

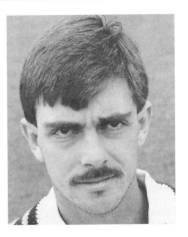

Name: Simon John Emmerson Brown
Role: Right-hand bat, left-arm medium pace bowler, gully fielder
Born: 29 June 1969, Cleadon Village, Sunderland
Height: 6ft 3in **Weight:** 13st
Nickname: Chubby
County debut: 1987 (Northamptonshire), 1992 (Durham)
50 wickets in a season: 2
1st-Class 50s: 1
1st-Class 5 w. in innings: 12
1st-Class catches: 23
Place in batting averages: 219th av. 17.86
Place in bowling averages:
47th av. 28.10 (1993 117th av. 39.59)
Strike rate: 46.30 (career 55.17)
Parents: Ernest and Doreen
Wife and date of marriage:
Sarah, 3 October 1992
Education: Boldon Comprehensive, Tyne & Wear; South Tyneside College
Qualifications: 6 O-levels, qualified electrician

Career outside cricket: Electrician
Off-season: Working for Northern Electric
Overseas tours: England YC to Sri Lanka 1986-87, to Australia for Youth World Cup 1987-88; MCC to Bahrain 1994-95
Overseas teams played for: Marist, Christchurch, New Zealand
Cricketers particularly admired: John Lever, Dennis Lillee
Other sports followed: Basketball and golf
Injuries: Damaged tendon in foot, missed one week
Relaxations: Playing basketball and golf
Extras: Offered basketball scholarship in America. Durham supporters' Player of the Year 1992. Durham Player of the Year 1994
Best batting: 69 Durham v Leicestershire, Durham University 1994
Best bowling: 7-70 Durham v Australians, Durham University 1993

1994 Season

	M	Inns	NO	Runs	HS	Avge	100s	50s	Ct	St	O	M	Runs	Wkts	Avge	Best	5wl	10wM
Test																		
All First	19	25	10	268	69	17.86	-	1	9	-	578.5	88	2108	75	28.10	6-68	6	-
1-day Int																		
NatWest	2	1	0	0	0	0.00	-	-	-	-	21.1	3	85	5	17.00	5-22	1	-
B & H	1	0	0	0	0	-	-	-	-	-	9.4	0	47	0	-	-	-	
Sunday	6	2	2	5	5 *	-	-	-	-	-	46.4	2	282	4	70.50	2-35	-	

Career Performances

	M	Inns	NO	Runs	HS	Avge	100s	50s	Ct	St	Balls	Runs	Wkts	Avge	Best	5wl	10wM
Test																	
All First	70	87	34	687	69	12.96	-	1	23	-	11310	6756	205	32.95	7-70	12	-
1-day Int																	
NatWest	5	3	2	10	7 *	10.00	-	-	-	-	340	254	8	31.75	5-22	1	-
B & H	7	2	2	6	4 *	-	-	-	-	-	376	241	6	40.16	2-32	-	
Sunday	39	10	4	24	7	4.00	-	-	6	-	1705	1478	38	38.89	3-26	-	

BURNS, M.   Warwickshire

Name: Michael Burns
Role: Right-hand bat, right-arm
medium bowler, wicket-keeper
Born: 6 February 1969, Barrow-in-Furness
Height: 6ft **Weight:** 13st
Nickname: George, Red Hot
County debut: 1991
1st-Class 50s: 1
1st-Class catches: 16
1st-Class stumpings: 2
Parents: Robert and Linda, stepfather Stan
Wife and date of marriage:
Carolyn, 9 October 1994
Family links with cricket: Grandfather was a
great back-garden bowler
Education: Walney Comprehensive;
Barrow College of Further Education
Qualifications: 'Few CSEs, couple of GCEs',
qualified fitter at VSEL in Barrow,
coaching award

Career outside cricket: Was a fitter, then a greengrocer
Off-season: Marriage, honeymoon. Working on family driving range
Overseas teams played for: Gill College, South Africa 1991-92; Motueka, Nelson, New
Zealand 1992-93; Alex CC, Harare
Cricketers particularly admired: Dermot Reeve, Tim Munton, Brian Lara, Pop Welch
Other sports followed: Rugby league and golf
Relaxations: 'Eating Indians, socialising with friends. One or two pints with Pop Welch'
Extras: Played for Cumberland 1989-90. Had a trial with Glamorgan, went to La Manga
with Lancashire junior side 1984.
Opinions on cricket: 'Tea should be longer because there is no time for wicket-keepers
to take gear off, get tea and relax.'
Best batting: 78 Warwickshire v Cambridge University, Fenner's 1992

1994 Season

	M	Inns	NO	Runs	HS	Avge	100s	50s	Ct	St	O	M	Runs	Wkts	Avge	Best	5wI	10wM
Test																		
All First	1	1	1	36	36 *	-	-	-	-	-								
1-day Int																		
NatWest																		
B & H	2	2	0	18	18	9.00	-	-	3	1								
Sunday	7	6	0	68	37	11.33	-	-	11	3								

Career Performances

	M	Inns	NO	Runs	HS	Avge	100s	50s	Ct	St	Balls	Runs	Wkts	Avge	Best	5wI	10wM
Test																	
All First	9	14	1	217	78	16.69	-	1	16	2	42	8	0	-		-	-	-
1-day Int																	
NatWest																	
B & H	4	4	0	43	22	10.75	-	-	4	1							
Sunday	17	14	2	150	37	12.50	-	-	19	7							

BUTCHER, G. P. — *Glamorgan*

Name: Gary Paul Butcher
Role: Right-hand opening bat,
right-arm medium bowler
Born: 11 March 1975, Clapham,
South London
Height: 5ft 9in **Weight:** 11st
Nickname: Butch, Bouché, The Meatseller
County debut: 1994
1st-Class catches: 2
Parents: Alan and Elaine
Marital status: Single
Family links with cricket: Father Alan
played for Surrey, Glamorgan and England
and is now with Essex; brother Mark plays
for Surrey and uncle Ian played for
Gloucestershire and Leicestershire
Education: Cumnor House; Trinity School;
Riddlesdown Comprehensive;
Heath Clark College
Qualifications: 4 GCSEs, BTEC 1st Diploma in Leisure Studies
Career outside cricket: Salesman
Overseas tours: England U18 to Denmark 1993; England U19 to Sri Lanka 1993-94
Cricketers particularly admired: David Gower, Viv Richards, Brian Lara, Curtly
Ambrose, Nick Moss
Other sports followed: Football, gymnastics, chess
Relaxations: 'Music, the slide, the economy and the odd night or two in Bridgend'
Extras: Won ASW Player of the Month, May 1993
Opinions on cricket: 'All 2nd XI games should be played at county grounds, with two
qualified umpires.'
Best batting: 41 Glamorgan v Leicestershire, Cardiff 1994
Best bowling: 2-36 Glamorgan v Oxford University, The Parks 1994

1994 Season

	M	Inns	NO	Runs	HS	Avge	100s	50s	Ct	St	O	M	Runs	Wkts	Avge	Best	5wl	10wM
Test																		
All First	3	3	0	50	41	16.66	-	-	2	-	37	5	148	2	74.00	2-36	-	-
1-day Int																		
NatWest																		
B & H																		
Sunday	3	0	0	0	0	-	-	-	-	-	10	0	66	2	33.00	2-8	-	

Career Performances

	M	Inns	NO	Runs	HS	Avge	100s	50s	Ct	St	Balls	Runs	Wkts	Avge	Best	5wl	10wM
Test																	
All First	3	3	0	50	41	16.66	-	-	2	-	222	148	2	74.00	2-36	-	-
1-day Int																	
NatWest																	
B & H																	
Sunday	3	0	0	0	0	-	-	-	-	-	60	66	2	33.00	2-8	-	

BUTCHER, M. A. Surrey

Name: Mark Alan Butcher
Role: Left-hand bat, right-arm medium bowler
Born: 23 August 1972, Croydon
Height: 5ft 11in **Weight:** 12st 7lbs
Nickname: Butch, Basil
County debut: 1991
1st-Class 50s: 4
1st-Class 100s: 1
1st-Class catches: 25
Place in batting averages: 86th av. 36.05 (1993 133rd av. 27.25)
Place in bowling averages: 125th av. 41.87 (1993 62nd av. 29.06)
Strike rate: 77.50 (career 72.12)
Parents: Alan and Elaine
Marital status: Engaged
Family links with cricket: Father Alan played for Glamorgan, Surrey and England and is now with Essex; brother Gary plays for Glamorgan; uncle Ian played for Gloucestershire and Leicestershire
Education: Cumnor House School; Trinity School; Archbishop Tenison's; Croydon

Qualifications: 5 O-levels, senior coaching award
Career outside cricket: Singer, guitar player, female impersonator
Off-season: Playing cricket in Australia
Overseas tours: England YC to New Zealand 1990-91; Surrey to Dubai 1990 and 1993
Overseas teams played for: South Melbourne, Australia 1993-94; North Perth 1994-95
Cricketers particularly admired: Graham Thorpe, Desmond Haynes, Ian Botham, David Gower, Joey Benjamin, Graham Dilley
Other sports followed: Football, tennis, golf
Injuries: Torn groin and hernia operation. Missed 6-7 weeks
Relaxations: 'Reading, films, music, bars that have live music'
Extras: Played his first game for Surrey against his father's Glamorgan in the Refuge Assurance League at The Oval, the first ever match of any sort between first-class counties in which a father and son have been in opposition
Opinions on cricket: 'In four-day cricket we are asked to bowl too many overs in a day. Test matches are 90 overs in 6 hours, yet in county games we are asked to bowl an extra 20 overs in half-an-hour extra time. Obviously this is to encourage the use of spin, but captains have to use the type of bowler that suits conditions, and for the majority of four-day matches that doesn't include spin.'
Best batting: 134 Surrey v Hampshire, Southampton 1994
Best bowling: 4-31 Surrey v Worcestershire, The Oval 1994

1994 Season

	M	Inns	NO	Runs	HS	Avge	100s	50s	Ct	St	O	M	Runs	Wkts	Avge	Best	5wI	10wM
Test																		
All First	12	19	2	613	134	36.05	1	3	21	-	206.4	50	670	16	41.87	4-31	-	-
1-day Int																		
NatWest																		
B & H	4	2	0	9	5	4.50	-	-	1	-	34.1	1	176	4	44.00	3-37	-	
Sunday	9	5	3	45	17 *	22.50	-	-	1	-	47	0	313	4	78.25	2-47	-	

Career Performances

	M	Inns	NO	Runs	HS	Avge	100s	50s	Ct	St	Balls	Runs	Wkts	Avge	Best	5wI	10wM
Test																	
All First	20	32	6	883	134	33.96	1	4	25	-	2308	1221	32	38.15	4-31	-	-
1-day Int																	
NatWest	2	2	1	19	15	19.00	-	-	2	-	144	93	2	46.50	2-57	-	
B & H	5	3	0	10	5	3.33	-	-	1	-	271	217	6	36.16	3-37	-	
Sunday	22	14	8	201	48 *	33.50	-	-	7	-	954	815	19	42.89	3-23	-	

BYAS, D.   Yorkshire

Name: David Byas
Role: Left-hand bat, right-arm medium bowler
Born: 26 August 1963, Middledale, Kilham
Height: 6ft 4in **Weight:** 15st
Nickname: Bingo
County debut: 1986
County cap: 1991
1000 runs in a season: 3
1st-Class 50s: 40
1st-Class 100s: 11
1st-Class catches: 146
One-Day 100s: 2
Place in batting averages: 74th av. 37.05
(1993 76th av. 35.76)
Parents: Richard and Anne
Wife and date of marriage:
Rachael, 27 October 1990
Children: Olivia Rachael, 16 December 1991;
Georgia Elizabeth, 30 December 1993
Family links with cricket: Father played in local league
Education: Scarborough College
Qualifications: 1 O-level (Engineering)
Career outside cricket: Farming
Off-season: Touring South Africa in March 1995 with YCC
Overseas teams played for: Papetoetoe, Auckland 1988
Cricketers particularly admired: David Gower, Viv Richards, Ian Botham
Other sports followed: Hockey, motor racing, rugby union
Relaxations: 'Looking after my two active daughters. Dining out with my wife. Shooting.'
Extras: Became youngest captain (aged 21) of Scarborough CC in 1985. Broke John
Hampshire's Sunday League record with 702 runs in 1994, which had stood since 1976.
Runner-up in the Sunday League averages 1994
Best batting: 156 Yorkshire v Essex, Chelmsford 1993
Best bowling: 3-55 Yorkshire v Derbyshire, Chesterfield 1990

1994 Season

	M	Inns	NO	Runs	HS	Avge	100s	50s	Ct	St	O	M	Runs	Wkts	Avge	Best	5wl	10wM
Test																		
All First	20	36	1	1297	104	37.05	2	9	23	-	16	4	52	2	26.00	1-16	-	-
1-day Int																		
NatWest	2	2	0	107	71	53.50	-	1	-	-								
B & H	1	1	0	10	10	10.00	-	-	-	-								
Sunday	16	16	2	702	101*	50.14	1	6	5	-	1	0	18	0	-		-	-

Career Performances

	M	Inns	NO	Runs	HS	Avge	100s	50s	Ct	St	Balls	Runs	Wkts	Avge	Best	5wI	10wM
Test																	
All First	139	232	22	6886	156	32.79	11	40	146	-	1056	682	12	56.83	3-55	-	-
1-day Int																	
NatWest	12	10	1	314	71	34.88	-	3	7	-	18	23	1	23.00	1-23	-	
B & H	20	18	1	413	92	24.29	-	2	4	-	283	155	5	31.00	2-38	-	
Sunday	106	103	17	2605	106 *	30.29	2	12	24	-	529	463	19	24.36	3-19	-	

CADDICK, A. R.   Somerset

Name: Andrew Richard Caddick
Role: Right-hand bat, right-arm
fast-medium bowler
Born: 21 November 1968, Christchurch,
New Zealand
Height: 6ft 8in **Weight:** 14st
Nickname: Kiwi, Vic, Doo,
Bean ('Quite a few')
County debut: 1991
Test debut: 1993
Tests: 8
One-Day Internationals: 5
50 wickets in a season: 3
1st-Class 50s: 2
1st-Class 5 w. in innings: 13
1st-Class 10 w. in match: 4
1st-Class catches: 21
One-Day 5 w. in innings: 2
Place in batting averages: 250th av. 13.68
(1993 232nd av. 14.45)
Place in bowling averages: 12th av. 23.25 (1993 41st av. 26.63)
Strike rate: 43.90 (50.70)
Parents: Christopher and Audrey
Marital status: Engaged
Education: Papanui High School, Christchurch, New Zealand
Qualifications: Qualified plasterer and tiler
Career outside cricket: Plasterer and tiler
Off-season: Recovering from shin operation (both legs), both in England and New
Zealand
Overseas tours: New Zealand YC to Australia (Youth World Cup) 1987-88, to England
1988; England A to Australia 1992-93; England to West Indies 1993-94

Cricketers particularly admired: Dennis Lillee, Richard Hadlee
Other sports followed: 'Mostly all'
Injuries: Shoulder and shins
Relaxations: Music, videos, golf, most sports
Extras: Rapid Cricketline Player of the Year 1991.
Opinions on cricket: 'For a bowler it's a very hard game.'
Best batting: 58* Somerset v Sussex, Hove 1994
Best bowling: 9-32 Somerset v Lancashire, Taunton 1993

1994 Season

	M	Inns	NO	Runs	HS	Avge	100s	50s	Ct	St	O	M	Runs	Wkts	Avge	Best	5wI	10wM
Test																		
All First	12	18	2	219	58 *	13.68	-	1	5	-	373.1	73	1186	51	23.25	6-51	3	-
1-day Int																		
NatWest	3	1	0	4	4	4.00	-	-	1	-	26	5	68	3	22.66	3-28	-	
B & H	1	1	1	4	4 *	-	-	-	-	-	11	0	62	0	-	-	-	
Sunday	6	4	1	8	7	2.66	-	-	-	-	43	4	176	6	29.33	3-41	-	

Career Performances

	M	Inns	NO	Runs	HS	Avge	100s	50s	Ct	St	Balls	Runs	Wkts	Avge	Best	5wI	10wM
Test	8	14	2	170	29 *	14.16	-	-	4	-	1940	1033	23	44.91	6-65	2	-
All First	58	74	13	919	58 *	15.06	-	2	21	-	11154	5922	220	26.91	9-32	13	4
1-day Int	5	3	3	23	20 *	-	-	-	1	-	318	258	6	43.00	3-39	-	
NatWest	9	5	1	12	8	3.00	-	-	2	-	533	282	18	15.66	6-30	2	
B & H	7	6	4	22	6 *	11.00	-	-	2	-	444	262	7	37.42	2-20	-	
Sunday	28	11	3	88	36 *	11.00	-	-	1	-	1194	921	31	29.70	4-18	-	

CAIRNS, C. L.   Nottinghamshire

Name: Christopher Lance Cairns
Role: Right-hand bat, right-arm fast-medium bowler
Born: 13 June 1970, Picton, New Zealand
Height: 6ft 2in **Weight:** 14st
Nickname: Sheep
County debut: 1988
County cap: 1993
Test debut: 1990-91
Tests: 10
One-Day Internationals: 22
50 wickets in a season: 2
1st-Class 50s: 23
1st-Class 100s: 3

1st-Class 5 w. in innings: 10
1st-Class 10 w. in match: 2
1st-Class catches: 39
One-Day 5 w. in innings: 1
Place in batting averages:
(1993 33rd av. 43.72)
Place in bowling averages:
(1993 18th av. 23.43)
Strike rate: (career 54.62)
Parents: Lance and Sue
Family links with cricket: Father played for
New Zealand, uncle played first-class cricket
in New Zealand
Education: Christchurch Boys' High School,
New Zealand
Qualifications: 5th and 6th form certificates
Marital status: Single
Off-season: Playing for New Zealand

Overseas tours: New Zealand YC to Australia
(Youth World Cup) 1987-88; New Zealand to Australia 1989-90, 1993-94
Overseas teams played for: Northern Districts 1988-89; Canterbury 1990-95
Cricketers particularly admired: Mick Newell, Richard Hadlee, Dennis Lillee
Other sports followed: Most sports
Opinions on cricket: 'Great game.'
Best batting: 110 Northern Districts v Auckland, Hamilton 1988-89
Best bowling: 7-34 Canterbury v Central Districts, New Plymouth 1991-92

1994 Season (did not make any first-class or one-day appearance)

Career Performances

	M	Inns	NO	Runs	HS	Avge	100s	50s	Ct	St	Balls	Runs	Wkts	Avge	Best	5wl	10wM
Test	10	17	0	349	78	20.52	-	2	6	-	1995	1207	28	43.10	6-52	2	-
All First	87	123	16	3415	110	31.91	3	23	39	-	14915	7975	273	29.21	7-34	10	2
1-day Int	22	19	4	360	70	24.00	-	1	12	-	954	736	22	33.45	4-55	-	
NatWest	4	4	0	226	77	56.50	-	3	1	-	266	123	9	13.66	4-18	-	
B & H	5	3	0	18	16	6.00	-	-	1	-	276	218	5	43.60	2-63	-	
Sunday	30	24	3	626	126 *	29.80	1	3	11	-	1336	998	41	24.34	6-52	1	

CAPEL, D. J.　　　　　　Northamptonshire

Name: David John Capel
Role: Right-hand bat, right-arm
medium bowler, all-rounder,
slip fielder
Born: 6 February 1963, Northampton
Height: 5ft 11in **Weight:** 12st 10lbs
Nickname: Capes, Fiery
County debut: 1981
County cap: 1986
Benefit: 1994
Test debut: 1987
Tests: 15
One-Day Internationals: 23
1000 runs in a season: 3
50 wickets in a season: 3
1st-Class 50s: 64
1st-Class 100s: 12
1st-Class 5 w. in innings: 12
1st-Class catches: 129
One-Day 100s: 3
Place in batting averages: (1993 212th av. 17.00)
Place in bowling averages: (1993 9th av. 21.00)
Strike rate: (career 62.40)
Parents: John and Janet
Wife and date of marriage: Debbie, 21 September 1985
Children: Jenny, 21 October 1987; Jordan, 18 May 1993
Family links with cricket: Father and brother Andrew both captained their local league
sides
Education: Roade Primary School; Roade Comprehensive School
Qualifications: 3 O-levels, 4 CSEs, NCA advanced coaching certificate
Overseas tours: England to Sharjah 1986-87, to Pakistan 1987-88, to New Zealand and
Australia 1987-88, to India (Nehru Cup) 1989-90, to West Indies 1989-90; England A to
Australia 1992-93
Overseas teams played for: Eastern Province, South Africa 1985-87; Petersham-
Marrickville, Sydney 1991-92
Other sports followed: 'Golf, local rugby and soccer teams'
Injuries: Knee and thumb (broken three times). Missed most of 1994 season from mid-July
Relaxations: 'Family, gardening, golf, walking, cycling, coarse fishing, most music'
Extras: Only second Northampton-born man to play for England. Two centuries in a
match against Sussex 1989. All-Rounder of the Year 'Wetherall Award' 1989. Broke
Northants records for fourth wicket in Sunday League with K.R. Curran and for fifth wicket
in NatWest Trophy with A.J. Lamb.

Best batting: 134 Eastern Province v Western Province, Port Elizabeth 1986-87
Best bowling: 7-46 Northamptonshire v Yorkshire, Northampton 1987

1994 Season

	M	Inns	NO	Runs	HS	Avge	100s	50s	Ct	St	O	M	Runs	Wkts	Avge	Best	5wl	10wM
Test																		
All First	2	3	0	43	29	14.33	-	-	1	-	33	7	89	0	-	-	-	-
1-day Int																		
NatWest																		
B & H																		
Sunday	3	3	1	42	29 *	21.00	-	-	-	-	9.5	0	54	2	27.00	1-20	-	

Career Performances

	M	Inns	NO	Runs	HS	Avge	100s	50s	Ct	St	Balls	Runs	Wkts	Avge	Best	5wl	10wM
Test	15	25	1	374	98	15.58	-	2	6	-	2000	1064	21	50.66	3-88	-	-
All First	272	411	61	10322	134	29.49	12	64	129	-	28519	14940	457	32.69	7-46	12	-
1-day Int	23	19	2	327	50 *	19.23	-	1	6	-	1038	805	17	47.35	3-38	-	
NatWest	32	28	8	845	101	42.25	1	4	8	-	1345	860	27	31.85	3-21	-	
B & H	46	40	5	716	97	20.45	-	1	9	-	2110	1332	50	26.64	4-29	-	
Sunday	148	136	29	3196	121	29.86	2	13	32	-	4375	3460	108	32.03	4-30	-	

CARR, J. D.   Middlesex

Name: John Donald Carr
Role: Right-hand bat, right-arm medium
bowler, county vice-captain
Born: 15 June 1963, St John's Wood
Height: 6ft **Weight:** 12st
Nickname: Carsy, Gold
County debut: 1983
County cap: 1987
1000 runs in a season: 3
1st-Class 50s: 43
1st-Class 100s: 20
1st-Class 200s: 1
1st-Class 5 w. in innings: 3
1st-Class catches: 193
One-day 100s: 1
Place in batting averages: 1st av. 90.70
(1993 25th av. 47.11)
Strike rate: (career 98.33)
Parents: Donald and Stella

Wife and date of marriage: Vicky, 5 May 1990

Children: Holly, 14 December 1992; Elinor, 6 August 1994

Family links with cricket: Father played for Derbyshire and England and is now secretary of the TCCB. Uncle, Major Douglas Carr, was secretary of Derbyshire CCC

Education: The Hall, Hampstead; Repton School; Worcester College, Oxford

Qualifications: Degree in Philosophy, Politics and Economics; senior coaching certificate

Career outside cricket: One year with Barclays Bank

Off-season: 'Close to home, working if possible!'

Overseas tours: Oxbridge to Australia and Hong Kong 1985-86; Troubadours to Argentina and Brazil 1990; MCC to Bahrain 1994-95

Overseas teams played for: Sydney University 1985-86; Weston Creek, Canberra 1987-88; Argentina Colts XI 1989-90

Cricketers particularly admired: Alan Border, Curtly Ambrose

Relaxations: Watching and playing a variety of sports – Eton fives, real tennis, golf, squash, football – good food and the cinema

Extras: Retired from first-class cricket at the end of 1990 season and played for Hertfordshire in 1991. Returned to full-time cricket in 1992

Opinions on cricket: 'I feel very strongly that there is a place for overseas players in county cricket. One per county is ideal. English players must be able to learn from playing with and against the world's top players. Overseas players greatly add to the entertainment value of county cricket. I am amazed by proposals to get rid of them.'

Best batting: 261* Middlesex v Gloucestershire, Lord's 1994

Best bowling: 6-61 Middlesex v Gloucestershire, Lord's 1985

1994 Season

	M	Inns	NO	Runs	HS	Avge	100s	50s	Ct	St	O	M	Runs	Wkts	Avge	Best	5wI	10wM
Test																		
All First	20	27	10	1542	261 *	90.70	6	7	31	-								
1-day Int																		
NatWest	2	1	0	16	16	16.00	-	-	-	-								
B & H	2	2	0	41	27	20.50	-	-	3	-								
Sunday	14	14	5	291	59 *	32.33	-	1	4	-	6	0	30	0	-	-	-	-

Career Performances

	M	Inns	NO	Runs	HS	Avge	100s	50s	Ct	St	Balls	Runs	Wkts	Avge	Best	5wI	10wM
Test																	
All First	175	274	44	9013	261 *	39.18	20	43	193	-	6687	2939	68	43.22	6-61	3	-
1-day Int																	
NatWest	17	16	0	363	83	22.68	-	1	4	-	204	93	4	23.25	2-19	-	
B & H	28	27	1	770	70	29.61	-	5	16	-	752	466	12	38.83	3-22	-	
Sunday	101	91	21	2244	104 *	32.05	1	10	45	-	1038	815	28	29.10	4-21	-	

CASSAR, M. E. Derbyshire

Name: Matthew Edward Cassar
Role: Right-hand bat,
right-arm fast-medium bowler
Born: 16 October 1972, Sydney, Australia
Height: 6ft **Weight:** 13st 5lbs
County debut: 1994
1st-Class 50s: 1
Parents: Edward and Joan
Marital status: Single
Education: Sir Joseph Banks High School,
Sydney
Qualifications: School certificate
Off-season: Playing grade cricket in
Australia
Overseas teams played for:
Petersham/Marrickville, Sydney
Cricketers particularly admired:
"My girlfriend Jane Smit (England Women's
wicket-keeper) and David Capel, who coached me while he was playing in Sydney'
Other sports followed: Football, rugby league, baseball, golf, tennis, snooker
Relaxations: Playing all sports, listening to music, watching television
Extras: Played for New South Wales Colts
Best batting: 66 Derbyshire v New Zealanders, Derby 1994
Best bowling: 3-65 Derbyshire v New Zealanders, Derby 1994

1994 Season

	M	Inns	NO	Runs	HS	Avge	100s	50s	Ct	St	O	M	Runs	Wkts	Avge	Best	5wl	10wM
Test																		
All First	1	1	0	66	66	66.00	-	1	-	-	24.2	3	94	3	31.33	3-65	-	-
1-day Int																		
NatWest																			
B & H																			
Sunday																			

Career Performances

	M	Inns	NO	Runs	HS	Avge	100s	50s	Ct	St	Balls	Runs	Wkts	Avge	Best	5wl	10wM
Test																	
All First	1	1	0	66	66	66.00	-	1	-	-	146	94	3	31.33	3-65	-	-
1-day Int																	
NatWest																	
B & H																	
Sunday																	

CAWDRON, M. J.　　　　　Gloucestershire

Name: Michael John Cawdron
Role: Left-hand bat,
right-arm medium bowler
Born: 7 October 1974, Luton
Height: 6ft 2in **Weight:** 12st
Nickname: Muscles
County debut: No first-team appearance
Parents: William and Mary
Marital status: Single
Family links with cricket: Father and
brother played local village cricket
Education: Cheltenham College
Qualifications: 10 GCSEs, 3 A-Levels
Career outside cricket: Coaching
Off-season: Tour to Zimbabwe with
Gloucestershire Gypsies
Overseas tours: West of England U14 to
Holland; Cheltenham College to
Zimbabwe 1992; Gloucestershire YC to Sri
Lanka 1993-94

Cricketers particularly admired:
David Gower, Richard Hadlee
Other sports followed: Rugby, hockey, racquets, clay-pigeon shooting, golf
Relaxations: 'Playing all sports'
Extras: Winner of the *Daily Telegraph* Regional Bowling Award 1993. Captain of MCC
Schools and ESCA U19, 1993

---

10. How was Brian Lara dismissed at the end of his record Test innings
of 375, and who were the England players involved in the dismissal?

Name: Colin Anthony Chapman
Role: Right-hand bat, wicket-keeper
Born: 8 June 1971, Bradford
Height: 5ft 8in **Weight:** 11st 7lbs
Nickname: Humpy, Turtle, Chappy
County debut: 1990
1st-Class catches: 5
1st-Class stumpings: 2
Parents: Mick and Joyce
Marital status: Single
Education: Nabwood Middle;
Beckfoot Grammar; Bradford & Ilkley
Community College
Qualifications: 5 O-levels, BTEC Diploma
in Graphic Design, coaching certificate
Career outside cricket:
Working in graphics
Overseas teams played for:
Waitamata, Auckland 1989-91
Cricketers particularly admired: Phil Carrick, Alan Knott
Other sports followed: 'Anything slightly interesting'
Relaxations: 'Spending a few hours at the pub'
Best batting: 20 Yorkshire v Middlesex, Uxbridge 1990

1994 Season (did not make any first team or one-day appearance)

Career Performances

	M	Inns	NO	Runs	HS	Avge	100s	50s	Ct	St	Balls	Runs	Wkts	Avge	Best	5wI	10wM
Test																	
All First	3	5	1	55	20	13.75	-	-	3	-							
1-day Int																		
NatWest																		
B & H																		
Sunday	5	4	1	52	36 *	17.33	-	-	1	-							

Name: Robert James Chapman
Role: Right-hand bat, right-arm
fast-medium bowler
Born: 28 July 1972, Nottingham
Height: 6ft 1in **Weight:** 13st
Nickname: Bob, Berty, Chapflap, Chappy
County debut: 1992
1st-Class catches: 1
Parents: Robert Dennis and Hazel Janice
Marital status: Single
Family links with cricket: Father plays club
cricket for Clifton Village CC
Education: South Wilford School;
Farnborough School, Clifton, Nottingham
Qualifications: 7 O-Levels, 2 A-Levels
Career outside cricket: Undecided
Off-season: Administration at Nottingham
Forest FC
Cricketers particularly admired: Allan
Donald, Derek Randall, Joe Thorpe, Kenny Wilson
Other sports followed: Football (Nottingham Forest, West Ham), indoor cricket (Scorers,
Nottingham)
Injuries: Shoulder muscle torn in two places, missed four weeks
Relaxations: Pearl Jam, Paul Weller, Nirvana, The Cure, U2. Indoor cricket, playing for
Nottingham Scorers in the national league
Extras: 'Father played for Nottingham Forest (Sammy). Brother-in-law Phil Starbuck
plays for Huddersfield Town. Nephew Daniel will soon play for England. Amy will be
Miss World.' Hit by an airgun pellet while fielding for Nottinghamshire 2nd XI in Bain
Clarkson match against Yorkshire
Opinions on cricket: 'There should be some effort to try and turn 2nd XI cricket into a
four-day game. Also there should be more television coverage of county games.'
Best batting: 25 Nottinghamshire v Lancashire, Trent Bridge 1994
Best bowling: 2-23 Nottinghamshire v Cambridge University, Fenner's 1994

1994 Season

	M	Inns	NO	Runs	HS	Avge	100s	50s	Ct	St	O	M	Runs	Wkts	Avge	Best	5wI	10wM
Test																		
All First	3	4	0	36	25	9.00	-	-	1	-	50.4	13	189	4	47.25	2-23	-	-
1-day Int																		
NatWest																			
B & H																			
Sunday	5	2	1	2	2*	2.00	-	-	-	-	29.3	0	156	3	52.00	2-44	-	

Career Performances

	M	Inns	NO	Runs	HS	Avge	100s	50s	Ct	St	Balls	Runs	Wkts	Avge	Best	5wI	10wM
Test																	
All First	4	4	0	36	25	9.00	-	-	1	-	382	266	6	44.33	2-23	-	-
1-day Int																	
NatWest																	
B & H																	
Sunday	5	2	1	2	2*	2.00	-	-	-	-	177	156	3	52.00	2-44	-	

CHAPPLE, G. Lancashire

Name: Glen Chapple
Role: Right-hand bat, right-arm
medium bowler
Born: 23 January 1974, Skipton, Yorkshire
Height: 6ft 2in **Weight:** 12st 7lbs
Nickname: Chappy, Boris, Boomor, Cheeky
County debut: 1992
50 wickets in a season: 1
1st-Class 100s: 1
1st-Class 5 w. in innings: 4
1st-Class catches: 11
Place in batting averages: 242nd av. 15.00
(1993 40th av. 42.66)
Place in bowling averages: 35th av. 26.80
(1993 130th av. 46.09)
Strike rate: 50.03 (career 55.91)
Parents: Eileen and Michael
Marital status: Single

Family links with cricket: Father played in
Lancashire League for Nelson and was a professional for Darwen and Earby
Education: West Craven High School; Nelson and Colne College
Qualifications: 8 GCSEs, 2 A-Levels in Geography and Economics
Off-season: Playing for England A
Overseas tours: England U18 to Canada 1991; England YC to New Zealand 1990-91;
England U19 to Pakistan 1991-92, to India 1992-93; England A to India 1994-95
Cricketers particularly admired: Dennis Lillee, Robin Smith
Other sports followed: Football (Liverpool), golf
Relaxations: 'Watching films, cinema, music, socialising'
Extras: Hit fastest century (21 minutes) against Glamorgan at Old Trafford 1993
Best batting: 109* Lancashire v Glamorgan, Old Trafford 1993
Best bowling: 6-48 Lancashire v Durham, Stockton 1994

1994 Season

	M	Inns	NO	Runs	HS	Avge	100s	50s	Ct	St	O	M	Runs	Wkts	Avge	Best	5wI	10wM
Test																		
All First	15	21	11	150	26 *	15.00	-	-	11	-	458.4	110	1474	55	26.80	6-48	4	-
1-day Int																		
NatWest	1	0	0	0	0	-	-	-	-	-	12	2	35	1	35.00	1-35	-	
B & H	1	0	0	0	0	-	-	-	-	-	11	1	30	2	15.00	2-30	-	
Sunday	12	2	2	4	3 *	-	-	-	2	-	82	6	329	10	32.90	3-29	-	

Career Performances

	M	Inns	NO	Runs	HS	Avge	100s	50s	Ct	St	Balls	Runs	Wkts	Avge	Best	5wI	10wM
Test																	
All First	25	36	19	425	109 *	25.00	1	-	11	-	3970	2109	71	29.70	6-48	4	-
1-day Int																	
NatWest	1	0	0	0	0		-	-	-	-	72	35	1	35.00	1-35	-
B & H	1	0	0	0	0	-	-	-	-	-	66	30	2	15.00	2-30	-
Sunday	17	4	3	16	9 *	16.00	-	-	2	-	580	413	12	34.41	3-29	-

CHILDS, J. H.   Essex

Name: John Henry Childs
Role: Left-hand bat, slow left-arm bowler
Born: 15 August 1951, Plymouth
Height: 6ft **Weight:** 12st 6lbs
Nickname: Charlie
County debut: 1975 (Gloucs), 1985 (Essex)
County cap: 1977 (Gloucs), 1986 (Essex)
Benefit: 1994
Testimonial: 1985
Test debut: 1988
Tests: 2
50 wickets in a season: 8
1st-Class 5 w. in innings: 50
1st-Class 10 w. in match: 8
1st-Class catches: 109
Place in batting averages:
(1993 257th av. 11.12)
Place in bowling averages: 81st av. 32.15
(1993 54th av. 27.88)
Strike rate: 71.51 (career 69.35)
Parents: Sydney and Barbara (both deceased)
Wife and date of marriage: Jane Anne, 11 November 1978

Children: Lee Robert, 28 November 1980; Scott Alexander, 21 August 1984
Education: Audley Park Secondary Modern, Torquay
Qualifications: Advanced cricket coach
Cricketers particularly admired: Gary Sobers, Mike Procter
Injuries: Broken right toe, missed two weeks
Relaxations: 'Watching rugby, decorating at home, walking on moors and beaches, enjoying my family'
Extras: Played for Devon 1973-74. Released by Gloucestershire at end of 1984 and joined Essex. One of *Wisden*'s Five Cricketers of the Year 1986. Selected for England's cancelled tour to India 1988-89. Essex Player of the Year 1992.
Best batting: 43 Essex v Hampshire, Chelmsford 1992
Best bowling: 9-56 Gloucestershire v Somerset, Bristol 1981

1994 Season

	M	Inns	NO	Runs	HS	Avge	100s	50s	Ct	St	O	M	Runs	Wkts	Avge	Best	5wl	10wM
Test																		
All First	15	17	12	96	42 *	19.20	-	-	1	-	464.5	122	1254	39	32.15	6-71	2	-
1-day Int																		
NatWest																		
B & H																		
Sunday																		

Career Performances

	M	Inns	NO	Runs	HS	Avge	100s	50s	Ct	St	Balls	Runs	Wkts	Avge	Best	5wl	10wM
Test	2	4	4	2	2 *	-	-	-	1	-	516	183	3	61.00	1-13	-	-
All First	358	326	159	1576	43	9.43	-	-	109	-	65263	28078	941	29.83	9-56	50	8
1-day Int																	
NatWest	10	5	4	35	14 *	35.00	-	-	-	-	646	378	10	37.80	2-15	-	
B & H	23	7	5	25	10	12.50	-	-	6	-	1272	688	21	32.76	3-36	-	
Sunday	84	32	18	117	16 *	8.35	-	-	16	-	3283	2494	64	38.96	4-15	-	

Name: Matthew John Church
Role: Right-hand bat,
right-arm medium bowler
Born: 26 July 1972, Guildford
Height: 6ft 2in **Weight:** 13st 7lbs
County debut: 1994
1st-Class catches: 1
Parents: Anthony and Annette
Marital status: Single
Education: St George's College, Weybridge
Qualifications: 4 GCSEs, 1 A-level
Off-season: Playing cricket in Australia
Overseas tours: St George's College to
Zimbabwe 1990-91; Surrey Young Cricketers
to Australia 1991-92
Overseas teams played for: Harmony,
Orange Free State 1991-92; North Shore,
Geelong 1992-93; Adelaide University 1994-95
Other sports followed: Rugby, hockey
Extras: Former MCC Young Cricketer, signed by Worcestershire at the beginning of the 1994 season. Sold scorecards at the 1993 Benson & Hedges Cup final and was 12th Man for Worcestershire at the NatWest final the following year. Fielded for England as substitute in 1995 Lord's Test against South Africa. Played for Surrey from U12 to U19.
Best batting: 38 Worcestershire v Yorkshire, Worcester 1994

1994 Season

	M	Inns	NO	Runs	HS	Avge	100s	50s	Ct	St	O	M	Runs	Wkts	Avge	Best	5wI	10wM
Test																		
All First	3	5	0	65	38	13.00	-	-	1	-	1	0	4	0	-	-	-	-
1-day Int																		
NatWest																		
B & H																		
Sunday	5	4	0	37	18	9.25	-	-	3	-								

Career Performances

	M	Inns	NO	Runs	HS	Avge	100s	50s	Ct	St	Balls	Runs	Wkts	Avge	Best	5wI	10wM
Test																	
All First	3	5	0	65	38	13.00	-	-	1	-	6	4	0	-	-	-	-
1-day Int																	
NatWest																	
B & H																	
Sunday	5	4	0	37	18	9.25	-	-	3	-							

CLARKE, V. P.   Somerset

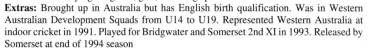

Name: Vincent Paul Clarke
Role: Right-hand bat, leg-break bowler
Born: 11 November 1971, Liverpool
Height: 6ft 3in **Weight:** 15st 10lbs
County debut: 1994
Parents: Vinnie and Sandra
Marital status: Single
Family links with cricket: Father played
representative schoolboy cricket
Education: Craigie Primary School;
Sacred Heart College, Sorrento;
Perth College, Western Australia
Qualifications: Diploma in Social Training
Overseas teams played for:
Wanneroo District, Perth 1990-94
Cricketers particularly admired:
Shane Warne, Ian Botham
Other sports followed: Windsurfing,
Aussie rules football, most sports
Relaxations: Playing the guitar, golf, watching sport
Extras: Brought up in Australia but has English birth qualification. Was in Western
Australian Development Squads from U14 to U19. Represented Western Australia at
indoor cricket in 1991. Played for Bridgwater and Somerset 2nd XI in 1993. Released by
Somerset at end of 1994 season
Best batting: 38 Somerset v Gloucestershire, Bristol 1994
Best bowling: 1-93 Somerset v Glamorgan, Swansea 1994

1994 Season

	M	Inns	NO	Runs	HS	Avge	100s	50s	Ct	St	O	M	Runs	Wkts	Avge	Best	5wI	10wM
Test																		
All First	2	4	0	46	38	11.50	-	-	-	-	23	4	105	1	105.00	1-93	-	-
1-day Int																		
NatWest																		
B & H	1	1	0	22	22	22.00	-	-	-	-								
Sunday	6	6	0	52	26	8.66	-	-	2	-	17.2	0	100	2	50.00	1-15	-	

11. Who was recently appointed as the first full-time General Secretary
of the Professional Cricketers' Association?

Career Performances

	M	Inns	NO	Runs	HS	Avge	100s	50s	Ct	St	Balls	Runs	Wkts	Avge	Best	5wI	10wM
Test																	
All First	2	4	0	46	38	11.50	-	-	-	-	138	105	1	105.00	1-93	-	-
1-day Int																	
NatWest																	
B & H	1	1	0	22	22	22.00	-	-	-	-							
Sunday	6	6	0	52	26	8.66	-	-	2	-	104	100	2	50.00	1-15	-	

CONNOR, C. A.   Hampshire

Name: Cardigan Adolphus Connor
Role: Right-hand bat, right-arm
fast-medium bowler
Born: 24 March 1961, The Valley, Anguilla
Height: 5ft 11in **Weight:** 12st 4lbs
Nickname: Cardi
County debut: 1984
County cap: 1988
50 wickets in a season: 4
1st-Class 50s: 2
1st-Class 5 w. in innings: 12
1st-Class 10 w. in match: 3
1st-Class catches: 54
Place in batting averages: 259th av. 11.31
(1993 193rd av. 20.00)
Place in bowling averages: 20th av. 24.50
(1993 138th av. 50.18)
Strike rate: 47.88 (career 62.58)
Parents: Ethleen
Marital status: Engaged to Jacqui
Education: The Valley Secondary School, Anguilla; Langley College
Qualifications: Engineer
Career outside cricket: Keep-fit instructor and masseur
Overseas tours: CCC to Australia 1983
Overseas teams played for: Merewether DCC, Newcastle, Australia 1983-92; Valley
Secondary School 1992-94
Cricketers particularly admired: Malcolm Marshall, Viv Richards, Richard Hadlee,
Kevan James
Other sports followed: All sports. Football (Arsenal)
Relaxations: Keeping fit and massage
Extras: Played for Buckinghamshire in Minor Counties before joining Hampshire. First

Anguillan-born player to appear in the County Championship
Best batting: 59 Hampshire v Surrey, The Oval 1993
Best bowling: 7-31 Hampshire v Gloucestershire, Portsmouth 1989

1994 Season

	M	Inns	NO	Runs	HS	Avge	100s	50s	Ct	St	O	M	Runs	Wkts	Avge	Best	5wI	10wM
Test																		
All First	15	22	3	215	25	11.31	-	-	4	-	574.4	131	1764	72	24.50	7-47	2	2
1-day Int																		
NatWest	2	1	0	5	5	5.00	-	-	-	-	20	5	61	4	15.25	4-11	-	
B & H	3	0	0	0	0	-	-	-	1	-	24	3	115	3	38.33	2-45	-	
Sunday	17	5	1	23	17 *	5.75	-	-	3	-	129.3	7	567	26	21.80	4-34	-	

Career Performances

	M	Inns	NO	Runs	HS	Avge	100s	50s	Ct	St	Balls	Runs	Wkts	Avge	Best	5wI	10wM
Test																	
All First	185	162	42	1304	59	10.86	-	2	54	-	30852	15893	493	32.23	7-31	12	4
1-day Int																	
NatWest	28	5	2	33	13	11.00	-	-	8	-	1810	1089	55	19.80	4-11	-	
B & H	45	9	4	19	5 *	3.80	-	-	9	-	2586	1695	70	24.21	4-19	-	
Sunday	159	44	14	206	25	6.86	-	-	30	-	7014	5113	196	26.08	4-11	-	

COOK, N. G. B.   Northamptonshire

Name: Nicholas Grant Billson Cook
Role: Right-hand bat, slow left-arm bowler
Born: 17 June 1956, Leicester
Height: 6ft **Weight:** 12st 8lbs
Nickname: Beast, Strop
County debut: 1978 (Leicestershire),
1986 (Northamptonshire)
County cap: 1982 (Leicestershire),
1987 (Northamptonshire)
Benefit: 1995
Test debut: 1983
Tests: 15
One-Day Internationals: 3
50 wickets in a season: 8
1st-Class 50s: 4
1st-Class 5 w. in innings: 31
1st-Class 10 w. in match: 4
1st-Class catches: 197

Place in bowling averages: 127th av. 42.05
Strike rate: 100.05 (career 73.34)
Parents: Peter and Cynthia
Wife and date of marriage: Shân, 20 September 1991
Family links with cricket: Father played club cricket
Education: Stokes Croft Junior; Lutterworth High; Lutterworth Upper
Qualifications: 7 O-levels, 1 A-level, advanced cricket coach
Off-season: Organising benefit for 1995
Overseas tours: England to New Zealand and Pakistan 1983-84, to Pakistan 1987-88, to India (Nehru Trophy) 1989-90; English Counties to Zimbabwe 1984-85; England B to Sri Lanka 1985-86; MCC to Bahrain 1994-95
Cricketers particularly admired: John Emburey, Phil Carrick
Other sports followed: Soccer (especially Leicester City), rugby, horse racing
Relaxations: Crosswords, reading (especially Wilbur Smith), good comedy programmes, good food
Extras: In 1975 played for English Schools and for Young England v Young West Indies. Left Leicestershire to join Northamptonshire in 1986
Opinions on cricket: 'Still of the opinion that groundsmen should be employed by the TCCB – with the object of making the best cricket pitch, i.e. pace, bounce and turn by the third day. Sunday League should again have good wickets and limited-over run-ups, therefore plenty of runs will be scored.'
Best batting: 75 Leicestershire v Somerset, Taunton 1980
Best bowling: 7-34 Leicestershire v Essex, Chelmsford 1992

1994 Season

	M	Inns	NO	Runs	HS	Avge	100s	50s	Ct	St	O	M	Runs	Wkts	Avge	Best	5wI	10wM
Test																		
All First	11	12	1	98	43 *	8.90	-	-	3	-	283.3	85	715	17	42.05	3-46	-	-
1-day Int																		
NatWest	3	1	0	1	1	1.00	-	-	-	-	25.1	0	93	2	46.50	1-39	-	
B & H																		
Sunday	16	7	3	33	21 *	8.25	-	-	7	-	100	1	480	10	48.00	3-19	-	

Career Performances

	M	Inns	NO	Runs	HS	Avge	100s	50s	Ct	St	Balls	Runs	Wkts	Avge	Best	5wI	10wM
Test	15	25	4	179	31	8.52	-	-	5	-	4172	1689	52	32.48	6-65	4	
All First	356	365	96	3137	75	11.66	-	4	197	-	64469	25507	879	29.01	7-34	31	4
1-day Int	3	0	0	0	0	-	-	-	2	-	144	95	5	19.00	2-18	-	
NatWest	28	9	2	44	13	6.28	-	-	8	-	1817	1046	28	37.35	4-24	-	
B & H	36	16	6	129	23	12.90	-	-	12	-	1849	1121	22	50.95	3-35	-	
Sunday	141	57	26	284	21 *	9.16	-	-	48	-	5479	4039	132	30.59	4-22	-	

COOPER, K. E.   Gloucestershire

Name: Kevin Edwin Cooper
Role: Left-hand bat, right-arm
fast-medium bowler
Born: 27 December 1957,
Sutton-in-Ashfield
Height: 6ft 1in **Weight:** 13st 2lbs
Nickname: Henry
County debut: 1976 (Nottinghamshire),
1993 (Gloucestershire)
County cap: 1980 (Nottinghamshire)
Benefit: 1990
50 wickets in a season: 8
1st-Class 50s: 1
1st-Class 5 w. in innings: 26
1st-Class 10 w. in match: 1
1st-Class catches: 92
Place in batting averages: 257th av. 12.00
(1993 255th av. 11.47)
Place in bowling averages: 50th av. 28.81
(1993 38th av. 26.23)
Strike rate: 66.05 (career 60.87)
Parents: Gerald Edwin and Margaret
Wife and date of marriage: Linda Carol, 14 February 1981
Children: Kelly Louise, 8 April 1982; Tara Amy, 22 November 1984
Family links with cricket: Father played local cricket
Education: Hucknall National Secondary School, Nottingham
Qualifications: Senior coach
Career outside cricket: Free trade sales rep. for local brewery. Worked in marketing
department for Nottinghamshire CCC
Off-season: 'Looking for employment.'
Overseas tours: Derrick Robins U23 to Australasia, 1979-80; Gloucestershire to Sri
Lanka, 1993; MCC to Bahrain 1994-95
Overseas teams played for: Nedlands CC, Perth, Australia 1978-79
Cricketers particularly admired: John Snow
Other sports followed: Golf, football
Relaxations: Golf
Extras: In 1974 took 10-6 in one innings for Hucknall Ramblers against Sutton College
in the Mansfield and District League. First bowler to 50 first-class wickets in 1988 season.
Took 101 first class wickets in 1988. Released by Notts at end of 1992 season
Best batting: 52 Gloucestershire v Lancashire, Cheltenham 1993
Best bowling: 8-44 Nottinghamshire v Middlesex, Lord's 1984

1994 Season

	M	Inns	NO	Runs	HS	Avge	100s	50s	Ct	St	O	M	Runs	Wkts	Avge	Best	5wl	10wM
Test																		
All First	12	16	9	84	18 *	12.00	-	-	2	-	418.2	99	1095	38	28.81	4-38	-	-
1-day Int																		
NatWest	1	0	0	0	0	-	-	-	-	-	12	1	30	2	15.00	2-30	-	
B & H	1	1	1	0	0 *	-	-	-	-	-	11	3	19	1	19.00	1-19	-	
Sunday	4	3	2	5	5 *	5.00	-	-	1	-	27	2	156	3	52.00	1-19	-	

Career Performances

	M	Inns	NO	Runs	HS	Avge	100s	50s	Ct	St	Balls	Runs	Wkts	Avge	Best	5wl	10wM
Test																	
All First	300	324	82	2443	52	10.09	-	1	92	-	48640	21700	799	27.15	8-44	26	1
1-day Int																	
NatWest	25	8	1	45	11	6.42	-	-	6	-	1712	782	37	21.13	4-49	-	
B & H	65	23	14	118	25 *	13.11	-	-	12	-	3799	2074	73	28.41	4-9	-	
Sunday	165	60	21	248	31	6.35	-	-	28	-	6922	5104	140	36.45	4-25	-	

CORK, D. G.   Derbyshire

Name: Dominic Gerald Cork
Role: Right-hand bat, right-arm
fast-medium bowler, slip fielder
Born: 7 August 1971,
Newcastle-under-Lyme, Staffordshire
Height: 6ft 3in **Weight:** 13st 4lbs
Nickname: Corky, Snaffler, Sherka, Golden
County debut: 1990
County cap: 1993
One-Day Internationals: 5
50 wickets in a season: 1
1st-Class 50s: 11
1st-Class 100s: 1
1st-Class 5 w. in innings: 5
1st-Class 10 w. in match: 1
1st-Class catches: 52
Place in batting averages: 172nd av. 24.14
(1993 131st av. 27.54)
Place in bowling averages: 58th av. 30.05 (1993 66th av. 29.78)
Strike rate: 53.37 (career 56.26)
Parents: Gerald and Mary
Wife and date of marriage: Jane, 2 October 1993

Children: Gregory Theodore Gerald, 29 September 1994
Family links with cricket: Father and two brothers, Simon and Jonathan, play in North Staffs & South Cheshire League. All four played for Betley at same time and mother made the teas
Education: St Joseph's College, Stoke-on-Trent; Newcastle College
Qualifications: History O-Level, leisure and recreation qualified coach
Off-season: Touring India with England A
Overseas tours: England YCs to Australia 1989-90; England A to Bermuda and West Indies 1991-92, to Australia 1992-93, to South Africa 1993-94, to India 1994-95
Overseas teams played for: East Shirley, Christchurch, New Zealand 1990-91
Cricketers particularly admired: Phillip DeFreitas, Ian Botham, Kim Barnett, Alan Warner
Other sports followed: Horse racing, football (Stoke), greyhounds and golf
Injuries: Knee problems, missed two months
Relaxations: 'Watching Stoke City go into the Premier League.'
Extras: First played cricket for Betley CC in the North Staffs & South Cheshire League. In 1990 he took a wicket in his first over in first-class cricket v New Zealand at Derby and scored a century as nightwatchman for England U19 v Pakistan at Taunton. Played Minor Counties cricket for Staffordshire in 1989 and 1990. Selected for England A in 1991 – his first full season of first-class cricket. The Cricket Association Young Player of 1991. Took eight wickets for 53 runs on 20th birthday. Achieved first-class hat-trick against Kent, 1994
Opinions on cricket: 'I'm very glad to see English cricket this season has hit a high again. Credit must go to the achievements of all those involved. Also I think the four-day game has helped players develop towards Test cricketers.'
Best batting: 104 Derbyshire v Gloucestershire, Cheltenham 1993
Best bowling: 8-53 Derbyshire v Essex, Derby 1991

1994 Season

	M	Inns	NO	Runs	HS	Avge	100s	50s	Ct	St	O	M	Runs	Wkts	Avge	Best	5wI	10wM
Test																		
All First	13	21	0	507	94	24.14	-	4	15	-	329.1	55	1112	37	30.05	6-29	2	-
1-day Int	2	0	0	0	0	-	-	-	-	-	22	1	95	4	23.75	3-49	-	
NatWest	2	2	0	81	62	40.50	-	1	-	-	23	4	67	7	9.57	5-43	1	
B & H	2	2	1	71	64 *	71.00	-	1	-	-	16	0	86	1	86.00	1-67	-	
Sunday	12	9	0	275	66	30.55	-	1	6	-	86.2	2	412	11	37.45	4-44	-	

Career Performances

	M	Inns	NO	Runs	HS	Avge	100s	50s	Ct	St	Balls	Runs	Wkts	Avge	Best	5wI	10wM
Test																	
All First	78	108	14	2195	104	23.35	1	11	52	-	11759	5846	209	27.97	8-53	5	1
1-day Int	5	1	0	11	11	11.00	-	-	-	-	318	213	5	42.60	3-49	-	
NatWest	6	6	0	133	62	22.16	-	1	-	-	389	194	20	9.70	5-18	2	
B & H	11	8	4	199	92 *	49.75	-	2	5	-	680	447	11	40.63	4-26	-	
Sunday	44	32	2	494	66	16.46	-	1	17	-	1884	1564	48	32.58	4-44	-	

COTTEY, P. A.   Glamorgan

Name: Phillip Anthony Cottey
Role: Right-hand bat
Born: 2 June 1966, Swansea
Height: 5ft 5in **Weight:** 11st
Nickname: Cotts, Baba
County debut: 1986
County cap: 1992
1000 runs in season: 4
1st-Class 50s: 35
1st-Class 100s: 10
1st-Class catches: 75
Place in batting averages: 17th av. 51.59
(1993 75th av. 35.82)
Parents: Bernard John and Ruth
Wife and date of marriage:
Gail, 5 October 1992
Children: Lowri, 16 October 1993
Family links with cricket: Father played
for Swansea
Education: Bishopston Comprehensive School, Swansea
Qualifications: 9 O-levels
Career outside cricket: Coaching in Wales with Robert Croft
Off-season: Coaching cricket
Overseas tours: Glamorgan to La Manga, Barbados, Trinidad, Zimbabwe and Cape Town
1987-92
Overseas teams played for: Penrith, Sydney 1986-88; Benoni, Johannesburg 1989-90;
Eastern Transvaal 1991-92
Cricketers particularly admired: John Steele, Alan Jones, Paul Johnson
Other sports followed: All sports, especially football
Relaxations: 'Watching films, training, lager tasting and spending time with new family.'
Extras: Left school at 16 to play for Swansea City FC for three years as a professional.
Three Welsh Youth caps (one as captain)
Opinions on cricket: 'Four-day cricket should be played on better wickets, but wickets
must be allowed to have some sideways movement (be it seam or spin). However the
pitches must be of even bounce and pace.'
Best batting: 191 Glamorgan v Somerset, Swansea 1994
Best bowling: 2-42 Eastern Transvaal v Western Transvaal, Potchefstroom 1991-92

---

12. Who did Shane Warne dismiss with his first ball in Test cricket in
England?

1994 Season

	M	Inns	NO	Runs	HS	Avge	100s	50s	Ct	St	O	M	Runs	Wkts	Avge	Best	5wI	10wM
Test																		
All First	19	33	6	1393	191	51.59	3	6	16	-	24.4	3	106	2	53.00	1-16	-	-
1-day Int																		
NatWest	3	3	1	100	57	50.00	-	1	-	-	6	0	30	1	30.00	1-12	-	
B & H	1	1	0	43	43	43.00	-	-	-	-								
Sunday	17	16	3	288	70	22.15	-	2	5	-	6	0	42	1	42.00	1-17	-	

Career Performances

	M	Inns	NO	Runs	HS	Avge	100s	50s	Ct	St	Balls	Runs	Wkts	Avge	Best	5wI	10wM
Test																	
All First	126	203	33	6014	191	35.37	10	35	75	-	682	532	8	66.50	2-42	-	-
1-day Int																	
NatWest	14	14	4	245	57	24.50	-	1	3	-	36	30	1	30.00	1-12	-	
B & H	14	14	1	243	68	18.69	-	1	4	-	6	1	0	-	-	-	-
Sunday	73	59	13	1100	92 *	23.91	-	6	23	-	108	94	3	31.33	2-30	-	

COUSINS, D. M.   Essex

Name: Darren Mark Cousins
Role: Right-hand bat, right-arm fast-medium bowler, outfielder
Born: 24 September 1971, Cambridge
Height: 6ft 1in **Weight:** 12st 7lbs
Nickname: Mad Dog, Cuz, Cuzza
County debut: 1993
1st-Class 5 w. in innings: 1
1st-Class catches: 2
Place in bowling averages: 30th av. 25.92
Strike rate: 51.69 (career 59.57)
Parents: Dennis Charles and Deanna Maureen
Marital status: Single
Family links with cricket: Father opened the bowling for Cambridgeshire until injury
Education: Milton Primary School; Impington Village College
Qualifications: 7 GCSEs; NCA coaching award
Career outside cricket: Teacing PE at a secondary school near Cambridge
Off-season: Teaching PE. Training for next season, playing football and possibly spending three months abroad playing cricket

Cricketers particularly admired: 'Too many to mention.'

Other sports followed: All sports apart from horse racing and motor racing

Relaxations: 'I spend most of my spare time with my young lady, Sarah Jayne. When I am not with her, I enjoy socialising with friends, going to pubs and clubs, playing sport, watching television and listening to music – all the usual things young men get up to.'

Extras: Represented Cambridgeshire at football and swimming and every level at cricket. Played for a Bull Development Squad against Australia in 1991, taking four wickets in each innings. Played 2nd XI cricket for Northants and Worcs. Holds the record for both number of wickets in any single Colts festival (21) and number of wickets taken in the Hilda Overy Festival overall (74). Awarded 2nd XI cap and Essex Young Player of the Year, 1994. Essex Cricket Society 2nd XI Player of the Year, 1994. Leading Essex wicket-taker in Sunday League and top of the bowling averages

Opinions on cricket: 'I think second-team cricket should be more like first-team cricket, eg first-class venues, pitches, balls, rules. This would help young players prepare for 1st class cricket.'

Best batting: 11 Essex v Leicestershire, Leicester 1994

Best bowling: 6-35 Essex v Cambridge University, Fenner's 1994

1994 Season

	M	Inns	NO	Runs	HS	Avge	100s	50s	Ct	St	O	M	Runs	Wkts	Avge	Best	5wI	10wM
Test																		
All First	4	5	0	24	11	4.80	-	-	2	-	112	21	337	13	25.92	6-35	1	-
1-day Int																		
NatWest	2	1	1	1	1*	-	-	-	-	-	10	1	57	1	57.00	1-33	-	
B & H																		
Sunday	11	5	1	9	6	2.25	-	-	1	-	73.3	5	351	18	19.50	3-18	-	

Career Performances

	M	Inns	NO	Runs	HS	Avge	100s	50s	Ct	St	Balls	Runs	Wkts	Avge	Best	5wI	10wM
Test																	
All First	5	7	1	24	11	4.00	-	-	2	-	834	446	14	31.85	6-35	1	-
1-day Int																	
NatWest	2	1	1	1	1*	-	-	-	-	-	60	57	1	57.00	1-33	-	
B & H																	
Sunday	12	6	1	10	6	2.00	-	-	1	-	483	382	19	20.10	3-18	-	

COWAN, A. P. Essex

Name: Ashley Preston Cowan
Role: Right-hand bat,
right-hand medium-fast bowler
Born: 7 May 1975, Hitchin, Hertfordshire
Height: 6ft 4in **Weight:** 13st 10lbs
Nickname: Victor
County debut: No first-team appearance
Parents: Jeff and Pam
Marital status: Single
Family links with cricket: Father played
Education: Kingshott Prep;
Framlingham College
Qualifications: 5 GCSEs, 1 A-level;
vocational business course
Career outside cricket: Family business
Off-season: Family business and travelling
Cricketers particularly admired: Ian Botham
and Graham Dilley
Other sports followed: Rugby, hockey, golf
Injuries: Stress fracture of spine, missed three-four months
Relaxations: Playing and coaching golf, pool, listening to music
Opinions on cricket: 'Due to the amount of matches and practices, players are suffering with injuries.'

13. Who is the only person to have scored a century in each innings for England in a Test match in the West Indies, where and when did he achieve this?

COWANS, N. G.　　　　　　　Hampshire

Name: Norman George Cowans
Role: Right-hand bat, right-arm fast bowler
Born: 17 April 1961,
Enfield St Mary, Jamaica
Height: 6ft 3in **Weight:** 14st 7lbs
Nickname: Flash, George, Seed
County debut: 1980 (Middlesex),
1994 (Hampshire)
County cap: 1984 (Middlesex)
Benefit: 1993
Test debut: 1982-83
Tests: 19
One-Day Internationals: 23
50 wickets in a season: 6
1st-Class 50s: 1
1st-Class 5 w. in innings: 23
1st-Class 10 w. in match: 1
1st-Class catches: 63
One-Day 5 w. in innings: 1

Place in bowling averages: 113th av. 37.92 (1993 1st av. 14.62)
Strike rate: 80.65 (career 49.88)
Parents: Gloria and Ivan
Children: Kimberley, 27 December 1983
Education: Park High Secondary, Stanmore, Middlesex
Qualifications: Qualified coach
Overseas tours: England YC to Australia 1978-79; England to Australia and New Zealand 1982-83, to New Zealand and Pakistan 1983-84, to India and Australia 1984-85; England B to Sri Lanka 1985-86
Cricketers particularly admired: Viv Richards, Malcolm Marshall
Other sports followed: Football (Arsenal FC), athletics, boxing
Relaxations: Fishing, photography, travelling, being with friends, listening to reggae and soul music
Extras: Played for England YC. Won athletics championships in sprinting and javelin throwing and was a squash and real tennis professional. Played 13 Tests for England before being awarded his Middlesex cap. Released by Middlesex at the end of the 1993 season
Best batting: 66 Middlesex v Surrey, Lord's 1984
Best bowling: 6-31 Middlesex v Leicestershire, Leicester 1985

---

14. In which countries is the next cricket World Cup to be held?

1994 Season

	M	Inns	NO	Runs	HS	Avge	100s	50s	Ct	St	O	M	Runs	Wkts	Avge	Best	5wI	10wM
Test																		
All First	12	15	6	51	19	5.66	-	-	3	-	349.3	93	986	26	37.92	4-76	-	-
1-day Int																		
NatWest	2	1	1	6	6 *	-	-	-	-	-	17	2	53	2	26.50	2-21	-	
B & H	3	0	0	0	0	-	-	-	-	-	26	3	97	7	13.85	4-36	-	
Sunday	12	3	1	1	1 *	0.50	-	-	2	-	89	7	394	10	39.40	2-21	-	

Career Performances

	M	Inns	NO	Runs	HS	Avge	100s	50s	Ct	St	Balls	Runs	Wkts	Avge	Best	5wI	10wM
Test	19	29	7	175	36	7.95	-	-	9	-	3452	2003	51	39.27	6-77	2	-
All First	239	248	68	1605	66	8.91	-	1	63	-	33023	16461	662	24.86	6-31	23	1
1-day Int	23	8	3	13	4 *	2.60	-	-	5	-	1282	913	23	39.69	3-44	-	
NatWest	35	14	3	51	12 *	4.63	-	-	9	-	2032	1118	50	22.36	4-24	-	
B & H	35	15	6	50	12	5.55	-	-	6	-	2017	1124	54	20.81	4-33	-	
Sunday	115	36	13	140	27	6.08	-	-	17	-	4999	3424	121	28.29	6-9	1	

COWDREY, G. R. Kent

Name: Graham Robert Cowdrey
Role: Right-hand bat, right-arm
medium bowler, cover fielder
Born: 27 June 1964, Farnborough, Kent
Height: 5ft 11in **Weight:** 13st 9lbs
Nickname: Van, Mervyn
County debut: 1984
County cap: 1988
1000 runs in season: 3
1st-Class 50s: 36
1st-Class 100s: 13
1st-Class catches: 77
One-Day 100s: 1
Place in batting averages: 119th av. 31.33
(1993 170th av. 22.76)
Parents: Michael Colin and Penelope Susan
Wife and date of marriage:
Maxine, 20 February 1993
Family links with cricket: Father (M.C.)
and brother (C.S.) played for, and captained, Kent and England
Education: Wellesley House, Broadstairs; Tonbridge School; Durham University
Qualifications: 8 O-levels, 3 A-levels, qualified electrician, completing plumbing exams

Off-season: Working for the Infocheck Group plc.
Overseas tours: Christians in Sport to India 1985-86, 1989-90; MCC to West Indies 1991-92
Overseas teams played for: Avendale, Cape Town 1983-84; Mossman, Sydney 1985-86; Randwick, Sydney 1986-87
Cricketers particularly admired: Wayne Larkins, Julian Wilson, John Longley, Nick Cook
Other sports followed: Horse racing, wife Maxine (Juster) is a jockey
Relaxations: 'Horse racing – watching wife winning races! Reading – Brian Moore and Jonathan Smith. Music – Van Morrison, Bob Dylan and Paul Brady.'
Extras: Played for England YC. Made 1000 runs for Kent 2nd XI first season on staff, and broke 2nd XI record with 1300 runs in 26 innings in 1985. Plays in contact lenses
Opinions on cricket: 'Four-day cricket is here to stay. I still see no proof that it has either improved standards or increased the entertainment. Convinced that when draw is made for one-day knockout matches, Kent are automatically drawn away to Warwickshire! Can we check this?'
Best batting: 147 Kent v Gloucestershire, Bristol 1992
Best bowling: 1-5 Kent v Warwickshire, Edgbaston 1988

1994 Season

	M	Inns	NO	Runs	HS	Avge	100s	50s	Ct	St	O	M	Runs	Wkts	Avge	Best	5wl	10wM
Test																		
All First	10	16	1	470	114	31.33	1	2	4	-	0.2	0	4	0	-	-	-	-
1-day Int																		
NatWest	3	3	1	68	35	34.00	-	-	-	-								
B & H	1	1	0	14	14	14.00	-	-	-	-								
Sunday	12	10	2	266	82	33.25	-	1	2	-								

Career Performances

	M	Inns	NO	Runs	HS	Avge	100s	50s	Ct	St	Balls	Runs	Wkts	Avge	Best	5wl	10wM
Test																	
All First	146	230	28	6957	147	34.44	13	36	77	-	1089	753	11	68.45	1-5	-	-
1-day Int																	
NatWest	19	16	4	288	37	24.00	-	-	2	-	285	130	8	16.25	2-4	-	
B & H	35	32	3	707	70 *	24.37	-	5	11	-	130	76	2	38.00	1-8	-	
Sunday	121	106	17	2222	102 *	24.96	1	9	41	-	600	458	21	21.80	4-15	-	

COX, D. M.   Durham

Name: David Matthew Cox
Role: Left-hand bat, slow left-arm bowler
Born: 2 March 1972, Southall, Middlesex
Height: 5ft 10in **Weight:** 11st
Nickname: Coxy, Arthur

County debut: 1994
1st-Class catches: 1
Parents: Charles and Georgina
Marital status: Hazel, 1 October 1994
Family links with cricket: Father played
for Guinness Brewery and Old Actonians
Education: Greenford High School
Qualifications: 5 GCSEs, cricket coaching
certificate
Career outside cricket: Plasterer
Off-season: Plastering and
trying to keep fit
Cricketers particularly admired:
Don Wilson, Clive Radley and Geoff Cooke
Other sports followed: Horse racing
Injuries: Chicken pox for two weeks while
playing against South Africa
Relaxations: Watching other sports, mainly
horse racing

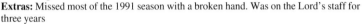

Extras: Missed most of the 1991 season with a broken hand. Was on the Lord's staff for
three years
Best batting: 26* Durham v South Africans, Chester-le-Street 1994
Best bowling: 1-92 Durham v South Africans, Chester-le-Street 1994

1994 Season

	M	Inns	NO	Runs	HS	Avge	100s	50s	Ct	St	O	M	Runs	Wkts	Avge	Best	5wI	10wM
Test																		
All First	3	4	1	32	26 *	10.66	-	-	1	-	74.5	11	345	1	345.00	1-92	-	-
1-day Int																		
NatWest																		
B & H																		
Sunday	3	0	0	0	0	-	-	-	-	-	20	2	89	1	89.00	1-25	-	

Career Performances

	M	Inns	NO	Runs	HS	Avge	100s	50s	Ct	St	Balls	Runs	Wkts	Avge	Best	5wI	10wM
Test																	
All First	3	4	1	32	26 *	10.66	-	-	1	-	449	345	1	345.00	1-92	-	-
1-day Int																	
NatWest																	
B & H																	
Sunday	3	0	0	0	0	-	-	-	-	-	120	89	1	89.00	1-25	-	

COX, R. M. F. Hampshire

Name: Rupert Michael Fiennes Cox
Role: Left-hand bat, off-spin bowler
Born: 20 August 1967, Guildford
Height: 5ft 9in **Weight:** 11st 7lbs
Nickname: Coxy, Ucca, MC and Nautilus
County debut: 1990
1st-Class 50s: 1
1st-Class 100s: 1
1st-Class catches: 12
Place in batting averages: 207th av. 19.00
(1993 174th av. 22.66)
Parents: Mike and Jo
Marital status: Single
Family links with cricket: Father played
for MCC and Hampshire Hogs
Education: Cheam Prep School;
Bradfield College
Qualifications: 8 O-levels, 2 A-levels
Overseas tours: Hampshire Hogs to
South Africa 1986, to Australia 1989
Overseas teams played for: Techs-Mutual, Cape Town 1986-92
Cricketers particularly admired: Geoffrey Boycott, Robin Smith, Malcolm Marshall
Other sports followed: Golf and football
Extras: Scored century in second first-class match. Wears one contact lens. Released by
Hampshire at end of 1994 season
Best batting: 104* Hampshire v Worcestershire, Worcester 1990

1994 Season

	M	Inns	NO	Runs	HS	Avge	100s	50s	Ct	St	O	M	Runs	Wkts	Avge	Best	5wl	10wM
Test																		
All First	4	7	1	114	46	19.00	-	-	3	-								
1-day Int																		
NatWest																		
B & H	1	0	0	0	0	-	-	-	-	-								
Sunday	6	5	1	46	23 *	11.50	-	-	2	-								

15. Without any change to its initials, under what three full names has
the ICC been know since its formation in 1909?

	M	Inns	NO	Runs	HS	Avge	100s	50s	Ct	St	Balls	Runs	Wkts	Avge	Best	5wl	10wM
Test																	
All First	19	29	4	605	104 *	24.20	1	1	12	-	6	1	0	-	-	-	-
1-day Int																	
NatWest																		
B & H	1	0	0	0	0	-	-	-	-	-							
Sunday	14	12	2	83	23 *	8.30	-	-	5	-							

CRAWLEY, J. P.   Lancashire

Name: John Paul Crawley
Role: Right-hand bat,
occasional wicket-keeper
Born: 21 September 1971, Malden, Essex
Height: 6ft 2in **Weight:** 14st
Nickname: Creeps, Jonty, JC
County debut: 1990
Test debut: 1994
Tests: 3
1000 runs in a season: 3
1st-Class 50s: 32
1st-Class 100s: 11
1st-Class 200s: 3
1st-Class catches: 65
Place in batting averages: 19th av. 50.64
(1993 22nd av. 47.54)
Parents: Frank and Jean
Marital status: Single
Family links with cricket: Father played in

Manchester Association; brother Mark played for Lancashire before moving to Nottinhamshire; other brother Peter plays for Warrington CC and has played for Scottish Universities and Cambridge University; uncle was excellent fast bowler; godfather umpires in Manchester Association
Education: Manchester Grammar School; Trinity College, Cambridge
Qualifications: 10 O-levels, 2 AO-Levels, 3 A-levels, 2 S-levels, BA in History, qualified cricket coach
Off-season: England tour to Australia
Overseas tours: England YC to Australia 1989-90, to New Zealand 1990-91; England A to South Africa 1993-94; England to Australia 1994-95
Overseas teams played for: Midland Guildford, Perth 1990
Cricketers particularly admired: Michael Atherton, Neil Fairbrother, Graham Gooch,

Alec Stewart, David Gower, Allan Donald, Ian Salisbury
Other sports followed: Football (Manchester United), golf
Relaxations: Music, foreign languages (French and Russian), dining out, golf, soccer and squash
Extras: Captained England YC (U19) to New Zealand 1990-91 and played for England YC in three home series v New Zealand 1989, Pakistan 1990 and Australia (as captain) 1991. Made his maiden first-class century for Cambridge University on the same day that brother Mark made his for Notts. First to score 1000 runs in U19 Tests. Scored 286 for England A against Eastern Province at Port Elizabeth in 1994, the highest score by an Englishman on an England or England A tour for almost 30 years.
Opinions on cricket: 'I think it's good that the four-day schedule has been introduced, and that the Sunday League has been commercialised.'
Best batting: 286 England A v Eastern Province, Port Elizabeth 1993-94
Best bowling: 1-90 Lancashire v Sussex, Hove 1992

1994 Season

	M	Inns	NO	Runs	HS	Avge	100s	50s	Ct	St	O	M	Runs	Wkts	Avge	Best	5wI	10wM
Test	3	5	0	59	38	11.80	-	-	4	-								
All First	20	34	3	1570	281 *	50.64	3	6	25	-	1	0	4	0	-	-	-	-
1-day Int																		
NatWest	2	2	0	31	22	15.50	-	-	1	-								
B & H	2	2	0	146	73	73.00	-	2	-	-								
Sunday	13	13	0	414	91	31.84	-	4	4	-								

Career Performances

	M	Inns	NO	Runs	HS	Avge	100s	50s	Ct	St	Balls	Runs	Wkts	Avge	Best	5wI	10wM
Test	3	5	0	59	38	11.80	-	-	4	-							
All First	80	133	13	5950	286	49.58	11	32	65	-	78	108	1	108.00	1-90	-	-
1-day Int																	
NatWest	2	2	0	31	22	15.50	-	-	1	-							
B & H	11	11	0	325	73	29.54	-	2	3	-							
Sunday	23	22	1	553	91	26.33	-	4	6	-							

CRAWLEY, M. A.   Nottinghamshire

Name: Mark Andrew Crawley
Role: Right-hand bat, right-arm medium bowler, slip fielder
Born: 16 December 1967, Newton-le-Willows
Height: 6ft 3¹/₂in **Weight:** 13st 8lbs
Nickname: Creeps, Flat-cap-whippet, Perch
County debut: 1990 (Lancashire), 1991 (Nottinghamshire)
1000 runs in a season: 1

1st-Class 50s: 14
1st-Class 100s: 8
1st-Class 5 w. in innings: 1
1st-Class catches: 59
Place in batting averages: 254th av. 13.23
(1993 200th av. 19.12)
Strike rate: (career 96.00)
Parents: Frank and Jean
Wife and date of marriage:
Natasha, 27 December 1991
Family links with cricket:
Father and uncle both excellent league players;
brother John plays for Lancashire; other brother
Peter plays for Warrington CC and has played
for Scottish Universities and Cambridge
University
Education: Manchester Grammar School;
Oxford University
Qualifications: 10 O-levels, 3 A-levels, BA
(Hons) in Chemistry, Special Diploma in Social Studies
Overseas tours: North of England U19 to Bermuda 1985; England YC to Sri Lanka
1986-87; Oxbridge to Holland 1987
Overseas teams played for: University of New South Wales, Sydney 1990-91
Cricketers particularly admired: Dennis Lillee, Jeff Thomson, David Gower, Jim Robson
Other sports followed: Football (Liverpool), golf, American football, rugby
Relaxations: Football, golf, squash and playing most sports, reading, crosswords
Extras: Third Notts player to score a century on his first-class debut. Nottinghamshire
Young Player of the Year 1992. Released by Nottinghamshire at end of 1994 season
Best batting: 160* Nottinghamshire v Derbyshire, Derby 1992
Best Bowling 6-92 Oxford University v Glamorgan, The Parks 1990

1994 Season

	M	Inns	NO	Runs	HS	Avge	100s	50s	Ct	St	O	M	Runs	Wkts	Avge	Best	5wI	10wM
Test																		
All First	8	14	1	172	45	13.23	-	-	7	-	77	33	132	1	132.00	1-48	-	-
1-day Int																		
NatWest	2	2	0	13	9	6.50	-	-	1	-	15	3	48	1	48.00	1-13	-	
B & H	3	3	0	73	37	24.33	-	-	1	-	25	3	101	5	20.20	4-43	-	
Sunday	12	11	2	222	42	24.66	-	-	5	-	43.4	0	241	3	80.33	1-25	-	

16. Who replaced Mike Procter as South Africa's coach/cricket manager?

Career Performances

	M	Inns	NO	Runs	HS	Avge	100s	50s	Ct	St	Balls	Runs	Wkts	Avge	Best	5wI	10wM
Test																	
All First	80	126	22	3378	160 *	32.48	8	14	66	-	6144	2985	64	46.64	6-92	1	-
1-day Int																	
NatWest	6	6	2	134	74 *	33.50	-	1	3	-	174	81	5	16.20	4-26	-	
B & H	22	21	3	472	58	26.22	-	3	5	-	986	608	12	50.66	4-43	-	
Sunday	45	38	9	634	94 *	21.86	-	1	14	-	1120	956	24	39.83	3-41	-	

CROFT, R. D. B.   Glamorgan

Name: Robert Damien Bale Croft
Role: Right-hand bat, off-spinner
Born: 25 May 1970, Swansea
Height: 5ft 11in **Weight:** 11st 5lbs
Nickname: Crofty
County debut: 1989
County cap: 1992
50 wickets in a season: 2
1st-Class 50s: 12
1st-Class 100s: 1
1st-Class 5 w. in innings: 10
1st-Class 10 w. in match: 1
1st-Class catches: 50
Place in batting averages: 152nd av. 26.08
(140th av. 26.59)
Place in bowling averages: 144th av. 52.82
(1993 103rd av. 35.37)
Strike rate: 104.70 (career 85.59)
Parents: Malcolm and Susan
Family links with cricket: Father and grandfather played local cricket
Education: St John Lloyd Catholic School; Neath Trinity College; West Glamorgan Institute of Higher Education
Qualifications: 6 O-levels; OND Business Studies; HND Business Studies; NCA senior coaching certificate
Career outside cricket: Personnel management ('not as yet!')
Overseas tours: England A to Bermuda and West Indies 1991-92, to South Africa 1993-94
Cricketers particularly admired: Alan Jones, Tom Cartwright, Don Shepherd, John Steele, John Emburey
Other sports followed: Rugby, soccer
Relaxations: Shooting, fishing, driving, music, golf
Extras: Captained England South to victory in International Youth Tournament 1989 and

was voted Player of the Tournament. Glamorgan Young Player of the Year 1992
Opinions on cricket: 'Enjoyment is of the utmost importance.'
Best batting: 107 Glamorgan v Cambridge University, Fenner's 1993
Best bowling: 8-66 Glamorgan v Warwickshire, Swansea 1992

1994 Season

	M	Inns	NO	Runs	HS	Avge	100s	50s	Ct	St	O	M	Runs	Wkts	Avge	Best	5wl	10wM
Test																		
All First	19	25	2	600	80	26.08	-	2	7	-	715.3	158	2166	41	52.82	5-80	1	-
1-day Int																		
NatWest	3	3	1	52	50	26.00	-	1	1	-	32.4	5	108	6	18.00	3-30	-	
B & H	1	1	1	23	23 *	-	-	-	-	-	11	2	29	2	14.50	2-29	-	
Sunday	17	13	4	125	29 *	13.88	-	-	5	-	101.4	2	470	21	22.38	6-20	1	

Career Performances

	M	Inns	NO	Runs	HS	Avge	100s	50s	Ct	St	Balls	Runs	Wkts	Avge	Best	5wl	10wM
Test																	
All First	117	163	37	3289	107	26.10	1	12	50	-	22170	10797	259	41.68	8-66	10	-
1-day Int																	
NatWest	13	11	3	158	50	19.75	-	1	2	-	718	418	12	34.83	3-30	-	
B & H	8	8	5	114	30 *	38.00	-	-	5	-	456	259	9	28.77	3-28	-	
Sunday	62	44	13	427	31 *	13.77	-	-	14	-	2404	1815	51	35.58	6-20	1	

CRONJE, W. J.   Leicestershire

Name: Wessel Johannes Cronje
Role: Right-hand bat, right-arm medium bowler
Born: 25 September 1969, Bloemfontein, South Africa
Nickname: Hansie
County debut: No first-team appearance
Test debut: 1992-93
1st-Class 50s: 19
1st-Class 100s: 13
1st-Class catches: 50
One-Day 100s: 1
Place in batting averages: 91st av. 34.78
Place in bowling averages: 61st av. 30.38
Strike rate: 73.76 (career 92.33)
Family links with cricket:
Father (N.E.) played for Orange Free State 1960-71 and elder brother (F.J.C) has also

played for Orange Free State
Education: Grey College, Bloemfontein; University of Orange Free State
Overseas tours: South Africa to India 1991-92, to Australia 1991-92, to West Indies 1991-92, to Sri Lanka 1993-94, to Australia 1993-94, to England 1994
Overseas teams played for: South African Universities; Orange Free State
Extras: Became captain of Orange Free State at age 21. Scored a century for South African Universities against Mike Gatting's England XI in 1989-90. Succeeded Kepler Wessels as captain of South Africa after the England tour in 1994
Best batting: 251 Orange Free State v Australia, Bloemfontein 1993-94
Best bowling: 4-47 South Africans v Kent, Canterbury 1994

1994 Season

	M	Inns	NO	Runs	HS	Avge	100s	50s	Ct	St	O	M	Runs	Wkts	Avge	Best	5wI	10wM
Test	3	6	1	90	38	18.00	-	-	2	-	37	9	94	0	-		-	-
All First	13	20	1	661	108	34.78	1	3	11	-	159.5	45	395	13	30.38	4-47	-	-
1-day Int	2	2	0	36	36	18.00	-	-	-	-	9	0	50	0	-		-	-
NatWest																		
B & H																		
Sunday																		

Career Performances

	M	Inns	NO	Runs	HS	Avge	100s	50s	Ct	St	Balls	Runs	Wkts	Avge	Best	5wI	10wM
Test	16	29	3	884	135	34.00	3	2	6	-	1153	351	5	70.20	2-17	-	-
All First	74	132	11	4689	251	38.75	13	19	50	-	2770	1117	30	37.23	4-47	-	-
1-day Int	51	48	9	1296	112	33.23	1	5	17	-	1622	1159	28	41.39	5-32	1	
NatWest																	
B & H																	
Sunday																	

CROWE, C. D.   Leicestershire

Name: Carl Daniel Crowe
Role: Right-hand bat, off-spin bowler
Born: 25 November 1975, Leicester
Height: 6ft **Weight:** 12st 7lbs
Nickname: Strutter
County debut: No first-team appearance
Parents: Edward and Jeannette
Marital status: Single
Family links with cricket: Younger brother has played for Leicestershire U15, U16 and U17
Education: Lutterworth Grammar School

Qualifications: 11 GCSEs, 2 A-levels, NCA Senior Coach
Off-season: Coaching and getting fit
Overseas tours: Leicestershire U19 to South Africa 1993-94
Cricketers particularly admired: All the staff at Leicestershire
Other sports followed: Football (Spurs) and most other sports
Relaxations: Eating out, going out with friends, sleeping
Extras: Played for Leicestershire U12-U19 and Midlands Schools U14-U19. One of the Cricketers of the Festival at Cambridge U19 Festival 1994

CUFFY, C. E. Surrey

Name: Cameron Eustace Cuffy
Role: Right-hand bat, right-arm fast bowler
Born: 8 February 1970, South Rivers, St Vincent
Height: 6ft 7in **Weight:** 13st 10lb
Nickname: Cammie
Place in bowling averages: 59th av. 30.05
Strike rate: 64.91 (career 57.97)
Parents: Eunice Campbell and Randolph Brewster
Family links with cricket: Three brothers all played for village team as fast bowlers
Education: South Rivers Methodist Primary School; Saint Martins Secondary School
Qualifications: 5 GCE/CXC O-levels
Career outside cricket: Tecnical Assistant at Cable and Wireless (W.J. Ltd)
Off-season: Touring with West Indies
Overseas tours: West Indies to India and New Zealand 1994-95
Cricketers particularly admired: Curtly Ambrose, Courtney Walsh
Other sports followed: Volleyball

Injuries: Muscle strain in shoulder, out for one month
Relaxations: Listening to reggae music, reading, meeting people and relaxing on the beach
Extras: Made his Test debut against India at Bombay in November 1994. Expected to be in West Indies party to tour England in 1995 and replaced by Waqar Younis as Surrey's overseas player.
Best batting: 14* Windward Islands v Leeward Islands, Castries 1992-93
Best bowling: 6-81 Windward Islands v Jamaica, Kingston 1993-94

1994 Season

	M	Inns	NO	Runs	HS	Avge	100s	50s	Ct	St	O	M	Runs	Wkts	Avge	Best	5wI	10wM
Test																		
All First	12	15	8	42	10	6.00	-	-	1	-	389.3	107	1082	36	30.05	4-70	-	-
1-day Int																		
NatWest	4	1	1	2	2*	-	-	-	1	-	42	11	133	6	22.16	4-43	-	
B & H	3	0	0	0	0	-	-	-	1	-	27	1	154	0	-		-	-
Sunday	1	0	0	0	0	-	-	-	-	-	6	0	43	0	-		-	-

Career Performances

	M	Inns	NO	Runs	HS	Avge	100s	50s	Ct	St	Balls	Runs	Wkts	Avge	Best	5wI	10wM
Test																	
All First	31	41	18	108	14*	4.69	-	-	4	-	5102	2398	88	27.25	6-81	3	-
1-day Int																	
NatWest	4	1	1	2	2*	-	-	-	1	-	252	133	6	22.16	4-43	-	
B & H	3	0	0	0	0	-	-	-	1	-	162	154	0	-		-	-
Sunday	1	0	0	0	0	-	-	-	-	-	36	43	0	-		-	-

17. Who captained England U19 on their 1994-95 tour to the West Indies and for which county did he play in 1994?

CULLINAN, D. J.   Derbyshire

Name: Daryll John Cullinan
Role: Right-hand bat, off-spin bowler
Born: 4 March 1967, East London
County debut: No first-team appearance
Test debut: 1992-93
1st-Class 50s: 32
1st-Class 100s: 11
1st-Class catches: 89
Place in batting averages: 62nd av. 38.90
Family links with cricket: Brother Ralph has played for Border and Orange Free State
Education: Queens College, Queenstown; Stellenbosch University
Overseas tours: South Africa to Australia 1991-92, to Sri Lanka 1993-94, to Australia 1993-94, to England 1994
Overseas teams played for: South African Universities; Border; Western Province
Extras: In 1983-84 became the youngest player to score a first-class century in South Africa. Holds record for the highest first-class score in South African cricket
Best batting: 337* Transvaal v Northern Transvaal, Johannesburg 1993-94
Best bowling: 2-27 Border v Natal B, East London 1983-84

1994 Season

	M	Inns	NO	Runs	HS	Avge	100s	50s	Ct	St	O	M	Runs	Wkts	Avge	Best	5wI	10wM
Test	1	2	0	101	94	50.50	-	1	-	-								
All First	9	14	3	428	94	38.90	-	4	5	-								
1-day Int	2	2	0	99	54	49.50	-	1	2	-								
NatWest																		
B & H																		
Sunday																		

Career Performances

	M	Inns	NO	Runs	HS	Avge	100s	50s	Ct	St	Balls	Runs	Wkts	Avge	Best	5wI	10wM
Test	8	14	0	438	102	31.28	1	2	2	-							
All First	95	167	24	5568	337*	38.93	11	32	89	-	138	70	3	23.33	2-27	-	-
1-day Int	22	21	2	450	70*	23.68	-	2	7	-							
NatWest																	
B & H																	
Sunday																	

CUMMINS, A. C.   Durham

Name: Anderson Cleophas Cummins
Role: Right-hand bat, right-arm
fast-medium bowler
Born: 7 April 1966, Packer's Valley,
Barbados
County debut: 1993
Test debut: 1992-93
Tests: 3
One-Day Internationals: 45
50 wickets in a season: 2
1st-Class 50s: 7
1st-Class 5 w. in innings: 3
1st-Class 10 w. in match: 1
1st-Class catches: 13
One-Day 5 w. in innings: 7
Place in batting averages: 177th av. 23.29
(1993 188th av. 20.91)
Place in bowling averages: 77th av. 31.57
(1993 74th av. 30.45)
Strike rate: 55.76 (career 55.94)
Education: Foundation School; Combermere School, Barbados
Career outside cricket: Works in a bank in Barbados, and spent summer 1992 working
for Barclays in Solihull
Off-season: Playing for West Indies
Overseas tours: West Indies to Australia and New Zealand (World Cup) 1991-92, to
Australia and South Africa 1992-93, to Sharjah, India (Hero Cup) and Sri Lanka 1993-94,
to India and New Zealand 1994-95
Overseas teams played for: YMPC, Barbados and Barbados 1989-92
Extras: Played for Blossomfield CC, Birmingham, during summer 1992. Was centre of
public boycott of historic West Indies v South Africa Test match, when not selected. Signed
for Durham in 1993 in place of Dean Jones, who was expected to be touring with Australia,
and retained for 1994. Made his Test debut against Australia on 1992-93 tour. Expected
to be in West Indies tour party to England in 1995, so replaced as Durham's overseas player
by Manoj Prabhakar
Best batting: 70 Durham v Worcestershire, Stockton-on-Tees 1993
Best bowling: 6-64 Durham v Somerset, Taunton 1994

---

18. Whose record did Graham Gooch pass in the last Test match of the
series against Australia in 1993 to become the most capped English Test
player?

1994 Season

	M	Inns	NO	Runs	HS	Avge	100s	50s	Ct	St	O	M	Runs	Wkts	Avge	Best	5wI	10wM
Test																		
All First	17	29	2	629	65	23.29	-	3	3	-	520.3	92	1768	56	31.57	6-64	4	1
1-day Int																		
NatWest	2	2	1	17	11	17.00	-	-	-	-	22	4	73	5	14.60	4-48	-	
B & H	1	1	0	21	21	21.00	-	-	-	-	11	0	37	1	37.00	1-37	-	
Sunday	14	10	2	337	67	42.12	-	2	4	-	110	4	571	20	28.55	3-32	-	

Career Performances

	M	Inns	NO	Runs	HS	Avge	100s	50s	Ct	St	Balls	Runs	Wkts	Avge	Best	5wI	10wM
Test	3	4	1	31	14 *	10.33	-	-	-	-	270	144	5	28.80	4-54	-	-
All First	55	82	10	1397	70	19.40	-	7	13	-	9790	5294	175	30.25	6-64	7	1
1-day Int	45	26	7	249	41	13.10	-	-	6	-	2326	1583	62	25.53	5-31	1	
NatWest	4	4	2	39	20 *	19.50	-	-	-	-	276	154	6	25.66	4-48	-	
B & H	2	2	1	24	21	24.00	-	-	-	-	132	73	4	18.25	3-36	-	
Sunday	31	22	3	438	67	23.05	-	2	5	-	1625	1253	49	25.57	4-24	-	

CUNLIFFE, R. J. Gloucestershire

Name: Robert John Cunliffe
Role: Right-hand bat, cover fielder,
occasional wicket-keeper
Born: 8 November 1973, Oxford
Height: 5ft 10in **Weight:** 12st 4lbs
Nickname: Arsie, Bertie
County debut: 1993 (one-day),
1994 (first-class)
1st-Class 100s: 1
1st-Class catches: 5
Place in batting averages: 133rd av. 29.50
Parents: Barry and Janet
Marital status: Single
Family links with cricket: 'Dad played
in his younger days for his wife's village
team and was groundsman for nine years
at Banbury Twenty CC'
Education: Banbury School and
Banbury Technical College
Qualifications: 'None (only GCSE in Physical Education)'
Off-season: Working in local sports centre in multi-gym
Overseas tours: England U19 to India 1992-93

Cricketers particularly admired: Robin Smith, David Gower, Graham Gooch
Other sports followed: Football
Extras: Played in England U19 home series against West Indies in 1993
Opinions on cricket: 'Maybe the 2nd XI games should be four days to get used to first-class cricket.'
Best batting: 177* Gloucestershire v Cambridge University, Bristol 1994

1994 Season

	M	Inns	NO	Runs	HS	Avge	100s	50s	Ct	St	O	M	Runs	Wkts	Avge	Best	5wI	10wM
Test																		
All First	7	13	1	354	177 *	29.50	1	-	5	-								
1-day Int																		
NatWest																		
B & H																		
Sunday																		

Career Performances

	M	Inns	NO	Runs	HS	Avge	100s	50s	Ct	St	Balls	Runs	Wkts	Avge	Best	5wI	10wM
Test																	
All First	7	13	1	354	177 *	29.50	1	-	5	-							
1-day Int																	
NatWest																	
B & H																	
Sunday	1	1	0	22	22	22.00	-	-	-	-							

CURRAN, K. M.   Northamptonshire

Name: Kevin Malcolm Curran
Role: Right-hand bat, right-arm fast-medium bowler
Born: 7 September 1959, Rusape, Rhodesia
Height: 6ft 2in **Weight:** 14st
Nickname: KC
County debut: 1985 (Gloucestershire), 1991 (Northamptonshire)
County cap: 1985 (Gloucestershire), 1992 (Northamptonshire)
One-Day Internationals: 11
1000 runs in a season: 5
50 wickets in a season: 5
1st-Class 50s: 55
1st-Class 100s: 19
1st-Class 5 w. in innings: 15
1st-Class 10 w. in match: 4
1st-Class catches: 131

One-Day 5 w. in innings: 1
Place in batting averages: 23rd av 48.65
(1993 100th av. 32.21)
Place in bowling averages: 137th av 47.19
(1993 3rd av. 19.29)
Strike rate: 82.03 (career 50.63)
Parents: Kevin and Sylvia
Marital status: Single
Family links with cricket: Father played for
Rhodesia 1947-54. Cousin Patrick Curran
played for Rhodesia 1975
Education: Marandellas High School,
Zimbabwe
Qualifications: 6 O-levels, 2 M-levels
Career outside cricket:
Tobacco buyer/farmer
Overseas tours: Zimbabwe to Sri Lanka
1982 and 1984, to England 1982 and for
World Cup 1983, to Pakistan and India for
World Cup 1987
Overseas teams played for: Zimbabwe and Natal 1988-92
Other sports followed: Rugby union
Relaxations: 'Game fishing, especially along the North Natal coast, the Mozambique
coast, and Magaruque Island'
Extras: First player to take a Sunday League hat-trick, and score 50 in the same match,
Gloucestershire v Warwickshire, Edgbaston 1989. Released by Gloucestershire at end of
1990 after he had completed the season's double of 1000 runs and 50 wickets. Chose to
join Northamptonshire for the 1991 season after he had been approached by several
counties.
Best batting: 144* Gloucestershire v Sussex, Bristol 1990
Best bowling: 7-47 Northamptonshire v Yorkshire, Harrogate 1993

1994 Season

	M	Inns	NO	Runs	HS	Avge	100s	50s	Ct	St	O	M	Runs	Wkts	Avge	Best	5wI	10wM
Test																		
All First	15	25	5	973	114	48.65	1	8	7	-	423.5	86	1463	31	47.19	4-65	-	-
1-day Int																		
NatWest	3	1	0	26	26	26.00	-	-	1	-	32	6	119	2	59.50	2-35	-	
B & H	1	1	0	5	5	5.00	-	-	-	-	10.5	0	65	0	-	-	-	
Sunday	14	14	2	414	88 *	34.50	-	2	7	-	85.1	6	423	12	35.25	3-26	-	

Career Performances

	M	Inns	NO	Runs	HS	Avge	100s	50s	Ct	St	Balls	Runs	Wkts	Avge	Best	5wI	10wM
Test																	
All First	241	368	62	11026	144 *	36.03	19	55	131	-	25672	13345	507	26.32	7-47	15	4
1-day Int	11	11	0	287	73	26.09	-	2	1	-	506	398	9	44.22	3-65	-	
NatWest	32	27	6	640	78 *	30.47	-	3	7	-	1655	948	32	29.62	4-34	-	
B & H	36	31	6	636	57	25.44	-	3	6	-	1758	1182	44	26.86	4-41	-	
Sunday	142	134	30	3249	92	31.24	-	18	29	-	4551	3620	134	27.01	5-15	1	

CURTIS, T. S. Worcestershire

Name: Timothy Stephen Curtis
Role: Right-hand bat, leg-spin bowler,
county captain
Born: 15 January 1960, Chislehurst, Kent
Height: 5ft 11in **Weight:** 12st 5lbs
Nickname: TC, Duracell, Professor
County debut: 1979
County cap: 1984
Benefit: 1994
Test debut: 1988
Tests: 5
1000 runs in a season: 10
1st-Class 50s: 92
1st-Class 100s: 35
1st-Class 200s: 2
1st-Class catches: 162
One-Day 100s: 5
Place in batting averages: 123rd av. 30.96
(1993 13th av. 53.55)
Strike rate: (career 92.36)
Parents: Bruce and Betty
Wife and date of marriage: Philippa, 21 September 1985
Children: Jennifer May, 9 February 1991; Andrew Stephen Neild, 17 February 1993
Family links with cricket: Father played good club cricket in Bristol and Stafford
Education: Royal Grammar School, Worcester; Durham University; Cambridge University
Qualifications: 12 O-levels, 4 A-levels, BA (Hons) in English, PCGE in English and Games
Off-season: Teaching at RGS, Worcester
Overseas tours: NCA U19 tour of Canada 1979
Other sports followed: Rugby, tennis, squash, golf
Extras: Captained Durham University to UAU Championship in 1981. Chairman of the
Professional Cricketers' Association. Appointed county captain in 1992. Worcestershire

supporters' Player of the Year 1992. A century against Durham in 1993 meant that he had scored a century against every other first-class county
Best batting: 248 Worcestershire v Somerset, Taunton 1991
Best bowling: 2-17 Worcestershire v Oxford University, The Parks 1991

1994 Season

	M	Inns	NO	Runs	HS	Avge	100s	50s	Ct	St	O	M	Runs	Wkts	Avge	Best	5wI	10wM
Test																		
All First	18	32	1	960	180	30.96	3	1	7	-	8	1	43	0	-		-	-
1-day Int																		
NatWest	5	5	1	245	136 *	61.25	1	1	2	-								
B & H	4	4	1	43	25 *	14.33	-	-	2	-								
Sunday	16	15	3	521	99 *	43.41	-	5	8	-								

Career Performances

	M	Inns	NO	Runs	HS	Avge	100s	50s	Ct	St	Balls	Runs	Wkts	Avge	Best	5wI	10wM
Test	5	9	0	140	41	15.55	-	-	3	-	18	7	0	-		-	-
All First	287	490	59	17910	248	41.55	35	92	162	-	1016	722	11	65.63	2-17	-	-
1-day Int																	
NatWest	36	35	4	1555	136 *	50.16	3	10	11	-	24	15	2	7.50	1-6	-	
B & H	52	52	4	1515	97	31.56	-	13	11	-	2	4	0	-		-	
Sunday	164	158	24	5551	124	41.42	2	47	50	-							

DAKIN, J. M.   Leicestershire

Name: Jonathan Michael Dakin
Role: Left-hand bat,
right-arm medium-fast bowler,
Born: 28 February 1973, Hitchin, Herts
Height: 6ft 5in **Weight:** 14st 4lb
Nickname: J.D., F.C., Half bat, The Sweep
County debut: 1993
Parents: Fred John and Gloria May
Marital status: Single
Family links with cricket: Brother plays club cricket for Wanderers 1st XI in South Africa
Education: King Edward VII School, Johannesburg, South Africa
Qualifications: Matriculation
Off-season: Playing cricket for Kaponga in New Zealand
Overseas tours: Rutland Tourists to Jersey 1992

Overseas teams played for:
Wanderers, South Africa, 1986-92; Alberts, South Africa 1993
Cricketers particularly admired:
Vince 'Clarke Kent' Wells, 'Roasting' Darren Maddy, Gordon 'F.M.' Parsons
Other sports followed: Most sports,
especially rugby (Tigers)
Injuries: Facets in back
Relaxations: Watching television, movies, listening to music, following sport and playing
golf
Extras: 'Only man to lose to David Millns in a two-mile race...ever.'
Opinions on cricket: 'Second-team games should be played on first-class wickets over
four days to allow for natural results. Two white balls should be used on Sundays to even
up the contest between bat and ball.'
Best batting: 18 Leicestershire v Hampshire, Leicester 1994
Best bowling: 4-45 Leicestershire v Cambridge University, Fenner's 1993

1994 Season

	M	Inns	NO	Runs	HS	Avge	100s	50s	Ct	St	O	M	Runs	Wkts	Avge	Best	5wI	10wM
Test																		
All First	2	3	0	29	18	9.66	-	-	-	-	11	1	36	1	36.00	1-36	-	-
1-day Int																		
NatWest																		
B & H																		
Sunday	14	12	0	96	41	8.00	-	-	4	-	33.3	0	198	10	19.80	3-32	-	

Career Performances

	M	Inns	NO	Runs	HS	Avge	100s	50s	Ct	St	Balls	Runs	Wkts	Avge	Best	5wI	10wM
Test																	
All First	3	4	0	34	18	8.50	-	-	-	-	270	120	5	24.00	4-45	-	-
1-day Int																	
NatWest																	
B & H																	
Sunday	22	18	1	174	41	10.23	-	-	6	-	595	573	16	35.81	3-32	-	

DALE, A.   Glamorgan

Name: Adrian Dale
Role: Right-hand bat, right-arm
medium bowler
Born: 24 October 1968, Germiston,
South Africa
Height: 5ft 11in **Weight:** 11st 10lbs
Nickname: Arthur
County debut: 1989
County cap: 1992
1000 runs in a season: 2
1st-Class 50s: 23
1st-Class 100s: 9
1st-Class 200s: 1
1st-Class 5 w. in innings: 1
1st-Class catches: 39
One-Day 5 w. in innings: 1
Place in batting averages: 161st av. 25.39
(1993 50th av. 39.78)
Place in bowling averages: 128th av. 42.39
(1993 98th av. 33.45)
Strike rate: 72.26 (career 70.09)
Parents: John and Maureen
Marital status: Single

Family links with cricket: Father played for Glamorgan 2nd XI and Chepstow CC
Education: Pembroke Primary; Chepstow Comprehensive; Swansea University
Qualifications: 9 O-levels, 3 A-levels, BA (Hons) in Economics
Off-season: Playing for Cornwall CCC in New Zealand
Overseas tours: Welsh Schools U16 to Australia 1986-87; Combined Universities to
Barbados 1988-89; Glamorgan to Trinidad 1989-90, to Zimbabwe 1990-91, to Trinidad
1991-92, to Cape Town 1992-93; England A to South Africa 1993-94
Overseas teams played for: Bionics, Zimbabwe 1990-91; Cornwall, New Zealand
1991-93
Cricketers particularly admired: Ian Botham, Michael Holding, Mike Gatting
Other sports followed: Football (Arsenal), athletics, US basketball
Injuries: Broken finger, out for three weeks
Relaxations: Learning to windsurf
Extras: Played in successful Combined Universities sides of 1989 and 1990. Only
batsman to score two half-centuries against the West Indies tourists in the same match in
1991. Took a wicket with his first delivery at Lord's. Recorded Glamorgan's best one-day
bowling figures, 6-22 against Durham 1993. Recorded Glamorgan's highest ever partnership,
425, with Viv Richards against Middlesex, 1993
Opinions on cricket: 'Zones is the best format for the B&H Cup with it coming so early

in the season. There is not enough value put on the use of coaching in the game.'
Best batting: 214* Glamorgan v Middlesex, Cardiff 1993
Best bowling: 6-18 Glamorgan v Warwickshire, Cardiff 1993

1994 Season

	M	Inns	NO	Runs	HS	Avge	100s	50s	Ct	St	O	M	Runs	Wkts	Avge	Best	5wl	10wM
Test																		
All First	18	29	1	711	131	25.39	2	2	3	-	277	65	975	23	42.39	2-7	-	-
1-day Int																		
NatWest	2	2	0	127	110	63.50	1	-	-	-	3	0	27	1	27.00	1-27	-	
B & H	1	1	0	23	23	23.00	-	-	-	-	5	0	40	0	-		-	
Sunday	13	13	1	304	61	25.33	-	1	2	-	34	1	198	6	33.00	2-21	-	

Career Performances

	M	Inns	NO	Runs	HS	Avge	100s	50s	Ct	St	Balls	Runs	Wkts	Avge	Best	5wl	10wM
Test																	
All First	98	161	16	4888	214 *	33.71	9	23	39	-	7640	4093	109	37.55	6-18	1	-
1-day Int																	
NatWest	16	14	1	366	110	28.15	1	1	4	-	784	534	17	31.41	3-54	-	
B & H	15	14	1	272	53	20.92	-	1	3	-	642	451	15	30.06	3-24	-	
Sunday	75	63	8	1438	67 *	26.14	-	9	21	-	2354	2093	68	30.77	6-22	1	

DALEY, J. A.   Durham

Name: James Arthur Daley
Role: Right-hand bat
Born: 24 September 1973, Sunderland
Height: 5ft 11in **Weight:** 12st
Nickname: Bebs, Jonty
County debut: 1992
1st-Class 50s: 8
1st-Class 100s: 1
1st-Class catches: 12
Place in batting averages: 112th av. 32.06
(1993 150th av. 25.59)
Parents: William and Christine
Marital status: Single
Family links with cricket: Brother played
representative cricket for Durham
Education: Hetton Comprehensive
Qualifications: 5 GCSEs
Career outside cricket: Travel agent

Off-season: In Australia
Overseas tours: Durham to Zimbabwe, 1991-92; England U19 to India 1992-93; England XI to Holland 1993
Cricketers particularly admired: David Graveney, Wayne Larkins, Jimmy Adams
Other sports followed: Most sports
Relaxations: Socialising, listening to all types of music
Extras: Scored three centuries in 1991 for MCC Young Cricketers at Lord's. Northern Electric Foundation for Sport award winner 1992
Best batting: 159* Durham v Hampshire, Portsmouth 1994

1994 Season

	M	Inns	NO	Runs	HS	Avge	100s	50s	Ct	St	O	M	Runs	Wkts	Avge	Best	5wI	10wM
Test																		
All First	10	18	2	513	159 *	32.06	1	3	3	-	2	0	9	0	-	-	-	-
1-day Int																		
NatWest																		
B & H																		
Sunday	8	6	2	218	98 *	54.50	-	2	1	-								

Career Performances

	M	Inns	NO	Runs	HS	Avge	100s	50s	Ct	St	Balls	Runs	Wkts	Avge	Best	5wI	10wM
Test																	
All First	25	44	3	1266	159 *	30.87	1	8	12	-	12	9	0	-	-	-	-
1-day Int																	
NatWest																	
B & H																	
Sunday	9	7	2	228	98 *	45.60	-	2	2	-							

19. Who in 1994 recorded the highest Championship-debut innings this century and the second highest of all time, what was his score, for which county and against whom?

DALTON, A. J.   Glamorgan

Name: Alistair John Dalton
Role: Right-hand bat, right-arm bowler
Born: 27 April 1973, Bridgend
Height: 5ft 7in **Weight:** 11st
Nickname: Ali, Dalts, A.J., Son of John
County debut: 1994
1st-Class 50s: 1
1st-Class catches: 5
Place in batting averages: 175th av. 23.50
Parents: John and Christine
Marital status: Single
Family links with cricket:
Father captained Bridgend Town 1st XI for
ten years; brother Simon now plays for the
same 1st XI and used to play for Welsh
Schools
Education: Brynteg Comprehensive School;
Millfield School; New College, Cardiff
Qualifications: 8 GCSEs, 3 A-levels, NCA Coach
Career outside cricket: Working for family business
Off-season: Playing and coaching in Durban
Overseas tours: Millfield School to Jamaica 1990; Glamorgan Schools to Singapore/
Malaysia 1992; Cardiff Eagles to Cape Town 1994; Glamorgan to Portugal 1994
Overseas teams played for: Paramatta, Sydney 1992-93; Crusaders, Durban 1994-95
Cricketers particularly admired: Tony Cottey, Mark Waugh, Jamie Bishop, all Cardiff
Eagles
Other sports followed: Rugby (played scrum-half for Millfield 1st XV and follows
Bridgend RFC)
Relaxations: All sports especially rugby, good films, Chinese food, travelling, 'a few pints
with the boys'
Extras: ASW Player of the Month, July 1994. ASW Young Player of the Year, 1994.
Glamorgan 2nd XI Player of the Year
Opinions on cricket: 'Good to see two bouncers allowed. Too much cricket played, so
the games are less intense and less appealing to spectators. Twelve-month employment
would be nice, financially.'
Best batting: 51* Glamorgan v South Africans, Pontypridd, 1994

20. Who topped the first-class batting averages in 1994?

1994 Season

	M	Inns	NO	Runs	HS	Avge	100s	50s	Ct	St	O	M	Runs	Wkts	Avge	Best	5wI	10wM
Test																		
All First	6	10	2	188	51 *	23.50	-	1	5	-								
1-day Int																		
NatWest																		
B & H																		
Sunday																		

Career Performances

	M	Inns	NO	Runs	HS	Avge	100s	50s	Ct	St	Balls	Runs	Wkts	Avge	Best	5wI	10wM
Test																	
All First	6	10	2	188	51 *	23.50	-	1	5	-							
1-day Int																	
NatWest																	
B & H																	
Sunday																	

DAVIES, A. P. Glamorgan

Name: Andrew Philip Davies
Role: Left-hand bat, right-arm medium-fast bowler
Born: 7 November 1976, Neath
Height: 5ft 11in **Weight:** 12st
Nickname: Davo
County debut: No first-team appearance
Parents: Phil and Anne
Marital status: Single
Family links with cricket: Father and brother play for BP Llandaray, mother makes the teas
Education: Dwr-y-felin Comprehensive School; Christ College, Brecon
Qualifications: 6 GCSEs
Career outside cricket: Studying for A-Levels
Off-season: 'Hopefully touring if I choose not to go to college.'
Overseas tours: Wales Minor Counties to Barbados
Cricketers particularly admired: Graeme Hick, Viv Richards
Other sports followed: Football (Swansea City)

Injuries: Broken thumb
Relaxations: 'Sleeping, playing golf (although I haven't got the patience)'
Extras: Trials at Birmingham City FC
Opinions on cricket: 'Too many games to play. Another league should be introduced with the bottom six or seven clubs of the original league going into the second division.'

DAVIES, M. Gloucestershire

Name: Mark Davies
Role: Right-hand bat, slow left-arm bowler
Born: 18 April 1969, Neath
Height: 5ft 8in **Weight:** 11st 6lb
Nickname: Sparky, Freddie,
'many other anti-Welsh names'
County debut: 1990 (Glamorgan),
1992 (Gloucestershire)
50 wickets in a season: 1
1st-Class 50s: 1
1st-Class 5 w. in innings: 3
1st-Class 10 w. in match: 1
1st-Class catches: 19
Place in batting averages: 138th av. 28.83
(1993 250th av. 12.22)
Place in bowling averages:
(1993 110th av. 38.16)
Strike rate: (career 70.70)
Parents: Peter Holbrook and Dorothy
Wife and date of marriage: Carol Elizabeth, 16 October 1993
Family links with cricket: Brother plays league cricket in Wales
Education: Cwrt Sart Comprehensive; Neath Tertiary College
Qualifications: 6 O-levels; BTEC ONC in Science; NCA advanced coach; qualified lifeguard
Off-season: Buying a house and playing in South Africa
Overseas tours: Fred Rumsey's XI to Barbados 1989; Gloucestershire to Sri Lanka 1992-93
Overseas teams played for: Newcastle City, New South Wales 1990-91; Villagers, Pretoria 1992-93
Cricketers particularly admired: Courtney Walsh, Tom Cartwright, John Steele
Other sports followed: Rugby union and league, boxing, athletics
Relaxations: 'Reading, good food and real ale, writing, listening to T.H.C. Hancock's opinions on everything from football to fudge-making.'
Extras: On the MCC groundstaff in 1987. Glamorgan 2nd XI Player of the Year 1991. Released by Glamorgan at the end of 1991. Gloucestershire Young Player of the Year 1993.
Opinions on cricket: 'Less secrecy and more openness regarding team selection. Keep

coloured clothing and use in 55-over cricket. Is Ricky Williams British or Bajan?'
Best batting: 54 Gloucestershire v Nottinghamshire, Trent Bridge 1994
Best bowling: 5-57 Gloucestershire v Northamptonshire, Northampton 1993

1994 Season

	M	Inns	NO	Runs	HS	Avge	100s	50s	Ct	St	O	M	Runs	Wkts	Avge	Best	5wI	10wM
Test																		
All First	4	8	2	173	54	28.83	-	1	1	-	104.3	14	370	6	61.66	3-53	-	-
1-day Int																		
NatWest																			
B & H																			
Sunday	9	5	1	40	14	10.00	-	-	2	-	57.2	2	285	8	35.62	2-23	-	

Career Performances

	M	Inns	NO	Runs	HS	Avge	100s	50s	Ct	St	Balls	Runs	Wkts	Avge	Best	5wI	10wM
Test																	
All First	39	57	18	555	54	14.23	-	1	19	-	7353	3590	104	34.51	5-57	3	1
1-day Int																	
NatWest																		
B & H																		
Sunday	16	8	2	66	14	11.00	-	-	2	-	458	405	12	33.75	2-23	-	

DAVIS, R. P. Warwickshire

Name: Richard Peter Davis
Role: Right-hand bat, slow left-arm bowler
Born: 18 March 1966, Westbrook, Margate
Height: 6ft 4in **Weight:** 14st 7lbs
Nickname: Dicky, Scud (missile)
County debut: 1986 (Kent), 1994 (Warwickshire)
County cap: 1990 (Kent), 1994 (Warwickshire)
50 wickets in season: 2
1st-Class 50s: 4
1st-Class 5 w. in innings: 15
1st-Class 10 w. in match: 2
1st-Class catches: 123
Place in batting averages: 212nd av. 18.71 (1993 253rd av. 11.71)
Place in bowling averages: 80th av. 31.80 (1993 80th av. 31.05)

Strike rate: 66.00 (career 74.28)
Parents: Brian and Silvia
Wife and date of marriage:
Samantha Jane, 3 March 1990
Family links with cricket: Father played club cricket and is an NCA coach; father-in-law Colin Tomlin helps with England's fitness training
Education: King Ethelbert's School, Birchington; Thanet Technical College, Broadstairs
Qualifications: 8 CSEs; NCA coaching certificate
Career outside cricket: Carpentry
Overseas tours: Kent Schools U17 to Canada 1983; Kent to Zimbabwe 1992-93
Overseas teams played for: Hutt Districts, New Zealand 1986-88
Cricketers particularly admired: Graham Gooch, Viv Richards
Other sports followed: Football, rugby, squash, golf
Relaxations: 'Any sport, television. Taking my wife out.'
Extras: Moved to Warwickshire at the end of the 1993 season after nine years at Kent
Best batting: 67 Kent v Hampshire, Southampton 1989
Best bowling: 7-64 Kent v Durham, Gateshead Fell 1992

1994 Season

	M	Inns	NO	Runs	HS	Avge	100s	50s	Ct	St	O	M	Runs	Wkts	Avge	Best	5wI	10wM
Test																		
All First	12	9	2	131	35 *	18.71	-	-	15	-	341	102	986	31	31.80	6-94	2	1
1-day Int																		
NatWest	1	0	0	0	0	-	-	-	-	-	6	1	20	1	20.00	1-20	-	-
B & H																		
Sunday	7	3	1	12	5	6.00	-	-	3	-	42.2	1	175	10	17.50	3-19	-	

Career Performances

	M	Inns	NO	Runs	HS	Avge	100s	50s	Ct	St	Balls	Runs	Wkts	Avge	Best	5wI	10wM
Test																	
All First	138	164	41	1930	67	15.69	-	4	123	-	26221	12260	353	34.73	7-64	15	2
1-day Int																	
NatWest	13	6	1	46	22	9.20	-	-	10	-	729	392	15	26.13	3-19	-	-
B & H	16	8	4	45	18 *	11.25	-	-	6	-	937	604	10	60.40	2-33	-	
Sunday	83	38	14	224	40 *	9.33	-	-	27	-	3128	2386	88	27.11	5-52	1	

DAWOOD, I.   Northamptonshire

Name: Ismail Dawood
Role: Right-hand bat, wicket-keeper
Born: 23 July 1976, Desbury, Yorks
Height: 5ft 8in **Weight:** 10st

Nickname: Hectic, Jive
County debut: 1994
Parents: Salim and Rashida
Marital status: Single
Family links with cricket: Father played local club cricket
Education: Batley Grammar School
Qualifications: 6 GCSEs (O-level passes)
Off-season: Touring with England U19
Overseas tours:
England U19 to Sri Lanka 1993-94,
to West Indies 1994-95
Overseas teams played for:
Grafton, Auckland 1992-93
Cricketers particularly admired:
Alan Knott, Ian Healy, Jack Russell,
Mohammad Azharuddin
Other sports followed: 'Local football team on a Saturday afternoon'
Relaxations: Watching football, spending time with family and friends
Extras: Went to the Yorkshire Cricket Academy
Opinions on cricket: 'I hope that the game of cricket is enjoyed by all who are associated with this fantastic game.'
Best batting: 2* Northamptonshire v Somerset, Taunton 1994

1994 Season

	M	Inns	NO	Runs	HS	Avge	100s	50s	Ct	St	O	M	Runs	Wkts	Avge	Best	5wl	10wM
Test																		
All First	1	1	1	2	2*	-	-	-	-	-	-							
1-day Int																		
NatWest																		
B & H																		
Sunday	1	1	0	2	2	2.00	-	-	-	-								

Career Performances

	M	Inns	NO	Runs	HS	Avge	100s	50s	Ct	St	Balls	Runs	Wkts	Avge	Best	5wl	10wM
Test																	
All First	1	1	1	2	2	* -	-	-	-	-							
1-day Int																	
NatWest																	
B & H																	
Sunday	1	1	0	2	2	2.00	-	-	-	-							

DAWSON, R. I.   Gloucestershire

Name: Robert Ian Dawson
Role: Right-hand bat, right-arm
medium bowler
Born: 29 March 1970, Exmouth, Devon
Height: 5ft 11in **Weight:** 12st
Nickname: Daws
County debut: 1991 (one-day),
1992 (first-class)
1000 runs in a season: 1
1st-Class 50s: 8
1st-Class 100s: 1
1st-Class catches: 21
Place in batting averages: 46th av. 42.76
(1993 182nd av. 21.87)
Parents: Barry and Shirley
Marital status: Single
Family links with cricket: Father and
brother both played club cricket
Education: Millfield School;
Newcastle Polytechnic
Qualifications: 8 O-levels, 3 A-levels
Overseas teams played for: Amanzimtoti, South Africa, 1993-94
Cricketers particularly admired: Ian Botham, David Gower, Viv Richards
Other sports followed: Football mainly and most other sports
Relaxations: 'Watching most sports and going down the pub for a pint'
Extras: Played in NatWest for Devon (from 1988), before joining Gloucestershire
Best batting: 127* Gloucestershire v Cambridge University, Bristol 1994
Best bowling: 2-38 Gloucestershire v Derbyshire, Chesterfield 1994

1994 Season

	M	Inns	NO	Runs	HS	Avge	100s	50s	Ct	St	O	M	Runs	Wkts	Avge	Best	5wI	10wM
Test																		
All First	16	30	4	1112	127 *	42.76	1	7	7	-	30	9	73	2	36.50	2-38	-	-
1-day Int																		
NatWest	1	1	0	60	60	60.00	-	1	-	-								
B & H																		
Sunday	16	15	0	268	45	17.86	-	-	3	-								

Career Performances

	M	Inns	NO	Runs	HS	Avge	100s	50s	Ct	St	Balls	Runs	Wkts	Avge	Best	5wI	10wM
Test																	
All First	31	55	5	1550	127 *	31.00	1	8	21	-	186	75	2	37.50	2-38	-	-
1-day Int																	
NatWest	4	3	0	73	60	24.33	-	1	-	-	24	37	1	37.00	1-37	-	
B & H																	
Sunday	33	28	2	428	45	16.46	-	-	9	-	48	36	0	-	-	-	-

DEFREITAS, P. A. J. Derbyshire

Name: Phillip Anthony Jason DeFreitas
Role: Right-hand bat, right-arm fast bowler
Born: 18 February 1966,
Scotts Head, Dominica
Height: 6ft **Weight:** 13st 7lbs
Nickname: Daffy, Lunchy
County debut: 1985 (Leics), 1989 (Lancs)
County cap: 1986 (Leics), 1989 (Lancs),
1994 (Derbys)
Test debut: 1986-87
Tests: 39
One-Day Internationals: 87
50 wickets in a season: 7
1st-Class 50s: 30
1st-Class 100s: 6
1st-Class 5 w. in innings: 36
1st-Class 10 w. in match: 3
1st-Class catches: 66
One-Day 5 w. in innings: 5
Place in batting averages: 139th av. 28.68 (1993 216th av. 16.60)
Place in bowling averages: 22nd av. 24.93 (1993 90th av. 32.83)
Strike rate: 48.92 (career 57.23)
Parents: Sybil and Martin
Wife and date of marriage: Nicola, 10 December 1990
Children: Alexandra Elizabeth Jane, 5 August 1991
Family links with cricket: Father played in Windward Islands. All six brothers play
Education: Willesden High School
Qualifications: 2 O-levels
Career outside cricket: 'Full-time dad!'
Off-season: Touring Australia with England
Overseas tours: England YC to West Indies 1984-85; England to Australia 1986-87, to

Pakistan, Australia and New Zealand 1987-88, to India and West Indies 1989-90, to Australia 1990-91, to New Zealand 1991-92, to India and Sri Lanka 1992-93, to Australia 1994-95

Overseas teams played for: Port Adelaide, South Australia 1985; Mossman, Sydney 1988; Boland, South Africa 1993-94

Cricketers particularly admired: Ian Botham, Graham Gooch, Geoff Boycott, Mike Gatting

Other sports followed: Football (Manchester City) and rugby league (Warrington)

Relaxations: 'Golf, gardening, visiting stately homes, spending spare time with wife and daughter Alexandra'

Extras: Left Leicestershire and joined Lancashire at end of 1988 season. Originally agreed to join unofficial English tour of South Africa 1989-90, but withdrew under pressure. Man of the Match in 1990 NatWest Trophy final. One of *Wisden*'s Five Cricketers of the Year 1992. Man of the Tournament in the Hong Kong Sixes 1993. Left Lancashire at the end of the 1993 season. Player of the Series against New Zealand 1994

Opinions on cricket: 'Pyjama cricket more interesting for children on a Sunday.'

Best batting: 113 Leicestershire v Nottinghamshire, Worksop 1988

Best bowling: 7-21 Lancashire v Middlesex, Lord's 1989

1994 Season

	M	Inns	NO	Runs	HS	Avge	100s	50s	Ct	St	O	M	Runs	Wkts	Avge	Best	5wl	10wM
Test	6	8	1	207	69	29.57	-	2	3	-	257	49	809	30	26.96	5-71	1	-
All First	14	21	2	545	108	28.68	1	3	5	-	530	108	1621	65	24.93	6-39	4	-
1-day Int	2	1	1	7	7 *	-	-	-	1	-	20	5	50	4	12.50	3-38	-	
NatWest	3	3	0	35	28	11.66	-	-	-	-	35	8	112	5	22.40	2-32	-	
B & H	2	2	0	25	16	12.50	-	-	1	-	15	2	75	1	75.00	1-29	-	
Sunday	11	5	2	105	33	35.00	-	-	2	-	83	6	314	11	28.54	4-9	-	

Career Performances

	M	Inns	NO	Runs	HS	Avge	100s	50s	Ct	St	Balls	Runs	Wkts	Avge	Best	5wl	10wM
Test	39	58	5	769	69	14.50	-	3	12	-	8572	4027	125	32.21	7-70	4	-
All First	212	291	30	5826	113	22.32	6	30	66	-	39323	19162	687	27.89	7-21	36	3
1-day Int	87	55	21	526	49 *	15.47	-	-	24	-	4861	3154	100	31.54	4-35	-	
NatWest	23	17	3	229	69	16.35	-	1	2	-	1397	699	35	19.97	5-13	3	
B & H	42	27	6	444	75 *	21.14	-	2	10	-	2484	1387	67	20.70	5-16	1	
Sunday	116	81	17	1043	49 *	16.29	-	-	16	-	4739	3514	142	24.74	5-26	1	

DE LA PENA, J. M.   Surrey

Name: Jason Michael de la Peña
Role: Right-hand bat,
right-arm fast-medium bowler
Born: 16 September 1972, Middlesex
Height: 6ft 5in **Weight:** 14st 7lb
Nickname: G.Wop, J, Stingray, Chewy, Les,
Leslie, Gin, De la Gin
County debut: 1991 (Gloucestershire),
1994 (Surrey – one-day)
Parents: Michael and Jacqueline
Marital status: Single
Education: Lambrook Prep School, Ascot;
Stowe School;
Bournside Sixth Form College, Cheltenham
Qualifications: 8 GCSEs, 2 A-Levels,
NCA Coach
Off-season: Playing in Australia
Overseas tours: England U19 to Pakistan
1991-92; Gloucestershire to Namibia 1990, Kenya 1991, Sri Lanka 1992-93
Overseas teams played for: North Hobart, Tasmania, Australia 1991-93; Mossman,
Sydney 1994-95
Cricketers particularly admired: David 'Syd' Lawrence, Dennis Lillee, Graham Dilley,
Michael Holding, Allan Donald and Richard Hadlee
Other sports followed: Golf, tennis, surfing, windsurfing, rugby union
Injuries: Ankle problem, out for three weeks; strained back ligament, out for one week
Relaxations: The cinema, music, girlfriend
Extras: England U19 against Young Australia. Selected for England U19 tour to Pakistan
1991-92, but had to pull out two hours before leaving owing to severe illness and underwent
an operation one day later. Joined Surrey for 1994 season
Opinions on cricket: 'It is still a batsman's game.'
Best batting: 7* Gloucestershire v Yorkshire, Sheffield 1993
Best bowling: 4-77 Gloucestershire v Australians, Bristol 1993

1994 Season

	M	Inns	NO	Runs	HS	Avge	100s	50s	Ct	St	O	M	Runs	Wkts	Avge	Best	5wl	10wM
Test																		
All First																		
1-day Int																		
NatWest																		
B & H																		
Sunday	1	1	1	0	0*	-	-	-	-	-	3	0	34	0	-		-	-

	M	Inns	NO	Runs	HS	Avge	100s	50s	Ct	St	Balls	Runs	Wkts	Avge	Best	5wl	10wM
Test																	
All First	4	4	2	8	7 *	4.00	-	-	-	-	354	294	7	42.00	4-77	-	-
1-day Int																	
NatWest																		
B & H																		
Sunday	1	1	1	0	0 *	-	-	-	-	-	18	34	0	-		-	-

DERBYSHIRE, N. A. Essex

Name: Nicholas Alexander Derbyshire
Role: Right-hand bat,
right-arm fast-medium bowler
Born: 11 September 1970, Ramsbottom
Height: 6ft **Weight:** 13st
Nickname: Derbs, Terrance, Spitfire,
The Count
County debut: 1994 (Lancashire)
Parents: Desmond and Pauline
Marital status: Single
Family links with cricket:
'My dad wishes he could play'
Education: Ampleforth College;
University of London
Qualifications: 4 A-levels, BA (Hons)
Career outside cricket: Part-time liquidator
Off-season: Playing in Australia
Overseas tours:
Lancashire to Johannesburg 1991-92
Overseas teams played for: DHS Old Boys, South Africa 1992-93; Manly, Sydney 1994-95
Cricketers particularly admired: Malcolm Marshall, Dennis Lillee, Allan Donald
Other sports followed: Rugby, skiing
Relaxations: Travelling
Extras: Moved from Lancashire to join Essex for 1995 season
Opinions on cricket: 'Too much cricket – other countries such as South Africa or Australia play far less and, therefore, are totally ready to play – no niggles, aches and pains or tiredness. There is no sense of monotony for them, whereas in our game it is a perpetual problem, leading to mediocrity on the field.'
Best batting: 5 Lancashire v Kent, Canterbury 1994
Best bowling: 1-48 Lancashire v Cambridge University, Fenner's 1994

1994 Season

	M	Inns	NO	Runs	HS	Avge	100s	50s	Ct	St	O	M	Runs	Wkts	Avge	Best	5wI	10wM
Test																		
All First	2	1	0	5	5	5.00	-	-	-	-	44	5	168	2	84.00	1-48	-	-
1-day Int																		
NatWest																		
B & H																		
Sunday																		

Career Performances

	M	Inns	NO	Runs	HS	Avge	100s	50s	Ct	St	Balls	Runs	Wkts	Avge	Best	5wI	10wM
Test																		
All First	2	1	0	5	5	5.00	-	-	-	-	264	168	2	84.00	1-48	-	-
1-day Int																		
NatWest																		
B & H																		
Sunday																		

DE SILVA, P. A. Kent

Name: Pinaduwage Aravinda de Silva
Role: Right-hand bat, off spin bowler
Born: 17 October 1965, Colombo, Sri Lanka
County debut: No first-team appearance
Test debut: 1984
Tests: 41
One-Day Internationals: 131
1st-Class 50s: 40
1st-Class 100s: 18
1st-Class 5 w. in innings: 3
1st-Class catches: 70
One-Day 100s: 2
Strike rate: (career 64.28)
Off-season: Playing for Sri Lanka
Overseas tours: Sri Lanka to England 1984, 1988, 1991, to Pakistan 1984-85, to India 1986-87, 1990-91, 1993-94, to Australia 1987-88, 1988-89, to New Zealand 1990-91, 1994-95, to Zimbabwe 1994-95, to India and Pakistan (World Cup) 1986-87, to Australia and New Zealand (World Cup) 1991-92
Overseas teams played for: Nondescripts, Colombo
Extras: Made his Test debut in Sri Lanka's first appearance at Lord's in 1984 and captained

Sri Lanka on their 1991 tour to England
Best batting: 267 Sri Lanka v New Zealand, Wellington 1990-91
Best bowling: 5-31 Nondescripts v Rio, Colombo 1992-93

1994 Season (did not make any first-class or one-day appearance)

Career Performances

	M	Inns	NO	Runs	HS	Avge	100s	50s	Ct	St	Balls	Runs	Wkts	Avge	Best	5wI	10wM
Test	41	70	3	2616	267	39.04	6	12	20	-	7732	384	11	34.90	3-39	-	-
All First	117	173	19	7466	267	48.48	18	40	70	-	3214	1399	50	27.98	5-31	3	-
1-day Int	131	127	12	3613	105	31.41	2	27	34	-	1846	1536	32	48.00	3-58	-	
NatWest																	
B & H																	
Sunday																	

DESSAUR, W. A.   Nottinghamshire

Name: Wayne Anthony Dessaur
Role: Right-hand bat, off-spin bowler
Born: 4 February 1971, Nottingham
Height: 6ft **Weight:** 12st
Nickname: Bed
County debut: 1992
1st-Class 50s: 2
1st-Class 100s: 2
1st-Class catches: 5
Place in batting averages: 204th av. 19.25
(1993 96th av. 32.50)
Parents: Pat and Tony
Marital status: Single
Family links with cricket: Father and
brother play local league cricket, father is
coach of county U15 side
Education: Loughborough Grammar School
Qualifications: 6 O-levels, 2 A-levels,
qualified coach
Off-season: Playing in Australia
Overseas teams played for: Grange, Adelaide 1991-94
Cricketers particularly admired: Tim Robinson, Derek Randall, Martin Crowe
Other sports followed: Football
Relaxations: Sleeping, reading, listening to music, 'receiving mail from Mick Newell'

Extras: Scored century in second first-class match. Nottinghamshire Young Player of the Year 1993. Released by Nottinghamshire at end of 1994 season
Best batting: 148 Nottinghamshire v Cambridge University, Trent Bridge 1992

1994 Season

	M	Inns	NO	Runs	HS	Avge	100s	50s	Ct	St	O	M	Runs	Wkts	Avge	Best	5wl	10wM
Test																		
All First	5	9	1	154	35	19.25	-	-	2	-								
1-day Int																		
NatWest																		
B & H																		
Sunday																		

Career Performances

	M	Inns	NO	Runs	HS	Avge	100s	50s	Ct	St	Balls	Runs	Wkts	Avge	Best	5wl	10wM
Test																		
All First	14	22	1	643	148	30.61	2	2	5	-	102	94	0	-	-	-	-
1-day Int																		
NatWest																		
B & H																		
Sunday	2	2	1	16	13 *	16.00	-	-	-	-								

DIMOND, M.   Somerset

Name: Matthew Dimond
Role: Right-hand bat, right-arm fast bowler
Born: 24 September 1975, Taunton
Height: 6ft 1in **Weight:** 11st 7lbs
Nickname: Dougie, Howser, Shearer
County debut: 1994
1st-Class catches: 4
Parents: Roger and Gillian
Marital status: Single
Education: Castle School, Taunton;
Richard Huish College, Taunton
Qualifications: 9 GCSEs, taking 2 A-levels in physical education and geology
Off-season: Touring with England U19 after finishing college
Overseas tours: West of England U15 to Trinidad and Tobago, 1991-92; Somerset Youth to Holland, 1992;

England U19 to West Indies 1994-95

Cricketers particularly admired: Allan Donald, Graham Thorpe
Other sports followed: Football (Yeovil Town), golf, American football
Injuries: Minor Achilles strain, missed one game at the end of the season
Relaxations: Golf, playing football, a night out with some college mates, music
Extras: Man of the Match for West of England U15 v Trinidad and Tobago, with a score of 56
Opinions on cricket: 'Too many games played in a short period of time, the end of the season tends to come earlier every year. So many games crammed into four-and-a-bit months, which gives the players barely any respite between games.'
Best batting: 25* Somerset v Yorkshire, Bradford 1994
Best bowling: 4-73 Somerset v Yorkshire, Bradford 1994

1994 Season

	M	Inns	NO	Runs	HS	Avge	100s	50s	Ct	St	O	M	Runs	Wkts	Avge	Best	5wI	10wM
Test																		
All First	3	2	1	34	25*	34.00	-	-	4	-	55.3	8	216	5	43.20	4-73	-	-
1-day Int																		
NatWest																		
B & H																		
Sunday	3	0	0	0	0	-	-	-	-	-	10	0	76	0	-		-	-

Career Performances

	M	Inns	NO	Runs	HS	Avge	100s	50s	Ct	St	Balls	Runs	Wkts	Avge	Best	5wI	10wM
Test																	
All First	3	2	1	34	25*	34.00	-	-	4	-	333	216	5	43.20	4-73	-	-
1-day Int																	
NatWest																	
B & H																	
Sunday	3	0	0	0	0	-	-	-	-	-	60	76	0	-		-	-

DITTA, A. I.   Leicestershire

Name: Adil Iqbal Ditta
Role: Right-hand bat, right-arm fast-medium bowler
Born: 10 October 1974, Middlesbrough
Height: 5ft 10in **Weight:** 11st
County debut: 1994 (one-day)
Parents: Ali and Naseem
Marital satus: Single
Education: Boynton Comprehensive School; Acklam College, Middlesbrough
Qualifications: 8 GCSEs
Off-season: Playing in South Africa
Overseas teams played for: CBC Old Boys, Orange Free State 1994-95
Cricketers particularly admired:
Hansie Cronje, Sachin Tendulkar, Allan Donald
Other sports followed:
Football (Middlesbrough), snooker, golf
Relaxations: Spending time with friends and family

Extras: Played for Yorkshire Cricket Association from U16 to U19, North of England U14 and U15 and for England U15. Played for England U17 against Zimbabwe and U19 against India

1994 Season

	M	Inns	NO	Runs	HS	Avge	100s	50s	Ct	St	O	M	Runs	Wkts	Avge	Best	5wI	10wM
Test																		
All First																		
1-day Int																		
NatWest																		
B & H																		
Sunday	1	1	1	1	1 *	-	-	-	-	-	-							

Career Performances

	M	Inns	NO	Runs	HS	Avge	100s	50s	Ct	St	Balls	Runs	Wkts	Avge	Best	5wI	10wM
Test																	
All First																		
1-day Int																		
NatWest																		
B & H																		
Sunday	1	1	1	1	1 *	-	-	-	-	-	-						

DIWAN, M.   Essex

Name: Muneeb Diwan
Born: 20 March 1972, St Stephens,
New Brunswick, Canada
Height: 5ft 10in **Weight:** 11st 6lbs
Nickname: Sammy
County debut: 1994
Parents: Azeem and Kishwar
Marital status: Single
Family links with cricket:
Father and uncles played club cricket
Education: Penge Primary School;
Haringey Cricket College
Qualifications: Qualified as player, coach
and umpire at Haringey Cricket College
Off-season: Four weeks in Kenya on a tour
sponsored by Sussex to play against Kenya XI
and Zimbabwe XI plus other top local teams.
Then from November onwards to a
training/ coaching camp in Pakistan.

Overseas teams played for: Nairobi Gymkhana, Kenya 1992-93
Cricketers particularly admired: Graeme Hick, Viv Richards, Dean Jones
Other sports followed: Tennis and football
Relaxations: Movies
Extras: 'My ambition is to play for England.' Scored 120 and 74* in his first game for Essex
2nd XI. Has also played for Derbyshire 2nd XI. Second successive year to score over 1500
runs for the 2nd XI at an average of over 40. Released by Essex at end of 1994 season
Opinions on cricket: 'A truly great and noble game! I believe in this game so much that
I intend to promote, dignify and popularise it wherever I can.'

1994 Season

	M	Inns	NO	Runs	HS	Avge	100s	50s	Ct	St	O	M	Runs	Wkts	Avge	Best	5wI	10wM
Test																		
All First	1	2	0	0	0	0.00	-	-	-	-								
1-day Int																		
NatWest																		
B & H																		
Sunday	4	4	0	31	14	7.75	-	-	-	-								

Career Performances

	M	Inns	NO	Runs	HS	Avge	100s	50s	Ct	St	Balls	Runs	Wkts	Avge	Best	5wI	10wM
Test																	
All First	1	2	0	0	0	0.00	-	-	-	-							
1-day Int																	
NatWest																	
B & H																	
Sunday	4	4	0	31	14	7.75	-	-	-	-							

D'OLIVEIRA, D. B.   Worcestershire

Name: Damian Basil D'Oliveira
Role: Right-hand bat, off-spin bowler,
slip or boundary fielder
Born: 19 October 1960, Cape Town,
South Africa
Height: 5ft 8in **Weight:** 11st 10lbs
Nickname: Dolly
County debut: 1982
County cap: 1985
Benefit: 1993 (£153,030 in joint benefit
with Martin Weston)
1000 runs in a season: 4
1st-Class 50s: 46
1st-Class 100s: 10
1st-Class 200s: 1
1st-Class catches: 203
One-Day 50s: 18
One-Day 100s: 1
Place in batting averages: (1993 186th av. 21.37)
Strike rate: (career 76.12)
Parents: Basil and Naomi
Wife and date of marriage: Tracey Michele, 26 September 1983
Children: Marcus Damian, 27 April 1986; Dominic James, 29 April 1988; Brett Louis, 28
February 1992
Family links with cricket: Father played for Worcestershire and England
Education: St George's RC Primary School; Blessed Edward Oldcorne Secondary School
Qualifications: 3 O-levels, 5 CSEs
Overseas tours: English Counties to Zimbabwe 1984-85
Overseas teams played for: West Perth, Australia 1980-81; East Christchurch, Shirley
1982-83, 1983-84
Cricketers particularly admired: Greg Chappell, Viv Richards, Dennis Lillee, Malcolm

Marshall, Richard Hadlee
Other sports followed: 'Most sport, but not horse racing'
Relaxations: Watching films, television, eating out, and playing with the kids
Best batting: 237 Worcestershire v Oxford University, The Parks 1991
Best bowling: 4-67 Worcestershire v Oxford University, Worcester 1994

1994 Season

	M	Inns	NO	Runs	HS	Avge	100s	50s	Ct	St	O	M	Runs	Wkts	Avge	Best	5wI	10wM
Test																		
All First	3	5	0	156	61	31.20	-	1	1	-	74	22	175	7	25.00	4-67	-	-
1-day Int																		
NatWest	1	1	0	12	12	12.00	-	-	-	-								
B & H	3	3	0	22	11	7.33	-	-	-	-								
Sunday	8	6	0	68	27	11.33	-	-	2	-								

Career Performances

	M	Inns	NO	Runs	HS	Avge	100s	50s	Ct	St	Balls	Runs	Wkts	Avge	Best	5wI	10wM
Test																	
All First	232	362	22	9445	237	27.77	10	46	203	-	3806	2110	50	42.20	4-67	-	-
1-day Int																	
NatWest	27	26	4	588	99	26.72	-	3	3	-	264	155	8	19.37	2-17	-	
B & H	51	46	4	818	66	19.47	-	4	20	-	234	150	5	30.00	3-12	-	
Sunday	174	154	17	3210	103	23.43	1	11	44	-	312	278	8	34.75	3-23	-	

DONALD, A. A.   Warwickshire

Name: Allan Anthony Donald
Role: Right-hand bat, right-arm fast bowler
Born: 20 October 1966, Bloemfontein, South Africa
Height: 6ft 3in **Weight:** 14st
County debut: 1987
County cap: 1989
Test debut: 1991-92
Tests: 17
One-Day Internationals: 46
50 wickets in a season: 3
1st-Class 5 w. in innings: 37
1st-Class 10 w. in match: 5
1st-Class catches: 76
One-Day 5 w. in innings: 4
Place in bowling averages: 68th av. 31.00 (1993 45th av. 27.03)
Strike rate: 50.96 (career 50.10)

Parents: Stuart and Francine
Wife and date of marriage:
Tina, 21 September 1991
Family links with cricket:
Father and uncle played club cricket
Education: Grey College High School;
Technical High School, Bloemfontein
Qualifications: Matriculation
Off-season: Playing cricket for South Africa
Overseas tours: South Africa to India
1991-92, to Australia and New Zealand (World
Cup) 1991-92, to West Indies 1991-92, to India
and Sri Lanka 1993-94, to Australia 1993-94
Overseas teams played for: Orange Free
State, South Africa 1985-93
Cricketers particularly admired: Richard
Hadlee, Malcolm Marshall, Gladstone Small,
Andy Lloyd, Eddie Barlow
Other sports followed: Rugby, golf, tennis
Relaxations: 'Listening to music, having a barbecue, playing golf and having a few beers
with my friends'
Extras: Played for South African XI v Australian XI in 1986-87 and v English XI in 1989-
90. Retained by Warwickshire for 1991 season ahead of Tom Moody. Toured with South
Africa on first-ever visit to India and to West Indies in 1991-92. One of *Wisden*'s Five
Cricketers of the Year 1992.
Best batting: 46* Orange Free State v Western Province, Cape Town 1990-91
Best bowling: 8-37 Orange Free State v Transvaal, Johannesburg 1986-87

1994 Season

	M	Inns	NO	Runs	HS	Avge	100s	50s	Ct	St	O	M	Runs	Wkts	Avge	Best	5wI	10wM
Test	3	4	2	46	27	23.00	-	-	1	-	89.3	15	410	12	34.16	5-74	1	-
All First	8	6	3	68	27	22.66	-	-	4	-	212.2	42	775	25	31.00	5-58	2	-
1-day Int	1	1	1	2	2 *	-	-	-	-	-	10.2	1	47	2	23.50	2-47	-	
NatWest																		
B & H																		
Sunday																		

Career Performances

	M	Inns	NO	Runs	HS	Avge	100s	50s	Ct	St	Balls	Runs	Wkts	Avge	Best	5wI	10wM
Test	17	23	13	75	27	7.50	-	-	5	-	4001	1978	75	26.37	7-84	4	1
All First	192	221	89	1470	46 *	11.13	-	-	76	-	34021	16510	679	24.31	8-37	37	5
1-day Int	46	15	8	29	7 *	4.14	-	-	5	-	2456	1614	62	26.03	5-29	1	
NatWest	19	7	4	28	14 *	9.33	-	-	1	-	1169	585	47	12.44	5-12	3	
B & H	17	9	5	57	23 *	14.25	-	-	3	-	1015	706	27	26.14	4-28	-	
Sunday	46	19	7	120	18 *	10.00	-	-	10	-	2086	1427	53	26.92	4-23	-	

DONELAN, B. T. P.   Somerset

Name: Bradleigh Thomas Peter Donelan
Role: Right-hand bat, off-spin bowler
Born: 3 January 1968, Park Royal,
Middlesex
Height: 6ft 1in **Weight:** 12st 7lbs
Nickname: Rooster, Freddie, Claw
County debut: 1989 (Sussex),
1994 (Somerset)
1st-Class 50s: 5
1st-Class 5 w. in innings: 4
1st-Class 10 w. in match: 1
1st-Class catches: 14
Strike rate: (career 81.37)
Parents: Terry and Patricia
Marital status: Single
Education: Our Lady of Grace Junior School;
Finchley Catholic High School
Qualifications: 8 CSEs, NCA coaching
certificate
Overseas tours: Christians in Sport to India 1989-90, to Zimbabwe 1994-95; MCC to Leeward Islands 1991-92
Overseas teams played for: Northcote, Melbourne 1987-88; Southland Cricket Association, New Zealand 1988-90; Otago B 1988-89; Wellington B 1990-91
Cricketers particularly admired: Martin Crowe, Dean Jones, John Emburey, Ian Botham
Other sports followed: Football, golf, tennis, snooker, darts
Extras: Was a product of the MCC groundstaff – there for 2$^{1}/_{2}$ years before joining Sussex in 1989. Released by Sussex at end of 1993 season. Played one Championship game for Somerset in 1994 but not retained for 1995 season
Best batting: 68* Sussex v Hampshire, Southampton 1992
Best bowling: 6-62 Sussex v Gloucestershire, Hove 1991

1994 Season

	M	Inns	NO	Runs	HS	Avge	100s	50s	Ct	St	O	M	Runs	Wkts	Avge	Best	5wI	10wM
Test																		
All First	1	1	0	0	0	0.00	-	-	-	-	15	2	59	1	59.00	1-27	-	-
1-day Int																		
NatWest																		
B & H																		
Sunday																		

Career Performances

	M	Inns	NO	Runs	HS	Avge	100s	50s	Ct	St	Balls	Runs	Wkts	Avge	Best	5wI	10wM
Test																	
All First	53	66	21	1105	68 *	24.55	-	5	14	-	8626	4627	106	43.65	6-62	4	1
1-day Int																	
NatWest																		
B & H	3	3	3	25	9 *	-	-	-	1	-	174	127	1	127.00	1-41	-	
Sunday	13	6	2	71	19	17.75	-	-	1	-	426	322	7	46.00	2-39	-	

DOWMAN, M. P. Nottinghamshire

Name: Mathew Peter Dowman
Role: Left-hand bat, right-arm medium
bowler
Born: 10 May 1974, Grantham, Lincs
Height: 5ft 10in **Weight:** 11st
Nickname: Doomer, Dowers
County debut: 1993 (one-day),
1994 (first-class)
Parents: Clive Stuart and Jackie Anne
Marital status: Single
Family links with cricket: Dad played
for Grantham Town. Three brothers also
play for Grantham, two of them representing
Lincolnshire Schools and Lincolnshire U19
Education: St Hugh's Comprehensive;
Grantham College
Qualifications: Senior Coach
Off-season: Having a back operation

Overseas tours: England U19 to India 1992-93; Lincolnshire U16 to Zimbabwe 1988-89;
Nottinghamshire to Cape Town 1992-93; also to Guernsey for Tim Robinson's benefit 1992
Cricketers particularly admired: Robin Smith, Mike Gatting, Malcolm Marshall, Andy
Afford 'for his wit'
Other sports followed: Most sports
Injuries: Back trouble, missed three and a half weeks
Relaxations: Watching television, playing golf, playing most sports, listening to music,
ballroom dancing
Extras: Played for England U19 in home series against West Indies in 1993, scoring 267 in
second 'Test'. Played in winning Midlands team at ESCA Festival 1989. Most runs in a season
for Lincolnshire Schools and holds record for most runs in Lincolnshire Schools career
Opinions on cricket: 'More 2nd XI fixtures should be played on county grounds.'
Best batting: 38 Nottinghamshire v Middlesex, Trent Bridge 1994

1994 Season

	M	Inns	NO	Runs	HS	Avge	100s	50s	Ct	St	O	M	Runs	Wkts	Avge	Best	5wI	10wM
Test																		
All First	3	5	0	111	38	22.20	-	-	-	-	12	2	45	0	-		-	-
1-day Int																		
NatWest																		
B & H																		
Sunday	6	6	1	86	52 *	17.20	-	1	1	-	4	0	23	0	-		-	-

Career Performances

	M	Inns	NO	Runs	HS	Avge	100s	50s	Ct	St	Balls	Runs	Wkts	Avge	Best	5wI	10wM
Test																	
All First	3	5	0	111	38	22.20	-	-	-	-	72	45	0	-		-	-
1-day Int																	
NatWest																	
B & H																	
Sunday	9	9	1	125	52 *	15.62	-	1	1	-	102	98	2	49.00	1-33	-	

DURANT, C. D.   Leicestershire

Name: Christian Dominic Durant
Role: Right-hand bat, wicket-keeper
Born: 23 January 1977, Leicester
Height: 5ft 11in **Weight:** 10st 11lbs
Nickname: Weggert
County debut: No first-team appearance
Parents: Roger and Sally
Marital satus: Single
Education: Stoneygate Prep School; Oakham School
Qualifications: 5 GCSEs
Overseas tours: Leicestershire Young Cricketers to South Africa 1993-94
Cricketers particularly admired: David Steele, Alex Stewart, Alan Knott
Other sports followed: Rugby union and football
Relaxations: Any sport
Extras: Leicestershire Schools and Cricket Association from U11 to U17, ESCA Midlands U14, HMC Schools U19. Holds all Oakham School wicket-keeping records (most dismissals in match, season, career)

174

DUTCH, K. P. Middlesex

Name: Keith Peter Dutch
Role: Right-hand bat, off-spin bowler
Born: 21 March 1973, Harrow, Middlesex
Height: 5ft 10in **Weight:** 11st 6lbs
Nickname: Dutchy, Kitten, Snout
County debut: 1993
1st-Class catches: 2
Parents: Alan and Ann
Marital status: Single
Family links with cricket: Father is a
qualified youth cricket coach at
Bessborough CC
Education: Nower Hill High School, Pinner;
Weald College, Harrow
Qualifications: 4 GCSEs and 1 A-level
Overseas teams played for:
Worcester United, South Africa 1992-93;
Geelong City, Australia, 1994
Cricketers particularly admired:
Desmond Haynes, John Emburey
Other sports followed: Most sports, especially football (Arsenal and Old Actonians FC)
Injuries: Rib injury, out for four weeks
Relaxations: Travelling, watching and playing other sports
Extras: On MCC groundstaff for one year before becoming a contracted player. Rapid
Cricketline 2nd XI Player of the Year 1993
Opinions on cricket: 'All 2nd XI Championship games should be allowed to be played on
county grounds with good wickets and one-day games should be spread around club
grounds if needed.'

1994 Season (did not make any first-class or one-day appearance)

Career Performances

	M	Inns	NO	Runs	HS	Avge	100s	50s	Ct	St	Balls	Runs	Wkts	Avge	Best	5wI	10wM
Test																	
All First	1	0	0	0	0	-	-	-	2	-	30	18	0	-	-	-	-
1-day Int																	
NatWest																	
B & H																	
Sunday																	

EALHAM, M. A.   Kent

Name: Mark Alan Ealham
Role: Right-hand bat,
right-arm medium bowler
Born: 27 August 1969, Ashford
Height: 5ft 10in **Weight:** 13st 9lbs
Nickname: Ealy
County debut: 1989
County cap: 1992
1st-Class 50s: 16
1st-Class 5 w. in innings: 5
1st-Class catches: 18
One-Day 5 w. in innings: 1
One-Day 50s: 1
Place in batting averages: 146th av. 26.58
(1993 19th av. 51.23)
Place in bowling averages: 48th av. 28.22
(1993 64th av. 29.58)
Strike rate: 59.03 (career 58.59)
Parents: Alan and Sue
Marital status: Single

Family links with cricket: Father played county cricket for Kent
Education: Stour Valley Secondary School
Qualifications: 9 CSEs
Off-season: Cricket coaching in Canterbury
Overseas teams played for: South Perth, Australia 1992-93
Cricketers particularly admired: Ian Botham, Viv Richards, Malcolm Marshall, Robin Smith, Paul Blackmore
Other sports followed: Golf, snooker and most other sports
Injuries: Groin strain, missed six weeks
Relaxations: Playing golf and snooker, watching films
Best batting: 85 Kent v Lancashire, Lytham 1993
Best bowling: 7-53 Kent v Hampshire, Canterbury 1994

1994 Season

	M	Inns	NO	Runs	HS	Avge	100s	50s	Ct	St	O	M	Runs	Wkts	Avge	Best	5wI	10wM
Test																		
All First	15	26	2	638	68 *	26.58	-	4	8	-	265.4	62	762	27	28.22	7-53	1	-
1-day Int																		
NatWest	4	4	2	52	26 *	26.00	-	-	2	-	35.5	3	107	7	15.28	4-10	-	
B & H	1	1	0	10	10	10.00	-	-	-	-	9	0	38	0	-	-	-	
Sunday	15	14	4	179	34	17.90	-	-	3	-	86	4	412	13	31.69	2-11	-	

Career Performances

	M	Inns	NO	Runs	HS	Avge	100s	50s	Ct	St	Balls	Runs	Wkts	Avge	Best	5wI	10wM
Test																	
All First	53	83	13	1988	85	28.40	-	16	18	-	6856	3550	117	30.34	7-53	5	-
1-day Int																	
NatWest	9	9	4	168	58 *	33.60	-	1	2	-	491	250	10	25.00	4-10	-	
B & H	14	12	4	117	26	14.62	-	-	8	-	738	465	19	24.47	4-29	-	
Sunday	67	51	17	662	43 *	19.47	-	-	19	-	2614	2001	64	31.26	6-53	1	

ECCLESTONE, S. C. Somerset

Name: Simon Charles Ecclestone
Role: Left-hand bat, right-arm
fast-medium bowler
Born: 16 July 1971, Great Dunmow, Essex
Height: 6ft 3in **Weight:** 14st 9lbs
Nickname: Eccles, The Beast
County debut: 1994
1st-Class 50s: 1
1st-Class catches: 3
Place in batting averages: 185th av. 22.26
Place in bowling averages: 111th av. 37.50
Strike rate: 81.40 (career 81.40)
Parents: Jonathan and Pippa
Marital satus: Single
Family links with cricket: Brother Giles played
for Essex, is vice-captain of Cambridgeshire
and won the *Daily Telegraph* Fantasy Cricket
League 1994

Education: Bryanston School;
Durham University; Keble College, Oxford
Qualifications: 9 O-levels, 3 A-levels, BA (Hons) Social Sciences, Dip Soc (Oxon)
Off-season: Playing in Australia
Overseas tours: Bryanston to West Indies 1989; Durham University to South Africa 1992-93
Cricketers particularly admired: David Gower
Other sports followed: Rugby and all other sports
Extras: Played for Essex from U11 to U19/2nd XI and for ESCA U19 v New Zealand 1989;
captained Durham University; played for Cambridgeshire; Blue for Oxford University
1994
Best batting: 80* Oxford University v Nottinghamshire, The Parks 1994
Best bowling: 4-66 Oxford University v Surrey, The Oval 1994

1994 Season

	M	Inns	NO	Runs	HS	Avge	100s	50s	Ct	St	O	M	Runs	Wkts	Avge	Best	5wI	10wM
Test																		
All First	13	19	4	334	80 *	22.26	-	1	3	-	298.3	70	825	22	37.50	4-66	-	-
1-day Int																		
NatWest																			
B & H	1	0	0	0	0	-	-	-	-	-	4	0	16	0	-		-	-
Sunday	8	8	1	218	66	31.14	-	1	-	-	45.2	1	238	11	21.63	4-31	-	

Career Performances

	M	Inns	NO	Runs	HS	Avge	100s	50s	Ct	St	Balls	Runs	Wkts	Avge	Best	5wI	10wM
Test																	
All First	13	19	4	334	80 *	22.26	-	1	3	-	1791	825	22	37.50	4-66	-	-
1-day Int																	
NatWest	1	1	0	1	1	1.00	-	-	-	-	18	22	0	-		-	-
B & H	1	0	0	0	0	-	-	-	-	-	24	16	0	-		-	-
Sunday	8	8	1	218	66	31.14	-	1	-	-	272	238	11	21.63	4-31	-	

EDWARDS, A. D. Sussex

Name: Alexander David Edwards
Role: Right-hand bat, right-arm fast-medium bowler
Born: 2 August 1975, Cuckfield, Sussex
Height: 6ft **Weight:** 12st 9lbs
Nickname: Al, Steady, Eddy
County debut: 1994 (one-day)
Parents: Richard John and Angela Janet
Marital status: Single
Family links with cricket: 'Parents drove me everywhere to play or practise cricket and have been absolutely wonderful'
Education: Felbridge Primary; Imberhorne Comprehensive; Loughborough University
Qualifications: 10 GCSEs, 4 A-levels
Career outside cricket:
Studying at Loughborough
Off-season: Studying for BSc in Physical Education and Sports Science
Overseas tours: Sussex U18 to India 1990-91; England U18 to South Africa 1992-93, to Denmark 1993
Cricketers particularly admired: Dennis Lillee, Michael Holding, Viv Richards, Stan

178

Berry and Pat Cale 'for their tremendous support, belief and encouragement'

Other sports followed: All sports except show jumping

Relaxations: Reading sports psychology, training, playing snooker, swimming, listening to a variety of music and watching sport on television

Extras: Lord's Taverners U15 Young Cricketer of the Year 1991 and a *Cricketer* magazine Young Cricketer of the Month in the same year. Played for England U19 against India U19 in 1994

Opinions on cricket: 'Second XI cricket should mirror the first-class game, e.g. same grounds, practice facilities and duration of matches in the championship (four days). This would help young players to make the transition from 2nd XI to first-class cricket. Young players should be given ample opportunity to prove themselves in first-class cricket. They shouldn't be afraid of initial failure.'

1994 Season

	M	Inns	NO	Runs	HS	Avge	100s	50s	Ct	St	O	M	Runs	Wkts	Avge	Best	5wI	10wM
Test																		
All First																		
1-day Int																		
NatWest																		
B & H																		
Sunday	1	0	0	0	0	-	-	-	-	-	5	1	24	0	-	-	-	-

Career Performances

	M	Inns	NO	Runs	HS	Avge	100s	50s	Ct	St	Balls	Runs	Wkts	Avge	Best	5wI	10wM
Test																	
All First																	
1-day Int																	
NatWest																	
B & H																	
Sunday	1	0	0	0	0	-	-	-	-	-	30	24	0	-	-	-	-

EDWARDS, T.   Worcestershire

Name: Timothy Edwards
Role: Right-hand bat, wicket-keeper
Born: 24 June 1974, Penzance, Cornwall
Height: 5ft 3in
Nickname: Ted, Pasty
County debut: 1993
1st-Class catches: 21
Parents: Chris and Heather
Marital status: Single
Family links with cricket: Father played
for Cornwall
Education: Mount's Bay School, Penzance
Off-season: Preparing for the new season
Overseas tours: West of England U14 to
Trinidad 1988; West of England U15 to
Holland 1989
Cricketers particularly admired:
Alan Knott, Ian Botham
Other sports followed: Football

Relaxations: 'Going out and enjoying myself'
Extras: Played for Somerset 2nd XI during two years with Somerset on YTS scheme
Best batting: 47 Worcestershire v Oxford University, 1994

1994 Season

	M	Inns	NO	Runs	HS	Avge	100s	50s	Ct	St	O	M	Runs	Wkts	Avge	Best	5wl	10wM
Test																		
All First	9	11	7	116	47	29.00	-	-	20	-								
1-day Int																		
NatWest																		
B & H																		
Sunday	5	3	3	20	16 *	-	-	-	6	-								

Career Performances

	M	Inns	NO	Runs	HS	Avge	100s	50s	Ct	St	Balls	Runs	Wkts	Avge	Best	5wl	10wM
Test																	
All First	10	11	7	116	47	29.00	-	-	21	-							
1-day Int																	
NatWest																	
B & H																	
Sunday	5	3	3	20	16 *	-	-	-	6	-							

ELLIS, S. W. K.   Worcestershire

Name: Scott William Kenneth Ellis
Role: Right-hand bat, right-arm fast-medium bowler
Born: 3 October 1975, Newcastle-under-Lyme
Height: 6ft 3in   **Weight:** 14st
County debut: No first-team appearance
Parents: Tony and Valerie Anne
Marital status: Single
Education: Shrewsbury School;
Warwick University
Qualifications: 9 GCSEs, 3 A-levels
Off-season: Studying ancient history and philosophy at university
Overseas tours: England U19 to West Indies 1994-95
Cricketers particularly admired:
Curtly Ambrose, Desmond Haynes, Robin Smith
Other sports followed: Football
Relaxations: Listening to music, reading
Extras: Played for England U18 against India U19 in 1994

EMBUREY, J. E.   Middlesex

Name: John Ernest Emburey
Role: Right-hand bat, off-spin bowler
Born: 20 August 1952, Peckham
Height: 6ft 2in **Weight:** 14st
Nickname: Embers, Ern
County debut: 1973
County cap: 1977
Benefit: 1986
Testimonial: 1995
Test debut: 1978
Tests: 63
One-Day Internationals: 61
50 wickets in a season: 16
1st-Class 50s: 53
1st-Class 100s: 7
1st-Class 5 w. in innings: 67
1st-Class 10 w. in match: 10

1st-Class catches: 434
One-Day 50s: 2
One-Day 5 w. in innings: 3
Place in batting averages: 245th av. 14.50 (1993 17th av. 52.14)
Place in bowling averages: 28th av. 25.66 (1993 4th av. 19.73)
Strike rate: 68.54 (career 70.26)
Parents: John (deceased) and Rose
Wife and date of marriage: Susie, 20 September 1980
Children: Clare, 1 March 1983; Chloë, 31 October 1985
Education: Peckham Manor Secondary School
Qualifications: O-levels, advanced cricket coaching certificate
Overseas tours: England to Australia 1978-79, to Australia and India 1979-80, to West Indies 1980-81, to India and Sri Lanka 1981-82, to West Indies 1985-86, to Australia 1986-87, to Pakistan, Australia and New Zealand 1987-88, to India 1992-93; unofficial English XI to South Africa 1981-82 and 1989-90
Overseas teams played for: Prahran, Melbourne 1977-78; St Kilda, Melbourne 1984-85; Western Province 1982-84
Cricketers particularly admired: Ken Barrington, Alan Knott
Other sports followed: Golf
Relaxations: Reading, golf
Extras: Played for Surrey YC 1969-70. Phil Edmonds of Middlesex and England was the best man at his wedding. Middlesex vice-captain 1983-93. One of *Wisden*'s Five Cricketers of the Year 1983. Captain of England v West Indies for two Tests in 1988. Banned from Test cricket for three years for touring South Africa in 1981-82, and for five more for touring in 1989-90, suspension remitted in 1992. Published autobiography *Emburey* in 1988. In the match against Somerset at Lord's in 1992 he became only the 9th player to take 1,000 wickets for Middlesex. Middlesex Player of the Year 1993
Opinions on cricket: 'Young players seem very uptight. They should relax and enjoy the game. The less pressure you put yourself under, the easier it will become. Good players don't become bad players, bad players can become good players. They just have to work a little harder.'
Best batting: 133 Middlesex v Essex, Chelmsford 1983
Best bowling: 8-40 Middlesex v Hampshire, Lord's 1993

1994 Season

	M	Inns	NO	Runs	HS	Avge	100s	50s	Ct	St	O	M	Runs	Wkts	Avge	Best	5wl	10wM
Test																		
All First	15	19	5	203	78 *	14.50	-	1	11	-	674	204	1514	59	25.66	6-89	2	-
1-day Int																		
NatWest	2	0	0	0	0	-	-	-	-	-	20.3	8	55	3	18.33	2-5	-	
B & H	2	1	0	0	0	0.00	-	-	-	-	22	6	56	4	14.00	3-37	-	
Sunday	7	3	0	23	16	7.66	-	-	-	-	53	2	212	4	53.00	2-46	-	

Career Performances

	M	Inns	NO	Runs	HS	Avge	100s	50s	Ct	St	Balls	Runs	Wkts	Avge	Best	5wI	10wM
Test	63	95	20	1705	75	22.73	-	10	33	-	15211	5564	147	37.85	7-78	6	-
All First	482	608	125	11395	133	23.59	7	53	434	-	105611	38956	1503	25.91	8-40	67	10
1-day Int	61	45	10	501	34	14.31	-	-	19	-	3425	2346	76	30.86	4-37	-	
NatWest	54	34	11	458	36 *	19.91	-	-	19	-	3615	1682	58	29.00	3-11	-	
B & H	75	53	14	626	50	16.05	-	1	39	-	4001	2079	79	26.31	5-37	1	
Sunday	243	161	56	1813	50	17.26	-	1	76	-	10445	7623	333	22.89	5-23	2	

EVANS, K. P. Nottinghamshire

Name: Kevin Paul Evans
Role: Right-hand bat, right-arm medium bowler
Born: 10 September 1963, Calverton, Nottingham
Height: 6ft 2in **Weight:** 13st
Nickname: Ghost, Texas
County debut: 1984
County cap: 1990
1st-Class 50s: 15
1st-Class 100s: 3
1st-Class 5 w. in innings: 4
1st-Class catches: 90
Place in batting averages: 126th av. 30.23 (1993 165th av. 23.10)
Place in bowling averages: 57th av. 30.02 (1993 39th av. 26.40)
Strike rate: 65.02 (career 66.89)
Parents: Eric and Eileen
Wife and date of marriage: Sandra, 19 March 1988
Family links with cricket: Brother Russell played for Nottinghamshire and still plays for Minor Counties and Lincolnshire. Father played local cricket
Education: William Lee Primary; Colonel Frank Seely Comprehensive, Calverton
Qualifications: 10 O-levels, 3 A-levels, qualified coach
Off-season: Working locally
Cricketers particularly admired: Richard Hadlee
Other sports followed: Football, tennis, squash
Injuries: Sore Achilles
Relaxations: Listening to music, reading, DIY, gardening
Extras: With brother, Russell, first brothers to bat together for Nottinghamshire in first-class cricket for 50 years. Kept wicket for the first time in the Championship match against

Essex at Colchester in 1992. Second Notts cricketer to bowl Sunday League hat-trick v Glamorgan at Trent Bridge, Mark Saxelby was the other
Opinions on cricket: 'Four-day format is very good. Also Sunday cricket is back to its best (40 overs).'
Best batting: 104 Nottinghamshire v Surrey, Trent Bridge 1992
104 Nottinghamshire v Sussex, Trent Bridge 1994
Best bowling: 6-67 Nottinghamshire v Yorkshire, Trent Bridge 1993

1994 Season

	M	Inns	NO	Runs	HS	Avge	100s	50s	Ct	St	O	M	Runs	Wkts	Avge	Best	5wI	10wM
Test																		
All First	16	21	4	514	104	30.23	1	3	12	-	411.5	105	1141	38	30.02	4-46	-	-
1-day Int																		
NatWest	2	1	0	21	21	21.00	-	-	-	-	17	4	34	7	4.85	6-10	1	
B & H	2	1	0	8	8	8.00	-	-	1	-	16	2	84	1	84.00	1-50	-	
Sunday	12	9	7	108	25 *	54.00	-	-	4	-	81	3	381	20	19.05	5-29	1	

Career Performances

	M	Inns	NO	Runs	HS	Avge	100s	50s	Ct	St	Balls	Runs	Wkts	Avge	Best	5wI	10wM
Test																	
All First	115	158	38	3119	104	25.99	3	15	90	-	16389	8206	245	33.49	6-67	4	-
1-day Int																	
NatWest	17	12	2	91	21	9.10	-	-	5	-	1018	525	23	22.82	6-10	1	
B & H	21	14	4	146	31 *	14.60	-	-	8	-	1170	810	25	32.40	4-43	-	
Sunday	102	62	26	626	30	17.38	-	-	16	-	4147	3595	110	32.68	5-29	1	

EYERS, C. J.   Worcestershire

Name: Christopher John Eyers
Role: Right-hand bat, right-arm medium bowler
Born: 28 March 1972, Aylesbury, Bucks
Height: 6ft 1in **Weight:** 13st 6lbs
Nickname: Pam
County debut: No first-team appearance
Parents: Brian and Jean
Marital status: Single
Education: Royal Grammar School, Worcester; Staffordshire University
Qualifications: 2 O-levels, 6 GCSEs, 3 A-levels, BA (Hons) in Geography, NCA coaching award
Off-season: Staying employed and fit
Cricketers particularly admired: David Gower, Sir Richard Hadlee, Malcolm Marshall, Tim Edwards

Other sports followed: Football (Liverpool), rugby, golf, tennis
Relaxations: Listening to music, cinema and films, playing golf
Opinions on cricket: 'Decrease the number of games in a season for the sake of players' fitness and mental state. Quality rather than quantity and all that.'

FAIRBROTHER, N. H. Lancashire

Name: Neil Harvey Fairbrother
Role: Left-hand bat, left-arm medium bowler
Born: 9 September 1963, Warrington, Cheshire
Height: 5ft 8in **Weight:** 11st
Nickname: Harvey
County debut: 1982
County cap: 1985
Benefit: 1995
Test debut: 1987
Tests: 10
One-Day Internationals: 42
1000 runs in a season: 9
1st-Class 50s: 77
1st-Class 100s: 31
1st-Class 200s: 2
1st-Class 300s: 1
1st-Class catches: 169
One-Day 50s: 54
One-Day 100s: 6
Place in batting averages: 20th av. 50.10 (1993 42nd av. 33.37)
Parents: Les and Barbara

Wife and date of marriage: Audrey, 23 September 1988
Children: Rachael Elizabeth, 4 April 1991
Family links with cricket: Father and two uncles played local league cricket
Education: St Margaret's Church of England School, Oxford; Lymn Grammar School
Qualifications: 5 O-levels
Overseas tours: England to Sharjah 1986-87, to India and Pakistan (World Cup), Australia and New Zealand 1987-88; England A to Pakistan 1990-91; England to New Zealand 1991-92, to India 1992-93, to Australia 1994-95
Cricketers particularly admired: Clive Lloyd, Allan Border, David Gower
Other sports followed: Football, rugby union, rugby league
Relaxations: Music and playing sport
Extras: 'I was named after the Australian cricketer Neil Harvey, who was my mum's favourite cricketer.' Played for England YC v Australia 1983. His innings of 366 in 1990 was the third highest score ever made in the County Championship, the second highest first-class score by a Lancashire batsman and the best at The Oval. Appointed Lancashire captain for 1992 but resigned in 1993. Called up to join England tour party as a replacement in Australia 1994-95 but was immediately injured in a collision with Steven Rhodes while fielding and forced to return home
Opinions on cricket: 'There is too much cricket. The game has to be made more entertaining.'
Best batting: 366 Lancashire v Surrey, The Oval 1990
Best bowling: 2-91 Lancashire v Nottinghamshire, Old Trafford 1987

1994 Season

	M	Inns	NO	Runs	HS	Avge	100s	50s	Ct	St	O	M	Runs	Wkts	Avge	Best	5wI	10wM
Test																		
All First	12	22	2	1002	204	50.10	4	1	16	-	1	0	3	0	-	-	-	-
1-day Int	2	2	1	22	19 *	22.00	-	-	-	-								
NatWest	2	2	0	28	28	14.00	-	-	1	-								
B & H	1	1	1	41	41 *	-	-	-	1	-								
Sunday	14	13	2	522	70	47.45	-	5	4	-								

Career Performances

	M	Inns	NO	Runs	HS	Avge	100s	50s	Ct	St	Balls	Runs	Wkts	Avge	Best	5wI	10wM
Test	10	15	1	219	83	15.64	-	1	4	-	12	9	0	-	-	-	-
All First	257	408	62	14317	366	41.37	31	77	169	-	662	426	5	85.20	2-91	-	-
1-day Int	42	40	9	1226	113	39.54	1	9	18	-	6	9	0	-	-	-	-
NatWest	27	26	4	1071	93 *	48.68	-	9	10	-	18	16	0	-	-	-	-
B & H	48	47	15	1637	116 *	51.15	1	12	22	-	36	50	0	-	-	-	-
Sunday	156	144	32	4186	116 *	37.37	4	24	44	-	12	15	0	-	-	-	-

FARBRACE, P.   Middlesex

Name: Paul Farbrace
Role: Right-hand bat, wicket-keeper
Born: 7 July 1967, Ash, nr Canterbury
Height: 5ft 10in **Weight:** 'Variable'
Nickname: Farby
County debut: 1987 (Kent),
1990 (Middlesex)
1st-Class 50s: 4
1st-Class catches: 86
1st-Class stumpings: 12
Parents: David and Betty
Wife and date of marriage: Elizabeth Jane,
27 July 1985
Children: Jemma Elizabeth, 30 March 1985;
Eleanor Kate, 3 September 1988
Family links with cricket: Father played
village cricket; two brothers play, Ian in
South Wales and Colin plays for Ash

Education: Ash CE Primary School;
Geoffrey Chaucer School, Canterbury
Qualifications: O-levels, NCA senior/advanced/staff coach
Career outside cricket: PE teacher, BBC radio reporter (Kent)
Off-season: Working as a PE teacher at Hampton School
Overseas tours: Kent Schools to Canada 1983; Middlesex to Portugal 1991, 1992
Cricketers particularly admired: Robin Sims, Nigel Mullarkey, Jason Harrison 'for his
ability to accept his dismissal with such good grace (normally LBW)'
Other sports followed: All sports except those with horses
Injuries: Patella injury to knee joint, missed two weeks
Relaxations: 'Football, reading about football, watching football (Gillingham and
occassionally Chelsea), my wife and children.'
Extras: Played County Schools football, had England Schools U18 trial, attracted attention
from Notts County and Coventry City. Captained Kent v Essex in a five-a-side cricket game
in Dartford Tunnel in February 1989 to raise money for Children in Need. Has bowled only
once in first-class cricket and took the wicket of Graham Gooch at Lord's. Middlesex
Uncapped Player of the Year 1993. Middlesex Young Player of the Year 1993. Chairman
of Ash CC, club captain of Mote CC (Maidstone).
Opinions on cricket: 'Due to rather a lengthy spell in 2nd XI cricket I have come to the
conclusion that two overseas players per county would benefit everybody. If young
overseas bowlers i.e Vasbert Drakes at Sussex, were to play for every 2nd XI it would raise
the standard of many 2nd XI attacks, helping to prepare young batters for first-class cricket.
The Gulf between the two is widening very quickly. Rather than knocking 2nd XI cricket
let's help to strengthen it.'

Best batting: 79 Middlesex v Cambridge University, Fenner's 1990
Best bowling: 1-64 Middlesex v Essex, Lord's 1991

1994 Season (did not make any first-class or one-day appearance)

Career Performances

	M	Inns	NO	Runs	HS	Avge	100s	50s	Ct	St	Balls	Runs	Wkts	Avge	Best	5wl	10wM
Test																	
All First	38	48	11	694	79	18.75	-	4	86	12	25	64	1	64.00	1-64	-	-
1-day Int																	
NatWest	6	4	1	41	17	13.66	-	-	8	1							
B & H																	
Sunday	18	12	4	73	26*	9.12	-		11	10							

FELTHAM, M. A. — Middlesex

Name: Mark Andrew Feltham
Role: Right-hand bat,
right-arm fast-medium bowler
Born: 26 June 1963, London
Height: 6ft 2in **Weight:** 13st 10lbs
Nickname: Felts, Felpsy, Boff or Douglas
County debut: 1983 (Surrey),
1993 (Middlesex)
County cap: 1990 (Surrey)
50 wickets in a season: 1
1st-Class 50s: 9
1st-Class 100s: 1
1st-Class 5 w. in innings: 7
1st-Class catches: 59
One-Day 50s: 3
One-Day 5 w. in innings: 2
Place in batting averages: 225th av. 17.06
(1993 199th av. 19.20)
Place in bowling averages: 86th av. 33.52
(1993 82nd av. 31.20)
Strike rate: 67.415 (career 61.92)
Parents: Leonard William and Patricia Louise
Wife and date of marriage: Debra Elizabeth, 22 September 1990
Children: Zoë Elizabeth, 23 June 1992
Family links with cricket: 'Mum responsible for fund-raising to build new development at Foster's Oval. Brother plays cricket in Middlesex League'

Education: Roehampton Church School; Tiffin Boys' School
Qualifications: 7 O-levels; advanced cricket coach
Career outside cricket: PR, marketing and media
Off-season: Coaching in inner London primary schools. Tours to Barbados and Malta with *Cricket World* magazine.
Overseas teams played for: Glenwood Old Boys, Durban, South Africa 1983-84, 1986-87
Cricketers particularly admired: Ian Botham, Gordon Greenidge, Waqar Younis and Sylvester Clarke
Other sports followed: Football, American football and most others
Injuries: Ankle, missed last two games
Relaxations: 'Music, particularly Luther Vandross, Woody Allen films and listening to Keith Brown and John Emburey talk chess.'
Extras: 'I write a weekly column in *Wandsworth Borough News*. Dismissed both Clive Rice and Richard Hadlee in their last innings in county cricket.' Released by Surrey at the end of 1992 season and signed by Middlesex for 1993. Writes monthly column in *Cricket World* magazine.
Opinions on cricket: 'In the Sunday League each team should have to field five players who are uncapped and under 25.'
Best batting: 101 Surrey v Middlesex, The Oval 1990
Best bowling: 6-53 Surrey v Leicestershire, The Oval 1990

1994 Season

	M	Inns	NO	Runs	HS	Avge	100s	50s	Ct	St	O	M	Runs	Wkts	Avge	Best	5wI	10wM
Test																		
All First	13	16	1	256	71	17.06	-	1	7	-	382.3	83	1140	34	33.52	5-69	1	-
1-day Int																		
NatWest	2	1	1	25	25 *	-	-	-	1	-	22	3	68	3	22.66	2-23	-	
B & H																		
Sunday	13	7	2	118	75	23.60	-	1	3	-	92	2	477	13	36.69	3-28	-	

Career Performances

	M	Inns	NO	Runs	HS	Avge	100s	50s	Ct	St	Balls	Runs	Wkts	Avge	Best	5wI	10wM
Test																	
All First	143	177	43	3070	101	22.91	1	9	59	-	21984	11311	355	31.86	6-53	7	-
1-day Int																	
NatWest	16	11	4	101	25 *	14.42	-	-	2	-	947	694	16	43.37	2-23	-	
B & H	32	21	4	207	35	12.17	-	-	10	-	1827	1193	53	22.50	5-28	2	
Sunday	116	79	23	1011	75	18.05	-	3	28	-	4590	3895	105	37.09	4-35	-	

FELTON, N. A.   Northamptonshire

Name: Nigel Alfred Felton
Role: Left-hand bat, 'Short-leg as nobody
else sees the role as theirs. Great!'
Born: 24 October 1960, Guildford
Height: 5ft 7in **Weight:** 11st
Nickname: Gringo, Ninja
County debut: 1982 (Somerset),
1989 (Northamptonshire)
County cap: 1986 (Somerset),
1990 (Northamptonshire)
1000 runs in a season: 5
1st-Class 50s: 61
1st-Class 100s: 15
1st-Class catches: 122
One-Day 50s: 22
Place in batting averages: 165th av. 24.72
(1993 69th av. 36.64)
Parents: Ralph and Enid
Wife and date of marriage: Jill-Marie,
October 1989

Family links with cricket: Father played non-white cricket in Cape Town and club cricket
in the UK
Education: Hawes Down Secondary School, Kent; Millfield School; Loughborough
University
Qualifications: 6 O-levels, 2 A-levels, BSc (Hons), Certificate of Education PE/Sports
Sciences, qualified teacher
Off-season: Promoting Tildent products throughout the UK
Overseas tours: English Schools to India 1976-77; England YC to Australia 1979;
Somerset to Barbados 1985-86; to Sierra Leone 1988; Northamptonshire to Cape Town
1992-93
Overseas teams played for: Waneroo, Perth, Western Australia 1984-86; Cape Town
1988; Primrose, Cape Town 1991-93
Cricketers particularly admired: 'Me, as nobody else seems to!!'
Other sports followed: 'Rugby, soccer and mainly looking foward to watching some rugby
at Franklin Gardens'
Relaxations: 'Spending time with my wife'
Extras: Played a season for Kent in 1980 after leaving Millfield and joined Somerset at end
of first year at Loughborough. Released by Somerset at end of 1988 season. Has written a
number of articles, including B&H Final programme and on unity in South African cricket.
Released by Northamptonshire at end of 1994 season
Opinions on cricket: 'Four-day cricket is a good idea. Groundsmen should be employed
by board, thereby decreasing clubs' influence on wickets. Press needs to be more sensitive

and positive about our game, as they all earn a nice living out of the game.'
Best batting: 173* Somerset v Kent, Taunton 1983
Best bowling: 1-48 Northamptonshire v Derbyshire, Northampton 1990

1994 Season

	M	Inns	NO	Runs	HS	Avge	100s	50s	Ct	St	O	M	Runs	Wkts	Avge	Best	5wI	10wM
Test																		
All First	10	19	1	445	87	24.72	-	2	5	-								
1-day Int																		
NatWest	2	2	0	57	37	28.50	-	-	1	-								
B & H	1	1	0	25	25	25.00	-	-	-	-								
Sunday	4	4	0	33	17	8.25	-	-	1	-								

Career Performances

	M	Inns	NO	Runs	HS	Avge	100s	50s	Ct	St	Balls	Runs	Wkts	Avge	Best	5wI	10wM
Test																	
All First	211	361	21	10242	173 *	30.12	15	61	122	-	288	345	2	172.50	1-48	-	-
1-day Int																	
NatWest	28	28	2	838	87	32.23	-	7	11	-	6	20	0	-		-	-
B & H	25	25	0	570	82	22.80	-	4	6	-							
Sunday	103	96	10	2056	96	23.90	-	11	30	-	6	7	0	-		-	-

FIELD-BUSS, M. G. Nottinghamshire

Name: Michael Gwyn Field-Buss
Role: Right-hand bat, off-spin bowler
Born: 23 September 1964, Malta
Height: 5ft 10in **Weight:** 11st
Nickname: Mouse
County debut: 1987 (Essex),
1989 (Nottinghamshire)
1st-Class 5 w. in innings: 1
1st-Class catches: 12
Place in batting averages:
(1993 249th av. 12.37)
Place in bowling averages: 133rd av. 45.00
(1993 43th av. 26.71)
Strike rate: 122.58 (career 84.33)
Parents: Gwyn and Monica
Marital status: Engaged to Paula
Family links with cricket: Father played local
cricket with Ilford RAFA

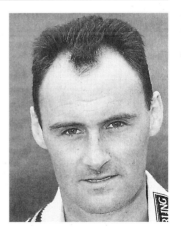

Education: Wanstead High School
Qualifications: Qualified coach
Off-season: Driving for local council
Overseas teams played for: Werribee, Melbourne 1987-88
Cricketers particularly admired:
'Bill Morris (coach at Ilford Cricket School) during my early years, Ray East and David Acfield at Essex, Eddie Hemmings at Notts'
Other sports followed:
'Watching Leyton Orient (although I support Arsenal). Keen on most other sports'
Relaxations: 'Spending as much time as possible with my fiancée, Paula, and my family, listening to music, playing with new kittens (Sam and Cassey)'
Opinions on cricket: 'More 2nd XI games should be played on first-class grounds.'
Best batting: 34* Essex v Middlesex, Lord's 1987
Best bowling: 6-42 Nottinghamshire v Kent, Trent Bridge 1993

1994 Season

	M	Inns	NO	Runs	HS	Avge	100s	50s	Ct	St	O	M	Runs	Wkts	Avge	Best	5wI	10wM
Test																		
All First	8	9	4	72	23	14.40	-	-	1	-	245.1	71	540	12	45.00	2-23	-	-
1-day Int																		
NatWest	2	1	1	4	4*	-	-	-	-	-	13	1	62	0	-		-	-
B & H	1	0	0	0	0	-	-	-	-	-	11	0	21	0	-		-	-
Sunday	9	4	3	5	3	5.00	-	-	2	-	55	1	333	7	47.57	2-27	-	

Career Performances

	M	Inns	NO	Runs	HS	Avge	100s	50s	Ct	St	Balls	Runs	Wkts	Avge	Best	5wI	10wM
Test																	
All First	36	41	14	307	34*	11.37	-	-	12	-	5229	2292	62	36.96	6-42	1	-
1-day Int																	
NatWest	5	3	2	10	5*	10.00	-	-	1	-	294	191	7	27.28	4-62	-	
B & H	1	0	0	0	0	-	-	-	-	-	66	21	0	-		-	
Sunday	33	16	6	46	10*	4.60	-	-	6	-	1398	1178	31	38.00	3-25	-	

FLEMING, M. V.   Kent

Name: Matthew Valentine Fleming
Role: Right-hand bat, right-arm medium bowler
Born: 12 December 1964, Macclesfield (by mistake - one month early!)
Height: 6ft **Weight:** 12st 6lbs
Nickname: Jazzer
County debut: 1988
County cap: 1990
1st-Class 50s: 27
1st-Class 100s: 5
1st-Class catches: 44
One-Day 50s: 11
Place in batting averages: 136th av. 28.92 (1993 83rd av. 34.41)
Place in bowling averages: (1993 88th av. 31.94)
Strike rate: (career 89.33)

Parents: Valentine and Elizabeth
Wife and date of marriage: Caroline, 23 September 1989
Children: Hannah and Victoria
Family links with cricket: Great-grandfather C.F. Leslie played for England in 1880s; father played for Eton 2nd XI; mother opened the bowling for Heathfield School
Education: St Aubyns School, Rottingdean; Eton College
Qualifications: 8 O-levels, 3 A-levels
Career outside cricket: 'Unemployable'
Off-season: 'Re-introducing myself to my daughters'
Overseas teams played for: Avendale, Cape Town 1983-84
Cricketers particularly admired: Matthew Walker, Eddie Stanford
Other sports followed: Football (Arsenal)
Injuries: 'Shoulder, did not miss any cricket, sadly. Operation this winter.'
Relaxations: Fishing, shooting, Arsenal FC
Extras: Ex-army officer in the Royal Green Jackets. First two scoring shots in Championship cricket were sixes. Vice-chairman of the Professional Cricketers' Association
Opinions on cricket: 'We're getting there slowly, but – short run-ups on Sundays should be re-introduced. Pitches must be improved. And Kent and Warwickshire should not have to play each other again until I've retired or been sacked.'
Best batting: 116 Kent v West Indies, Canterbury 1991
Best bowling: 4-31 Kent v Gloucestershire, Tunbridge Wells 1993

1994 Season

	M	Inns	NO	Runs	HS	Avge	100s	50s	Ct	St	O	M	Runs	Wkts	Avge	Best	5wI	10wM
Test																		
All First	16	29	1	810	73	28.92	-	6	3	-	239.5	48	746	9	82.88	2-36	-	-
1-day Int																		
NatWest	4	4	0	52	22	13.00	-	-	4	-	21.1	0	97	6	16.16	3-28	-	
B & H	1	1	1	36	36 *	-	-	-	1	-	11	0	39	2	19.50	2-39	-	
Sunday	17	15	0	458	79	30.53	-	3	7	-	79	2	411	21	19.57	4-36	-	

Career Performances

	M	Inns	NO	Runs	HS	Avge	100s	50s	Ct	St	Balls	Runs	Wkts	Avge	Best	5wI	10wM
Test																	
All First	103	167	20	4597	116	31.27	5	27	44	-	10006	4661	112	41.61	4-31	-	-
1-day Int																	
NatWest	13	13	1	231	53	19.25	-	1	9	-	471	295	16	18.43	3-28	-	
B & H	21	20	1	476	69	25.05	-	3	5	-	1020	690	23	30.00	3-52	-	
Sunday	90	82	11	1713	79	24.12	-	7	29	-	3382	2891	104	27.79	4-36	-	

FLETCHER, I.   Somerset

Name: Iain Fletcher
Role: Right-hand bat, right-arm medium bowler
Born: 31 August 1971, Sawbridgeworth, Herts
Height: 5ft 9in **Weight:** 13st 11lbs
County debut: 1991
1st-Class 50s: 5
1st-Class catches: 4
Place in batting averages: 201st av. 19.88 (1993 157th av. 24.77)
Parents: Roy and Maureen
Family links with cricket: Father qualified coach; all brothers played when younger
Education: Millfield School; Loughborough University
Qualifications: 3 A-Levels, BA (Hons) in Politics
Overseas tours:
Millfield School to Australia 1988-89
Cricketers particularly admired: Peter Roebuck, Ken McEwan, Malcolm Marshall
Relaxations: 'In search of the perfect pint of bitter, Guinness or Murphy's. Reading –

authors Allan Massie, George McDonald Fraser, Gabriel Garcia Marquez'
Extras: Played for Hertfordshire in NatWest Trophy 1990 and for Combined Universities in B&H Cup 1991. Schools *Daily Telegraph* award winner 1989. Released by Somerset at end of 1994 season
Opinions on cricket: 'Senior players have much to offer us younger players in different circumstances, yet so often they are shouted down without proper thought in a manner that belongs to the long gone repressive era and not the 1990s. Opinions aren't there to be correct, they are there to be aired.'
Best batting: 65* Somerset v Middlesex, Bath 1993

1994 Season

	M	Inns	NO	Runs	HS	Avge	100s	50s	Ct	St	O	M	Runs	Wkts	Avge	Best	5wI	10wM
Test																		
All First	6	10	1	179	54 *	19.88	-	2	3	-								
1-day Int																		
NatWest																		
B & H																		
Sunday	3	3	0	15	10	5.00	-	-	3	-								

Career Performances

	M	Inns	NO	Runs	HS	Avge	100s	50s	Ct	St	Balls	Runs	Wkts	Avge	Best	5wI	10wM
Test																	
All First	14	22	3	460	65 *	24.21	-	5	4	-							
1-day Int																	
NatWest	1	1	0	1	1	1.00	-	-	-	-							
B & H	1	1	0	9	9	9.00	-	-	1	-							
Sunday	8	8	0	72	26	9.00	-	-	3	-							

21. In 1994, Richard Johnson took 10-45 for Middlesex in a single innings. Which Sussex bowler was the last to take 10 wickets in an innings in county cricket?

FLINT, D. P. J.   Hampshire

Name: Darren Peter John Flint
Role: Right-hand bat, slow left-arm bowler
Born: 14 June 1970, Basingstoke
Height: 6ft **Weight:** 14st
County debut: 1993
1st-Class 5 w. in innings: 1
1st-Class catches: 8
Place in bowling averages:
(1993 102nd av. 34.38)
Strike rate: (career 82.00)
Parents: Peter and Linda
Marital status: Engaged
Education: Cranbourne Comprehensive;
Queen Mary's College, Basingstoke
Qualifications: 5 O-levels, NCA senior
coach
Off-season: Coaching and working for the
family business
Overseas tours: Hampshire to Isle of Wight
1990, 1991, 1992, 1993
Cricketers particularly admired: Derek Underwood, John Emburey, Malcolm Marshall,
Sean 'The Pedigree' Morris and Rupert 'Mature' Cox
Other sports followed: Rugby, shooting, fishing
Relaxations: Enjoying good food and drink, especially sampling real ales
Extras: Thames Valley League Bowler of the Year 1989. Rapid Cricketline Player of the
Month August/September 1991. Took 5 wickets in an innings on his first-class debut
Opinions on cricket: 'Left-arm bowlers should be able to bowl over the wicket and get an
lbw decision if the ball pitches outside the leg stump.'
Best batting: 14* Hampshire v Worcestershire, Portsmouth 1993
Best bowling: 5-32 Hampshire v Gloucestershire, Bristol 1993

1994 Season

	M	Inns	NO	Runs	HS	Avge	100s	50s	Ct	St	O	M	Runs	Wkts	Avge	Best	5wI	10wM
Test																		
All First	3	2	1	8	5	8.00	-	-	1	-	49	13	129	1	129.00	1-12	-	-
1-day Int																		
NatWest																		
B & H																		
Sunday																		

Career Performances

	M	Inns	NO	Runs	HS	Avge	100s	50s	Ct	St	Balls	Runs	Wkts	Avge	Best	5wl	10wM
Test																	
All First	13	15	6	55	14 *	6.11	-	-	8	-	2624	1195	32	37.34	5-32	1	-
1-day Int																	
NatWest																	
B & H																	
Sunday																	

FLINTOFF, A. Lancashire

Name: Andrew Flintoff
Role: Right-hand bat, right-arm medium bowler
Born: 6 December 1977, Preston
Height: 6ft 4in **Weight:** 12st 7lb
County debut: No first-team appearance
Parents: Colin and Susan
Family links with cricket: Father and brother both play local club cricket
Education: Ribbleton Hall High School
Qualifications: 9 GCSEs
Off-season: Touring with England U19
Overseas tours: England Schools U15 to South Africa 1993; England U19 to West Indies 1994-95
Cricketers particularly admired: Graeme Hick, Robin Smith, Peter Sleep, Peter Seal
Other sports followed:
Football (Preston North End)
Relaxations: Listening to music, sleeping, good food
Extras: Won a *Daily Telegraph* award for batting. Represented England U14 to U19 and played for U17 against India in 1994
Opinions on cricket: 'I think more measures should be taken to attract larger crowds.'

22. Who was quoted as saying 'Venus is in the wrong juxtaposition with something else' when explaining another England defeat in 1993?

FOLLAND, N. A.   Somerset

Name: Nicholas Arthur Folland
Role: Left-hand bat, right-arm medium
bowler
Born: 17 September 1963, Bristol
Height: 6ft **Weight:** 13st
County debut: 1992
1st-Class 50s: 10
1st-Class 100s: 2
1st-Class catches: 20
One-Day 50s: 14
One-Day 100s: 2
Place in batting averages: 113th av. 31.95
(1993 99th av. 32.29)
Parents: Geoffrey and Maureen
Wife and date of marriage:
Diane, 4 April 1992
Family links with cricket: Brother Neil
played for Devon and now plays for Beds
Education: Exmouth School; Loughborough University
Qualifications: Degree in Sports Science and Recreation Management, PGCE PE/Geography
Career outside cricket: Teaching PE and geography at Blundells School, Tiverton
Off-season: Teaching
Overseas teams played for: Claremont Cottesloe, Perth, Western Australia 1985
Cricketers particularly admired: David Gower, Viv Richards, Malcolm Marshall, Alan Border
Other sports followed: All sports, especially rugby
Relaxations: Watching sport, reading, good food
Extras: Had trial for Gloucestershire in 1979. Played for Devon in the NatWest Trophy
since 1984 and Minor Counties in the B&H Cup 1989-1992. Captained Minor Counties to
victory over Pakistanis 1992. Devon RFC squad 1988-89. Scored his first two first-class
centuries in the same match against Sussex at Taunton in 1993. Retired from first-class
cricket at end of 1994 season
Best batting: 108* Somerset v Sussex, Taunton 1993

1994 Season

	M	Inns	NO	Runs	HS	Avge	100s	50s	Ct	St	O	M	Runs	Wkts	Avge	Best	5wl	10wM
Test																		
All First	13	22	1	671	91	31.95	-	4	6	-								
1-day Int																		
NatWest	3	3	0	36	18	12.00	-	-	-	-								
B & H	1	1	0	38	38	38.00	-	-	-	-								
Sunday	11	11	0	309	75	28.09	-	2	4	-								

Career Performances

	M	Inns	NO	Runs	HS	Avge	100s	50s	Ct	St	Balls	Runs	Wkts	Avge	Best	5wI	10wM
Test																	
All First	32	56	5	1755	108 *	34.41	2	10	20	-							
1-day Int																	
NatWest	14	14	0	326	63	23.28	-	3	11	-	20	55	1	55.00	1-52	-	
B & H	19	19	3	781	100 *	48.81	1	7	11	-							
Sunday	25	24	1	671	107 *	29.17	1	4	10	-							

FOLLETT, D. Middlesex

Name: David Follett
Role: Right-hand bowler, right-arm fast bowler
Born: 14 October 1968, Hanley,
Stoke-on-Trent
Height: 6ft 2in **Weight:** 12st
Nickname: Foll
County debut: No first-team appearance
Parents: Gordon and Sandra
Marital status: Single
Family links with cricket: Father played club
cricket for Burslem
Education: Moorland Road Hight School,
Burslem, Stoke-on-Trent
Qualifications: Engineer
Career outside cricket: Engineer
Off-season: Playing cricket in Australia
Overseas teams played for: Queenbeyan, New
South Wales, Australia, 1994-95
Cricketers particularly admired: Imran Khan, Ian Botham
Other sports followed: Football, motor racing
Relaxations: Keeping fit, music
Opinions on cricket: 'The fielding standards have dropped and have been shown up by
England in the Test matches in Australia.'

FORDHAM, A.   Northamptonshire

Name: Alan Fordham
Role: Right-hand bat, occasional right-arm medium bowler
Born: 9 November 1964, Bedford
Height: 6ft 1in **Weight:** 13st
Nickname: Forders
County debut: 1986
County cap: 1990
1000 runs in a season: 4
1st-Class 50s: 42
1st-Class 100s: 20
1st-Class 200s: 1
1st-Class catches: 84
One-Day 50s: 24
One-Day 100s: 4
Place in batting averages: 36th av. 44.42
(1993 65th av. 37.57)
Parents: Clifford and Ruth
Marital status: Single
Family links with cricket: Brother John played school and college cricket
Education: Bedford Modern School; Durham University
Qualifications: 9 O-levels, 3 A-levels, BSc (Hons) Chemistry, NCA senior coaching award
Career outside cricket: 'A few plans brewing'
Off-season: Captaining Christians in Sport tour to Zimbabwe, then working in England
Overseas tours: Bedford Modern to Barbados 1983; Gentlemen of Leicestershire to Jersey and Guernsey 1987; International Ambassadors XI/Christians in Sport to India 1989-90, to Zimbabwe 1994-95; MCC to Leeward Islands 1991-92; Northamptonshire to Natal 1991-92
Overseas teams played for: Richmond, Melbourne 1983-84; Camberwell, Melbourne 1987-88; Curtin University, Perth, Western Australia 1988; Nirman Schools XI, Dhaka, Bangladesh 1989-90; Montrose, Cape Town, South Africa 1992-93
Cricketers particularly admired: Allan Lamb, Bob Willis, Mike Brearley
Other sports followed: Rugby union
Injuries: Appendicitis, missed five weeks
Relaxations: Television, music, travel
Extras: Has appeared for Bedfordshire in Minor Counties Championship. Played for Combined Universities in B&H Cup 1987. Shared county third-wicket record stand of 393 with Allan Lamb v Yorkshire at Headingley in 1990. Only white man to have played league cricket in Bangladesh. Treasurer of the Professional Cricketers' Association
Opinions on cricket: 'Now the improved television deal has been negotiated, surely we can be paid sufficiently so that a benefit year is not essential for long-term security.'
Best batting: 206* Northamptonshire v Yorkshire, Headingley 1990
Best bowling: 1-25 Northamptonshire v Yorkshire, Northampton 1990

1994 Season

	M	Inns	NO	Runs	HS	Avge	100s	50s	Ct	St	O	M	Runs	Wkts	Avge	Best	5wI	10wM
Test																		
All First	11	20	1	844	158	44.42	3	4	7	-								
1-day Int																		
NatWest	1	1	0	0	0	0.00	-	-	-	-								
B & H	1	1	0	38	38	38.00	-	-	1	-								
Sunday	13	13	0	262	111	20.15	1	-	1	-								

Career Performances

	M	Inns	NO	Runs	HS	Avge	100s	50s	Ct	St	Balls	Runs	Wkts	Avge	Best	5wI	10wM
Test																	
All First	131	231	18	8655	206 *	40.63	20	42	84	-	362	238	3	79.33	1-25	-	-
1-day Int																	
NatWest	18	18	1	821	132 *	48.29	2	5	3	-	21	6	1	6.00	1-3	-	
B & H	19	18	1	575	103	33.82	1	4	3	-							
Sunday	87	82	1	2210	111	27.28	1	15	21	-	6	10	0	-	-	-	-

FOSTER, M. J.   Northamptonshire

Name: Michael James Foster
Role: Right-hand bat,
right-arm medium bowler
Born: 17 September 1972, Leeds
Height: 6ft 2in **Weight:** 14st 7lbs
Nickname: Foz, Baar, Hooligan
County debut: 1993 (Yorkshire)
1st-Class 50s: 1
1st-Class catches: 6
One-Day 100s: 1
Parents: Paul and Margaret
Marital status: Single
Family links with cricket: Grandfather and
father play local cricket; sister played for
Yorkshire
Education: Park High School, Pontefract;
New College, Pontefract
Qualifications: 7 GCSEs, 2 A-levels
Overseas tours: England U19 to
Pakistan 1991-92

Overseas teams played for: Freemantle, Western Australia 1991-92; Ringwood, Victoria
1992-93, 1993-94

Cricketers particularly admired: Ian Botham, Alan Border, Geoff Thomson, Steve Waugh, Richie Richardson
Other sports followed: Rugby, boxing
Relaxations: Gym, running, socialising
Extras: Captained Yorkshire at all junior age levels. Moved to Northamptonshire for 1995 season
Opinions on cricket: 'All games should be played with coloured clothing. Sometimes there is too much cricket. Shouldn't the emphasis be on quality as well as quantity?'
Best batting: 63* Yorkshire v Oxford University, The Parks 1994
Best bowling: 3-39 Yorkshire v Hampshire, Southampton 1993

1994 Season

	M	Inns	NO	Runs	HS	Avge	100s	50s	Ct	St	O	M	Runs	Wkts	Avge	Best	5wl	10wM
Test																		
All First	4	6	1	159	63 *	31.80	-	1	5	-	37.5	12	100	3	33.33	2-4	-	-
1-day Int																		
NatWest																		
B & H																		
Sunday	9	6	1	26	9	5.20	-	-	3	-	22	0	161	2	80.50	2-74	-	

Career Performances

	M	Inns	NO	Runs	HS	Avge	100s	50s	Ct	St	Balls	Runs	Wkts	Avge	Best	5wl	10wM
Test																	
All First	5	7	1	165	63 *	27.50	-	1	6	-	329	150	6	25.00	3-39	-	-
1-day Int																	
NatWest																	
B & H																	
Sunday	20	14	1	199	118	15.30	1	-	6	-	396	370	6	61.66	2-74	-	

FOWLER, G.   Durham

Name: Graeme Fowler
Role: Left-hand opening bat, occasional wicket-keeper, first slip, 'slow right-arm declaration bowler'
Born: 20 April 1957, Accrington
Height: 5ft 9in **Weight:** 'Near 11st'
Nickname: Fow, Foxy
County debut: 1979 (Lancashire), 1993 (Durham)
County cap: 1981 (Lancashire)
Benefit: 1991 (£152,000)
Test debut: 1982
Tests: 21

One-Day Internationals: 26
1000 runs in a season: 8
1st-Class 50s: 85
1st-Class 100s: 36
1st-Class 200s: 2
1st-Class catches: 152
1st-Class stumpings: 5
One-Day 50s: 51
One-Day 100s: 9
Place in batting averages: 110th av. 32.42
(1993 142nd av. 26.37)
Education: Accrington Grammar School; Bede
College, Durham University
Qualifications: Certificate of Education,
advanced cricket coach
Career outside cricket: 'Some radio and
television work'
Overseas tours: England to Australia and
New Zealand 1982-83, to New Zealand and
Pakistan 1983-84, to India and Australia 1984-85
Overseas teams played for: Tasmania 1981-82
Cricketers particularly admired: David Lloyd and Paul Allott
Other sports followed: 'Bits of everything'
Relaxations: Music, gardening, playing drums
Extras: Played for Accrington and Rawtenstall in Lancashire League: at 15 he was the
youngest opener in the League. Played for England YC in 1976. Published *Fox on the Run*,
a cricketing diary from 1984 to 1986, which won Channel 4's Sports Book of the Year
award. First Englishman to score a double century in India. Released by Lancashire at the
end of the 1992 season and joined Durham. Released by Durham at end of 1994 season
Opinions on cricket: 'Good game isn't it!'
Best batting: 226 Lancashire v Kent, Maidstone 1984
Best bowling: 2-34 Lancashire v Warwickshire, Old Trafford 1986

1994 Season

	M	Inns	NO	Runs	HS	Avge	100s	50s	Ct	St	O	M	Runs	Wkts	Avge	Best	5wI	10wM
Test																		
All First	4	7	0	227	68	32.42	-	3	2	-								
1-day Int																		
NatWest																		
B & H																		
Sunday	2	2	0	0	0	0.00	-	-	-	-								

Career Performances

	M	Inns	NO	Runs	HS	Avge	100s	50s	Ct	St	Balls	Runs	Wkts	Avge	Best	5wl	10wM
Test	21	37	0	1307	201	35.32	3	8	10	-	18	11	0	-	-	-	-
All First	292	495	27	16663	226	35.60	36	85	152	5	407	366	10	36.60	2-34	-	-
1-day Int	26	26	2	744	81 *	31.00	-	4	4	2							
NatWest	31	31	0	904	122	29.16	2	4	9	2							
B & H	62	61	1	1696	136	28.26	1	12	18	1							
Sunday	183	177	12	5325	124	32.27	6	31	65	-	6	1	0	-	-	-	-

FRASER, A. R. C.   Middlesex

Name: Angus Robert Charles Fraser
Role: Right-hand bat, right-arm medium-fast bowler
Born: 8 August 1965, Billinge, Lancashire
Height: 6ft 5in **Weight:** 15st 7lbs
Nickname: Gus, Lard
County debut: 1984
County cap: 1988
Test debut: 1989
Tests: 21
One-Day Internationals: 29
50 wickets in a season: 5
1st-Class 50s: 1
1st-Class 5 w. in innings: 19
1st-Class 10 w. in match: 2
1st-Class catches: 31
Place in batting averages:
(1993 258th av. 10.80)
Place in bowling averages:
36th av. 26.86 (1993 15th av. 22.75)
Strike rate: 63.94 (career 61.59)
Parents: Don and Irene
Marital status: Engaged to Denise
Children: Alexander Charles Mitchell Fraser, 4 May 1993
Family links with cricket: Brother Alastair played for Middlesex and Essex. Parents are keen followers
Education: Gayton High School, Harrow; Orange Senior High School, Edgware
Qualifications: 7 O-levels, qualified cricket coach
Career outside cricket: Learning about investments with Whittingdale
Off-season: Playing for Western Suburbs in Sydney
Overseas tours: Thames Valley Gentlemen to Barbados 1985; Middlesex to La Manga

1985 and 1986, to Portugal 1991-93; England to India (Nehru Cup) 1989-90, to West Indies 1989-90, to Australia 1990-91, to West Indies 1993-94, to Australia 1994-95

Overseas teams played for: Plimmerton, Wellington 1985-86 and 1987-88; Western Suburbs, Sydney 1988-89, 1994-95

Cricketers particularly admired: Richard Hadlee, Allan Border, Graham Gooch and Dennis Lillee

Other sports followed: 'Watch Liverpool FC when I can, follow local rugby club, Harrow, watch rugby internationals when I can get tickets, golf'

Injuries: Broken finger ('thank you Allan Donald'), out for ten days

Relaxations: Watching Liverpool FC, rugby internationals and Harrow RFC. 'Playing with my son, Alex'

Extras: Middlesex Player of the Year 1988 and 1989. Selected for England tour to New Zealand 1991-92 but ruled out by injury. Originally left out of England tour party to Australia 1994-95 but called up when Martin McCague was injured 'Got an LBW out of Dickie Bird this year.'

Opinions on cricket: 'Always look on the bright side of life. It's a funny old game.'

Best batting: 92 Middlesex v Surrey, The Oval 1990

Best bowling: 8-75 England v West Indies, Bridgetown, 1994

1994 Season

	M	Inns	NO	Runs	HS	Avge	100s	50s	Ct	St	O	M	Runs	Wkts	Avge	Best	5wl	10wM
Test	5	7	0	40	10	5.71	-	-	2	-	211.5	56	541	14	38.64	3-72	-	-
All First	14	15	1	80	16	5.71	-	-	3	-	532.5	142	1343	50	26.86	3-16	-	-
1-day Int	1	0	0	0	0	-	-	-	-	-	10	0	37	1	37.00	1-37	-	
NatWest	2	0	0	0	0	-	-	-	1	-	22	5	63	2	31.50	2-21	-	
B & H	2	1	1	1	1 *	-	-	-	-	-	22	7	58	2	29.00	1-26	-	
Sunday	9	3	2	14	11 *	14.00	-	-	2	-	69	9	262	9	29.11	3-31	-	

Career Performances

	M	Inns	NO	Runs	HS	Avge	100s	50s	Ct	St	Balls	Runs	Wkts	Avge	Best	5wl	10wM
Test	21	29	4	180	29	7.20	-	-	6	-	5665	2370	85	27.88	8-75	6	-
All First	157	173	40	1502	92	11.29	-	1	31	-	29937	12646	486	26.02	8-75	19	-
1-day Int	29	5	5	74	38 *	10.57	-	-	1	-	1630	1002	29	34.55	3-22	-	
NatWest	20	5	4	30	19	30.00	-	-	2	-	1377	700	33	21.21	4-34	-	
B & H	24	12	6	40	13 *	6.66	-	-	5	-	1477	852	28	30.42	3-30	-	
Sunday	103	35	15	213	30 *	10.65	-	-	16	-	4504	3011	98	30.72	4-17	-	

FRENCH, B. N.   Nottinghamshire

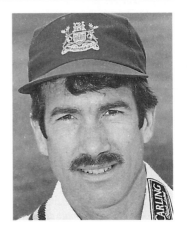

Name: Bruce Nicholas French
Role: Right-hand bat, wicket-keeper
Born: 13 August 1959, Warsop, Notts
Height: 5ft 8in **Weight:** 10st
Nickname: Frog
County debut: 1976
County cap: 1980
Benefit: 1991
Test debut: 1986
Tests: 16
One-Day Internationals: 13
1st-Class 50s: 25
1st-Class 100s: 2
1st-Class catches: 812
1st-Class stumpings: 100
Place in batting averages:
(1993 194th av. 20.00)
Parents: Maurice and Betty
Wife and date of marriage:
Ellen Rose, 9 March 1978
Children: Charles Daniel, 31 August 1978; Catherine Ellen, 28 December 1980
Family links with cricket: Brothers, Neil, David, Charlie, Joe, play for Welbeck and father is treasurer. Neil also plays for Lincolnshire
Education: Meden School, Warsop
Qualifications: O-level and CSE
Overseas tours: England to India and Sri Lanka 1984-85, to West Indies 1985-86, to Australia 1986-87, to India and Pakistan (World Cup), Australia and New Zealand 1987-88; unofficial England XI to South Africa 1989-90
Cricketers particularly admired: Bob Taylor
Other sports followed: Rock climbing, fell walking and all aspects of mountaineering
Injuries: Missed most of 1988 season following operations in May on index finger of left hand, and in 1989 broke the same finger again, missing end of season. Previously, French was bitten by a dog whilst jogging in the Caribbean in 1985-86; had to be carried off the field with a cut head and concussion after being struck by a short-pitched delivery from Richard Hadlee at Lord's in 1986; contracted a chest infection after being hit in the chest by a ball in Australia in 1986-87; in Pakistan in 1987-88, he needed stitches in a cut eye and on the way to hospital a car struck his legs
Relaxations: Reading, pipe smoking and drinking Theakston's Ale
Extras: Youngest player to play for Nottinghamshire, aged 16 years 10 months. Equalled Nottinghamshire record for dismissals in match with 10 (7ct, 3st), and in innings with 6 catches; also set new county record in 1984 for dismissals in a season with 87 (75ct, 12st). Banned from Test cricket for touring South Africa in 1989-90, suspension remitted in 1992.

Made his maiden first-class century in 1990 in 15th season of county cricket
Best batting: 123 Nottinghamshire v Durham, Chester-le-Street 1993
Best bowling: 1-37 Nottinghamshire v Derbyshire, Derby 1991

1994 Season

	M	Inns	NO	Runs	HS	Avge	100s	50s	Ct	St	O	M	Runs	Wkts	Avge	Best	5wI	10wM
Test																		
All First	1	0	0	0	0	-	-	-	2	-								
1-day Int																		
NatWest																		
B & H																		
Sunday																		

Career Performances

	M	Inns	NO	Runs	HS	Avge	100s	50s	Ct	St	Balls	Runs	Wkts	Avge	Best	5wI	10wM
Test	16	21	4	308	59	18.11	-	1	38	1							
All First	358	468	91	7141	123	18.94	2	25	814	100	90	70	1	70.00	1-37	-	-
1-day Int	13	8	3	34	9 *	6.80	-	-	13	3							
NatWest	32	27	6	368	49	17.52	-	-	47	4							
B & H	61	42	12	416	48 *	13.86	-	-	62	11							
Sunday	177	111	38	1103	37	15.10	-	-	141	17							

FROST, A.   Warwickshire

Name: Anthony Frost
Role: Right-hand bat, wicket-keeper
Born: 17 November 1975, Stoke-on-Trent
Height: 5ft 10in **Weight:** 10st 6lbs
County debut: No first-team apppearance
Parents: Ivan and Christine
Marital status: Single
Family links with cricket:
Father played for Staffordshire
Education: James Brinkley High School;
Stoke-on-Trent College
Qualifications: 5 GCSEs
Off-season: Training
Overseas tours:
Kidsgrove U18 to Australia 1990-91
Cricketers particularly admired:
Alan Knott, Viv Richards, Gary Sobers
Other sports followed: Football, golf

Relaxations: Listening to music, watching films, reading aircraft magazines
Extras: Has represented Staffordshire at all levels from U11 to U19. Won Texaco U16 competition with Staffordshire in 1992. Played for Development of Excellence XI U17 v South Africa and U18 v West Indies and U19 v India
Opinions on cricket: 'What a great game but I think that the amount of overs in a day should be reduced. '

FULTON, D. P. Kent

Name: David Paul Fulton
Role: Right-hand bat, slow left-arm bowler
Born: 15 November 1971, Lewisham
Height: 6ft 2in **Weight:** 12st
Nickname: Rave
County debut: 1992
1st-Class 50s: 3
1st-Class 100s: 1
1st-Class catches: 30
Place in batting averages: 145th av. 27.06
(1993 151st av. 25.58)
Parents: John and Ann
Marital status: Single
Family links with cricket: Father plays for
Otford village side
Education: Otford County Primary; The Judd
School, Tonbridge; Kent University
Qualifications: 10 GCSEs, 3 A-levels,
BA (Hons) Politics and International Relations;
senior NCA coach
Off-season: In South Africa, Cape Town
Overseas tours: Kent Schools U17 to Singapore and New Zealand 1986-87
Overseas teams played for: Avendale, Cape Town 1993-94; Victoria, Cape Town 1994-95
Cricketers particularly admired: David Gower, Gordon Greenidge, Michael Atherton, Graham Gooch, Carl Hooper, Steve Waugh
Other sports followed: Rugby (Harlequins) and football (Nottingham Forest)
Injuries: 'Blow to back of elbow at silly point due to a Nigel Llong waist-high full toss, off for 45 minutes'
Relaxations: 'Other kinds of sport, soccer, snooker, chess, weight training. Socialising with team-mates and girlfriend (the lovely Janine at time of writing)'
Extras: Played mainly Kent 2nd XI in 1992 scoring 1022 runs at 63.87 after returning from university in June and being voted Rapid Cricketline Player of the Month for July. Helped Kent University reach the final of UAU that year and felt that 1992 was his best season yet.
Opinions on cricket: 'Winning has become too important in our county game. Bad cricket

played on bad pitches has become acceptable as long as the right result ensues. County captains will seek to negate a Donald, a Mushtaq or a Walsh through pitch preparation. Wickets have to become harder, bouncier and flatter (where possible) to encourage the batsman, the seamer and the spinner alike. Only then will our county game improve.'

Best batting: 109 Kent v Cambridge University, Fenner's 1994

1994 Season

	M	Inns	NO	Runs	HS	Avge	100s	50s	Ct	St	O	M	Runs	Wkts	Avge	Best	5wl	10wM
Test																		
All First	10	16	0	433	109	27.06	1	1	17	-	0.1	0	0	0	-	-	-	-
1-day Int																		
NatWest	1	1	0	18	18	18.00	-	-	-	-								
B & H																		
Sunday																		

Career Performances

	M	Inns	NO	Runs	HS	Avge	100s	50s	Ct	St	Balls	Runs	Wkts	Avge	Best	5wl	10wM
Test																	
All First	18	31	1	798	109	26.60	1	3	30	-	1	0	0	-	-	-	-
1-day Int																	
NatWest	1	1	0	18	18	18.00	-	-	-	-							
B & H																	
Sunday	3	3	0	35	29	11.66	-	-	2	-							

23. Which Test cricketer had to curtail his tour of England in 1993 for a serious bowel operation?

GALLIAN, J. E. R.   Lancashire

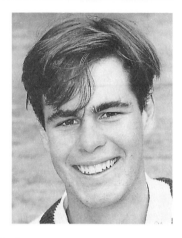

Name: Jason Edward Riche Gallian
Role: Right-hand bat, right-arm medium
bowler
Born: 25 June 1971, Manly, NSW, Australia
Height: 6ft **Weight:** 13st
Nickname: Gally
County debut: 1990
County cap: 1994
1st-Class 50s: 11
1st-Class 100s: 5
1st-Class catches: 17
One-Day 50s: 4
Place in batting averages: 39th av. 43.70
(1993 32nd av. 43.87)
Place in bowling averages: 105th av. 36.80
(1993 141st av. 53.18)
Strike rate: 57.00 (career 77.85)
Parents: Ray and Marilyn
Marital status: Single
Family links with cricket: Father played for Stockport
Education: The Pittwater House Schools, Australia; Oxford University
Qualifications: Higher School Certificate, Diploma in Social Studies (Keble College, Oxford)
Off-season: England A to India
Overseas tours: Australia U20 to West Indies 1989-90; England A to India 1994-95
Overseas teams played for: NSW and Australia U19 1988-89; NSW Colts and NSW 2nd
XI 1990-91; Australia U20 and U21 1991-92; Manly 1993-94
Cricketers particularly admired: Desmond Haynes, Mike Gatting
Other sports followed: Rugby league and union, football
Injuries: Fractured thumb, missed four weeks; twisted ankle, missed three weeks
Relaxations: Listening to music, playing golf
Extras: Played for Oxford University in 1992 and for Combined Universities in the B&H
Cup. Captained Oxford University 1993
Best batting: 171 Lancashire v Surrey, Old Trafford 1994
Best bowling: 4-29 Oxford University v Lancashire, The Parks 1992

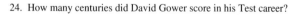

24. How many centuries did David Gower score in his Test career?

1994 Season

	M	Inns	NO	Runs	HS	Avge	100s	50s	Ct	St	O	M	Runs	Wkts	Avge	Best	5wI	10wM
Test																		
All First	12	20	0	874	171	43.70	2	5	6	-	95	10	368	10	36.80	2-27	-	-
1-day Int																		
NatWest	1	1	0	1	1	1.00	-	-	-	-	6	1	21	0	-		-	-
B & H	2	2	0	48	39	24.00	-	-	-	-	9	0	53	0	-		-	-
Sunday	9	9	2	260	84	37.14	-	2	1	-	32.4	0	172	9	19.11	2-10	-	

Career Performances

	M	Inns	NO	Runs	HS	Avge	100s	50s	Ct	St	Balls	Runs	Wkts	Avge	Best	5wI	10wM
Test																	
All First	33	55	4	2061	171	40.41	5	11	17	-	3114	1646	40	41.15	4-29	-	-
1-day Int																	
NatWest	1	1	0	1	1	1.00	-	-	-	-	36	21	0	-		-	-
B & H	6	6	0	162	50	27.00	-	2	-	-	192	155	2	77.50	1-26	-	
Sunday	9	9	2	260	84	37.14	-	2	1	-	196	172	9	19.11	2-10	-	

GARAWAY, M.   Hampshire

Name: Mark Garaway
Role: Right-hand bat, wicket-keeper
Born: 20 July 1973, Swindon, Wilts
Height: 5ft 7in **Weight:** 11st 8lbs
Nickname: Garas, Wolf, Hair, Val de Lobo
County debut: No first-team appearance
Parents: Michael and Valerie Anne
Marital status: 'Very single'
Family links with cricket: 'Grandfather
kept wicket for 40 years for Glamorgan.
Father regularly outscores and outclasses me at
club level for Ventnor 1st XI. Sister captains
Ventnor U14'
Education: Carhampton Primary, Somerset;
Ventnor Middle and Sandown High School,
Isle of Wight, 'Ventnor CC, the Astoria
(Hermanus, SA)'
Qualifications: 10 O-levels, 3 A-levels,
NCA cricket coach
Career outside cricket: 'Fitness instructor to Chris "Oggie" Sketchley, disc jockey, babysitter'
Off-season: 'Resting on holiday, improving my footwork on the dance floors of the Isle of

Wight and coaching on the island and in Hampshire.'

Overseas tours: Isle of Wight U14 and U17 to Jersey and Guernsey 1988-91; Ventnor to Winchester 1994; Hampshire to Val de Lobo 1994

Overseas teams played for: Worcester, Boland, South Africa 1991-93; Hermanus, South Africa 1993; 'Ventnor, Isle of Wight 1982-94'

Cricketers particularly admired: Ian Botham, Robin Smith, Rupert Cox, Jeff Hose, Adam Hose and Mark Brumer (Hermanus CC)

Other sports followed: Rugby, football, hockey and any sport on television

Injuries: Groin injury, missed one day

Relaxations: 'Music, socialising over a "quiet beer" at the local nitespot and watching Ventnor Youth 93 in Division 3 of the Sunday Football League.'

Extras: Represented England at U15, U17 and U19 level. Played for Isle of Wight at U16, U17, U21 and senior level in the same season. Spent two years (1991 and 1992) as MCC Young Professional. Hampshire Schools Wicketkeepers Award 1988. Andrew Swallow Memorial Cup 1987. Wight Waters Sports Award 1989-91

Opinions on cricket: 'The extra hour ruling in the 2nd team should be abolished as it not only makes players and spectators alike extremely cold, bored and irritable but it also deprives the cricketer of that extra hour of sleep which is important at most times for the development of a player but essential on the long, hard and totally lifeless away trips which many of us suffer at regular intervals during the summer.'

GARNHAM, M. A.   Essex

Name: Michael Anthony Garnham
Role: Right-hand bat, wicket-keeper
Born: 20 August 1960, Johannesburg
Height: 5ft 11in **Weight:** 12st
Nickname: Bones, Fred
County debut: 1979 (Gloucestershire), 1980 (Leicestershire), 1989 (Essex)
County cap: 1989 (Essex)
1st-Class 50s: 33
1st-Class 100s: 5
1st-Class catches: 428
1st-Class stumpings: 41
One-Day 50s: 3
One-Day 100s: 1
Place in batting averages: 191st av. 21.68
(1993 127th av. 27.76)
Parents: Pauline Anne and Robert Arthur
Wife and date of marriage: Lorraine,
15 September 1984
Children: Laura Clare, 3 November 1988;

Eleanor Louise, 22 October 1990
Family links with cricket: Father was a club cricketer in Essex. He lost the sight of an eye keeping wicket
Education: Camberwell Grammar, Melbourne, Australia; Scotch College, Perth, Australia; Park School, Barnstaple, North Devon; North Devon College; University of East Anglia (for one year)
Qualifications: 10 O-levels, 2 A-levels
Off-season: 'Driving the length of Africa in a 4-wheel-drive with some friends to raise money for Oxfam. Six months of playing boy scouts!'
Overseas tours: English Schools to India 1977-78; England YC to Australia 1978-79
Cricketers particularly admired: Bob Taylor
Other sports followed: Squash
Injuries: Dislocated finger and 18-20 stitches in an eye injury but missed no cricket
Relaxations: Carpentry – furniture making, building and DIY
Extras: Moved to England in 1975 after living in South Africa for four years and in Australia for ten years. Played for Devon in 1976 and 1977 before joining Gloucestershire. Signed for Leicestershire in 1980 and was banned by the registration committee from competitive first-team cricket for a month for breach of registration regulations. Retired at end of 1985, but returned for one one-day and one three-day game in 1988 following injury to Phil Whitticase. Signed for Essex in 1989, having been playing for Cambridgeshire. 'Having run a business making 'keeping gloves, I wear gloves I have made myself.'
Opinions on cricket: 'The only piece of cricket equipment without advertising on it is now the bails – couldn't someone veto some of the suggestions from the marketing men?'
Best batting: 123 Essex v Leicestershire, Leicester 1991

1994 Season

	M	Inns	NO	Runs	HS	Avge	100s	50s	Ct	St	O	M	Runs	Wkts	Avge	Best	5wl	10wM
Test																		
All First	18	30	5	542	62	21.68	-	4	33	5								
1-day Int																		
NatWest	2	2	1	3	2 *	3.00	-	-	1	1								
B & H	2	1	1	14	14 *	-	-	-	2	-								
Sunday	9	9	1	186	39	23.25	-	-	10	-								

Career Performances

	M	Inns	NO	Runs	HS	Avge	100s	50s	Ct	St	Balls	Runs	Wkts	Avge	Best	5wl	10wM
Test																	
All First	206	280	55	6192	123	27.52	5	33	428	41	24	39	0	-	-	-	-
1-day Int																	
NatWest	27	22	7	393	110	26.20	1	1	20	6							
B & H	57	40	16	536	55	22.33	-	1	53	7							
Sunday	163	122	28	1555	79 *	16.54	-	1	140	23							

GATTING, M. W.   Middlesex

Name: Michael William Gatting
Role: Right-hand bat, right-arm medium
bowler, slip fielder
Born: 6 June 1957, Kingsbury, Middlesex
Height: 5ft 10in **Weight:** 15st
Nickname: Gatt, Jabba
County debut: 1975
County cap: 1977
Benefit: 1988 (£205,000)
Test debut: 1977-78
Tests: 74

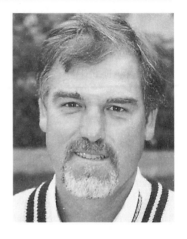

One-Day Internationals: 92
1000 runs in a season: 16
1st-Class 50s: 158
1st-Class 100s: 82
1st-Class 200s: 8
1st-Class 5 w. in innings: 2
1st-Class catches: 423
One-Day 50s: 74
One-Day 100s: 12
Place in batting averages: 3rd av. 69.62 (1993 11th av. 56.60)
Strike rate: (career 63.68)
Parents: Bill and Vera
Wife and date of marriage: Elaine, September 1980
Children: Andrew, 21 January 1983; James, 11 July 1986
Family links with cricket: Father used to play club cricket. Brother Steve played for
Middlesex 2nd XI
Education: Wykeham Primary School; John Kelly Boys' High School
Qualifications: 4 O-levels
Off-season: Touring Australia with England
Overseas tours: England to New Zealand and Pakistan 1977-78, to West Indies 1980-81,
to India and Sri Lanka 1981-82, to New Zealand and Pakistan 1983-84, to India 1984-85,
to West Indies 1985-86, to Australia 1986-87, to India and Pakistan (World Cup), Australia
and New Zealand 1987-88; unofficial English XI to South Africa 1989-90; England to India
and Sri Lanka 1992-93, to Australia 1994-95
Cricketers particularly admired: Gary Sobers, Len Hutton
Other sports followed: Football, golf, tennis, etc.
Relaxations: Golf, swimming, reading, music
Extras: Awarded OBE in Queen's Birthday Honours 1987 for services to cricket. Captain
of Middlesex since 1983. Captain of England from 1986 to 1988. Published autobiography
Leading From the Front in 1988. Won a bronze medal for ballroom dancing at the Neasden
Ritz. Played football for Edgware Town as a teenager. Started as a goalkeeper, but also

played centre-half for Middlesex Schools. Was recommended to West Ham, had a trial with QPR and offered an apprenticeship by Watford. His brother Steve has had a successful football career with Arsenal and Brighton. Mike started his cricket career as wicket-keeper for his school team. He toured West Indies with England Young Cricketers in 1976 and 'to my immense pleasure (and to most other people's total disbelief) I was given the job of opening the bowling in the "Test" matches.' One of *Wisden*'s Five Cricketers of the Year 1983. His finest achievement was as captain of England on victorious tour of Australia, 1986-87, when they won the Ashes, the Perth Challenge Cup and World Series Cup. Was relieved of England captaincy after the First Test against West Indies in 1988. Captain of unofficial English team in South Africa in 1989-90 and was banned from Test cricket for five years; suspension remitted in 1992. Captained Middlesex to Championship title in 1990 and 1993. Retired from Test cricket after the final Test of the 1994-95 series against Australia

Opinions on cricket: 'Four-day cricket has been an eye-opener.'

Best batting: 258 Middlesex v Somerset, Bath 1984

Best bowling: 5-34 Middlesex v Glamorgan, Swansea 1982

1994 Season

	M	Inns	NO	Runs	HS	Avge	100s	50s	Ct	St	O	M	Runs	Wkts	Avge	Best	5wI	10wM
Test																		
All First	19	27	3	1671	225	69.62	6	6	28	-	26	4	97	2	48.50	1-10	-	-
1-day Int																		
NatWest	2	1	0	11	11	11.00	-	-	2	-								
B & H	2	2	0	28	28	14.00	-	-	-	-								
Sunday	16	10	1	180	51	20.00	-	1	5	-	6.2	0	58	1	58.00	1-58	-	

Career Performances

	M	Inns	NO	Runs	HS	Avge	100s	50s	Ct	St	Balls	Runs	Wkts	Avge	Best	5wI	10wM
Test	74	129	14	4227	207	36.75	9	21	56	-	752	317	4	79.25	1-14	-	-
All First	474	740	116	31785	258	50.93	82	158	423	-	9935	4592	156	29.43	5-34	2	-
1-day Int	92	88	17	2095	115 *	29.50	1	9	22	-	392	336	10	33.60	3-32	-	
NatWest	57	55	13	1964	132 *	46.76	2	14	24	-	1004	643	19	33.84	2-14	-	
B & H	81	75	17	2578	143 *	44.44	3	17	24	-	1382	940	41	22.92	4-49	-	
Sunday	235	210	28	5834	124 *	32.05	6	34	78	-	3138	2677	86	31.12	4-30	-	

GIBSON, O. D.   Glamorgan

Name: Ottis Delroy Gibson
Role: Right-hand bat, right-arm fast bowler
Born: 16 March 1969, St James, Barbados
Height: 6ft 2in   **Weight:** 13st 3lb
County debut: 1994
50 wickets in a season: 1
1st-Class 50s: 9
1st-Class 5 w. in innings: 8
1st-Class 10 w. in match: 2
1st-Class catches: 15
Place in batting averages: 148th av. 26.29
Place in bowling averages: 101st av. 36.15
Strike rate: 57.96 (career 51.96)
Marital status: Single
Education: St Silas Primary;
Ellerslie Secondary
Qualifications: 3 O-levels
Off-season: Playing in South Africa
Overseas teams played for: Fremantle, Perth
1989-90; Spartan, Barbados and Barbados 1991-94 ; Border, South Africa 1992-95
Cricketers particularly admired: Malcolm Marshall, Ian Botham, Viv Richards, Brian Lara.
Other sports followed: All sports
Relaxations: Sleep
Extras: Played for Farnworth in the Bolton League 1992 and 1993. South African Player of the Year 1992-93. Has played for West Indies A. Reported to have hit a straight six 150 yards over the pavilion at Buffalo Park, East London (South Africa) and into a car park
Opinions on cricket: 'We play too much cricket. The matches are so close together that if you are injured or off form you are not given enough time to recover or practise.'
Best batting: 85 Glamorgan v New Zealanders, Swansea 1994
Best bowling: 7-78 Barbados v Trinidad, Port of Spain 1991-92

1994 Season

	M	Inns	NO	Runs	HS	Avge	100s	50s	Ct	St	O	M	Runs	Wkts	Avge	Best	5wI	10wM
Test																		
All First	20	31	4	710	85	26.29	-	7	7	-	579.4	100	2169	60	36.15	6-64	4	1
1-day Int																		
NatWest	3	3	0	68	44	22.66	-	-	1	-	27	3	116	5	23.20	3-34	-	
B & H	1	1	0	37	37	37.00	-	-	-	-	8.4	0	50	2	25.00	2-50	-	
Sunday	17	15	7	206	33	25.75	-	-	4	-	92.5	5	446	12	37.16	2-35	-	

Career Performances

	M	Inns	NO	Runs	HS	Avge	100s	50s	Ct	St	Balls	Runs	Wkts	Avge	Best	5wI	10wM
Test																	
All First	46	68	11	1241	85	21.77	-	9	15	-	8367	4754	161	29.52	7-78	8	2
1-day Int																	
NatWest	3	3	0	68	44	22.66	-	-	1	-	162	116	5	23.20	3-34	-	
B & H	1	1	0	37	37	37.00	-	-	-	-	52	50	2	25.00	2-50	-	
Sunday	17	15	7	206	33	25.75	-	-	4	-	557	446	12	37.16	2-35	-	

GIDDINS, E. S. H. Sussex

Name: Edward Simon Hunter Giddins
Role: Right-hand bat, right-arm medium-fast bowler
Born: 20 July 1971, Eastbourne
Height: 6ft 4in **Weight:** 13st 7lb
Nickname: Geezer
County debut: 1991
County cap: 1994
50 wickets in a season: 1
1st-Class 5 w. in innings: 6
1st-Class catches: 9
Place in bowling averages: 19th av. 24.38
(1993 140th av. 51.37)
Strike rate: 45.06 (career 55.76)
Parents: Simon and Pauline
Marital status: Single
Family links with cricket:
Great-grandmother played cricket for
England Ladies. 'Family members George and
Misty have a fantastic eye for the ball'
Education: St Bede's Prep School;Eastbourne College
Qualifications: 'Various O and A-levels, national coaching certificate, recorder (grade 2), shorthand and typing 100/60.'
Career outside cricket: 'PR for Executive Search companies'
Off-season: 'I intend to train in Sydney (Jan, Feb, March) and intend to play cricket as well'
Overseas tours: Eastbourne College cricket/drama/debating tour to New Zealand 1988
Overseas teams played for: Discovery Bay Hotel, Barbados 1991; Bondi Surf, Sydney 1991-92; Bayswater Morley, Perth 1992
Cricketers particularly admired: Eddie Hemmings
Other sports followed: Brighton & Hove Albion, football; 'the sport in Browns Bar, Shoreditch'

Relaxations: *Neighbours*, *Home and Away*, Guinness
Extras: Took four wickets for no runs in ten balls against Derbyshire at Eastbourne in 1992. Sussex U23 Player of the Year 1992 and 1994. Nominated as one of England's three most eligible bachelors in *Company* magazine, March 1995
Opinions on cricket: 'Top drawer.'
Best batting: 24 Sussex v Essex, Chelmsford 1994
Best bowling: 5-32 Sussex v Derbyshire, Eastbourne 1992

1994 Season

	M	Inns	NO	Runs	HS	Avge	100s	50s	Ct	St	O	M	Runs	Wkts	Avge	Best	5wI	10wM
Test																		
All First	17	22	4	83	24	4.61	-	-	2	-	450.4	89	1463	60	24.38	5-38	3	-
1-day Int																		
NatWest	1	1	0	13	13	13.00	-	-	-	-	12	1	56	2	28.00	2-56	-	
B & H	2	0	0	0	0	-	-	-	1	-	20.2	2	88	1	88.00	1-29	-	
Sunday	15	6	3	5	2	1.66	-	-	2	-	102	6	522	20	26.10	4-23	-	

Career Performances

	M	Inns	NO	Runs	HS	Avge	100s	50s	Ct	St	Balls	Runs	Wkts	Avge	Best	5wI	10wM
Test																	
All First	45	50	19	124	24	4.00	-	-	9	-	6803	3996	122	32.75	5-32	6	-
1-day Int																	
NatWest	6	2	1	13	13	13.00	-	-	-	-	420	245	6	40.83	2-21	-	
B & H	5	1	0	0	0	0.00	-	-	1	-	286	209	4	52.25	2-42	-	
Sunday	40	18	8	20	9 *	2.00	-	-	8	-	1745	1439	50	28.78	4-23	-	

> 25. Which Durham bowler delivered the ball from which Brian Lara reached 501*?

GILES, A. F. Warwickshire

Name: Ashley Fraser Giles
Role: Right-hand bat, slow left-arm bowler
Born: 19 March 1973, Chertsey, Surrey
Height: 6ft 4in **Weight:** 14st
Nickname: Splash, Skater, Shanks
County debut: 1993
Parents: Michael and Paula
Marital status: Single
Family links with cricket: Brother and other family members play local club cricket
Education: George Abbot County Secondary, Guildford
Qualifications: 9 GCSEs, 1 A-level
Off-season: Playing for Vredenburg/ Saldanha, South Africa
Overseas tours: Surrey U19 to Barbados 1990-91
Overseas teams played for: Vredenburg/ Saldanha, South Africa 1992-94
Cricketers particularly admired:
Ian Botham, David Gower, Waqar Younis, Brian Lara, 'my girlfriend'
Other sports followed: Football, golf, basketball
Relaxations: Golf, relaxing with girlfriend Melanie, socialising
Extras: Surrey Young Cricketer Player of the Year 1991
Opinions on cricket: 'Four-day cricket is probably great for spin bowlers, but I haven't played too much yet. I believe, to give young players the best experience, that the 2nd XI Championship games should be played over four days.'
Best batting: 23 Warwickshire v Kent, Canterbury 1993
Best bowling: 1-27 Warwickshire v Durham, Darlington 1993

1994 Season (did not make any first-class or one-day appearance)

Career Performances

	M	Inns	NO	Runs	HS	Avge	100s	50s	Ct	St	Balls	Runs	Wkts	Avge	Best	5wI	10wM
Test																	
All First	2	4	1	53	23	17.66	-	-	-	-	249	128	3	42.66	1-27	-	-
1-day Int																	
NatWest																		
B & H																		
Sunday																		

GOOCH, G. A.   Essex

Name: Graham Alan Gooch
Role: Right-hand bat, right-arm medium bowler
Born: 23 July 1953, Leytonstone
Height: 6ft **Weight:** 13st
Nickname: Zap, Goochie
County debut: 1973
County cap: 1975
Benefit: 1985 (£153,906)
Testimonial: 1995
Test debut: 1975
Tests: 113
One-Day Internationals: 121
1000 runs in a season: 18
1st-Class 50s: 198
1st-Class 100s: 112
1st-Class 200s: 11
1st-Class 5 w. in innings: 3
1st-Class catches: 510
One-Day 50s: 119
One-Day 100s: 38
Place in batting averages: 4th av. 64.70 (1993 7th av. 63.21)
Strike rate: (career 77.57)
Parents: Alfred and Rose
Wife and date of marriage: Brenda, 23 October 1976
Children: Hannah; Megan and Sally (twins)
Family links with cricket: Father played local cricket for East Ham Corinthians. Second cousin, Graham Saville, played for Essex CCC and is now England YC team manager
Education: Cannhall School and Norlington Junior High School, Leytonstone; Redbridge Technical College
Qualifications: 6 CSEs; four-year apprenticeship in tool-making
Off-season: Touring Australia with England
Overseas tours: England YC to West Indies 1971-72; England to Australia 1978-79, to Australia and India 1979-80, to West Indies 1980-81, to India and Sri Lanka 1981-82, to World Cup and Pakistan 1987-88, to India and West Indies 1989-90, to Australia 1990-91, to New Zealand 1991-92, to Australia (World Cup) 1991-92, to India 1992-93, to Australia 1994-95; unofficial English XI to South Africa 1981-82
Overseas teams played for: Western Province, South Africa 1982-84
Cricketers particularly admired: Bob Taylor, a model sportsman; Mike Procter for his enthusiasm; Barry Richards for his ability
Other sports followed: Squash, soccer, golf. Has trained with West Ham United FC
Relaxations: 'Relaxing at home'

Extras: One of *Wisden*'s Five Cricketers of the Year 1979. Captained English rebel team in South Africa in 1982 and was banned from Test cricket for three years. Hit a hole in one at Tollygunge Golf Club during England's tour in India, 1981-82. Appointed Essex captain 1986, but resigned captaincy at end of 1987, being reappointed in 1989 following retirement of Keith Fletcher. Captain of England for last two Tests of 1988 season against West Indies and Sri Lanka in 1988 and chosen to captain England on the cancelled tour of India in 1988-89. Reappointed captain for the tour to India and West Indies in 1989-90, and led England to their first Test victory over West Indies for 16 years. His 333 in the Lord's Test v India was the third highest score ever by an England batsman in a Test match, and by hitting 123 in the second innings he created a record Test aggregate of 456 runs and became the first man to hit a triple century and a century in the same first-class match. His aggregate for the season (2746 runs at 101.70) was the best since 1961 and he was only the fourth batsman to finish an English season with an average better than 100. When he first joined Essex, he was a wicket-keeper and batted at No 11 in his first match. He went on a Young England tour to the West Indies as second wicket-keeper to Andy Stovold of Gloucestershire. Autobiography *Out of the Wilderness* published in 1988; *Test of Fire,* an account of the West Indies tour, published in 1990; *Captaincy* published in 1992. Scored his 100th century in 1993. Resigned as England captain after Australia had retained the Ashes in 1993. Became the 15th player to pass 40,000 runs in first-class cricket. Resigned as Essex captain at end of 1994 season. Retired from Test cricket after final Test of 1994-95 series against Australia. *Graham Gooch: My Autobiography* written with Frank Keating to be published in 1995
Best batting: 333 England v India, Lord's 1990
Best bowling: 7-14 Essex v Worcestershire, Ilford 1982

1994 Season

	M	Inns	NO	Runs	HS	Avge	100s	50s	Ct	St	O	M	Runs	Wkts	Avge	Best	5wI	10wM
Test	6	10	0	362	210	36.20	1	-	4	-	10	1	35	0	-	-	-	-
All First	17	29	2	1747	230	64.70	0	6	15	,	31.3	11	60	3	20.00	1-0	-	-
1-day Int	1	1	0	23	23	23.00	-	-	-	-								
NatWest	2	2	0	96	86	48.00	-	1	2	-								
B & H	2	2	1	151	130 *	151.00	1	-	-	-								
Sunday	11	11	0	415	101	37.72	1	2	1	-								

Career Performances

	M	Inns	NO	Runs	HS	Avge	100s	50s	Ct	St	Balls	Runs	Wkts	Avge	Best	5wI	10wM
Test	113	205	6	8655	333	43.49	20	45	103	-	2505	995	22	45.22	3-39	-	-
All First	525	888	72	40174	333	49.23	112	198	510	-	18307	8206	236	34.77	7-14	3	-
1-day Int	121	118	6	4229	142	37.75	8	23	44	-	1958	1436	36	39.88	3-19	-	
NatWest	50	49	4	2383	144	52.95	6	15	24	-	1639	847	28	30.25	3-31	-	
B & H	101	100	11	4607	198 *	51.76	12	29	62	-	3641	2118	69	30.69	3-24	-	
Sunday	249	244	21	7906	176	35.45	12	52	91	-	2474	4143	139	29.80	4-33	-	

GOUGH, D.   Yorkshire

Name: Darren Gough
Role: Right-hand bat, right-arm fast bowler
Born: 18 September 1970, Barnsley
Height: 5ft 11in **Weight:** 12st 7lbs
Nickname: Dazzler, Rhino
County debut: 1989
County cap: 1993
Test debut: 1994
Tests: 4
One-Day Internationals: 3
50 wickets in a season: 2
1st-Class 50s: 4
1st-Class 5 w. in innings: 8
1st-Class 10 w. in innings: 1
1st-Class catches: 10
One-Day 50s: 1
Place in batting averages: 186th av. 22.18
(1993 251st av. 11.81)
Place in bowling averages: 21st av. 24.61
(1993 40th av. 26.61)
Strike rate: 46.38 (career 56.30)
Parents: Trevor and Christine
Wife and date of marriage: Anna, 16 October 1993
Family links with cricket: Brother plays for Barnsley in Yorkshire League
Education: St Helens Junior; Priory Comprehensive; Airedale and Wharfdale College
(part-time)
Qualifications: 2 O-levels, 5 CSEs, BTEC Leisure, distinction coaching award 1
Career outside cricket: Coaching
Off-season: Touring Australia with England
Overseas tours: England YC to Australia 1989-90; Yorkshire to Barbados 1989-90, to
South Africa 1991-92 and 1992-93; England A to South Africa 1993-94; England to
Australia 1994-95
Overseas teams played for: East Shirley, Christchurch, New Zealand 1991-92
Cricketers particularly admired: Ian Botham, Richard Hadlee and Malcolm Marshall
Other sports followed: Football, golf
Injuries: Torn rib muscle, out for five weeks. Stress fracture of foot on England tour to
Australia and had to fly home
Relaxations: Cinema, 'walking with my wife Anna and dog, Jack the Jack Russell'
Extras: 'Had trials with Rotherham United FC but wasn't good enough'. Whittingdale
Player of the Month, July 1993. Yorkshire Player of the Year 1993
Opinions on cricket: 'County cricketers are not paid enough compared to other pro
sportsmen and should be given a 12-month contract or 9-month.'

Best batting: 72 Yorkshire v Northamptonshire, Northampton 1991
Best bowling: 7-42 Yorkshire v Somerset, Taunton 1993

1994 Season

	M	Inns	NO	Runs	HS	Avge	100s	50s	Ct	St	O	M	Runs	Wkts	Avge	Best	5wI	10wM
Test	4	5	2	146	65	48.66	-	1	-	-	170.2	28	566	17	33.29	4-46	-	-
All First	13	19	3	355	65	22.18	-	2	1	-	479.2	100	1526	62	24.61	6-66	3	-
1-day Int	3	0	0	0	0	-	-	-	1	-	32	4	115	4	28.75	2-36	-	
NatWest	2	1	0	2	2	2.00	-	-	-	-	24	1	101	4	25.25	3-51	-	
B & H	1	0	0	0	0	-	-	-	-	-	9	1	34	0	-	-	-	
Sunday	10	5	2	74	39	24.66	-	-	1	-	76.3	5	309	15	20.60	5-13	1	

Career Performances

	M	Inns	NO	Runs	HS	Avge	100s	50s	Ct	St	Balls	Runs	Wkts	Avge	Best	5wI	10wM
Test	4	5	2	146	65	48.66	-	1	-	-	1022	566	17	33.29	4-46	-	-
All First	76	98	23	1228	72	16.37	-	4	13	-	12557	6803	223	30.50	7-42	8	-
1-day Int	3	0	0	0	0	-	-	-	1	-	192	115	4	28.75	2-36	-	
NatWest	10	5	0	26	16	5.20	-	-	1	-	646	373	17	21.94	3-31	-	
B & H	8	5	1	20	7 *	5.00	-	-	-	-	402	253	9	28.11	2-29	-	
Sunday	54	32	10	274	72 *	12.45	-	1	11	-	2339	1715	60	28.58	5-13	1	

GRAVENEY, D. A.   Durham

Name: David Anthony Graveney
Role: Right-hand bat, slow left-arm bowler
Born: 2 January 1953, Bristol
Height: 6ft 4in **Weight:** 14st
Nickname: Gravity, Grav
County debut: 1972 (Gloucestershire),
1991 (Somerset), 1992 (Durham)
County cap: 1976 (Gloucestershire)
Benefit: 1986
50 wickets in a season: 7
1st-Class 50s: 16
1st-Class 100s: 2
1st-Class 5 w. in innings: 40
1st-Class 10 w. in match: 7
1st-Class catches: 241
One-Day 50s: 1
One-Day 5 w. in innings: 1
Place in batting averages: 202nd av. 19.68
(1993 190th av. 20.64)

Place in bowling averages: 120th av. 40.22 (1993 101st av. 34.36)
Strike rate: 88.25 (career 70.84)
Parents: Ken and Jeanne (deceased)
Wife and date of marriage: Julie, 23 September 1978
Children: Adam, 13 October 1982
Family links with cricket: Son of J.K. Graveney, captain of Gloucestershire, who took 10 wickets for 66 runs v Derbyshire at Chesterfield in 1949, and nephew of Tom Graveney of Gloucestershire, Worcestershire and England. Brother, John, selected for English Public Schools v English Schools at Lord's
Education: Millfield School
Career outside cricket: Company director, accountant
Overseas tours: Unofficial English XI to South Africa 1989-90; MCC to Bahrain 1994-95
Other sports followed: Golf, soccer, squash
Relaxations: 'Playing sport, television and cinema. Relaxing at a good pub'
Extras: Treasurer of Cricketers' Association. Captain of Gloucestershire, 1981 to 1988. Third member of the Graveney family to be dismissed by Gloucester CCC – Uncle Tom as captain in 1960 and father Ken as chairman in 1982 – when he was sacked as captain. Player-manager of unofficial tour to South Africa 1989-90, banned for five years but suspension remitted in 1992. Left Gloucestershire at end of 1990 season and joined Somerset, but left after a year to captain Durham in their first season as a first-class county. Co-author with Jack Bannister of *Durham CCC: Past, Present and Future* published in 1993. Resigned as captain of Durham at the end of the 1993 season. Retired from first-class cricket at end of 1994 season and appointed General Secretary of the Professional Cricketers' Association
Best batting: 119 Gloucestershire v Oxford University, The Parks 1980
Best bowling: 8-85 Gloucestershire v Nottinghamshire, Cheltenham 1974

1994 Season

	M	Inns	NO	Runs	HS	Avge	100s	50s	Ct	St	O	M	Runs	Wkts	Avge	Best	5wI	10wM
Test																		
All First	13	22	6	315	65 *	19.68	-	1	5	-	456	121	1247	31	40.22	6-80	1	-
1-day Int																		
NatWest	2	1	1	16	16 *	-	-	-	1	-	20	6	51	2	25.50	1-7	-	
B & H	1	1	1	4	4 *	-	-	-	-	-	11	0	36	0	-	-	-	
Sunday	12	6	5	54	25 *	54.00	-	-	1	-	89	3	388	10	38.80	3-49	-	

Career Performances

	M	Inns	NO	Runs	HS	Avge	100s	50s	Ct	St	Balls	Runs	Wkts	Avge	Best	5wI	10wM
Test																	
All First	457	580	178	7105	119	17.67	2	16	241	-	69496	29867	981	30.44	8-85	40	7
1-day Int																	
NatWest	46	26	10	308	44	19.25	-	-	20	-	2549	1363	54	25.24	5-11	1	
B & H	73	46	17	463	49 *	15.96	-	-	19	-	3026	1836	51	36.00	3-13	-	
Sunday	260	152	64	1467	56 *	16.67	-	1	63	-	7725	5928	180	32.93	4-22	-	

GRAYSON, A. P.   Yorkshire

Name: Adrian Paul Grayson
Role: Right-hand bat, slow left-arm bowler
Born: 31 March 1971, Ripon
Height: 6ft 2in **Weight:** 11st 7lb
Nickname: PG, Laz, Ravi, BK
County debut: 1990
1000 runs in a season: 1
1st-Class 50s: 10
1st-Class 100s: 1
1st-Class catches: 13
One-Day 50s: 1
Place in batting averages: 64th av. 38.74
(1993 172nd av. 22.70)
Strike rate: (career 146.45)
Parents: Adrian and Carol
Wife and date of marriage:
Alison, 30 September 1994
Family links with cricket: 'Dad played
good league cricket and is also an NCA staff
coach; brother also plays when free from football commitments'
Education: Bedale Comprehensive School
Qualifications: 8 CSEs, BTEC in Leisure, NCA Senior Coaching Award
Career outside cricket: Coaching at Yorkshire Cricket School
Off-season: Touring Cape Town with Lancashire and playing football
Overseas tours: England YC to Australia 1989-90; Yorkshire to Barbados 1989-90, to
Cape Town 1991-92, to Cape Town 1992-93, to Cape Town 1994-95
Overseas teams played for: Petone, Wellington 1991-92
Cricketers particularly admired: Graham Gooch, Martyn Moxon
Other sports followed: Any sport on television, football (Leeds United)
Relaxations: Playing golf, eating out
Extras: Played for England YC v New Zealand 1989 and Pakistan 1990. Turned down an
offer by Middlesex. Brother plays football for Leicester City. Scored 1000 runs for first time
this season (1994)
Opinions on cricket: 'More cricket should be played in schools. The reverse sweep should
be banned.'
Best batting: 100 Yorkshire v Worcestershire, Worcester 1994
Best bowling: 2-43 Yorkshire v Hampshire, Headingley 1994

---

26. Which one player took the most wickets, scored the most runs, and took
the most catches in Test matches on England's tour to India in 1992-93?

1994 Season

	M	Inns	NO	Runs	HS	Avge	100s	50s	Ct	St	O	M	Runs	Wkts	Avge	Best	5wl	10wM
Test																		
All First	19	31	4	1046	100	38.74	1	7	19	-	103.3	34	236	8	29.50	2-43	-	-
1-day Int																		
NatWest	2	2	0	47	29	23.50	-	-	1	-	17	1	75	2	37.50	1-25	-	
B & H	1	1	1	22	22 *	-	-	-	-	-	9	1	30	1	30.00	1-30	-	
Sunday	16	12	3	123	55	13.66	-	1	8	-	67	2	370	12	30.83	4-25	-	

Career Performances

	M	Inns	NO	Runs	HS	Avge	100s	50s	Ct	St	Balls	Runs	Wkts	Avge	Best	5wl	10wM
Test																	
All First	43	66	9	1723	100	30.22	1	10	32	-	1611	766	11	69.63	2-43	-	-
1-day Int																	
NatWest	4	4	0	64	29	16.00	-	-	1	-	114	81	2	40.50	1-25	-	
B & H	5	5	1	85	22 *	21.25	-	-	-	-	102	62	1	62.00	1-30	-	
Sunday	35	25	4	280	55	13.33	-	1	11	-	834	722	20	36.10	4-25	-	

GREEN, R. J.   Lancashire

Name: Richard James Green
Role: Right-hand bat
Born: 13 March 1976, Warrington, Cheshire
Height: 6ft **Weight:** 13st
County debut: No first-team appearance
Parents: Jim and Christina
Marital status: Single
Family links with cricket:
Grandfather and father both played
Education: Bridgewater County
High School, Warrington; Hartford College
Qualifications: 5 GCSEs, studying
Business Studies at college
Off-season: Playing in Australia
Overseas teams played for: Pro Waratah,
Newcastle, NSW
Cricketers particularly admired:
Steve Waugh and David Gower
Other sports followed: Rugby league (Warrington)
Relaxations: Driving and music
Extras: Cheshire County League's youngest century-maker. Played for England U17
Opinions on cricket: 'Cricket should be adopted by many more schools.'

GREENFIELD, K.   Sussex

Name: Keith Greenfield
Role: Right-hand bat,
right-arm off-spin bowler
Born: 6 December 1968, Brighton
Height: 6ft **Weight:** 12st 12lbs
Nickname: Grubby
County debut: 1987
1st-Class 50s: 5
1st-Class 100s: 4
1st-Class catches: 32
One-Day 50s: 11
Place in batting averages:
(1993 54th av. 39.22)
Parents: Leslie Ernest and Sheila
Wife and date of marriage:
Caroline Susannah, 22 February 1992
Family links with cricket: Father keen
spectator, father-in-law played club cricket
for 20 years and now umpires
Education: Coldean First and Middle Schools; Falmer High School
Qualifications: 3 O-levels, BTEC National Diploma in Leisure and Management, junior,
senior and advanced coaching certificates
Career outside cricket: Cricket coach
Off-season: Coaching at Hove for Sussex
Overseas tours: Sussex U16 to Guernsey 1985; Select XI to Malaga 1993; Sussex to
Malaga 1993-94; David Smith Testimonial XI to Malaga 1994
Overseas teams played for: Cornwall, Auckland 1988-90
Cricketers particularly admired: Derek Randall, Ian Botham, Chris Tugwell and
Malcolm Eldridge (St Peters) and Ray Bierber (Brighton & Hove)
Other sports followed: 'All sports interest me', Liverpool FC
Relaxations: 'Eating out with friends, music (Dire Straits, UB40), spending time with Caz'
Extras: First person taken on Youth Training Scheme to become a professional cricketer
at Sussex. Only uncapped player to have captained Sussex at Hove (v Cambridge U), scored
century in this game. Captained 2nd XI to Championship title in 1990. Sussex Team Man
of the Year 1990, 1993
Best batting: 127* Sussex v Cambridge University, Hove 1991
Best bowling: 2-40 Sussex v Essex, Hove 1993

---

27. Which two Glamorgan cricketers played for Old Cliftonians in
the 1994 *Cricketer* Cup final?

1994 Season

	M	Inns	NO	Runs	HS	Avge	100s	50s	Ct	St	O	M	Runs	Wkts	Avge	Best	5wI	10wM
Test																		
All First	1	2	2	61	35 *	-	-	-	-	-	16	1	76	0	-		-	-
1-day Int																		
NatWest																		
B & H	1	1	0	27	27	27.00	-	-	-	-								
Sunday	16	16	2	372	61	26.57	-	1	3	-	12	0	103	0	-		-	-

Career Performances

	M	Inns	NO	Runs	HS	Avge	100s	50s	Ct	St	Balls	Runs	Wkts	Avge	Best	5wI	10wM
Test																	
All First	34	56	10	1409	127 *	30.63	4	5	32	-	489	345	5	69.00	2-40	-	-
1-day Int																	
NatWest	6	5	2	124	96 *	41.33	-	1	2	-	246	146	3	48.66	2-35	-	
B & H	10	10	1	263	62	29.22	-	2	5	-	180	141	1	141.00	1-35	-	
Sunday	63	61	7	1377	79	25.50	-	8	17	-	624	651	9	72.33	3-44	-	

GRIFFITH, F. A.   Derbyshire

Name: Frank Alexander Griffith
Role: Right-hand bat, right-arm medium bowler
Born: 15 August 1968, Leyton
Height: 6ft **Weight:** 12st
Nickname: Sir Learie
County debut: 1988
1st-Class 50s: 3
1st-Class catches: 18
Place in batting averages:
(1993 204th av. 18.35)
Place in bowling averages:
(1993 123rd av. 42.35)
Strike rate: (career 58.25)
Parents: Alex and Daisy
Marital status: Single
Education: William Morris High School, Walthamstow
Qualifications: Food and Nutrition and Art O-levels; NCA coaching certificate
Cricketers particularly admired: Collis King, Franklyn Stephenson
Other sports followed: Table tennis, basketball, football

Relaxations: Listening to music
Extras: Attended Haringey Cricket College
Best batting: 81 Derbyshire v Glamorgan, Chesterfield 1992
Best bowling: 4-33 Derbyshire v Leicestershire, Ilkeston 1992

1994 Season

	M	Inns	NO	Runs	HS	Avge	100s	50s	Ct	St	O	M	Runs	Wkts	Avge	Best	5wI	10wM
Test																		
All First	3	5	1	123	36	30.75	-	-	2	-	67.4	12	210	8	26.25	3-32	-	-
1-day Int																		
NatWest	3	2	0	8	8	4.00	-	-	2	-	21	6	73	2	36.50	1-18	-	
B & H	1	1	0	4	4	4.00	-	-	-	-	0.2	0	5	0	-	-	-	-
Sunday	7	3	0	68	31	22.66	-	-	2	-	46	1	246	7	35.14	2-27	-	

Career Performances

	M	Inns	NO	Runs	HS	Avge	100s	50s	Ct	St	Balls	Runs	Wkts	Avge	Best	5wI	10wM
Test																	
All First	34	50	5	847	81	18.82	-	3	18	-	3204	1820	55	33.09	4-33	-	-
1-day Int																	
NatWest	5	4	0	16	8	4.00	-	-	2	-	224	132	4	33.00	1-13	-	
B & H	6	5	1	35	13*	8.75	-	-	3	-	254	211	7	30.14	2-48	-	
Sunday	34	26	4	238	31	10.81	-	-	5	-	1315	1170	35	33.42	4-48	-	

HABIB, A.   Middlesex

Name: Aftab Habib
Role: Right-hand bat,
right-arm medium bowler
Born: 7 February 1972, Reading, Berks
Height: 5ft 11in
County debut: 1992
Parents: Hussain and Tahira
Marital status: Single
Family links with cricket: Cousin of
Zahid Sadiq (ex-Surrey and Derbyshire)
Education: Millfield School;
Taunton School
Qualifications: 7 GCSEs,
NCA coaching certificate
Career outside cricket: Salesman for Sewards
Overseas tours: England YC to Australia 1989-
90, to New Zealand 1990-91

Overseas teams played for: Gloobe Wakatu, Nelson, New Zealand, 1992-93
Cricketers particularly admired: Desmond Haynes, Javed Miandad, Dean Jones and Mark Waugh
Other sports followed: All sports
Relaxations: Music, videos, reading and magazines
Extras: 2nd XI Seaxe Player of the Year 1992. Released by Middlesex at end of 1994 season
Best batting: 12 Middlesex v Surrey, The Oval 1992

1994 Season

	M	Inns	NO	Runs	HS	Avge	100s	50s	Ct	St	O	M	Runs	Wkts	Avge	Best	5wI	10wM
Test																		
All First																		
1-day Int																		
NatWest																		
B & H																		
Sunday	1	1	0	11	11	11.00	-	-	-	-								

Career Performances

	M	Inns	NO	Runs	HS	Avge	100s	50s	Ct	St	Balls	Runs	Wkts	Avge	Best	5wI	10wM
Test																	
All First	1	2	1	19	12	19.00	-	-	-	-							
1-day Int																	
NatWest																	
B & H																	
Sunday	2	2	0	26	15	13.00	-	-	-	-							

HALL, J. W.   Sussex

Name: James William Hall
Role: Right-hand opening batsman
Born: 30 March 1968, Chichester
Height: 6ft 4in **Weight:** 13st 7lbs
Nickname: Gus
County debut: 1990
County cap: 1992
1000 runs in a season: 2
1st-Class 50s: 25
1st-Class 100s: 5
1st-Class catches: 36
Place in batting averages: 135th av. 29.22 (1993 146th av. 26.00)
Parents: Maurice and Marlene (deceased)
Marital status: Single

Family links with cricket: Father played club cricket for Chichester Priory Park. Brother David a very keen supporter
Education: Chichester Boys' High School
Qualifications: 9 O-levels, level 1 and 2 Coaching Awards
Career outside cricket: Coach
Off-season: Coaching at the Scots College in Sydney, Australia
Overseas tours: Malaga Select XI, Spain, 1993
Overseas teams played for: Southern Districts, Perth, Western Australia 1986-87; Swanbourne, Perth 1988-89; University St Helliers, Auckland 1991-92; Malaga Select XI, 1993-94
Cricketers particularly admired: Alan Wells, Ritchie Laing, John Crumplin, Alec Stewart, Peter Moores, Barry Hutton
Other sports followed: Football (Brighton & Hove Albion and Carlisle United), kick-boxing
Injuries: Rib cartilage and intercostal strain, missed three weeks
Relaxations: 'Spending numerous hours at the following places: The Royal Escape, The Zap, The Shark Bar and Slid Row Bar. Being entertained by Ed Giddins batting'
Extras: Scored 53 on 1st XI debut v Zimbabwe and scored maiden first-class century in same week (120* v New Zealand) in 1990, going on to make over 1000 runs in debut season of first-class cricket. Run out without facing a ball on NatWest debut v Glamorgan ('thanks Neil'). Whittingdale Young Cricketer of the Month for May 1991. Scorer of slowest ever Championship 50 v Surrey, The Oval 29 July 1994.
Best batting: 140* Sussex v Lancashire, Hove 1992

1994 Season

	M	Inns	NO	Runs	HS	Avge	100s	50s	Ct	St	O	M	Runs	Wkts	Avge	Best	5wI	10wM
Test																		
All First	14	27	0	789	85	29.22	-	7	9	-								
1-day Int																		
NatWest																		
B & H																		
Sunday	4	4	0	120	69	30.00	-	1	1	-								

28. Which company sponsors the International Test Umpires Panel?

Career Performances

	M	Inns	NO	Runs	HS	Avge	100s	50s	Ct	St	Balls	Runs	Wkts	Avge	Best	5wl	10wM
Test																	
All First	78	140	10	4130	140 *	31.76	5	25	36	-	12	14	0	-	-	-	-
1-day Int																	
NatWest	4	4	0	50	47	12.50	-	-	-	-							
B & H	9	9	0	339	81	37.66	-	3	1	-							
Sunday	23	22	0	625	77	28.40	-	6	6	-							

HALLETT, J. C. Somerset

Name: Jeremy Charles Hallett
Role: Right-hand bat,
right-arm medium-fast bowler
Born: 18 October 1970, Yeovil
Height: 6ft 2in **Weight:** 12st
Nickname: Chicks, Pikey
County debut: 1990
1st-Class 50 scored: 1
1st-Class catches: 6
Place in batting averages: 261st av. 11.28
Strike rate: (career 73.37)
Parents: Glyn and Rosemarie
Marital status: Single
Family links with cricket: 'Father has
played Somerset League cricket for years,
and sister plays for Sussex Ladies and English
Universities.'
Education: Wells Cathedral Junior School;
Millfield School; Durham University
Qualifications: 10 O-levels, 3 A-levels, degree in economics, management, history
Off-season: Playing in New Zealand
Overseas tours: England YC to Australia, 1989-90; Durham University to South Africa
1992-93
Cricketers particularly admired: Malcolm Marshall, Viv Richards, Terry Alderman,
Richard Hadlee, Martin Crowe, Jimmy Cook
Other sports followed: Football (Yeovil Town), golf, Bath RFC, 'all sports really'
Relaxations: 'Films, music, playing golf, a good pub, food!'
Extras: Cricketer of the Series, England YC in Australia 1989-90. Also played v New
Zealand YC 1989 and Pakistan YC 1990. Somerset Young Player of the Year 1990. Played
for Combined Universities in B&H Cup 1991,1992 and 1993 and v Australians 1993
Opinions on cricket: 'Limited run-ups should be re-introduced to the Sunday League.'

Best batting: 52 Combined University v New Zealand, Fenner's 1994
Best bowling: 4-59 Somerset v Kent, Canterbury 1994

1994 Season

	M	Inns	NO	Runs	HS	Avge	100s	50s	Ct	St	O	M	Runs	Wkts	Avge	Best	5wI	10wM
Test																		
All First	4	8	1	79	52	11.28	-	1	1	-	84.2	24	270	8	33.75	4-59	-	-
1-day Int																		
NatWest																		
B & H	1	0	0	0	0	-	-	-	-	-	10	1	40	0	-	-	-	-
Sunday	3	3	0	37	16	12.33	-	-	1	-	14.5	0	93	2	46.50	2-40	-	

Career Performances

	M	Inns	NO	Runs	HS	Avge	100s	50s	Ct	St	Balls	Runs	Wkts	Avge	Best	5wI	10wM
Test																	
All First	16	15	3	120	52	10.00	-	1	6	-	2128	1256	29	43.31	4-59	-	-
1-day Int																	
NatWest	1	0	0	0	0	-	-	-	-	-	72	31	0	-	-	-	-
B & H	11	5	1	13	5 *	3.25	-	-	1	-	541	342	7	48.85	3-36	-	-
Sunday	19	8	3	71	26	14.20	-	-	2	-	638	598	15	39.86	3-41	-	

HAMILTON, G. M. Yorkshire

Name: Gavin Mark Hamilton
Role: Right-hand bat,
right-arm fast bowler
Born: 16 September 1974, Broxburn
Height: 6ft 2in **Weight:** 12st 7lb
Nickname: Hammy
County debut: 1994
Parents: Gavin and Wendy
Marital status: Single
Family links with cricket: Brother plays for
Scotland and dad is a long-term club cricketer
for Sidcup and West Lothian
Education: Hurstmere School, Sidcup
Qualifications: 9 GCSEs
Off-season: Playing for Wellington in Cape
Town
Overseas teams played for: Municipals,
Orange Free State, South Africa; Wellington,
Cape Town, South Africa

Cricketers particularly admired: Mark Robinson, David Gower
Other sports followed: Golf
Injuries: Shin splints, missed two weeks
Relaxations: 'Sunbathing or day out on the waterfront'
Extras: Has played first-class cricket for Scotland
Opinions on cricket: 'Quite happy with the situation.'
Best batting: 48 Yorkshire v Kent, Maidstone 1994
Best bowling: 5-65 Scotland v Ireland, Eglinton 1993

1994 Season

	M	Inns	NO	Runs	HS	Avge	100s	50s	Ct	St	O	M	Runs	Wkts	Avge	Best	5wl	10wM
Test																		
All First	4	4	0	70	48	17.50	-	-	2	-	100.2	20	364	5	72.80	2-76	-	-
1-day Int																		
NatWest	1	1	0	2	2	2.00	-	-	-	-	11	4	42	2	21.00	2-42	-	
B & H	1	1	1	8	8 *	-	-	-	-	-	9	2	27	0	-		-	-
Sunday	6	3	2	41	16 *	41.00	-	-	-	-	40.1	0	242	8	30.25	2-27	-	

Career Performances

	M	Inns	NO	Runs	HS	Avge	100s	50s	Ct	St	Balls	Runs	Wkts	Avge	Best	5wl	10wM
Test																	
All First	5	5	0	70	48	14.00	-	-	2	-	815	464	10	46.40	5-65	1	-
1-day Int																	
NatWest	2	1	0	2	2	2.00	-	-	1	-	120	86	4	21.50	2-42	-	
B & H	2	1	1	8	8 *	-	-	-	-	-	78	42	0	-		-	-
Sunday	6	3	2	41	16 *	41.00	-	-	-	-	241	242	8	30.25	2-27	-	

HANCOCK, T. H. C.   Gloucestershire

Name: Timothy Harold Coulter Hancock
Role: Right-hand bat, occasional right-arm medium bowler, short-leg or cover fielder
Born: 20 April 1972, Reading
Height: 5ft 11in **Weight:** 12st 12lb
Nickname: Herbie
County debut: 1991
1st-Class 50s: 14
1st-Class 100s: 2
1st-Class catches: 31
Place in batting averages: 159th av. 25.55 (1993 136th av. 26.77)
Parents: John and Jennifer
Marital status: Single
Family links with cricket: 'Dad still plays.'

Education: St Edward's, Oxford; Henley College
Qualifications: 8 GCSEs
Off-season: In Durban, South Africa
Overseas tours: Gloucestershire to Kenya 1991, to Sri Lanka 1993
Overseas teams played for: CBC Old Boys, Bloemfontein 1991-92; Wynnum Manley, Brisbane 1992-93
Cricketers particularly admired: Ian Botham, Viv Richards
Other sports followed: Rugby union, golf, hockey
Relaxations: Playing golf, watching television, 'having a pint or two with friends'
Extras: Played hockey for Oxfordshire U19
Opinions on cricket: 'Four-day cricket I think will work out for the best. I can't say I'm too

sure about Sundays still with coloured clothing etc. I wish people who made a good living out of county cricket would stop moaning that the reason our national side is playing badly is because of county cricket. We have some superb international players who will in time bring us back up the ladder.'
Best batting: 123 Gloucestershire v Essex, Chelmsford 1994
Best bowling: 3-10 Gloucestershire v Glamorgan, Abergavenny 1993

1994 Season

	M	Inns	NO	Runs	HS	Avge	100s	50s	Ct	St	O	M	Runs	Wkts	Avge	Best	5wI	10wM
Test																		
All First	20	37	1	920	123	25.55	1	7	10	-	47	7	207	3	69.00	2-16	-	-
1-day Int																		
NatWest	1	1	0	29	29	29.00	-	-	-	-	5	0	32	0	-		-	-
B & H	1	1	0	13	13	13.00	-	-	-	-								
Sunday	16	16	0	253	43	15.81	-	-	6	-	15	0	105	3	35.00	2-31	-	

Career Performances

	M	Inns	NO	Runs	HS	Avge	100s	50s	Ct	St	Balls	Runs	Wkts	Avge	Best	5wI	10wM
Test																	
All First	52	94	6	2177	123	24.73	2	14	31	-	748	479	13	36.84	3-10	-	-
1-day Int																	
NatWest	2	2	0	74	45	37.00	-	-	1	-	41	39	2	19.50	2-7	-	
B & H	7	5	0	61	23	12.20	-	-	2	-							
Sunday	39	36	1	499	46	14.25	-	-	15	-	114	121	3	40.33	2-31	-	

HARDEN, R. J.   Somerset

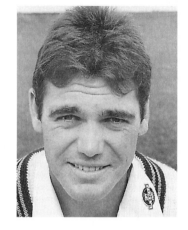

Name: Richard John Harden
Role: Right-hand bat, left-arm medium
bowler
Born: 16 August 1965, Bridgwater
Height: 5ft 11¹/₂in **Weight:** 13st 7lbs
Nickname: Sumo, Curtis
County debut: 1985
County cap: 1989
1000 runs in a season: 5
1st-Class 50s: 53
1st-Class 100s: 20
1st-Class catches: 145
One-Day 50s: 20
One-Day 100s: 2
Place in batting averages: 53rd av. 40.80
(1993 57th av. 39.06)
Parents: Chris and Anne
Wife and date of marriage:
Nicki Rae, 25 September 1992
Family links with cricket: Grandfather played club cricket for Bridgwater
Education: King's College, Taunton
Qualifications: 8 O-levels, 2 A-levels, coaching award
Career outside cricket: Print broker for Pennine Dataforms
Off-season: Working for Pennine Dataforms
Overseas teams: Central Districts, New Zealand
Cricketers particularly admired: Viv Richards, Jimmy Cook
Other sports followed: Squash, golf, rugby
Relaxations: 'Love my domestic duties (dusting, Hoovering, etc.) rather than golf. Good food and the odd drink.'
Opinions on cricket: 'The four-day game has been excellent with the best team winning. We must make sure we don't go back to playing four-day cricket on three-day result wickets though, which would defeat the object of four-day cricket.'
Best batting: 187 Somerset v Nottinghamshire, Taunton 1992
Best bowling: 2-7 Central Districts v Canterbury, Blenheim 1987-88

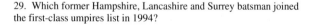

29. Which former Hampshire, Lancashire and Surrey batsman joined the first-class umpires list in 1994?

1994 Season

	M	Inns	NO	Runs	HS	Avge	100s	50s	Ct	St	O	M	Runs	Wkts	Avge	Best	5wl	10wM
Test																		
All First	18	31	5	1061	131 *	40.80	2	7	13	-								
1-day Int																		
NatWest	3	3	1	178	105 *	89.00	1	1	3	-								
B & H	1	1	0	34	34	34.00	-	-	-	-								
Sunday	14	14	1	331	59	25.46	-	2	7	-								

Career Performances

	M	Inns	NO	Runs	HS	Avge	100s	50s	Ct	St	Balls	Runs	Wkts	Avge	Best	5wl	10wM
Test																	
All First	191	308	49	10096	187	38.98	20	53	145	-	1400	952	19	50.10	2-7	-	-
1-day Int																	
NatWest	18	16	2	595	108 *	42.50	2	2	10	-	18	23	0	-		-	-
B & H	36	35	3	648	76	20.25	-	2	8	-							
Sunday	127	121	21	2953	90 *	29.53	-	16	37	-	1	0	0	-		-	-

HARRIS, A. J.   Derbyshire

Name: Andrew James Harris
Role: Right-hand bat, right-arm fast bowler
Born: 26 June 1973, Ashton-under-Lyne
Height: 6ft **Weight:** 11st 7lbs
Nickname: AJ 'and the odd person resorts to Rolf'
County debut: 1994
Parents: Norman and Joyce
Marital status: Single
Education: Tintwistle Primary School; Hadfield Comprehensive School; Glossopdale Community College
Qualifications: 6 GCSEs, 1 A-Level
Off-season: 'Winterrring in Australia or in the event of a job not arising I may well return to my last job in the close season which was retail sales – dept assistant manager (foil packer) – in a local firm'
Overseas teams played for: Ginninderra, West Belconnen, Australia 1992-93
Cricketers particularly admired: 'Being a bowler by trade I particularly admire Kim Barnett, obviously (I have to stay in his good books), Brian Lara – he's top

drawer – and Merv Hughes for his effort and determination'

Other sports followed: 'Soccer, as my brother plays for Altrincham, but I support the True Blues, Man City, and every sport I will view with great determination'

Relaxations: 'Playing any sport, golf in particular. As relaxing goes, watching television, playing on my Sega, and how could I forget having quite a few beers, although I have never been to the Pink Coconut'

Best batting: 10 Derbyshire v Surrey, The Oval 1994

Best bowling: 3-40 Derbyshire v Worcestershire, Derby 1994

1994 Season

	M	Inns	NO	Runs	HS	Avge	100s	50s	Ct	St	O	M	Runs	Wkts	Avge	Best	5wI	10wM
Test																		
All First	2	3	0	11	10	3.66	-	-	-	-	32	1	165	5	33.00	3-40	-	-
1-day Int																		
NatWest																		
B & H																		
Sunday	1	0	0	0	0	-	-	-	-	-	8	0	49	2	24.50	2-49	-	

Career Performances

	M	Inns	NO	Runs	HS	Avge	100s	50s	Ct	St	Balls	Runs	Wkts	Avge	Best	5wI	10wM
Test																	
All First	2	3	0	11	10	3.66	-	-	-	-	192	165	5	33.00	3-40	-	-
1-day Int																	
NatWest																	
B & H																	
Sunday	1	0	0	0	0	-	-	-	-	-	48	49	2	24.50	2-49	-	

HARRIS, G. A. R.   Middlesex

Name: Gordon Andrew Robert Harris

Role: Right-hand bat, right-arm fast bowler

Born: 11 January 1964, Tottenham, London

Height: 6ft 3in **Weight:** 13st 7lb

Nickname: Flash

County debut: 1986 (Leicestershire), 1994 (Middlesex)

Parents: Colin and Yvonne

Wife and date of marriage: Clare, September 1994

Family links with cricket: Father is an MCC member and is a former club cricketer

Education: Merchant Taylors; Northwood; Uxbridge TCC; Leicester Polytechnic

Qualifications: 9 O-levels, 2 A-levels, BSc (Hons) in Physics and Computing

Career outside cricket: Systems analyst

Off-season: Permanent job at Lloyd's Bank in information systems

Overseas tours: CCC to Australia 1991, to South Africa 1994; Teddington to Barbados 1990 as National Club Champions
Cricketers particularly admired: Richard Hadlee, Dennis Lillee, Ian Botham, Viv Richards
Other sports followed: Football (Spurs), hockey, golf, rugby, skiing
Relaxations: Classic cars, DIY, hockey, socialising, golf, swimming and fitness training
Extras: MCC member. Played one Championship and one Sunday League game for Leicestershire in 1986. Played Minor Counties for Bedfordshire and Hertfordshire
Opinions on cricket: 'I would like to see the English game structured similar to that

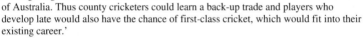

of Australia. Thus county cricketers could learn a back-up trade and players who develop late would also have the chance of first-class cricket, which would fit into their existing career.'
Best batting: 11 Middlesex v Glamorgan, Lord's 1994
Best batting: 1-61 Middlesex v Glamorgan, Lord's 1994

1994 Season

	M	Inns	NO	Runs	HS	Avge	100s	50s	Ct	St	O	M	Runs	Wkts	Avge	Best	5wI	10wM
Test																		
All First	2	2	1	16	11	16.00	-	-	-	-	51	11	215	1	215.00	1-61	-	-
1-day Int																		
NatWest																		
B & H																		
Sunday	3	0	0	0	0	-	-	-	-	-	21.1	1	101	6	16.83	5-26	1	

Career Performances

	M	Inns	NO	Runs	HS	Avge	100s	50s	Ct	St	Balls	Runs	Wkts	Avge	Best	5wI	10wM
Test																	
All First	3	4	2	22	11	11.00	-	-	-	-	354	249	1	249.00	1-61	-	-
1-day Int																	
NatWest	3	2	0	10	10	5.00	-	-	-	-	168	116	2	58.00	2-32	-	
B & H																	
Sunday	4	0	0	0	0	-	-	-	-	-	175	128	7	18.28	5-26	1	

HARRISON, J. C.   Middlesex

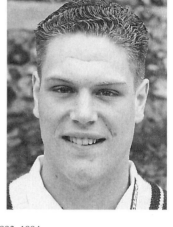

Name: Jason Christian Harrison
Role: Right-hand bat, off-spin bowler, short-leg fielder
Born: 15 January 1972, Amersham, Bucks
Height: 6ft 3in **Weight:** 13st 10lbs
Nickname: Harry
County debut: 1994
1st-Class catches: 2
Parents: Paul and Carey
Marital status: Single
Education: Great Marlow, Bucks, College of Higher Education
Qualifications: 6 GCSEs, NCA coaching certificate, City & Guilds apprenticeship in sheet metal fabrication
Career outside cricket:
Sheet metal fabricator
Off-season: Playing and coaching for Bellville in South Africa
Overseas tours: Middlesex to Portugal 1992, 1993, 1994
Overseas teams played for: Bellville, South Africa 1993-95
Cricketers particularly admired: Malcolm Roberts, Mike Roseberry, Keith Brown, Mike Gatting, Jason Pooley
Other sports followed: Football (Wycombe Wanderers)
Relaxations: Listening to music, spending time with friends, gym work
Extras: Played for Buckinghamshire 1991 and 1992 and for NCA U19 and NAYC in 1991. Holds the record for the highest score in the Thames Valley League. Offered contract by Leicestershire as well as Middlesex. Was out first ball in first-class cricket
Opinions on cricket: 'All 2nd XI games, whether Championship or Bain Clarkson, should be played on first-class grounds.'
Best batting: 4 Middlesex v Cambridge University, Fenner's 1994

1994 Season

	M	Inns	NO	Runs	HS	Avge	100s	50s	Ct	St	O	M	Runs	Wkts	Avge	Best	5wI	10wM
Test																		
All First	1	2	0	4	4	2.00	-	-	2	-								
1-day Int																		
NatWest																		
B & H																		
Sunday	1	1	0	2	2	2.00	-	-	-	-								

	M	Inns	NO	Runs	HS	Avge	100s	50s	Ct	St	Balls	Runs	Wkts	Avge	Best	5wI	10wM
Test																	
All First	1	2	0	4	4	2.00	-	-	2	-							
1-day Int																	
NatWest																	
B & H																	
Sunday	1	1	0	2	2	2.00	-	-	-	-							

HARTLEY, P. J. *Yorkshire*

Name: Peter John Hartley
Role: Right-hand bat,
right-arm medium-fast bowler
Born: 18 April 1960, Keighley
Height: 6ft **Weight:** 13st 2lbs
Nickname: Jack
County debut: 1982 (Warwickshire),
1985 (Yorkshire)
County cap: 1987 (Yorkshire)
50 wickets in a season: 4
1st-Class 50s: 10
1st-Class 100s: 2
1st-Class 5 w. in innings: 14
1st-Class catches: 49
One-Day 50s: 2
One-Day 5 w. in innings: 4
Place in batting averages: 224th av. 17.15

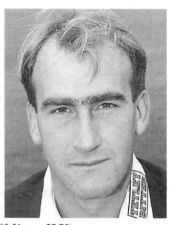

(1993 138th av. 26.66)
Place in bowling averages: 46th av. 27..88 (1993 51st av. 27.75)
Strike rate: 55.29 (career 58.17)
Parents: Thomas and Molly
Wife and date of marriage: Sharon, 12 March 1988
Children: Megan Grace, 25 April 1992
Family links with cricket: Father played local league cricket
Education: Keighley Grammar School; Bradford College
Qualifications: City & Guilds in textile design and management
Career outside cricket: Textile design and management and coaching
Off-season: Coaching, working on golf game
Overseas tours: Yorkshire pre-season tours to Barbados 1986-87, to South Africa 1991-92, 1992-93
Overseas teams played for: Melville, New Zealand 1983-84; Adelaide, Australia 1985-

86; Harmony and Orange Free State, South Africa 1988-89

Cricketers particularly admired: Dennis Lillee, Malcolm Marshall, Richard Hadlee

Other sports followed: Golf, American football (Minnesota Vikings), rugby league (Keighley Cougars)

Injuries: Broken thumb, missed one match; inflamed knee, one match

Relaxations: Golf (handicap of 4), walking the dog

Opinions on cricket: 'Too many overs to play in Sunday League. B&H should still be in league form due to the early fixture of the first round, because if you lose that match then you are out of one of the major competitions of the season, thus losing revenue both to the club and the players.'

Best batting: 127* Yorkshire v Lancashire, Old Trafford 1988

Best bowling: 8-111 Yorkshire v Sussex, Hove 1992

1994 Season

	M	Inns	NO	Runs	HS	Avge	100s	50s	Ct	St	O	M	Runs	Wkts	Avge	Best	5wI	10wM
Test																		
All First	16	23	3	343	61	17.15	-	1	3	-	562.1	116	1701	61	27.88	5-89	1	-
1-day Int																		
NatWest	2	2	1	12	7*	12.00	-	-	-	-	21	3	80	0	-		-	-
B & H	1	1	1	19	19*	-	-	-	-	-	9	1	31	0	-		-	-
Sunday	16	13	2	213	40*	19.36	-	-	3	-	113.2	10	541	15	36.06	2-21	-	

Career Performances

	M	Inns	NO	Runs	HS	Avge	100s	50s	Ct	St	Balls	Runs	Wkts	Avge	Best	5wI	10wM
Test																	
All First	154	184	45	3022	127*	21.74	2	10	49	-	24202	13591	416	32.67	8-111	14	-
1-day Int																	
NatWest	17	11	5	140	52	23.33	-	1	-	-	1055	694	30	23.13	5-46	1	
B & H	27	16	6	97	29*	9.70	-	-	8	-	1531	993	41	24.21	5-43	1	
Sunday	103	72	22	733	51	14.66	-	1	15	-	4507	3448	123	28.03	5-36	2	

HARVEY, M. E.   Lancashire

Name: Mark Edward Harvey
Role: Right-hand bat
Born: 26 June 1974, Burnley, Lancs
Height: 5ft 9in **Weight:** 12st
Nickname: Harv, Vadge, Baz, Angry
County debut: 1994
1st-Class catches: 1
Parents: David and Wendy
Marital status: Single
Family links with cricket:
Brother Jonathan was on MCC
groundstaff 1989-92 and professional
for Greenmount CC in the Bolton
League 1993; father played local
club cricket
Education: Worsthorne County Primary;
Habergham High School, Burnley;
Loughborough University
Qualifications: 8 GCSEs, 3 A-levels
Off-season: Studying Physical Education,
Sports Science and Recreation Management at university
Overseas tours: England U19 to India 1992-93
Cricketers particularly admired: 'David Gower (someone who makes it all look so easy),
Dean Jones (exciting both batting and fielding), Mudassar Nazar (an admired professional
for many years at Burnley), Peter Sleep, Les "The Whirlwind" Seal'
Other sports followed: Football (Burnley and Oxford United), golf and 'anything else that
keeps me interested'
Relaxations: Football, golf, most sports, listening to music (especially New Order),
watching comedies, sleeping in and watching any films with Demi Moore in them
Extras: Captained England U17, represented England at U17, U18 and U19 levels,
represented Lancashire from U13 to U19. In an attempt to produce a result in a rain-affected
2nd XI match v Yorkshire at Todmorden, he bowled an over costing 108 runs from 18 no-
balls, all of which went for four without hitting the bat. 'This allowed both teams to contrive
a game in five rather than 50 minutes. A claim to fame which earns me never-ending stick
at the local pub!'
Best batting: 23 Lancashire v Nottinghamshire, Trent Bridge 1994

---

30. How did a glove delay play in a Red Stripe match between
Jamaica and Guyana?

1994 Season

	M	Inns	NO	Runs	HS	Avge	100s	50s	Ct	St	O	M	Runs	Wkts	Avge	Best	5wI	10wM
Test																		
All First	2	3	0	44	23	14.66	-	-	1	-								
1-day Int																		
NatWest																		
B & H																		
Sunday																		

Career Performances

	M	Inns	NO	Runs	HS	Avge	100s	50s	Ct	St	Balls	Runs	Wkts	Avge	Best	5wI	10wM
Test																	
All First	2	3	0	44	23	14.66	-	-	1	-							
1-day Int																	
NatWest																	
B & H																	
Sunday																	

HARVEY, N. P.   Lancashire

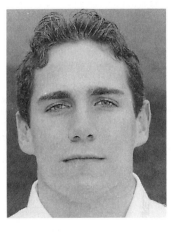

Name: Nicholas Paul Harvey
Role: Right-hand bat, wicket-keeper
Born: 21 November 1973, Ascot, Berks
Height: 5ft 7in **Weight:** 11st
Nickname: Del Boy, No Legs
County debut: No first-team appearance
Parents: Trevor and Moya
Marital status: Single
Family links with cricket: Older brother Andy plays for Hurst CC and played County Youth cricket; grandfather was an opening batsman and wicket-keeper in local club cricket
Education: Forest Comprehensive, Winnersh, Berks
Qualifications: 9 GCSEs, 3 A-levels, NCA coaching award
Overseas tours: Berkshire U19 to Australia 1990-91
Cricketers particularly admired: Ian Healy, Steve Rhodes, Peter Seal 'for his infectious enthusiasm for the game', Alan Rodhouse
Other sports followed: Football (Southampton and Reading), golf, boxing
Relaxations: Music, cinema, pubs, good food (Indian, Chinese, steaks)

Extras: MCC Young Pro 1993; played for England U17 in 1991 and for Berkshire in 1993
Opinions on cricket: 'Four-day 2nd XI Championship should be played on better wickets. More money should be put into the promotion of cricket in the state education system as a vast amount of future talent is presently being lost through lack of opportunity for most youngsters.'

HAYE, A. F.   Leicestershire

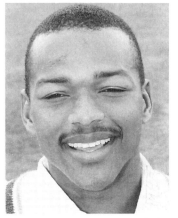

Name: Andrew Fitzpatrick Haye
Role: Right-hand bat, right-arm fast-medium bowler
Born: 10 November 1972, St Anne, Jamaica
Height: 6ft 2in **Weight:** 13st 7lbs
Nickname: Ninja Man, Turtle
County debut: 1994 (one-day)
Parents: Vera and Claude Duncan
Marital status: Single
Education: Copeland Community High School, Wembley
Qualifications: 1 O-level, 4 GCSEs, BTEC Business Studies
Off-season: Studying
Overseas tours: England U18 to Canada 1991
Cricketers particularly admired:
Graham Gooch, Malcolm Marshall, Justin Benson ('Rambo')
Other sports followed: Football (Aston Villa)
Relaxations: Watching television, music, eating out
Extras: Was on MCC groundstaff and has played for Middlesex 2nd XI. Released by Leicestershire at end of 1994 season

1994 Season

	M	Inns	NO	Runs	HS	Avge	100s	50s	Ct	St	O	M	Runs	Wkts	Avge	Best	5wI	10wM
Test																		
All First																			
1-day Int																			
NatWest																			
B & H																				
Sunday	1	1	0	0	0	0.00	-	-	-	-								

	M	Inns	NO	Runs	HS	Avge	100s	50s	Ct	St	Balls	Runs	Wkts	Avge	Best	5wI	10wM
Test																	
All First																	
1-day Int																	
NatWest																	
B & H																	
Sunday	1	1	0	0	0	0.00	-	-	-	-							

HAYHURST, A. N. Somerset

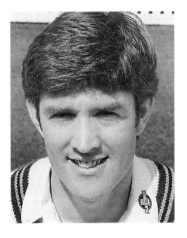

Name: Andrew Neil Hayhurst
Role: Right-hand bat, right-arm medium bowler, county captain
Born: 23 November 1962, Davyhulme, Manchester
Height: 6ft **Weight:** 13st 7lbs
Nickname: Bully, Sponge
County debut: 1985 (Lancashire), 1990 (Somerset)
County cap: 1990 (Somerset)
1000 runs in a season: 3
1st-Class 50s: 33
1st-Class 100s: 13
1st-Class catches: 48
One-Day 5 w. in innings: 1
Place in batting averages: 14th av. 52.08 (1993 111th av. 30.40)
Strike rate: (career 80.81)
Parents: William and Margaret
Wife and date of marriage: April, 17 February 1990
Children: Myles William David, 31 March 1992
Family links with cricket: Father played club cricket for Worsley in the Manchester and District Cricket Association, grew up in house lived in by Tyldesley brothers (Lancashire and England)
Education: St Mark's Primary School; Worsley Wardley High; Eccles Sixth Form College; Leeds Polytechnic (Carnegie College of PE)
Qualifications: 8 O-levels, 4A-levels, BA (Hons) Human Movement, advanced cricket coach, qualified financial consultant
Career outside cricket: Financial consultant
Off-season: Working as financial consultant and in local media
Overseas tours: Lancashire to Jamaica 1986-87 and 1987-88, to Zimbabwe 1988-89;

Somerset to Bahamas 1989-90

Overseas teams played for: South Launceston, Tasmania 1987-89

Cricketers particularly admired: Viv Richards, Ian Botham, Clive Lloyd, Malcolm Marshall, Dermot Reeve

Other sports followed: All sports, especially football (Manchester United) and rugby league (Salford)

Relaxations: Animals, gardening, decorating

Extras: Played football for Greater Manchester U19. Scored a record 197 runs whilst playing for North of England v South, Southampton 1982. Held record for number of runs in Manchester and District Cricket Association League, whilst playing for Worsley in 1984 (Mudassar Nazar beat it with 1197, 1994): 1193 runs (av. 70.17). Released by Lancashire at the end of 1989 season and joined Somerset on a three-year contract in 1990. Made 110* on his first-class debut for Somerset and was appointed captain for the 1994 season

Opinions on cricket: 'Four-day cricket has worked. Best team actually wins the Championship! County staffs are still too big, youngsters should back themselves to make it with shorter contracts.'

Best batting: 172* Somerset v Gloucestershire, Bath 1991

Best bowling: 4-27 Lancashire v Middlesex, Old Trafford 1987

1994 Season

	M	Inns	NO	Runs	HS	Avge	100s	50s	Ct	St	O	M	Runs	Wkts	Avge	Best	5wI	10wM
Test																		
All First	18	30	6	1250	121	52.08	2	10	10	-	87.3	25	265	9	29.44	2-5	-	-
1-day Int																		
NatWest	3	3	2	91	38 *	91.00	-	-	1	-	10.5	0	49	5	9.80	4-29	-	
B & H	1	1	0	7	7	7.00	-	-	-	-	8	0	38	0	-	-	-	-
Sunday	15	15	3	309	49	25.75	-	-	4	-	52.5	0	320	10	32.00	2-15	-	

Career Performances

	M	Inns	NO	Runs	HS	Avge	100s	50s	Ct	St	Balls	Runs	Wkts	Avge	Best	5wI	10wM
Test																	
All First	138	221	28	6770	172 *	35.07	13	33	48	-	7920	4351	98	44.39	4-27	-	-
1-day Int																	
NatWest	19	18	4	563	91 *	40.21	-	3	4	-	761	502	24	20.91	5-60	1	
B & H	24	22	1	506	95	24.09	-	4	2	-	818	580	22	26.36	4-50	-	
Sunday	102	86	17	1901	84	27.55	-	9	15	-	2538	2260	59	38.30	4-37	-	

HAYNES, D. L.   Middlesex

Name: Desmond Leo Haynes
Role: Right-hand bat,
right-arm medium/leg-break bowler
Born: 15 February 1956, St James,
Barbados
County debut: 1989
County cap: 1989
Test debut: 1977-78
Tests: 116
One-Day Internationals: 238
1000 runs in a season: 3
1st-Class 50s: 126
1st-Class 100s: 59
1st-Class 200s: 4
1st-Class catches: 184
1st-Class stumpings: 1
One-Day 100s: 23
Place in batting averages: 61st av 38.92
(1993 51st av. 39.65)
Wife and date of marriage: Dawn, 14 September 1991
Education: Federal HS, Barbados
Off-season: Playing for West Indies
Overseas teams played for: Barbados 1976-92; Western Province, South Africa 1994-95
Overseas tours: World Series Cricket (Kerry Packer) 1978-79; Young West Indies to Zimbabwe 1981-82; West Indies to Australia 1979-80, 1981-82, 1984-85, 1988-89, (World Cup) 1991-92, 1992-93, to New Zealand 1979-80, 1986-87, to England 1980, 1984, 1988, 1991, to Pakistan 1980-81, 1986-87, 1990-91, 1991-92, to India 1983-84, 1987-88, 1989-90, to South Africa 1992-93, to Sharjah, India (Hero Cup) and Sri Lanka 1993-94
Extras: Played for Scotland in the B&H Cup. Captained West Indies v England, Port-of-Spain 1989-90, and on tour of Pakistan 1990-91. Vice-captain (to Viv Richards) on England tour 1991 and promoted to vice-captain (to Richie Richardson) on tours to Pakistan and Australia 1991-92, when Gus Logie was ruled out after being injured in a car accident. Britannic Assurance Player of the Year 1990
Best batting: 255* Middlesex v Sussex, Lord's 1990
Best bowling: 1-2 West Indies v Pakistan, Lahore 1980-81

---

31. Which current English player has been selected for Test cricket while contracted to three different counties?

1994 Season

	M	Inns	NO	Runs	HS	Avge	100s	50s	Ct	St	O	M	Runs	Wkts	Avge	Best	5wl	10wM
Test																		
All First	17	27	2	973	134	38.92	5	2	6	-	2	2	0	0	-	-	-	-
1-day Int																		
NatWest	2	2	1	101	64 *	101.00	-	1	-	-								
B & H	1	1	0	6	6	6.00	-	-	-	-								
Sunday	12	11	0	320	52	29.09	-	1	5	-	0.4	0	3	0	-	-	-	

Career Performances

	M	Inns	NO	Runs	HS	Avge	100s	50s	Ct	St	Balls	Runs	Wkts	Avge	Best	5wl	10wM
Test	116	202	25	7487	184	42.29	18	39	65	-	18	8	1	8.00	1-2	-	-
All First	351	528	69	24219	255 *	52.76	59	126	184	1	488	268	8	33.50	1-2	-	-
1-day Int	238	237	28	8649	152 *	41.38	17	57	59	-	30	24	0	-	-	-	
NatWest	14	14	3	838	149 *	76.18	2	7	2	-	132	66	1	66.00	1-41	-	
B & H	15	15	1	773	131	55.21	1	7	7	-	192	110	3	36.66	1-9	-	
Sunday	68	66	6	2445	142 *	40.75	3	20	23	-	306	287	3	95.66	1-17	-	

HAYNES, G. R.   Worcestershire

Name: Gavin Richard Haynes
Role: Right-hand bat, right-arm medium bowler
Born: 29 September 1969, Stourbridge
Height: 5ft 10in **Weight:** 12st
Nickname: Splash
County debut: 1991
County cap: 1994
1000 runs in a season: 1
1st-Class 50s: 9
1st-Class 100s: 3
1st-Class catches: 21
Place in batting averages: 101st av. 34.03
(1993 115th av. 29.46)
Strike rate: (career 116.21)
Parents: Nicholas and Dorothy
Marital status: Single
Family links with cricket: Father played club
cricket and manages Worcester U14 side
Education: Gigmill Junior School; High Park
Comprehensive; King Edward VI College, Stourbridge
Qualifications: 5 O-levels, 1 A-level, senior cricket coaching award
Off-season: Coaching in England, resting

Overseas tours: Worcestershire to Zimbabwe and South Africa
Overseas teams played for:
Sunrise Sports Club, Zimbabwe 1989-90
Cricketers particularly admired:
Ian Botham, Graham Dilley, Graham Gooch,
Malcolm Marshall, Viv Richards,
Graeme Hick
Other sports followed:
Football (Aston Villa), golf
Injuries: Infection, missed two days
Relaxations: Playing golf or squash,
watching videos, eating out
Extras: Represented England Schools U15.
Worcestershire Uncapped Player of the
Year 1993
Opinions on cricket: 'Four-day cricket has been a great success as results now come without contrived games. The standard of 2nd XI wickets should be improved especially at out grounds.'
Best batting: 158 Worcestershire v Kent, Worcester 1993
Best bowling: 3-19 Worcestershire v Hampshire, Worcester 1994

1994 Season

	M	Inns	NO	Runs	HS	Avge	100s	50s	Ct	St	O	M	Runs	Wkts	Avge	Best	5wI	10wM
Test																		
All First	20	32	2	1021	141	34.03	2	4	12	-	108.3	23	319	7	45.57	3-19	-	-
1-day Int																		
NatWest	5	3	0	154	98	51.33	-	1	1	-	20	2	63	3	21.00	1-9	-	
B & H	3	2	0	87	65	43.50	-	1	1	-	2	0	26	0	-		-	-
Sunday	16	13	0	306	83	23.53	-	2	6	-	15	0	79	3	26.33	1-10	-	

Career Performances

	M	Inns	NO	Runs	HS	Avge	100s	50s	Ct	St	Balls	Runs	Wkts	Avge	Best	5wI	10wM
Test																	
All First	44	65	6	1893	158	32.08	3	9	21	-	1627	803	14	57.35	3-19	-	-
1-day Int																	
NatWest	6	4	0	159	98	39.75	-	1	1	-	180	143	3	47.66	1-9	-	
B & H	6	5	2	123	65	41.00	-	1	3	-	192	119	3	39.66	2-22	-	
Sunday	33	26	2	557	83	23.20	-	2	9	-	774	517	11	47.00	2-21	-	

HEADLEY, D. W. Kent

Name: Dean Warren Headley
Role: Right-hand bat, right-arm medium-fast bowler
Born: 27 January 1970, Stourbridge
Height: 6ft 5in **Weight:** 13st 8lbs
Nickname: Frog
County debut: 1991 (Middlesex), 1993 (Kent)
County cap: 1993 (Kent)
1st-Class 50s: 2
1st-Class 5 w. in innings: 6
1st-Class catches: 24
One-Day 5 w. in innings: 1
Place in batting averages: 228th av. 16.75 (1993 185th av. 21.61)
Place in bowling averages: 43rd av. 27.47 (1993 57th av. 28.35)
Strike rate: 49.25 (career 63.50)
Parents: Ronald George Alphonso and Gail
Marital status: Single
Family links with cricket: Father Ron played for Worcestershire, Jamaica and West Indies and grandfather George played for Jamaica and West Indies
Education: Gigmill Junior School; Oldswinford Hospital School; Royal Grammar School, Worcester
Qualifications: 7 O-levels
Career outside cricket: 'Not yet established'
Off-season: Playing and holidaying in South Africa
Overseas tours: RGS Worcester to Zimbabwe 1988; Christians in Sport to India 1989-90
Overseas teams played for: Melbourne, Jamaica 1991-92; Primrose CC, South Africa 1993-95
Cricketers particularly admired: Clive Lloyd, Minal Patel, Ian Botham, Robin Smith, Malcolm Marshall, Carl Hooper
Other sports followed: Any sport
Injuries: Double hernia, missed six weeks
Relaxations: Sleeping, socialising with friends and colleagues
Extras: Took five wickets on debut including a wicket with his first ball in Championship cricket. Played for Worcestershire 2nd XI 1988-89. Left Middlesex at the end of 1992 season and signed for Kent
Opinions on cricket: 'Four-day cricket must be played on wickets that last four days. Games should never finish in two days. Thanks for the lie-in on Sunday.'
Best batting: 91 Middlesex v Leicestershire, Leicester 1992
Best bowling: 7-79 Kent v Gloucestershire, Tunbridge Wells 1993

1994 Season

	M	Inns	NO	Runs	HS	Avge	100s	50s	Ct	St	O	M	Runs	Wkts	Avge	Best	5wl	10wM
Test																		
All First	9	13	5	134	46 *	16.75	-	-	5	-	295.3	48	989	36	27.47	5-60	2	-
1-day Int																		
NatWest	4	1	1	7	7 *	-	-	-	-	-	37	2	155	5	31.00	3-44	-	
B & H	1	0	0	0	0	-	-	-	-	-	10.4	0	36	2	18.00	2-36	-	
Sunday	10	4	1	4	1 *	1.33	-	-	2	-	64.4	5	342	15	22.80	3-27	-	

Career Performances

	M	Inns	NO	Runs	HS	Avge	100s	50s	Ct	St	Balls	Runs	Wkts	Avge	Best	5wl	10wM
Test																	
All First	53	62	16	887	91	19.28	-	2	24	-	8764	4723	138	34.22	7-79	6	-
1-day Int																	
NatWest	8	5	4	26	11 *	26.00	-	-	-	-	481	319	14	22.78	5-20	1	
B & H	9	4	0	41	26	10.25	-	-	2	-	503	339	9	37.66	4-19	-	
Sunday	46	13	7	57	10 *	9.50	-	-	9	-	1901	1511	50	30.22	4-23	-	

HEGG, W. K. Lancashire

Name: Warren Kevin Hegg
Role: Right-hand bat, wicket-keeper
Born: 23 February 1968, Radcliffe, Lancashire
Height: 5ft 9in **Weight:** 12st 4lbs
Nickname: Chucky
County debut: 1986
1st-Class 50s: 20
1st-Class 100s: 2
1st-Class catches: 379
1st-Class stumpings: 47
Place in batting averages: 200th av. 19.92 (1993 175th av. 22.64)
Parents: Kevin and Glenda
Wife and date of marriage: Joanne, 29 October 1994
Family links with cricket: Father and brother Martin play in local leagues
Education: Unsworth High School; Stand College, Whitefield
Qualifications: 5 O-levels, 7 CSEs, qualified coach
Career outside cricket: Groundsman – worked in textile warehouse

Off-season: 'Cocktail waiter'

Overseas tours: NCA North U19 to Bermuda 1985; England YC to Sri Lanka 1986-87, to Australia (Youth World Cup) 1987-88; England A to Pakistan and Sri Lanka 1990-91

Overseas teams played for: Sheffield, Tasmania 1988-90, 1992-93

Cricketers particularly admired: Ian Botham, Alan Knott, Bob Taylor, Gehan Mendis (for perseverance)

Other sports followed: Football, golf, fishing, Aussie rules football

Relaxations: Listening to music, walking on my own

Extras: First player to make county debut from Lytham CC. Youngest player for 30 years to score a century for Lancashire, 130 v Northamptonshire in his fourth first-class game. Eleven victims in match v Derbyshire, equalling world record. Wombwell Cricket Lovers' Society joint Wicket-keeper of the Year 1993

Opinions on cricket: '100-over games with three two-hour sessions. NatWest final should start at 11.00 am.'

Best batting: 130 Lancashire v Northamptonshire, Northampton 1987

1994 Season

	M	Inns	NO	Runs	HS	Avge	100s	50s	Ct	St	O	M	Runs	Wkts	Avge	Best	5wI	10wM
Test																		
All First	19	30	4	518	66	19.92	-	2	46	3								
1-day Int																		
NatWest	2	1	0	32	32	32.00	-	-	1	1								
B & H	2	0	0	0	0	-	-	-	1	-								
Sunday	17	12	8	164	52	41.00	-	1	16	-								

Career Performances

	M	Inns	NO	Runs	HS	Avge	100s	50s	Ct	St	Balls	Runs	Wkts	Avge	Best	5wI	10wM
Test																	
All First	167	243	47	4782	130	24.39	2	20	379	47	6	7	0	-		-	-
1-day Int																	
NatWest	17	9	1	150	32	18.75	-	-	22	2							
B & H	34	13	5	123	31*	15.37	-	-	46	2							
Sunday	112	59	32	610	52	22.59	-	1	113	13							

HEMMINGS, E. E.   Sussex

Name: Edward Ernest Hemmings
Role: Right-hand bat, off-spin bowler
Born: 20 February 1949, Leamington Spa, Warwickshire
Height: 5ft 10in **Weight:** 14st 7lb
Nickname: Sideways, Yakka
County debut: 1966 (Warwickshire), 1979 (Nottinghamshire), 1993 (Sussex)
County cap: 1974 (Warwickshire), 1980 (Nottinghamshire), 1993 (Sussex)
Benefit: 1987
Test debut: 1982
Tests: 16
One-Day Internationals: 33
50 wickets in a season: 15
1st-Class 50s: 27
1st-Class 100s: 1
1st-Class 5 w. in innings: 70
1st-Class 10 w. in match: 15
1st-Class catches: 211
One-Day 5 w. in innings: 4

Place in bowling averages: 53rd av. 29.06 (1993 27th av. 24.46)
Strike rate: 76.72 (career 67.08)
Parents: Edward and Dorothy Phyllis
Wife and date of marriage: Christine Mary, 23 October 1971
Children: Thomas Edward, 26 July 1977; James Oliver, 9 September 1979
Family links with cricket: Father and father's father played Minor Counties and league cricket
Education: Campion School, Leamington Spa
Overseas tours: England to Australia and New Zealand 1982-83, to Pakistan (World Cup), Australia and New Zealand 1987-88, to India and West Indies 1989-90, to Australia 1990-91
Other sports followed: Golf, football, rugby
Relaxations: Coaching cricket at all levels and working with off-spin bowlers
Extras: Took a hat-trick for Warwickshire in 1977; hit first (and only) century – 127* for Nottinghamshire v Yorkshire at Worksop, July 1982 – after 16 years in first-class game. Released by Notts end of the 1992 season and signed by Sussex
Best batting: 127* Nottinghamshire v Yorkshire, Worksop 1982
Best bowling: 10-175 International XI v West Indies XI, Kingston 1982-83

1994 Season

	M	Inns	NO	Runs	HS	Avge	100s	50s	Ct	St	O	M	Runs	Wkts	Avge	Best	5wI	10wM
Test																		
All First	14	24	12	88	14 *	7.33	-	-	5	-	422	140	959	33	29.06	7-66	2	-
1-day Int																		
NatWest	1	1	0	6	6	6.00	-	-	-	-	12	1	53	0	-	-	-	-
B & H	2	1	0	0	0	0.00	-	-	1	-	22	1	67	0	-	-	-	-
Sunday	4	1	1	6	6 *	-	-	-	3	-	32	2	127	5	25.40	3-23	-	

Career Performances

	M	Inns	NO	Runs	HS	Avge	100s	50s	Ct	St	Balls	Runs	Wkts	Avge	Best	5wI	10wM
Test	16	21	4	383	95	22.52	-	2	5	-	4437	1825	43	42.44	6-58	1	-
All First	511	671	162	9463	127 *	18.59	1	27	211	-	100621	43961	1500	29.30	10-175	70	15
1-day Int	33	12	6	30	8 *	5.00	-	-	5	-	1752	1293	37	34.94	4-52	-	
NatWest	44	31	11	261	31 *	13.05	-	-	8	-	2938	1659	47	35.29	3-27	-	
B & H	92	54	17	505	61 *	13.64	-	1	21	-	5533	2951	83	35.55	4-47	-	
Sunday	275	170	54	1606	44 *	13.84	-	-	86	-	10792	8274	281	29.44	5-22	4	

HEMP, D. L.   Glamorgan

Name: David Lloyd Hemp
Role: Left-hand bat, right-arm medium bowler
Born: 15 November 1970, Bermuda
Height: 6ft **Weight:** 12st 7lbs
Nickname: Hempy, Soc, Mad Dog
County debut: 1991
1000 runs in a season: 1
1st-Class 50s: 15
1st-Class 100s: 4
1st-Class catches: 28
Place in batting averages: 48th av. 42.70
(1993 112th av. 29.88)
Parents: Clive and Elisabeth
Marital status: Single
Family links with cricket: Father plays for
Ffynone and brother plays for Swansea
Education: Olchfa Comprehensive School;
Millfield School
Qualifications: 5 O-levels, 2 A-levels
Off-season: Touring with England A
Overseas tours: Welsh Schools U19 to Australia 1986-87; Welsh Cricket Association U18
to Barbados 1987; Glamorgan to Trinidad 1990; South Wales Cricket Association to New

Zealand and Australia 1991-92; England A to India 1994-95
Overseas teams played for: Hirsh Crusaders 1992-94
Cricketers particularly admired: Viv Richards, David Gower, Keith Arthurton
Other sports followed: Football
Relaxations: Watching football and TV, going to movies
Extras: Scored 258* for Wales v MCC 1991. In 1990 scored 104* and 101* for Welsh Schools U19 v Scottish Schools U19 and 120 & 102* v Irish Schools U19
Opinions on cricket: 'All 2nd XI games should be played on county grounds rather than club grounds as the quality of wickets is usually poorer at clubs, also they do not have such good facilities for covering wickets.'
Best batting: 136 Glamorgan v Gloucestershire, Bristol 1994

1994 Season

	M	Inns	NO	Runs	HS	Avge	100s	50s	Ct	St	O	M	Runs	Wkts	Avge	Best	5wI	10wM
Test																		
All First	21	38	4	1452	136	42.70	4	8	16	-	8	0	41	0	-	-	-	-
1-day Int																		
NatWest	2	2	0	19	13	9.50	-	-	-	-								
B & H																			
Sunday	12	11	0	253	73	23.00	-	1	6	-	0.2	0	1	0	-	-	-	

Career Performances

	M	Inns	NO	Runs	HS	Avge	100s	50s	Ct	St	Balls	Runs	Wkts	Avge	Best	5wI	10wM
Test																	
All First	44	76	9	2298	136	34.29	4	15	28	-	48	41	0	-	-	-	-
1-day Int																	
NatWest	2	2	0	19	13	9.50	-	-	-	-							
B & H																		
Sunday	24	18	1	305	73	17.94	-	1	10	-	2	1	0	-	-	-	

HEPWORTH, P. N.   Leicestershire

Name: Peter Nash Hepworth
Role: Right-hand bat, off-spin bowler
Born: 4 May 1967, Ackworth, West Yorkshire
Height: 6ft 1in **Weight:** 12st 7lbs
Nickname: Nash
County debut: 1988
1st-Class 50s: 8
1st-Class 100s: 3
1st-Class catches: 30
One-Day 5 w. in innings: 1

Place in batting averages: 260th av. 11.30
(1993 132nd av. 27.33)
Strike rate: (career 64.80)
Parents: George and Zena
Marital status: Single
Family links with cricket: Father and
uncle played cricket for Ackworth
Education: Bell Lane School, Ackworth;
Ackworth Middle School;
Hemsworth High School
Qualifications: 8 CSEs, NCA senior
coaching certificate
Career outside cricket: Builder (with family
firm), cricket coach
Off-season: Coaching
Overseas tours: Hull CC to Barbados
Overseas teams played for: Played a season in
Bloemfontein 1991-92
Cricketers particularly admired: David Gower, Geoff Boycott
Other sports followed: Football (Leeds United), rugby and most other sports
Relaxations: Music and movies
Extras: Started playing for Ackworth Cricket Club following the likes of Neil Lloyd ('the
best young cricketer I've ever seen'), Graham Stevenson, Tim Boon, Geoff Boycott.
Released by Leicestershire at end of 1994 season
Best batting: 129 Leicestershire v Glamorgan, Leicester 1993
Best bowling: 3-30 Leicestershire v Kent, Leicester 1994

1994 Season

	M	Inns	NO	Runs	HS	Avge	100s	50s	Ct	St	O	M	Runs	Wkts	Avge	Best	5wI	10wM
Test																		
All First	5	10	0	113	60	11.30	-	1	1	-	72	14	253	9	28.11	3-30	-	-
1-day Int																		
NatWest	1	0	0	0	0	-	-	-	-	-								
B & H																		
Sunday	12	12	1	152	49	13.81	-	-	2	-	42	0	255	10	25.50	5-51	1	

Career Performances

	M	Inns	NO	Runs	HS	Avge	100s	50s	Ct	St	Balls	Runs	Wkts	Avge	Best	5wI	10wM
Test																	
All First	59	98	8	2113	129	23.47	3	8	30	-	1944	1269	30	42.30	3-30	-	-
1-day Int																	
NatWest	1	0	0	0	0	-	-	-	-	-							
B & H	4	3	1	53	33	26.50	-	-	2	-	186	127	7	18.14	4-39	-	
Sunday	32	28	4	341	49	14.20	-	-	5	-	570	536	18	29.77	5-51	1	

HEWSON, D. R. — Gloucestershire

Name: Dominic Robert Hewson
Role: Right-hand bat,
right-arm medium bowler
Born: 3 October 1974
Height: 5ft 10in **Weight:** 12st 12lbs
County debut: No first-team appearance
Parents: Robert and Julie
Marital status: Single
Education: Cheltenham College;
University of West of England
Qualifications: 10 GCSEs, 3 A-levels
Career outside cricket: Studying to be
a surveyor
Off-season: Student
Cricketers particularly admired:
David Gower, Robin Smith
Other sports followed: Rugby
Relaxations: Seeing friends
Extras: Made debut for Gloucestershire 2nd XI in July 1993

HIBBERT, A. J. E. — Essex

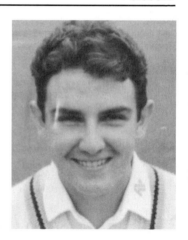

Name: Andrew James Edward Hibbert
Role: Right-hand bat, off-spin bowler
Born: 17 December 1974, Harold Wood, Essex
Height: 6ft **Weight:** 13st 2lbs
Nickname: Buns
County debut: No first-team appearance
Parents: Thelma
Marital status: Single
Education: St Edward's C of E
Comprehensive, Romford
Qualifications: 8 GCSEs, NCA Senior
Coaching Award
Off-season: Coaching for Essex CCC at
Chelmsford
Overseas tours: England U18 to Denmark
(International Youth Tournament) 1993
Cricketers particularly admired:
'Carl Hooper batting'

Other sports followed: Golf, football (Spurs)
Relaxations: Music
Extras: Played for Essex from U16 to 2nd XI

HICK, G. A. Worcestershire

Name: Graeme Ashley Hick
Role: Right-hand bat, off-spin bowler
Born: 23 May 1966, Salisbury, Rhodesia
Height: 6ft 3in **Weight:** 14st 7lbs
Nickname: Hicky, Ash
County debut: 1984
County cap: 1986
Test debut: 1991
Tests: 29
One-Day Internationals: 40
1000 runs in a season: 10
1st-Class 50s: 90
1st-Class 100s: 77
1st-Class 200s: 9
1st-Class 400s: 1
1st-Class 5 w. in innings: 4
1st-Class 10 w. in match: 1
1st-Class catches: 330
One-Day 100s: 13

Place in batting averages: 9th av. 54.92 (1993 12th av. 54.35)
Place in bowling averages: 126th av. 42.00 (1993 146th av. 60.30)
Strike rate: 94.36 (career 85.03)
Parents: John and Eve
Wife and date of marriage: Jackie, 5 October 1991
Children: Lauren Amy, 12 September 1992
Family links with cricket: Father served on Zimbabwe Cricket Union Board of Control since 1984 and played representative cricket in Zimbabwe
Education: Banket Primary; Prince Edward Boys' High School, Zimbabwe
Qualifications: 4 O-levels, NCA coaching award
Off-season: Touring Australia with England
Overseas tours: Zimbabwe to England (World Cup) 1983, to Sri Lanka 1983-84, to England 1985; England to New Zealand and Australia (World Cup) 1991-92, to India and Sri Lanka 1992-93, to West Indies 1993-94, to Australia 1994-95
Overseas teams played for: Old Hararians, Zimbabwe 1982-90; Northern Districts, New Zealand 1987-89; Queensland, Australia 1990-91
Cricketers particularly admired: Duncan Fletcher (Zimbabwe captain) for approach and understanding of the game, David Houghton, Basil D'Oliveira

Other sports followed: Follows Liverpool FC, golf, tennis, squash, hockey
Injuries: Back injury forced him to return home before the end of the England tour to Australia
Relaxations: 'Leaning against Steve Rhodes at first-slip'
Extras: Made first century aged six for school team; youngest player participating in 1983 Prudential World Cup (aged 17); youngest player to represent Zimbabwe. Scored 1234 runs in Birmingham League and played for Worcestershire 2nd XI in 1984 – hitting six successive centuries. In 1986, at age 20, he became the youngest player to score 2000 runs in an English season. One of *Wisden*'s Five Cricketers of the Year 1986. In 1988 he made 405* v Somerset at Taunton, the highest individual score in England since 1895, and scored 1000 first-class runs by end of May, hitting a record 410 runs in April. In 1990 became youngest batsman ever to make 50 first-class centuries and scored 645 runs without being dismissed – a record for English cricket. Also in 1990 became the fastest to 10,000 runs in county cricket (179 innings). Qualified as an English player in 1991. Scored first Test century v India in Bombay 1992-93 and was England's leading batsman, bowler and fielder. Published *Hick 'n' Dilley Circus* and *A Champion's Diary*. Also played hockey for Zimbabwe
Opinions on cricket: 'What a great game.'
Best batting: 405* Worcestershire v Somerset, Taunton 1988
Best bowling: 5-37 Worcestershire v Gloucestershire, Worcester 1990

1994 Season

	M	Inns	NO	Runs	HS	Avge	100s	50s	Ct	St	O	M	Runs	Wkts	Avge	Best	5wl	10wM
Test	6	10	1	437	110	48.55	1	2	11	-	66	31	119	3	39.66	1-12	-	-
All First	17	29	1	1538	215	54.92	5	5	22	-	173.2	55	462	11	42.00	3-64	-	-
1-day Int	3	3	0	99	81	33.00	-	1	2	-	15	1	64	2	32.00	2-31	-	
NatWest	5	5	1	203	97	50.75	-	2	6	-	23	0	88	5	17.60	4-54	-	
B & H	4	4	2	211	104*	105.50	1	-	3	-	4	0	23	0	-		-	-
Sunday	10	9	2	356	103	50.85	1	2	2	-	19	0	109	0	-		-	-

Career Performances

	M	Inns	NO	Runs	HS	Avge	100s	50s	Ct	St	Balls	Runs	Wkts	Avge	Best	5wl	10wM
Test	29	50	1	1725	178	35.20	2	9	41	-	2303	915	19	48.15	4-126	-	-
All First	276	450	46	23124	405*	57.23	77	90	330	-	14967	7265	176	41.27	5-37	4	1
1-day Int	40	39	6	1304	105*	39.51	1	10	22	-	396	338	8	42.25	2-7	-	
NatWest	29	29	6	1254	172*	54.52	3	7	15	-	897	533	15	35.53	4-54	-	
B & H	43	43	9	1828	109	53.76	4	13	29	-	450	316	7	45.14	3-36	-	
Sunday	129	124	21	4660	120*	45.24	5	36	29	-	1796	1573	47	33.46	4-42	-	

HINDSON, J. E.   Nottinghamshire

Name: James Edward Hindson
Role: Right-hand bat, slow left-arm bowler
Born: 13 September 1973,
Huddersfield, Yorkshire
Height: 6ft 1in **Weight:** 11st 8lbs
Nickname: Jim, Muppet, Hindmarsh
County debut: 1992
1st-Class 5 w. in innings: 2
1st-Class catches: 2
Parents: Robert and Gloria
Marital status: Single
Education: Robert Sherborne Infants School,
Rolleston, Staffs; Ernhale Junior School,
Arnold; St Peter's Primary School,
East Bridgford; Toot Hill Comprehensive
School, Bingham
Qualifications: 10 GCSEs, 3 A-levels, senior
cricket coach
Career outside cricket: Employed by
Nottinghamshire to coach in the winter

Off-season: Coaching at Trent Bridge
Overseas tours: England U19 to India 1992-93
Cricketers particularly admired: Richard Hadlee, Derek Randall, Robin Smith
Other sports followed: Ice hockey, football
Injuries: Open dislocation of little finger, missed two weeks
Relaxations: Anything to do with ice hockey, reading, socialising and keeping fit
Extras. Took five wickets on first-class debut (eight in the match) v Cambridge University.
Converted from right-arm to left-arm bowler at age six, still throws right-handed and
bowled left-arm medium until 15 years old. Received 2nd team cap at end of 1993 season
Opinions on cricket: 'Richard Bates should lose weight. Limit bat weights to 2lb 2oz.'
Best batting: 11 Nottinghamshire v Lancashire, Trent Bridge 1994
Best bowling: 5-42 Nottinghamshire v Cambridge University, Trent Bridge 1992

1994 Season

	M	Inns	NO	Runs	HS	Avge	100s	50s	Ct	St	O	M	Runs	Wkts	Avge	Best	5wI	10wM
Test																		
All First	4	3	0	20	11	6.66	-	-	2	-	106	27	344	8	43.00	5-53	1	-
1-day Int																		
NatWest																		
B & H																		
Sunday	4	2	1	24	21	24.00	-	-	1	-	26	0	112	5	22.40	4-19	-	

Career Performances

	M	Inns	NO	Runs	HS	Avge	100s	50s	Ct	St	Balls	Runs	Wkts	Avge	Best	5wI	10wM
Test																	
All First	7	4	0	21	11	5.25	-	-	2	-	1077	532	17	31.29	5-42	2	-
1-day Int																	
NatWest																		
B & H																		
Sunday	4	2	1	24	21	24.00	-	-	1	-	156	112	5	22.40	4-19	-	

HINKS, S. G. Gloucestershire

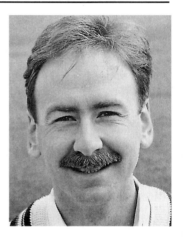

Name: Simon Graham Hinks
Role: Left-hand opening bat,
right-arm medium bowler
Born: 12 October 1960, Northfleet, Kent
Height: 6ft 2in **Weight:** 13$^{1}/_{2}$-14st
Nickname: Shaba, Shinks, Hinksy
County debut: 1982 (Kent),
1992 (Gloucestershire)
County cap: 1985 (Kent)
1000 runs in a season: 3
1st-Class 50s: 43
1st-Class 100s: 11
1st-Class 200s: 1
1st-Class catches: 114
Place in batting averages: 170th av. 24.20
(1993 187th av. 20.95)
Parents: Mary and Graham
Wife and date of marriage:
Vicki, September 1990
Children: Megan Rose, 15 June 1991
Family links with cricket: Father captained Gravesend and is now chairman; brother
Jonathan captains Gravesend and has played for Kent U19
Education: Dover Road Infant and Junior Schools, Northfleet; St George's C of E School,
Gravesend; Sheffield University
Qualifications: 5 O-levels, 1 A-level, senior cricket coach, Diploma in Leisure Management
Overseas teams played for: Pirates, Johannesburg 1980-81; University of Tasmania,
Australia 1983-86: Durbanville, South Africa 1992-93
Cricketers particularly admired: Courtney Walsh, Viv Richards
Other sports followed: All sports
Relaxations: Sport, television, DIY, gardening
Extras: Left Kent at the end of 1991 season and signed three-year contract with

Gloucestershire. Released by Gloucestershire at end of 1994 season

Opinions on cricket: 'Media interest is now focusing on individual and team behaviour on the field, the majority of which is overblown. Would it not be a good idea for the players to police themselves, setting up disciplinary rules and regulations with a level of fines etc. to be implemented by fellow-professionals. It is quite amazing that the professional players have so little to say in the running of the game they love. The media have also mentioned that current players do not seem to be enjoying themselves: we are, but we cannot afford to be seen to be, otherwise we are accused of being less than professional. Give us more say and you would be surprised how many so-called "traditionalists" you would find.'

Best batting: 234 Kent v Middlesex, Canterbury 1990
Best bowling: 2-18 Kent v Nottinghamshire, Trent Bridge 1989

1994 Season

	M	Inns	NO	Runs	HS	Avge	100s	50s	Ct	St	O	M	Runs	Wkts	Avge	Best	5wI	10wM
Test																		
All First	5	10	0	242	74	24.20	-	2	4	-	-							
1-day Int																		
NatWest																		
B & H	1	1	0	4	4	4.00	-	-	-	-								
Sunday	8	6	0	95	31	15.83	-	-	1	-								

Career Performances

	M	Inns	NO	Runs	HS	Avge	100s	50s	Ct	St	Balls	Runs	Wkts	Avge	Best	5wI	10wM
Test																	
All First	182	319	19	8715	234	29.05	11	43	114	-	603	383	8	47.87	2-18	-	-
1-day Int																	
NatWest	13	13	3	500	95	50.00	-	4	3	-	18	23	0	-	-	-	-
B & H	39	38	1	845	85	22.83	-	4	7	-	246	198	5	39.60	1-15	-	
Sunday	118	116	6	2654	99	24.12	-	18	34	-	150	139	4	34.75	1-3	-	

32. Which famous South African cricketer shares the record for the most consecutive centuries in first-class cricket?

HODGSON, G. D.   Gloucestershire

Name: Geoffrey Dean Hodgson
Role: Right-hand opening bat
Born: 22 October 1966, Carlisle
Height: 6ft 1in **Weight:** 13st 7lbs
Nickname: Deano, Harrable
County debut: 1987 (Warwickshire),
1989 (Gloucestershire)
County cap: 1992
1000 runs in a season: 4
1st-Class 50s: 33
1st-Class 100s: 8
1st-Class catches: 42
One-Day 100s: 2
Place in batting averages: 167th av. 24.46
(1993 37th av. 43.16)
Parents: John and Dorothy
Marital status: Single
Education: Nelson Thomlinson

Comprehensive, Wigton; Loughborough University
Qualifications: 11 O-levels, 4 A-levels, BSc (Hons) Human Biological Sciences, NCA qualified cricket coach, PFA qualified football coach, LTA qualified tennis coach
Off-season: Public relations, promotions and sales support for Müller dairy products
Overseas tours: NCA North U19 to Bermuda 1985; Geoff Humpage Benefit Tour to Barbados 1987; Gloucestershire to Namibia 1990, to Kenya 1991, to Sri Lanka 1992-93
Overseas teams played for: Southern Districts, Queensland 1988-89; Wests, Brisbane 1990-91; Belgrano, Buenos Aires, Argentina 1991-93
Cricketers particularly admired: Dennis Amiss, Ian Botham, Malcolm Marshall, David Gower and other players who make the most of their abilities
Other sports followed: Football, international rugby (league & union), golf, tennis, skiing
Injuries: Groin strain and back spasms, chronic throughout July
Relaxations: Listening to music ('all types depending on mood'), reading thrillers and autobiographies, watching comedies and thrillers, going to wine bars
Extras: Played Minor County Cricket for Cumberland 1982-88; played in 2nd XI for Lancashire 1985-87 and Worcestershire 1989, also played for Warwickshire 1987-88; first-class debut for Gloucestershire in 1989. Rapid Cricketline Player of the Month August/September 1989 while on trial with Gloucestershire and voted Gloucestershire Supporters Player of the Year 1990. Two B&H Man of the Match awards. Shared in record opening stand of 279 v Hampshire at Bristol with Chris Broad in July 1993
Opinions on cricket: 'Perhaps the time has come to extend contracts from six to at least nine months, with players employed by counties to promote and coach cricket in local schools. Wickets need improving for four-day cricket with more pace and an even bounce.'
Best batting: 147 Gloucestershire v Essex, Southend 1992

1994 Season

	M	Inns	NO	Runs	HS	Avge	100s	50s	Ct	St	O	M	Runs	Wkts	Avge	Best	5wl	10wM
Test																		
All First	9	16	1	367	113	24.46	1	1	3	-								
1-day Int																		
NatWest																		
B & H	1	1	0	3	3	3.00	-	-	-	-								
Sunday	3	3	0	42	29	14.00	-	-	-	-								

Career Performances

	M	Inns	NO	Runs	HS	Avge	100s	50s	Ct	St	Balls	Runs	Wkts	Avge	Best	5wl	10wM
Test																	
All First	94	162	10	5151	166	33.88	8	33	42	-	24	65	0	-	-	-	-
1-day Int																	
NatWest	10	10	0	300	62	30.00	-	2	1	-							
B & H	9	9	1	286	103 *	35.75	1	2	1	-							
Sunday	41	39	4	881	104 *	25.17	1	2	14	-							

HOLLIOAKE, A. J.   Surrey

Name: Adam John Hollioake
Role: Right-hand bat, right-arm
fast-medium bowler
Born: 5 September 1971, Melbourne, Australia
Height: 5ft 11in **Weight:** 13st
Nickname: Smokey, Smokin' Joe, Wolf,
Rock, Rambo, Holly, Strong Dance,
Millionaire, Oaky, The Oak, Hokey Cokey,
Abo, Bong
County debut: 1992 (one-day),
1993 (first-class)
1st-Class 50s: 5
1st-Class 100s: 4
1st-Class catches: 16
Place in batting average: 83rd av. 36.10
(1993 55th av. 39.11)
Place in bowling averages: 107th av. 36.84)
Strike rate: 60.96 (career 70.96)
Parents: John and Daria
Marital status: Single
Family links with cricket: Brother plays for Western Australia U17
Education: St Joseph's College, Sydney; St Patrick's College, Ballarat, Australia; St

George's School, Weybridge; Surrey Tutorial College, Guildford

Qualifications: 'Some GCSEs and A-levels'

Off-season: 'A few Fosters, a few barbies, a few late nights out, a few operations and spending time with a delightful little wood nymph called Judy'

Overseas tours: School trip to Zimbabwe; Surrey YC to Australia; England YC to New Zealand 1990-91

Overseas teams played for: Fremantle, Western Australia 1990-91; North Shore, Sydney 1992-93; Geelong; Victoria; North Perth

Cricketers particularly admired:

'All my North Perth colleagues, Alec Stewart, Graham Thorpe, Joey Benjamin'

Other sports followed: Rugby, boxing, Aussie rules football, American football

Injuries: Hernia or Guilmores groin and broken bone in ankle

Relaxations: 'A fine bottle of wine, a fine piece of art, a fine piece of jewellery, watching Graham Thorpe compile an innings.'

Extras: Played rugby for London Counties, Middlesex and South of England as well as having a trial for England U18. Scored a century on first-class debut against Derbyshire. Surrey Young Player of the Year 1993. Fastest ever one-day 50 – in 15 balls v Yorkshire

Opinions on cricket: 'Too boring for spectators. If you hit the ball out of the ground you should get 12. In addition I believe that the short-pitched bowling law as it stands can be a help to players who struggle in this area, allowing them to compete where they may not previously have been capable of competing, and also a hindrance to people who thrive on this type of bowling. I also feel the game would be quite interesting if in one-day games it was made compulsory for two spinners to bowl in each innings with the straight boundary reduced to 20 yards.'

Best batting: 138 Surrey v Leicestershire, The Oval 1994

Best bowling: 4-48 Surrey v Sussex, The Oval 1994

1994 Season

	M	Inns	NO	Runs	HS	Avge	100s	50s	Ct	St	O	M	Runs	Wkts	Avge	Best	5wl	10wM
Test																		
All First	17	23	3	722	138	36.10	3	3	12	-	264.1	44	958	26	36.84	4-48	-	-
1-day Int																		
NatWest	4	3	1	116	60	58.00	-	1	3	-	21.4	1	116	4	29.00	2-40	-	
B & H	4	3	1	14	6	7.00	-	-	1	-	23	0	123	4	30.75	3-48	-	
Sunday	17	14	3	329	72 *	29.90	-	2	2	-	98.4	0	650	14	46.42	3-39	-	

Career Performances

	M	Inns	NO	Runs	HS	Avge	100s	50s	Ct	St	Balls	Runs	Wkts	Avge	Best	5wl	10wM
Test																	
All First	22	32	3	1074	138	37.03	4	5	16	-	2200	1263	31	40.74	4-48	-	-
1-day Int																	
NatWest	4	3	1	116	60	58.00	-	1	3	-	130	116	4	29.00	2-40	-	
B & H	4	3	1	14	6	7.00	-	-	1	-	138	123	4	30.75	3-48	-	
Sunday	28	23	5	515	72 *	28.61	-	3	3	-	1161	1113	33	33.72	4-33	-	

HOLLOWAY, P. C. L.   Somerset

Name: Piran Christopher Laity Holloway
Role: Left-hand bat, wicket-keeper
Born: 1 October 1970,
Helston, Cornwall
Height: 5ft 8in **Weight:** 11st
Nickname: Pils, Piras, Villager, Vill
County debut: 1988 (Warwickshire),
1994 (Somerset)
1st-Class 50s: 3
1st-Class 100s: 1
1st-Class catches: 32
1st-Class stumpings: 1
Place in batting averages: 205th av. 19.00
Parents: Chris and Mary
Marital status: Single
Family links with cricket:
'Mum and Dad are keen supporters
of Helston CC'
Education: Nansloe CP School, Helston;
Millfield School; Taunton School;
Loughborough University
Qualifications: 6 O-levels, 2 A-levels
Overseas tours: Millfield School to Barbados 1986; England YC to Australia 1989-90
Cricketers particularly admired: Alan Knott, Roger Twose, Dermot Reeve, Bob Woolmer
Other sports followed: Rugby (union and league), fishing, squash
Relaxations: Keeping fit, training at the gym, having a few beers with the Loughborough
rugby league team on a Wednesday night, reading
Extras: Joined Somerset for the 1995 season
Best batting: 102* Warwickshire v Worcestershire, Edgbaston 1992

1994 Season

	M	Inns	NO	Runs	HS	Avge	100s	50s	Ct	St	O	M	Runs	Wkts	Avge	Best	5wI	10wM
Test																		
All First	4	6	0	114	50	19.00	-	1	1	-								
1-day Int																		
NatWest																		
B & H																		
Sunday	7	7	1	90	29	15.00	-	-	-	-								

Career Performances

	M	Inns	NO	Runs	HS	Avge	100s	50s	Ct	St	Balls	Runs	Wkts	Avge	Best	5wI	10wM
Test																	
All First	18	27	7	618	102 *	30.90	1	3	32	1							
1-day Int																	
NatWest	3	2	0	18	16	9.00	-	-	3	1							
B & H	6	6	1	67	27	13.40	-	-	7	-							
Sunday	32	25	6	354	51	18.63	-	1	23	6							

HOOPER, C. L.   Kent

Name: Carl Llewellyn Hooper
Role: Right-hand bat, off-spin bowler
Born: 15 December 1966, Guyana
Height: 6ft **Weight:** 13st
County debut: 1992
County cap: 1992
Test debut: 1987-88
Tests: 40
One-Day Internationals: 115
1000 runs in a season: 4
1st-Class 50s: 53
1st-Class 100s: 25
1st-Class 200s: 1
1st-Class 5 w. in innings: 9
1st-Class catches: 181
One-Day 100s: 5
One-Day 5 w. in innings: 1
Place in batting averages: 10th av. 54.44

(1993 8th av. 59.27)
Place in bowling averages: 104th av. 36.37 (1993 113th av. 38.81)
Strike rate: 85.68 (career 79.18)
Off-season: Playing for West Indies
Overseas tours: West Indies to India and Pakistan 1987-88, to Australia 1988-89, to Pakistan 1990-91, to England 1991, to Pakistan and Australia (World Cup) 1991-92, to Australia and South Africa 1992-93, to Sharjah, India (Hero Cup) and Sri Lanka 1993-94, to India 1994-95
Overseas teams played for: Guyana 1984-94
Extras: AXA Equity & Law Award 1993
Best batting: 236* Kent v Glamorgan, Canterbury 1993
Best bowling: 5-33 West Indies v Queensland, Brisbane 1988-89

1994 Season

	M	Inns	NO	Runs	HS	Avge	100s	50s	Ct	St	O	M	Runs	Wkts	Avge	Best	5wl	10wM
Test																		
All First	16	29	0	1579	183	54.44	5	7	26	-	414.1	93	1055	29	36.37	5-52	1	-
1-day Int																		
NatWest	4	4	1	228	136 *	76.00	1	-	5	-	35	1	113	1	113.00	1-37	-	
B & H	1	1	0	4	4	4.00	-	-	2	-	11	0	31	1	31.00	1-31	-	
Sunday	17	17	2	773	122	51.53	2	6	5	-	122.4	5	558	20	27.90	4-37	-	

Career Performances

	M	Inns	NO	Runs	HS	Avge	100s	50s	Ct	St	Balls	Runs	Wkts	Avge	Best	5wl	10wM
Test	40	67	6	1832	178 *	30.03	4	8	40	-	4565	2010	36	55.83	5-40	1	-
All First	167	259	28	10448	236 *	45.22	25	53	181	-	22569	9841	285	34.52	5-33	9	-
1-day Int	115	100	24	2177	113 *	28.64	1	9	57	-	4636	3300	110	30.00	4-34	-	
NatWest	9	9	1	395	136 *	49.37	1	1	7	-	507	284	5	56.80	2-12	-	
B & H	6	6	0	177	50	29.50	-	1	3	-	396	188	9	20.88	3-28	-	
Sunday	48	46	6	1903	122	47.57	3	15	25	-	2203	1431	47	30.44	5-41	1	

HUGHES, J. G.   Northamptonshire

Name: John Gareth Hughes
Role: Right-hand bat, right-arm medium-fast bowler
Born: 3 May 1971, Wellingborough
Height: 6ft 2in **Weight:** 14st
Nickname: Yozzer
1st Class 5 w. in innings: 1
1st-Class catches: 3
Place in bowling averages: 63rd av. 30.57
Strike rate: 58.85 (career 68.38)
Parents: John and Jennifer
Marital status: Engaged to Helen
Family links with cricket: 'My grandad, dad and brother all play or have played for Little Harrowden, whilst two of my uncles umpire for the same club'
Education: Little Harrowden Primary School; Westfield Boys/Sir Christopher Hatton School, Wellingborough; Sheffield Hallam University
Qualifications: 7 O-levels, 2 A-levels, BEd (Hons) in Physical Education
Off-season: Playing and coaching in Wellington, New Zealand
Overseas tours: Northamptonshire CA

U15 to Holland 1986; Northamptonshire to Durban 1991-92, to Cape Town 1992-93
Cricketers particularly admired: Nick Cook, Alan Walker, David Capel, Greg Thomas, Bob Carter, Curtly Ambrose
Other sports followed: 'Football especially, but I enjoy most sports'
Injuries: Torn muscle in ribcage, missed final four weeks of season
Relaxations: Going out for a pint and a meal
Extras: Represented both English Schools and England YC at various age groups. Also represented Northamptonshire at football and basketball at schoolboy level. Grandfather played international football for Wales.
Best batting: 17 Northamptonshire v Hampshire, Southampton 1994
Best bowling: 5-69 Northamptonshire v Hampshire, Southampton 1994

1994 Season

	M	Inns	NO	Runs	HS	Avge	100s	50s	Ct	St	O	M	Runs	Wkts	Avge	Best	5wI	10wM
Test																		
All First	4	6	0	47	17	7.83	-	-	2	-	137.2	38	428	14	30.57	5-69	1	-
1-day Int																		
NatWest																		
B & H	1	0	0	0	0	-	-	-	-	-	4.3	0	27	0	-	-	-	-
Sunday	2	1	0	9	9	9.00	-	-	1	-	11	0	40	0	-	-	-	-

Career Performances

	M	Inns	NO	Runs	HS	Avge	100s	50s	Ct	St	Balls	Runs	Wkts	Avge	Best	5wI	10wM
Test																	
All First	10	15	0	58	17	3.86	-	-	3	-	1436	878	21	41.80	5-69	1	-
1-day Int																	
NatWest																	
B & H	1	0	0	0	0	-	-	-	-	-	27	27	0	-	-	-	-
Sunday	4	3	1	31	21	15.50	-	-	1	-	90	56	0	-	-	-	-

33. Who, in 1993-94, took 10 wickets in the match to give South Africa their first Test victory in Australia for 30 years?

Name: Shaun Humphries
Role: Right-hand bat, wicket-keeper
Born: 11 January 1973, Horsham, West Sussex
Height: 5ft 11in **Weight:** 10st
Nickname: Stan, Gooner
County debut: 1993
1st-Class catches: 2
Parents: Peter and Marilyn
Marital status: Single
Education: The Weald School, Billingshurst;
Kingston College of Further Education
Qualifications: 5 GCSEs, BTEC National
Diploma in Leisure Studies
Off-season: Playing in Sydney
Overseas tours: Sussex U13 to Barbados
1987; Sussex U18 to India 1990-91
Overseas teams played for:
Sutherland, Sydney 1994-95
Cricketers particularly admired:
Peter Moores, Alec Stewart, John Berry
Other sports followed: Football (Arsenal)
Relaxations: Music, raves, 'laughing at Tottenham'
Opinions on cricket: 'More attention should be given to the quality of pitches used by
youngsters – improve safety.'

1994 Season (did not make any first-class or one-day appearance)

Career Performances

	M	Inns	NO	Runs	HS	Avge	100s	50s	Ct	St	Balls	Runs	Wkts	Avge	Best	5wI	10wM
Test																	
All First	1	0	0	0	0	-	-	-	2	-							
1-day Int																	
NatWest																	
B & H																	
Sunday																	

> 34. How many matches did it take for Shane Warne to reach 100
> Test wickets?

HUSSAIN, N.   Essex

Name: Nasser Hussain
Role: Right-hand bat, leg-spin bowler
Born: 28 March 1968, Madras, India
Height: 6ft **Weight:** 12st
Nickname: Bunny
County debut: 1987
Test debut: 1989-90
Tests: 7
One-Day Internationals: 4
1000 runs in a season: 2
1st-Class 50s: 36
1st-Class 100s: 20
1st-Class catches: 174
One-Day 100s: 2
Place in batting averages: 115th av. 31.79
(1993 14th av. 53.46)
Parents: Joe and Shireen
Wife and date of marriage:
Karen, 24 September 1993

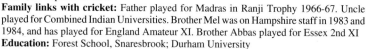

Family links with cricket: Father played for Madras in Ranji Trophy 1966-67. Uncle played for Combined Indian Universities. Brother Mel was on Hampshire staff in 1983 and 1984, and has played for England Amateur XI. Brother Abbas played for Essex 2nd XI
Education: Forest School, Snaresbrook; Durham University
Qualifications: 10 O-levels, 3 A-levels; BSc (Hons) in Geology; NCA cricket coaching award
Overseas tours: England YC to Sri Lanka 1986-87, to Australia (Youth World Cup) 1987-88; England to India (Nehru Cup) 1989-90, to West Indies 1989-90 and 1993-94; England A to Pakistan and Sri Lanka 1990-91, to Bermuda and West Indies 1991-92
Overseas teams played for: Madras 1986-87; Petersham, Sydney 1992-93; Adelaide University 1990
Cricketers particularly admired: David Gower, Mark Waugh, Don Topley
Other sports followed: Golf, football (Leeds)
Relaxations: Watching football, playing golf, listening to music and falling asleep watching old black and white movies
Extras: Played for England Schools U15 for two years (one as captain). Youngest player to play for Essex Schools U11 at the age of eight and U15 at the age of 12. At 15, was considered the best young leg-break bowler in the country. Cricket Writers' Club Young Cricketer of the Year, 1989. Holds record for third, fourth and fifth wicket partnerships for Essex (with Mark Waugh, Salim Malik and Mike Garnham). Essex Player of the Year 1993
Best batting: 197 Essex v Surrey, The Oval 1990
Best bowling: 1-38 Essex v Worcestershire, Kidderminster 1992

1994 Season

	M	Inns	NO	Runs	HS	Avge	100s	50s	Ct	St	O	M	Runs	Wkts	Avge	Best	5wI	10wM
Test																		
All First	19	31	2	922	115 *	31.79	2	5	34	-	1	0	1	0	-	-	-	-
1-day Int																		
NatWest	2	2	0	73	47	36.50	-	-	2	-								
B & H	2	2	1	89	59	89.00	-	1	1	-								
Sunday	16	16	1	504	76	33.60	-	4	8	-								

Career Performances

	M	Inns	NO	Runs	HS	Avge	100s	50s	Ct	St	Balls		Runs	Wkts	Avge	Best	5wI	10wM
Test	7	13	2	284	71	25.81	-	1	3	-								
All First	141	213	31	7833	197	43.03	20	36	174	-	276		307	2	153.50	1-38	-	-
1-day Int	4	4	1	43	16	14.33	-	-	2	-								
NatWest	12	11	1	458	108	45.80	1	2	9	-								
B & H	27	24	4	687	118	34.35	1	5	11	-								
Sunday	83	73	14	1609	76	27.27	-	7	35	-								

HUTTON, S.   Durham

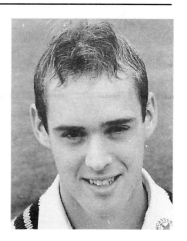

Name: Stewart Hutton
Role: Left-hand bat, cover fielder
Born: 30 November 1969, Stockton-on-Tees
Height: 6ft **Weight:** 12st
Nickname: Len
County debut: 1992
1st-Class 50s: 7
1st-Class 100s: 1
1st-Class catches: 21
Place in batting averages: 128th av. 30.09
(1993 130th av. 27.58)
Parents: Leonard and Mavis
Marital status: Single
Education: De Brus Comprehensive;
Cleveland Technical College
Qualifications: 6 O-levels (equivalent),
A-level Economics
Overseas tours: Durham to
Zimbabwe 1991-92
Cricketers particularly admired: Mike Gatting
Other sports followed: Golf, football
Relaxations: Playing golf

Extras: Scored century for Durham on pre-season tour to Zimbabwe in 1991-92
Best batting: 101 Durham v Northamptonshire, Hartlepool 1994

1994 Season

	M	Inns	NO	Runs	HS	Avge	100s	50s	Ct	St	O	M	Runs	Wkts	Avge	Best	5wl	10wM
Test																		
All First	14	24	2	662	101	30.09	1	3	10	-								
1-day Int																		
NatWest	2	2	0	11	10	5.50	-	-	1	-								
B & H	1	1	0	8	8	8.00	-	-	-	-								
Sunday	9	7	0	121	42	17.28	-	-	-	-								

Career Performances

	M	Inns	NO	Runs	HS	Avge	100s	50s	Ct	St	Balls	Runs	Wkts	Avge	Best	5wl	10wM
Test																	
All First	32	56	2	1537	101	28.46	1	7	21	-	13	5	0	-	-	-	-
1-day Int																	
NatWest	4	4	1	124	95	41.33	-	1	2	-							
B & H	1	1	0	8	8	8.00	-	-	-	-							
Sunday	25	23	4	506	70	26.63	-	1	7	-							

IGGLESDEN, A. P. Kent

Name: Alan Paul Igglesden
Role: Right-hand bat, right-arm
fast-medium bowler
Born: 8 October 1964, Farnborough, Kent
Height: 6ft 6in **Weight:** 15st
Nickname: Iggy, Norm, Ivor
County debut: 1986
Test debut: 1989
Tests: 3
One-Day Internationals: 4
50 wickets in a season: 4
1st-Class 5 w. in innings: 22
1st-Class 10 w. in match: 4
1st-Class catches: 36
One-Day 5 w. in innings: 2
Place in bowling averages: 117th av. 38.70
(1993 5th av. 19.77)
Strike rate: 79.04 (career 52.42)
Parents: Alan Trevor and Gillian Catharine

Wife and date of marriage: Hilary Moira, 20 January 1990
Family links with cricket: Brother Kevin plays for Holmesdale in the Kent League
Education: St Mary's Primary School; Hosey School; Churchill Secondary School, Westerham
Qualifications: 9 CSEs, coaching certificate
Off-season: Working for the Infocheck Group, charity cricket match in Hollywood
Overseas tours: With England A to Zimbabwe and Kenya 1989-90; Fred Rumsey's XI to Barbados 1990; Boland Cricket Union and Kraaifontein 1992-93;England to West Indies 1993-94
Overseas teams played for: Avendale, Cape Town 1985-89; Western Province 1987-91; Green Point, Cape Town 1991-92; Boland Cricket Union 1992-93
Cricketers particularly admired: Terry Alderman, Dennis Lillee, Carl Hooper, Graeme Hick
Other sports followed: 'Very keen Crystal Palace supporter'
Injuries: Slipped disc, missed last five weeks of season
Relaxations: 'Golf, walking "Lillee", our pet cocker spaniel, with Hilary and drinking'
Opinions on cricket: 'Bring in two extra minor counties or a Combined Universities side, put all the names in a hat. Draw out two leagues of ten. The two winners of the groups play a five-day final at Lords/Oval/Old Trafford for the County Championship. That means only nine first-class games, bringing us more into line with the other countries concerning the amount of cricket we play. Then have one, six-Test match series with a triangular World Series Cup. Now that's fallen on deaf ears – it was great to be able to read the Sunday papers at your leisure again!'
Best batting: 41 Kent v Surrey, Canterbury 1988
Best bowling: 7-28 Boland v Griqualand West, Kimberley 1992-93

1994 Season

	M	Inns	NO	Runs	HS	Avge	100s	50s	Ct	St	O	M	Runs	Wkts	Avge	Best	5wI	10wM
Test																		
All First	11	16	8	61	15 *	7.62	-	-	2	-	316.1	75	929	24	38.70	5-38	1	-
1-day Int																		
NatWest	3	0	0	0	0	-	-	-	-	-	24	5	67	5	13.40	3-37	-	
B & H	1	0	0	0	0	-	-	-	-	-	11	1	26	3	8.66	3-26	-	
Sunday	9	2	2	4	3 *	-	-	-	1	-	68.2	5	244	10	24.40	3-22	-	

Career Performances

	M	Inns	NO	Runs	HS	Avge	100s	50s	Ct	St	Balls	Runs	Wkts	Avge	Best	5wI	10wM
Test	3	5	3	6	3 *	3.00	-	-	1	-	555	329	6	54.83	2-91	-	-
All First	138	149	55	800	41	8.51	-	-	36	-	24219	12185	462	26.37	7-28	22	4
1-day Int	4	3	1	20	18	10.00	-	-	1	-	168	122	2	61.00	2-12	-	
NatWest	13	4	3	23	12 *	23.00	-	-	3	-	686	353	18	19.61	4-29	-	
B & H	24	10	7	43	26 *	14.33	-	-	5	-	1391	847	34	24.91	3-24	-	
Sunday	70	24	16	77	13 *	9.62	-	-	16	-	3240	2167	94	23.05	5-13	2	

ILLINGWORTH, R. K. Worcestershire

Name: Richard Keith Illingworth
Role: Right-hand bat, slow left-arm bowler
Born: 23 August 1963, Bradford
Height: 6ft **Weight:** 13st
Nickname: Lucy, Harry
County debut: 1982
County cap: 1986
Test debut: 1991
Tests: 2
One-Day Internationals: 18
50 wickets in a season: 4
1st-Class 50s: 14
1st-Class 100s: 3
1st-Class 5 w. in innings: 22
1st-Class 10 w. in match: 5
1st-Class catches: 122
One-Day 5 w. in innings: 2
Place in batting averages: 179th av. 23.05
(1993 155th av. 25.06)
Place in bowling averages: 64th av. 30.59 (1993 34th av. 25.52)
Strike rate: 83.14 (career 77.25)
Parents: Keith and Margaret
Wife and date of marriage: Anne, 20 September 1985
Children: Miles, 28 August 1987; Thomas, 20 April 1989
Family links with cricket: Father played Bradford League cricket
Education: Wrose Brow Middle; Salts Grammar School ('same school as the late Jim Laker')
Qualifications: 6 O-levels, senior coaching award
Overseas tours: England A to Zimbabwe and Kenya 1989-90, to Pakistan and Sri Lanka 1990-91; England to New Zealand and Australia (World Cup) 1991-92
Overseas teams played for: Natal 1988-89
Cricketers particularly admired: Ian Botham
Other sports followed: Most sports – football, golf and rugby
Relaxations: 'Golf, playing with my two children, cycling, reading autobiographies, DIY and gardening.'
Extras: Took 11 for 108 on South African first-class debut for Natal B v Boland 1988. Scored 120 not out as nightwatchman for Worcestershire v Warwickshire 1988 and 106 for England A v Zimbabwe 1989-90. In 1991, v West Indies, became 11th person in history to take a wicket with first ball in Test cricket. Took a hat-trick in Sunday League v Sussex in 1993, the first Worcestershire player to do this in one-day cricket. Won 1993 Dick Lygon award for contribution to Worcestershire CCC
Best batting: 120* Worcestershire v Warwickshire, Worcester 1987
Best bowling: 7-50 Worcestershire v Oxford University, The Parks 1985

1994 Season

	M	Inns	NO	Runs	HS	Avge	100s	50s	Ct	St	O	M	Runs	Wkts	Avge	Best	5wI	10wM
Test																		
All First	20	25	6	438	59 *	23.05	-	3	8	-	679	212	1499	49	30.59	4-51	-	-
1-day Int																		
NatWest	5	1	1	0	0 *	-	-	-	2	-	48	6	163	3	54.33	2-26	-	
B & H	4	2	1	18	18	18.00	-	-	-	-	31	1	128	3	42.66	3-51	-	
Sunday	16	8	2	62	31	10.33	-	-	2	-	111	6	444	18	24.66	4-23	-	

Career Performances

	M	Inns	NO	Runs	HS	Avge	100s	50s	Ct	St	Balls	Runs	Wkts	Avge	Best	5wI	10wM
Test	2	4	2	31	13	15.50	-	-	1	-	340	213	4	53.25	3-110	-	-
All First	283	314	84	4941	120 *	21.48	3	14	122	-	49597	19833	642	30.89	7-50	22	5
1-day Int	18	7	2	61	14	12.20	-	-	8	-	1093	760	24	31.66	3-33	-	
NatWest	30	13	5	97	22	12.12	-	-	10	-	1783	917	25	36.68	4-20	-	
B & H	44	23	13	200	36 *	20.00	-	-	10	-	2205	1294	39	33.17	4-36	-	
Sunday	155	72	36	490	31	13.61	-	-	36	-	5889	4252	181	23.49	5-24	2	

ILOTT, M. C.   Essex

Name: Mark Christopher Ilott
Role: Left-hand bat (tail end), left-arm
fast-medium bowler
Born: 27 August 1970, Watford
Height: 6ft 1in **Weight:** 13st
Nickname: Ramble, Choock, Headless
County debut: 1988
County cap: 1993
Test debut: 1993
Tests: 3
50 wickets in a season: 2
1st-Class 50s: 2
1st-Class 5 w. in innings: 11
1st-Class 10 w. in match: 1
1st-Class catches: 23
One-Day 5 w. in innings: 1
Place in batting averages: 221st av. 17.63
(1993 237th av. 14.00)
Place in bowling averages: 15th av. 23.57
(1993 95th av. 33.25)
Strike rate: 50.63 (career 58.79)
Parents: John and Glenys

Wife and date of marriage: Sandra Bishop, 14 October 1994
Family links with cricket: Brother plays Minor Counties for Hertfordshire, father is qualified umpire and grandfather played for Ruislip Manor for many years
Education: Francis Combe School
Qualifications: 8 O-levels, 2 A-levels, coaching qualification, Diploma in Fitness and Nutrition
Career outside cricket: Working for car sponsors, RS Kennedy – Civil Engineers and Contractors
Off-season: Touring with England A to India
Overseas tours: England A to Sri Lanka 1990-91, to Australia 1992-93, to South Africa 1993-94, to India 1994-95
Overseas teams played for: East Torrens District, Adelaide 1989-91
Cricketers particularly admired: John Lever, Malcolm Marshall, Dennis Lillee, Graham Gooch
Other sports followed: Golf, tennis, football, snooker
Injuries: Groin strain, missed eight weeks. England A tour cut short through injury
Relaxations: Listening to music, reading, snooker, cycling, golf
Extras: Youngest player ever to play for Hertfordshire. Missed almost all 1991 season with stress fracture of the back
Best batting: 51 Essex v Sussex, Hove 1993
Best bowling: 7-85 Essex v Surrey, The Oval 1993

1994 Season

	M	Inns	NO	Runs	HS	Avge	100s	50s	Ct	St	O	M	Runs	Wkts	Avge	Best	5wI	10wM
Test																		
All First	14	16	5	194	45 *	17.63	-	-	3	-	497.5	115	1391	59	23.57	6-24	3	1
1-day Int																		
NatWest	2	1	0	26	26	26.00	-	-	1	-	23.2	3	87	2	43.50	2-43	-	
B & H	2	0	0	0	0	-	-	-	-	-	15	3	45	3	15.00	3-28	-	
Sunday	9	5	2	43	24	14.33	-	-	2	-	66.2	5	303	12	25.25	4-25	-	

Career Performances

	M	Inns	NO	Runs	HS	Avge	100s	50s	Ct	St	Balls	Runs	Wkts	Avge	Best	5wI	10wM
Test	3	5	1	28	15	7.00	-	-	-	-	774	412	8	51.50	3-108	-	-
All First	82	88	24	883	51	13.79	-	2	23	-	16110	8045	274	29.36	7-85	11	1
1-day Int																	
NatWest	8	4	2	50	26	25.00	-	-	2	-	505	324	10	32.40	2-23	-	
B & H	12	3	1	19	14	9.50	-	-	-	-	635	320	20	16.00	5-21	1	
Sunday	46	23	6	139	24	8.17	-	-	5	-	2040	1481	58	25.53	4-15	-	

INNES, K. J.   Northamptonshire

Name: Kevin John Innes
Role: Right-hand bat, right-arm medium
bowler
Born: 24 September 1975, Wellingborough
Height: 5ft 10in **Weight:** 10st 7lbs
Nickname: Ernie, Milkman
County debut: 1994
Parents: Peter and Jane
Marital status: Single
Education: Boothville Middle School;
Weston Favell Upper School, Northampton
Qualifications: 6 GCSEs, 4 O-levels
Overseas tours:
England U18 to South Africa 1992-93;
England U19 to Sri Lanka 1993-94
Cricketers particularly admired:
Carl Hooper, Viv Richards

Other sports followed: Snooker, football, golf
Relaxations: Watching and playing most sport,
music
Extras: Played for England U19 in home series against India in 1994
Opinions on cricket: 'It is a shame that employment is not found at the end of the season
for a lot more cricketers.'

1994 Season

	M	Inns	NO	Runs	HS	Avge	100s	50s	Ct	St	O	M	Runs	Wkts	Avge	Best	5wI	10wM
Test																		
All First	1	2	0	0	0	0.00	-	-	-	-	10	3	33	0	-	-	-	-
1-day Int																		
NatWest																		
B & H	1	0	0	0	0	-	-	-	-	-	6	1	25	1	25.00	1-25	-	
Sunday	5	2	0	8	5	4.00	-	-	2	-	26	1	187	2	93.50	1-35	-	

Career Performances

	M	Inns	NO	Runs	HS	Avge	100s	50s	Ct	St	Balls	Runs	Wkts	Avge	Best	5wI	10wM
Test																	
All First	1	2	0	0	0	0.00	-	-	-	-	60	33	0	-	-	-	-
1-day Int																	
NatWest																	
B & H	1	0	0	0	0	-	-	-	-	-	36	25	1	25.00	1-25	-	
Sunday	5	2	0	8	5	4.00	-	-	2	-	156	187	2	93.50	1-35	-	

IRANI, R.　　　　　　　　　　　　　　Essex

Name: Ronnie Irani
Role: Right-hand bat,
right-arm medium bowler
Born: 26 October 1971,
Leigh, Lancashire
Height: 6ft 4in **Weight:** 13st 8lbs
Nickname: Reggie, Eric
County debut: 1990 (Lancashire),
1994 (Essex)
County cap: 1994
1st-Class 50s: 8
1st-Class 100s: 2
1st-Class catches: 11
Place in batting averages: 52nd av. 41.93
Place in bowling averages: 56th av. 29.78
Strike rate: 53.50 (career 61.43)
Parents: Jimmy and Anne
Marital status: Single
Family links with cricket: 'Father played local

league cricket in Bolton for 30 years; mother did teas for many years!'
Education: Church Road Primary School;
Smithills Comprehensive School
Qualifications: 9 GCSEs
Career outside cricket: 'Watching football'
Off-season: Watching football
Overseas tours: England YC to Australia 1989-90
Overseas teams played for: Technicol Natal, Durban, South Africa 1992-93; Eden-Roskill, Auckland 1993-94
Cricketers particularly admired: Mark Waugh, Javed Miandad, Wasim Akram, John Crawley
Other sports followed: Football, boxing, Muay Thai boxing
Injuries: Back (through bowling), stopped bowling but kept batting
Relaxations: Music, gym work
Extras: Played for England U19 in home series v Australia 1991, scoring a century and three 50s in six innings and being named Bull Man of the Series
Opinions on cricket: 'Too much cricket played by English county cricket professionals'
Best batting: 119 Essex v Worcestershire, Worcester 1994
Best bowling: 4-27 Essex v Kent, Chelmsford 1994

1994 Season

	M	Inns	NO	Runs	HS	Avge	100s	50s	Ct	St	O	M	Runs	Wkts	Avge	Best	5wl	10wM
Test																		
All First	18	29	6	965	119	41.95	2	8	6	-	249.4	42	834	28	29.78	4-27	-	-
1-day Int																		
NatWest	2	2	0	41	30	20.50	-	-	-	-	24	2	121	4	30.25	4-55	-	
B & H	2	0	0	0	0	-	-	-	-	-	14	1	89	1	89.00	1-61	-	
Sunday	16	16	0	185	33	11.56	-	-	2	-	61.1	6	248	11	22.54	3-22	-	

Career Performances

	M	Inns	NO	Runs	HS	Avge	100s	50s	Ct	St	Balls		Runs	Wkts	Avge	Best	5wl	10wM
Test																		
All First	27	40	7	1108	119	33.57	2	8	11	-	2028		1132	33	34.30	4-27	-	-
1-day Int																		
NatWest	2	2	0	41	30	20.50	-	-	-	-	144		121	4	30.25	4-55	-	
B & H	2	0	0	0	0	-	-	-	-	-	84		89	1	89.00	1-61	-	
Sunday	24	20	0	255	34	12.75	-	-	3	-	453		321	15	21.40	3-22	-	

JAMES, K. D.   Hampshire

Name: Kevan David James
Role: Left-hand bat, left-arm medium bowler
Born: 18 March 1961, Lambeth, South London
Height: 6ft ½in **Weight:** 13st 8lbs
Nickname: Jambo, Jaimo, Jockey
County debut: 1980 (Middlesex), 1985 (Hampshire)
County cap: 1989
1000 runs in a season: 2
1st-Class 50s: 30
1st-Class 100s: 8
1st-Class 5 w. in innings: 7
1st-Class catches: 54
Place in batting averages: 196th av. 20.85 (1993 128th av. 27.76)
Place in bowling averages: 94th av. 34.61 (1993 37th av. 26.16)
Strike rate: 64.65 (career 64.51)
Parents: David (deceased) and Helen
Wife and date of marriage: Debbie, October 1987
Children: Natalie Ann, 8 October 1992

Family links with cricket: Late father played club cricket in North London; brother Martin plays for Hertfordshire
Education: Edmonton County High School
Qualifications: 5 O-levels; qualified coach
Off-season: Working for Southern Electric contracting
Overseas tours: England YC to Australia 1978-79, to West Indies 1979-80
Overseas teams played for: Wellington, New Zealand 1982-83, 1983-84
Cricketers particularly admired: Chris Smith
Other sports followed: Football (Spurs)
Injuries: Bruised ego
Extras: Released by Middlesex at end of 1984 season and joined Hampshire
Opinions on cricket: 'Sick and tired of journalists who slag off professional cricket. If they don't enjoy watching it then they should move over and let others who do enjoy it write about it. We all have a duty to promote county cricket, especially those who earn a living from it and don't even play the game.'
Best batting: 162 Hampshire v Glamorgan, Cardiff 1989
Best bowling: 6-22 Hampshire v Australia, Southampton 1985

1994 Season

	M	Inns	NO	Runs	HS	Avge	100s	50s	Ct	St	O	M	Runs	Wkts	Avge	Best	5wI	10wM
Test																		
All First	13	22	2	417	53	20.85	-	2	2	-	280.1	56	900	26	34.61	4-78	-	-
1-day Int																		
NatWest	2	1	0	11	11	11.00	-	-	1	-	22	7	50	5	10.00	3-36	-	
B & H	3	1	1	5	5 *	-	-	-	1	-	21	1	76	0	-	-	-	-
Sunday	16	11	2	122	39 *	13.55	-	-	3	-	112	6	508	21	24.19	5-42	1	

Career Performances

	M	Inns	NO	Runs	HS	Avge	100s	50s	Ct	St	Balls	Runs	Wkts	Avge	Best	5wI	10wM
Test																	
All First	170	248	42	6490	162	31.50	8	30	54	-	18130	9070	281	32.27	6-22	7	-
1-day Int																	
NatWest	19	11	2	147	42	16.33	-	-	3	-	1162	751	24	31.29	3-22	-	
B & H	35	24	5	334	45	17.57	-	-	7	-	1765	1154	28	41.21	3-31	-	
Sunday	128	86	25	1240	66	20.32	-	3	35	-	5113	3653	115	31.76	5-42	1	

JAMES, S. P.   Glamorgan

Name: Stephen Peter James
Role: Right-hand opening bat
Born: 7 September 1967, Lydney
Height: 6ft **Weight:** 12st 7lbs
Nickname: Sid, Sog
County debut: 1985
County cap: 1992
1000 runs in a season: 2
1st-Class 50s: 22
1st-Class 100s: 14
1st-Class catches: 88
One-Day 100s: 4
Place in batting averages: 67th av. 38.13
(1993 119th av. 28.55)
Parents: Peter and Margaret
Marital status: Single
Family links with cricket: Father played
for Gloucestershire 2nd XI. Distant relative of
Dominic Ostler

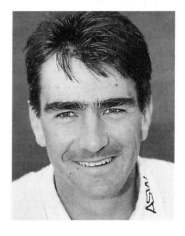

Education: Monmouth School; University College, Swansea; Cambridge University
Qualifications: BA (Hons) Wales – Classics; BA (Hons) Cantab – Land Economy
Off-season: Playing and coaching in Zimbabwe
Overseas tours: Welsh Schools to Barbados 1984; Monmouth Schools to Sri Lanka 1985;
Combined Universities to Barbados 1989; Glamorgan to Trinidad 1989-90, to Zimbabwe
1990-91, Cape Town 1993-94
Overseas teams played for: Bionics, Zimbabwe 1990-92; Universals Sports Club,
Zimbabwe 1992-94
Cricketers particularly admired: Michael Atherton, Graham Burgess
Other sports followed: Rugby union
Relaxations: Reading, crosswords, videos, weight training
Extras: Scored maiden century in only second first-class game. Played rugby for Lydney,
Gloucestershire and Cambridge University and was on the substitutes' bench for 1988 and
1989 Varsity matches
Opinions on cricket: 'The position of Test match referees needs to be looked at because
there is no consistency in their decisions at present.'
Best batting: 152* Glamorgan v Lancashire, Colwyn Bay 1992

---

35. Which television commentator and former Australian Test
captain was born on 6 October 1930?

1994 Season

	M	Inns	NO	Runs	HS	Avge	100s	50s	Ct	St	O	M	Runs	Wkts	Avge	Best	5wl	10wM
Test																		
All First	16	28	5	877	150	38.13	3	1	18	-	-							
1-day Int																		
NatWest	2	2	0	141	123	70.50	1	-	-	-								
B & H	1	1	0	12	12	12.00	-	-	-	-								
Sunday	15	15	0	452	102	30.13	1	2	4	-								

Career Performances

	M	Inns	NO	Runs	HS	Avge	100s	50s	Ct	St	Balls	Runs	Wkts	Avge	Best	5wl	10wM
Test																		
All First	109	189	17	5772	152 *	33.55	14	22	88	-	-							
1-day Int																		
NatWest	10	10	0	355	123	35.50	1	1	-									
B & H	14	14	0	445	135	31.78	1	3	4	-								
Sunday	48	46	1	1423	107	31.62	2	9	11	-								

JARVIS, P. W.   Sussex

Name: Paul William Jarvis
Role: Right-hand bat,
right-arm fast-medium bowler
Born: 29 June 1965, Redcar,
North Yorkshire
Height: 5ft 11in **Weight:** 12st 7lbs
Nickname: Jarv, Harvey, Gnasher
County debut: 1981 (Yorkshire),
1994 (Sussex)
County cap: 1986 (Yorkshire)
Test debut: 1987-88
Tests: 9
One-Day Internationals: 16
50 wickets in a season: 4
1st-Class 50s: 6
1st-Class 5 w. in innings: 19
1st-Class 10 w. in match: 3
1st-Class catches: 43
One-Day 5 w. in innings: 4
Place in batting averages: 230th av. 16.52 (1993 222nd av. 15.92)
Place in bowling averages: 96th av. 34.76 (1993 46th av. 27.11)
Strike rate: 70.15 (career 53.39)

Parents: Malcolm and Marjorie
Wife and date of marriage: Wendy Jayne, 3 December 1988
Children: Alexander Michael, 13 July 1989; Isabella Grace, 21 March 1993
Family links with cricket: Father plays league cricket for Sudbrooke in Gwent; brother Andrew plays for Methley CC, Lord's finalists in 1992 National Village Championship
Education: Bydales Comprehensive School, Marske, Cleveland
Qualifications: 4 O-levels, advanced coaching awards
Off-season: Playing and coaching for Onslow, Wellington, New Zealand
Overseas tours: Yorkshire to St Lucia and Barbados 1987, to South Africa 1991; England to India/Pakistan (World Cup) and Pakistan 1986-87, to Australia and New Zealand 1987-88, to India and Sri Lanka 1992-93; unofficial English XI to South Africa 1989-90
Overseas teams played for: Mossman Middle Harbour, Sydney 1984-85; Avendale, Cape Town 1985-86; Manly Warringah, Sydney 1987
Cricketers particularly admired: Richard Hadlee, Malcolm Marshall, Ian Botham
Other sports followed: Most sports
Injuries: Slight groin strain, missed one Championship match
Relaxations: Fishing, golf, DIY, cooking
Extras: Youngest player ever to play for Yorkshire in County Championship (16 years, 2 months, 13 days) and youngest player to take hat-trick in Sunday League (1982) and Championship (1985). Played for England YC v West Indies 1982 and Australia 1983. Banned from Test cricket for joining 1989-90 tour of South Africa, suspension remitted in 1992
Opinions on cricket: 'Four-day game appears to be a much fairer competition. Sunday League should be scrapped altogether. B&H should go back to group system, creating more cricket at the start of the season, as quite a bit of cricket is lost to bad weather.'
Best batting: 80 Yorkshire v Northamptonshire, Scarborough 1992
Best bowling: 7-55 Yorkshire v Surrey, Headingley 1986

1994 Season

	M	Inns	NO	Runs	HS	Avge	100s	50s	Ct	St	O	M	Runs	Wkts	Avge	Best	5wI	10wM
Test																		
All First	17	27	6	347	70 *	16.52	-	1	4	-	496.2	89	1773	51	34.76	7-58	1	-
1-day Int																		
NatWest	1	1	0	1	1	1.00	-	-	-	-	12	1	53	0	-	-	-	-
B & H	2	1	1	21	21 *	-	-	-	-	-	20	3	63	3	21.00	2-34	-	
Sunday	12	9	1	78	17	9.75	-	-	2	-	83.5	3	381	14	27.21	3-40	-	

Career Performances

	M	Inns	NO	Runs	HS	Avge	100s	50s	Ct	St	Balls	Runs	Wkts	Avge	Best	5wI	10wM
Test	9	15	2	132	29 *	10.15	-	-	2	-	1912	965	21	45.95	4-107	-	-
All First	173	210	58	2474	80	16.27	-	6	43	-	29151	15384	546	28.17	7-55	19	3
1-day Int	16	8	2	31	16 *	5.16	-	-	1	-	879	672	24	28.00	5-35	1	
NatWest	17	10	2	87	16	10.87	-	-	3	-	1129	708	19	37.26	4-41	-	
B & H	34	15	5	131	42	13.10	-	-	4	-	1946	1069	55	19.43	4-34	-	
Sunday	106	58	22	394	38 *	10.94	-	-	27	-	4574	3295	152	21.67	6-27	3	

JEAN-JACQUES, M.   Hampshire

Name: Martin Jean-Jacques
Role: Right-hand bat,
right-arm fast-medium bowler
Born: 2 August 1960,
Soufrière, Dominica
Height: 5ft 11in **Weight:** 12st 7lbs
Nickname: JJ
County debut: 1986 (Derbyshire),
1993 (Hampshire)
1st-Class 50s: 1
1st-Class 5 w. in innings: 2
1st-Class 10 w. in match: 1
1st-Class catches: 15
Strike rate: (career 60.88)
Education: Scotts Head Primary, Dominica;
Aylestone High, London
Career outside cricket: Electrician
Cricketers particularly admired:
Michael Holding
Other sports followed: Football
Relaxations: Listening to music – reggae and soul
Extras: Played Minor Counties cricket for Buckinghamshire. On debut for Derbyshire (v Yorkshire) put on a county record 132 with Alan Hill for the tenth wicket. Released by Derbyshire at the end of 1992 season. Knee injury brought about retirement at the end of 1994 season
Best batting: 73 Derbyshire v Yorkshire, Sheffield 1986
Best bowling: 8-77 Derbyshire v Kent, Derby 1986

1994 Season

	M	Inns	NO	Runs	HS	Avge	100s	50s	Ct	St	O	M	Runs	Wkts	Avge	Best	5wl	10wM
Test																		
All First	3	5	1	52	22 *	13.00	-	-	1	-	53.1	4	242	5	48.40	3-44	-	-
1-day Int																		
NatWest																		
B & H	1	0	0	0	0	-	-	-	-	-	2	0	20	0	-		-	-
Sunday	3	2	1	12	8	12.00	-	-	-	-	24	0	122	5	24.40	3-44	-	

> 36. In 1993-94 which Australian became the fourth batsman to score
> 1000 runs in the Sheffield Shield for three consecutive seasons,
> joining Sir Donald Bradman, Greg Chappell and Allan Border?

Career Performances

	M	Inns	NO	Runs	HS	Avge	100s	50s	Ct	St	Balls	Runs	Wkts	Avge	Best	5wI	10wM
Test																	
All First	60	74	17	681	73	11.94	-	1	15	-	7550	4514	124	36.40	8-77	2	1
1-day Int																	
NatWest	8	5	3	28	16	14.00	-	-	1	-	444	310	12	25.83	3-23	-	
B & H	6	2	1	4	2*	4.00	-	-	2	-	258	243	6	40.50	3-22	-	
Sunday	37	18	2	108	23	6.75	-	-	5	-	1362	1268	35	36.22	3-36	-	

JOHNSON, P. Nottinghamshire

Name: Paul Johnson
Role: Right-hand bat, right-arm medium 'occasional' bowler
Born: 24 April 1965, Newark
Height: 5ft 7in 'below average'
Weight: 11st 11lbs 'above average'
Nickname: Johno, Midget
County debut: 1982
County cap: 1986
Benefit: 1995
1000 runs in a season: 7
1st-Class 50s: 75
1st-Class 100s: 31
1st-Class catches: 157
1st-Class stumpings: 1
One-Day 100s: 8
Place in batting averages: 43rd av. 43.33 (1993 42nd av. 42.26)
Parents: Donald Edward and Joyce
Wife's name and date of marriage: Jackie, 24 December 1993
Family links with cricket: Father played local cricket and is a qualified coach
Education: Grove Comprehensive School, Newark
Qualifications: 9 CSEs, NCA advanced coach
Off-season: Organising 1995 benefit
Overseas tours: England A to Bermuda and West Indies 1991-92
Overseas teams played for: RAU Johannesburg, 1985-86; Hutt District, Wellington, New Zealand 1988-89
Cricketers particularly admired: Clive Rice
Other sports followed: Watches ice-hockey (Nottingham Panthers), football (Nottingham Forest and Notts County)
Injuries: Irritable bowel syndrome and right knee problem, missed three weeks in all

Relaxations: 'Listening to music, crosswords and reading autobiographies'
Extras: Played for English Schools in 1980-81 and England YC 1982 and 1983. Youngest player ever to join the Nottinghamshire staff. Made 235 for Nottinghamshire 2nd XI, July 1982, aged 17. Won Man of the Match award in his first NatWest game (101* v Staffordshire) in 1985, but missed the final owing to appendicitis. Sunday morning soccer referee in Nottingham
Opinions on cricket: 'Who would take any notice?'
Best batting: 187 Nottinghamshire v Lancashire, Old Trafford 1993
Best bowling: 1-9 Nottinghamshire v Oxford University, Trent Bridge 1984

1994 Season

	M	Inns	NO	Runs	HS	Avge	100s	50s	Ct	St	O	M	Runs	Wkts	Avge	Best	5wI	10wM
Test																		
All First	17	29	2	1170	132	43.33	4	5	6	-	-							
1-day Int																		
NatWest	2	2	0	183	146	91.50	1	-	1	-								
B & H	3	3	1	63	35 *	31.50	-	-	-	-								
Sunday	13	13	1	436	90	36.33	-	4	3	-								

Career Performances

	M	Inns	NO	Runs	HS	Avge	100s	50s	Ct	St	Balls	Runs	Wkts	Avge	Best	5wI	10wM
Test																	
All First	248	409	40	13736	187	37.22	31	75	157	1	478	510	5	102.00	1-9	-	-
1-day Int																	
NatWest	26	26	2	760	146	31.66	2	1	7	-	12	16	0	-		-	-
B & H	41	39	6	1048	104 *	31.75	2	6	14	-							
Sunday	159	149	16	3825	167 *	28.75	4	22	54	-							

JOHNSON, R. L.   Middlesex

Name: Richard Leonard Johnson
Role: Right-hand bat, right-arm fast-medium bowler, outfielder
Born: 29 December 1974, Chertsey, Surrey
Height: 6ft 2in **Weight:** 13st 6lbs
Nickname: Jono, Lenny
County debut: 1992
1st-Class 50s: 1
1st-Class 5 w. in innings: 1
1st-Class 10 w. in match: 1
1st-Class catches: 1
Place in batting averages: 198th av. 20.50
Place in bowling averages: 33rd av. 26.47

Strike rate: 52.60 (career 54.38)
Parents: Roger and Mary Ann
Marital status: Single
Family links with cricket: Father and grandfather played club cricket
Education: Sunbury Manor School; Spelthorne College
Qualifications: 9 GCSEs, A-Level in Physical Education
Off-season: Touring with England A
Overseas tours: England U18 to South Africa 1992-93; England U19 to South Africa 1993-94; England A to India 1994-95
Cricketers particularly admired: Ian Botham, Richard Hadlee
Other sports followed: Basketball, soccer, snooker and most other sports
Injuries: Knee injury, missed six weeks
Relaxations: Sport and music

Extras: Plays for Sunbury CC, has represented Middlesex at all levels since U11. Took 10 for 45 v Derbyshire in July, first person to take 10 wickets in an innings since Ian Thomson (Sussex) in 1964, also most economical figures since Hedley Verity's 10 for 10.
Best batting: 50* Middlesex v Cambridge University, Fenner's 1994
Best bowling: 10-45 Middlesex v Derbyshire, Derby 1994

1994 Season

	M	Inns	NO	Runs	HS	Avge	100s	50s	Ct	St	O	M	Runs	Wkts	Avge	Best	5wl	10wM
Test																		
All First	11	13	3	205	50 *	20.50		1	5	*	390.4	85	1059	40	26.47	10-45	1	1
1-day Int																		
NatWest	2	1	1	12	12 *	-	-	-	-	-	20	2	68	1	68.00	1-22	-	
B & H	2	1	0	1	1	1.00	-	-	-	-	20	4	62	1	62.00	1-17	-	
Sunday	11	7	3	52	14 *	13.00	-	-	2	-	84.5	3	458	14	32.71	3-32	-	

Career Performances

	M	Inns	NO	Runs	HS	Avge	100s	50s	Ct	St	Balls	Runs	Wkts	Avge	Best	5wl	10wM
Test																	
All First	13	16	3	214	50 *	16.46	-	1	6	-	2284	1188	42	28.28	10-45	1	1
1-day Int																	
NatWest	3	2	1	17	12 *	17.00	-	-	-	-	180	112	1	112.00	1-22	-	
B & H	2	1	0	1	1	1.00	-	-	-	-	120	62	1	62.00	1-17	-	
Sunday	21	11	6	89	18	17.80	-	-	2	-	943	825	24	34.37	4-66	-	

JONES, P. S.   Glamorgan

Name: Philip Steffan Jones
Role: Right-hand bat, right-arm fast-medium bowler
Born: 9 February 1974, Llanelli
Height: 6ft 1in **Weight:** 13st
Nickname: Cracker
County debut: No first-team appearance
Parents: Lyndon and Ann
Marital status: Single
Family links with cricket: Father played cricket for Welsh Secondary Schools, Glamorgan 2nd XI, Dafen, Hendy
Education: Ysgol Gyfun Y Strade (Strade Comp.); Neath Tertiary College
Qualifications: Student
Career outside cricket: PE teacher
Off-season: Playing rugby and returning to Loughborough University
Cricketers particularly admired: Michael Holding, Richard Hadlee
Other sports followed: Plays rugby
Relaxations: Listening to music, art and painting, eating Italian food
Extras: Played rugby at U18 and U19 for Wales. Top of the bowling and batting averages for Wales Minor Counties and played for them in the 1994 NatWest Trophy

1994 Season

	M	Inns	NO	Runs	HS	Avge	100s	50s	Ct	St	O	M	Runs	Wkts	Avge	Best	5wI	10wM
Test																		
All First																		
1-day Int																		
NatWest	1	1	1	26	26*	-	-	-	-	-	3	0	30	0	-		-	-
B & H																		
Sunday																		

Career Performances

	M	Inns	NO	Runs	HS	Avge	100s	50s	Ct	St	Balls	Runs	Wkts	Avge	Best	5wI	10wM
Test																	
All First																	
1-day Int																	
NatWest	1	1	1	26	26*	-	-	-	-	-	18	30	0	-		-	-
B & H																	
Sunday																	

KASPROWICZ, M. S. Essex

Name: Michael Scott Kasprowicz
Role: Right-hand bat, right-arm fast-medium bowler
Born: 10 February 1972, Brisbane, Australia
Height: 6ft 3in
County debut: 1994
County cap: 1994
50 wickets in season: 1
1st-Class 5w. in innings: 7
1st-Class catches: 19
Place in batting averages: 231st av. 16.30
Place in bowling averages: 71st av. 31.15
Strike rate: 52.75 (career 61.67)
Marital status: Single
Education: Brisbane State High School
Overseas tours:
Australian YC to England 1991
Overseas teams played for:
Queensland, Australia 1989-94
Extras: Was captain of cricket for four years at Brisbane State High School and played for Queensland U17 and U19. Played for Australia U17 and made his Queensland debut aged 17. Took nine wickets in first 'Test' at Grace Road, Leicester on Australian YC tour to England 1991. Was second leading wicket-taker in the Sheffield Shield 1992-93 with 51 wickets at an average of 24.13. Toured New Zealand with Australian Schoolboys rugby team in 1989. Not retained for 1995 season
Best batting: 49 Queensland v Western Australia, Perth 1989-90
Best bowling: 7-83 Essex v Somerset, Weston-super-Mare 1994

1994 Season

	M	Inns	NO	Runs	HS	Avge	100s	50s	Ct	St	O	M	Runs	Wkts	Avge	Best	5wI	10wM
Test																		
All First	17	24	4	326	44	16.30	-	-	9	-	527.3	92	1869	60	31.15	7-83	3	-
1-day Int																		
NatWest	1	1	0	13	13	13.00	-	-	-	-	12	2	60	5	12.00	5-60	1	
B & H	2	0	0	0	0	-	-	-	1	-	15	0	76	2	38.00	2-52	-	
Sunday	15	12	0	61	17	5.08	-	-	2	-	94.4	6	458	11	41.63	2-38	-	

37. Which England player helped to shave Chris Lewis's head which led to Lewis getting sunstroke and missing the start of the 1993-94 West Indies tour?

Career Performances

	M	Inns	NO	Runs	HS	Avge	100s	50s	Ct	St	Balls	Runs	Wkts	Avge	Best	5wI	10wM
Test																	
All First	46	64	8	810	49	14.46	-	-	19	-	8696	4674	141	33.14	7-83	7	-
1-day Int																	
NatWest	1	1	0	13	13	13.00	-	-	-	-	72	60	5	12.00	5-60	1	
B & H	2	0	0	0	0	-	-	-	1	-	90	76	2	38.00	2-52	-	
Sunday	15	12	0	61	17	5.08	-	-	2	-	568	458	11	41.63	2-38	-	

KEECH, M. Hampshire

Name: Matthew Keech
Role: Right-hand bat, right-arm medium bowler
Born: 21 October 1970, Hampstead
Height: 6ft **Weight:** 13st 6lbs
County debut: 1991 (Middlesex), 1994 (Hampshire)
1st-Class 50s: 3
1st-Class catches: 15
Place in batting averages: 234th av. 15.66 (1993 206th av. 18.22)
Parents: Ron and Brenda
Marital status: Single
Education: Northumberland Park School, Tottenham
Qualifications: 5 O-levels, NCA coaching certificate
Overseas tours: England YC to Australia 1989-90
Overseas teams played for: Mossman, Sydney 1988-89; Lancaster Park, Christchurch NZ 1990-91
Cricketers particularly admired: Mike Gatting, Richard Hadlee, Paul Downton
Other sports followed: Most other sports except horse racing
Relaxations: Listening to music, watching videos
Extras: Left Middlesex and moved to Hampshire for 1994 season
Best batting: 58* Middlesex v Nottinghamshire, Lord's 1991
Best bowling: 2-28 Middlesex v Gloucestershire, Bristol 1993

---

38. Which current Test captain has been the youngest captain of both his state and his national side?

1994 Season

	M	Inns	NO	Runs	HS	Avge	100s	50s	Ct	St	O	M	Runs	Wkts	Avge	Best	5wI	10wM
Test																		
All First	5	9	0	141	57	15.66	-	1	6	-	9.3	2	39	0	-	-	-	-
1-day Int																		
NatWest	1	0	0	0	0	-	-	-	2	-	1	0	3	0	-	-	-	
B & H	2	1	0	37	37	37.00	-	-	2	-	3	0	10	0	-	-	-	
Sunday	9	7	0	80	27	11.42	-	-	1	-	6.2	0	43	0	-	-	-	

Career Performances

	M	Inns	NO	Runs	HS	Avge	100s	50s	Ct	St	Balls	Runs	Wkts	Avge	Best	5wI	10wM
Test																	
All First	25	43	4	725	58 *	18.58	-	3	15	-	453	188	5	37.60	2-28	-	-
1-day Int																	
NatWest	2	1	0	3	3	3.00	-	-	2	-	60	41	0	-	-	-	
B & H	5	4	0	128	47	32.00	-	-	3	-	66	47	1	47.00	1-37	-	
Sunday	33	28	6	373	49 *	16.95	-	-	5	-	398	286	6	47.66	2-22	-	

KEEDY, G.   Lancashire

Name: Gary Keedy
Role: Left-hand bat, slow left-arm bowler
Born: 27 November 1974, Wakefield
Height: 6ft **Weight:** 11st 2lbs
County debut: 1994 (Yorkshire)
Nickname: Bod, Keeds
Parents: Roy and Pat
Marital status: Single
Education: Garforth Comprehensive
Qualifications: 4 GCSEs, junior coaching award
Off-season: Coaching and looking for additional work
Overseas tours: England U18 to South Africa 1992-93, to Denmark 1994; England U19 to Sri Lanka 1993-94
Cricketers particularly admired: Shane Warne, Graham Gooch
Other sports followed: Rugby league
Extras: Player of the Series for England U19 v West Indies U19 in 1993. Graduate of the Yorkshire Cricket Academy. Played for England U19 in the home series against India in 1994. Signed a three-year contract to play for Lancashire from 1995
Best batting: 1 Yorkshire v Sussex, Hove 1994

1994 Season

	M	Inns	NO	Runs	HS	Avge	100s	50s	Ct	St	O	M	Runs	Wkts	Avge	Best	5wl	10wM
Test																		
All First	1	1	0	1	1	1.00	-	-	-	-								
1-day Int																		
NatWest																		
B & H																		
Sunday																		

Career Performances

	M	Inns	NO	Runs	HS	Avge	100s	50s	Ct	St	Balls	Runs	Wkts	Avge	Best	5wl	10wM
Test																	
All First	1	1	0	1	1	1.00	-	-	-	-							
1-day Int																	
NatWest																	
B & H																	
Sunday																	

KELLETT, S. A.   Yorkshire

Name: Simon Andrew Kellett
Role: Opening bat, occasional right-arm medium bowler
Born: 16 October 1967, Mirfield
Height: 6ft 1in **Weight:** 12st 7lbs
Nickname: Kel, Ginner
County debut: 1989
County cap: 1992
1000 runs in a season: 2
1st-Class 50s: 28
1st-Class 100s: 2
1st-Class catches: 73
One-Day 100s: 1
Place in batting averages: 229th av. 16.62 (1993 91st av. 33.44)
Parents: Brian and Valerie
Marital status: Girlfriend, Sarah
Family links with cricket: Father played local league cricket
Education: Whitcliffe Mount High School; Huddersfield Technical College
Qualifications: 5 CSEs, Sports Management course
Overseas tours: Yorkshire U17 to West Indies

Overseas teams played for: Upper Hutt, New Zealand 1991-92; Wellington State 1992
Cricketers particularly admired: Martyn Moxon, Graham Gooch, Tony Greig
Other sports followed: Rugby league (Bradford Northern)
Relaxations: Watching Bradford Northern
Extras: Captained NAYC against MCC; captained Yorkshire to win U19 County Festival at Cambridge; was out to first ball in first-class cricket
Opinions on cricket: 'Make balls bigger and bats wider!'
Best batting: 125* Yorkshire v Derbyshire, Chesterfield 1991

1994 Season

	M	Inns	NO	Runs	HS	Avge	100s	50s	Ct	St	O	M	Runs	Wkts	Avge	Best	5wI	10wM
Test																		
All First	9	16	0	266	50	16.62	-	1	11	-								
1-day Int																		
NatWest																		
B & H																		
Sunday	2	2	0	74	58	37.00	-	1	-	-								

Career Performances

	M	Inns	NO	Runs	HS	Avge	100s	50s	Ct	St	Balls	Runs	Wkts	Avge	Best	5wI	10wM
Test																	
All First	81	138	9	4006	125 *	31.05	2	28	73	-	30	19	0	-	-	-	-
1-day Int																	
NatWest	6	4	0	41	38	10.25	-	-	3	-							
B & H	13	11	1	233	45	23.30	-	-	-	-							
Sunday	28	28	2	667	118 *	25.65	1	3	5	-	18	16	0	-	-	-	

39. Which Australian scored 164 and took 4-26 in helping his team square the home series with South Africa at Adelaide in 1993-94?

KENDALL, W. S. Hampshire

Name: William Salwey Kendall
Role: Right-hand bat, right-arm medium bowler
Born: 18 December 1973, Wimbledon
Height: 5ft 10in **Weight:** 12st 7lb
County debut: No first-team appearance
1st-Class 100s: 1
1st-Class catches: 8
Place in batting averages: 81st av. 36.14
Parents: Tom and Sue
Marital status: Single
Family links with cricket: Father played
club cricket with East Horsley, Incogniti and
Hampshire Hogs. Older brother James plays
for Durham University and played for Surrey
Junior team and both are MCC members.
Education: Bradfield College, Berkshire;
Keble College, Oxford University
Qualifications: 10 GCSEs, 3 A-levels,
1 AS-level
Career outside cricket: Student
Off-season: Completing 2nd year at Oxford
Overseas tours: Bradfield College to Barbados, 1991
Cricketers particularly admired: Bob Taylor, Robin Smith, Jonty Rhodes, Ian Botham
Other sports followed: Interested in most other sports especially golf, football and rugby
Injuries: Broken hand, missed obtaining his Blue in the Varsity match and was off for two
and a half months
Relaxations: Hockey (for Oxford), football, golf, socialising with friends, watching sport,
relaxing at home
Extras: Surrey Young Cricketer of the Year 1992. Awarded Gray-Nicolls Trophy for
Schoolboy Cricketer of the Year in memory of Len Newbury 1992. Made first-class debut
for Oxford University in 1994. Played football for Independent Schools 1992. Offered one-
year contract with Reading FC
Opinions on cricket: 'Fielders should not be penalised for good throws that hit the stumps
when the batsman is in his ground by giving away overthrows. Instead the ball should be
declared dead. Otherwise no real complaints. The game does not seem in as bad a state as
many suggest.'
Best batting: 113* Oxford University v Surrey, The Oval 1994

---

40. Who topped the first-class batting averages on the England A
tour to South Africa in 1993-94?

1994 Season

	M	Inns	NO	Runs	HS	Avge	100s	50s	Ct	St	O	M	Runs	Wkts	Avge	Best	5wI	10wM
Test																		
All First	9	10	3	253	113 *	36.14	1	-	8	-								
1-day Int																		
NatWest																		
B & H																		
Sunday																		

Career Performances

	M	Inns	NO	Runs	HS	Avge	100s	50s	Ct	St	Balls	Runs	Wkts	Avge	Best	5wI	10wM
Test																	
All First	9	10	3	253	113 *	36.14	1	-	8	-							
1-day Int																	
NatWest																	
B & H																	
Sunday																	

KENDRICK, N. M.   Surrey

Name: Neil Michael Kendrick
Role: Right-hand bat, slow left-arm bowler, gully fielder
Born: 11 November 1967, Bromley
Height: 5ft 10in **Weight:** 12st
Nickname: Kendo, Rat, Merson
County debut: 1988
50 wickets in a season: 1
1st-Class 50s: 3
1st-Class 5 w. in innings: 6
1st-Class 10 w. in match: 1
1st-Class catches: 47
Place in batting averages: 256th av. 12.44
(1993 223rd av. 15.80)
Place in bowling averages:
(1993 93rd av. 33.10)
Strike rate: (career 76.35)
Parents: Michael Hall and Anne Patricia
Marital status: Single
Family links with cricket: Father plays club cricket for Old Wilsonians, and sister has represented Kent Ladies
Education: Hayes Primary; Wilson's Grammar School and 'the Surrey dressing-room'

Qualifications: 7 O-levels, 1 A-level, senior coaching certificate
Career outside cricket: Selling duplicating machines
Off-season: Playing cricket, 'trying to convince people to buy machines from me'
Overseas tours: Surrey U19 to Australia 1985-86; Surrey to Dubai
Cricketers particularly admired: Ian Botham, Bishen Bedi
Other sports followed: Football
Relaxations: 'Sleeping, acid jazz music, listening to Ed Piller's views on cricket'
Extras: Released by Surrey at the end of the 1994 season
Opinions on cricket: 'More sponsorship could be found if the game's marketing people looked beyond insurance companies and photocopier salesmen!'
Best batting: 55 Surrey v Middlesex, Lord's 1992
Best bowling: 7-115 Surrey v Nottinghamshire, The Oval 1993

1994 Season

	M	Inns	NO	Runs	HS	Avge	100s	50s	Ct	St	O	M	Runs	Wkts	Avge	Best	5wI	10wM
Test																		
All First	7	11	2	112	25	12.44	-	-	6	-	185.3	36	606	9	67.33	3-159	-	-
1-day Int																		
NatWest																		
B & H																		
Sunday	2	2	2	14	13*	-	-	-	-	-	12.3	0	86	3	28.66	2-48	-	

Career Performances

	M	Inns	NO	Runs	HS	Avge	100s	50s	Ct	St	Balls	Runs	Wkts	Avge	Best	5wI	10wM
Test																	
All First	55	72	19	862	55	16.26	-	3	47	-	10155	4825	133	36.27	7-115	6	1
1-day Int																	
NatWest	1	0	0	0	0	-	-	-	-	-	72	51	1	51.00	1-51	-	
B & H	2	2	1	25	24	25.00	-	-	1	-	132	98	3	32.66	2-47	-	
Sunday	6	4	3	17	13*	17.00	-	-	2	-	237	215	4	53.75	2-48	-	

KENLOCK, S. G.   Surrey

Name: Stratford (Mark) G. Kenlock
Role: Right-hand bat, left-arm medium bowler
Born: 16 April 1965, Jamaica
Height: 5ft 11in **Weight:** 12st
Nickname: Kenny
County debut: 1994
1st-Class catches: 1
Parents: Vincent and Lynette
Marital status: Single

Children: Brandon, 13 February 1994
Family links with cricket: Brother plays league cricket
Education: Stockwell Manor School; Vauxhall College
Career outside cricket: Engineer
Off-season: Coaching children
Overseas tours: Surrey to Australia 1995
Cricketers particularly admired: Viv Richards, Michael Holding
Other sports followed: Football, American football
Injuries: Split webbing on left hand, out for six weeks
Relaxations: Listening to music
Extras: Received 2nd XI cap in 1994 and 2nd XI Bowler of the Year
Opinions on cricket: 'Four-day cricket is now proving to be better cricket. Sunday League cricket should remain 40-over game – coloured clothing is good for the game.'
Best bowling: 3-104 Surrey v Kent, The Oval 1994

1994 Season

	M	Inns	NO	Runs	HS	Avge	100s	50s	Ct	St	O	M	Runs	Wkts	Avge	Best	5wI	10wM
Test																		
All First	2	0	0	0	0	-	-	-	1	-	53	10	186	3	62.00	3-104	-	-
1-day Int																		
NatWest																		
B & H																		
Sunday	5	0	0	0	0	-	-	-	3	-	36.2	3	171	10	17.10	4-30	-	

Career Performances

	M	Inns	NO	Runs	HS	Avge	100s	50s	Ct	St	Balls	Runs	Wkts	Avge	Best	5wI	10wM
Test																	
All First	2	0	0	0	0	-	-	-	1	-	318	186	3	62.00	3-104	-	
1-day Int																	
NatWest																	
B & H																	
Sunday	5	0	0	0	0	-	-	-	3	-	218	171	10	17.10	4-30	-	

KENNIS, G. J. Surrey

Name: Gregor John Kennis
Role: Right-hand bat, right-arm off-spin bowler
Born: 9 March 1974, Yokohama, Japan
Height: 6ft 1in **Weight:** 12st
County debut: 1994
Parents: Michael and Sally
Marital status: Single
Family links with cricket: 'Father plays for
Lloyds Register of Shipping CC (his
company side) and is NCA Senior Coach.
Mother made the teas when I was at school.'
Education: Tiffin Boys' School; Stewart
Cricket Academy; 'Matt Church's room (on
the MCC groundstaff)'
Qualifications: 9 GCSEs, 1 A-level,
NCA senior coach
Career outside cricket: 'All I ever wanted
to do was to play cricket'
Off-season: 'Coaching at the Stewart
Cricket Academy'
Overseas tours: Surrey U19 to Barbados 1991
Cricketers particularly admired: Neil Stewart, David Gower, Allan Border, David Boon
Other sports followed: Horse racing and football (West Ham)
Relaxations: Golf and listening to music
Extras: Got hit for the biggest six ever seen at The Oval by David Ward
Opinions on cricket: 'I think more should be done to encourage cricket to be played in schools.'
Best batting: 23 Surrey v Oxford University, The Oval 1994

1994 Season

	M	Inns	NO	Runs	HS	Avge	100s	50s	Ct	St	O	M	Runs	Wkts	Avge	Best	5wI	10wM
Test																		
All First	1	2	0	41	23	20.50	-	-	2	-								
1-day Int																		
NatWest																		
B & H																		
Sunday																		

	M	Inns	NO	Runs	HS	Avge	100s	50s	Ct	St	Balls	Runs	Wkts	Avge	Best	5wI	10wM
Test																	
All First	1	2	0	41	23	20.50	-	-	2	-							
1-day Int																	
NatWest																	
B & H																	
Sunday																	

KERR, J. I. D.   Somerset

Name: Jason Ian Douglas Kerr
Role: Right-hand bat, right-arm fast-medium bowler
Born: 7 April 1974, Bolton, Lancashire
Height: 6ft 3in **Weight:** 12st 6lbs
Nickname: Norman, Normski, Stretchy
County debut: 1993
1st-Class catches: 4
Place in bowling averages:
(1993 44th av. 27.00)
Strike rate: (career 52.06)
Parents: Len and Janet
Marital status: Single
Family links with cricket: 'Father manages my league club, Tonge'
Education: Withins High School; Bolton Met College
Qualifications: 5 GCSEs, BTEC National Diploma in Business Studies, cricket coach
Off-season: Playing first-grade cricket in Sydney, Australia
Overseas tours: England U19 to India 1992-93
Cricketers particularly admired: David Gower, Viv Richards, Ian Botham
Other sports followed: Golf, football (all sports)
Injuries: Ripped cartilage on left lower rib, missed four months
Relaxations: Playing golf, socialising, squash, TV, swimming, sleeping, listening to music, spending time with friends and girlfriend Emma
Opinions on cricket: 'Too much cricket is played. Teams can be playing for weeks on the run. This is too much for any player. 2nd XI cricket should be played on county wickets as 2nd XI is preparation for first-class.'
Best batting: 19* Somerset v Essex, Chelmsford 1993
Best bowling: 3-47 Somerset v Essex, Chelmsford 1993

1994 Season

	M	Inns	NO	Runs	HS	Avge	100s	50s	Ct	St	O	M	Runs	Wkts	Avge	Best	5wI	10wM
Test																		
All First	1	2	0	5	4	2.50	-	-	1	-	21	3	91	0	-		-	-
1-day Int																		
NatWest	1	1	0	0	0	0.00	-	-	-	-								
B & H																		
Sunday	5	4	2	6	3	3.00	-	-	-	-	29.2	2	158	4	39.50	2-45	-	

Career Performances

	M	Inns	NO	Runs	HS	Avge	100s	50s	Ct	St	Balls	Runs	Wkts	Avge	Best	5wI	10wM
Test																	
All First	8	13	3	72	19 *	7.20	-	-	4	-	781	496	15	33.06	3-47	-	-
1-day Int																	
NatWest	1	1	0	0	0	0.00	-	-	-	-							
B & H																	
Sunday	14	12	4	66	17	8.25	-	-	1	-	596	513	17	30.17	3-34	-	

KERSEY, G. J.   Surrey

Name: Graham James Kersey
Role: Right-hand bat, wicket-keeper
Born: 19 May 1971, Greenwich
Height: 5ft 8in **Weight:** 10st 7lbs
Nickname: Scuz
County debut: 1991 (Kent), 1993 (Surrey)
1st-Class catches: 64
1st-Class stumpings: 6
Place in batting averages: 249th av. 14.11
(1993 228th av. 15.11)
Parents: Don and Beryl
Marital status: Single
Family links with cricket: Brother Ian
played for Kent U19 and UAU 2nd XI
Education: Bexley-Erith Technical
High School
Qualifications: 6 O-levels, 1 A-level,
NCA coaching certificate
Overseas tours: Kent Schools U17 to
Singapore and New Zealand 1987-88
Overseas teams played for: Eastern Suburbs District, Brisbane 1989-91; Windhoek
College of Education, Namibia 1992-93; Easts, Brisbane 1993-94

Cricketers particularly admired: Alan Knott, Jack Russell, David Gower, Steve Waugh, Carl Hooper
Other sports followed: Football, rugby
Relaxations: 'A pint of Guinness and port with Tony Murphy'
Opinions on cricket: 'Rules about qualifying for England are not nearly strict enough. 2nd XI cricket should be played on same standard wickets as first-class.'
Best batting: 39 Surrey v Durham, Darlington 1994

1994 Season

	M	Inns	NO	Runs	HS	Avge	100s	50s	Ct	St	O	M	Runs	Wkts	Avge	Best	5wI	10wM
Test																		
All First	7	11	2	127	39	14.11	-	-	16	2								
1-day Int																		
NatWest																		
B & H																		
Sunday	5	2	0	37	37	18.50	-	-	7	-								

Career Performances

	M	Inns	NO	Runs	HS	Avge	100s	50s	Ct	St	Balls	Runs	Wkts	Avge	Best	5wI	10wM
Test																	
All First	23	34	6	468	39	16.71	-	-	64	6							
1-day Int																	
NatWest																	
B & H																	
Sunday	13	7	1	165	50	27.50	-	1	18	4							

41. Who took the most first-class wickets on the England A tour to South Africa in 1993-94?

KETTLEBOROUGH, R. A. Yorkshire

Name: Richard Allan Kettleborough
Role: Left-hand bat, right-arm medium
bowler
Born: 15 March 1973, Sheffield
Height: 5ft 10in **Weight:** 12st 7lbs
Nickname: Ketts, Rusty
County debut: 1994
Parents: Allan and Pat
Marital status: Single
Family links with cricket: Father represented
Yorkshire and Nottinghamshire and is now
coach at Worksop College
Education: Laughton All Saints
Junior School; Worksop College;
Dinnington Comprehensive School
Qualifications: 5 GCSEs, City & Guilds in
Recreational Management, Senior Coaching
Award
Career outside cricket: 'I would love to
run my own pub and nightclub'
Off-season: 'Coaching schools for Yorkshire, coaching at Headingley, getting fit for 1995'
Overseas tours: Worksop College to Australia 1988-89; England U18 to Canada 1991
Overseas teams played for: Somerset West, Cape Town 1993-94
Cricketers particularly admired: David Gower 'was and still is a childhood hero', David
Byas, Curtly Ambrose, Michael Vaughan
Other sports followed: Football, 'I follow Sheffield Wednesday at home and away'
Relaxations: Watching Sheffield Wednesday all over the country. Spending time with
girlfriend, Sarah, and going to the pub with friends
Extras: Won the Lord's Taverners U15 award for the Most Promising Young Cricketer in
1988. 2nd XI cap at Yorkshire
Opinions on cricket: 'More 2nd XI cricket should be played on county grounds.'
Best batting: 25 Yorkshire v Northamptonshire, Luton 1994

1994 Season

	M	Inns	NO	Runs	HS	Avge	100s	50s	Ct	St	O	M	Runs	Wkts	Avge	Best	5wI	10wM
Test																		
All First	1	2	1	49	25	49.00	-	-	-	-	6	2	18	0	-		-	-
1-day Int																		
NatWest																		
B & H																		
Sunday	3	2	1	32	28	32.00	-	-	-	-	5	0	29	1	29.00	1-17	-	

Career Performances

	M	Inns	NO	Runs	HS	Avge	100s	50s	Ct	St	Balls	Runs	Wkts	Avge	Best	5wI	10wM
Test																	
All First	1	2	1	49	25	49.00	-	-	-	-	36	18	0	-		-	-
1-day Int																	
NatWest																	
B & H																	
Sunday	3	2	1	32	28	32.00	-	-	-	-	30	29	1	29.00	1-17	-

KHAN, G. A. Essex

Name: Gul Abbass Khan
Role: Right-hand bat, leg-break bowler
Born: 31 December 1973, Gujrat, Pakistan
Height: 5ft 9in **Weight:** 11st
Nickname: Gulie
County debut: No first-team appearance
Parents: Mohammed Qufait and
Shahnaz Aslam
Marital status: Single
Family links with cricket: Father played
cricket in Pakistan
Education: Valentines High School;
Ipswich School; Swansea University
Qualifications: 8 GCSEs, 3 A-levels,
studying for a degree
Career outside cricket: Student
Off-season: Final year at Swansea
Overseas tours: English Schools U17,
U18 and U19 tours; Ipswich School
to Australia
Overseas teams played for: P&T Gymkhana, Lahore, Pakistan
Cricketers particularly admired: Brian Lara, Sachin Tendulkar, Javed Miandad, Duncan
Verry (Butch), Andrew Alexander
Other sports followed: Rugby and golf
Relaxations: Reading, music, spending time with family
Extras: *Daily Telegraph* Batsman of the Year (South of England) at U15 and U19
Opinions on cricket: 'Coaches put too much emphasis on the A technique.'

---

42. In 1993-94 each game in a 3-0 three-match Test series was won
by an innings, who won and who was the defeated country?

KHAN, W. G.   Warwickshire

Name: Wasim Gulzar Khan
Role: Left-hand bat, right-arm leg-break bowler
Born: 26 February 1971, Birmingham
Height: 6ft 2in **Weight:** 11st 7lbs
Nickname: Mowgli, Wasby, Dog
County debut: 1992 (one-day)
Parents: Raja Gulzar (deceased) and Zarina Begum
Marital status: Single
Education: Small Heath Secondary School, Birmingham; Josiah Mason Sixth Form College, Birmingham
Qualifications: 6 O-levels, 1 A-level
Off-season: Playing in Melbourne
Overseas tours: Warwicks to Cape Town 1993
Overseas teams played for: Western Suburbs, Sydney 1990-91; North Perth, Western Australia 1991-93; Albion, Melbourne 1993-95
Cricketers particularly admired: Wasim Akram, Brian Lara, Andy Moles, Graham Thorpe, Paul Terry, Gladstone Small
Other sports followed: Football (Leeds United), boxing
Relaxations: Listening to music, spending time with family and friends, playing golf, 'listening to Michael Bell's chat-up lines'
Extras: Most Promising Young Cricketer 1990. Scored four centuries in a row for Warwickshire U19. Scored 171* v Northants in second trial game for Warwickshire 2nd XI. England Schools U19. Won Oxford/Cambridge U19 Festival 1989, 1990
Opinions on cricket: '2nd XI wickets should be similar to first-class wickets in their preparation and covering. Maybe through no fault of their own players' progression in the game is seriously restricted by the lack of opportunity given to them!'

1994 Season (did not make any first-class or one-day appearance)

Career Performances

	M	Inns	NO	Runs	HS	Avge	100s	50s	Ct	St	Balls	Runs	Wkts	Avge	Best	5wI	10wM
Test																	
All First																	
1-day Int																	
NatWest																	
B & H																	
Sunday	1	1	0	7	7	7.00	-	-	-	-							

KIRTLEY, R. J. Sussex

Name: Robert James Kirtley
Role: Right-hand bat, right-arm fast-medium bowler
Born: 10 January 1975, Eastbourne
Height: 5ft 11in **Weight:** 11st 11lbs
Nickname: Amby
County debut: No first-team appearance
Parents: Bob and Pip
Marital status: Single
Family links with cricket: Brother plays league cricket for Eastbourne
Education: St Andrews School, Eastbourne; Clifton College, Bristol
Qualifications: 9 GCSEs, 2 A-levels
Off-season: Playing abroad and touring in Sri Lanka
Overseas tours: Sussex U19 to Barbados 1992-93, Sussex Youth XI to Sri Lanka 1994-95
Cricketers particularly admired: Curtly Ambrose, Jim Andrew and Darren Gough
Other sports followed: Rugby, hockey and football (Brighton & Hove Albion)
Relaxations: Sleeping

43. Who has taken over from Graham Gooch as Essex captain for 1995?

KNIGHT, N. V.   Warwickshire

Name: Nicholas Verity Knight
Role: Left-hand bat,
right-arm medium-fast bowler,
close fielder
Born: 28 November 1969, Watford
Height: 6ft 1in **Weight:** 12st 7lbs
Nickname: Knighty, Stitch
County debut: 1991 (Essex)
County cap: 1994 (Essex)
1st-Class 50s: 11
1st-Class 100s: 7
1st-Class catches: 59
Place in batting averages: 26th av. 47.20
(1993 173rd av. 22.69)
Parents: John and Rosemary
Marital status: Single
Family links with cricket: Father played
for Cambridgeshire, brother plays club
cricket for St Giles in Cambridge

Education: St John's School, Cambridge; Felsted Prep; Felsted School; Loughborough University
Qualifications: 9 O-levels, 3 A-levels, BSc (Hons) Sociology, coaching qualification
Off-season: Touring India with England A
Overseas tours: Felsted School to Australia 1986-87; England A to India 1994-95
Overseas teams played for: Northern Districts, Sydney 1991-92; East Torrens, Adelaide 1992-94
Cricketers particularly admired: David Gower
Other sports followed: Most sports
Injuries: Ruptured thigh muscle, missed one month
Relaxations: 'Eating nice food, playing golf, listening to Kylie Minogue, Gloria Estefan, Sonia'
Extras: Captained English Schools 1987 and 1988, England YC v New Zealand 1989 and Combined Universities 1991. Played hockey for Essex and Young England. Played rugby for Eastern Counties. Won *Daily Telegraph* award 1988; voted Gray-Nicolls Cricketer of the Year 1988, Cricket Society Cricketer of the Year 1989, Essex Young Player of the Year 1991 and Essex U19 Player of the Year. Left Essex at the end of 1994 season to join Warwickshire
Opinions on cricket: 'Longer tea break. Too many overs in a day.'
Best batting: 157 Essex v Sussex, Chelmsford 1994
Best bowling: 1-61 Essex v Middlesex, Uxbridge 1994

1994 Season

	M	Inns	NO	Runs	HS	Avge	100s	50s	Ct	St	O	M	Runs	Wkts	Avge	Best	5wI	10wM
Test																		
All First	12	21	1	944	157	47.20	4	3	22	-	11.4	0	61	1	61.00	1-61	-	-
1-day Int																		
NatWest	1	1	0	23	23	23.00	-	-	-	-								
B & H	2	1	1	26	26 *	-	-	-	-	-								
Sunday	13	13	1	275	61 *	22.91	-	1	3	-	6	0	41	1	41.00	1-41	-	

Career Performances

	M	Inns	NO	Runs	HS	Avge	100s	50s	Ct	St	Balls	Runs	Wkts	Avge	Best	5wI	10wM
Test																	
All First	46	74	8	2454	157	37.18	7	11	59	-	100	93	1	93.00	1-61	-	-
1-day Int																	
NatWest	4	4	1	113	81 *	37.66	-	1	-	-							
B & H	13	11	2	140	36	15.55	-	-	7	-	6	4	0	-		-	-
Sunday	45	39	7	746	61 *	23.31	-	2	19	-	84	85	2	42.50	1-14	-	

KRIKKEN, K. M.   Derbyshire

Name: Karl Matthew Krikken
Role: Right-hand bat, wicket-keeper
Born: 9 April 1969, Bolton
Height: 5ft 10in **Weight:** 12st
Nickname: Krikk
County debut: 1987 (one-day),
1989 (first-class)
County cap: 1992
1st-Class 50s: 8
1st-Class catches: 223
1st-Class stumpings: 19
Place in batting averages: 162nd av. 25.05
(1993 219th av. 16.21)
Parents: Brian and Irene
Marital status: Engaged to Liz
Family links with cricket: Father kept
wicket for Lancashire and Worcestershire
Education: Horwich Parish Church School;
Rivington and Blackrod High School and 6th
Form College
Qualifications: 6 O-levels, 3 A-levels, cricket coaching certificates
Career outside cricket: Matthew Vandrau's fitness trainer

Overseas tours: Derbyshire to Bermuda 1993

Overseas teams played for: CBC Old Boys, Kimberley, South Africa 1988-89; Green Island, Dunedin, New Zealand 1990-91; United, Cape Town 1992-93: Rivertonians, Cape Town 1993-94

Cricketers particularly admired: Bob Taylor, Bruce French, Derek Randall, Ray Eccleshare, Jack Russell

Other sports followed: Football (Wigan FC, Bolton FC – 'someone's got to do it'), any ball sports

Injuries: Torn hamstring – out for four weeks

Relaxations: Golf, Chinese meals, videos, cricket, most sports, 'winding Corky up, getting wound up by Corky'

Extras: Derbyshire Supporters' Player of the Year 1991, Derbyshire Clubman of the Year 1993, 'the Phillip DeFreitas "shirking" award for June 1994'

Opinions on cricket: 'It's the best game in the world.'

Best batting: 85* Derbyshire v Glamorgan, Cardiff 1994

1994 Season

	M	Inns	NO	Runs	HS	Avge	100s	50s	Ct	St	O	M	Runs	Wkts	Avge	Best	5wl	10wM
Test																		
All First	15	27	10	426	85 *	25.05	-	2	26	2								
1-day Int																		
NatWest	2	2	2	14	8 *	-	-	-	2	-								
B & H	2	1	0	0	0	0.00	-	-	-	1								
Sunday	13	4	3	30	15	30.00	-	-	22	-								

Career Performances

	M	Inns	NO	Runs	HS	Avge	100s	50s	Ct	St	Balls	Runs	Wkts	Avge	Best	5wl	10wM
Test																	
All First	102	149	30	2329	85 *	19.57	-	8	223	19	36	40	0	-		-	-
1-day Int																	
NatWest	5	4	3	41	18	41.00	-	-	4	-							
B & H	11	8	3	94	37 *	18.80	-	-	16	1							
Sunday	53	29	9	315	44 *	15.75	-	-	66	4							

KUMBLE, A.   Northamptonshire

Name: Anil Kumble
Role: Right-hand bat,
leg-spin bowler
Born: 17 December 1969, Bangalore
County debut: No first-team appearance
Test debut: 1990
Tests: 17
One-Day Internationals: 46
1st-Class 50s: 5
1st-Class 100s: 3
1st-Class 5 w. in innings: 14
1st-Class 10 w. in match: 3
1st-Class catches: 24
One-Day 5 w. in innings: 2
Strike rate: (career 61.36)
Off-season: Playing for India
Overseas tours: India to England 1990,
to Australia 1991-92, to South Africa 1992-93,
to Zimbabwe 1992-93, to Sri Lanka 1993-94
Overseas teams played for: Karnataka, India
Best batting: 154* Karnataka v Kerala, Bijapur 1991-92
Best bowling: 7-59 India v Sri Lanka, Lucknow 1993-94

1994 Season (did not make any first-class or one-day appearance)

Career Performances

	M	Inns	NO	Runs	HS	Avge	100s	50s	Ct	St	Balls	Runs	Wkts	Avge	Best	5wI	10wM
Test	17	15	2	132	21 *	10.15	-	-	8	-	5692	2101	86	24.43	7-59	5	1
All First	53	62	14	1377	154 *	28.68	3	5	24	-	13808	5576	225	24.78	7-59	14	3
1-day Int	46	21	8	133	24	10.23	-	-	13	-	2563	1683	54	31.16	6-12	2	
NatWest																	
B & H																	
Sunday																	

LAMB, A. J. Northamptonshire

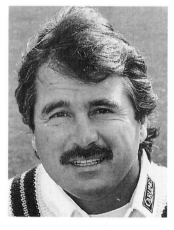

Name: Allan Joseph Lamb
Role: Right-hand bat, right-arm medium bowler, county captain
Born: 20 June 1954, Langebaanweg, Cape Province, South Africa
Height: 5ft 8in **Weight:** 12st
Nickname: Lambie, Legger, Joe
County debut: 1978
County cap: 1978
Benefit: 1988 (£134,000)
Test debut: 1982
Tests: 79
One-Day Internationals: 122
1000 runs in a season: 13
1st-Class 50s: 158
1st-Class 100s: 86
1st-Class 200s: 4
1st-Class catches: 353
One-Day 100s: 18
Place in batting averages: 44th av. 43.23 (1993 46th av. 40.44)
Parents: Michael and Joan
Wife and date of marriage: Lindsay, 8 December 1979
Children: Katie-Ann and Richard Edward Thomas
Family links with cricket: Father and brother played in the B section of the Currie Cup
Education: Wynberg Boys' High School; Abbotts College
Qualifications: Matriculation
Career outside cricket: Promotions company
Overseas tours: With England to Australia and New Zealand 1982-83, to New Zealand and Pakistan 1983-84, to India and Australia 1984-85, to West Indies 1985-86, to Australia 1986-87, to India and Pakistan (World Cup) 1987-88, to India and West Indies 1989-90, to Australia 1990-91, to New Zealand 1991-92
Overseas teams played for: Western Province 1972-81, 1992-93; Orange Free State 1987-88
Cricketers particularly admired: Dennis Lillee, Viv Richards
Other sports followed: Tennis, golf, rugby and horse racing
Relaxations: Fly-fishing (trout and salmon)
Extras: Was primarily a bowler when he first played school cricket in South Africa. Made first-class debut for Western Province in 1972-73. Top of first-class batting averages in 1980, when he was one of *Wisden*'s Five Cricketers of the Year. Qualified to play for England in 1982. Appointed Northamptonshire captain 1989. Captained England in Tests v West Indies in 1989-90 and v Australia in 1990-91 after injuries to Graham Gooch. Hit three centuries in consecutive Tests v West Indies 1984 and, in his first Test as captain, made a century v West Indies at Bridgetown. Northamptonshire Player of the Year 1992

Opinions on cricket: 'Get our one-day domestic game in line with overseas, i.e. we should play 50 overs as they do abroad. Our longer competition could be 55 not 60.'
Best batting: 294 Orange Free State v Eastern Province, Bloemfontein 1987-88
Best bowling: 2-29 Northamptonshire v Lancashire, Lytham 1991

1994 Season

	M	Inns	NO	Runs	HS	Avge	100s	50s	Ct	St	O	M	Runs	Wkts	Avge	Best	5wI	10wM
Test																		
All First	15	22	1	908	131	43.23	2	5	17	-								
1-day Int																		
NatWest	3	3	1	142	129 *	71.00	1	-	1	-								
B & H	1	1	0	25	25	25.00	-	-	-	-								
Sunday	12	11	1	304	78	30.40	-	2	2	-								

Career Performances

	M	Inns	NO	Runs	HS	Avge	100s	50s	Ct	St	Balls	Runs	Wkts	Avge	Best	5wI	10wM
Test	79	139	10	4656	142	36.09	14	18	75	-	30	23	1	23.00	1-6	-	
All First	450	744	104	31131	294	48.64	86	158	353	-	305	199	8	24.87	2-29	-	-
1-day Int	122	118	16	4010	118	39.31	4	26	31	-	6	3	0	-	-	-	
NatWest	50	49	5	1895	129 *	43.06	4	12	14	-	8	12	1	12.00	1-4	-	
B & H	70	64	11	2557	126 *	48.24	5	17	25	-	6	11	1	11.00	1-11	-	
Sunday	186	178	24	5439	132 *	35.31	5	30	49	-							

LAMPITT, S. R.   Worcestershire

Name: Stuart Richard Lampitt
Role: Right-hand bat, right-arm fast-medium bowler
Born: 29 July 1966, Wolverhampton
Height: 5ft 11in **Weight:** 13st 10lb
Nickname: Jed
County debut: 1985
County cap: 1989
50 wickets in a season: 3
1st-Class 50s: 12
1st-Class 100s: 1
1st-Class 5 w. in innings: 10
1st-Class catches: 75
One-Day 5 w. in innings: 3
Place in batting averages: 131st av. 29.71
(1993 201st av. 19.04)
Place in bowling averages: 11th av. 23.18
(1993 83rd av. 31.23)

Strike rate: 48.06 (career 55.68)
Parents: Joseph Charles and Muriel Ann
Marital status: Single
Education: Kingswinford Secondary School; Dudley Technical College
Qualifications: 7 O-levels; Diploma in Business Studies
Career outside cricket: 'Various, too many to mention'
Off-season: 'Good question. Staying in UK and trying to find work'
Overseas tours: NCA U19 to Bermuda; Worcestershire to Bahamas 1990, to Zimbabwe 1990-91, to South Africa 1991-92
Overseas teams played for: Mangere, Auckland 1986-88; University CC, Perth 1991-93
Cricketers particularly admired: All first-class cricketers
Other sports followed: Football (Wolves), golf, and most ball sports
Relaxations: 'Playing golf. Play football for Oldbury Utd in West Midlands Premier League.'
Extras: Took five wickets and made 42 for Stourbridge in final of the William Younger Cup at Lord's in 1986. One of the Whittingdale Young Players of the Year 1990. 'Must be the only bowler to be hit for six first ball by Adrian Jones and Phil Tufnell (two master batsmen)'
Opinions on cricket: 'Four-day cricket is a winner. Better quality of games, and the cricket is better. However, I feel there is room for improvement in pitches.'
Best batting: 122 Worcestershire v Middlesex, Lord's 1994
Best bowling: 5-32 Worcestershire v Kent, Worcester 1989

1994 Season

	M	Inns	NO	Runs	HS	Avge	100s	50s	Ct	St	O	M	Runs	Wkts	Avge	Best	5wI	10wM
Test																		
All First	17	26	5	624	122	29.71	1	2	12	-	512.4	127	1484	64	23.18	5-33	2	-
1-day Int																		
NatWest	5	3	1	34	16 *	17.00	-	-	3	-	37.3	4	192	6	32.00	3-44	-	
B & H	4	2	1	7	6 *	7.00	-	-	-	-	42.2	4	158	9	17.55	6-26	1	
Sunday	16	12	4	197	35 *	24.62	-	-	3	-	99.2	7	435	23	18.91	4-22	-	

Career Performances

	M	Inns	NO	Runs	HS	Avge	100s	50s	Ct	St	Balls	Runs	Wkts	Avge	Best	5wI	10wM
Test																	
All First	124	153	30	2761	122	22.44	1	12	75	-	15897	8355	286	29.21	5-32	10	-
1-day Int																	
NatWest	17	10	3	88	17	12.57	-	-	5	-	899	642	27	23.77	5-22	1	
B & H	22	11	3	127	41	15.87	-	-	7	-	1197	840	36	23.33	6-26	1	
Sunday	91	50	18	612	41 *	19.12	-	-	27	-	3081	2533	92	27.53	5-67	1	

LANEY, J. S.   Hampshire

Name: Jason Scott Laney
Role: Right-hand bat,
right-arm off-spin bowler
Born: 24 April 1973, Winchester
Height: 5ft 10in **Weight:** 12st 7lbs
Nickname: Chucky, Hurler
County debut: 1993 (one-day)
Parents: Geoff and Pam
Marital status: Single
Family links with cricket: Grandfather
played good club cricket
Education: Pewsey Vale Comprehensive;
St John's, Marlborough;
Leeds Metropolitan University
Qualifications: 8 GCSEs, 2 A-levels, BA
(Hons) in Sports Science
Off-season: Spending winter in Nelson, New
Zealand
Overseas tours: England U18 to
Canada 1991
Overseas teams played for: Wakatu , New Zealand 1994-95
Cricketers particularly admired: Rupert Cox 'for his madcap attitude at times', Paul
Terry, Kevan James
Other sports followed: Football (Swindon Town), golf
Relaxations: Playing golf whenever possible, eating out, relaxing with a beer or two
Opinions on cricket: 'The extra hour in 2nd XI cricket has a good purpose but is disliked
by 99% of players. Tea and lunch intervals could be a bit longer.'

1994 Season (did not make any first-class or one-day appearance)

Career Performances

	M	Inns	NO	Runs	HS	Avge	100s	50s	Ct	St	Balls	Runs	Wkts	Avge	Best	5wI	10wM
Test																	
All First																		
1-day Int																		
NatWest																			
B & H																			
Sunday	1	1	0	12	12	12.00	-	-	-	-							

LARA, B. C. Warwickshire

Name: Brian Charles Lara
Role: Left-hand bat, leg-spin bowler
Born: 2 May 1969, Port of Spain, Trinidad
County debut: 1994
County cap: 1994
Test debut: 1990-91
Tests: 16
One-Day Internationals: 68
1000 runs in a season: 1
1st-Class 50s: 26
1st-Class 100s: 22
1st-Class 200s: 2
1st-Class 300s: 1
1st-Class 500s: 1
1st-Class catches: 102
One-Day 100s: 4
Place in batting averages: 2nd av. 89.82
Overseas tours: With West Indies to
Pakistan 1990-91, to England 1991, to Australia
1992-93, to Sri Lanka 1993-94, to India 1994-95, to New Zealand 1994-95
Overseas teams played for: Trinidad
Extras: In an amazing few weeks in 1994 he broke the record for the highest Test score 375,
v England at Antigua, and the highest first-class score 501*, for Warwickshire v Durham
at Edgbaston, he also passed 1000 runs in an English season in only seven innings equalling
the record held by Don Bradman, scoring a record seven centuries in his first eight innings.
He also created a record by scoring centuries in his first four Championship innings. Signed
new contract with Warwickshire to start in 1996.
Best batting: 501* Warwickshire v Durham, Edgbaston 1994
Best bowling: 1-22 Trinidad v Leeward Islands, Plymouth (Montserrat) 1993-94

1994 Season

	M	Inns	NO	Runs	HS	Avge	100s	50s	Ct	St	O	M	Runs	Wkts	Avge	Best	5wI	10wM
Test																		
All First	15	25	2	2066	501 *	89.82	9	3	11	-	21	1	112	0	-	-	-	-
1-day Int																		
NatWest	5	5	0	158	81	31.60	-	1	3	-								
B & H	3	3	0	112	70	37.33	-	1	-	-								
Sunday	14	14	0	364	75	26.00	-	3	6	-								

Career Performances

	M	Inns	NO	Runs	HS	Avge	100s	50s	Ct	St	Balls	Runs	Wkts	Avge	Best	5wI	10wM
Test	16	26	0	1628	375	62.61	3	8	27	-	12	4	0	-	-	-	
All First	80	130	4	7320	501 *	58.09	22	26	102	-	257	215	1	215.00	1-22	-	
1-day Int	68	68	5	2529	153	40.14	4	18	38	-	12	5	0	-	-	-	
NatWest	5	5	0	158	81	31.60	-	1	3	-							
B & H	3	3	0	112	70	37.33	-	1	-	-							
Sunday	14	14	0	364	75	26.00	-	3	6	-							

LARKINS, W. Durham

Name: Wayne Larkins
Role: Right-hand bat, right-arm medium bowler
Born: 22 November 1953, Roxton, Beds
Height: 5ft 11in **Weight:** 12st
Nickname: Ned
County debut: 1972 (Northamptonshire), 1992 (Durham)
County cap: 1976
Benefit: 1986
Test debut: 1979-80
Tests: 13
One-Day Internationals: 25
1000 runs in a season: 13
1st-Class 50s: 115
1st-Class 100s: 57
1st-Class 200s: 3
1st-Class 5 w. in innings: 1
1st-Class catches: 295
One-Day 100s: 23
One-Day 5 w. in innings: 1

Place in batting averages: 54th av 40.66 (1993 58th av. 38.70)
Parents: Mavis (father deceased)
Wife and date of marriage: Jane Elaine, 22 March 1975
Children: Philippa Jane, 30 May 1981
Family links with cricket: Father was umpire. Brother, Melvin, played for Bedford Town for many years
Education: Bushmead, Eaton Socon, Huntingdon
Overseas tours: England to Australia and India 1979-80, to India and Sri Lanka 1981-82, to India and West Indies 1989-90, to Australia 1990-91; unofficial English XI to South Africa 1981-82
Other sports followed: Golf, football (was on Notts County's books), squash

Relaxations: Gardening
Extras: Banned from Test cricket for three years for joining rebel tour of South Africa in 1982. Recalled to Test team in 1986 but withdrew owing to thumb injury and missed another Test recall in 1987 because of a football injury. Eventually returned to Test cricket in the West Indies in 1989-90, nine years after his last appearance. Moved to Durham at the beginning of the 1992 season
Best batting : 252 Northamptonshire v Glamorgan, Cardiff 1983
Best bowling : 5-59 Northamptonshire v Worcestershire, Worcester 1984

1994 Season

	M	Inns	NO	Runs	HS	Avge	100s	50s	Ct	St	O	M	Runs	Wkts	Avge	Best	5wI	10wM
Test																		
All First	16	27	3	976	158 *	40.66	1	6	11	-	5	0	39	0	-	-	-	-
1-day Int																		
NatWest	2	2	0	64	34	32.00	-	-	1	-								
B & H	1	1	0	19	19	19.00	-	-	-	-								
Sunday	12	11	1	421	131 *	42.10	2	1	4	-								

Career Performances

	M	Inns	NO	Runs	HS	Avge	100s	50s	Ct	St	Balls	Runs	Wkts	Avge	Best	5wI	10wM
Test	13	25	1	493	64	20.54	-	3	8	-							
All First	469	819	54	26405	252	34.51	57	115	295	-	3517	1915	42	45.59	5-59	1	-
1-day Int	25	24	0	591	124	24.62	1	-	9	-	15	22	0	-	-	-	
NatWest	51	50	3	1764	121 *	37.53	2	12	21	-	455	274	4	68.50	2-38	-	
B & H	77	73	4	2409	132	34.91	6	10	18	-	675	444	16	27.75	4-37	-	
Sunday	280	269	17	7378	172 *	29.27	14	36	86	-	2033	1679	57	29.45	5-32	1	

LATHWELL, M. N.   Somerset

Name: Mark Nicholas Lathwell
Role: Right-hand bat, right-arm medium and off-break bowler
Born: 26 December 1971, Bletchley, Bucks
Height: 5ft 8in **Weight:** 11st 6lbs
Nickname: Lathers, Rowdy
County debut: 1991
County cap: 1992
Test debut: 1993
Tests: 2
1000 runs in a season: 2
1st-Class 50s: 25
1st-Class 100s: 7
1st-Class 200s: 1

1st-Class catches: 52
One-Day 100s: 1
Place in batting averages: 57th av. 39.67
(1993 90th av. 33.63)
Parents: Derek Peter and Valerie
Marital status: Single
Family links with cricket: Brother plays local
club cricket; father is a 'retired' club cricketer
and now senior coach
Education: Overstone Primary, Wing,
Bucks; Southmead Primary, Braunton, N
Devon; Braunton Comprehensive
Qualifications: 5 GCSEs
Career outside cricket: Bank clerk
Overseas tours: England A to Australia
1992-93, to South Africa 1993-94
Cricketers particularly admired: Ian Botham,
Graham Gooch
Other sports followed: Snooker, darts
Relaxations: Fishing, darts, playing cards, eating, swimming
Extras: Spent one season on Lord's groundstaff. Played for England U19 v Australia U19
1991. Young Player of the Year and Somerset Player of the Year 1992: Cricket Writers'
Club Young Cricketer of the Year 1993
Best batting: 206 Somerset v Surrey, Bath 1994
Best bowling: 2-21 Somerset v Sussex, Hove 1994

1994 Season

	M	Inns	NO	Runs	HS	Avge	100s	50s	Ct	St	O	M	Runs	Wkts	Avge	Best	5wI	10wM
Test																		
All First	18	32	1	1230	206	39.67	2	9	10	-	29	6	119	3	39.66	2-21	-	
1-day Int																		
NatWest	3	3	0	98	64	32.66	-	1	1	-								
B & H	1	1	0	120	120	120.00	1	-	-	-								
Sunday	17	17	0	472	117	27.76	1	2	3	-								

Career Performances

	M	Inns	NO	Runs	HS	Avge	100s	50s	Ct	St	Balls	Runs	Wkts	Avge	Best	5wI	10wM
Test	2	4	0	78	33	19.50	-	-	-	-							
All First	67	119	4	4025	206	35.00	7	25	52	-	876	515	9	57.22	2-21	-	
1-day Int																	
NatWest	10	10	0	368	103	36.80	1	2	3	-	66	23	1	23.00	1-23	-	-
B & H	5	5	0	295	120	59.00	1	2	-	-	24	49	0	-	-	-	-
Sunday	45	44	1	1286	117	29.90	1	6	12	-	102	85	0	-	-	-	-

LAW, D. R. C.   Sussex

Name: Danny Richard Charles Law
Role: Right-hand bat, right-arm fast bowler
Born: 15 July 1975, Lambeth, London
Height: 6ft 5in **Weight:** 13st 7lbs
Nickname: Decas, Desperate
County debut: 1993
Parents: Richard (deceased) and Claudette
Marital status: 'Attached'
Education: Wolverton Hall School;
Steyning Grammar School
Qualifications: Cricket coach
Off-season: Playing and training in Barbados
Overseas tours: Sussex Schools U16 to
Jersey 1991; England U18 to South
Africa 1992-93, to Denmark 1993;
England U19 to Sri Lanka 1993-94
Cricketers particularly admired:
Michael Holding, Allan Donald,
Courtney Walsh, Franklyn Stephenson,
John North, Chris Tugwell
Other sports followed: Most sports
Injuries: Slight back problem, missed two to three weeks
Relaxations: Listening to music, spending time at home
Opinions on cricket: 'The 2nd XI Championship should be increased from a three-day game to a four-day game so that younger players are used to playing four-day cricket and are not thrown in at the deep end if they progress to first-class cricket.'
Best batting: 11 Sussex v Gloucestershire, Hove 1993
Best bowling: 2-38 Sussex v Worcestershire, Hove 1993

1994 Season (did not make any first-class or one-day appearance)

Career Performances

	M	Inns	NO	Runs	HS	Avge	100s	50s	Ct	St	Balls	Runs	Wkts	Avge	Best	5wI	10wM
Test																	
All First	3	2	0	11	11	5.50	-	-	-	-	382	216	5	43.20	2-38	-	-
1-day Int																	
NatWest																	
B & H																	
Sunday																	

LEATHERDALE, D. A. — Worcestershire

Name: David Anthony Leatherdale
Role: Right-hand bat, right-arm medium
bowler, cover fielder
Born: 26 November 1967, Bradford
Height: 5ft 10in **Weight:** 11st
Nickname: Lugsy, Spock
County debut: 1988
County cap: 1994
1st-Class 50s: 15
1st-Class 100s: 5
1st-Class catches: 73
Place in batting averages: 34th av. 44.86
(1993 154th av. 25.28)
Parents: Paul and Rosalyn
Wife's name: Vanessa
Children: Callum Edward, 6 July 1990
Family links with cricket: Father played
local cricket; brother plays for East Bierley
in Bradford League; brother-in-law played for England YC in 1979
Education: Bolton Royd Primary School; Pudsey Grangefield Secondary School
Qualifications: 8 O-levels, 2 A-levels; NCA coaching award (stage 1)
Career outside cricket: Marketing executive for Worcestershire CCC
Off-season: Touring with England Indoor cricket team and working for Worcestershire
Overseas tours: England Indoor to Australia and New Zealand 1994-95
Overseas teams played for: Pretoria Police, South Africa 1987-88
Cricketers particularly admired: Mark Scott, George Batty, Peter Kippax
Other sports followed: Football, American football
Relaxations: Golf
Opinions on cricket: 'With the injection of money coming into the game with more
television coverage/rights, hopefully county playing staffs will see the benefits of salary
increases in line with professionals of other sports.'
Best batting: 157 Worcestershire v Somerset, Worcester 1991
Best bowling: 2-11 Worcestershire v Cambridge University, Fenner's 1994

1994 Season

	M	Inns	NO	Runs	HS	Avge	100s	50s	Ct	St	O	M	Runs	Wkts	Avge	Best	5wI	10wM
Test																		
All First	17	25	3	987	139	44.86	2	3	17	-	108.1	22	339	5	67.80	2-11	-	
1-day Int																		
NatWest	5	3	0	28	21	9.33	-	-	2	-	8.4	1	37	3	12.33	3-14	-	-
B & H	4	2	0	34	30	17.00	-	-	1	-	7	0	39	0	-	-	-	
Sunday	16	13	1	208	41	17.33	-	-	12	-	11.3	1	46	4	11.50	2-15	-	

Career Performances

	M	Inns	NO	Runs	HS	Avge	100s	50s	Ct	St	Balls	Runs	Wkts	Avge	Best	5wI	10wM
Test																	
All First	78	118	11	3297	157	30.81	5	15	73	-	769	398	6	66.33	2-11	-	
1-day Int																	
NatWest	16	13	1	232	43	19.33	-	-	5	-	64	45	3	15.00	3-14	-	-
B & H	11	7	0	81	30	11.57	-	-	2	-	42	39	0	-	-	-	-
Sunday	69	60	8	773	62 *	14.86	-	2	37	-	129	107	4	26.75	2-15	-	

LEFEBVRE, R. P. Glamorgan

Name: Roland Phillippe Lefebvre
Role: Right-hand bat, right-arm medium bowler
Born: 7 February 1963, Rotterdam
Height: 6ft 1in **Weight:** 12st 6lbs
Nickname: Tulip
County debut: 1990 (Somerset), 1993 (Glamorgan)
County cap: 1991 (Somerset), 1993 (Glamorgan)
1st-Class 50s: 3
1st-Class 100s: 1
1st-Class 5 w. in innings: 2
1st-Class catches: 36
One-Day 5 w. in innings: 1
Place in batting averages:
190th av. 21.81 (1993 197th av. 19.36)
Place in bowling averages:
98th av. 35.84 (1993 86th av. 31.34)
Strike rate: 87.68 (career 90.71)
Parents: Pierre Joseph Ernest

Wife's name and date of marriage: Sandy, 12 August 1994
Children: Kirsty, 9 February 1990
Family links with cricket: Father plays for 'Still Going Strong' CC and brother plays for The Wanderers in Johannesburg
Education: Montessori Lyceum, Rotterdam; The Hague Academy of Physiotherapy
Qualifications: Qualified physiotherapist
Career outside cricket: Physiotherapy
Off-season: Hong Kong Sixes, physiotherapy, coaching, indoor cricket
Overseas tours: Holland tours to England, Canada, Denmark, New Zealand, Barbados, Zimbabwe, Dubai and South Africa, to New Zealand 1991-92, to South Africa 1992-93, to

Kenya (ICC Trophy) 1993-94, to Hong Kong Sixes 1994; MCC to Leeward Islands 1991-92
Overseas teams played for: VOC Rotterdam, Flamingos; East Coast Bays Cricket Club, Auckland 1987-89; Woolston Working Men's Club, Christchurch, New Zealand 1990-91; Canterbury, New Zealand 1990-91; Alma Marist CC, Cape Town 1993-94
Cricketers particularly admired: Vivian Richards, Ian Botham
Other sports followed: Most other sports
Injuries: Little groin strain/niggle
Relaxations: Playing the piano, music of various kinds, reading, the countryside, travelling
Extras: More than 80 caps for Holland. Played in 1986 and 1990 ICC Trophy competitions – voted Player of Tournament 1990; was a member of the Dutch teams that beat England (captained by Peter Roebuck) in 1989 and West Indies in 1991. First Dutch player to score a first-class century. Moved to Glamorgan for the 1993 season
Opinions on cricket: 'Taking all the money that has recently come into the game into consideration, capped players should be better rewarded for their services. There is too much of a wage gap between certain players. It's very good to see Holland being entered in the NatWest and hopefully it won't take long for them to join the B & H Cup as well.'
Best batting: 100 Somerset v Worcestershire, Weston-super-Mare 1991
Best bowling: 6-53 Canterbury v Auckland, Auckland 1990-91

1994 Season

	M	Inns	NO	Runs	HS	Avge	100s	50s	Ct	St	O	M	Runs	Wkts	Avge	Best	5wI	10wM
Test																		
All First	12	14	3	240	33	21.81	-	-	5	-	365.2	108	896	25	35.84	4-63	-	-
1-day Int																		
NatWest	3	2	1	15	15	15.00	-	-	3	-	35	7	89	4	22.25	3-28	-	
B & H	1	1	1	6	6 *	-	-	-	-	-	11	0	43	1	43.00	1-43	-	
Sunday	17	10	3	102	25	14.57	-	-	6	-	117	6	438	24	18.25	4-23	-	

Career Performances

	M	Inns	NO	Runs	HS	Avge	100s	50s	Ct	St	Balls	Runs	Wkts	Avge	Best	5wI	10wM
Test																	
All First	74	86	16	1439	100	20.55	1	3	36	-	12972	5220	143	36.50	6-53	2	-
1-day Int																	
NatWest	12	6	4	65	21 *	32.50	-	-	8	-	825	321	25	12.84	7-15	1	
B & H	13	10	5	154	37	30.80	-	-	3	-	746	471	12	39.25	3-44	-	
Sunday	66	42	13	416	36 *	14.34	-	-	31	-	2889	1943	81	23.98	4-23	-	

LENHAM, N. J.   Sussex

Name: Neil John Lenham
Role: Right-hand bat, right-arm medium bowler
Born: 17 December 1965, Worthing
Height: 5ft 11in **Weight:** 11st
Nickname: Pin
County debut: 1984
County cap: 1990
1000 runs in a season: 3
1st-Class 50s: 38
1st-Class 100s: 16
1st-Class 200s: 1
1st-Class catches: 58
One-Day 5 w. in innings: 1
Place in batting averages: 121st av. 31.11 (1993 63rd av. 38.04)
Strike rate: (career 85.89)
Parents: Leslie John and Valerie Anne
Marital status: Single
Family links with cricket: Father played for Sussex and is now one of the NCA's national coaches
Education: Broadwater Manor Prep School; Brighton College
Qualifications: 5 O-levels, 2 A-levels, NCA Senior Staff Coach
Off-season: Coaching in Namibia
Overseas tours: England YC to West Indies (as captain) 1985
Overseas teams played for: Port Elizabeth, South Africa 1987-88; Brighton, Tasmania 1989-91; United, Namibia 1994-95
Cricketers particularly admired: Ken McEwan, Barry Richards
Other sports followed: Golf, horse racing, rugby and fishing
Relaxations: Fishing, horse racing, tropical fish, gherkins, wine
Extras: Made debut for England YC in 1983. Broke record for number of runs scored in season at a public school in 1984 (1534 av. 80.74). Youngest player to appear for Sussex 2nd XI at 14 years old. Appointed as Eastbourne's first Cricket Development Officer for 1992
Opinions on cricket: 'Bouncer ruling should be left to the umpire's discretion. Four-day matches should not be split by Sunday league competition.'
Best batting: 222* Sussex v Kent, Hove 1992
Best bowling: 4-13 Sussex v Durham, Durham University 1993

---

44. Who was Warwickshire's original overseas signing for 1994 before injury led to him being replaced by Brian Lara?

1994 Season

	M	Inns	NO	Runs	HS	Avge	100s	50s	Ct	St	O	M	Runs	Wkts	Avge	Best	5wI	10wM
Test																		
All First	14	27	1	809	102	31.11	1	5	2	-	9	0	24	0	-	-	-	-
1-day Int																		
NatWest	1	1	1	82	82 *	-	-	1	-	-								
B & H	2	1	0	44	44	44.00	-	-	-	-	11	0	58	0	-	-	-	-
Sunday	7	7	2	120	58 *	24.00	-	1	1	-	2	0	17	1	17.00	1-17	-	

Career Performances

	M	Inns	NO	Runs	HS	Avge	100s	50s	Ct	St	Balls	Runs	Wkts	Avge	Best	5wI	10wM
Test																	
All First	154	267	23	8075	222 *	33.09	16	38	58	-	3264	1674	38	44.05	4-13	-	-
1-day Int																	
NatWest	11	10	2	397	82 *	49.62	-	3	-	-	369	222	9	24.66	2-12	-	
B & H	19	18	4	392	82	28.00	-	2	2	-	258	211	4	52.75	1-3	-	
Sunday	78	67	15	1519	86	29.21	-	10	16	-	822	821	27	30.40	5-28	1	

LEWIS, C. C.   Nottinghamshire

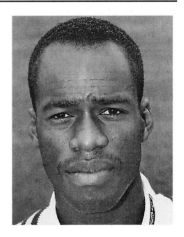

Name: Christopher Clairmonte Lewis
Role: Right-hand bat, right-arm fast-medium
bowler
Born: 14 February 1968, Georgetown,
Guyana
Height: 6ft 2in **Weight:** 13st
Nickname: Carl
County debut: 1987 (Leicestershire),
1992 (Nottinghamshire)
County cap: 1990 (Leicestershire),
1992 (Nottinghamshire)
Test debut: 1990
Tests: 25
One-Day Internationals: 48
50 wickets in a season: 2
1st-Class 50s: 23
1st-Class 100s: 7
1st-Class 200s: 2
1st-Class 5 w. in innings: 15
1st-Class 10 w. in match: 3
1st-Class catches: 103
One-Day 50s: 8

One-Day 5 w. in innings: 1
Place in batting averages: 5th av. 58.73 (1993 102nd av. 32.04)
Place in bowling averages: 13th av. 23.52 (1993 112th av. 38.54)
Strike rate: 45.04 (career 59.98)
Parents: Philip and Patricia
Marital status: Single
Education: Willesden High School
Qualifications: 2 O-levels
Overseas tours: England YC to Australia (Youth World Cup) 1987; England A to Kenya and Zimbabwe 1989-90; England to West Indies 1989-90, to Australia and New Zealand 1990-91, to New Zealand 1991-92, to India and Sri Lanka 1992-93, to West Indies 1993-94, to Australia 1994-95
Cricketers particularly admired: Graham Gooch, Robin Smith
Other sports followed: Snooker, football, darts, American football, basketball
Relaxations: Music, sleeping
Extras: Joined England's tour of West Indies in 1989-90 as a replacement for Ricky Ellcock. Suffers from Raynaud's disease, a problem of blood circulation, and has to spend one night in hospital every two months to have the disease treated. Left Leicestershire at the end of 1991 season and signed for Nottinghamshire. Hit first Test century v India at Madras in 1992-93 tour to India and Sri Lanka. Joined England tour party in Australia following injury to Darren Gough
Best batting: 247 Nottinghamshire v Durham, Chester-le-Street 1993
Best bowling: 6-22 Leicestershire v Oxford University, The Parks 1988

1994 Season

	M	Inns	NO	Runs	HS	Avge	100s	50s	Ct	St	O	M	Runs	Wkts	Avge	Best	5wI	10wM
Test																		
All First	12	19	4	881	220 *	58.73	2	5	18	-	345.2	69	1082	46	23.52	5-55	2	-
1-day Int	3	2	1	36	19	36.00	-	-	4	-	26.5	2	96	6	16.00	3-20	-	
NatWest	2	2	0	112	89	56.00	-	1	1	-	18	2	68	1	68.00	1-48	-	
B & H	2	1	1	48	48 *	-	-	-	1	-	17	2	76	2	38.00	1-33	-	
Sunday	8	7	1	190	75	31.66	-	2	3	-	57	1	317	10	31.70	3-29	-	

Career Performances

	M	Inns	NO	Runs	HS	Avge	100s	50s	Ct	St	Balls	Runs	Wkts	Avge	Best	5wI	10wM
Test	25	40	2	941	117	24.76	1	4	20	-	5163	2621	66	39.71	6-111	2	-
All First	132	196	25	5343	247	31.24	7	23	103	-	23514	11550	392	29.46	6-22	15	3
1-day Int	48	36	11	315	33	12.60	-	-	20	-	2350	1735	61	28.44	4-30	-	
NatWest	15	13	0	294	89	22.61	-	2	9	-	810	473	16	29.56	3-24	-	
B & H	20	16	6	264	48 *	26.40	-	-	7	-	1143	784	27	29.03	5-46	1	
Sunday	80	69	15	1413	93 *	26.16	-	6	21	-	3178	2353	83	28.34	4-13	-	

LEWIS, J. J. B.   Essex

Name: Jonathan James Benjamin Lewis
Role: Right-hand bat,
right-arm slow-medium net bowler
Born: 21 May 1970, Middlesex
Height: 5ft 9in **Weight:** 11st 7lbs
Nickname: Scrubby, Judgey, The Drinks
Machine
County debut: 1990
County cap: 1994
1st-Class 50s: 16
1st-Class 100s: 4
1st-Class catches: 29
Place in batting averages: 137th av. 28.88
(1993 66th av. 36.80)
Parents: Graham Edward and Regina Mary
Marital status: 'Happily single'
Family links with cricket: Father played for
Warwickshire Schools. Sister 'bowled a bit'.
Uncle a lifelong supporter of Somerset

Education:
King Edward VI School, Chelmsford; Roehampton Institute of Higher Education
Qualifications: 5 O-levels, 3 A-levels, BSc (Hons) Sports Science, NCA Senior Coach
Off-season: Playing and coaching in Natal, South Africa
Overseas teams played for: Old Hararians, Zimbabwe 1991-92; Taita District, New
Zealand 1992-93
Cricketers particularly admired: John Childs, Graham Gooch, Greg Matthews, Keith
Fletcher
Other sports followed: Soccer, rugby, basketball, 'most sports really'
Relaxations: 'Pubs with real ale'
Extras: Hit century on first-class debut in Essex's final Championship match of the 1990
season
Best batting: 136* Essex v Nottinghamshire, Trent Bridge 1993

1994 Season

	M	Inns	NO	Runs	HS	Avge	100s	50s	Ct	St	O	M	Runs	Wkts	Avge	Best	5wI	10wM
Test																		
All First	16	29	3	751	109	28.88	1	4	9	-	8	1	32	0	-		-	-
1-day Int																		
NatWest	2	2	1	25	24*	25.00	-	-	1	-								
B & H																		
Sunday	6	6	2	70	23	17.50	-	-	1	-								

Career Performances

	M	Inns	NO	Runs	HS	Avge	100s	50s	Ct	St	Balls	Runs	Wkts	Avge	Best	5wI	10wM
Test																	
All First	45	76	12	2422	136 *	37.84	4	16	29	-	48	32	0	-	-	-	-
1-day Int																	
NatWest	3	3	1	46	24 *	23.00	-	-	1	-							
B & H																	
Sunday	19	14	3	149	23	13.54	-	-	5	-							

LEWRY, J. D. Sussex

Name: Jason David Lewry
Role: Left-hand bat,
left-arm fast-medium bowler
Born: 2 April 1971, Worthing, West Sussex
Height: 6ft 2in **Weight:** 14st 4lb
County debut: 1994
Parents: David and Veronica
Marital status: Single
Family links with cricket: Father coaches
Education: Durrington High School,
Worthing; Sixth Form College, Worthing
Qualifications: 6 O-levels, 3 GCSEs,
City & Guilds, NCA Award Course
Career outside cricket: Salesman and stores
manager for City Electrical Factors Ltd,
Chichester branch
Off-season: 'Hoping to return to old employers
but open to offers'
Cricketers particularly admired: The Sussex staff, David Gower, Wasim Akram, Martin Andrews
Other sports followed: Rugby union and league, golf
Injuries: 'Everything (first seasonitis), missed two weeks in total'
Relaxations: Golf, eating out, going out
Extras: Selected in a 15-man England indoor cricket squad for the series against South
Africa in England, alongside Mike Gatting and Asif Din, and for the tour of New Zealand
and Australia during 1991-92. The tour was cancelled due to a lack of funds of the UKICF
(UK Indoor Cricket Federation)
Opinions on cricket: 'Should be an hour for lunch and 30 minutes for tea. 2nd XI cricket
should be four-day. More should be done for players during close season, either 12-monthly
salary or club could help to find individuals winter employment.'
Best batting: 6* Sussex v Northamptonshire, Northampton 1994
Best bowling: 4-40 Sussex v Middlesex, Arundel 1994

1994 Season

	M	Inns	NO	Runs	HS	Avge	100s	50s	Ct	St	O	M	Runs	Wkts	Avge	Best	5wI	10wM
Test																		
All First	4	6	4	14	6 *	7.00	-	-	-	-	96	20	315	7	45.00	4-40	-	-
1-day Int																		
NatWest																		
B & H																		
Sunday	5	1	1	1	1 *	-	-	-	-	1	-	33.3	3	159	4	39.75	2-43	-

Career Performances

	M	Inns	NO	Runs	HS	Avge	100s	50s	Ct	St	Balls	Runs	Wkts	Avge	Best	5wI	10wM
Test																	
All First	4	6	4	14	6 *	7.00	-	-	-	-	576	315	7	45.00	4-40	-	-
1-day Int																	
NatWest																	
B & H																	
Sunday	5	1	1	1	1 *	-	-	-	-	1	-	201	159	4	39.75	2-43	-

LIGERTWOOD, D. G. C. Durham

Name: David George Coutts Ligertwood
Role: Right-hand bat, off-spin bowler, wicket-keeper
Born: 16 May 1969, Oxford
Height: 6ft 1in **Weight:** 12st
Nickname: Hippy, Woody, Syph
County debut: 1992 (Surrey)
1st-Class catches: 7
1st-Class stumpings: 1
Parents: Andrew and Virginia
Marital status: Single
Children: Charlene, 3 September 1990
Family links with cricket: Brother played for South Australia U17 'and grandmother is a fanatic'
Education:
Rose Park Primary School; Wootton School; Magdalen College School, Oxford; University of Adelaide
Qualifications: BA
Career outside cricket: Cricket coach
Overseas teams played for: Adelaide University 1987-92

Extras: Played for Hertfordshire in 1991 NatWest Trophy. Played for Surrey in 1992
Best batting: 28 Surrey v Sussex, The Oval 1992

1994 Season (did not make any first-class or one-day appearance)

Career Performances

	M	Inns	NO	Runs	HS	Avge	100s	50s	Ct	St	Balls	Runs	Wkts	Avge	Best	5wI	10wM
Test																	
All First	4	7	0	63	28	9.00	-	-	7	1							
1-day Int																	
NatWest	1	1	1	37	37 *	-	-	-	-	-							
B & H																	
Sunday	1	0	0	0	0 -	-	-	-	-	1							

LLONG, N. J. Kent

Name: Nigel James Llong
Role: Left-hand bat, off-spin bowler
Born: 11 February 1969, Ashford, Kent
Height: 6ft **Weight:** 11st 6lb
Nickname: Nidge, Lloyd
County debut: 1991
County cap: 1993
1st-Class 50s: 8
1st-Class 100s: 2
1st-Class 5 w. in innings: 1
1st-Class catches: 25
Place in batting averages: 206th av. 19.00
(1993 39th av. 42.86)
Strike rate: (career 61.35)
Parents: Richard and Peggy (deceased)
Marital status: Single
Family links with cricket: Father and
brother played local club cricket
Education:
Ashford North Secondary School

Qualifications: 6 CSEs, NCA coaching award
Career outside cricket: Assistant groundsman, barman
Off-season: Playing in South Africa
Overseas tours: Kent to Zimbabwe 1992-93
Overseas teams played for: Ashburton, Melbourne 1988-90; Green Point, Cape Town
1990-95

Cricketers particularly admired: David Gower
Other sports followed: American football, golf
Relaxations: Listening to music
Extras: Kent Supporters Club Young Player of the Year Award 1993
Opinions on cricket: 'The TCCB should have total control on pitch preparation, making sure that pitches are of the best quality possible.'
Best batting: 116* Kent v Cambridge University, Fenner's 1993
Best bowling: 5-63 Kent v Cambridge University, Fenner's 1994

1994 Season

	M	Inns	NO	Runs	HS	Avge	100s	50s	Ct	St	O	M	Runs	Wkts	Avge	Best	5wI	10wM
Test																		
All First	7	11	0	209	44	19.00	-	-	3	-	41.3	11	113	6	18.83	5-63	1	-
1-day Int																		
NatWest																		
B & H																		
Sunday	16	12	6	211	55	35.16	-	1	5	-	13	0	67	4	16.75	2-25	-	

Career Performances

	M	Inns	NO	Runs	HS	Avge	100s	50s	Ct	St	Balls	Runs	Wkts	Avge	Best	5wI	10wM
Test																	
All First	35	52	8	1435	116 *	32.61	2	8	25	-	1043	537	17	31.58	5-63	1	-
1-day Int																	
NatWest	3	3	2	41	27 *	41.00	-	-	1	-	24	11	1	11.00	1-11	-	
B & H	1	1	0	5	5	5.00	-	-	1	-							
Sunday	43	36	13	640	64 *	27.82	-	2	11	-	254	209	11	19.00	4-24	-	

45. Who retired from international cricket at the end of 1994 as the record wicket-taker in Test cricket and how many wickets had he taken?

LLOYD, G. D.   Lancashire

Name: Graham David Lloyd
Role: Right-hand bat, right-arm medium bowler
Born: 1 July 1969, Accrington
Height: 5ft 7in **Weight:** 13st
Nickname: Bumble
County debut: 1988
County cap: 1992
1000 runs in a season: 2
1st-Class 50s: 35
1st-Class 100s: 10
1st-Class catches: 67
One-Day 100s: 1
Place in batting averages: 140th av. 28.50
(1993 64th av. 37.75)
Parents: David and Susan
Marital status: Single
Family links with cricket: Father played for Lancashire and England
Education: Hollins County High School, Accrington
Qualifications: 3 O-levels, NCA coaching certificate
Off-season: Playing in Queensland
Overseas tours: England A to Australia 1992-93
Overseas teams played for: Maroochydore, Queensland 1988-89 and 1991-95
Cricketers particularly admired: Gordon Parsons, David Millns, Nigel Briers
Other sports followed: Football (Manchester United), horse and greyhound racing
Relaxations: 'Playing pool and cards'
Extras: His school did not play cricket, so he learnt at Accrington, playing in the same team as his father
Opinions on cricket: 'NatWest Final should start at 11.00 am.'
Best batting: 132 Lancashire v Kent, Old Trafford 1992
Best bowling: 1-57 Lancashire v Yorkshire, Old Trafford 1991

1994 Season

	M	Inns	NO	Runs	HS	Avge	100s	50s	Ct	St	O	M	Runs	Wkts	Avge	Best	5wI	10wM
Test																		
All First	16	27	3	684	112	28.50	1	5	11	-								
1-day Int																		
NatWest	1	1	0	19	19	19.00	-	-	-	-								
B & H	2	2	1	39	31 *	39.00	-	-	-	-								
Sunday	17	16	3	351	77	27.00	-	2	5	-								

Career Performances

	M	Inns	NO	Runs	HS	Avge	100s	50s	Ct	St	Balls	Runs	Wkts	Avge	Best	5wl	10wM
Test																	
All First	99	163	19	5397	132	37.47	10	35	67	-	151	186	1	186.00	1-57	-	-
1-day Int																	
NatWest	6	6	0	126	39	21.00	-	-	-	-							
B & H	14	13	5	206	34	25.75	-	-	1	-							
Sunday	78	74	10	1895	100*	29.60	1	12	17	-							

LONGLEY, J. I.   Durham

Name: Jonathan Ian Longley
Role: Right-hand bat
Born: 12 April 1969, New Brunswick, USA
Height: 5ft 8in **Weight:** 11st 10lbs
County debut: 1989 (Kent), 1994 (Durham)
1st-Class 50s: 6
1st-Class 100s: 2
1st-Class catches: 15
Place in batting averages: 155th av. 25.82
Parents: Dick and Helen
Marital status: Single
Education: Tonbridge School; Durham University
Qualifications: 9 O-levels, 3 A-levels, BA Sociology
Overseas teams played for:
Prospect District, Adelaide 1991-92;
Green Point, Cape Town 1992-93

Cricketers particularly admired:
Robin Smith, Gordon Greenidge, Allan Border
Other sports followed: Rugby, golf, squash, tennis
Relaxations: 'Love listening to music (Bob Dylan, Van Morrison and the Rolling Stones). Also love old English pubs, Australian beaches and socialising with friends and family'
Extras: Member of the Combined Universities team which reached the quarter-finals of the B&H Cup in 1989. Moved from Kent to Durham for 1994 season
Best batting: 110 Kent v Cambridge University, Fenner's 1992

---

46. In the Test match against Australia at Lord's in 1993 which two batsmen were dismissed on 99?

1994 Season

	M	Inns	NO	Runs	HS	Avge	100s	50s	Ct	St	O	M	Runs	Wkts	Avge	Best	5wI	10wM
Test																		
All First	14	25	2	594	100 *	25.82	1	5	7	-								
1-day Int																		
NatWest	2	2	0	14	9	7.00	-	-	-	-								
B & H	1	1	0	33	33	33.00	-	-	-	-								
Sunday	13	12	2	342	88	34.20	-	3	1	-								

Career Performances

	M	Inns	NO	Runs	HS	Avge	100s	50s	Ct	St	Balls	Runs	Wkts	Avge	Best	5wI	10wM
Test																	
All First	24	42	2	955	110	23.87	2	6	15	-							
1-day Int																	
NatWest	2	2	0	14	9	7.00	-	-	-	-							
B & H	17	17	1	319	57	19.93	-	1	1	-							
Sunday	23	22	3	539	88	28.36	-	5	4	-							

LOYE, M. B.   Northamptonshire

Name: Malachy Bernard Loye
Role: Right-hand bat, off-spin bowler
Born: 27 September 1972, Northampton
Height: 6ft 2in **Weight:** 13st 7lb
Nickname: Mal, Mad Jack, Fruit Bat
County debut: 1991
County cap: 1994
1st-Class 50s: 13
1st-Class 100s: 5
1st-Class catches: 39
One-Day 100s: 1
Place in batting averages: 56th av. 39.73
(1993 62nd av. 38.24)
Parents: Patrick and Anne
Marital status: Single
Family links with cricket: Father and
brother both play for Cogenhoe CC
in Northampton
Education: Moulton Comprehensive School
Qualifications: GCSEs and senior coaching certificate
Off-season: 'Waiting for the pins to come out of my thumb and then playing and coaching
in New Zealand'

Overseas tours: England U18 to Canada 1991; England U19 to Pakistan 1991-92; England A to South Africa 1993-94

Overseas teams played for: Riccarton, New Zealand and Canterbury B 1992-93

Cricketers particularly admired: Gordon Greenidge, Wayne Larkins, Curtly Ambrose

Other sports followed: Football, golf, basketball and boxing

Injuries: Broken thumb, missed two months

Relaxations: Watching films, listening to music, and going out with friends

Extras: Played for England U19 in the home series against Australia U19 in 1991 and against Sri Lanka U19 1992. Voted Professional Cricket Association's Young Player of the Year 1993 and Whittingdale Young Player of the Year 1993

Opinions on cricket: 'Too many overs are bowled in a day, they should be reduced to 100. I can't understand how a player can represent one country and then another.'

Best batting: 153* Northamptonshire v Kent, Canterbury 1993

1994 Season

	M	Inns	NO	Runs	HS	Avge	100s	50s	Ct	St	O	M	Runs	Wkts	Avge	Best	5wI	10wM
Test																		
All First	15	26	3	914	132	39.73	3	5	7	-								
1-day Int																		
NatWest	3	3	2	62	34	62.00	-	-	1	-								
B & H	1	1	1	68	68 *	-	-	1	-	-								
Sunday	13	13	0	225	64	17.30	-	1	-	-								

Career Performances

	M	Inns	NO	Runs	HS	Avge	100s	50s	Ct	St	Balls	Runs	Wkts	Avge	Best	5wI	10wM
Test																	
All First	52	81	9	2507	153 *	34.81	5	13	39	-	1	1	0	-	-	-	-
1-day Int																	
NatWest	6	6	2	129	66	34.75		1	1	-							
B & H	4	4	2	116	68 *	58.00	-	1	2	-							
Sunday	28	26	1	752	122	30.08	1	4	6	-							

LUGSDEN, S.   Durham

Name: Steven Lugsden
Role: Right-hand bat, right-arm fast bowler
Born: 10 July 1976, Gateshead
Height: 6ft 2in **Weight:** 12st 7lbs
County debut: 1993
Parents: William and Nora
Marital status: Single
Education: St Edmund Campion RC School,
Wrekenton, Gateshead
Qualifications: 7 GCSEs,
BTEC Business and Finance
Career outside cricket: Works in
a sports shop
Off-season: Touring with England U19
Overseas tours: England U19 to West Indies
1994-95
Cricketers particularly admired:
Curtly Ambrose, Graeme Hick, Tom Moody
Other sports followed: Football (Newcastle
United)
Injuries: Shin soreness, missed four weeks
Relaxations: Football
Extras: Youngest player (17 years 27 days) to make first-class debut for Durham. Played
against India for England U19 in home series 1994
Opinions on cricket: 'Wickets are getting better to bat on but still need improving.'
Best batting: 5* Durham v Derbyshire, Durham University 1993
Best bowling: 2-43 Durham v Derbyshire, Durham University 1993

1994 Season

	M	Inns	NO	Runs	HS	Avge	100s	50s	Ct	St	O	M	Runs	Wkts	Avge	Best	5wl	10wM
Test																		
All First	5	5	2	2	2	0.66	-	-	-	-	106.2	16	412	3	137.33	1-15	-	-
1-day Int																		
NatWest																		
B & H																		
Sunday	1	0	0	0	0	-	-	-	-	-	8	0	55	1	55.00	1-55	-	

> 47. Who played the most first-class innings of 100 and over in the
> 1993 English season, and how many?

	M	Inns	NO	Runs	HS	Avge	100s	50s	Ct	St	Balls	Runs	Wkts	Avge	Best	5wI	10wM
Test																	
All First	6	6	3	7	5 *	2.33	-	-	-	-	794	497	5	99.40	2-43	-	-
1-day Int																	
NatWest																	
B & H																	
Sunday	1	0	0	0	0	-	-	-	-	-	48	55	1	55.00	1-55	-	

LYNCH, M. A. — Gloucestershire

Name: Monte Allan Lynch
Role: Right-hand bat, right-arm medium and off-spin bowler
Born: 21 May 1958, Georgetown, Guyana
Height: 5ft 9in **Weight:** 13st 3lbs
Nickname: Mont
County debut: 1977 (Surrey)
County cap: 1982 (Surrey)
Benefit: 1991 (£107,000)
One-Day Internationals: 3
1000 runs in a season: 9
1st-Class 50s: 78
1st-Class 100s: 34
1st-Class catches: 323
One-Day 100s: 5
Place in batting averages:
58th av. 39.66 (1993 158th av. 24.66)
Parents: Lawrence and Doreen Austin
Marital status: Single
Children: Lours, 31 September 1983; Marissa, 30 July 1989
Family links with cricket: 'Father and most of family played at some time or another'
Education: Ryden's School, Walton-on-Thames
Overseas tours: Unofficial West Indies XI to South Africa 1983-84
Overseas teams played for: Guyana 1982-83
Other sports followed: Football, table tennis
Extras: When he made 141* for Surrey v Glamorgan at Guildford in August 1982, off 78 balls in 88 minutes, one six hit his captain Roger Knight's car. Joined West Indies rebels in South Africa 1983-84, although qualified for England. Appeared in all three One-Day Internationals v West Indies 1988. Moved to Gloucestershire for 1994 season
Best batting: 172* Surrey v Kent, The Oval 1989
Best bowling: 3-6 Surrey v Glamorgan, Swansea 1981

1994 Season

	M	Inns	NO	Runs	HS	Avge	100s	50s	Ct	St	O	M	Runs	Wkts	Avge	Best	5wl	10wM
Test																		
All First	4	7	1	238	60	39.66	-	1	6	-	10	2	35	0	-	-	-	-
1-day Int																		
NatWest																		
B & H																		
Sunday	3	2	0	0	0	0.00	-	-	4	-								

Career Performances

	M	Inns	NO	Runs	HS	Avge	100s	50s	Ct	St	Balls	Runs	Wkts	Avge	Best	5wl	10wM
Test																		
All First	319	518	60	16281	172 *	35.54	34	78	323	-	2183	1395	26	53.65	3-6	-	-
1-day Int	3	3	0	8	6	2.66	-	-	1	-							
NatWest	37	32	5	779	129	28.85	1	3	18	-	282	168	6	28.00	2-28	-	
B & H	57	52	3	1312	112 *	26.77	2	7	26	-	132	121	0	-	-	-	
Sunday	209	191	26	4675	136	28.33	2	29	74	-	149	182	7	26.00	2-2	-	

MACMILLAN, G. I.   Leicestershire

Name: Gregor Innes Macmillan
Role: Right-hand bat, off-spin bowler
Born: 7 August 1969, Guildford
Height: 6ft 5in **Weight:** 12st 10lbs
County debut: 1994 (one-day)
1st-Class 50s: 6
1st-Class catches: 25
Place in batting averages: 142nd av. 28.21
Strike rate: (career 69.14)
Parents: Angus and Evelyn
Marital status: Single
Family links with cricket: Father played club cricket at Odiham and Midsomer Norton
Education: Guildford County School; Charterhouse; Southampton University; Oxford University
Qualifications: 3 A-levels, BA Phil, Certificate in Social Administration
Career outside cricket: Studying
Off-season: Doing a postgraduate degree in South African Politics at Oxford University
Overseas teams played for: Harvinia, Orange Free State 1988-89, 1993-94
Other sports followed: All sport

338

Extras: Captained Southampton University to the UAU final 1991. Played for Surrey from U11 to U19. Captain of Oxford University for 1995 season
Best batting: 69 Oxford University v Cambridge University, Lord's 1994
Best bowling: 3-13 Oxford University v Cambridge University, Lord's 1993

1994 Season

	M	Inns	NO	Runs	HS	Avge	100s	50s	Ct	St	O	M	Runs	Wkts	Avge	Best	5wI	10wM
Test																		
All First	10	17	3	395	69	28.21	-	3	20	-	94	17	324	7	46.28	1-15	-	
1-day Int																		
NatWest																		
B & H	1	1	0	19	19	19.00	-	-	-	-								
Sunday	4	4	0	113	48	28.25	-	-	1	-								

Career Performances

	M	Inns	NO	Runs	HS	Avge	100s	50s	Ct	St	Balls	Runs	Wkts	Avge	Best	5wI	10wM
Test																	
All First	19	31	4	731	69	27.07	-	6	25	-	968	535	14	38.21	3-13	-	
1-day Int																	
NatWest																	
B & H	3	3	0	38	19	12.66	-	-	-	-	31	18	1	18.00	1-18	-	
Sunday	4	4	0	113	48	28.25	-	-	1	-							

MADDY, D. L.　　　　　　　　Leicestershire

Name: Darren Lee Maddy
Role: Right-hand bat,
right-arm medium bowler
Born: 23 May 1974, Leicester
Height: 5ft 9in **Weight:** 11st
Nickname: Dazza, Roasting
County debut: 1993 (one-day), 1994
(first-class)
1st-Class catches: 3
Place in batting averages: 252nd av. 13.33
Parents: Bill and Hilary
Marital status: Single
Family links with cricket: Father and younger
brother play club cricket
Education: Herrick Junior School, Leicester;
Roundhills, Thurmaston;
Wreake Valley, Syston

Qualifications: 8 GCSEs
Off-season: Playing cricket in Orange
Free State, South Africa
Overseas teams played for:
Wanderers, Johannesburg 1992-93; Northern Free State, Orange Free State 1993-95
Cricketers particularly admired: Brian Lara, Michael Atherton, Richard Hadlee, Justin
Benson, Darren Jolly, Viv Richards
Other sports followed: Rugby union, golf, American football, Baseball
Relaxations: Scuba diving, bungee jumping, listening to music
Extras: 'Voted having the biggest thighs in Leicester by team-mates.' Set a new 2nd XI
Championship run aggregate record (1498) beating the previous one which had stood since
1961. Rapid Cricketline 2nd XI Player of the Year 1994
Opinions on cricket: '2nd XI cricket should be played on good, first-class wickets.'
Best batting: 34 Leicestershire v Worcestershire, Leicester 1994

1994 Season

	M	Inns	NO	Runs	HS	Avge	100s	50s	Ct	St	O	M	Runs	Wkts	Avge	Best	5wI	10wM
Test																		
All First	3	6	0	80	34	13.33	-	-	3	-								
1-day Int																		
NatWest																		
B & H																		
Sunday	11	11	1	213	54	21.30	-	2	9	-								

Career Performances

	M	Inns	NO	Runs	HS	Avge	100s	50s	Ct	St	Balls	Runs	Wkts	Avge	Best	5wI	10wM
Test																	
All First	3	6	0	80	34	13.33	-	-	3	-							
1-day Int																	
NatWest																	
B & H																	
Sunday	12	12	1	216	54	19.63	-	2	10	-							

MAHER, B. J. M.   Derbyshire

Name: Bernard Joseph Michael Maher
Role: Right-hand bat, wicket-keeper
Born: 11 February 1958, Hillingdon,
Middlesex
Height: 5ft 10in **Weight:** 13st
Nickname: BJ
County debut: 1981
County cap: 1987
1st-Class 50s: 17
1st-Class 100s: 4
1st-Class catches: 289
1st-Class stumpings: 14
Parents: Francis (deceased) and
Mary Anne
Wife and date of marriage: Janet,
February 1995
Family links with cricket: Brother kept
wicket for school, father was a keen
follower of Derbyshire
Education: St Bernadette's RC Primary;
Abbotsfield Comprehensive; Bishopshalt GS; Harrow College; Loughborough University
Qualifications: 10 O-levels, 3 A-levels,
Association of Certified Accountants Examinations, BSc (Hons) Accountancy/Economics
Career outside cricket: Accountancy, marketing and part-time radio work
Off-season: Working in sales and marketing for Derbyshire CCC and coaching
Overseas tours: Middlesex Cricket League to West Indies 1978; Loughborough University
to Amsterdam 1981; Derbyshire to Denmark 1994
Overseas teams played for: Zingari, Pietermaritzburg, South Africa 1982-84; Ellerslie,
Auckland 1984-85; Northland Cricket Association, New Zealand 1985-88; Tairi, Dunedin,
New Zealand 1989-93; Otago, New Zealand 1992-93
Cricketers particularly admired: Malcolm Marshall, Richard Hadlee
Other sports followed: Rugby, boxing, athletics
Relaxations: Fly-fishing in England and New Zealand for trout and salmon
Opinions on cricket: '1. Two-division championship with three promoted (three demoted)
each season would provide a very competitive competition; 2. If we can improve the bounce
of pitches in all standards of cricket better players will emerge; 3. I would like to see the word
"born" deleted from all English qualification regulations and the word "bred" substituted
– eg. a person would have had to have lived in England from the age of 15 to be able to be
an English-qualified player!'
Best batting: 126 Derbyshire v New Zealand, Derby 1986
Best bowling: 2-69 Derbyshire v Glamorgan, Abergavenny 1986

Career Performances

	M	Inns	NO	Runs	HS	Avge	100s	50s	Ct	St	Balls	Runs	Wkts	Avge	Best	5wI	10wM
Test																	
All First	133	205	36	3689	126	21.82	4	17	289	14	270	234	4	58.50	2-69		
1-day Int																	
NatWest	10	10	2	99	44	12.37	-	-	17	-							
B & H	20	13	2	256	50	23.27	-	1	25	1							
Sunday	79	68	14	799	78	14.79	-	1	63	10							

MALCOLM, D. E. Derbyshire

Name: Devon Eugene Malcolm
Role: Right-hand bat, right-arm fast bowler
Born: 22 February 1963, Kingston, Jamaica
Height: 6ft 2in **Weight:** 15st
Nickname: Dude
County debut: 1984
County cap: 1989
Test debut: 1989
Tests: 28
One-Day Internationals: 10
50 wickets in a season: 3
1st-Class 50s: 1
1st-Class 5 w. in innings: 16
1st-Class 10 w. in innings: 2
1st-Class catches: 28
One-Day 5 w. in innings: 1
Place in bowling averages: 54th av. 29.20
(1993 79th av. 30.78)
Strike rate: 47.92 (career 53.90)
Parents: Albert and Brendalee (deceased)
Wife and date of marriage: Jennifer, October 1989
Children: Erica Cian, 11 June 1991; Natile Jade, 25 June 1993
Education: St Elizabeth Technical High School; Richmond College; Derby College of Higher Education
Qualifications: College certificates, O-levels, coaching certificate
Off-season: England tour to Australia
Overseas tours: England to West Indies 1989-90, to Australia 1990-91, to India and Sri Lanka 1992-93, to West Indies 1993-94, to Australia 1994-95; England A to Bermuda and West Indies 1991-92

Overseas teams played for: Ellerslie, Auckland 1985-87
Cricketers particularly admired: Michael Holding, Richard Hadlee, Malcolm Marshall, Alan Warner, Viv Richards
Other sports followed: Football, boxing
Relaxations: Music and movies, eating
Extras: Played league cricket for Sheffield Works and Sheffield United. Became eligible to play for England in 1987. Took 10 for 137 v West Indies in Port-of-Spain Test, 1989-90. Struck down with chickenpox early in the England tour to Australia 1994-95
Best batting: 51 Derbyshire v Surrey, Derby 1989
Best bowling: 9-57 England v South Africa, The Oval 1994

1994 Season

	M	Inns	NO	Runs	HS	Avge	100s	50s	Ct	St	O	M	Runs	Wkts	Avge	Best	5wI	10wM
Test	2	1	0	4	4	4.00	-	-	1	-	69.1	14	222	12	18.50	9-57	1	1
All First	18	22	9	89	15 *	6.84	-	-	2	-	551.3	97	2015	69	29.20	9-57	3	1
1-day Int																		
NatWest	3	1	0	0	0	0.00	-	-	-	-	36	4	132	3	44.00	2-50	-	
B & H	1	1	0	2	2	2.00	-	-	-	-	4	1	14	0	-	-	-	
Sunday	11	0	0	0	0	-	-	-	1	-	75.2	1	419	16	26.18	3-41	-	

Career Performances

	M	Inns	NO	Runs	HS	Avge	100s	50s	Ct	St	Balls	Runs	Wkts	Avge	Best	5wI	10wM
Test	28	40	13	158	18	5.85	-	-	4	-	6190	3438	98	35.08	9-57	5	2
All First	168	191	58	1035	51	7.78	-	1	28	-	28462	16613	528	31.46	9-57	16	2
1-day Int	10	5	2	9	4	3.00	-	-	1	-	526	404	16	25.25	3-40	-	
NatWest	14	9	1	21	10 *	2.62	-	-	-	-	904	596	20	29.80	3-29	-	
B & H	21	10	2	54	15	6.75	-	-	-	-	1200	817	29	28.17	5-27	1	
Sunday	52	18	7	78	18	7.09	-	-	6	-	2335	1996	73	27.34	4-21	-	

48. Where did South Africa play the first friendly match of their 1994 tour to England and against what oppposition?

MALLENDER, N. A.   Northamptonshire

Name: Neil Alan Mallender
Role: Right-hand bat,
right-arm fast-medium bowler
Born: 13 August 1961, Kirk Sandall,
Doncaster
Height: 6ft **Weight:** 13st
Nickname: Ghostie
County debut: 1980 (Northamptonshire),
1987 (Somerset)
County cap: 1984 (Northamptonshire),
1987 (Somerset)
Tests: 2
50 wickets in a season: 6
1st-Class 50s: 10
1st-Class 100s: 1
1st-Class 5 w. in innings: 36
1st-Class 10 w. in match: 5
1st-Class catches: 107
One-Day 5 w. in innings: 3
Place in batting averages: 129th av. 30.00 (1993 156th av. 25.00)
Place in bowling averages: 112th av. 37.62 (1993 23rd av. 24.12)
Strike rate: 72.56 (career 56.77)
Parents: Ron and Jean
Wife and date of marriage: Caroline, 1 October 1984
Children: Kirstie Jane, 18 May 1988; Dominic James, 21 September 1991
Family links with cricket: Brother Graham used to play good representative cricket
before joining the RAF
Education: Beverley Grammar School, East Yorkshire
Qualifications: 7 O-levels, NCA preliminary coaching course
Overseas tours: England YC to West Indies 1979-80
Overseas teams played for: Otago, New Zealand 1983-93; Kalkorai, New Zealand 1983-93
Cricketers particularly admired: Richard Hadlee, Dennis Lillee, Peter Willey
Other sports followed: Golf, rugby league, football
Injuries: Thigh strain, missed one month; groin strain, missed six weeks
Relaxations: Golf
Extras: Joined Somerset in 1987. Equalled Somerset first-class record for ninth wicket v
Sussex at Hove in 1990 – batting with Chris Tavaré. Called up to join England tour squad
in New Zealand 1991-92 as cover for injured fast bowlers. On debut for England v Pakistan
in 1992 at Headingley, he achieved a new bowling record for a Test debutant at that ground
by taking eight wickets in the game. At school opened both the batting and the bowling.
Plans to return to Northamptonshire for 1995 season, subject to fitness
Opinions on cricket: 'Still believe that new ball should be available to be taken after 85

overs in first-class cricket (as in Test cricket).'
Best batting: 100* Otago v Central Districts, Palmerston North 1991-92
Best bowling: 7-27 Otago v Auckland, Auckland 1984-85

1994 Season

	M	Inns	NO	Runs	HS	Avge	100s	50s	Ct	St	O	M	Runs	Wkts	Avge	Best	5wI	10wM
Test																		
All First	8	12	3	270	43 *	30.00	-	-	1	-	193.3	50	602	16	37.62	3-23	-	-
1-day Int																		
NatWest	2	1	1	0	0 *	-	-	-	-	-	17	3	52	1	52.00	1-20	-	
B & H	1	1	0	2	2	2.00	-	-	-	-	11	0	44	0	-	-	-	
Sunday	9	5	3	42	19 *	21.00	-	-	-	-	67.2	0	381	16	23.81	4-38	-	

Career Performances

	M	Inns	NO	Runs	HS	Avge	100s	50s	Ct	St	Balls	Runs	Wkts	Avge	Best	5wI	10wM
Test	2	3	0	8	4	2.66	-	-	-	-	449	215	10	21.50	5-50	1	-
All First	334	382	119	4557	100 *	17.32	1	10	107	-	52009	24022	916	26.22	7-27	36	5
1-day Int																	
NatWest	30	13	6	63	11 *	9.00	-	-	5	-	1856	865	43	20.11	7-37	1	
B & H	54	26	10	93	16 *	5.81	-	-	14	-	3033	1889	64	29.51	5-53	1	
Sunday	174	81	44	557	31 *	15.05	-	-	31	-	7103	5240	193	27.15	5-34	1	

MARC, K. Middlesex

Name: Kervin Marc
Role: Left-hand bat,
left-arm fast bowler
Born: 9 January 1975, Monrepos, St Lucia
Height: 6ft 5in **Weight:** 14st
Nickname: Kerv, Swerv
County debut: 1994
Parents: Linda and Pima
Marital status: Single
Family links with cricket: Uncle Terry plays
for Monrepos
Education: The London Oratory School; Central
St Martin College of Art and Design
Qualifications: 7 GCSEs, 2 A-levels
Career outside cricket: Art and design
Off-season: Relaxing, getting fit for next season
Cricketers particularly admired: Brian Lara,
Desmond Haynes, Alf Langley

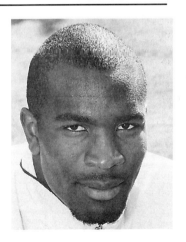

Injuries: Palela tendonitis, missed three weeks
Relaxations: Drawing, painting, designing, music (hip hop, R&B, Ragga)
Opinions on cricket: 'Something drastic needs to be done to create interest in the game within the school system, e.g. coloured clothing could be worn. There should be a greater involvement of countries worldwide, hence creating a bigger World Cup. The game should incorporate American-style marketing involving bigger multinational sports companies.'
Best batting: 9 Middlesex v Lancashire, Old Trafford 1994
Best bowling: 2-52 Middlesex v Lancashire, Old Trafford 1994

1994 Season

	M	Inns	NO	Runs	HS	Avge	100s	50s	Ct	St	O	M	Runs	Wkts	Avge	Best	5wl	10wM
Test																		
All First	1	2	0	17	9	8.50	-	-	-	-	29	4	133	3	44.33	2-52	-	-
1-day Int																		
NatWest																		
B & H																		
Sunday																		

Career Performances

	M	Inns	NO	Runs	HS	Avge	100s	50s	Ct	St	Balls	Runs	Wkts	Avge	Best	5wl	10wM
Test																	
All First	1	2	0	17	9	8.50	-	-	-	-	174	133	3	44.33	2-52	-	-
1-day Int																	
NatWest																	
B & H																	
Sunday																	

49. Which country recorded their highest Test innings total of 544-4 declared against Pakistan in 1994-95?

MARLAND, L. Lancashire

Name: Lee John Marland
Role: Right-hand bat
Born: 21 September 1975, Withington,
Manchester
Nickname: Marlene, Marlo, Charlie Chan
County debut: No first-team appearance
Parents: Liz and Jeff
Marital status: Single
Family links with cricket: Father has played
for Brooklands for many years
Education: Worthington Primary; Manchester
Grammar School; Northumbria University
Qualifications: 10 GCSEs, 3 A-levels
Off-season: At university
Cricketers particularly admired:
Graham Gooch 'and my Dad'
Other sports followed: Rugby league, football
Relaxations: Eating, sleeping, listening to music
Extras: *Daily Telegraph* U15 batting award

MARSH, S. A. Kent

Name: Steven Andrew Marsh
Role: Right-hand bat, wicket-keeper,
county vice-captain
Born: 27 January 1961, Westminster
Height: 5ft 11in **Weight:** 13st
Nickname: Marshy
County debut: 1982
County cap: 1986
Benefit: 1995
1st-Class 50s: 39
1st-Class 100s: 7
1st-Class catches: 497
1st-Class stumpings: 40
Place in batting averages: 111th av. 32.28
(1993 137th av. 26.68)
Parents: Melvyn Graham and Valerie Ann
Wife and date of marriage:
Julie, 27 September 1986

Children: Hayley Ann, 15 May 1987;
Christian James Robert, 20 November 1990
Family links with cricket: Father played local cricket for Lordswood. Father-in-law, Bob Wilson, played for Kent 1954-66
Education: Walderslade Secondary School for Boys; Mid-Kent College of Higher and Further Education
Qualifications: 6 O-levels, 2 A-levels, OND in Business Studies
Career outside cricket: Jazz singer
Off-season: 'Relaxing before my benefit year, by becoming a couch potato'
Overseas tours: Fred Rumsey XI to Barbados 1986-87
Overseas teams played for: Avendale CC, Cape Town 1985-86
Cricketers particularly admired: Robin Smith, Graham Cowdrey, Ian Botham
Other sports followed: Golf
Injuries: 'Missed one day, one session and five minutes'
Extras: Appointed Kent vice-captain in 1991. In the match v Middlesex at Lord's in 1991 he held a world record eight catches in an innings and scored 113*. 'Cycling proficiency'
Opinions on cricket: 'Generally very tedious, brought on by four-day cricket. Unless of course you watch Kent who will either be bowled out for 150 in a session or score 450 in a day. Now that's what I call cricket. Boredom bores me!'
Best batting: 125 Kent v Yorkshire, Canterbury 1992
Best bowling: 2-20 Kent v Warwickshire, Edgbaston 1990

1994 Season

	M	Inns	NO	Runs	HS	Avge	100s	50s	Ct	St	O	M	Runs	Wkts	Avge	Best	5wI	10wM
Test																		
All First	19	31	6	807	88	32.28	-	5	69	5								
1-day Int																		
NatWest	4	3	2	28	22	28.00	-	-	6	1								
B & H	1	1	1	15	15*	-	-	-	1	-								
Sunday	16	11	7	125	28	31.25	-	-	16	3								

Career Performances

	M	Inns	NO	Runs	HS	Avge	100s	50s	Ct	St	Balls	Runs	Wkts	Avge	Best	5wI	10wM
Test																	
All First	211	300	53	7009	125	28.37	7	39	497	40	154	227	2	113.50	2-20	-	-
1-day Int																	
NatWest	19	13	3	128	24*	12.80	-	-	27	3							
B & H	39	30	7	380	71	16.52	-	1	45	2							
Sunday	135	97	24	1409	59	19.30	-	4	130	18							

Name: Peter James Martin
Role: Right-hand bat, right-arm
fast-medium bowler
Born: 15 November 1968, Accrington
Height: 6ft 5in **Weight:** 15st 4lbs
Nickname: Digger, Long John, Rolf
County debut: 1989
County cap: 1994
50 wickets in season: 1
1st-Class 50s: 3
1st-Class 100s: 1
1st-Class 5 w. in innings: 3
1st-Class catches: 21
Place in batting averages:
232nd av. 15.95 (1993 120th av. 28.50)
Place in bowling averages:
55th av. 29.25 (1993 84th av. 31.26)
Strike rate: 68.29 (career 73.88)
Parents: Keith and Catherine Lina
Marital status: Single
Education: Danum School, Doncaster
Qualifications: 6 O-levels, 2 A-levels

Overseas tours: England YC to Australia (Youth World Cup) 1988; 'and various other tours with English Schools and NAYC'
Overseas teams played for: Southern Districts, Queensland 1988-89; South Launceston, Tasmania 1989-90; South Canberra, ACT 1990-92
Cricketers particularly admired: 'Loads'
Other sports followed: Football (Manchester United), rugby league (St Helens)
Relaxations: Music, painting, golf, cooking, walking
Extras: Plays district football and basketball for Doncaster. Played for England A v Sri Lankans 1991
Opinions on cricket: 'Should only be six-hour days with 100 overs a day.'
Best batting: 133 Lancashire v Durham, Gateshead Fell 1992
Best bowling: 5-35 Lancashire v Yorkshire, Headingley 1993

50. Which West Indian member of the International Panel of umpires officiated in England for the first two Test matches against New Zealand in 1994?

1994 Season

	M	Inns	NO	Runs	HS	Avge	100s	50s	Ct	St	O	M	Runs	Wkts	Avge	Best	5wI	10wM
Test																		
All First	18	27	3	383	57	15.95	-	1	4	-	614.4	177	1580	54	29.25	5-61	2	-
1-day Int																		
NatWest	2	1	0	16	16	16.00	-	-	-	-	24	2	96	4	24.00	3-63	-	
B & H	2	0	0	0	0	-	-	-	-	-	20	4	66	1	66.00	1-35	-	
Sunday	17	5	2	14	8 *	4.66	-	-	3	-	117.4	11	488	25	19.52	5-32	1	

Career Performances

	M	Inns	NO	Runs	HS	Avge	100s	50s	Ct	St	Balls	Runs	Wkts	Avge	Best	5wI	10wM
Test																	
All First	84	94	27	1423	133	21.23	1	3	21	-	13890	6582	188	35.01	5-35	3	-
1-day Int																	
NatWest	6	1	0	16	16	16.00	-	-	1	-	318	194	8	24.25	3-63	-	
B & H	4	1	1	10	10 *	-	-	-	1	-	252	145	4	36.25	2-50	-	
Sunday	40	12	7	76	18 *	15.20	-	-	7	-	1498	1133	43	26.34	5-32	1	

MARU, R. J. Hampshire

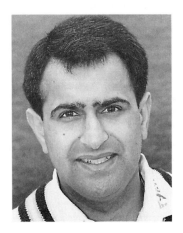

Name: Rajesh Jamnadass Maru
Role: Right-hand bat, slow left-arm bowler, close fielder
Born: 28 October 1962, Nairobi, Kenya
Height: 5ft 6in **Weight:** 11st
Nickname: Raj
County debut: 1980 (Middlesex), 1984 (Hampshire)
County cap: 1986 (Hampshire)
50 wickets in a season: 4
1st-Class 50s: 6
1st-Class 5 w. in innings: 15
1st-Class 10 w. in match: 1
1st-Class catches: 225
Place in batting averages: 209th av. 18.81
Place in bowling averages: 123rd av. 41.40
Strike rate: 101.66 (career 73.76)
Parents: Jamnadass and Prabhavati
Wife and date of marriage:
Amanda Jane, 21 September 1991
Children: Christopher Patrick
Family links with cricket: Father played in Kenya and in England for North London

Polytechnic. Brother Pradip plays for Wembley in the Middlesex League and has played for Middlesex 2nd XI, Middlesex U19 and for Middlesex Colts & Schools
Education: Rooks Heath High School, Harrow; Pinner Sixth Form College
Qualifications: NCA advanced coach
Career outside cricket: Cricket coach
Off-season: Coaching for Hampshire
Overseas tours: England YC South to Canada 1979; England YC to West Indies 1979-80; Middlesex to Zimbabwe 1980; Hampshire to Barbados 1987,1988,1990; Hampshire to Dubai 1989; Barbican International XI to Dubai 1981; MCC to Leeward Islands 1992
Overseas teams played for: Marlborough CA, Blenheim, New Zealand 1985-87
Cricketers particularly admired: David Gower, Bishen Bedi, Richard Hadlee, Phil Edmonds, John Emburey, Malcolm Marshall
Other sports followed: Football, rugby, 'would watch any sport'
Relaxations: Spending time with wife and son, DIY at home
Extras: Played for Middlesex 1980-83; has taken over 400 County Championship wickets
Opinions on cricket: 'Four-day cricket has been good for the game, but the standard of wickets have to change. You have to produce good wickets to make the game last the full four days.'
Best batting: 74 Hampshire v Gloucestershire, Gloucester 1988
Best bowling: 8-41 Hampshire v Kent, Southampton 1989

1994 Season

	M	Inns	NO	Runs	HS	Avge	100s	50s	Ct	St	O	M	Runs	Wkts	Avge	Best	5wI	10wM
Test																		
All First	9	15	4	207	38 *	18.81	-	-	13	-	254.1	75	621	15	41.40	3-61	-	-
1-day Int																		
NatWest																			
B & H																			
Sunday	4	2	2	13	7 *	-	-	-	-	-	28.4	0	188	7	26.85	3-33	-	

Career Performances

	M	Inns	NO	Runs	HS	Avge	100s	50s	Ct	St	Balls	Runs	Wkts	Avge	Best	5wI	10wM
Test																	
All First	210	205	50	2560	74	16.51	-	6	225	-	36515	16278	495	32.88	8-41	15	1
1-day Int																	
NatWest	13	5	2	43	22	14.33	-	-	11	-	822	492	12	41.00	3-46	-	
B & H	10	2	0	13	9	6.50	-	-	5	-	495	330	9	36.66	3-46	-	
Sunday	49	21	12	135	33 *	15.00	-	-	18	-	1618	1406	39	36.05	3-30	-	

MASON, T. J.   Leicestershire

Name: Timothy James Mason
Role: Right-hand bat, right-arm off-spin
bowler
Born: 12 April 1975, Leicester
Height: 5ft 8in **Weight:** 10st 2lbs
Nickname: Perry, Rowdy, Stone
County debut: 1994
1st-Class catches: 2
Parents: Phil and Anthea
Marital status: Single
Family links with cricket: Father has
played club cricket, is manager and coach
of Leicester U11 and chairman of
Leicestershire Schools CA 1993-94
Education: Brookvale High School,
Leicester; Denstone College
Qualifications: 9 GCSEs, 3 A-levels
Off-season: Coaching
Overseas tours: Denstone College to
South Africa 1993; England U19 to Sri Lanka 1993-94
Cricketers particularly admired: Allan Lamb, Malcolm Marshall
Other sports followed: Rugby union, football
Relaxations: Listening to music, watching most sports
Extras: Captained Leicestershire Schools at all age levels. 1992 *Daily Telegraph* U19
Midlands Bowler of the Year; 1993 *Daily Telegraph* U19 National Bowler of the Year;
1993 Gray-Nicolls Outstanding Schoolboy Player of the Year. Dislocated shoulder prevented
him from going on England U18 tour to South Africa 1992-93.
Opinions on cricket: 'Cricket has already provided me with the opportunity to travel to
places around the world which otherwise I wouldn't have been able to do.'
Best batting: 3 Leicestershire v Essex, Leicester 1994
Best bowling: 1-22 Leicestershire v Essex, Leicester 1994

1994 Season

	M	Inns	NO	Runs	HS	Avge	100s	50s	Ct	St	O	M	Runs	Wkts	Avge	Best	5wI	10wM
Test																		
All First	1	1	0	3	3	3.00	-	-	2	-	7	0	22	1	22.00	1-22	-	-
1-day Int																		
NatWest																		
B & H																		
Sunday																		

	M	Inns	NO	Runs	HS	Avge	100s	50s	Ct	St	Balls	Runs	Wkts	Avge	Best	5wI	10wM
Test																	
All First	1	1	0	3	3	3.00	-	-	2	-	42	22	1	22.00	1-22	-	-
1-day Int																	
NatWest																	
B & H																	
Sunday																	

MAYNARD, M. P. Glamorgan

Name: Matthew Peter Maynard
Role: Right-hand bat, right-arm medium
'declaration' bowler, cover fielder
Born: 21 March 1966, Oldham, Lancashire
Height: 5ft 11in **Weight:** 13st
Nickname: Ollie
County debut: 1985
County cap: 1987
Test debut: 1988
Tests: 4
One-Day Internationals: 5
1000 runs in a season: 8
1st-Class 50s: 75
1st-Class 100s: 30
1st-Class 200s: 2
1st-Class catches: 204
1st-Class stumpings: 3
One-Day 100s: 7
Place in batting averages: 84th av. 36.07
(1993 29th av. 44.45)
Parents: Ken (deceased) and Pat
Wife and date of marriage: Susan, 27 September 1986
Children: Tom, 25 March 1989; Ceri Lloyd, 5 August 1993
Family links with cricket: Father played for many years for Duckinfield. Brother Charlie
plays for St Fagans
Education: Ysgol David Hughes, Menai Bridge, Anglesey
Qualifications: Cricket coach
Career outside cricket: Marketing for Glamorgan CCC
Off-season: As above
Overseas tours: North Wales XI to Barbados 1982; Glamorgan to Barbados 1982, to South
Africa 1993; unofficial England XI to South Africa 1989-90; HKCC (Australia) to Bangkok

and Hong Kong, 1990; England VI to Hong Kong Sixes 1992 and 1994; England to West Indies 1993-94

Overseas teams played for: St Joseph's, Whakatane, New Zealand 1986-88; Gosnells, Perth, Western Australia 1988-89; Papakura and Northern Districts, New Zealand 1990-92; Morrinsville College and Northern Districts 1991-92

Cricketers particularly admired: Ian Botham, Viv Richards

Other sports followed: 'Most'

Injuries: Broken knuckle in right hand, missed four weeks

Relaxations: 'Spending time with my wife and family. Playing golf and having the odd pint.'

Extras: Scored century on first-class debut v Yorkshire at Swansea in 1985, when he became the youngest centurion for Glamorgan, and scored 1000 runs in first full season. In 1987 scored the fastest ever 50 for Glamorgan (14 mins) v Yorkshire and was youngest player to be awarded Glamorgan cap. Voted Young Cricketer of the Year 1988 by the Cricket Writers' Club. Banned from Test cricket for five years for joining 1989-90 tour of South Africa, ban remitted 1992. Scored 987 runs in July 1991, including a century in each innings v Gloucestershire at Cheltenham. Captained Glamorgan for most of 1992 in Alan Butcher's absence. Second child was born on the morning of the fifth Test against Australia at Edgbaston 1993 – he had a daughter and a duck on the same day.

Opinions on cricket: 'Four-day cricket should be here to stay, but start on a Wednesday and finish on a Saturday.'

Best batting: 243 Glamorgan v Hampshire, Southampton 1991

Best bowling: 3-21 Glamorgan v Oxford University, The Parks 1987

1994 Season

	M	Inns	NO	Runs	HS	Avge	100s	50s	Ct	St	O	M	Runs	Wkts	Avge	Best	5wI	10wM
Test																		
All First	16	28	1	974	118	36.07	2	5	18	1	1	0	10	0	-		-	-
1-day Int																		
NatWest	3	3	0	166	78	55.33	-	2	5	-								
B & H	1	1	0	19	19	19.00	-	-	-	-								
Sunday	15	15	1	349	65	24.92	-	2	10	-								

Career Performances

	M	Inns	NO	Runs	HS	Avge	100s	50s	Ct	St	Balls	Runs	Wkts	Avge	Best	5wI	10wM
Test	4	8	0	87	35	10.87	-	-	3	-							
All First	227	372	39	13817	243	41.49	30	75	204	3	816	686	6	114.33	3-21	-	-
1-day Int	5	5	1	59	22 *	14.75	-	-	1	-							
NatWest	25	25	2	1200	151 *	52.17	2	10	9	-							
B & H	31	31	3	1065	115	38.03	2	6	8	-	24	32	0	-		-	-
Sunday	133	128	8	3623	122 *	30.19	3	24	43	-	16	27	0	-		-	-

McCAGUE, M. J.   Kent

Name: Martin John McCague
Role: Right-hand bat, right-arm
fast bowler
Born: 24 May 1969,
Larne, Northern Ireland
Height: 6ft 5in **Weight:** 17st
Nickname: Stinger, Pigsy
County debut: 1991
County cap: 1992
Test debut: 1993
Tests: 2
50 wickets in season: 2
1st-Class 50s: 1
1st-Class 5 w. in innings: 14
1st-Class 10 w. in match: 2
1st-Class catches: 33
One-Day 5 w. in innings: 2
Place in bowling averages: 189th av. 21.92
Place in bowling averages:
4th 19.01 (1993 59th av. 28.64)
Strike rate: 35.91 (career 51.21)
Parents: Mal and Mary
Marital status: Single
Education: Hedland Senior High School
Qualifications: Electrician
Off-season: Touring with England
Overseas tours: England A to South Africa 1993-94, England to Australia 1994-95
Overseas teams played for: Western Australia 1990-91
Cricketers particularly admired: Dennis Lillee, Curtly Ambrose
Other sports followed: Football (Crystal Palace and Gillingham)
Injuries: Rotator cuff joint in right shoulder, missed 12 weeks. Suffered from shin splints
on England tour to Australia and forced to return home early
Relaxations: Music and sport on television
Opinions on cricket: 'Bowl-outs in finals to be reviewed. Games should be rescheduled
if possible.'
Best batting: 56 Kent v Durham, Canterbury 1994
Best bowling: 9-86 Kent v Derbyshire, Derby 1994

---

51. Who are the only two bowlers to have been hit for six sixes in
one over in first-class cricket?

1994 Season

	M	Inns	NO	Runs	HS	Avge	100s	50s	Ct	St	O	M	Runs	Wkts	Avge	Best	5wI	10wM
Test																		
All First	10	16	3	285	56	21.92	-	1	5	-	341.1	67	1084	57	19.01	9-86	5	1
1-day Int																		
NatWest	2	1	0	1	1	1.00	-	-	1	-	22	1	73	4	18.25	2-36	-	
B & H	1	0	0	0	0	-	-	-	-	-	2.2	0	10	0	-	-	-	
Sunday	9	3	1	13	7	6.50	-	-	2	-	55.5	1	223	18	12.38	4-19	-	

Career Performances

	M	Inns	NO	Runs	HS	Avge	100s	50s	Ct	St	Balls	Runs	Wkts	Avge	Best	5wI	10wM
Test	2	3	0	20	11	6.66	-	-	1	-	477	294	4	73.50	4-121	-	
All First	59	73	16	771	56	13.52	-	1	33	-	10449	5403	204	26.48	9-86	14	2
1-day Int																	
NatWest	8	6	3	37	14	12.33	-	-	1	-	474	304	16	19.00	5-26	1	-
B & H	11	8	3	83	30	16.60	-	-	2	-	508	344	22	15.63	5-43	1	
Sunday	38	19	9	123	22 *	12.30	-	-	7	-	1567	1317	65	20.26	4-19	-	

McCORKILL, B. M.   Worcestershire

Name: Benjamin Michael McCorkill
Role: Left-arm spin bowler
Born: 18 September 1976, Truro, Cornwall
Height: 5ft 9in **Weight:** 10st 7lbs
County debut: No first-team appearance
Parents: Michael and Elaine
Marital status: Single
Education: Mullion CP; Cury CP;
Mullion Camp; Millfield School
Qualifications: 9 GCSEs
Career outside cricket: School
Off-season: At school and living in Ghana
during the holidays
Overseas tours: Millfield School U15 to
Zimbabwe 1991; Millfield School to
Sri Lanka 1993
Cricketers particularly admired:
Richard Illingworth, Graeme Hick
Other sports followed: Football
Injuries: Dislodged disc in back, missed six weeks
Relaxations: Weights, visiting the beach
Extras: Played football for SW England U15 and cricket for England U17 against India

Opinions on cricket: 'I believe overseas players improve English cricket, not just because they are good players, but it gives English cricketers the chance to play against Test players and also listen to what they have to say when practising.'

McGRATH, A.   Yorkshire

Name: Anthony McGrath
Role: Right-hand bat, off-spin bowler
Born: 6 October 1975, Bradford
Height: 6ft 2in **Weight:** 13st
Nickname: Mags
County debut: No first-team appearance
Parents: Terry and Kathleen
Marital status: Single
Family links with cricket: Brother Dermot plays in the Bradford League
Education: St Winefride's; St Blaise; Yorkshire Martyrs Collegiate School
Qualifications: 9 GCSEs, National Diploma in Leisure Studies
Off-season: Touring with England U19
Overseas tours: England U19 to West Indies 1994-95
Cricketers particularly admired: Martyn Moxon, Graham Gooch, Ashley Metcalfe, Graham Thorpe
Other sports followed: Football (Manchester United), and most other sports
Relaxations: Music, playing other sports
Extras: Captained Yorkshire Schools U13, U14, U15 and U16; captained English Schools U17. Bradford League Young Cricketer of the Year 1992 and 1993. Played for England U17, and for England U19 in home series against India 1994
Opinions on cricket: 'Too much cricket is played during the season. This results in players becoming tired, thus affecting their performance.'

---

52. Which county has won the County Championship most times since 1890 and when did they last win it?

McKEOWN, P. C. — Lancashire

Name: Patrick Christopher McKeown
Role: Right-hand bat
Born: 1 June 1976, Liverpool
Height: 6ft 3in **Weight:** 13st
Nickname: Paddy
Parents: Paddy and Cathy
Marital status: Single
Education: Rossall School (Blackpool)
Qualifications: 7 GCSEs, 3 A-levels
Off-season: Playing cricket in Australia
Cricketers particularly admired:
Graeme Hick and Neil Fairbrother
Other sports followed: Football and rugby
Relaxations: 'Playing most sports, especially
football and rugby. I enjoy spending time on the
golf course.'
Extras: Represented England Schools U19 ,
and U18 versus India. Played for Development
of Excellence U19, National Cricket Association
U19, Headmasters' Conference U19

METCALFE, A. A. — Yorkshire

Name: Ashley Anthony Metcalfe
Role: Right-hand opening bat, off-spin bowler
Born: 25 December 1963, Horsforth, Leeds
Height: 5ft 9½in **Weight:** 11st 7lbs
County debut: 1983
County cap: 1986
Benefit: 1995
1000 runs in a season: 6
1st-Class 50s: 51
1st-Class 100s: 24
1st-Class 200s: 1
1st-Class catches: 69
One-Day 100s: 4
Place in batting averages: (1993 107th av. 31.13)
Parents: Tony and Ann
Wife and date of marriage: Diane, 20 April 1986
Children: Zoë, 18 July 1990; Amy, 22 August 1993

Family links with cricket: Father played in local league; father-in-law Ray Illingworth (Yorkshire and England)
Education: Ladderbanks Middle School; Bradford Grammar School; University College, London
Qualifications: 9 O-levels, 3 A-levels, NCA coaching certificate
Career outside cricket: 'Metcalfe & Sidebottom Associates – sports promotion company'
Off-season: Selling leisurewear
Overseas teams played for: Orange Free State 1988-89
Cricketers particularly admired: Barry Richards, Doug Padgett, Don Wilson, Arnie Sidebottom, Pete Hartley, Paul Jarvis
Other sports followed: Most, particularly golf
Relaxations: 'Relaxing at home with my family'

Extras: Making 122 on first-class debut v Nottinghamshire at Park Avenue in 1983 he became the youngest Yorkshire player to achieve the feat and recorded the highest debut score by a Yorkshireman. Reached 2000 runs for the season in the last match of 1990 with 194* and 107 v Nottinghamshire at Trent Bridge.
Best batting: 216* Yorkshire v Middlesex, Headingley 1988
Best bowling: 2-18 Yorkshire v Warwickshire, Scarborough 1987

1994 Season

	M	Inns	NO	Runs	HS	Avge	100s	50s	Ct	St	O	M	Runs	Wkts	Avge	Best	5wI	10wM
Test																		
All First	2	4	0	15	12	3.75	-	-	1	-								
1-day Int																		
NatWest																		
B & H																		
Sunday	9	8	3	230	65 *	46.00	-	2	1	-								

Career Performances

	M	Inns	NO	Runs	HS	Avge	100s	50s	Ct	St	Balls	Runs	Wkts	Avge	Best	5wI	10wM
Test																	
All First	190	329	19	10692	216 *	34.49	24	51	69	-	392	316	4	79.00	2-18	-	-
1-day Int																	
NatWest	18	18	3	681	127 *	45.40	1	5	4	-	42	44	2	22.00	2-44	-	
B & H	31	31	4	1277	114	47.29	1	8	8	-							
Sunday	131	128	5	3398	116	27.62	2	22	30	-							

METSON, C. P.   Glamorgan

Name: Colin Peter Metson
Role: Right-hand bat, wicket-keeper, bowl-out specialist bowler (at one stump)
Born: 2 July 1963, Cuffley, Herts
Height: 5ft 6in **Weight:** 11st
Nickname: Meto, Stumpie
County debut: 1981 (Middlesex), 1987 (Glamorgan)
County cap: 1987 (Glamorgan)
1st-Class 50s: 7
1st-Class catches: 491
1st-Class stumpings: 41
Place in batting averages: 187th av. 22.11 (1993 230th av. 14.69)
Parents: Denis Alwyn and Jean Mary
Wife and date of marriage: Stephanie Leslie Astrid, 13 October 1991
Family links with cricket: Father captained Winchmore Hill
Education: Stanborough School, Welwyn Garden City; Enfield Grammar School; Durham University
Qualifications: 10 O-levels, 5 A-levels, BA (Hons) Economic History, advanced cricket coach
Career outside cricket: Project co-ordinator with Castle Services
Off-season: As above
Overseas teams played for: Payneham, Adelaide 1986-88; Rostrevor Old Boys, Adelaide 1987-88
Cricketers particularly admired: Bob Taylor, Rod Marsh, Ian Botham
Other sports followed: Football, golf, most sports except wrestling
Injuries: Broken finger, missed two weeks
Relaxations: Watching sport, videos, good wine, port
Extras: Played for England YC v India YC 1981 and was voted Young Wicket-keeper of the Year. In 1984 captained Durham University, losing finalists in UAU competition. Left Middlesex at end of 1986 season. Holds the Glamorgan record for most catches in an innings (7) and match (9). Played 160 consecutive Championship matches for Glamorgan, 1987-94. Wombwell Cricket Lovers' Society Wicket-keeper of the Year 1993
Opinions on cricket: 'Cricket must find ways to market itself better, and must give the sponsors value for money. The 25-point deduction regarding "unfit" pitches should be more widely used so that the counties will prepare the best possible pitches. Counties should take more interest in the winter and future careers of its players (regarding placements, qualifications, etc). Use of the third umpire in semi-finals as well as the finals.'
Best batting: 96 Middlesex v Gloucestershire, Uxbridge 1984

1994 Season

	M	Inns	NO	Runs	HS	Avge	100s	50s	Ct	St	O	M	Runs	Wkts	Avge	Best	5wl	10wM
Test																		
All First	18	22	4	398	51	22.11	-	1	54	7								
1-day Int																		
NatWest	3	2	0	11	7	5.50	-	-	4	-								
B & H	1	0	0	0	0	-	-	-	1	1								
Sunday	16	8	3	60	26 *	12.00	-	-	19	5								

Career Performances

	M	Inns	NO	Runs	HS	Avge	100s	50s	Ct	St	Balls	Runs	Wkts	Avge	Best	5wl	10wM
Test																	
All First	204	265	58	3737	96	18.05	-	7	491	41	6	0	0	-	-	-	
1-day Int																	
NatWest	23	13	2	69	21	6.27	-	-	23	2							
B & H	27	18	3	153	23	10.20	-	-	14	4							
Sunday	134	81	41	640	30 *	16.00	-	-	129	39							

MIDDLETON, T. C. Hampshire

Name: Tony Charles Middleton
Role: Right-hand bat, slow left-arm bowler
Born: 1 February 1964, Winchester
Height: 5ft 10in **Weight:** 11st
Nickname: Dogun
County debut: 1984
County cap: 1990
1000 runs in a season: 2
1st-Class 50s: 24
1st-Class 100s: 13
1st-Class 200s: 1
1st-Class catches: 78
Place in batting averages: 150th av. 26.20
(1993 147th av. 25.95)
Parents: Peter and Molly
Wife and date of marriage:
Sherralyn, 23 September 1989
Family links with cricket: Brother plays
local club cricket
Education: Weeke Infants and Junior Schools; Montgomery of Alamein Comprehensive;
Peter Symonds Sixth Form College, Winchester
Qualifications: 5 O-levels, 1 A-level

Overseas tours: Hampshire to Barbados 1989; England A to Australia 1992-93
Overseas teams played for: South African Police, Durban 1984-86; Belmont, Newcastle, NSW, Australia 1987-89
Cricketers particularly admired: Barry Richards, Gordon Greenidge, 'I was particularly helped by Neville Rodgers and Tim Tremlett'
Other sports followed: Football, rugby union, badminton, squash
Relaxations: Watching sport, gardening, real ale pubs, holidays
Extras: Played for English Schools 1982. Scored six consecutive centuries for Hampshire in May 1990: 104 and 144 v Somerset II; 121 v Yorkshire II; 100 and 124 v Leicestershire II; 104* for 1st XI v Essex. Scored 78 in NatWest final 1991, on his first appearance in the competition. Was first batsman to 1000 first-class runs in 1992
Best batting: 221 Hampshire v Surrey, Southampton 1992
Best bowling: 2-41 Hampshire v Kent, Canterbury 1991

1994 Season

	M	Inns	NO	Runs	HS	Avge	100s	50s	Ct	St	O	M	Runs	Wkts	Avge	Best	5wI	10wM
Test																		
All First	13	23	3	524	102	26.20	1	1	8	-								
1-day Int																		
NatWest																		
B & H	2	2	1	80	63 *	80.00	-	1	2	-								
Sunday	11	11	1	334	73	33.40	-	4	3	-								

Career Performances

	M	Inns	NO	Runs	HS	Avge	100s	50s	Ct	St	Balls	Runs	Wkts	Avge	Best	5wI	10wM
Test																	
All First	107	183	16	5705	221	34.16	13	24	78	-	236	241	5	48.20	2-41	-	-
1-day Int																	
NatWest	5	5	0	202	78	40.40	-	1	-	-							
B & H	15	15	2	522	91 *	40.15	-	5	5	-							
Sunday	41	40	4	1415	98	39.30	-	14	13	-							

MIKE, G. W.   Nottinghamshire

Name: Gregory Wentworth Mike
Role: Right-hand bat, right-arm medium-fast bowler
Born: 14 July 1966, Nottingham
Height: 6ft 1in **Weight:** 14st
Nickname: Wenters
County debut: 1989
1st-Class 50s: 4
1st-Class 5 w. in innings: 2

1st-Class catches: 10
Place in batting averages: 233rd av. 15.86
(1993 195th av. 20.00)
Place in bowling averages: 78th av. 31.60
(1993 121th av. 41.64)
Strike rate: 54.11 (career 62.32)
Parents: Clinton and Kathleen
Marital status: Single
Family links with cricket: Father played
Education: Claremont Comprehensive;
Basford College
Qualifications: 5 CSEs, 2 O-levels
Career outside cricket: Youth worker
Off-season: Coaching at Trent Bridge
Overseas tours: Nottinghamshire to Barbados
1987, 1988, 1991
Overseas teams played for:
Geelong City, Australia 1990-91;
Lancaster Park, New Zealand 1992-93

Cricketers particularly admired: Viv Richards, Ian Botham, Richard Hadlee
Other sports followed: All sports
Relaxations: Listening to music (swing beat, soul and reggae music)
Opinions on cricket: 'Great game.'
Best batting: 61* Nottinghamshire v Warwickshire, Edgbaston 1992
Best bowling: 5-44 Nottinghamshire v Yorkshire, Middlesbrough 1994

1994 Season

	M	Inns	NO	Runs	HS	Avge	100s	50s	Ct	St	O	M	Runs	Wkts	Avge	Best	5wI	10wM
Test																		
All First	17	26	3	365	60 *	15.86	-	1	1	-	405.5	92	1422	45	31.60	5-44	1	-
1-day Int																		
NatWest	2	2	1	8	5 *	8.00	-	-	-	-	18	2	84	1	84.00	1-71	-	
B & H	3	2	1	21	15 *	21.00	-	-	1	-	26	1	121	3	40.33	2-35	-	
Sunday	15	9	2	61	29 *	8.71	-	-	2	-	96.3	5	555	20	27.75	4-41	-	

Career Performances

	M	Inns	NO	Runs	HS	Avge	100s	50s	Ct	St	Balls	Runs	Wkts	Avge	Best	5wI	10wM
Test																	
All First	35	52	8	851	61 *	19.34	-	4	10	-	4737	2814	76	37.02	5-44	2	-
1-day Int																	
NatWest	2	2	1	8	5 *	8.00	-	-	-	-	108	84	1	84.00	1-71	-	
B & H	4	3	2	46	25 *	46.00	-	-	2	-	222	165	7	23.57	4-44	-	
Sunday	48	32	6	291	51 *	11.19	-	1	10	-	1886	1767	52	33.98	4-41	-	

MILBURN, S. M.   Yorkshire

Name: Stuart Mark Milburn
Role: Right-hand bat, right-arm
medium-fast bowler
Born: 29 September 1972, Harrogate
Height: 6ft 1in **Weight:** 13st 3lbs
Nickname: Millers
County debut: 1992
Parents: Ken and Pam
Marital status: Engaged
Education: Upper Nidderdale High School,
Pateley Bridge, Harrogate
Qualifications: 7 GCSEs,
Diploma in Catering
Overseas teams played for:
Somerset West, South Africa 1992-93
Cricketers particularly admired:
Ian Botham, Richard Hadlee
Other sports followed: Golf, snooker

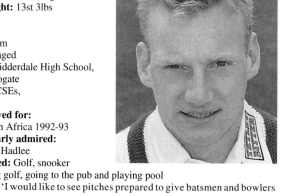

Relaxations: Playing golf, going to the pub and playing pool
Opinions on cricket: 'I would like to see pitches prepared to give batsmen and bowlers an equal chance.'
Best batting: 5 Yorkshire v Worcestershire, Worcester 1992
Best bowling: 2-74 Yorkshire v Worcestershire, Worcester 1994

1994 Season

	M	Inns	NO	Runs	HS	Avge	100s	50s	Ct	St	O	M	Runs	Wkts	Avge	Best	5wI	10wM
Test																		
All First	1	0	0	0	0	-	-	-	-	-	24.2	4	77	3	25.66	2-74	-	-
1-day Int																		
NatWest																		
B & H																		
Sunday																		

Career Performances

	M	Inns	NO	Runs	HS	Avge	100s	50s	Ct	St	Balls	Runs	Wkts	Avge	Best	5wI	10wM
Test																	
All First	3	2	1	7	5	7.00	-	-	-	-	421	227	4	56.75	2-74	-	-
1-day Int																	
NatWest																	
B & H																	
Sunday																	

MILLNS, D. J.   Leicestershire

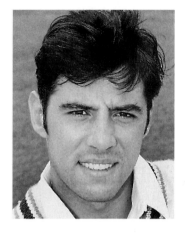

Name: David James Millns
Role: Left-hand bat, right-arm fast bowler, slip fielder
Born: 27 February 1965, Clipstone, Nottinghamshire
Height: 6ft 3in **Weight:** 14st 10lbs
Nickname: Trigger
County debut: 1988 (Nottinghamshire), 1990 (Leicestershire)
County cap: 1991
50 wickets in a season: 3
1st-Class 50s: 1
1st-Class 5 w. in innings: 17
1st-Class 10 w. in match: 2
1st-Class catches: 48
Place in batting averages: 199th av. 20.47
Place in bowling averages: 24th av. 25.01
(1993 17th av. 23.36)
Strike rate: 42.00 (career 46.78)
Parents: Bernard and Brenda
Wife and date of marriage: Wanda, 25 September 1993
Family links with cricket: Nottinghamshire's Andy Pick is brother-in-law. Great-uncle Richard played against the Australians for Saskatoon University, Canada in 1932 and bowled Don Bradman. Grandfather had ten brothers who all played in the same chapel team. Father played in club cricket and Notts Over 50s. Brother Paul plays for Clipstone
Education: Samuel Barlow Junior; Garibaldi Comprehensive; North Notts College of Further Education; Nottingham Trent Polytechnic
Qualifications: 9 CSEs, qualified coach
Career outside cricket: 'Yet to be decided'
Off-season: 'Making babies. Playing in Auckland, New Zealand.'
Overseas tours: England A to Australia 1992-93; Leicestershire to South Africa and Holland 1994
Overseas teams played for: Uitenhage, Port Elizabeth, South Africa 1988-89; Birkenhead, Auckland 1989-91; Cornwall CC, Auckland, New Zealand 1994-95
Cricketers particularly admired: Richard Hadlee, Franklyn Stephenson
Other sports followed: Football (Leicester City and Leicester Tigers)
Relaxations: Playing golf, movies and reading
Extras: Harold Warwood Bowling Award 1984. Asked to be released by Nottinghamshire at the end of 1989 season and joined Leicestershire in 1990. Finished third in national bowling averages in 1990. Britannic Assurance Player of the Month in August 1991 after taking 9-37 v Derbyshire, the best Leicestershire figures since George Geary's 10-18 v Glamorgan in 1929. Players' representative on Cricketers' Association Executive for

Leicestershire. Leicestershire Cricketer of the Year 1992. Leicestershire Bowling Award 1990, 1991 and 1992

Opinions on cricket: 'We are entrusted with this game for the few years we play it, so let's keep the standard of sportsmanship high for future generations to enjoy.'

Best batting: 64* Leicestershire v Worcestershire, Leicester 1994

Best bowling: 9-37 Leicestershire v Derbyshire, Derby 1991

1994 Season

	M	Inns	NO	Runs	HS	Avge	100s	50s	Ct	St	O	M	Runs	Wkts	Avge	Best	5wI	10wM
Test																		
All First	19	27	10	348	64 *	20.47	-	1	12	-	532	99	1901	76	25.01	6-44	4	-
1-day Int																		
NatWest	2	1	1	7	7 *	-	-	-	-	-	24	3	92	3	30.66	2-35	-	
B & H	2	1	0	10	10	10.00	-	-	-	-	19	1	76	2	38.00	2-32	-	
Sunday	4	2	1	5	3 *	5.00	-	-	-	-	24	0	107	3	35.66	2-11	-	

Career Performances

	M	Inns	NO	Runs	HS	Avge	100s	50s	Ct	St	Balls	Runs	Wkts	Avge	Best	5wI	10wM
Test																	
All First	92	108	42	1007	64 *	15.25	-	1	48	-	13896	7977	297	26.85	9-37	17	2
1-day Int																	
NatWest	7	2	2	36	29 *	-	-	-	2	-	438	273	11	24.81	3-22	-	
B & H	10	5	4	30	11 *	30.00	-	-	1	-	522	384	15	25.60	4-51	-	
Sunday	34	17	8	98	20 *	10.88	-	-	8	-	1296	1145	25	45.80	2-11	-	

53. Which country has won the women's World Cup three times since its introduction in 1973?

MIRZA, P.   Worcestershire

Name: Parvaz Mirza
Role: Right-hand opening bat, right-arm fast-medium bowler
Born: 17 December 1970, Birmingham
Height: 5ft 11in **Weight:** 11st 8lbs
Nickname: Parv
County debut: 1994
1st-Class catches: 1
Parents: Mirza Sher Baz (deceased) and Zarda Bi
Marital status: Single
Family links with cricket: Younger brother, Maneer, is a talented all-rounder
Education: Small Heath School, East Birmingham College
Qualifications: 5 GCSEs, City & Guilds in Recreation and Leisure
Off-season: Playing some cricket abroad

Cricketers particularly admired: Wasim Akram, Martin Crowe, David Houghton
Other sports followed: Snooker, football and boxing
Relaxations: Watching films and spending time with friends
Opinions on cricket: 'It would be better for bowlers if we played on wickets with a bit more life.'
Best batting: 40 Worcestershire v Kent, Canterbury 1994
Best bowling: 4-29 Worcestershire v Oxford University, Worcester 1994

1994 Season

	M	Inns	NO	Runs	HS	Avge	100s	50s	Ct	St	O	M	Runs	Wkts	Avge	Best	5wI	10wM
Test																		
All First	3	5	1	47	40	11.75	-	-	1	-	61.4	14	193	9	21.44	4-29	-	-
1-day Int																		
NatWest																		
B & H																		
Sunday	3	1	0	0	0	0.00	-	-	-	-	17	1	82	3	27.33	2-41	-	

Career Performances

	M	Inns	NO	Runs	HS	Avge	100s	50s	Ct	St	Balls	Runs	Wkts	Avge	Best	5wI	10wM
Test																	
All First	3	5	1	47	40	11.75	-	-	1	-	370	193	9	21.44	4-29	-	-
1-day Int																	
NatWest																	
B & H																	
Sunday	3	1	0	0	0	0.00	-	-	-	-	102	82	3	27.33	2-41	-	

MOLES, A. J.   Warwickshire

Name: Andrew James Moles
Role: Right-hand opening bat, right-arm
medium bowler
Born: 12 February 1961, Solihull
Height: 5ft 10in **Weight:** 'Above average'
Nickname: Moler
County debut: 1986
County cap: 1987
1000 runs in a season: 6
1st-Class 50s: 76
1st-Class 100s: 25
1st-Class 200s: 4
1st-Class catches: 124
One-Day 100s: 2
Place in batting averages: 18th av. 50.76
(1993 52nd av. 39.61)
Strike rate: (career 83.85)
Parents: Stuart Francis and Gillian Margaret
Wife and date of marriage:
Jacquie, 17 December 1988
Children: Daniel

Family links with cricket: Brother plays club cricket
Education: Finham Park Comprehensive, Coventry; Henley College of Further Education;
Butts College of Further Education
Qualifications: 3 O-levels, 4 CSEs, Toolmaker/Standard Room Inspector City & Guilds
Career outside cricket: Selling corporate hospitality
Overseas teams played for: Griqualand West, South Africa 1986-88
Cricketers particularly admired: Dennis Amiss, Fred Gardner, Tom Moody
Other sports followed: Football, golf
Relaxations: Playing golf and spending time with family
Best batting: 230* Griqualand West v Northern Transvaal B, Verwoerdburg 1988-89
Best bowling: 3-21 Warwickshire v Oxford University, The Parks 1987

1994 Season

	M	Inns	NO	Runs	HS	Avge	100s	50s	Ct	St	O	M	Runs	Wkts	Avge	Best	5wI	10wM
Test																		
All First	11	20	3	863	203 *	50.76	1	5	5	-								
1-day Int																		
NatWest	3	3	2	154	105 *	154.00	1	-	-	-								
B & H																		
Sunday	2	2	0	51	31	25.50	-	-	2	-								

Career Performances

	M	Inns	NO	Runs	HS	Avge	100s	50s	Ct	St	Balls	Runs	Wkts	Avge	Best	5wI	10wM
Test																	
All First	195	351	37	12964	230 *	41.28	25	76	124	-	3354	1860	40	46.50	3-21	-	-
1-day Int																	
NatWest	28	28	3	872	127	34.88	2	4	4	-	90	81	0	-	-	-	
B & H	25	24	0	694	72	28.91	-	8	7	-	300	224	4	56.00	1-11	-	
Sunday	86	81	4	2036	96 *	26.44	-	15	25	-	446	415	7	59.28	2-24	-	

MONTGOMERIE, R. R.   Northamptonshire

Name: Richard Robert Montgomerie
Role: Right-hand opening bat, right-arm off-spin bowler
Born: 3 July 1971, Rugby
Height: 5ft 11in **Weight:** 12st
Nickname: Albert, Chesh, Sheep's Head, Monty
County debut: 1991
1000 runs in season: 1
1st-Class 50s: 16
1st-Class 100s: 4
1st-Class catches: 29
Place in batting averages: 96th av. 34.25 (1993 77th av. 35.53)
Parents: Robert and Gillian
Marital status: Single
Family links with cricket: Father captained Oxfordshire
Education: Rugby School; Worcester College, Oxford University
Qualifications: 12 O-levels, 4 A-levels, BA (Chemistry)
Off-season: Working for Scott Bader, Wollaston
Overseas tours: Oxford University to Namibia 1991
Cricketers particularly admired: Curtly Ambrose
Other sports followed: All sports, particularly hockey, rackets and real tennis
Relaxations: Any sport
Extras: Scored unbeaten 50 in each innings of 1991 Varsity match and was Oxford captain in 1994. Oxford rackets Blue 1990. Captain Combined Universities 1994
Opinions on cricket: 'I have enjoyed four-day cricket immensely. It seems a true test of the two teams and we have played some very good games. From the Combined Universities' point of view, it is a very good thing that the B&H Cup has gone zonal in 1995.'
Best batting: 151 Northamptonshire v Derbyshire, Northampton 1994

1994 Season

	M	Inns	NO	Runs	HS	Avge	100s	50s	Ct	St	O	M	Runs	Wkts	Avge	Best	5wI	10wM
Test																		
All First	19	34	3	1062	151	34.25	2	8	12	-	4	0	28	0	-	-	-	-
1-day Int																		
NatWest																		
B & H	1	1	0	52	52	52.00	-	1	-	-								
Sunday	4	4	0	136	74	34.00	-	1	1	-								

Career Performances

	M	Inns	NO	Runs	HS	Avge	100s	50s	Ct	St	Balls	Runs	Wkts	Avge	Best	5wI	10wM
Test																	
All First	45	76	9	2310	151	34.47	4	16	29	-	96	65	0	-	-	-	-
1-day Int																	
NatWest																	
B & H	6	6	0	209	75	34.83	-	2	-	-	6	0	0	-	-	-	
Sunday	5	5	0	136	74	27.20	-	1	1	-								

MOODY, T. M. Worcestershire

Name: Thomas Masson Moody
Role: Right-hand bat, right-arm medium bowler
Born: 2 October 1965, Adelaide
Height: 6ft 7in **Weight:** 16st
Nickname: Moods, Tex
County debut: 1990 (Warwickshire), 1991 (Worcestershire)
County cap: 1990 (Warwickshire), 1991 (Worcestershire)
Test debut: 1989-90
Tests: 5
One-Day Internationals: 34
1000 runs in a season: 3
1st-Class 50s: 54
1st-Class 100s: 37
1st-Class 200s: 2
1st-Class 5 w. in innings: 1
1st-Class 10 w. in match: 1
1st-Class catches: 154
One-Day 100s: 8
Place in batting averages: 31st av. 46.40

Place in bowling averages: 116th av. 38.13
Strike rate: 78.00 (career 74.17)
Parents: John and Janet
Marital status: Single
Family links with cricket: Father played A Grade cricket in South Australia
Education: Guildford Grammar School, Western Australia
Qualifications: HSE
Career outside cricket: 'Entrepreneur'
Off-season: Playing cricket in Australia
Overseas tours: Australia to India/Pakistan (World Cup) 1987, to England 1989, to India 1989-90, to Sri Lanka 1992
Overseas teams played for: Western Australia 1985-95
Cricketers particularly admired: Dennis Lillee, Allan Border
Other sports followed: Aussie rules football, football, golf, tennis
Injuries: Hamstring and back, missed two weeks
Relaxations: Golf, swimming and films
Extras: Scored 150s in both innings of 1988-89 Sheffield Shield final for Western Australia v Queensland. Hit a century against Warwickshire during Australia's 1989 tour and signed on a one-year contract with them for 1990. Hit centuries in first three first-class matches for Warwickshire, and seven in first eight matches – a unique achievement. Scored the (then) fastest ever first-class century v Glamorgan in 26 minutes – taking advantage of declaration bowling. Reached 1000 first-class runs in first season of county cricket in only 12 innings – another record. Released by Warwickshire at the end of the 1990 season after they had chosen Allan Donald as their one overseas player and was signed by Worcestershire for 1991 when Graeme Hick was no longer considered an overseas player. Not re-signed for 1993 season because he was expected to be touring with the Australian team, although in the event he was not selected. Re-signed for 1994 season. Scored 180* and shared record unbeaten partnership with Tim Curtis in the semi-final of the NatWest Trophy 1994
Opinions on cricket: 'You play too much county cricket.'
Best batting: 210 Worcestershire v Warwickshire, Worcester 1991
Best bowling: 7-43 Western Australia v Victoria, Perth 1990-91

1994 Season

	M	Inns	NO	Runs	HS	Avge	100s	50s	Ct	St	O	M	Runs	Wkts	Avge	Best	5wl	10wM
Test																		
All First	18	28	3	1160	159	46.40	3	6	20	-	195	48	572	15	38.13	4-24	-	-
1-day Int																		
NatWest	5	5	2	350	180 *	116.66	1	1	4	-	52	12	141	7	20.14	2-33	-	
B & H	4	3	1	168	65 *	84.00	-	2	2	-	44	13	84	5	16.80	3-14	-	
Sunday	16	16	2	448	107	32.00	1	2	5	-	119	11	362	17	21.29	3-18	-	

Career Performances

	M	Inns	NO	Runs	HS	Avge	100s	50s	Ct	St	Balls	Runs	Wkts	Avge	Best	5wI	10wM
Test	8	14	0	456	106	32.57	2	3	9	-	432	147	2	73.50	1-17	-	-
All First	175	288	22	12128	210	45.59	37	54	154	-	8679	3858	117	32.97	7-43	1	1
1-day Int	34	32	3	751	89	25.89	-	7	10	-	894	651	16	40.68	3-56	-	
NatWest	9	9	3	538	180 *	89.66	1	3	7	-	373	182	8	22.75	2-33	-	
B & H	19	18	4	892	110 *	63.71	2	7	6	-	600	351	12	29.25	4-59	-	
Sunday	58	56	6	2216	160	44.32	5	17	15	-	1251	842	28	30.07	3-18	-	

MOORES, P. Sussex

Name: Peter Moores
Role: Right-hand bat, wicket-keeper
Born: 18 December 1962,
Macclesfield, Cheshire
Height: 6ft **Weight:** 13st
Nickname: Billy
County debut: 1983 (Worcestershire),
1985 (Sussex)
County cap: 1989
1st-Class 50s: 23
1st-Class 100s: 4
1st-Class catches: 370
1st-Class stumpings: 40
Place in batting averages:
160th av. 25.53 (1993 152nd av. 25.34)
Parents: Bernard and Winifred
Wife and date of marriage:
Karen Jane, 28 September 1989

Children: Natalie Marie, 4 August 1993
Family links with cricket: Brothers, Anthony, Stephen and Robert, all play club cricket
Education: King Edward VI School, Macclesfield
Qualifications: 7 O-levels, 3 A-levels, advanced cricket coach
Career outside cricket: Coach for Sussex in off-season
Overseas tours: Christians in Sport to India 1989-90; MCC to Namibia 1990-91, to
Leeward Islands 1991-92, to Bahrain 1994-95
Overseas teams played for: Orange Free State, South Africa 1988-89
Cricketers particularly admired: Bob Taylor, Alan Knott, Clive Lloyd
Other sports followed: Football, golf
Relaxations: Golf, wine and old films
Extras: On MCC groundstaff in 1982 before joining Worcestershire in latter half of 1982
season. Joined Sussex in 1985

Opinions on cricket: 'I feel we need to split the Sunday and the four-day game for two reasons: 1. It would prevent injuries in the Sunday game affecting the result in the four-day game. 2. It would benefit players not to have to switch "codes" halfway through a game.'
Best batting: 116 Sussex v Somerset, Hove 1989

1994 Season

	M	Inns	NO	Runs	HS	Avge	100s	50s	Ct	St	O	M	Runs	Wkts	Avge	Best	5wI	10wM
Test																		
All First	18	32	2	766	70 *	25.53	-	4	61	1								
1-day Int																		
NatWest	1	1	0	11	11	11.00	-	-	3	-								
B & H	2	1	0	6	6	6.00	-	-	2	-								
Sunday	16	14	5	164	41 *	18.22	-	-	11	-								

Career Performances

	M	Inns	NO	Runs	HS	Avge	100s	50s	Ct	St	Balls	Runs	Wkts	Avge	Best	5wI	10wM
Test																	
All First	173	247	31	5282	116	24.45	4	23	370	40	18	16	0	-	-	-	-
1-day Int																	
NatWest	19	13	3	145	26	14.50	-	-	27	2							
B & H	22	17	2	232	76	15.46	-	1	19	2							
Sunday	121	92	26	1095	57	16.59	-	3	108	17							

MORRIS, A. C.   Yorkshire

Name: Alexander Corfield Morris
Role: Left-hand bat, right-arm medium bowler
Born: 4 October 1976, Barnsley
Height: 6ft 3in   **Weight:** 12st 12lbs
County debut: No first-team appearance
Parents: Chris and Janet
Marital status: Single
Education: Holgate School, Barnsley; Barnsley College
Qualifications: 4 GCSEs, NCA coaching
Off-season: Studying and touring with England U19
Overseas tours: England U19 to West Indies 1994-95
Cricketers particularly admired: Brian Lara, Martyn Moxon
Relaxations: Listening to music
Extras: Played for Yorkshire U11-U19. Played

for England U15 against Barbados and in 1994 for both England U17 and U19 against India. Played junior football with both Barnsley and Rotherham and had trials for Nottingham Forest and Leeds

MORRIS, H. — Glamorgan

Name: Hugh Morris
Role: Left-hand bat, right-arm medium bowler, county captain
Born: 5 October 1963, Cardiff
Height: 5ft 8in **Weight:** 13st 4lbs
Nickname: Banners
County debut: 1981
County cap: 1986
Benefit: 1994
Test debut: 1991
Tests: 3
1000 runs in a season: 7
1st-Class 50s: 77
1st-Class 100s: 37
1st-Class catches: 163
One-Day 100s: 9
Place in batting averages: 124th av. 30.51 (1993 48th av. 40.18)
Parents: Roger and Anne
Wife: Debra Jane
Children: Bethan Louise; Emily Charlotte
Family links with cricket: Brother played for Glamorgan U19 and currently plays local league cricket. Father played local club cricket
Education: Blundells School; South Glamorgan Institute of Higher Education
Qualifications: 9 O-levels, 3 A-levels, 1 AO-level, BA (Hons) in Physical Education, NCA coaching award
Career outside cricket: Journalism; sales and marketing
Off-season: Resting or recuperating after knee operation
Overseas tours: English Public Schoolboys to West Indies 1980-81, to Sri Lanka 1982-83; England A to Pakistan 1990-91 (called up to join England tour party in Australia), to Bermuda and West Indies 1991-92, to South Africa 1993-94; England to Australia 1990-91;
Overseas teams played for: CBC Old Boys, Pretoria 1985-87
Cricketers particularly admired: Viv Richards, Ian Botham, Jimmy Cook
Other sports followed: Rugby, golf
Injuries: Knee cartilage, missed four weeks
Relaxations: Music, watching movies, travelling and holiday at end of the season

Extras: Highest schoolboy cricket average in 1979 (89.71), 1981 (184.60) and 1982 (149.20). Captain of English Schools U19 in 1981 and 1982; played for England YC v West Indies 1982, and captain v Australia 1983. Appointed youngest ever Glamorgan captain 1986, but resigned in 1989 to concentrate on batting. In 1990 scored most runs in a season by a Glamorgan player (2276) and hit most centuries (10). After missing selection for the tour of Australia, appointed captain for England A tour of Pakistan in 1990-91; then, after Gooch had required a hand operation and England had lost the first Test to Australia, he flew out to join the senior tour until the England captain recovered. Glamorgan Player of the Year. Captained the England A tour to South Africa 1993-94 and Wombwell Cricket Lovers' Society Captain of the Year 1993. Played first-class rugby for Aberavon 1984-85 and South Glamorgan Institute, scoring over 150 points

Best batting: 160* Glamorgan v Derbyshire, Cardiff 1990
Best bowling: 1-6 Glamorgan v Oxford University, The Parks 1987

1994 Season

	M	Inns	NO	Runs	HS	Avge	100s	50s	Ct	St	O	M	Runs	Wkts	Avge	Best	5wl	10wM
Test																		
All First	16	31	2	885	106	30.51	1	6	13	-								
1-day Int																		
NatWest	3	3	0	32	24	10.66	-	-	-	-	2	0	12	0	-		-	-
B & H	1	1	0	55	55	55.00	-	1	1	-								
Sunday	13	13	2	530	127 *	48.18	1	3	2	-								

Career Performances

	M	Inns	NO	Runs	HS	Avge	100s	50s	Ct	St	Balls	Runs	Wkts	Avge	Best	5wl	10wM
Test	3	6	0	115	44	19.16	-	-	3	-							
All First	260	447	43	15192	160 *	37.60	37	77	163	-	348	380	2	190.00	1-6	-	-
1-day Int																	
NatWest	27	26	3	1095	154 *	47.60	3	4	9	-	12	12	0	-		-	-
B & H	34	34	2	898	143 *	28.06	3	3	13	-	18	15	1	15.00	1-14	-	
Sunday	144	140	15	4461	127 *	35.68	3	32	48	-							

MORRIS, J. E.   Durham

Name: John Edward Morris
Role: Right-hand bat, right-arm medium bowler
Born: 1 April 1964, Crewe
Height: 5ft 10in **Weight:** 13st 6lbs
Nickname: Animal
County debut: 1982 (Derbyshire),
1994 (Durham)
County cap: 1986 (Derbyshire)
Test debut: 1990
Tests: 3
One-Day Internationals: 8
1000 runs in a season: 9
1st-Class 50s: 79
1st-Class 100s: 39
1st-Class 200s: 2
1st-Class catches: 109
One-Day 100s: 6
Place in batting averages: 51st av. 42.14
(1993 16th av. 52.17)
Parents: George (Eddie) and Jean
Wife and date of marriage: Sally, 30 September 1990
Children: Tom, 27 June 1991
Family links with cricket: Father played for Crewe for many years as an opening bowler
Education: Shavington Comprehensive School; Dane Bank College of Further Education
Qualifications: O-levels
Overseas tours: England to Australia 1990-91; MCC to Bahrain 1994-95
Overseas teams played for: Griqualand West, South Africa 1988-89, 1993-94
Other sports followed: Athletics, motor racing, football, snooker
Relaxations: Golf
Extras: Youngest player to score a Sunday League century. Left Derbyshire at end of 1993 season.
Best batting: 229 Derbyshire v Gloucestershire, Cheltenham 1993
Best bowling: 1-6 Derbyshire v Cambridge University, Fenner's 1993

1994 Season

	M	Inns	NO	Runs	HS	Avge	100s	50s	Ct	St	O	M	Runs	Wkts	Avge	Best	5wI	10wM
Test																		
All First	20	35	1	1433	204	42.14	4	6	8	-	27.5	3	125	1	125.00	1-37	-	-
1-day Int																		
NatWest	2	2	0	92	67	46.00	-	1	1	-								
B & H	1	1	0	23	23	23.00	-	-	-	-								
Sunday	15	13	1	189	77 *	15.75	-	1	5	-								

Career Performances

	M	Inns	NO	Runs	HS	Avge	100s	50s	Ct	St	Balls	Runs	Wkts	Avge	Best	5wl	10wM
Test	3	5	2	71	32	23.66	-	-	3	-							
All First	260	431	28	16004	229	39.71	39	79	109	-	986	902	7	128.85	1-6	-	-
1-day Int	8	8	1	167	63 *	23.85	-	1	2	-							
NatWest	22	21	3	565	94 *	31.38	-	4	6	-							
B & H	45	41	5	1024	123	28.44	2	4	9	-	24	14	0	-		-	-
Sunday	159	151	11	3658	134	26.12	4	16	35	-	3	7	0	-		-	-

MORRIS, R. S. M. Hampshire

Name: Robert Sean Milner Morris
Role: Right-hand bat, off-spin
bowler, occasional wicket-keeper
Born: 10 September 1968,
Great Horwood, Buckinghamshire
Height: 6ft **Weight:** 12st 7lbs
Nickname: Stowers, Mozza
County debut: 1992
1st-Class 50s: 7
1st-Class 100s: 2
1st-Class catches: 25
Place in batting averages: 22nd av. 49.00
(1993 141st av. 26.57)
Parents: Stuart and Sue
Marital status: Single
Family links with cricket: Great-grandfather
played for Worcestershire

Education: Swanbourne House School;
Stowe School; Durham University 'and Yung's Bar, Bangkok'
Qualifications: 8 O-levels, 2 A-levels, BA (Dunelm) Sociology
Career outside cricket: 'Beach bumming'
Overseas tours: Stowe to Australia 1982; Combined Universities to Barbados 1990
Overseas teams played for: Midland Guildford, Perth, Western Australia 1987-88; St Albans, Buenos Aires 1991-92; Tigers Parow, Cape Town 1993-94
Cricketers particularly admired: Malcolm Marshall, Robin Smith, James Bovill 'for his team's enjoyment'
Other sports followed: Hockey, rugby, skiing
Relaxations: 'Fast food, fast cars and fast women and pushing myself through a rigorous fitness regime'
Extras: Captained Durham University hockey and cricket, played hockey for County Durham and the North

377

Best batting: 174 Hampshire v Nottinghamshire, Basingstoke 1994

1994 Season

	M	Inns	NO	Runs	HS	Avge	100s	50s	Ct	St	O	M	Runs	Wkts	Avge	Best	5wI	10wM
Test																		
All First	9	17	3	686	174	49.00	2	3	4	-								
1-day Int																		
NatWest	2	2	1	63	34 *	63.00	-	-	-	-								
B & H																			
Sunday	4	4	0	55	34	13.75	-	-	2	-								

Career Performances

	M	Inns	NO	Runs	HS	Avge	100s	50s	Ct	St	Balls	Runs	Wkts	Avge	Best	5wI	10wM
Test																	
All First	22	40	4	1267	174	35.19	2	7	25	-	4	1	0	-	-	-	-
1-day Int																	
NatWest	2	2	1	63	34 *	63.00	-	-	-	-							
B & H																		
Sunday	5	5	1	59	34	14.75	-	-	2	-							

MORTENSEN, O. H — Derbyshire

Name: Ole Henrik Mortensen
Role: Right-hand bat, right-arm
fast-medium bowler
Born: 29 January 1958, Vejle, Denmark
Height: 6ft 4in **Weight:** 14st 2lbs
Nickname: Stan, Blood-axe, The Great Dane
County debut: 1983
County cap: 1986
Benefit: 1994
50 wickets in a season: 3
1st-Class 50s: 1
1st-Class 5 w. in innings: 16
1st-Class 10 w. in match: 1
1st-Class catches: 47
One-day 5 w. in innings: 2
Place in bowling averages:
(1993 76th av. 30.61)
Strike rate: (career 55.02)
Parents: Willy and Inge
Wife: Jette Jepmond

Children: Julie Jepmond, 30 August 1982 and Emilia

Family links with cricket: 'My brother, Michael, is a very talented cricketer but gave the game up to concentrate on tennis. He has played in the Davis Cup for Denmark'

Education: Brondbyoster School; Avedore College of Higher Education, Copenhagen

Overseas tours: Denmark to East Africa, England, Scotland, Wales, Ireland and Holland

Overseas clubs played for: Ellerslie, Auckland 1983-84; Brighton, Melbourne 1984-1992

Cricketers particularly admired: 'Anyone who is successful at first-class and Test level over a number of years'

Other sports played: Tennis, golf, football, Australian rules football

Relaxations: Collecting stamps (only Danish) and coins, reading books about wine, sleeping in in the morning, reading newspapers

Extras: *Derbyshire's Dane* by Peter Hargreaves, published 1984. Played for Denmark in the ICC Trophy. Most economical bowler in Refuge League 1990. Played for Rest of the World XI v Australian XI in Melbourne 1990 (organised by Lord's Taverners of Australia). Released by Derbyshire at end of 1994 season

Best batting: 74* Derbyshire v Yorkshire, Chesterfield 1987

Best bowling: 6-27 Derbyshire v Yorkshire, Sheffield 1983

1994 Season

	M	Inns	NO	Runs	HS	Avge	100s	50s	Ct	St	O	M	Runs	Wkts	Avge	Best	5wI	10wM
Test																		
All First	2	0	0	0	0	-	-	-	-	-	23	5	48	2	24.00	1-18	-	-
1-day Int																		
NatWest																		
B & H	1	0	0	0	0	-	-	-	-	-	11	1	50	0	-		-	-
Sunday	3	0	0	0	0	-	-	-	-	-	21	1	122	2	61.00	2-53	-	

Career Performances

	M	Inns	NO	Runs	HS	Avge	100s	50s	Ct	St	Balls	Runs	Wkts	Avge	Best	5wI	10wM
Test																	
All First	157	173	94	709	74 *	8.97	-	1	47	-	23883	10364	434	23.88	6-27	16	1
1-day Int																	
NatWest	17	12	7	28	11	5.60	-	-	7	-	1086	495	29	17.06	6-14	2	
B & H	39	11	6	23	5 *	4.60	-	-	2	-	2372	1179	53	22.24	3-17	-	
Sunday	139	50	34	93	11	5.81	-	-	17	-	6287	3825	135	28.33	4-10	-	

MOXON, M. D.   Yorkshire

Name: Martyn Douglas Moxon
Role: Right-hand bat, right-arm medium
bowler, county captain
Born: 4 May 1960, Barnsley
Height: 6ft 1in **Weight:** 14st
Nickname: Frog
County debut: 1981
County cap: 1984
Benefit: 1993
Test debut: 1986
Tests: 10
One-Day Internationals: 8
1000 runs in a season: 11
1st-Class 50s: 98
1st-Class 100s: 38
1st-Class 200s: 3
1st-Class catches: 203
One-Day 100s: 6
One-Day 5 w. in innings: 1
Place in batting averages: 7th av. 56.07 (1993 41st av. 42.48)
Strike rate: (career 94.64)
Parents: Audrey and Derek (deceased)
Wife and date of marriage: Sue, October 1985
Children: Charlotte Louise, 13 March 1990; Jonathan James, 6 May 1993
Family links with cricket: Father and grandfather played local league cricket
Education: Holgate Grammar School, Barnsley
Qualifications: 8 O-levels, 3 A-levels, HNC in Business Studies, NCA coaching award
Off-season: Hosting tour to Australia – coaching in schools
Overseas tours: England to India and Australia 1984-85, to Australia and New
Zealand 1987-88; England B to Sri Lanka 1985-86; England A to Bermuda and West
Indies 1991-92, to Australia 1992-93
Overseas teams played for: Griqualand West, South Africa 1982-83 and 1983-84
Cricketers particularly admired: Viv Richards
Other sports followed: Football (supporter of Barnsley FC) and golf
Injuries: Displaced disc and patella tendonitis, missed two weeks
Relaxations: Listening to most types of music, having a drink with friends
Extras: Captained Yorkshire Schools U15, North of England U15 and Yorkshire Senior
Schools. Played for Wombwell Cricket Lovers' Society U18 side. First Yorkshire player
to make centuries in his first two Championship games in Yorkshire, 116 v Essex at
Headingley (on debut) and 111 v Derbyshire at Sheffield, and scored 153 in his first innings
in a Roses match. Picked for Lord's Test of 1984 v West Indies, but withdrew through injury
and had to wait until 1986 to make Test debut. Appointed Yorkshire captain in 1990.

Appointed captain of England A team to tour Bermuda and West Indies 1991-92, but played no first-class cricket owing to injury. Wombwell Cricket Lovers' Society Cricketer of the Year 1991. Scored 274* against Worcester which is the highest individual score for Yorkshire since the war

Best batting: 274* Yorkshire v Worcestershire, Worcester 1994
Best bowling: 3-24 Yorkshire v Hampshire, Southampton 1989

1994 Season

	M	Inns	NO	Runs	HS	Avge	100s	50s	Ct	St	O	M	Runs	Wkts	Avge	Best	5wl	10wM
Test																		
All First	17	30	4	1458	274 *	56.07	4	6	8	-								
1-day Int																		
NatWest	2	2	0	72	49	36.00	-	-	-	-								
B & H	1	1	0	40	40	40.00	-	-	-	-								
Sunday	12	12	1	331	58	30.09	-	2	5	-								

Career Performances

	M	Inns	NO	Runs	HS	Avge	100s	50s	Ct	St	Balls	Runs	Wkts	Avge	Best	5wl	10wM
Test	10	17	1	455	99	28.43	-	3	10	-							
All First	276	472	36	18301	274 *	41.97	38	98	203	-	2650	1481	28	52.89	3-24	-	-
1-day Int	8	8	0	174	70	21.75	-	1	5	-							
NatWest	26	26	6	946	107 *	47.30	1	8	12	-	156	85	5	17.00	2-19	-	
B & H	39	39	5	1546	141 *	45.47	2	11	16	-	342	242	9	26.88	5-31	1	
Sunday	135	127	8	3820	129 *	32.10	3	23	42	-	984	868	21	41.33	3-29	-	

54. Who topped the first-class bowling averages in England in 1994?

MULLALLY, A. D. Leicestershire

Name: Alan David Mullally
Role: Right-hand bat, left-arm fast bowler
Born: 12 July 1969, Southend
Height: 6ft 5in **Weight:** 14st
Nickname: Bob, Bryan, Eric, Spider,
'too many to mention'
County debut: 1988 (Hampshire),
1990 (Leicestershire)
County cap: 1993
50 wickets in a season: 1
1st-Class 5 w. in innings: 4
1st-Class 10 w. in match: 1
1st-Class catches: 23
Place in bowling averages: 115th av. 38.03
(1993 26th av. 24.29)
Strike rate: 81.47 (career 73.21)
Parents: Michael and Ann
Marital status: Single
Family links with cricket: 'Dad bowls a

vicious arm ball on the back patio, two brothers play club cricket in Perth and sister fancied David Gower'
Education: Cannington High School and Primary, Perth, Australia; Wembley and Carlisle Technical College
Qualifications: 'Jack-of-all-trades'
Career outside cricket: As above
Off-season: Getting a rock/reggae band together
Overseas tours: Western Australia to India 1990-91; Leicestershire to Jamaica 1992-93
Overseas teams played for: Western Australia; Victoria; Australian YC
Cricketers particularly admired: Curtly Ambrose, Brian Lara – 'those who get to the very top'
Other sports followed: Australian rules football, basketball, most sports
Injuries: Sprained ankle, side strain. 'Hit on top of foot by Courtney. Missed too much cricket.'
Relaxations: Music, playing the guitar. 'Doing things in my own time'
Extras: English-qualified as he was born in Southend, he made his first-class debut for Western Australia in the 1987-88 Sheffield Shield final, and played for Australian YC 1988-89. Played one match for Hampshire in 1988 before joining Leicestershire
Opinions on cricket: 'Batsmen should try to use wider bats against us left-handers (maybe they'll be able to edge it more often). Phil Simmons should be given a fishing net when fielding at second slip .'
Best batting: 34 Western Australia v Tasmania, Perth 1989-90
Best bowling: 7-72 Leicestershire v Gloucestershire, Leicester 1993

1994 Season

	M	Inns	NO	Runs	HS	Avge	100s	50s	Ct	St	O	M	Runs	Wkts	Avge	Best	5wI	10wM
Test																		
All First	14	19	4	114	23	7.60	-	-	6	-	448.1	121	1255	33	38.03	5-85	1	-
1-day Int																		
NatWest	2	1	0	0	0	0.00	-	-	-	-	24	5	70	3	23.33	2-35	-	
B & H	2	1	1	0	0*	-	-	-	-	-	21	7	59	2	29.50	2-30	-	
Sunday	10	10	2	101	38	12.62	-	-	3	-	76.2	6	336	13	25.84	3-9	-	

Career Performances

	M	Inns	NO	Runs	HS	Avge	100s	50s	Ct	St	Balls	Runs	Wkts	Avge	Best	5wM	10wM
Test																	
All First	88	94	25	560	34	8.11	-	-	23	-	15667	7462	214	34.86	7-72	4	1
1-day Int																	
NatWest	10	5	2	24	19*	8.00	-	-	2	-	612	339	14	24.21	2-22	-	
B & H	16	6	2	18	11	4.50	-	-	-	-	894	550	10	55.00	2-30	-	
Sunday	55	27	13	156	38	11.14	-	-	12	-	2421	1802	58	31.06	3-9	-	

MUNTON, T. A.   Warwickshire

Name: Timothy Alan Munton
Role: Right-hand bat, right-arm
fast-medium bowler, county vice-captain
Born: 30 July 1965, Melton Mowbray
Height: 6ft 6in **Weight:** 15st 7lbs
Nickname: Harry, Captain Sensible
County debut: 1985
County cap: 1990
Test debut: 1991
Tests: 2
50 wickets in a season: 5
1st-Class 5 w. in innings: 22
1st-Class 10 w. in match: 5
1st-Class catches: 63
One-Day 5 w. in innings: 2
Place in batting averages: 264th av. 10.60
Place in bowling averages: 8th av. 21.58
(1993 48th av. 27.40)
Strike rate: 51.80 (career 60.91)
Parents: Alan and Brenda
Wife and date of marriage: Helen, 20 September 1986
Children: Camilla Dallas, 13 August 1988; Harrison George Samuel, 17 February 1992

Family links with cricket: Father played for Buckminster CC
Education: Sarson High School; King Edward VII Upper School, Melton Mowbray
Qualifications: CSE grade 1, 9 O-levels, 1 A-level,
Off-season: Salesman for Bass Brewers. Salesman for Warwickshire CC
Overseas tours: England A to Pakistan 1990-91, to Bermuda and West Indies 1991-92
Overseas teams played for: Victoria University, Wellington, New Zealand 1985-86; Witwatersrand University, Johannesburg, South Africa 1986-87
Cricketers particularly admired: Richard Hadlee, David Gower
Other sports followed: Basketball, soccer, golf
Relaxations: 'Playing golf, spending time with my family'
Extras: Appeared for Leicestershire 2nd XI 1982-84. Second highest wicket-taker in 1990 with 78. Called into England A squad to tour Bermuda and West Indies 1991-92 when Dermot Reeve replaced the injured Angus Fraser on the senior tour. Was voted Warwickshire Player of the Season 1990, 1991 and 1994
Opinions on cricket: 'NatWest Trophy semi-finals and final should be played in one week in mid-August, to reduce the effect of the toss! Attempts should be made to play all one-day domestic cricket at weekends. More money from television deals should go to the players.'
Best batting: 47 Warwickshire v Kent, Edgbaston 1992
Best bowling: 8-89 Warwickshire v Middlesex, Edgbaston 1991

1994 Season

	M	Inns	NO	Runs	HS	Avge	100s	50s	Ct	St	O	M	Runs	Wkts	Avge	Best	5wI	10wM
Test																		
All First	18	17	7	106	36	10.60	-	-	4	-	699.4	181	1748	81	21.58	7-52	6	2
1-day Int																		
NatWest	5	1	1	0	0 *	-	-	-	-	-	54	13	138	8	17.25	2-14	-	
B & H	3	0	0	0	0	-	-	-	1	-	33	8	92	4	23.00	3-27	-	
Sunday	17	2	2	16	15 *	-	-	-	4	-	117	12	501	16	31.31	3-57	-	

Career Performances

	M	Inns	NO	Runs	HS	Avge	100s	50s	Ct	St	Balls	Runs	Wkts	Avge	Best	5wI	10wM
Test	2	2	1	25	25 *	25.00	-	-	-	-	405	200	4	50.00	2-22	-	-
All First	180	182	71	1096	47	9.87	-	-	63	-	30581	13417	502	26.72	8-89	22	5
1-day Int																	
NatWest	27	9	5	9	5	2.25	-	-	4	-	1624	804	29	27.72	3-36	-	
B & H	27	13	8	52	13	10.40	-	-	6	-	1702	969	33	29.36	4-35	-	
Sunday	122	33	24	122	15 *	13.55	-	-	20	-	5255	3386	118	28.69	5-23	2	

MURPHY, A. J.   Surrey

Name: Anthony John Murphy
Role: Right-hand bat, right-arm
fast-medium bowler
Born: 6 August 1962, Manchester
Height: 5ft 11in **Weight:** 'Getting larger
by the year'
Nickname: Headless, Murph
County debut: 1985 (Lancashire),
1989 (Surrey)
50 wickets in a season: 1
1st-Class 5 w. in innings: 6
1st-Class catches: 17
One-Day 5 w. in innings: 1
Place in bowling averages:
(1993 89th av. 32.59)
Strike rate: (career 71.92)
Parents: John Desmond and Elizabeth
Catherine
Marital status: 'Definitely single'
Family links with cricket: Brother captains
Maori club in London; 'distant cousin's grandfather captained Southern Ireland. Distant
cousin plays in Canada and girlfriend's grandmother made tea for tourists to Northern
Rhodesia'
Education: Xaverian College, Manchester; Swansea University
Qualifications: 9 O-levels, 4 A-levels
Overseas tours: MCCA U25 to Kenya
1986; Lancashire to Jamaica 1986 and 1987; Surrey to Sharjah 1989, 1990, 1993, to
Barbados 1989, 1990, to Lanzarote 1991, to Rhodes 1992; MCC to Bahrain 1994-95
Overseas teams played for: Central Districts, New Zealand 1986-87; Hawkes Bay, New
Zealand 1985-87; Brazil 1992-93
Cricketers particularly admired: Ken Marshall, Bill Dewsall, Bill Ellis
Other sports followed: American football, chess, rugby, ballooning, 'any game that
Manchester United lose'
Extras: Surrey Bowler of the Year 1989, Man of the Match for League Cricket Conference against
West Indies 1984, captain of Swansea University. Released by Surrey at end of 1994 season
Best batting: 38 Surrey v Gloucestershire, The Oval 1989
Best bowling: 6-97 Surrey v Derbyshire, Derby 1989

---

55. Which Pakistani has the best bowling figures in international
one-day cricket, what were the figures and against whom?

1994 Season

	M	Inns	NO	Runs	HS	Avge	100s	50s	Ct	St	O	M	Runs	Wkts	Avge	Best	5wI	10wM
Test																		
All First	1	1	1	10	10 *	-	-	-	-	-	22	8	50	2	25.00	2-42	-	-
1-day Int																		
NatWest	1	0	0	0	0	-	-	-	-	-	12	3	26	6	4.33	6-26	1	
B & H	1	0	0	0	0	-	-	-	-	-	11	0	67	2	33.50	2-67	-	
Sunday	11	1	1	1	1 *	-	-	-	-	-	78.3	7	391	10	39.10	3-35	-	

Career Performances

	M	Inns	NO	Runs	HS	Avge	100s	50s	Ct	St	Balls	Runs	Wkts	Avge	Best	5wI	10wM
Test																	
All First	84	86	39	323	38	6.87	-	-	17	-	14961	7934	208	38.14	6-97	6	
1-day Int																	
NatWest	10	2	2	1	1 *	-	-	-	-	-	662	391	16	24.43	6-26	1	
B & H	11	6	3	6	5 *	2.00	-	-	-	-	648	452	10	45.20	2-23	-	
Sunday	64	15	8	32	9 *	4.57	-	-	5	-	2851	2241	81	27.66	4-22	-	

MUSHTAQ AHMED   Somerset

Name: Mushtaq Ahmed
Role: Right-hand bat, leg-break
and googly bowler
Born: 28 June 1970, Sahiwal, Pakistan
Height: 5ft 4in **Weight:** 13st
Nickname: Mushy
County debut: 1993
County cap: 1993
Test debut: 1991-92
Tests: 13
One-Day Internationals: 77
50 wickets in a season: 2
1st-Class 50s: 4
1st-Class 5w. in innings: 25
1st-Class 10w. in match: 6
1st-Class catches: 53
Place in batting averages:
237th av. 15.27 (1993 196th av. 19.92)
Place in bowling averages:
34th av. 26.57 (1993 8th av. 20.85)
Strike rate: 53.86 (career 51.40)
Marital status: Married

Career outside cricket: Banking
Off-season: On tour with Pakistan
Overseas tours: Pakistan to Australia 1989-90, to New Zealand and Australia (World Cup) 1991-92, to England 1992, to New Zealand, Australia and South Africa 1992-93, to New Zealand 1993-94, to Sri Lanka 1994
Overseas teams played for: United Bank, Pakistan
Cricketers particularly admired: Bob Cottam and Peter Anderson
Extras: Took 6-81 against England for Punjab Chief Minister's XI 1987. Finished second to Wasim Akram as Pakistan's highest wicket-taker in the World Cup 1991-92 with 16 wickets. Received specialist coaching from Intikhab Alam. Named Somerset Player of the Year 1993
Opinions on cricket: 'I like the four-day county championship because it gives spin bowlers a good chance to bowl long spells. One-day cricket is exciting to watch and play in. A good cricketer can play all types of cricket successfully. Most of those against that view have never played it.'
Best batting: 90 Somerset v Sussex, Taunton 1993
Best bowling: 9-93 Multan v Peshawar, Sahiwal 1986-87

1994 Season

	M	Inns	NO	Runs	HS	Avge	100s	50s	Ct	St	O	M	Runs	Wkts	Avge	Best	5wI	10wM
Test																		
All First	9	14	3	168	38	15.27	-	-	4	-	404	114	1196	45	26.57	7-94	4	1
1-day Int																		
NatWest	2	1	0	0	0	0.00	-	-	-	-	21	7	60	3	20.00	3-26	-	
B & H	1	1	0	3	3	3.00	-	-	-	-	7	0	33	0	-	-	-	
Sunday	7	6	3	29	12 *	9.66	-	-	1	-	47	0	225	6	37.50	2-41	-	

Career Performances

	M	Inns	NO	Runs	HS	Avge	100s	50s	Ct	St	Balls	Runs	Wkts	Avge	Best	5wI	10wM
Test	13	18	3	95	18	6.33	-	-	3	-	2410	1074	29	37.03	3-32	-	
All First	90	111	14	1309	90	13.49	-	4	53	-	19175	9168	373	24.57	9-93	25	6
1-day Int	77	39	15	200	17 *	8.33	-	-	16	-	3813	2847	89	31.98	3-14	-	
NatWest	6	4	1	54	35	18.00	-	-	1	-	394	196	8	24.50	3-26	-	
B & H	2	2	0	10	7	5.00	-	-	-	-	108	83	0	-	-	-	
Sunday	20	18	3	118	32	7.86	-	-	1	-	927	588	23	25.56	3-17	-	

NASH, D. C.   Middlesex

Name: David Charles Nash
Role: Right-hand bat, wicket-keeper
Born: 19 January 1978, Chertsey, Surrey
Height: 5ft 7in **Weight:** 9st 7lbs
Nickname: Nashy
County debut: No first-team appearance
Parents: Dave and Chris
Marital status: Single
Family links with cricket:
Father played club cricket
Education: Sunbury Manor; Malvern College,
Worcestershire
Qualifications: 10 GCSEs
Off-season: Studying A-levels at Malvern
Overseas tours: England U15 to South
Africa 1993; British Airways Youth Team to
West Indies 1993-94
Cricketers particularly admired:
Colin Metson, Mark Ramprakash, and
George Simons 'for his big heart'
Other sports followed: Football (Brentford) and most other sports
Relaxations: Listening to music, playing golf and going out with friends
Extras: A qualified referee. Represented Middlesex at all ages. Played for England U14,
U15, U17 and U18. Once took six wickets in six balls when aged 11 – 'when I could bowl!'.
Daily Telegraph Southern England Batting Award 1993. Seaxe Young Player of the Year 1993
Opinions on cricket: 'I would like to see county 2nd XI matches extended to four days so
there is more chance of a result. I would also like to see day/night cricket introduced into
the English game.'

NASH, D. J.   Middlesex

Name: Dion Joseph Nash
Role: Right-hand bat, right arm medium-fast bowler
Born: 20 November 1971, Auckland, New Zealand
Height: 6ft 2in **Weight:** 13st 5lbs
Nickname: Nashi
County debut: No first-team appearance
Test debut: 1992
Tests: 6
One-Day Internationals: 10

1st-Class 50s: 3
1st-Class 5 w. in innings: 7
1st-Class 10 w. in match: 1
1st-Class catches: 22
Place in bowling averages: 69th av. 31.00
Parents: Paul and Joan
Marital status: Single
Education: Pargaville High School; Auckland Grammar School; Otago University
Qualifications: School Certificate, 6th Form Certificate, University Bursary Bachelor of Arts
Career outside cricket: 'Yet to pursue one.'
Off-season: Playing cricket for and in New Zealand
Overseas tours: New Zealand Youth to India 1991-92; New Zealand to Zimbabwe and Sri Lanka 1992, to England 1994, to South Africa 1994-95
Cricketers particularly admired: Dennis Lillee, Dean Jones
Other sports followed: Rugby, surfing
Injuries: Small rib cartilage tear, missed two weeks. Broke finger playing against West Indies in New Zealand 1994-95
Relaxations: Reading, music, all sports
Opinions on cricket: 'More Test cricket should be played as opposed to increasing the number of one-day games.'
Best batting: 56 New Zealand v England, Lord's 1994
Best bowling: 6-30 New Zealand Academy XI v Northern Districts, Rotorua 1993-94

1994 Season

	M	Inns	NO	Runs	HS	Avge	100s	50s	Ct	St	O	M	Runs	Wkts	Avge	Best	5wl	10wM
Test	3	5	2	94	56	31.33	-	1	3	-	129	28	429	17	25.23	6-76	2	1
All First	8	11	6	177	56	35.40	-	1	5	-	228.4	51	775	25	31.00	6-76	2	1
1-day Int	1	1	0	0	0	0.00	-	-	1	-	6	1	20	0	-	-	-	
NatWest																		
B & H																		
Sunday																		

Career Performances

	M	Inns	NO	Runs	HS	Avge	100s	50s	Ct	St	Balls	Runs	Wkts	Avge	Best	5wl	10wM
Test	6	9	5	128	56	32.00	-	1	6	-	1296	651	21	31.00	6-76	2	1
All First	38	57	19	853	56	22.44	-	3	22	-	5784	2761	99	27.88	6-30	7	1
1-day Int	10	9	2	71	40 *	10.14	-	-	4	-	366	315	6	52.50	3-43	-	
NatWest																	
B & H																	
Sunday																	

NEWELL, K.   Sussex

Name: Keith Newell
Role: Right-hand bat, occasional
medium-pace bowler
Born: 25 March 1972, Crawley
Height: 6ft **Weight:** 11st 10lbs
Nickname: Ede, Prac, Wheely, Emerson
County debut: 1993 (one-day)
Parents: Peter Charles and Julie Anne
Marital status: Single
Family links with cricket: Brother Mark is
on Sussex staff. Other brother plays club
cricket for Three Bridges. Father used to play
Education: Gossops Green Junior School;
Ifield Community College
Qualifications: 10 GCSEs, coaching
certificate
Career outside cricket: 'Survival'
Off-season: 'Surviving'

Overseas teams played for: Zimbabwe Universals 1989-90; Bulawayo Athletic Club
1991-92; Lower Hutt, New Zealand 1993-94; Riverside CC, Wellington
Cricketers particularly admired: Ian Botham, Matthew Church, John Marchant, Toby Peirce
Relaxations: 'The movies and an occasional drink'
Extras: 'A couple of table tennis awards'

1994 Season

	M	Inns	NO	Runs	HS	Avge	100s	50s	Ct	St	O	M	Runs	Wkts	Avge	Best	5wI	10wM
Test																		
All First																		
1-day Int																		
NatWest																		
B & H																		
Sunday	1	1	0	10	10	10.00	-	-	-	-	4	0	25	0	-		-	-

Career Performances

	M	Inns	NO	Runs	HS	Avge	100s	50s	Ct	St	Balls	Runs	Wkts	Avge	Best	5wI	10wM
Test																	
All First																	
1-day Int																	
NatWest																	
B & H																	
Sunday	2	1	0	10	10	10.00	-	-	-	-	60	69	0	-		-	-

NEWELL, M.   Sussex

Name: Mark Newell
Role: Right-hand bat, right-arm
fast-medium bowler
Born: 19 December 1973, Crawley
Height: 6ft 1in **Weight:** 12st 2lbs
Nickname: Bambi, Little Ede, Linford
County debut: No first-team appearance
Parents: Peter Charles and Julie Anne
Marital status: Single
Family links with cricket: Brother Keith
also on the Sussex staff, father and younger
brother Jonathan both play league cricket
Education: Hazelwick Comprehensive; City
of Westminster College
Qualifications: 9 GCSEs, NCA Senior
Coaching Award
Career outside cricket: 'Opening up a "Ricky
Fay" school of swing bowling'
Off-season: Studying advanced GNVQ in
Leisure and Tourism in the inaugural course set up by MCC for their Young Cricketers
Overseas tours: Sussex U19 to India 1990-91, to Barbados (as captain) 1993-94
Overseas teams played for: Bulawayo Athletic Club, Zimbabwe 1991-92
Cricketers particularly admired: Mark Waugh, Darren Gough, Justin Bates
Other sports followed: 'I walk around with a glow if Arsenal or Tottenham lose'
Relaxations: Films and the film industry
Extras: MCC Young Cricketer in 1994. Was on a sponsored scholarship at Arundel Castle
which enabled him and two others to work, play and coach all over Sussex for two years.
Opinions on cricket: 'Young cricketers are ill-prepared for their introduction into three or
four-day cricket due to the nature of youth cricket. U19 cricket should be extended to give
good YCs some experience of championship-style conditions before they actually make the
step up.'

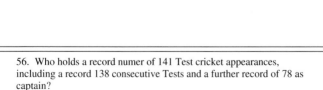

56. Who holds a record numer of 141 Test cricket appearances,
including a record 138 consecutive Tests and a further record of 78 as
captain?

NEWELL, M.   Nottinghamshire

Name: Michael Newell
Role: Right-hand opening bat, leg-break
bowler, occasional wicket-keeper
Born: 25 February 1965, Blackburn
Height: 5ft 10in **Weight:** 11st
Nickname: Mugly, Tricky, Animal
County debut: 1984
County cap: 1987
1000 runs in a season: 1
1st-Class 50s: 24
1st-Class 100s: 6
1st-Class 200s: 1
1st-Class catches: 93
1st-Class stumpings: 1
One-Day 100s: 1
Parents: Barry and Janet
Wife and date of marriage:
Jayne, 23 September 1989
Children: Elizabeth Rose, 1 September 1993
Family links with cricket: Father chairman of Notts Unity CC and brother, Paul, is the captain
Education: West Bridgford Comprehensive
Qualifications: 8 O-levels, 3 A-levels. NCA advanced coach
Off-season: Part-time at Trent Bridge on the development side
Cricketers particularly admired: Mathew Dowman, Dominic Cork, James Hindson
Other sports followed: Rugby union, football, darts
Relaxations: 'Feet up, slippers on in front of the television. Spending time with my family.'
Extras: Captain and coach of Nottinghamshire 2nd XI (The Stiffs)
Opinions on cricket: 'There has been a lot of scornful criticism of county cricket and its players from press people who have been too quick to moan. There are a lot of very good players in this country and some excellent young ones. Four-day cricket should lead to a revival in our Test fixtures and should sort out the better players from the average ones.'
Best batting: 203* Nottinghamshire v Derbyshire, Derby 1987
Best bowling: 2-38 Nottinghamshire v Sri Lankans, Trent Bridge 1988

1994 Season (did not make any first-class or one-day appearance)

---

57. Which former Australia U19 player represented England A on their 1994-95 tour to India?

Career Performances

	M	Inns	NO	Runs	HS	Avge	100s	50s	Ct	St	Balls	Runs	Wkts	Avge	Best	5wI	10wM
Test																	
All First	102	178	26	4636	203 *	30.50	6	24	93	1	363	282	7	40.28	2-38	-	-
1-day Int																	
NatWest	5	5	0	136	60	27.20	-	1	3	-	6	10	0	-		-	-
B & H	10	10	1	205	39	22.77	-	-	2	-							
Sunday	24	21	4	611	109 *	35.94	1	3	8	-							

NEWPORT, P. J.   Worcestershire

Name: Philip John Newport
Role: Right-hand bat, right-arm
fast-medium bowler, outfielder
Born: 11 October 1962, High Wycombe
Height: 6ft 2in **Weight:** 13st 7lbs
Nickname: Schnozz, Newps
County debut: 1982
County cap: 1986
Test debut: 1988
Tests: 3
50 wickets in a season: 7
1st-Class 50s: 18
1st-Class 5 w. in innings: 29
1st-Class 10 w. in match: 3
1st-Class catches: 69
One-Day 5 w. in innings: 2
Place in batting averages:
218th av. 18.15 (1993 104th av. 31.50)
Place in bowling averages:
72nd av. 31.20 (1993 24th av. 24.23)
Strike rate: 58.45 (career 52.80)
Parents: John and Sheila Diana
Wife and date of marriage: Christine Anne, 26 October 1985
Children: Nathan Alexander, 10 May 1989
Family links with cricket: Brother Stewart is captain of Octopus CC in North London
Education: Royal Grammar School, High Wycombe; Portsmouth University
Qualifications: 8 O-levels, 3 A-levels, BA (Hons) Geography, coaching qualification
Overseas tours: NCA to Denmark 1981; England A to Pakistan 1990-91; England to
Australia 1990-91
Overseas teams played for: Vogeltown, New Plymouth, New Zealand 1986; Boland, South
Africa 1987-88; Ginnenderra and ACT, Australia 1991; Northern Transvaal, South Africa 1992-93

Other sports followed: American football, basketball, golf
Relaxations: 'Cinema, spending time with my son (improving his golf swing and cover drive)'
Extras: Had trial as schoolboy for Southampton FC. Played cricket for NAYC England Schoolboys 1981 and for Buckinghamshire in Minor Counties Championship in 1981 and 1982. Selected for cancelled England tour to India 1988-89 and selected as a replacement for England's tour to Australia in 1990-91. Winner of Worcestershire's Dick Lygon Award 1992 and voted Worcestershire Player of the Year 1992 and 1993
Opinions on cricket: 'County staffs will diminish in size as four-day cricket is bound to shrink each club's income.'
Best batting: 98 Worcestershire v New Zealanders, Worcester 1990
Best bowling: 8-52 Worcestershire v Middlesex, Lord's 1988

1994 Season

	M	Inns	NO	Runs	HS	Avge	100s	50s	Ct	St	O	M	Runs	Wkts	Avge	Best	5wI	10wM
Test																		
All First	17	24	5	345	41	18.15	-	-	3	-	516.2	103	1654	53	31.20	4-50	-	-
1-day Int																		
NatWest	5	1	0	14	14	14.00	-	-	1	-	37.1	4	143	11	13.00	4-30	-	
B & H	4	1	1	1	1 *	-	-	-	-	-	38	8	98	6	16.33	3-14	-	
Sunday	15	5	2	23	17	7.66	-	-	5	-	114.2	8	453	25	18.12	3-21	-	

Career Performances

	M	Inns	NO	Runs	HS	Avge	100s	50s	Ct	St	Balls	Runs	Wkts	Avge	Best	5wI	10wM
Test	3	5	1	110	40 *	27.50	-	-	1	-	669	417	10	41.70	4-87	-	-
All First	233	270	79	4798	98	25.12	-	18	69	-	37066	19377	702	27.60	8-52	29	3
1-day Int																	
NatWest	25	12	3	98	25	10.88	-	-	2	-	1323	788	34	23.17	4-30	-	
B & H	40	21	6	149	28	9.93	-	-	9	-	2561	1293	59	21.91	5-22	2	
Sunday	134	62	23	415	26 *	10.64	-	-	30	-	5284	3788	140	27.05	4-18	-	

NICHOLAS, M. C. J.   Hampshire

Name: Mark Charles Jefford Nicholas
Role: Right-hand bat, 'I think I bowl, but no one else does', county captain
Born: 29 September 1957, London
Height: 6ft **Weight:** 12st 5lbs
Nickname: Skip, Dougie, Cappy
County debut: 1978
County cap: 1982
Benefit: 1991 (£174,260)
1000 runs in a season: 9

1st-Class 50s: 77
1st-Class 100s: 32
1st-Class 200s: 1
1st-Class 5 w. in innings: 2
1st-Class catches: 210
One-Day 100s: 1
Place in batting averages: 33rd av. 45.46
(1993 67th av. 36.72)
Strike rate: (career 80.73)
Parents: Anne
Marital status: Single
Family links with cricket: Grandfather
(F.W.H.) played for Essex as batsman and
wicket-keeper and toured with MCC. Father
played for Navy
Education: Fernden Prep School;
Bradfield College
Qualifications: 9 O-levels, 3 A-levels
Career outside cricket: Broadcasting
and journalism
Off-season: Working as journalist and broadcaster on England tour to Australia
Overseas tours: English Counties XI to Zimbabwe 1984-85; England B to Sri Lanka
(captain) 1985-86; England A to Zimbabwe and Kenya (captain) 1989-90
Cricketers particularly admired: Barry Richards, John Snow, Mike Brearley
Other sports followed: Most – football, golf, fives, squash
Relaxations: Theatre, music, golf, going out to dinner
Extras: Hampshire captain since 1985 but missed Hampshire's first NatWest final in 1994
after having his knuckle and finger broken a few days earlier by a delivery from Surrey's
Waqar Younis in the Championship game between the two NatWest finalists
Opinions on cricket: 'Four-day cricket should be played during the week and two, not
three, one-day competitions should be played at weekends: 1. A B&H-style 50-over Sunday
league with semi-finals and finals; 2. NatWest Trophy .'
Best batting: 206* Hampshire v Oxford University, The Parks 1982
Best bowling: 6-37 Hampshire v Somerset, Southampton 1989

1994 Season

	M	Inns	NO	Runs	HS	Avge	100s	50s	Ct	St	O	M	Runs	Wkts	Avge	Best	5wI	10wM
Test																		
All First	19	32	6	1182	145	45.46	3	5	7	-	4	2	7	0	-	-	-	-
1-day Int																		
NatWest	2	1	0	62	62	62.00	-	1	-	-								
B & H	3	3	2	119	46 *	119.00	-	-	1	-								
Sunday	17	15	3	285	47	23.75	-	-	8	-								

Career Performances

	M	Inns	NO	Runs	HS	Avge	100s	50s	Ct	St	Balls	Runs	Wkts	Avge	Best	5wI	10wM
Test																	
All First	358	587	86	17052	206 *	34.03	32	77	210	-	5813	3219	72	44.70	6-37	2	-
1-day Int																	
NatWest	43	37	6	972	71	31.35	-	7	14	-	521	346	9	38.44	2-39	-	-
B & H	63	56	9	1221	74	25.97	-	4	19	-	1020	759	24	31.62	4-34	-	
Sunday	218	197	39	4474	108	28.31	1	26	70	-	1902	1783	59	30.22	4-30	-	

NIXON, P. A.   Leicestershire

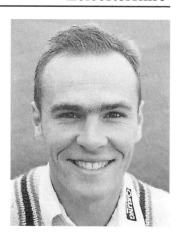

Name: Paul Andrew Nixon
Role: Left-hand bat, wicket-keeper
Born: 21 October 1970, Carlisle
Height: 5ft 11in **Weight:** 12st 7lbs
Nickname: Nico, Murdock
County debut: 1989
1000 runs in a season: 1
1st-Class 50s: 8
1st-Class 100s: 5
1st-Class catches: 211
1st-Class stumpings: 17
Place in batting averages: 63rd 38.74
(1993 169th av. 22.77)
Parents: Brian and Sylvia
Marital status: Single
Family links with cricket: 'Grandfather and
father played local club cricket and mum
made teas for Edenhall, Penrith.'
Education: Langwathby Primary;
Ullswater High
Qualifications: 2 O-levels, 8 CSEs, NCA cricket coaching certificate
Career outside cricket: Farmer on father's farm. Bricklayer and landscape gardener in
Australia. Cricket coach at Leicestershire CCC
Off-season: England A tour to India. Kick-boxing in Leicester
Overseas tours: Cumbria to Denmark 1985; Leicestershire to Holland 1991, to Montego
Bay, to Bloemfontein; England A to India 1994-95
Overseas teams played for: Melville and North Fremantle, Perth, Western Australia 1989-
92; Mitchells Rain, Cape Town 1992
Cricketers particularly admired: David Gower, Jack Russell, Ralphy Roseberry
Other sports followed: Everything
Injuries: Broken thumb, bursa in groin, did not miss any cricket

Relaxations: Bungee jumping, kick-boxing, rally driving
Extras: Youngest person to score a century against Yorkshire (at U15). Played for England U15 and played in Minor Counties Championship for Cumberland at 16, MCC Young Pro in 1988. Took eight catches in debut match v Warwickshire at Hinckley in 1989. Played for Carlisle United and 'once got lost in South African township at 3.30am'. Leicester Young Player of the Year two years running. Second Leicester wicket-keeper to score 1000 runs in a season
Opinions on cricket: 'Umpires should have lighter coloured trousers on.'
Best batting: 131 Leicestershire v Hampshire, Leicester 1994

1994 Season

	M	Inns	NO	Runs	HS	Avge	100s	50s	Ct	St	O	M	Runs	Wkts	Avge	Best	5wI	10wM
Test																		
All First	19	30	3	1046	131	38.74	3	4	60	2								
1-day Int																		
NatWest	2	1	0	2	2	2.00	-	-	1	1								
B & H	2	1	0	5	5	5.00	-	-	1	-								
Sunday	17	16	2	318	72	22.71	-	3	13	4								

Career Performances

	M	Inns	NO	Runs	HS	Avge	100s	50s	Ct	St	Balls	Runs	Wkts	Avge	Best	5wI	10wM
Test																	
All First	83	117	28	2628	131	29.52	5	8	211	17							
1-day Int																	
NatWest	10	8	2	91	32	15.16	-	-	11	2							
B & H	7	6	0	58	27	9.66	-	-	3	1							
Sunday	65	54	9	880	72	19.55	-	4	51	9							

58. Who recorded the slowest-ever first-class fifty in 1994 and how long did it take?

Name: Wayne Michael Noon
Role: Right-hand bat, wicket-keeper
Born: 5 February 1971, Grimsby
Height: 5ft 9¹/₂in **Weight:** 11st 7lbs
Nickname: Noonie
County debut: 1988 (one-day),
1989 (first-class) (Northamptonshire),
1994 (Nottinghamshire)
1st-Class 50s: 3
1st-Class catches: 61
1st-Class stumpings: 8
Place in batting averages: 157th av. 25.70
Parents: Trafford and Rosemary
Marital status: Single
Education: Caistor Grammar School
Qualifications: 5 O-levels
Off-season: Playing cricket in Christchurch
NZ and working for Canterbury CA
Overseas tours: Lincolnshire U15 to Pakistan
1984; England YC to Australia 1989-90; Rutland tourists to South Africa 1988
Overseas teams played for: Burnside West, Christchurch, New Zealand 1989-90 and
1993-94; Rivertonians, Cape Town 1992-93
Cricketers particularly admired: Ian Botham, Graham Gooch
Other sports followed: Football, horse racing, any sport with British interest
Injuries: Thumb, missed one game
Relaxations: 'Follow Lincoln City FC. The occasional bet.'
Extras: Played for England YC v New Zealand YC 1989; captain v Australian YC
1989-90 and Pakistan YC 1990. Was the 1000th player to appear in the Sunday League
competition. Broke the Northants record for most 2nd XI hundreds in one season in 1993
Opinions on cricket: 'Keep Sunday League the same except use a red ball. Tea should be
half an hour. The B&H Cup should be 50 overs to bring in line with other countries.'
Best batting: 75 Nottinghamshire v Northamptonshire, Trent Bridge 1994

1994 Season

	M	Inns	NO	Runs	HS	Avge	100s	50s	Ct	St	O	M	Runs	Wkts	Avge	Best	5wI	10wM
Test																		
All First	18	30	6	617	75	25.70	-	3	38	5								
1-day Int																		
NatWest	2	1	0	34	34	34.00	-	-	2	1								
B & H	3	2	0	12	9	6.00	-	-	3	1								
Sunday	14	10	1	71	27	7.88	-	-	9	3								

Career Performances

	M	Inns	NO	Runs	HS	Avge	100s	50s	Ct	St	Balls	Runs	Wkts	Avge	Best	5wI	10wM
Test																	
All First	30	46	8	767	75	20.18	-	3	61	8							
1-day Int																	
NatWest	2	1	0	34	34	34.00	-	-	2	1							
B & H	4	2	0	12	9	6.00	-	-	3	1							
Sunday	30	21	3	151	27	8.38	-	-	19	5							

NORTH, J. A. Sussex

Name: John Andrew North
Role: Right-hand bat, right-arm
medium bowler, outfielder
Born: 19 November 1970, Slindon
Height: 5ft 11in **Weight:** 12st
Nickname: Ollie
County debut: 1990
1st-Class 50s: 3
1st-Class 100s: 1
1st-Class catches: 4
Place in batting averages:
(1993 121st av. 28.50)
Strike rate: (career 60.02)
Parents: John Allan and Margaret Anne
Marital status: Single
Family links with cricket: Brother Mark
played county schoolboy cricket. Father plays
club cricket
Education: Bishop Luffa Comprehensive
School; Slindon College
Qualifications: 10 O-levels, 2 A-levels, senior coaching award
Career outside cricket: Electrician
Off-season: Working for Fording Bridge Engineering
Overseas tours: Buckingham Cavaliers to Cape Town, South Africa 1989 and 1992;
Sussex Martlets to Zimbabwe 1991
Overseas teams played for: University St Heliers, Auckland 1989-90
Cricketers particularly admired: Mahmoud Nassarian, Daniel Oliver
Other sports followed: 'Football and anything without horses.'
Relaxations: 'Eating out, watching movies'
Extras: Played for English Schools U15 and U17, NAYC and for England YC v Pakistan
YC 1990

Opinions on cricket: 'Tea intervals should be extended. Young players are important to a county's future and should be treated in accordance.'
Best batting: 114 Sussex v Essex, Hove 1993
Best bowling: 4-47 Sussex v Sri Lankans, Hove 1991

1994 Season

	M	Inns	NO	Runs	HS	Avge	100s	50s	Ct	St	O	M	Runs	Wkts	Avge	Best	5wI	10wM
Test																		
All First																		
1-day Int																		
NatWest																		
B & H																		
Sunday	7	6	0	17	7	2.83	-	-	1	-	20.1	1	80	0	-		-	-

Career Performances

	M	Inns	NO	Runs	HS	Avge	100s	50s	Ct	St	Balls	Runs	Wkts	Avge	Best	5wI	10wM
Test																	
All First	23	31	6	513	114	20.52	1	3	4	-	2641	1577	44	35.84	4-47	-	-
1-day Int																	
NatWest	2	2	0	31	20	15.50	-	-	-	-	12	17	0	-		-	-
B & H	7	5	1	64	22	16.00	-	-	-	-	348	300	8	37.50	3-24	-	
Sunday	29	26	6	269	56	13.45	-	1	8	-	614	590	18	32.77	3-29	-	

NOWELL, R. W. Surrey

Name: Richard William Nowell
Role: Left-hand bat, slow left-arm bowler
Born: 29 December 1975, Croydon
Height: 6ft **Weight:** 12st 7lbs
County debut: No first-team appearance
Nickname: Nowlsie, Muesli, Nosebleed
Parents: Bill and June
Marital status: Single
Education: Cumnor House Prep School; Trinity School, Croydon
Qualifications: 10 GCSEs, 3 A-levels, coaching certificate
Off-season: Playing in South Africa
Overseas tours: England U18 to South Africa 1992-93
Overseas teams played for: Technikon, Natal 1994-95

Cricketers particularly admired: Phil Tufnell, Merv Hughes
Other sports followed: Football (Arsenal), rugby
Relaxations: 'Enjoying life'
Extras: Played for Surrey from U11 to U19. Played England U15, U17 and U18. Holds record for highest aggregate of runs in school cricket.

O'GORMAN, T. J. G. Derbyshire

Name: Timothy Joseph Gerard O'Gorman
Role: Right-hand bat, off-spin bowler
Born: 15 May 1967, Woking
Height: 6ft 2in **Weight:** 12st
County debut: 1987
County cap: 1992
1000 runs in a season: 2
1st-Class 50s: 22
1st-Class 100s: 9
1st-Class catches: 66
Place in batting averages: 104th av. 33.53
(1993 122nd av. 28.38)
Parents: Brian and Kathleen
Marital status: Single
Family links with cricket:
Grandfather Joe O'Gorman played for Surrey;
father Brian played for Nigeria, for Sussex 2nd
XI and Middlesex 2nd XI
Education: St George's College, Weybridge;
St Chad's College, Durham University; College of Law, Guildford
Qualifications: 12 O-levels, 3 A-levels, BA (Hons) Law; Law Society finals
Career outside cricket: Solicitor
Overseas tours: Troubadours to Argentina 1987, to Brazil 1989; Christians in Sport to Zimbabwe 1994-95
Overseas teams played for: Alexandra, Zimbabwe; Southern Hawkes Bay, New Zealand
Cricketers particularly admired: David Gower, Greg Chappell, Richard Hadlee
Other sports followed: Tennis, golf, hockey, rugby, football
Relaxations: Arts, theatre, music, reading
Extras: Surrey Young Cricketer of the Year 1984. Captained Surrey Young Cricketers for three years. Trials for England schoolboys at hockey
Best batting: 148 Derbyshire v Lancashire, Old Trafford 1991
Best bowling: 1-7 Derbyshire v Cambridge University, Fenner's 1992

1994 Season

	M	Inns	NO	Runs	HS	Avge	100s	50s	Ct	St	O	M	Runs	Wkts	Avge	Best	5wI	10wM
Test																		
All First	16	28	2	872	145	33.53	3	3	12	-	0.5	0	8	0	-	-	-	-
1-day Int																		
NatWest	3	3	0	94	89	31.33	-	1	-	-								
B & H	2	2	0	26	24	13.00	-	-	-	-								
Sunday	16	15	6	309	63 *	34.33	-	1	2	-								

Career Performances

	M	Inns	NO	Runs	HS	Avge	100s	50s	Ct	St	Balls	Runs	Wkts	Avge	Best	5wI	10wM
Test																	
All First	101	169	21	4611	148	31.15	9	22	66	-	265	215	3	71.66	1-7	-	-
1-day Int																	
NatWest	7	7	1	164	89	27.33	-	2	1	-							
B & H	22	19	1	387	49	21.50	-	-	4	-	6	1	0	-	-	-
Sunday	76	71	14	1445	69	25.35	-	4	13	-							

OSTLER, D. P.   Warwickshire

Name: Dominic Piers Ostler
Role: Right-hand bat, right-arm medium bowler
Born: 15 July 1970, Solihull
Height: 6ft 2in **Weight:** 12st
Nickname: Ossie, Blondie
County debut: 1990
County cap: 1991
1000 runs in a season: 4
1st-Class 50s: 32
1st-Class 100s: 7
1st-Class catches: 85
One-Day 100s: 1
Place in batting averages: 45th av. 43.00
(1993 87th av. 33.93)
Parents: Mike and Ann
Marital status: Single
Family links with cricket: Brother plays for Knowle and Dorridge
Education: Princethorpe College; Solihull Technical College
Qualifications: 4 O-levels
Career outside cricket: Businessman (Executive)

Off-season: 'Earnings lots of money and playing golf.'
Overseas tours: Gladstone Small's Benefit Tour to Barbados, 1992
Overseas teams played for: Avendale CC, South Africa 1991-92
Cricketers particularly admired: Gladstone Small, Graeme Welsh
Other sports followed: Football, golf, snooker
Relaxations: 'Looking after brother's little boy. Cinema and spending time with girlfriend, Sam.'
Extras: Played club cricket for Moseley in the Birmingham League; made his Warwickshire 2nd XI debut in 1989 and was a member of Warwickshire U19 side that won Esso U19 County Festivals in 1988 and 1989. Has collected winner's medals for B&H Cup, Britannic Assurance County Championship, NatWest Trophy and Sunday League
Opinions on cricket: 'Not enough prize money for major trophies – triple the prize money!'
Best batting: 192 Warwickshire v Surrey, Guildford 1992

1994 Season

	M	Inns	NO	Runs	HS	Avge	100s	50s	Ct	St	O	M	Runs	Wkts	Avge	Best	5wI	10wM
Test																		
All First	18	29	2	1161	186	43.00	2	6	14	-	1.1	0	13	0	-	-	-	-
1-day Int																		
NatWest	5	5	0	163	81	32.60	-	1	2	-								
B & H	3	3	0	110	55	36.66	-	1	2	-								
Sunday	17	17	1	530	84 *	33.12	-	5	4	-								

Career Performances

	M	Inns	NO	Runs	HS	Avge	100s	50s	Ct	St	Balls	Runs	Wkts	Avge	Best	5wI	10wM
Test																	
All First	93	160	14	5288	192	36.21	7	32	85	-	143	122	0	-	-	-	-
1-day Int																	
NatWest	19	18	2	449	104	28.06	1	2	8	-	9	4	1	4.00	1-4	-	
B & H	13	13	1	351	65 *	29.25	,	2	6	,							
Sunday	72	66	9	1794	84 *	31.47	-	14	19	-	6	4	0	-	-	-	

OWEN, J. E.   Derbyshire

Name: John Edward Owen
Role: Right-hand bat
Born: 7 August 1971
Height: 5ft 10in **Weight:** 11st 7lbs
County debut: No first-team appearance
Parents: David Horton and Carole
Marital status: Single
Family links with cricket: Father played in Derbyshire League for Alvaston, Boulton and Spondon. Grandfather played for Crewe
Education: Spondon School, Derby
Qualifications: Qualified green-keeper
Career outside cricket: Green-keeper
Off-season: Groundstaff at Derbyshire
Cricketers particularly admired:
Ian Botham, Viv Richards
Other sports followed: Football, golf, rugby union
Relaxations: Football, golf

Opinions on cricket: 'I think that the third umpire is a good idea because there is no arguing with the television screen on slow motion replay. I do think that overseas players should stay in first-class cricket because they keep the standard high, which would drop if they were not here, plus the interest from the public would not be as great.'

PARKER, B.   Yorkshire

Name: Bradley Parker
Role: Right-hand bat, right-arm medium bowler, cover point fielder
Born: 23 June 1970, Mirfield
Height: 5ft 10in **Weight:** 12st 7lbs
Nickname: Nesty, Ceefax, Floyd
County debut: 1992
1st-Class 50s: 4
1st-Class 100s: 1
1st-Class catches: 7
Place in batting averages: 82nd av. 36.12
Parents: Diane and David
Marital status: Single
Family links with cricket: Father played club cricket and Lincolnshire U23
Education: Bingley Grammar School

Qualifications: 'None worth mentioning from school.' Cricket coaching awards

Career outside cricket: 'Training, and keeping to my strict diet'

Off-season: 'Going on holiday, coaching in local schools. Hoping to make it on to pre-season tour to South Africa'

Overseas teams played for: Ellerslie, Auckland 1988-90

Cricketers particularly admired: Chris Spence, Alec Stewart, Graham Thorpe, Viv Richards

Other sports followed: Rugby league, boxing

Relaxations: Films, eating out, drinking and socialising

Opinions on cricket: 'Far too much cricket played in too short a time.'

Best batting: 127 Yorkshire v Surrey, Scarborough 1994

1994 Season

	M	Inns	NO	Runs	HS	Avge	100s	50s	Ct	St	O	M	Runs	Wkts	Avge	Best	5wI	10wM
Test																		
All First	10	18	2	578	127	36.12	1	4	6	-								
1-day Int																		
NatWest																		
B & H																		
Sunday	10	9	1	164	36	20.50	-	-	2	-								

Career Performances

	M	Inns	NO	Runs	HS	Avge	100s	50s	Ct	St	Balls	Runs	Wkts	Avge	Best	5wI	10wM
Test																	
All First	11	20	2	615	127	34.16	1	4	7	-							
1-day Int																	
NatWest																	
B & H																	
Sunday	11	10	1	169	36	18.77	-	-	2	-							

PARKIN, O. T. Glamorgan

Name: Owen Thomas Parkin
Role: Right-hand bat, right-arm medium-fast bowler
Born: 24 August 1972, Coventry
Height: 6ft 2in **Weight:** 11st 6lbs
Nickname: Parallel, Reverse, Tickets, Cars, Longterm, Disabled
County debut: 1994
Parents: Vernon Cyrus and Sarah Patricia
Marital status: Single
Family links with cricket: Younger brother Morgan plays for the county in his age group
Education: Bournemouth Grammar School; Bath University
Qualifications: 9 GCSEs, 4 A-levels, 1 S-level
Career outside cricket: Student, reading Mathematics
Off-season: Final year at university
Overseas tours: Dorset Youth to Denmark
Overseas teams played for: Kew, Melbourne 1992-93; North Balwyn, Melbourne 1993-94
Cricketers particularly admired: Malcolm Marshall, Richard Hadlee
Other sports followed: Rugby, football (Nottingham Forest), golf
Injuries: Pulled side muscle, missed three-four weeks. Lower back problem, missed one month at end of season
Relaxations: Squash, golf, listening to The Stranglers, socialising and finishing degree
Extras: Played for Dorset in the NatWest Trophy 1992 and 1993. ASW Young Player of the Month July 1994
Opinions on cricket: 'I feel that something should be given for a draw in the Championship especially now it is four days. With 16 points for a win, the incentive to win would still be there even if, say three or four points were given for a drawn game.'
Best batting: 2* Glamorgan v Middlesex, Lord's 1994
Best bowling: 2-45 Glamorgan v Middlesex, Lord's 1994

1994 Season

	M	Inns	NO	Runs	HS	Avge	100s	50s	Ct	St	O	M	Runs	Wkts	Avge	Best	5wI	10wM
Test																		
All First	2	2	2	2	2*	-	-	-	-	-	54	9	170	4	42.50	2-45	-	-
1-day Int																		
NatWest																		
B & H																		
Sunday																		

Career Performances

	M	Inns	NO	Runs	HS	Avge	100s	50s	Ct	St	Balls	Runs	Wkts	Avge	Best	5wI	10wM
Test																	
All First	2	2	2	2	2*	-	-	-	-	-	324	170	4	42.50	2-45	-	-
1-day Int																	
NatWest	2	1	0	0	0	0.00	-	-	-	-	48	54	0	-		-	-
B & H																	
Sunday																	

PARSONS, G. J.   Leicestershire

Name: Gordon James Parsons
Role: Left-hand bat, right-arm medium bowler
Born: 17 October 1959, Slough
Height: 6ft 1in **Weight:** 13st 'on a good day'
Nickname: Bullhead,
County debut: 1978 (Leicestershire), 1986 (Warwickshire)
County cap: 1984 (Leicestershire), 1987 (Warwickshire)
Benefit: 1994
50 wickets in a season: 2
1st-Class 50s: 25
1st-Class 5 w. in innings: 19
1st-Class 10 w. in match: 1
1st-Class catches: 106
Place in batting averages: 154th av. 25.84 (1993 153rd av. 25.31)
Place in bowling averages: 42nd av. 27.45 (1993 30th av. 24.68)
Strike rate: 63.04 (career 59.98)
Parents: Dave and Evelyn
Wife and date of marriage: Hester Sophia, 8 February 1991
Children: Alexandra Suzanna, 5 June 1992
Family links with cricket: Father played club cricket , brother-in-law, Hansie Cronje, is captain of South Africa
Education: Woodside County Secondary School, Slough
Qualifications: 6 O-levels
Career outside cricket: 'Open to offers.'
Off-season: Coaching Orange Free State B side in South Africa and finishing benefit
Overseas tours: English Schools to India 1977-78; Derrick Robins XI to Australasia 1980;

Leicestershire to Zimbabwe 1981, to Jamaica 1993
Overseas teams played for: Maharaja's, Sri Lanka 1979,1987; Boland, South Africa 1982-83; Griqualand West, South Africa 1984-85; Orange Free State, South Africa 1986-92
Cricketers particularly admired: Graham 'the bookies' hero' Lloyd, Alan 'waca nets' Mullally, Jonathan 'fat boy' Dakin, David 'Thompson holidays' Millns, Ben 'gadget' Smith
Other sports followed: Golf
Relaxations: 'My wife and daughter'
Extras: Played for Leicester 2nd XI from 1976 and for Buckinghamshire in 1977. Left Leicestershire after 1985 season and joined Warwickshire. Capped by Warwickshire while in plaster and on crutches. Released at end of 1988 season and returned to his old county. Justin Benson was best man at his wedding, 'contradiction in terms, though it is!'
Best batting: 76 Boland v Western Province B, Cape Town 1984-85
Best bowling: 9-72 Boland v Transvaal B, Johannesburg 1984-85

1994 Season

	M	Inns	NO	Runs	HS	Avge	100s	50s	Ct	St	O	M	Runs	Wkts	Avge	Best	5wl	10wM
Test																		
All First	16	25	6	491	70	25.84	-	2	17	-	462.2	131	1208	44	27.45	5-34	1	-
1-day Int																		
NatWest	2	1	0	2	2	2.00	-	-	1	-	24	4	65	2	32.50	1-19	-	
B & H	2	1	0	1	1	1.00	-	-	-	-	20.5	5	66	1	66.00	1-21	-	
Sunday	15	12	3	109	29	12.11	-	-	4	-	113	5	415	16	25.93	4-50	-	

Career Performances

	M	Inns	NO	Runs	HS	Avge	100s	50s	Ct	St	Balls	Runs	Wkts	Avge	Best	5wl	10wM
Test																	
All First	294	389	90	5825	76	19.48	-	25	106	-	41692	20755	695	29.86	9-72	19	1
1-day Int																	
NatWest	28	18	5	139	23	10.69	-	-	6	-	1532	968	21	46.09	2-11	-	
B & H	50	26	11	266	63 *	17.73	-	1	11	-	2703	1574	57	27.61	4-12	-	
Sunday	173	108	42	1009	38 *	15.28	-	-	24	-	7111	5252	167	31.44	4-19	-	

PARSONS, K. A.   Somerset

Name: Keith Alan Parsons
Role: Right-hand bat, right-arm medium bowler
Born: 2 May 1973, Taunton
Height: 6ft 1in **Weight:** 13st
Nickname: Pilot, Pars, Orv
County debut: 1992
1st-Class 50s: 1
1st-Class catches: 5
Place in batting averages:
(1993 215th av. 16.75)
Parents: Alan and Lynne
Marital status: Single
Family links with cricket: Identical twin brother, Kevin, was on the Somerset staff. Father played six seasons for Somerset 2nd XI and captained National Civil Service XI
Education: Castle School, Taunton; Richard Huish Sixth Form College, Taunton
Qualifications: 8 GCSEs, 3 A-levels, NCA coaching award
Off-season: Coaching and playing for Taita in Hutt Valley, Wellington, New Zealand
Overseas tours: Castle School to Barbados 1989
Overseas teams played for: Kapiti Old Boys, New Zealand 1992-93; Harowhenera, New Zealand 1992-93; Taita District, Wellington, New Zealand 1993-95
Cricketers particularly admired: Viv Richards, Richard Hadlee, Robin Smith
Other sports followed: Rugby union, soccer, golf
Relaxations: 'All sports'
Extras: Captained two National Cup winning sides – Taunton St Andrews in National U15 Club Championship and Richard Huish College in National U17 School Championship. Represented English Schools at U15 and U19 level. Somerset Young Player of the Year 1993
Opinions on cricket: 'Now that the first-class Championship has been changed to four-day games, in order to improve the Test team and reduce the amount of contrived finishes, shouldn't the next step be to change the 2nd XI competition to a four-day Championship also, to help the younger players, in 2nd XI, become better four-day cricketers?'
Best batting: 63 Somerset v Sussex, Taunton 1993

---

59. In 1994 Alex Kelly, 17, set a new world record in a Milburngate County Junior League match — what was it?

1994 Season

	M	Inns	NO	Runs	HS	Avge	100s	50s	Ct	St	O	M	Runs	Wkts	Avge	Best	5wI	10wM
Test																		
All First	3	5	1	38	16	9.50	-	-	2	-	4	0	21	0	-		-	-
1-day Int																		
NatWest																		
B & H																		
Sunday	1	1	0	18	18	18.00	-	-	-	-								

Career Performances

	M	Inns	NO	Runs	HS	Avge	100s	50s	Ct	St	Balls	Runs	Wkts	Avge	Best	5wI	10wM
Test																	
All First	9	16	2	173	63	12.35	-	1	5	-	30	35	0	-		-	-
1-day Int																	
NatWest	2	2	1	33	33	33.00	-	-	-	-	72	47	2	23.50	2-47	-	
B & H																	
Sunday	8	8	0	101	34	12.62	-	-	1	-	54	49	1	49.00	1-19	-	

PATEL, M. M.   Kent

Name: Minal Mahesh Patel
Role: Right-hand bat, slow left-arm bowler
Born: 7 August 1970, Bombay, India
Height: 5ft 9in **Weight:** 9st 7lbs
Nickname: Min
County debut: 1989
County cap: 1994
1st-Class 5 w. in innings: 10
1st-Class 10 w. in match: 5
1st-Class catches: 20
Place in batting averages: 266th av. 10.24
Place in bowling averages: 9th av. 22.86
(1993 86th av. 31.35)
Strike rate: 54.08 (career 63.92)
Parents: Mahesh and Aruna
Marital status: Single
Family links with cricket: Father played good club cricket in India, Africa and England
Education: Dartford GS; Erith College of Technology; Manchester Polytechnic
Qualifications: 6 O-levels, 3 A-levels
Off-season: Touring with England A

Overseas tours: Dartford GS to Barbados 1988; England A to India 1994-95
Cricketers particularly admired: Bishen Bedi, Derek Underwood, Sunil Gavaskar
Other sports followed: 'All except anything to do with horses'
Relaxations: Listening to soul and dance music, playing snooker
Extras: Played for English Schools 1988,1989 and NCA England South 1989. Was voted Kent League Young Player of the Year 1987 while playing for Blackheath. First six overs in NatWest Trophy were all maidens. Whittingdale Young Player of the Year 1994
Best batting: 43 Kent v Leicestershire, Leicester 1991
Best bowling: 7-75 Kent v Lancashire, Lytham 1993

1994 Season

	M	Inns	NO	Runs	HS	Avge	100s	50s	Ct	St	O	M	Runs	Wkts	Avge	Best	5wI	10wM
Test																		
All First	18	27	2	256	39	10.24	-	-	12	-	811.2	202	2058	90	22.86	8-96	6	3
1-day Int																		
NatWest	2	0	0	0	0	-	-	-	2	-	24	4	71	1	71.00	1-27	-	
B & H																		
Sunday	6	2	0	6	5	3.00	-	-	1	-	29.2	0	191	6	31.83	3-50	-	

Career Performances

	M	Inns	NO	Runs	HS	Avge	100s	50s	Ct	St	Balls	Runs	Wkts	Avge	Best	5wI	10wM
Test																	
All First	40	54	12	453	43	10.78	-	-	20	-	9014	3919	141	27.79	8-96	10	5
1-day Int																	
NatWest	3	0	0	0	0	-	-	-	2	-	216	100	3	33.33	2-29	-	
B & H																	
Sunday	6	2	0	6	5	3.00	-	-	1	-	176	191	6	31.83	3-50	-	

PAYNE, A.   Somerset

Name: Andrew Payne
Role: Right-hand bat, right arm medium-fast bowler
Born: 20 October 1973, Rawtenstall, Lancs
Height: 5ft 10in **Weight:** 12st 6lbs
Nickname: Beastie
County debut: 1992
1st-Class 50s: 1
1st-Class catches: 2
Parents: Brian and Margaret
Marital status: Single
Family links with cricket: Brother represented County Junior Leagues (Lancashire); father captained Rawtenstall in Lancashire League

Education: Bacup and Rawtenstall Grammar School; Accrington and Rossendale College
Qualifications: 8 GCSEs, BTEC in Human Biology, BTEC in Art and Design, qualified cricket coach
Career outside cricket: In the police force
Off-season: Playing in Pretoria, South Africa and coaching
Overseas tours: England U19 to Pakistan 1991-92, to India 1992-93
Overseas teams played for: Villagers, Pretoria, South Africa 1993-94
Cricketers particularly admired: Chris Tavaré, David Gower, Robin Smith, Allan Donald
Other sports followed: 'Most sports, especially football'
Relaxations: Playing golf, watching football and socialising
Extras: Youngest ever pro in the Ribblesdale cricket league. One of the few players to play for all Lancashire junior teams (U11-U19). Released by Lancashire at end of 1994 season
Opinions on cricket: 'I think that the one bouncer per over rule should either be tightened up on or totally abolished because there is still uncertainty to both batsmen, bowlers and umpires as to what should be classed as a bouncer and what shouldn't.'
Best batting: 51* Somerset v Gloucestershire, Taunton 1992
Best bowling: 2-15 Somerset v Worcestershire, Worcester 1993

---

60. Who held the record for the highest innings in first-class cricket before Brian Lara's 501*?

1994 Season

	M	Inns	NO	Runs	HS	Avge	100s	50s	Ct	St	O	M	Runs	Wkts	Avge	Best	5wI	10wM
Test																		
All First	1	1	0	34	34	34.00	-	-	-	-	12	2	54	0	-		-	-
1-day Int																		
NatWest																		
B & H																		
Sunday	4	4	1	44	32 *	14.66	-	-	1	-	13.1	0	95	4	23.75	4-37	-	

Career Performances

	M	Inns	NO	Runs	HS	Avge	100s	50s	Ct	St	Balls	Runs	Wkts	Avge	Best	5wI	10wM
Test																	
All First	4	4	2	124	51 *	62.00	-	1	2	-	344	187	5	37.40	2-15	-	-
1-day Int																	
NatWest																	
B & H																	
Sunday	16	15	4	159	55 *	14.45	-	1	2	-	540	450	10	45.00	4-37	-	

PEARSON, R. M. Essex

Name: Richard Michael Pearson
Role: Right-hand bat, right arm off-spin bowler
Born: 27 January 1972, Batley, Yorkshire
Height: 6ft 3in **Weight:** 13st 5lbs
Nickname: Batley, Pancho
County debut: 1992 (Northamptonshire),
1994 (Essex)
1st-Class 5 w. In Innings: 1
1st-Class catches: 11
Place in batting averages:
(1993 261st av. 10.44)
Place in bowling averages:
(1993 134th av. 48.57)
Strike rate: (career 114.46)
Parents: Mike and Carol
Marital status: Single
Family links with cricket: Father played in
Yorkshire League
Education: Batley Grammar School;
St John's, Cambridge
Qualifications: 2 O-levels, 9 GCSEs,
4 A-levels, BA Hons in History

Off-season: Working for HMV in London
Overseas tours: England U19 to Pakistan 1991-92
Cricketers particularly admired: Darren Robinson, Paul Dowson, Mick Kaye, Paul Marlow
Other sports followed: Football (Leeds), rugby league (Batley)
Relaxations: Playing football, drinking good beer
Extras: Made first-class debut for Cambridge University in 1991 and has played for Combined Universities in the Benson & Hedges Cup since 1991. Football and cricket Blues at Cambridge. Moved to Essex for the 1994 season
Opinions on cricket: 'We should be able to play in shorts when it is hot. Second team matches should go back to the end of the week – Monday nights are too quiet.'
Best batting: 33* Cambridge University v Surrey, Fenner's 1992
Best bowling: 5-108 Cambridge University v Warwickshire, Fenner's 1992

1994 Season

	M	Inns	NO	Runs	HS	Avge	100s	50s	Ct	St	O	M	Runs	Wkts	Avge	Best	5wI	10wM
Test																		
All First	3	4	0	45	20	11.25	-	-	2	-	74.4	17	226	4	56.50	1-39	-	-
1-day Int																		
NatWest	1	0	0	0	0	-	-	-	-	-	12	0	47	1	47.00	1-47	-	
B & H																		
Sunday	9	6	5	23	7	23.00	-	-	-	-	55.2	2	259	8	32.37	3-33	-	

Career Performances

	M	Inns	NO	Runs	HS	Avge	100s	50s	Ct	St	Balls	Runs	Wkts	Avge	Best	5wI	10wM
Test																	
All First	34	39	7	305	33 *	9.53	-	-	11	-	6868	3615	60	60.25	5-108	1	-
1-day Int																	
NatWest	1	0	0	0	0	-	-	-	-	-	72	47	1	47.00	1-47	-	
B & H	6	2	1	10	8	10.00	-	-	-	-	366	235	4	58.75	2-31	-	
Sunday	10	6	5	23	7	23.00	-	-	-	-	344	277	8	34.62	3-33	-	

61. On which cricket ground did England end a 59-year-old unbeaten run by defeating the West Indies in a Test match in 1993-94?

Name: Michael Toby Edward Peirce
Role: Left-hand bat, slow left-arm bowler
Born: 14 June 1973, Maidenhead
Height: 5ft 10in **Weight:** 11st
Nickname: Beastie
County debut: 1994 (one-day)
1st-Class catches: 1
Parents: Michael Robert and Katherine Ross
Marital status: Single
Education: Ardingly College; Durham University
Qualifications: 9 GCSEs, 3 A-levels, 1 S-level
Career outside cricket: Student
Off-season: Studying
Overseas tours: Sussex Schools U14 to Barbados 1987; Sussex Schools U18 to India 1990-91; Ardingly College to India 1988-89
Overseas teams played for: Kilbirnie, Wellington, New Zealand 1991-92; Wellington B, New Zealand 1991-92
Cricketers particularly admired: David Smith, David Gower, Phil Edmonds, 'J. Batty Esq'
Other sports followed: Most
Relaxations: 'Drinks with mates (both of them), music'
Best batting: 24 Combined Universities v New Zealand, Fenner's 1994

1994 Season

	M	Inns	NO	Runs	HS	Avge	100s	50s	Ct	St	O	M	Runs	Wkts	Avge	Best	5wI	10wM
Test																		
All First	1	2	0	24	24	12.00	-	-	1	-	-							
1-day Int																		
NatWest																		
B & H																		
Sunday	1	1	0	6	6	6.00	-	-	2	-								

Career Performances

	M	Inns	NO	Runs	HS	Avge	100s	50s	Ct	St	Balls	Runs	Wkts	Avge	Best	5wl	10wM
Test																	
All First	1	2	0	24	24	12.00	-	-	1	-	-						
1-day Int																	
NatWest																	
B & H																	
Sunday	1	1	0	6	6	6.00	-	-	2	-							

Name: Anthony Leonard Penberthy
Role: Left-hand bat, right-arm medium bowler
Born: 1 September 1969, Troon, Cornwall
Height: 6ft 1in **Weight:** 12st 7lbs
Nickname: Berth, Penbers, After
County debut: 1989
County cap: 1994
1st-Class 50s: 10
1st-Class 100s: 1
1st-Class 5 w. in innings: 2
1st-Class catches: 39
One-Day 5 w. in innings: 1
Place in batting averages: 106th av. 32.80
(1993 240th av. 13.66)
Place in bowling averages: 110th av. 37.13
(1993 60th av. 29.00)
Strike rate: 64.89 (career 65.03)
Parents: Gerald and Wendy
Marital status: Single

Family links with cricket: Father played in local leagues in Cornwall and is now a qualified umpire instructor
Education: Troon County Primary; Camborne Comprehensive
Qualifications: 3 O-levels, 3 CSEs, coaching certificate
Off-season: Working locally
Overseas tours: Druids to Zimbabwe 1988; Northants to Durban 1992, to Cape Town 1993
Cricketers particularly admired: Ian Botham, David Gower, Dennis Lillee, Viv Richards, Eldine Baptiste
Other sports followed: Football, snooker, rugby, golf
Relaxations: Listening to music, watching videos and comedy programmes
Extras: Had football trials for Plymouth Argyle but came to Northampton for cricket trials instead. Took wicket with first ball in first-class cricket – Mark Taylor caught behind, June 1989. Played for England YC v New Zealand YC 1989
Opinions on cricket: 'Back to short run-ups on Sundays. Lunch and tea intervals should be longer. Over-rate fines are too strict, and I feel that 100 overs a day would be ample.'
Best batting: 101* Northamptonshire v Cambridge University, Fenner's 1990
Best bowling: 5-37 Northamptonshire v Glamorgan, Swansea 1993

---

62. Which county recorded a Sunday League record total of 375 for 4 in September 1994 and against whom?

1994 Season

	M	Inns	NO	Runs	HS	Avge	100s	50s	Ct	St	O	M	Runs	Wkts	Avge	Best	5wI	10wM
Test																		
All First	17	25	5	658	88 *	32.90	-	5	9	-	400.1	83	1374	37	37.13	5-54	1	-
1-day Int																		
NatWest	3	1	0	18	18	18.00	-	-	1	-	24	3	100	1	100.00	1-28	-	
B & H	1	1	0	24	24	24.00	-	-	-	-	11	1	40	1	40.00	1-40	-	
Sunday	16	13	2	181	69 *	16.45	-	1	2	-	92	4	532	16	33.25	3-48	-	

Career Performances

	M	Inns	NO	Runs	HS	Avge	100s	50s	Ct	St	Balls	Runs	Wkts	Avge	Best	5wI	10wM
Test																	
All First	65	95	14	1727	101 *	21.32	1	10	39	-	6829	3805	105	36.23	5-37	2	-
1-day Int																	
NatWest	10	6	1	113	41 *	22.60	-	-	3	-	457	294	6	49.00	2-29	-	
B & H	7	5	1	46	24	11.50	-	-	1	-	342	243	4	60.75	2-22	-	
Sunday	52	38	6	495	69 *	15.46	-	1	12	-	1668	1524	44	34.63	5-36	1	

PENN, C.   Kent

Name: Christopher Penn
Role: Left-hand bat, right-arm fast-medium bowler
Born: 19 June 1963, Dover
Height: 6ft 1in **Weight:** 14-15st
Nickname: Penny, Gazza
County debut: 1982
County cap: 1987
50 wickets in a season: 2
1st-Class 50s: 6
1st-Class 100s: 1
1st-Class 5 w. in innings: 12
1st-Class catches: 56
Place in bowling averages: (1993 29th av. 24.66)
Strike rate: (career 62.90)
Parents: Reg and Brenda
Wife and date of marriage:
Caroline Ann, 22 March 1986
Children: Matthew Thomas,
14 September 1987; David Thomas, 30 March 1990; Robert Thomas, 6 March 1993
Family links with cricket: Father played club cricket for Dover for 26 years; mother made the teas

Education: River Primary School; Dover Grammar School
Qualifications: 9 O-levels, 3 A-levels, coaching awards
Career outside cricket: Financial consultant, sports development, cricket coaching, consultant for the Infocheck Group
Off-season: Working for Infocheck on new products and coaching in Kent
Overseas tours: NCA South of England U19 to Denmark 1981; Whitbread Scholarship to Australia 1982-83; Kent to Zimbabwe 1992-93
Overseas teams played for: Koh-i-Noor Crescents, Johannesburg 1981-82, 1983-84 (part); West Perth, Australia 1982-83; Johannesburg Municipals 1983-84 (part); Witwatersrand University, Johannesburg 1984-85; Green Point, Cape Town 1990-91
Cricketers particularly admired: Dennis Lillee, Robin Smith, 'plus those I learnt from – my father, Geoff Arnold, Colin Page, Graham Johnson, Barney Lock, Graham Mart, Darryl Foster, Bob Lee and many, many more'
Other sports followed: Football (Dover FC) and all sports
Injuries: Shoulder operation, missed three weeks
Relaxations: Family, music (rock), art and art history mainly Impressionism, eating out, wine and keeping fit
Extras: Played for England YC and English Schools. Took hat-trick in first 2nd XI match v Middlesex when 16 years old. Bowled two consecutive overs in 2nd XI game against Sussex at Hastings – last over one evening, first over next morning. Coached for Transvaal Cricket Council in the Johannesburg townships during the early 1980s. Kent Player of the Year 1988
Opinions on cricket: 'Perhaps there are more injuries now, not because we train too much, but we don't train specifically for the job we do. We are athletes, let's face it, and the demands of the modern game need more than just practice to keep us in tune. Most of the training we do perhaps shouldn't be done pre-season, but before that!'
Best batting: 115 Kent v Lancashire, Old Trafford 1984
Best bowling: 7-70 Kent v Middlesex, Lord's 1988

1994 Season

	M	Inns	NO	Runs	HS	Avge	100s	50s	Ct	St	O	M	Runs	Wkts	Avge	Best	5wI	10wM
Test																		
All First	1	1	0	0	0	0.00	-	-	-	-	13	4	51	1	51.00	1-51	-	-
1-day Int																		
NatWest																		
B & H																		
Sunday																		

> 63. Which county deprived Warwickshire of the Grand Slam of all four domestic competitons in 1994?

	M	Inns	NO	Runs	HS	Avge	100s	50s	Ct	St	Balls	Runs	Wkts	Avge	Best	5wI	10wM
Test																	
All First	128	146	36	2048	115	18.61	1	6	56	-	18611	9840	296	33.24	7-70	12	-
1-day Int																	
NatWest	8	4	1	28	20 *	9.33	-	-	1	-	480	249	10	24.90	3-30	-	-
B & H	24	16	7	97	24 *	10.77	-	-	4	-	1278	834	25	33.36	4-34	-	
Sunday	65	33	9	231	40	9.62	-	-	16	-	2605	2109	67	31.47	4-15	-	

PENNETT, D. B.   Nottinghamshire

Name: David Barrington Pennett
Role: Right-hand bat, right-arm fast-medium bowler
Born: 26 October 1969, Leeds
Height: 6ft **Weight:** 12st 7lbs
Nickname: Yorkie, Fiery
County debut: 1992
1st-Class 5 w. in innings: 1
1st-Class catches: 3
Place in bowling averages: (1993 75th av. 30.58)
Strike rate: (career 65.76)
Parents: Barrie and Valerie
Marital status: Engaged to Helen Flesher
Education: Benton Park Grammar School
Qualifications: 5 O-levels, ASA teacher's certificate (swimming), coaching certificate, senior coaching certificate
Career outside cricket: 'Modelling, coaching at Trent Bridge'
Off-season: Playing in New Zealand or modelling and coaching at home
Overseas tours: Nottinghamshire to Cape Town, South Africa 1992-93
Overseas teams played for: Hamilton Star University, New Zealand 1993-94
Cricketers particularly admired: Malcolm Marshall, Ian Botham, Viv Richards
Other sports followed: Football (Manchester Utd), rugby union (Otley)
Injuries: Stress fracture, missed twelve weeks
Relaxations: Night clubs, playing football, fashion
Extras: At Yorkshire Cricket Academy in 1990 for two years. Took hat-trick in a Bain Clarkson game for Yorkshire v Nottinghamshire, and one for Nottinghamshire v Herefordshire
Opinions on cricket: 'Four-day games should be played in a more positive fashion, with captains being prepared to lose to win. Sunday League clothing should have stayed adventurous, rather than conforming to traditionalists' ideas. The old styles allowed clubs

to market themselves better, bringing in wanted revenue and a fun element to the game.'
Best batting: 29 Nottinghamshire v Derbyshire, Trent Bridge 1992
Best bowling: 5-36 Nottinghamshire v Durham, Chester-le-Street 1993

1994 Season

	M	Inns	NO	Runs	HS	Avge	100s	50s	Ct	St	O	M	Runs	Wkts	Avge	Best	5wl	10wM
Test																		
All First	1	0	0	0	0	-	-	-	-	-	3	1	9	0	-	-	-	-
1-day Int																		
NatWest																		
B & H																		
Sunday	8	0	0	0	0	-	-	-	2	-	47	1	229	7	32.71	2-26	-	

Career Performances

	M	Inns	NO	Runs	HS	Avge	100s	50s	Ct	St	Balls	Runs	Wkts	Avge	Best	5wl	10wM
Test																	
All First	20	15	3	80	29	6.66	-	-	3	-	2828	1510	43	35.11	5-36	1	-
1-day Int																	
NatWest																	
B & H																	
Sunday	21	5	4	18	12*	18.00	-	-	4	-	846	677	17	39.82	3-32	-	

PENNEY, T. L. Warwickshire

Name: Trevor Lionel Penney
Role: Right-hand bat, right-arm leg-break
bowler
Born: 12 June 1968, Salisbury, Rhodesia
Height: 6ft **Weight:** 11st
Nickname: TP, Lemon Kop
County debut: 1992
County cap: 1994
1st-Class 50s: 10
1st-Class 100s: 6
1st-Class catches: 31
Place in batting averages: 70th av. 38.00
(1993 84th av. 34.26)
Parents: George and Bets
Wife and date of marriage:
Deborah Anne, 19 December 1992
Family links with cricket: Brother Stephen
played for Zimbabwe U25

Education: Blakiston Primary; Prince Edward Boys High School, Zimbabwe
Qualifications: 3 O-levels
Career outside cricket: Tobacco buyer
Off-season: Playing hockey and coaching cricket
Overseas tours: Zimbabwe to Sri Lanka 1987; ICC Associates to Australia (Youth World Cup)
Overseas teams played for: Old Hararians, Zimbabwe 1983-89 and 1993-94; Scarborough, Australia 1989-90; Boland, South Africa 1991-92; Avendale, South Africa 1992-93
Cricketers particularly admired: Colin Bland, Ian Botham, Graeme Hick, Brian Lara
Other sports followed: Football, golf, hockey, tennis, squash
Relaxations: Playing golf and drinking Castle on Lake Kariba. White-water rafting at Victoria Falls
Extras: Captained the ICC Associates team at the Youth World Cup in 1987-88. Played for Zimbabwe against Sri Lanka in 1987. Played hockey for Zimbabwe from 1984-87 and also made the African team who played Asia in 1987. Qualified to play for England in 1992
Opinions on cricket: 'The four-day cricket is fine but it should be 100 overs per day, especially with the 40-over game in between.'
Best batting: 151 Warwickshire v Middlesex, Lord's 1992

1994 Season

	M	Inns	NO	Runs	HS	Avge	100s	50s	Ct	St	O	M	Runs	Wkts	Avge	Best	5wI	10wM
Test																		
All First	16	24	3	798	111	38.00	1	1	14	-								
1-day Int																		
NatWest	5	5	2	116	65 *	38.66	-	1	2	-	1.4	0	12	1	12.00	1-8	-	
B & H	3	2	1	51	39	51.00	-	-	3	-								
Sunday	15	13	9	229	55	57.25	-	1	4	-								

Career Performances

	M	Inns	NO	Runs	HS	Avge	100s	50s	Ct	St	Balls	Runs	Wkts	Avge	Best	5wI	10wM
Test																	
All First	57	89	20	2862	151	41.47	6	10	31	-	103	107	1	107.00	1-40	-	-
1-day Int																	
NatWest	12	12	3	172	65 *	19.11	-	1	8	-	10	12	1	12.00	1-8	-	
B & H	6	5	1	95	39	23.75	-	-	5	1							
Sunday	42	35	17	726	83 *	40.33	-	3	16	-	6	2	0	-	-	-	-

PHELPS, B. S.   Glamorgan

Name: Byron Stuart Phelps
Role: Right-hand bat, slow left-arm bowler
Born: 16 December 1975, Neath
Height: 5ft 5in **Weight:** 10st 6lbs
Nickname: Phelpsy, Phelps, Racquel
County debut: 1993
Parents: Byron and Barbara
Marital status: Single
Family links with cricket: Elder brother,
Andrew, played for Welsh Schools
Education: Glanafan Comprehensive;
Neath Tertiary College
Qualifications: GCSE Art
Off-season: Training ('Honestly')
Overseas tours: Welsh U18 to
Australia 1992-93
Overseas teams played for: Balmaine,
Sydney 1994-95
Cricketers particularly admired:
Viv Richards, Allan Border
Other sports followed: Any sport except show jumping
Relaxations: 'Listening to music, playing the guitar. Convincing Adrian Shaw that not all his bats are made of balsa wood.'
Extras: Took ten wickets for Wales U16 at the Jersey Festival 1992. Played for Wales 1993
Opinions on cricket: '2nd XI cricket should be four days and played on first-class pitches.'
Best batting: 11 Glamorgan v Somerset, Swansea 1994
Best bowling: 2-70 Glamorgan v Somerset, Swansea 1994

1994 Season

	M	Inns	NO	Runs	HS	Avge	100s	50s	Ct	St	O	M	Runs	Wkts	Avge	Best	5wI	10wM
Test																		
All First	2	4	1	18	11	6.00	-	-	-	-	86	22	241	4	60.25	2-70	-	-
1-day Int																		
NatWest																		
B & H																		
Sunday																		

> 64. How many runs did Devon Malcolm concede when he took nine
> South African wickets in August 1994?

Career Performances

	M	Inns	NO	Runs	HS	Avge	100s	50s	Ct	St	Balls	Runs	Wkts	Avge	Best	5wI	10wM
Test																	
All First	3	4	1	18	11	6.00	-	-	-	-	672	363	5	72.60	2-70	-	-
1-day Int																	
NatWest																	
B & H																	
Sunday																	

PHILLIPS, N. C. Sussex

Name: Nicholas Charles Phillips
Role: Right-hand bat, off-spin bowler
Born: 10 May 1974, Pembury, Kent
Height: 5ft 11in **Weight:** 11st
County debut: 1994
1st-Class catches: 1
Parents: Robert and Joan
Marital status: Single
Family links with cricket: Father represented Kent Association and the Kent League while playing for Tunbridge Wells, and has scored over 100 club centuries
Education:
Hilden Grange School, Tonbridge;
St Thomas's School, Winchelsea;
William Parker School, Hastings
Qualifications: 8 GCSEs, NCA coaching certificate
Off-season: Coaching and playing hockey
Overseas tours: Sussex U18 to India 1990-91
Cricketers particularly admired: Eddie Hemmings, Derek Randall
Other sports followed: Hockey, football (West Ham)
Relaxations: Playing hockey for South Saxons, music (The Stone Roses), spending time with friends
Extras: Represented England U19 in home series against West Indies U19 1993. Has played hockey for Sussex U14 and U16
Best batting: 37* Sussex v South Africans, Hove 1994

---

65. Who is the world's leading run-maker in one-day Internationals?

1994 Season

	M	Inns	NO	Runs	HS	Avge	100s	50s	Ct	St	O	M	Runs	Wkts	Avge	Best	5wI	10wM
Test																		
All First	1	2	1	37	37 *	37.00	-	-	1	-	36	5	127	2	63.50	2-127	-	-
1-day Int																		
NatWest																			
B & H																			
Sunday	6	3	2	22	11 *	22.00	-	-	-	-	33	2	154	4	38.50	2-19	-	

Career Performances

	M	Inns	NO	Runs	HS	Avge	100s	50s	Ct	St	Balls	Runs	Wkts	Avge	Best	5wI	10wM
Test																	
All First	2	2	1	37	37 *	37.00	-	-	1	-	474	230	5	46.00	3-39	-	-
1-day Int																	
NatWest																	
B & H																	
Sunday	6	3	2	22	11 *	22.00	-	-	-	-	198	154	4	38.50	2-19	-

PICK, R. A.   Nottinghamshire

Name: Robert Andrew Pick
Role: Left-hand bat, right-arm fast-medium bowler, gully fielder
Born: 19 November 1963, Nottingham
Height: 5ft 10in **Weight:** 13st
Nickname: Dad
County debut: 1983
County cap: 1987
50 wickets in a season: 3
1st-Class 50s: 4
1st-Class 5 w. in innings: 14
1st-Class 10 w. in match: 3
1st-Class catches: 36
One-Day 5 w. in innings: 1
Place in batting averages: 240th av. 15.13 (1993 191st av. 13.62)
Place in bowling averages: 31st av. 26.16 (1993 125th av. 42.80)
Strike rate: 56.37 (career 59.45)
Parents: Bob and Lillian
Wife and date of marriage: Jennie Ruth, 8 April 1989
Family links with cricket: Father, uncles and cousins all play local cricket; David Millns

(Leicestershire) is brother-in-law
Education: Alderman Derbyshire Comprehensive; High Pavement College
Qualifications: 7 O-levels, 1 A-level, coaching qualification
Overseas tours: England A to Pakistan 1990-91, to Bermuda and West Indies 1991-92
Overseas teams played for: Wellington, New Zealand 1989-90
Cricketers particularly admired: Bob White, Mike Hendrick, Mike Harris, Franklyn Stephenson
Other sports followed: Ice hockey, soccer and American football
Relaxations: 'As much fishing as possible and listening to a wide range of music; eating and drinking; going to the pictures'
Extras: Played for England YC v Australia YC 1983. Played football for Nottingham Schoolboys
Opinions on cricket: 'Coloured clothing should be introduced for all one-day cricket.'
Best batting: 65* Nottinghamshire v Northamptonshire, Trent Bridge 1994
Best bowling: 7-128 Nottinghamshire v Leicestershire, Leicester 1990

1994 Season

	M	Inns	NO	Runs	HS	Avge	100s	50s	Ct	St	O	M	Runs	Wkts	Avge	Best	5wl	10wM
Test																		
All First	16	22	7	227	65 *	15.13	-	1	4	-	507.2	122	1413	54	26.16	6-62	2	-
1-day Int																		
NatWest	2	1	0	10	10	10.00	-	-	-	-	18	1	70	4	17.50	2-25	-	
B & H	3	2	2	26	16 *	-	-	-	1	-	31	2	134	0	-	-	-	-
Sunday	7	3	1	27	17 *	13.50	-	-	3	-	48.3	2	292	8	36.50	3-24	-	

Career Performances

	M	Inns	NO	Runs	HS	Avge	100s	50s	Ct	St	Balls	Runs	Wkts	Avge	Best	5wl	10wM
Test																	
All First	167	169	50	1766	65	14.84		4	10		25625	14004	431	32.49	7-128	14	3
1-day Int																	
NatWest	25	15	11	120	34 *	30.00	-	-	4	-	1627	1025	40	25.62	5-22	1	
B & H	34	14	9	76	25 *	15.20	-	-	4	-	2067	1422	42	33.85	4-42	-	
Sunday	97	34	15	232	24	12.21	-	-	21	-	4239	3591	107	33.56	4-32	-	

PIERSON, A. R. K.   Leicestershire

Name: Adrian Roger Kirshaw Pierson
Role: Right-hand bat,
right-arm off-spin bowler
Born: 21 July 1963, Enfield, Middlesex
Height: 6ft 4in **Weight:** 12st
Nickname: Stick, Skirlogue, Bunny
County debut: 1985 (Warwickshire),
1993 (Leicestershire)
1st-Class 50s: 1
1st-Class 5 w. in innings: 8
1st-Class catches: 35
Place in batting averages: 184th av. 22.26
(1993 238th av. 14.00)
Place in bowling averages: 91st av. 34.24
(19993 81st av. 31.15)
Strike rate: 81.18 (career 78.75)
Parents: Patrick and Patricia
Wife and date of marriage:
Helen Majella, 29 September 1990
Education: Lochinver House Primary School; Kent College, Canterbury; Hatfield
Polytechnic
Qualifications: 8 O-levels, 2 A-levels, senior coaching award
Career outside cricket: Production editor for a graphic design company
Off-season: 'Working in London for Tobasgo Design Consultants – a sports magazine
publishing company that produces the Test match programmes'
Cricketers particularly admired: John Emburey, Phil Edmonds, Tony Greig, Clive Rice
Other sports followed: All sports except horse racing, but especially golf
Injuries: 'Too many to list'
Relaxations: Golf, driving and squash
Extras: On Lord's groundstaff 1984-85 and on Warwickshire staff from 1985-91. First
Championship wicket was Viv Richards
Opinions on cricket: 'Sunday League should be two 20-over games per Sunday afternoon
– the shorter the game, the more appeal it has for the Sunday public. Four-day Championship
is the best format if pitch standards can be raised to enable the game to reach the fourth day.
Cricketers' benefits may improve financially if they were to be taxed, for it would enable
beneficiaries to run the benefit as a business, i.e. advertise events and sell. Counties rely too
heavily on income generated by the TCCB. Perhaps more use could be made of grounds
while not being used for cricket?'
Best batting: 58 Leicestershire v Lancashire, Leicester 1993
Best bowling: 8-42 Leicestershire v Warwickshire, Edgbaston 1994

1994 Season

	M	Inns	NO	Runs	HS	Avge	100s	50s	Ct	St	O	M	Runs	Wkts	Avge	Best	5wI	10wM
Test																		
All First	15	20	5	334	43 *	22.26	-	-	15	-	500.4	131	1267	37	34.24	8-42	1	-
1-day Int																		
NatWest	1	1	0	0	0	0.00	-	-	-	-	1	0	6	0	-		-	-
B & H	2	1	1	3	3 *	-	-	-	2	-	22	4	70	3	23.33	2-54	-	
Sunday	11	8	4	55	29 *	13.75	-	-	5	-	72.1	2	302	11	27.45	4-29	-	

Career Performances

	M	Inns	NO	Runs	HS	Avge	100s	50s	Ct	St	Balls	Runs	Wkts	Avge	Best	5wI	10wM
Test																	
All First	90	107	40	999	58	14.91	-	1	35	-	13073	6391	166	38.50	8-42	8	-
1-day Int																	
NatWest	8	4	1	3	1 *	1.00	-	-	2	-	468	227	5	45.40	3-20	-	
B & H	12	9	5	26	11	6.50	-	-	4	-	678	377	12	31.41	3-34	-	
Sunday	52	28	12	146	29 *	9.12	-	-	21	-	2139	1660	45	36.88	4-29	-	

PIGOTT, A. C. S.   Surrey

Name: Anthony Charles Shackleton Pigott
Role: Right-hand bat, right-arm
fast-medium bowler, slip fielder
Born: 4 June 1958, London
Height: 6ft 1in **Weight:** 12st 9lbs
Nickname: Lester
County debut: 1978 (Sussex), 1994 (Surrey)
County cap: 1982 (Sussex)
Benefit: 1991 (£60,025)
Test debut: 1983-84
Tests: 1
50 wickets in a season: 5
1st-Class 50s: 20
1st-Class 100s: 1
1st-Class 5 w. in innings: 24
1st-Class 10 w. in match: 1
1st-Class catches: 120
One-Day 5 w. in innings: 3
Place in batting averages: 244th av. 14.54
(1993 239th av. 13.90)
Place in bowling averages: 26th av. 25.41 (1993 132nd av. 47.66)
Strike rate: 55.55 (career 56.60)

Parents: Tom and Juliet
Marital status: Divorced
Children: Elliot Sebastian, 15 March 1983
Family links with cricket: Father captained village side, mother played at school 'and claims I got my cricket ability from her'
Education: Holmwood House, Kent; Harrow School
Qualifications: 5 O-levels, 2 A-levels; junior coaching certificate
Career outside cricket: Has own squash club in Brighton
Overseas tours: England to New Zealand 1983-84; MCC to Leeward Islands 1991-92, to West Africa 1993-94; *Cricket World* to Barbados 1993-94
Overseas teams played for: Wellington, New Zealand 1982-83 and 1983-84
Cricketers particularly admired: Ian Botham, Geoff Arnold, John Snow, Mike Gatting
Other sports followed: Squash, soccer, golf, rugby
Extras: Public schools rackets champion 1975. First three wickets in first-class cricket were a hat-trick. Had operation on back, April 1981, missing most of season, and was told by a specialist he would never play cricket again. Postponed wedding to make Test debut when called into England party on tour of New Zealand 1983-84. Originally going to Somerset for 1984 season, but remained with Sussex. Was diagnosed as a diabetic after he lost 11lbs in two weeks in 1987, but recovered to take 74 wickets in 1988 season. Moved to Surrey at end of 1993 season after 18 years with Sussex
Best batting: 104* Sussex v Warwickshire, Edgbaston 1986
Best bowling: 7-74 Sussex v Northamptonshire, Eastbourne 1982

1994 Season

	M	Inns	NO	Runs	HS	Avge	100s	50s	Ct	St	O	M	Runs	Wkts	Avge	Best	5wI	10wM
Test																		
All First	8	11	0	160	40	14.54	-	-	1	-	268.3	73	737	29	25.41	6-46	1	-
1-day Int																		
NatWest	4	2	1	4	4 *	4.00	-	-	-	-	46	4	189	7	27.00	3-32	-	
B & H	1	1	1	13	13 *	-	-	-	-	-	11	0	43	3	14.33	3-43	-	
Sunday	15	8	4	59	15	14.75	-	-	4	-	107.2	8	478	17	28.11	3-48	-	

Career Performances

	M	Inns	NO	Runs	HS	Avge	100s	50s	Ct	St	Balls	Runs	Wkts	Avge	Best	5wI	10wM
Test	1	2	1	12	8 *	12.00	-	-	-	-	102	75	2	37.50	2-75	-	
All First	254	306	65	4765	104 *	19.77	1	20	120	-	36790	20164	650	31.02	7-74	24	1
1-day Int																	
NatWest	30	16	2	170	53	12.14	-	1	6	-	1679	1036	42	24.66	3-4	-	
B & H	40	28	9	276	49 *	14.52	-	-	15	-	2211	1541	52	29.63	3-29	-	
Sunday	175	103	39	1110	51 *	17.34	-	1	55	-	7118	5795	250	23.18	5-24	3	

PIKE, V. J.   Gloucestershire

Name: Vyvian John Pike
Role: Right-hand bat, leg-spin bowler
Born: 13 August 1969, Taunton
Height: 6ft 1in **Weight:** 14st
Nickname: Magnus
County debut: 1994
1st-Class 5 w. in innings: 1
1st-Class catches: 2
Place in bowling averages: 51st av. 28.90
Strike rate: 59.70 (career 59.70)
Parents: Stephen and Diane
Marital status: Engaged
Education: Taunton School
Qualifications: 8 O-levels, 2 A-levels, degree
in Civil Engineering
Career outside cricket: Bridge engineer
Off-season: Working as above
Cricketers particularly admired: Courtney
Walsh
Other sports followed: Rugby union and all other sports
Relaxations: Eating out and photography
Best batting: 27 Gloucestershire v Derbyshire, Chesterfield 1994
Best bowling: 6-41 Gloucestershire v Cambridge University, Bristol 1994

1994 Season

	M	Inns	NO	Runs	HO	Avge	100s	50s	Ct	St	O	M	Runs	Wkts	Avge	Best	5wI	10wM
Test																		
All First	9	12	4	114	27	14.25	-	-	2	-	199	51	578	20	28.90	6-41	1	-
1-day Int																		
NatWest																		
B & H																		
Sunday																		

Career Performances

	M	Inns	NO	Runs	HS	Avge	100s	50s	Ct	St	Balls	Runs	Wkts	Avge	Best	5wI	10wM
Test																	
All First	9	12	4	114	27	14.25	-	-	2	-	1194	578	20	28.90	6-41	1	-
1-day Int																	
NatWest																	
B & H																	
Sunday																	

PIPER, K. J.   Warwickshire

Name: Keith John Piper
Role: Right-hand bat, wicket-keeper
Born: 18 December 1969, Leicester
Height: 5ft 7in **Weight:** 10st 8lbs
Nickname: Tubbsy, Garden Boy
County debut: 1989
County cap: 1992
1st-Class 50s: 6
1st-Class 100s: 2
1st-Class catches: 236
1st-Class stumpings: 15
Place in batting averages: 180th av. 22.70
(1993 236th av. 14.07)
Parents: John and Charlotte
Marital status: Single
Family links with cricket: Father plays
club cricket in Leicester
Education: Seven Sisters Junior;
Somerset Senior
Qualifications: Cricket senior coaching award, basketball coaching award, volleyball coaching award
Overseas tours: Haringey Cricket College to Barbados 1986, to Trinidad 1987, to Jamaica 1988; Warwickshire to La Manga 1989, to St Lucia 1990; England A to India 1994-95
Overseas teams played for: Desmond Haynes's XI, Barbados v Haringey Cricket College
Cricketers particularly admired: Jack Russell, Alec Stewart, Dermot Reeve, Colin Metson
Other sports followed: Snooker, football, tennis
Relaxations: Music, eating
Extras: London Young Cricketer of the Year 1989 and in the last five 1992. Played for England YC 1989. Was batting partner (116*) to Brian Lara when he reached his 501*
Best batting: 116* Warwickshire v Durham, Edgbaston 1994
Best bowling: 1-57 Warwickshire v Nottinghamshire, Edgbaston 1992

1994 Season

	M	Inns	NO	Runs	HS	Avge	100s	50s	Ct	St	O	M	Runs	Wkts	Avge	Best	5wI	10wM
Test																		
All First	17	24	4	454	116 *	22.70	1	1	61	5								
1-day Int																		
NatWest	5	3	3	29	16 *	-	-	-	7	2								
B & H	1	0	0	0	0	-	-	-	2	-								
Sunday	10	7	4	31	13 *	10.33	-	-	11	4								

430

	M	Inns	NO	Runs	HS	Avge	100s	50s	Ct	St	Balls	Runs	Wkts	Avge	Best	5wI	10wM
Test																	
All First	93	126	20	2114	116 *	19.94	2	6	236	15	28	57	1	57.00	1-57	-	-
1-day Int																	
NatWest	16	9	4	65	16 *	13.00	-	-	24	2							
B & H	7	6	3	36	11 *	12.00	-	-	8	-							
Sunday	42	23	11	144	30	12.00	-	-	30	11							

POLLARD, P. R. Nottinghamshire

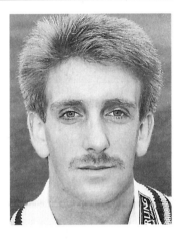

Name: Paul Raymond Pollard
Role: Left-hand opening bat, right-arm medium bowler
Born: 24 September 1968, Carlton, Nottinghamshire
Height: 5ft 11in **Weight:** 12st
Nickname: Polly, Sugar Ray
County debut: 1987
County cap: 1992
1000 runs in a season: 3
1st-Class 50s: 29
1st-Class 100s: 11
1st-Class catches: 113
One-Day 100s: 3
Place in batting averages: 127th av. 30.16 (1993 20th av. 50.44)
Parents: Eric (deceased) and Mary
Wife's name and date of marriage: Kate, 14 March 1992
Education: Gedling Comprehensive
Off-season: Coaching and training at Trent Bridge
Overseas teams played for: Southern Districts, Brisbane 1988; North Perth 1990
Cricketers particularly admired: David Gower, Derek Randall, Ian Botham, Graham Gooch
Other sports followed: Football, golf, ice hockey
Relaxations: Watching videos, playing golf and music
Extras: Made debut for Nottinghamshire 2nd XI in 1985. Worked in Nottinghamshire CCC office on a Youth Training Scheme. Shared stands of 222 and 282 with Tim Robinson in the same game v Kent 1989. Youngest player to reach 1000 runs for Nottinghamshire
Opinions on cricket: 'The one bouncer rule should be abolished.'
Best batting: 180 Nottinghamshire v Derbyshire, Trent Bridge 1993
Best bowling: 2-79 Nottinghamshire v Gloucestershire, Bristol 1993

1994 Season

	M	Inns	NO	Runs	HS	Avge	100s	50s	Ct	St	O	M	Runs	Wkts	Avge	Best	5wI	10wM
Test																		
All First	18	31	1	905	134	30.16	2	4	11	-	2	0	20	1	20.00	1-20	-	-
1-day Int																		
NatWest	2	2	0	23	13	11.50	-	-	-	-								
B & H	3	3	0	125	104	41.66	1	-	1	-								
Sunday	14	12	0	274	53	22.83	-	1	5	-								

Career Performances

	M	Inns	NO	Runs	HS	Avge	100s	50s	Ct	St	Balls	Runs	Wkts	Avge	Best	5wI	10wM
Test																	
All First	118	206	11	6424	180	32.94	11	29	113	-	274	268	4	67.00	2-79	-	-
1-day Int																	
NatWest	8	8	0	123	28	15.37	-	-	2	-	18	9	0	-		-	-
B & H	16	16	1	438	104	29.20	1	3	7	-							
Sunday	65	58	6	1576	123 *	30.30	2	7	22	-							

POOLEY, J. C.   Middlesex

Name: Jason Calvin Pooley
Role: Left-hand bat, right-arm slow bowler
Born: 8 August 1969, Hammersmith
Height: 6ft **Weight:** 13st 4lbs
County debut: 1989
1st-Class 50s: 4
1st-Class catches: 12
One-Day 100s: 1
Parents: Dave and Kath
Marital status: Engaged to Justine
Family links with cricket: Father and older
brother play club cricket. Younger brother
Gregg has played for Middlesex YC, Middlesex
2nd XI and Derbyshire 2nd XI
Education: Acton High School
Career outside cricket: Working for
father's building firm
Off-season: As above
Overseas teams played for:
St George's, Sydney 1988-89; Western Suburbs, Sydney 1991-92
Cricketers particularly admired: David Gower, Desmond Haynes, Mark Ramprakash
Other sports followed: Horse racing and football (Portsmouth)

Relaxations: Watching all sports, eating out with my fiancée
Extras: Voted Rapid Cricketline 2nd XI Player of the Year in 1989, his first year on the Middlesex staff
Opinions on cricket: 'Teams should have to play a certain number of uncapped players in the Sunday League, to allow younger players to come through.'
Best batting: 88 Middlesex v Derbyshire, Lord's 1991

1994 Season

	M	Inns	NO	Runs	HS	Avge	100s	50s	Ct	St	O	M	Runs	Wkts	Avge	Best	5wI	10wM
Test																		
All First	3	4	0	77	40	19.25	-	-	2	-								
1-day Int																		
NatWest	1	1	0	33	33	33.00	-	-	-	-								
B & H																		
Sunday	9	8	1	228	77	32.57	-	3	1	-								

Career Performances

	M	Inns	NO	Runs	HS	Avge	100s	50s	Ct	St	Balls	Runs	Wkts	Avge	Best	5wI	10wM
Test																	
All First	22	37	2	794	88	22.68	-	4	12	-	12	11	0	-	-	-	-
1-day Int																	
NatWest	1	1	0	33	33	33.00	-	-	-	-							
B & H	3	3	0	11	8	3.66	-	-	-	-							
Sunday	15	14	1	418	109	32.15	1	3	1	-							

66. Who broke the record for the highest score on a first-class debut with 260* in February 1994?

Name: Michael James Powell
Role: Right-hand bat,
right arm medium bowler
Born: 5 April 1975, Bolton
Height: 5ft 11in **Weight:** 11st 2lbs
Nickname: Powelly, Arthur
County debut: No first-team appearance
Parents: Terry and Pat
Marital status: Single
Education: Rivington and Blackrod
High School, Horwich;
Lawrence Sheriff School, Rugby
Qualifications: 6 GCSEs, 2 A-levels
Career outside cricket: Part-time PE teacher
Off-season: Playing in South Africa
Overseas tours: England U18 (captain) to
South Africa 1992-93, to Denmark (captain)
1993; England U19 to Sri Lanka 1993-94
Overseas teams played for: Avendale CC,
Cape Town, 1994-95

Cricketers particularly admired: Ian Botham, Tim Munton, Roger Twose
Other sports followed: Rugby, football
Relaxations: Playing golf, snooker and spending time with family, friends, particularly
girlfriend, Sarah
Opinions on cricket: 'Second-class cricket should be played in conditions identical to the
first-class game, including pitches and length of games.'

---

67. Which former England fast bowler retired in March 1994, having
never fully recovered from a knee injury sustained on an England tour?

PRABHAKAR, M.   Durham

Name: Manoj Prabhakar
Role: Right-hand bat,
right-arm fast-medium bowler
Born: 15 April 1963
County debut: No first-team appearance
Test debut: 1984-85
Tests: 27
One-Day Internationals: 102
1st-Class 50s: 25
1st-Class 100s: 15
1st-Class 5 w. in innings: 9
1st-Class 10 w. in match: 1
1st-Class catches: 49
One-Day 100s: 1
One-Day 5 w. in innings: 1
Strike rate: (career 61.59)
Off-season: Playing for India
Overseas tours: India to England 1986,
to Pakistan 1989-90, New Zealand 1989-90,

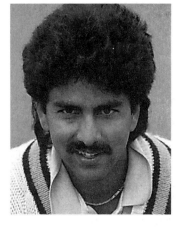

to England 1990, to Australia and New Zealand (World Cup) 1991-92, to Zimbabwe and
South Africa 1992-93, to Sri Lanka and New Zealand 1993-94
Overseas teams played for: Delhi and Districts, India
Extras: Scored maiden Test century against West Indies at Chandigarh in December 1994.
Was due to play for Warwickshire in 1994 but was injured and replaced by Brian Lara
Best batting: 229* Delhi v Himachal Pradesh, Delhi 1989-90
Best bowling: 6-36 Delhi v Orissa, Delhi 1989-90

1994 Season (did not make any first-class or one-day appearance)

Career Performances

	M	Inns	NO	Runs	HS	Avge	100s	50s	Ct	St	Balls	Runs	Wkts	Avge	Best	5wI	10wM
Test	33	48	7	1338	95	32.63	-	9	18	-	7121	3384	92	36.78	6-132	3	-
All First	118	156	28	5609	229 *	43.82	15	25	49	-	18541	8764	301	29.11	6-36	9	1
1-day Int	102	72	15	1253	106	21.98	1	6	21	-	-	5062	3457	129	26.79	5-35	1
NatWest																	
B & H																	
Sunday																	

PRESTON, N. W.   Kent

Name: Nicholas William Preston
Role: Right-hand bat,
right-arm medium-fast bowler
Born: 22 January 1972, Dartford
Height: 6ft 1in **Weight:** 11st 5lbs
Nickname: North End, Jagback
County debut: No first-team appearance
Parents: Susan and Geoffrey
Marital status: Single
Family links with cricket: Grandfather
played for Leicestershire. Brother plays
for Kent youth teams
Education: Gravesend Grammar School;
Exeter University
Qualifications:
BSc (Hons) Biology/Geography
Off-season: Playing and coaching in
Cape Town, South Africa
Overseas teams played for:
Avendale, Cape Town 1993-94; Green Point, Cape Town 1994-95
Cricketers particularly admired: Richard Hadlee, Allan Donald, Carl Hooper
Other sports followed: Rugby, tennis, football, golf
Relaxations: Golf, listening to music, watching movies, spending time with close friends
Extras: Kent League record of five wickets in five balls for Sevenoaks Vine v Midland Bank, 1994
Opinions on cricket: 'All 2nd XI cricket should be played on first-class grounds. Four-day cricket is good, but pitches need to last four days, not two or three. The structure of league cricket needs to be improved, as does the quality of pitches played on.'

PRICHARD, P. J.   Essex

Name: Paul John Prichard
Role: Right-hand bat, cover/mid-wicket fielder, county captain
Born: 7 January 1965, Brentwood, Essex
Height: 5ft 10in **Weight:** 11st 7lbs
Nickname: Pablo
County debut: 1984
County cap: 1986
1000 runs in a season: 6
1st-Class 50s: 66

1st-Class 100s: 23
1st-Class 200s: 2
1st-Class catches: 146
One-Day 100s: 3
Place in batting averages: 71st av. 37.93
(1993 49th av. 39.97)
Parents: John and Margaret
Wife's name and date of marriage:
Jo-Anne, 24 November 1991
Children: Danielle Jade, 23 April 1993
Family links with cricket: Father played
club cricket in Essex
Education: Brentwood County High School
Qualifications: NCA coaching certificate
Career outside cricket: Marketing executive
with T.D. Ridley & Sons
Off-season: As above
Overseas tours: England A to Australia
1992-93
Overseas teams played for: VOB Cavaliers, Cape Town 1981-82; Sutherland, Sydney
1984-87; Waverley, Sydney 1987-92
Cricketers particularly admired: Malcolm Marshall, Allan Border, David Gower, Mark Waugh
Other sports followed: Football (West Ham)
Injuries: Broken thumb, missed three months
Relaxations: 'Golf, sleeping, watching television, odd pint of real ale'
Extras: Shared county record second wicket partnership of 403 with Graham Gooch v
Leicestershire in 1990. Britannic Assurance Cricketer of the Year 1992. Essex joint Player
of the Year 1993. Appointed Essex captain for 1995
Best batting: 245 Essex v Leicestershire, Chelmsford 1990
Best bowling: 1-20 Essex v Hampshire, Chelmsford 1991

1994 Season

	M	Inns	NO	Runs	HS	Avge	100s	50s	Ct	St	O	M	Runs	Wkts	Avge	Best	5wl	10wM
Test																		
All First	11	17	2	569	119	37.93	3	2	6	-	1	0	11	0	-	-	-	-
1-day Int																		
NatWest																		
B & H	2	2	0	29	23	14.50	-	-	1	-								
Sunday	7	7	1	154	65 *	25.66	-	1	5	-								

> 68. Who won the 1994 ICC Trophy, who did they beat in the final
> and where was the tournament held?

Career Performances

	M	Inns	NO	Runs	HS	Avge	100s	50s	Ct	St	Balls	Runs	Wkts	Avge	Best	5wI	10wM
Test																	
All First	226	363	43	11546	245	36.08	23	66	146	-	289	497	2	248.50	1-28	-	-
1-day Int																	
NatWest	21	20	2	675	94	37.50	-	5	9	-
B & H	41	39	8	929	107	29.96	1	4	10	-
Sunday	126	108	9	2506	107	25.31	2	11	39	-

RADFORD, N. V.   Worcestershire

Name: Neal Victor Radford
Role: Right-hand bat, right-arm fast-medium bowler, gully fielder
Born: 7 June 1957, Luanshya, Zambia
Height: 5ft 11in **Weight:** 12st 8lbs
Nickname: Radiz, Vic
County debut: 1980 (Lancashire), 1985 (Worcestershire)
County cap: 1985 (Worcestershire)
Benefit: 1995
Test debut: 1986
Tests: 3
One-Day Internationals: 6
100 wickets in a season: 2
50 wickets in a season: 6
1st-Class 50s: 7
1st-Class 5 w. in innings: 47
1st-Class 10 w. in match: 7
1st-Class catches: 130
One-Day 5 w. in innings: 2
Place in batting averages: 270th av. 10.06 (1993 252nd av. 11.77)
Place in bowling averages: 100th av. 36.10 (1993 77th av. 30.66)
Strike rate: 87.56 (career 50.75)
Parents: Victor Reginald and Edith Joyce
Wife: Lynne
Children: Luke Anthony, 3 June 1988; Josh Deckland, 12 February 1990
Family links with cricket: Brother Wayne is pro for Gowerton (SWCA) and plays for Glamorgan 2nd XI. Also played for Orange Free State in Currie Cup
Education: Athlone Boys High School, Johannesburg
Qualifications: Matriculation and university entrance, NCA advanced coach
Off-season: 'Running my own business, spending time with my family and recharging the

batteries for the next season'

Overseas teams played for: Transvaal 1979-89
Overseas tours: England to New Zealand and Australia 1987-88
Cricketers particularly admired: Vintcent van der Bijl
Other sports followed: All sports
Relaxations: Music, television, films, golf
Extras: Only bowler to take 100 first-class wickets in 1985 and was first to 100 wickets in 1987, taking most first-class wickets both years. One of *Wisden*'s Five Cricketers of the Year 1985. The Cricketers' Association Cricketer of the Year 1985
Opinions on cricket: 'The balance in one-day cricket has swayed considerably in favour of the batsmen with the introduction of the no-ball for height ruling. The bouncer can be a wicket-taking delivery and same rule should be applied as that of the first-class game.'
Best batting: 76* Lancashire v Derbyshire, Blackpool 1981
Best bowling: 9-70 Worcestershire v Somerset, Worcestershire 1986

1994 Season

	M	Inns	NO	Runs	HS	Avge	100s	50s	Ct	St	O	M	Runs	Wkts	Avge	Best	5wI	10wM
Test																		
All First	15	20	4	161	25	10.06	-	-	6	-	459.1	106	1408	39	36.10	5-93	1	-
1-day Int																		
NatWest	4	1	1	0	0 *	-	-	-	3	-	40	9	135	5	27.00	2-3	-	
B & H	4	1	1	23	23 *	-	-	-	1	-	30	5	123	2	61.50	1-11	-	
Sunday	15	11	6	78	23 *	15.60	-	-	4	-	101.3	5	491	24	20.45	4-36	-	

Career Performances

	M	Inns	NO	Runs	HS	Avge	100s	50s	Ct	St	Balls	Runs	Wkts	Avge	Best	5wI	10wM
Test	3	4	1	21	12 *	7.00	-	-	-	-	678	351	4	87.75	2-131	-	-
All First	286	287	71	3407	76 *	15.77	-	7	130	-	49331	25927	972	26.67	9-70	47	7
1-day Int	0	3	2	0	0 *	0.00	-		2		040	200	2	110.00	1 00		
NatWest	34	18	6	151	37	12.58	-	-	13	-	1974	1118	48	23.29	7-19	1	
B & H	47	28	15	375	40	28.84	-	-	12	-	2579	1552	68	22.82	4-25	-	
Sunday	152	93	39	1081	70	20.01	-	2	36	-	6077	4615	202	22.84	5-32	1	

RADFORD, T. A.   Middlesex

Name: Toby Alexander Radford
Role: Right-hand bat, 'occasional right-arm off-spin bowler'
Born: 3 December 1971, Caerphilly, Wales
Height: 5ft 10in **Weight:** 10st 4lbs
Nickname: Trawlerman, Radders
County debut: 1993 (one-day), 1994 (first-class)
1st-Class catches: 1
Parents: Brian and Jill
Marital status: Single
Family links with cricket: Dad is a senior coach
Education: Park House School, Newbury; St Bartholomew's School, Newbury; City University, London
Qualifications: 9 O-levels, 3 A-levels, BA (Hons) in Journalism, qualified coach
Career outside cricket: Journalism
Off-season: Coaching and writing features
Overseas tours: England YC to Australia 1989-90, to New Zealand 1990-91
Cricketers particularly admired: Dean Jones, Desmond Haynes
Other sports followed: Football, snooker, speedway
Relaxations: Music (U2), cinema
Extras: *Daily Telegraph* U15 Batsman of the Year 1987; MCC/Lord's Taverners' Player of the Year at U13, U15 and U19 age-groups
Opinions on cricket: 'More and better training facilities needed. An English equivalent of the Adelaide Academy might be a good idea to bring on talented youngsters.'
Best batting: 4 Middlesex v England A, Lord's 1994

1994 Season

	M	Inns	NO	Runs	HS	Avge	100s	50s	Ct	St	O	M	Runs	Wkts	Avge	Best	5wl	10wM
Test																		
All First	1	1	0	4	4	4.00	-	-	1	-								
1-day Int																		
NatWest																		
B & H																		
Sunday																		

Career Performances

	M	Inns	NO	Runs	HS	Avge	100s	50s	Ct	St	Balls	Runs	Wkts	Avge	Best	5wI	10wM
Test																	
All First	1	1	0	4	4	4.00	-	-	1	-							
1-day Int																	
NatWest																	
B & H																	
Sunday	1	1	0	38	38	38.00	-	-	-	-							

RAMPRAKASH, M. R.   Middlesex

Name: Mark Ravindra Ramprakash
Role: Right-hand bat, right-arm off-spin bowler
Born: 5 September 1969, Bushey, Herts
Height: 5ft 10in **Weight:** 12st 4lbs
Nickname: Ramps, Bloodaxe
County debut: 1987
County cap: 1990
Test debut: 1991
Tests: 10
One-Day Internationals: 4
1000 runs in a season: 5
1st-Class 50s: 46
1st-Class 100s: 19
1st-Class 200s: 1
1st-Class catches: 83
One-Day 100s: 5
One-Day 5 w. in innings: 1
Place in batting averages: 13th av. 52.95
(1993 59th av. 38.39)

Parents: Deonarine and Jennifer
Date of marriage: 24 September 1993
Family links with cricket: Father played club cricket in Guyana
Education: Gayton High School; Harrow Weald Sixth Form College
Qualifications: 6 O-levels, 2 A-levels
Career outside cricket: 'Any ideas welcome.'
Off-season: England A to India
Overseas tours: England YC to Sri Lanka 1986-87, to Australia (Youth World Cup) 1987-88; England A to Pakistan 1990-91; to West Indies 1991-92, to India (vice captain) 1994-95; England to New Zealand 1991-92, to West Indies 1993-94, to Australia 1994-95; Lion Cubs to Barbados 1993
Overseas teams played for: Nairobi Jafferys, Kenya 1988; North Melbourne 1989

Cricketers particularly admired: 'All the great all-rounders'
Other sports followed: Snooker, football
Relaxations: 'Being at home with the family, going to movies, eating out'
Extras: Did not begin to play cricket until he was nine years old; played for Bessborough CC at age 13, played for Middlesex 2nd XI aged 16 and made first-team debut for Middlesex aged 17. Scored 204* in NCA Guernsey Festival Tournament and in 1987 made 186* on his debut for Stanmore CC. Voted Best U15 Schoolboy of 1985 by Cricket Society, Best Young Cricketer of 1986 and Most Promising Player of the Year in 1988. Played for England YC v New Zealand YC in 1989. Man of the Match in Middlesex's NatWest Trophy final win in 1988, on his debut in the competition. While on tour with England A in India was called up as replacement for Graeme Hick on the senior tour to Australia 1994-95
Opinions on cricket: 'To lose overseas players would lower playing standards greatly. People should think about the positive things that 99% of them bring to county cricket. Why do the powers that be feel that they must constantly tamper with the rules, i.e. bouncers etc?'
Best batting: 233 Middlesex v Surrey, Lord's 1992
Best bowling: 1-0 Middlesex v Northamptonshire, Uxbridge 1991

1994 Season

	M	Inns	NO	Runs	HS	Avge	100s	50s	Ct	St	O	M	Runs	Wkts	Avge	Best	5wI	10wM
Test																		
All First	18	26	2	1271	135	52.95	4	6	13	-	2	0	6	0	-		-	-
1-day Int																		
NatWest	1	1	1	0	0*	-	-	-	1	-								
B & H	2	2	1	161	119*	161.00	1	-	-	-								
Sunday	17	16	1	561	97	37.40	-	3	3	-	4	0	21	0	-		-	-

Career Performances

	M	Inns	NO	Runs	HS	Avge	100s	50s	Ct	St	Balls	Runs	Wkts	Avge	Best	5wI	10wM
Test	14	24	1	384	64	16.69	-	1	9	-	127	56	0	-	-	-	-
All First	160	257	37	8938	233	40.62	19	46	83	-	1183	678	8	84.75	1-0	-	-
1-day Int	4	4	2	47	31	23.50	-	-	3	-							
NatWest	16	15	1	426	104	30.42	1	1	5	-	174	98	4	24.50	2-15	-	
B & H	22	21	5	618	119*	38.62	2	1	7	-							
Sunday	91	85	17	2960	147*	43.52	2	21	28	-	195	185	9	20.55	5-38	1	

RATCLIFFE, J. D.   Surrey

Name: Jason David Ratcliffe
Role: Right-hand opening bat, right-arm medium/off-spin bowler, slip fielder
Born: 19 June 1969, Solihull
Height: 6ft 3in **Weight:** 14st 7lbs
Nickname: Ratters

County debut: 1988 (Warwickshire)
1st-Class 50s: 21
1st-Class 100s: 3
1st-Class catches: 47
One-Day 100s: 1
Place in batting averages:
(1993 116th av. 29.38)
Parents: David and Sheila
Wife and date of marriage:
Andrea, 7 January 1995
Family links with cricket: Father
(D.P. Ratcliffe) played for Warwickshire
1956-62
Education: Meadow Green Primary School;
Sharmans Cross Secondary School; Solihull
Sixth Form College
Qualifications: 6 O-levels; NCA staff coach
Career outside cricket: Working for
Birmingham City FC marketing team
Off-season: Playing cricket in Australia
Overseas tours: NCA (South) to Ireland 1988; Warwickshire to South Africa 1991-92
Overseas teams played for: West End, Kimberley, South Africa 1987-88; Belmont,
Newcastle, NSW 1990-91; Penrith, Sydney 1992-94
Cricketers particularly admired: Geoff Boycott, Jimmy Cook, Allan Donald, Paul
Booth, Andy Moles, Tim Munton, Roger Twose, Gladstone Small, Dominic Ostler
Other sports followed: Football (Birmingham City) and most other sports
Injuries: Broken thumb, did not miss any cricket
Relaxations: Music, reading, eating out
Extras: Scored a century against Boland on Warwickshire tour to South Africa 1991-92.
Released by Warwickshire at end of 1994 season and signed for Surrey
Best batting: 127* Warwickshire v Cambridge University, Fenner's 1989
Best bowling: 1-6 Warwickshire v Gloucestershire, Edgbaston 1993

1994 Season

	M	Inns	NO	Runs	HS	Avge	100s	50s	Ct	St	O	M	Runs	Wkts	Avge	Best	5wI	10wM
Test																		
All First	3	5	0	87	69	17.40	-	1	1	-								
1-day Int																		
NatWest																		
B & H																		
Sunday																		

	M	Inns	NO	Runs	HS	Avge	100s	50s	Ct	St	Balls	Runs	Wkts	Avge	Best	5wl	10wM
Test																	
All First	78	144	8	3863	127 *	28.40	3	21	47	-	343	235	4	58.75	1-4	-	-
1-day Int																	
NatWest	8	8	1	333	105	47.57	1	2	1	-	30	20	0	-	-	-	
B & H	1	1	0	29	29	29.00	-	-	-	-							
Sunday	13	12	1	145	37	13.18	-	-	5	-	85	69	4	17.25	2-11	-	

REES, G. H. J. Glamorgan

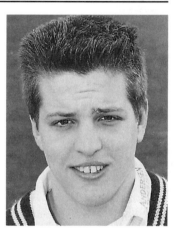

Name: Gareth Henry John Rees
Role: Right-hand bat, right-arm 'net' bowler
Born: 24 October 1974, Clifton, Bristol
Height: 6ft 2in **Weight:** 14st 12lb
Nickname: Greeser, Sponge
County debut: No first-team appearance
Parents: John and Sue
Marital status: Single
Family links with cricket: Father played
for Cheltenham College
Education: Clifton College Preparatory
School; Clifton College; Durham University
Qualifications: 10 GCSEs, 3 A-levels
Off-season: At university
Overseas tours: West of England U14 to
Holland 1990; Clifton College to Barbados
1991 and 1993
Cricketers particularly admired:
Jim Andrew, Peter Hall, Chris St John
Other sports followed: Rugby union
Relaxations: 'An avid supporter of Bristol rugby club, although I support Wales'
Extras: Record run-scorer at Clifton College, National Schools Fives Champion, played
for Clifton Flax Bourton in Western League. Made debut for Glamorgan 2nd XI at 16.
Played rugby for Gloucestershire Schools, Glamorgan U19 and Glamorgan Colts.

REEVE, D. A. Warwickshire

Name: Dermot Alexander Reeve
Role: Right-hand bat, right-arm fast-medium
bowler, county captain
Born: 2 April 1963, Hong Kong
Height: 6ft **Weight:** 11st 11lbs
Nickname: Legend
County debut: 1983 (Sussex),
1988 (Warwickshire)
County cap: 1986 (Sussex),
1989 (Warwickshire)
Tests: 3
One-Day Internationals: 25
1000 runs in a season: 2
50 wickets in a season: 2
1st-Class 50s: 47
1st-Class 100s: 5
1st-Class 200s: 1
1st-Class 5 w. in innings: 6
1st-Class catches: 172
One-Day 100s: 1
One-Day 5 w. in innings: 1

Place in batting averages: 255th av. 12.88 (1993 71st av. 36.42)
Place in bowling averages: 66th av. 30.80 (1993 22nd av. 24.00)
Strike rate: 86.40 (career 66.03)
Parents: Alexander James and Monica
Marital status: Divorced
Children: Emily Kaye, 14 September 1988
Family links with cricket: Father was captain of his school XI; brother Mark is an
improving club cricketer. Mother took over as scorer during the England tour to India and
Sri Lanka 1992-93 when Clem Driver was taken ill
Education: King George V School, Kowloon, Hong Kong
Qualifications: 7 O-levels
Off-season: 'Doing some after-dinner speaking and then visiting my daughter in Australia.
Lots of sitting on the beach and golf.'
Overseas tours: England to New Zealand and Australia (World Cup) 1991-92, to India and
Sri Lanka 1992-93
Overseas teams played for: Hong Kong
Cricketers particularly admired: 'John Barclay (enthusiasm), Wasim Akram (talent),
Tim Munton (committment), Malcolm Marshall (power with grace), Alec Stewart (timing),
Ray Alikhan (guts), Graham Gooch and Mike Gatting (dedication)'
Other sports followed: Football (Manchester United)
Injuries: Tear to groin, missed the odd game

Relaxations: Swimming, golf, eating out, music, movies and popcorn
Extras: Formerly on Lord's groundstaff. Represented Hong Kong in ICC Trophy June 1982. Hong Kong Cricketer of the Year 1980-81 and Hong Kong's Cricket Sports Personality of the Year 1981. Twice Western Australian CA Cricketer of the Year. Man of the Match in 1986 NatWest final for Sussex and 1989 final for Warwickshire. Originally selected for England A tour to Bermuda and West Indies 1991-92 but promoted to senior tour to New Zealand when Angus Fraser was ruled out by injury. Appointed Warwickshire captain for 1993 and was voted their Player of the Year 1993 after leading them to victory in the NatWest Trophy. On the Sky Sports commentary team for the England tour of Australia 1994-95
Opinions on cricket: 'More one-day internationals should be played in England. Four-day cricket is good for the game, but needs to be played on better wickets. Change the one bouncer per batsmen, per over rule back and leave intimidation in the hands of the umpires in first-class cricket.'
Best batting: 202* Warwickshire v Northamptonshire, Northampton 1990
Best bowling: 7-37 Sussex v Lancashire, Lytham 1987

1994 Season

	M	Inns	NO	Runs	HS	Avge	100s	50s	Ct	St	O	M	Runs	Wkts	Avge	Best	5wI	10wM
Test																		
All First	9	10	1	116	33	12.88	-	-	18	-	144	48	308	10	30.80	2-9	-	-
1-day Int	1	1	0	16	16	16.00	-	-	-	-	4	0	15	0	-	-		
NatWest	5	4	0	107	37	26.75	-	-	-	-	48	8	153	8	19.12	3-44	-	
B & H	3	3	3	78	46 *	-	-	-	1	-	31	4	114	5	22.80	3-48	-	
Sunday	16	16	4	378	65 *	31.50	-	3	2	-	91.3	8	328	10	32.80	2-16	-	

Career Performances

	M	Inns	NO	Runs	HS	Avge	100s	50s	Ct	St	Balls	Runs	Wkts	Avge	Best	5wI	10wM
Test	3	5	0	124	59	24.80	-	1	1	-	149	60	2	30.00	1-4	-	-
All First	219	291	72	7431	202 *	33.93	5	47	172	-	27007	11354	409	27.76	7-37	6	-
1-day Int	25	17	9	241	33 *	30.12	-	-	11	-	969	686	18	38.11	3-20	-	
NatWest	38	30	11	715	81 *	37.63	-	4	14	-	2176	1079	40	26.97	4-20	-	
B & H	33	28	11	423	80	24.88	-	1	6	-	1719	1209	37	32.67	4-42	-	
Sunday	152	110	28	2112	100	25.75	1	8	43	-	5364	4029	137	29.40	5-23	1	

REMY, C. C.   Sussex

Name: Carlos Charles Remy
Role: Right-hand bat, right-arm
fast-medium bowler
Born: 24 July 1968, Castries, St Lucia
Height: 5ft 10in **Weight:** 11st

Nickname: Dredd
County debut: 1989
1st-Class 50s: 2
1st-Class catches: 7
Place in batting averages: 203rd av. 19.40
Parents: Mary Annette
Marital status: Single
Family links with cricket: Stepfather
played club cricket for STC in Morrant
League
Education: St William of York School,
London
Qualifications: 1 O-level, 3 CSEs, NCA
coaching certificate
Career outside cricket: 'Doing any job'
Overseas tours: Haringey Cricket College to
West Indies 1988, 1989
Overseas teams played for: Bionics, Harare
1989-90; Parnell, Auckland 1990-91

Cricketers particularly admired: Franklyn Stephenson, Robin Smith, Allan Border,
Malcolm Marshall
Other sports followed: Football and rugby
Relaxations: Listening to music (soul, swing, rap and ragga), dancing
Extras: 'Scored my very first hundred for Sussex in my first game for the 2nd XI'
Best batting: 60 Sussex v Northamptonshire, Northampton 1994
Best bowling: 4-63 Sussex v Cambridge University, Hove 1990

1994 Season

	M	Inns	NO	Runs	HS	Avge	100s	50s	Ct	St	O	M	Runs	Wkts	Avge	Best	5wI	10wM
Test																		
All First	6	11	1	194	60	19.40	-	2	3	-	61	6	241	5	48.20	2-67	-	-
1-day Int																		
NatWest																			
B & H																			
Sunday	13	10	1	57	14	6.33	-	-	4	-	92	3	427	14	30.50	4-43	-	

Career Performances

	M	Inns	NO	Runs	HS	Avge	100s	50s	Ct	St	Balls	Runs	Wkts	Avge	Best	5wI	10wM
Test																	
All First	20	27	3	475	60	19.79	-	2	7	-	1502	937	19	49.31	4-63	-	-
1-day Int																	
NatWest	1	1	0	1	1	1.00	-	-	-	-	60	30	0	-		-	-
B & H																	
Sunday	28	22	2	151	19	7.55	-	-	7	-	994	812	29	28.00	4-31	-	

RHODES, S. J.   Worcestershire

Name: Steven John Rhodes
Role: Right-hand bat, wicket-keeper,
county vice-captain
Born: 17 June 1964, Bradford
Height: 5ft 8in **Weight:** 12st
Nickname: Bumpy
County debut: 1981 (Yorkshire),
1985 (Worcestershire)
County cap: 1986 (Worcestershire)
Test debut: 1994
Tests: 6
One-Day Internationals: 6
1st-Class 50s: 37
1st-Class 100s: 7
1st-Class catches: 643
1st-Class stumpings: 83
Place in batting averages: 8th av. 56.00
(1993 79th av. 35.33)
Parents: William Ernest and
Norma Kathleen

Wife and date of marriage: Judy Ann, 6 March 1993
Children: Holly Jade, 20 August 1985; George Harry, 26 October 1993
Family links with cricket: Father played for Nottinghamshire 1959-64
Education: Bradford Moor Junior School; Lapage St Middle; Carlton-Bolling Comprehensive, Bradford
Qualifications: 4 O-levels, coaching certificate
Career outside cricket: Labourer; trainee sports shop manager
Off-season: Ashes tour
Overseas tours: England A to Sri Lanka 1986-86; England A to Zimbabwe and Kenya 1989-90, to Pakistan 1990-91, to West Indies 1991-92, to South Africa 1993-94; England to Australia 1994-95
Overseas teams played for: Past Bros, Bundaberg, Queensland; Avis Vogeltown, New Plymouth, New Zealand; Melville, Perth, Australia
Cricketers particularly admired: Graeme Hick, Richard Hadlee
Other sports followed: Rugby league, horse racing and golf
Injuries: 'Niggles'
Relaxations: Keeping and breeding tropical fish ('very therapeutic')
Extras: Played for England YC v Australia YC in 1983 and holds record for most victims in an innings for England YC. Youngest wicket-keeper to play for Yorkshire. Released by Yorkshire to join Worcestershire at end of 1984 season. Selected for cancelled England tour to India 1988-89 and was one of four players put on stand-by as reserves for 1992 World Cup squad. Writes a weekly cricket column for a Birmingham newspaper.

Opinions on cricket: 'How England Test bowlers can stay fresh in between Test matches is beyond me. They bowl their hearts out in a Test and then go straight into five tough days county cricket. The next day they report to the next Test venue for another gruelling match. No wonder we can't sustain the same high level in the second consecutive bowling day of a Test. Don't ask me how we achieve the perfect answer to the problem. Extending the four-foot rule to six feet would be worth experimenting with, to help spinners on flat pitches.'
Best batting: 116* Worcestershire v Warwickshire, Worcester 1992

1994 Season

	M	Inns	NO	Runs	HS	Avge	100s	50s	Ct	St	O	M	Runs	Wkts	Avge	Best	5wI	10wM
Test	6	8	4	222	65 *	55.50	-	1	26	2								
All First	18	27	11	896	100 *	56.00	1	5	59	8								
1-day Int	3	3	1	68	56	34.00	-	1	1	1								
NatWest	5	3	2	66	36	66.00	-	-	8	1								
B & H	4	2	0	12	12	6.00	-	-	7	-								
Sunday	10	7	3	85	46 *	21.25	-	-	17	4								

Career Performances

	M	Inns	NO	Runs	HS	Avge	100s	50s	Ct	St	Balls	Runs	Wkts	Avge	Best	5wI	10wM
Test	6	8	4	222	65 *	55.50	-	1	26	2							
All First	259	344	105	7988	116 *	33.42	7	37	643	83	6	30	0	-	-	-	-
1-day Int	6	5	2	77	56	25.66	-	1	4	1							
NatWest	33	24	8	363	61	22.68	-	2	39	5							
B & H	47	34	6	445	51 *	15.89	-	1	64	7							
Sunday	149	94	21	1424	48 *	19.50	-	-	155	43							

69. Which Pakistani opener scored 169 in the Second Test against New Zealand in 1993-94 to help his country to an innings victory?

RICHARDSON, A.   Derbyshire

Name: Alan Richardson
Role: Right-hand bat, right-arm medium bowler
Born: 6 May 1975, Newcastle-under-Lyme
Height: 6ft 2in **Weight** 12st 7lbs
Nickname: YP, Darren, Shaggy, Ladder,
Steffs, Son of Lovell
County debut: No first-team appearance
Parents: Roy and Sandra
Marital status: Single
Family links with cricket: Father played club
cricket
Education: Alleyne's High School, Stone;
Stafford College of Further Education;
Roehampton Institute
Qualifications: 8 GCSEs, 2 A-levels,
2 AS-levels, Advanced Cricket Coach
Off-season: 'Doing lots of stretching and
running. Visiting friends at university. Training
with Gary Steer at Cheltenham University as
he is a model professional.'
Cricketers particularly admired: David Lovell, Greg Pooley, Gary Steer
Other sports followed: Football (Stoke City)
Relaxations: Any sport, especially golf, badminton and volleyball, listening to music
Extras: *The Cricketer*/Slazenger Cricketer of the Month June 1991 and *Cricket World*
award for best bowling performance in Oxford U19 Festival (8-60 v Devon)

RICHARDSON, R. B.   Yorkshire

Name: Richard Benjamin Richardson
Role: Right-hand bat, right-arm medium bowler
Born: 12 January 1962, Five Islands, Antigua
Nickname: Richie
County debut: 1993
County cap: 1993
Test debut: 1983-84
Tests: 76
One-Day Internationals: 202
1st-Class 50s: 55
1st-Class 100s: 30
1st-Class 5 w. in innings: 1

1st-Class catches: 173
One-Day 100s: 6
Place in batting averages: 95th av. 34.43
(1993 81st av. 34.50)
Career outside cricket: Owns duty-free
shop – 'Richie Rich' – on St John's
waterfront (Antigua)
Overseas tours: West Indies to India
1983-84, to England 1984, to Australia
1984-85, to Pakistan and New Zealand
1986-87, to India 1987-88, to England
1988, to Australia 1988-89, to England
1991, to Pakistan 1991-92, to Australia and
New Zealand (World Cup) 1991-92, to
Australia 1992-93, to South Africa 1992-93,
to Sharjah, India (Hero Cup) and Sri Lanka
1993-94
Overseas teams played for: Leeward Islands
1981-1995
Relaxations: Plays guitar

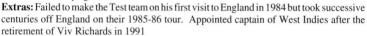

Extras: Failed to make the Test team on his first visit to England in 1984 but took successive
centuries off England on their 1985-86 tour. Appointed captain of West Indies after the
retirement of Viv Richards in 1991
Best batting: 194 West Indies v India, Georgetown 1988-89
Best bowling: 5-40 Leeward Islands v England XI, St John's 1985-86

1994 Season

	M	Inns	NO	Runs	HS	Avge	100s	50s	Ct	St	O	M	Runs	Wkts	Avge	Best	5wI	10wM
Test																		
All First	0	10	0	551	76	34.43	-	5	9	-								
1-day Int																		
NatWest	2	2	0	42	27	21.00	-	-	-	-								
B & H	1	1	0	7	7	7.00	-	-	-	-								
Sunday	8	8	2	203	55	33.83	-	1	1	-								

Career Performances

	M	Inns	NO	Runs	HS	Avge	100s	50s	Ct	St	Balls	Runs	Wkts	Avge	Best	5wI	10wM
Test	76	130	11	5445	194	45.75	15	25	82	-	66	18	0	-	-	-	-
All First	191	318	25	12280	194	41.91	30	55	173	-	480	235	6	39.16	5-40	1	-
1-day Int	202	195	27	5641	122	33.57	5	41	70	-	58	46	1	46.00	1-4	-	
NatWest	5	5	0	194	90	38.80	-	2	-	-							
B & H	2	2	0	59	52	29.50	-	1	-	-							
Sunday	21	21	6	740	103	49.33	1	5	5	-							

RICKETTS, C. I.   Essex

Name: Courtney Ian Ricketts
Role: Right-hand bat, slow left-arm bowler
Born: 26 April 1967, Kennington, London
Height: 5ft 10in **Weight:** 11st 7lbs
County debut: 1987 (Sussex)
1st-Class catches: 1
Parents: Owen Rickets and Merle Thompson
Marital status: Engaged
Children: Richie, 15 July 1990; Martina, 14
April 1992
Education: St Andrew Technical College,
Kingston, Jamaica
Qualifications: 4 Caribbean GCSE
equivalents, 1 O-level, cricket coach
Overseas tours: Haingey Cricket College to
Barbados/Trinidad and Tobago 1987
Overseas teams played for: Kensington,
Jamaica 1982-85

Cricketers particularly admired: Desmond Haynes, Gordon Greenidge, David Gower
Other sports followed: Football, golf, tennis, athletics, boxing, motor racing, snooker,
show jumping, American football, basketball, baseball, gymnastics, winter sports
Relaxations: Watching action and thriller movies, listening to soul and reggae music
Extras: The first Haringey Cricket College recruit to score a century on a West Indies tour.
Was previously with Sussex (1987) and Gloucestershire (1988)
Opinions on cricket: 'I think English county cricketers are too uptight, making the game
seem like a matter of life and death. My opinion is that cricket should be played extremely
hard and to win, but with a smile on your face to indicate that you are enjoying it. A good
example – Darren Gough.'
Best batting: 29 Sussex v Worcestershire, Worcester 1987
Best bowling: 2-40 Sussex v Worcestershire, Worcester 1987

1994 Season (did not make any first-class or one-day appearance)

Career Performances

	M	Inns	NO	Runs	HS	Avge	100s	50s	Ct	St	Balls	Runs	Wkts	Avge	Best	5wl	10wM
Test																	
All First	3	1	0	29	29	29.00	-	-	1	-	430	253	5	50.60	2-40	-	-
1-day Int																	
NatWest	1	-	-	-	-	-	-	-	-	-	24	11	0	-	-	-	-
B & H	2	1	-	-	-	-	-	-	1	-	132	67	2	33.50	1-30	-	
Sunday	3	2	0	10	9	5.00	-	-	-	-	66	74	1	74.00	1-25	-	

Name: David Ripley
Role: Right-hand bat, wicket-keeper
Born: 13 September 1966, Leeds
Height: 5ft 11in **Weight:** 11st 10lbs
Nickname: Rips, Spud
County debut: 1984
County cap: 1987
1st-Class 50s: 12
1st-Class 100s: 6
1st-Class catches: 464
1st-Class stumpings: 65
Place in batting averages: 210th av. 18.78
(1993 181st av. 22.11)
Parents: Arthur and Brenda
Wife and date of marriage:
Jackie, 24 September 1988
Children: Joe David, 11 October 1989; George

William, 5 March 1994
Education: Woodlesford Primary;
Royds High, Leeds
Qualifications: 5 O-levels, NCA advanced coach
Career outside cricket: Director of Gard Sports, Northampton
Off-season: Coaching in schools
Overseas tours: England YC to West Indies 1984-85; Northants to Durban, South Africa
1991-92, to Cape Town 1992-93
Overseas teams played for: Marists and Poverty Bay, New Zealand 1985-87
Cricketers particularly admired: Alan Knott, Bob Taylor 'and many other keepers',
Clive Radley, Ian Botham, Geoff Boycott
Other sports followed: Football (Leeds United) and rugby league (Castleford)
Injuries: Back injury, missed two weeks
Relaxations: 'Eating out, enjoying a couple of pints with the lads'
Extras: Finished top of wicket-keepers' dismissals list for 1988 and 1992 and was voted
Wombwell Cricket Lovers' Society Best Wicket-keeper 1992. Played for England YC v
Sri Lanka 1986
Opinions on cricket: 'Four-day cricket is working well. I would like to see short run-ups
on Sundays as there are too many low-scoring games.'
Best batting: 134* Northamptonshire v Yorkshire, Scarborough 1986
Best bowling: 2-89 Northamptonshire v Essex, Ilford 1987

---

70. Which New Zealander scored his first Test hundred to help his
country to square the series against Pakistan in 1993-94?

1994 Season

	M	Inns	NO	Runs	HS	Avge	100s	50s	Ct	St	O	M	Runs	Wkts	Avge	Best	5wI	10wM
Test																		
All First	16	23	9	263	36 *	18.78	-	-	40	6								
1-day Int																		
NatWest	3	1	0	0	0	0.00	-	-	2	-								
B & H	1	1	1	1	1 *	-	-	-	2	-								
Sunday	11	7	1	65	21	10.83	-	-	9	2								

Career Performances

	M	Inns	NO	Runs	HS	Avge	100s	50s	Ct	St	Balls	Runs	Wkts	Avge	Best	5wI	10wM
Test																	
All First	212	276	72	4929	134 *	24.16	6	12	464	65	60	103	2	51.50	2-89	-	-
1-day Int																	
NatWest	35	20	9	130	27 *	11.81	-	-	36	3							
B & H	37	25	9	305	36 *	19.06	-	-	37	4							
Sunday	124	77	35	822	52 *	19.57	-	1	87	13							

ROBERTS, A. R. — Northamptonshire

Name: Andrew Richard Roberts
Role: Right-hand bat, leg-break bowler
Born: 16 April 1971, Kettering
Height: 5ft 5in **Weight:** 10st 7lbs
Nickname: Reggie
County debut: 1989
1st-Class 50s: 2
1st-Class 5 w. in innings: 1
1st-Class catches: 22
Place in batting averages: 109th av. 32.62
Place in bowling averages: 142nd av. 51.17
(1993 120th av. 40.00)
Strike rate: 85.41 (career 83.50)
Parents: David and Shirley
Marital status: Single
Family links with cricket: Father (Dave) played a few games for Northants 2nd XI; brother Tim won the Lord's Taverners U13 award in 1991, played Midlands Schools U14 and England Schoolboys U15
Education: Bishop Stopford Comprehensive, Kettering
Qualifications: 3 O-levels, 5 CSEs, Carpentry and Joinery City & Guilds

Career outside cricket: Carpenter
Off-season: Playing for Eastern Suburbs, Wellington, New Zealand
Overseas tours: Northamptonshire to Durban, South Africa 1991-92, to Cape Town, South Africa 1992-93
Overseas teams played for: Woolston Working Men's Club, Christchurch, New Zealand 1989-91; Eastern Suburbs, Wellington 1993-94
Cricketers particularly admired: Richard Williams, Wayne Larkins, Dennis Lillee
Other sports followed: Rugby and golf
Relaxations: 'Music, sleeping, eating, a good pint of bitter!'
Extras: Played for England YC v Pakistan YC 1990
Opinions on cricket: 'In favour of uncovered wickets, which would produce better technique and more exciting cricket.'
Best batting: 62 Northamptonshire v Nottinghamshire, Trent Bridge 1992
Best bowling: 6-72 Northamptonshire v Lancashire, Lytham 1991

1994 Season

	M	Inns	NO	Runs	HS	Avge	100s	50s	Ct	St	O	M	Runs	Wkts	Avge	Best	5wl	10wM
Test																		
All First	9	12	4	261	51	32.62	-	1	3	-	242	49	870	17	51.17	3-106	-	-
1-day Int																		
NatWest																		
B & H																		
Sunday	2	2	0	20	20	10.00	-	-	1	-	8	0	51	3	17.00	2-40	-	

Career Performances

	M	Inns	NO	Runs	HS	Avge	100s	50s	Ct	St	Balls	Runs	Wkts	Avge	Best	5wl	10wM
Test																	
All First	54	73	18	1011	62	18.38	-	2	22	-	8100	4257	97	43.88	6-72	1	-
1-day Int																	
NatWest	1	0	0	0	0	-	-	-	1	-	72	23	1	23.00	1-23	-	
B & H																	
Sunday	10	4	0	38	20	9.50	-	-	4	-	240	218	9	24.22	3-26	-	

ROBERTS, D. J.   Northamptonshire

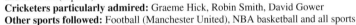

Name: David James Roberts
Role: Right-hand bat
Born: 29 December 1976, Truro, Cornwall
Height: 6ft **Weight:** 11st
Nickname: Robo
County debut: No first-team appearance
Parents: Dennis and Pam
Marital status: Single
Family links with cricket: Cousin, Chris
Bullen, played for Surrey. Father played
cricket for local club and is also a youth
coach. Mother is a keen supporter!
Education: Mullion County Primary;
Mullion Comprehensive
Qualifications: 9 GCSEs
Career outside cricket: Helping on the
family farm
Overseas tours: West of England to
Barbados, Trinidad and Tobago 1990-91
and 1991-92 (captain)
Cricketers particularly admired: Graeme Hick, Robin Smith, David Gower
Other sports followed: Football (Manchester United), NBA basketball and all sports
Injuries: Tennis elbow – out for five weeks
Relaxations: Watching television, listening to music, playing football
Extras: Played for English Schools since the age of 14, including matches against South
Africa in 1992. Represented England U17 v India U17 in 1994
Opinions on cricket: 'Too much one-day cricket is played, which is bad preparation for
Test matches. Four-day games should improve Test performances.'

ROBINSON, D. D. J.   Essex

Name: Darren David John Robinson
Role: Right-hand opening bat, occasional
right-arm medium bowler
Born: 2 March 1973, Braintree, Essex
Height: 5ft 10in **Weight:** 12st 8lbs
Nickname: Robbo
County debut: 1993
1st-Class 50s: 1
1st-Class catches: 3

Parents: David John and Dorothy May

Marital status: Single

Family links with cricket: Father local club cricketer for 35 years, supporter of England and Essex. 'Mother very supportive of my cricketing endeavours'

Education: Tabor High School, Braintree; Chelmsford College of Further Education

Qualifications: 5 GCSEs, BTEC National Diploma in Building and Construction

Overseas tours: England U18 to Canada 1991; England U19 to Pakistan 1991-92

Overseas teams played for: Waverley, Sydney 1992-94

Cricketers particularly admired: Geoff Boycott, Graham Gooch, Keith Fletcher

Other sports followed: Rugby union, swimming, golf

Relaxations: Listening to music and socialising

Extras: *Daily Telegraph* batting award 1988 and International Youth Tournament in Canada batting award 1991

Opinions on cricket: 'A very gratifying sport, which is demanding, requires dedication and considerable powers of concentration. Is frustrating at times when things are not working out. Is a good character builder, providing experience of team spirit, comradeship, independence, socialising and the opportunity of international travel.'

Best batting: 67 Essex v Gloucestershire, Bristol 1993

1994 Season

	M	Inns	NO	Runs	HS	Avge	100s	50s	Ct	St	O	M	Runs	Wkts	Avge	Best	5wl	10wM
Test																		
All First	1	1	0	38	38	38.00	-	-	1	-								
1-day Int																		
NatWest																		
B & H																		
Sunday																		

Career Performances

	M	Inns	NO	Runs	HS	Avge	100s	50s	Ct	St	Balls	Runs	Wkts	Avge	Best	5wl	10wM
Test																	
All First	3	5	0	150	67	30.00	-	1	3	-							
1-day Int																	
NatWest																	
B & H																	
Sunday	1	1	0	2	2	2.00	-	-	-	-							

ROBINSON, M. A.   Yorkshire

Name: Mark Andrew Robinson
Role: Right-hand bat, right-arm
fast-medium bowler
Born: 23 November 1966, Hull
Height: 6ft 3in **Weight:** 13st 3lbs
Nickname: Jessie, Coddy, Scoope
County debut: 1987 (Northamptonshire),
1991 (Yorkshire)
County cap: 1990 (Northamptonshire)
1992 (Yorkshire)
50 wickets in season: 1
1st-Class 5 w. in innings: 7
1st-Class 10 w. in match: 2
1st-Class catches: 27
Place in bowling averages: 106th av. 36.84
(1993 50th av. 27.46)
Strike rate: 82.53 (career 69.27)
Parents: Joan Margarette and Malcolm
Wife and date of marriage: Julia, 8 October 1994
Family links with cricket: Grandfather a prominent local cricketer;
father was hostile bowler in back garden
Education: Fifth Avenue Primary; Endike Junior High; Hull Grammar School
Qualifications: 6 O-levels, 2 A-levels, senior coach
Career outside cricket: Self-employed cricket coach
Off-season: 'Coaching in Hull, watching the Tigers at Boothferry Park and walking dog, Molly'
Overseas tours: England U19 North to Bermuda; Yorkshire to Cape Town 1991-92 and
1992-93, to West Indies 1994
Overseas teams played for: East Shirley, Canterbury, New Zealand 1987-89; Canterbury,
New Zealand 1989-90
Cricketers particularly admired: Dennis Lillee, Mike Gatting, John Emburey
Other sports followed: Hull City FC ('The Tigers')
Injuries: Floating ligament in back of right knee. 'Dodgy' right hamstring. Did not miss
any cricket
Relaxations: Reading, music, 'long walks with my dog', all sports
Extras: Took hat-trick with first three balls of innings in Yorkshire League, playing for Hull
v Doncaster. First player to win Yorkshire U19 Bowler of the Season award in two
successive years. Northamptonshire Uncapped Player of the Year 1989. Endured a world
record 11 innings without scoring a run during 1990 season. Took 9 for 37 v Northamptonshire
at Harrogate 1993, 12 for 109 in match
Opinions on cricket: 'Lunch interval should be shorter and tea interval should be extended'
Best batting: 19* Northamptonshire v Essex, Chelmsford 1988
Best bowling: 9-37 Yorkshire v Northamptonshire, Harrogate 1993

458

1994 Season

	M	Inns	NO	Runs	HS	Avge	100s	50s	Ct	St	O	M	Runs	Wkts	Avge	Best	5wI	10wM
Test																		
All First	19	23	8	58	9	3.86	-	-	5	-	619	171	1658	45	36.84	5-48	1	-
1-day Int																		
NatWest	2	1	0	0	0	0.00	-	-	-	-	24	4	65	2	32.50	1-23	-	
B & H	1	0	0	0	0	-	-	-	-	-	7	0	12	1	12.00	1-12	-	
Sunday	16	4	3	2	1 *	2.00	-	-	1	-	119	7	451	17	26.52	3-28	-	

Career Performances

	M	Inns	NO	Runs	HS	Avge	100s	50s	Ct	St	Balls	Runs	Wkts	Avge	Best	5wI	10wM
Test																	
All First	137	141	60	237	19 *	2.92	-	-	27	-	22377	10684	323	33.07	9-37	7	2
1-day Int																	
NatWest	14	6	4	4	3 *	2.00	-	-	2	-	980	516	21	24.57	4-32	-	
B & H	15	6	4	5	3 *	2.50	-	-	-	3	838	523	18	29.05	3-20	-	
Sunday	82	25	11	23	6 *	1.64	-	-	10	-	3577	2669	71	37.59	4-23	-	

ROBINSON, P. E. Leicestershire

Name: Phillip Edward Robinson
Role: Right-hand bat,
left-arm 'declaration' bowler
Born: 3 August 1963, Keighley,
West Yorkshire
Height: 5ft 9in **Weight:** 13st 7lbs
Nickname: Robbo
County debut: 1984 (Yorkshire),
1992 (Leicestershire)
County cap: 1988 (Yorkshire)
1000 runs in a season: 3
1st-Class 50s: 50
1st-Class 100s: 7
1st-Class catches: 125
One-Day 100s: 1
Place in batting averages: 40th av. 43.57
(1993 192nd av. 20.23)
Parents: Keith and Lesley
Wife and date of marriage:
Jane, 19 September 1986
Family links with cricket: Brother Richard at Yorkshire Cricket Academy; mother
secretary of Baldwin CC; father played and is now umpire in Bradford League; elder brother

459

plays in the same league and both brothers-in-law play local league cricket
Education: Long Lee Primary; Hartington Middle; Greenhead Comprehensive
Qualifications: 2 O-levels
Off-season: Working for Leicestershire CCC
Overseas tours: Southland CC to Tasmania 1987; Yorkshire to St Lucia and Barbados 1988
Overseas teams played for: Southland, New Zealand 1987; Eastern Southland cricket coach 1987; Eden Roskill, Auckland 1989-90; Riverside, Wellington 1990
Cricketers particularly admired: Geoff Boycott, Richard Hadlee
Other sports followed: Keighley rugby league, Manchester United, Meadowbank in Scotland, golf
Injuries: Impingement in left shoulder, did not miss any cricket. Intercostal rib cartilage, missed three weeks
Relaxations: War-gaming, watching sports, playing golf and other sports
Extras: Made the highest score by a Yorkshire 2nd XI player with 233 in 1983. Scored most runs by an overseas player in the Auckland Cricket League for Eden Roskill 1989-90 (1200 runs). Hit the fastest televised 50 in the Sunday League (19 balls) v Derbyshire at Chesterfield 1991. Released by Yorkshire at his own request at the end of the 1991 season. Played for Cumberland in 1992 and could play only limited-overs for Leicestershire in 1992 (apart from one match) but on full contract from 1993
Opinions on cricket: 'Cricket should be played in three days on uncovered pitches – standards of pitches for four-day matches are not good enough, generally.'
Best batting: 189 Yorkshire v Lancashire, Scarborough 1991
Best bowling: 1-10 Yorkshire v Somerset, Scarborough 1990

1994 Season

	M	Inns	NO	Runs	HS	Avge	100s	50s	Ct	St	O	M	Runs	Wkts	Avge	Best	5wl	10wM
Test																		
All First	5	7	0	305	86	43.57	-	3	8	-								
1-day Int																		
NatWest	1	0	0	0	0	-	-	-	-	-								
B & H	1	1	0	27	27	27.00	-	-	-	-								
Sunday	11	10	1	220	39 *	24.44	-	-	8	-								

Career Performances

	M	Inns	NO	Runs	HS	Avge	100s	50s	Ct	St	Balls	Runs	Wkts	Avge	Best	5wl	10wM
Test																	
All First	156	255	34	7518	189	34.01	7	50	125	-	296	329	3	109.66	1-10	-	-
1-day Int																	
NatWest	15	11	0	376	73	34.18	-	3	3	-							
B & H	26	22	3	554	73 *	29.15	-	3	9	-							
Sunday	138	133	13	3025	104	25.20	1	14	52	-							

ROBINSON, R. T.   Nottinghamshire

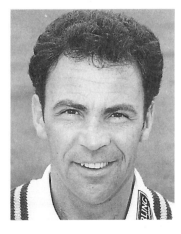

Name: Robert Timothy Robinson
Role: Right-hand opening bat, right-arm medium bowler, county captain
Born: 21 November 1958, Sutton-in-Ashfield, Nottinghamshire
Height: 6ft **Weight:** 12st 6lbs
Nickname: Robbo
County debut: 1978
County cap: 1983
Benefit: 1992 (£90,040)
Test debut: 1984-85
Tests: 29
One-Day Internationals: 26
1000 runs in a season: 12
1st-Class 50s: 117
1st-Class 100s: 51
1st-Class 200s: 2
1st-Class catches: 219
One-Day 100s: 9
Place in batting averages: 49th av. 42.53 (1993 30th av. 44.30)
Parents: Eddy and Christine
Wife and date of marriage: Patricia, 2 November 1985
Children: Philip Thomas; Alex James
Family links with cricket: Father, uncle, cousin and brother all played local cricket
Education: Dunstable Grammar School; High Pavement College, Nottingham; Sheffield University
Qualifications: BA (Hons) in Accountancy and Financial Management
Off-season: Runs his own sports shop
Overseas tours: England to India and Australia 1984-85, to West Indies 1985-86, to India and Pakistan (World Cup) 1987-88, to New Zealand 1987-88; unofficial English XI to South Africa 1989-90
Cricketers particularly admired: Geoffrey Boycott
Other sports followed: Golf, squash
Injuries: Tennis elbow
Relaxations: Spending time with family
Extras: Played for Northamptonshire 2nd XI in 1974-75 and for Nottinghamshire 2nd XI in 1977. Had soccer trials with Portsmouth, Chelsea and QPR. One of *Wisden*'s Five Cricketers of the Year 1985. Banned from Test cricket for joining 1989-90 tour of South Africa, remitted in 1992
Best batting: 220* Nottinghamshire v Yorkshire, Trent Bridge 1990
Best bowling: 1-22 Nottinghamshire v Northamptonshire, Northampton 1982

1994 Season

	M	Inns	NO	Runs	HS	Avge	100s	50s	Ct	St	O	M	Runs	Wkts	Avge	Best	5wI	10wM
Test																		
All First	19	31	1	1276	182	42.53	2	10	7	-	2.1	0	31	1	31.00	1-31	-	-
1-day Int																		
NatWest	2	2	0	67	62	33.50	-	1	-	-								
B & H	3	3	1	129	91 *	64.50	-	1	-	-								
Sunday	12	12	2	381	119 *	38.10	1	1	2	-								

Career Performances

	M	Inns	NO	Runs	HS	Avge	100s	50s	Ct	St	Balls	Runs	Wkts	Avge	Best	5wI	10wM
Test	29	49	5	1601	175	36.38	4	6	8	-	6	0	0	-	-	-	-
All First	349	605	76	22637	220 *	42.79	51	117	219	-	253	285	4	71.25	1-22	-	-
1-day Int	26	26	0	597	83	22.96	-	3	6	-							
NatWest	35	35	2	1365	139	41.36	2	6	14	-							
B & H	61	60	8	2182	120	41.96	3	15	15	-							
Sunday	192	186	24	5238	119 *	32.33	4	32	60	-							

ROLLINS, A. S.   Derbyshire

Name: Adrian Stewart Rollins
Role: Right-hand bat, right-arm medium bowler, occasional wicket-keeper
Born: 8 February 1972, Barking, Essex
Height: 6ft 5in **Weight:** 16st 4lbs
Nickname: Rollie, The Truth, Stinkmout, Full, Max, Charles Atlas
County debut: 1993
1st-Class 50s: 8
1st-Class catches: 23
1st-Class stumpings: 1
Place in batting averages: 149th av. 26.22 (1993 34th av. 43.55)
Parents: Marva
Marital status: Single
Family links with cricket: Brother Robert on Essex staff. Brother Gary at London Cricket College. Uncles play in Essex League.
Education: Little Ilford Comprehensive School, Manor Park, London
Qualifications: 10 GCSEs, 4 A-levels, CCPR Community Sports Leaders Award, BAWLA Leaders Award, NCA coaching award

Career outside cricket: Fitness instructor
Off-season: Relaxing and playing in New Zealand
Overseas tours: London Federation of Boys Clubs to Barbados 1987
Overseas teams played for: Kaponga, New Zealand 1993-94
Cricketers particularly admired: Dominic Cork, Philip DeFreitas, Chris Adams, Lee Tatam
Other sports followed: 'Big basketball fan'
Injuries: Knee ligament damage, missed two weeks
Relaxations: 'Weight-training and photography. A strict hip-hop, swingbeat, soul and ragga listener'
Extras: Made Championship debut on same day as brother. Became 500th first-class player for Derbyshire, for whom he was named Young Player of the Year 1993
Opinions on cricket: 'I am happy with the current format with four-dayers and Sunday League 40 overs. Over-rates in Championship are a bit of a task with an all-seam attack.'
Best batting: 97 Derbyshire v Lancashire, Blackpool 1994

1994 Season

	M	Inns	NO	Runs	HS	Avge	100s	50s	Ct	St	O	M	Runs	Wkts	Avge	Best	5wl	10wM
Test																		
All First	16	29	2	708	97	26.22	-	6	18	-	4	0	32	0	-	-	-	-
1-day Int																		
NatWest	1	1	0	6	6	6.00	-	-	2	-								
B & H	1	1	0	70	70	70.00	-	1	-	-								
Sunday	9	7	0	122	35	17.42	-	-	10	-								

Career Performances

	M	Inns	NO	Runs	HS	Avge	100s	50s	Ct	St	Balls	Runs	Wkts	Avge	Best	5wl	10wM
Test																	
All First	23	42	6	1100	97	30.55	-	8	23	1	24	32	0	-	-	-	-
1-day Int																	
NatWest	1	1	0	6	6	6.00	-	-	2	-							
B & H	1	1	0	70	70	70.00	-	1	-	-							
Sunday	17	14	1	250	57	19.23	-	1	11	-							

ROLLINS, R. J.   Essex

Name: Robert John Rollins
Role: Right-hand bat, wicket-keeper
Born: 30 January 1974, Plaistow, London
Height: 5ft 9in **Weight:** 12st 8lbs
Nickname: Rollie
County debut: 1992
1st-Class catches: 6
1st-Class stumpings: 3
Parents: Marva
Marital status: Single
Family links with cricket: Brother, Adrian,
on Derbyshire staff
Education: Little Ilford
Comprehensive School
Qualifications: 6 GCSEs
Off-season: 'Relaxing, coaching and lots
of practising; also playing on Megadrive'
Overseas tours: England U18 to Canada
1991; England U19 to Pakistan 1991-92, to
India 1992-93
Cricketers particularly admired: Keith Hurst 'my uncle, who is still a very good club
cricketer', all of the Clayhall indoor cricket team – N. Pace, G. Rollins, A. Ahmed, J. French,
T. Cutbill, D. McEwan
Other sports followed: All sports except anything to do with horses
Relaxations: 'I love swimming, because I'm so good at it, and I enjoy reading all books'
Extras: Named Essex Young Player of the Year 1992 and awarded his 2nd XI cap in
September of that year
Opinions on cricket: 'Four-day cricket is enjoyable.'
Best batting: 13 Essex v Pakistanis, Chelmsford 1992

1994 Season

	M	Inns	NO	Runs	HS	Avge	100s	50s	Ct	St	O	M	Runs	Wkts	Avge	Best	5wI	10wM
Test																		
All First	1	1	0	9	9	9.00	-	-	1	-								
1-day Int																		
NatWest																		
B & H																		
Sunday	9	8	4	27	9*	6.75	-	-	8	3								

	M	Inns	NO	Runs	HS	Avge	100s	50s	Ct	St	Balls	Runs	Wkts	Avge	Best	5wI	10wM
Test																	
All First	5	7	1	42	13	7.00	-	-	6	3							
1-day Int																	
NatWest																	
B & H																	
Sunday	11	9	4	27	9 *	5.40	-	-	11	4							

ROSE, G. D.   Somerset

Name: Graham David Rose
Role: Right-hand bat, right-arm fast-medium
bowler, first slip
Born: 12 April 1964, Tottenham
Height: 6ft 4in **Weight:** 15st
Nickname: Hagar
County debut: 1985 (Middlesex),
1987 (Somerset)
County cap: 1988 (Somerset)
1000 runs in a season: 1
50 wickets in a season: 2
1st-Class 50s: 24
1st-Class 100s: 6
1st-Class 5 w. in innings: 7
1st-Class catches: 83
One-Day 100s: 2
Place in batting averages: 163rd av. 24.90
(1993 103rd av. 32.03)
Place in bowling averages: 29th av. 25.81
(1993 32nd av. 25.34)
Strike rate: 46.93 (career 56.45)
Parents: William and Edna

Wife and date of marriage: Teresa Julie, 19 September 1987
Children: Georgina Charlotte, 6 December 1990
Family links with cricket: Father and brothers have played club cricket
Education: Northumberland Park School, Tottenham
Qualifications: 6 O-levels, 4 A-levels, NCA coaching certificate
Off-season: Local government officer with Somerset County Council
Overseas teams played for: Carey Park, Bunbury, Western Australia 1984-85; Fremantle,
Perth 1986-87; Paarl, Cape Town 1988-89
Cricketers particularly admired: Richard Hadlee, Jimmy Cook, Mushtaq Ahmed

Other sports followed: Football, rugby, golf
Injuries: Left knee, missed two Championship and three Sunday League matches
Relaxations: Wine, music, gardening, playing golf and 'my daughter, Georgina'
Extras: Played for England YC v Australia YC 1983. Took 6-41 on Middlesex debut in 1985, then scored 95 on debut for Somerset in 1987. Completed double of 1000 runs and 50 wickets in first-class cricket in 1990 and scored fastest recorded centuries in NatWest Trophy (v Devon) and Sunday League (v Glamorgan)
Opinions on cricket: 'With the B&H competition returning to the zonal format, I feel we are playing the right balance of games in our domestic programme. The only thing I would like to see changed is leg-byes – are they necessary, particularly in one-day games?'
Best batting: 138 Somerset v Sussex, Taunton 1993
Best bowling: 6-41 Middlesex v Worcestershire, Worcester 1985

1994 Season

	M	Inns	NO	Runs	HS	Avge	100s	50s	Ct	St	O	M	Runs	Wkts	Avge	Best	5wI	10wM
Test																		
All First	16	24	2	548	121	24.90	1	2	16	-	344.1	70	1136	44	25.81	4-40	-	-
1-day Int																		
NatWest	3	3	1	26	19 *	13.00	-	-	-	-	23	3	68	2	34.00	2-35	-	
B & H	1	1	0	0	0	0.00	-	-	-	-	9	1	42	1	42.00	1-42	-	
Sunday	13	13	2	451	91 *	41.00	-	5	3	-	83.1	4	356	15	23.73	4-35	-	

Career Performances

	M	Inns	NO	Runs	HS	Avge	100s	50s	Ct	St	Balls	Runs	Wkts	Avge	Best	5wI	10wM
Test																	
All First	155	212	40	5139	138	29.87	6	24	83	-	19815	10566	351	30.10	6-41	7	-
1-day Int																	
NatWest	16	14	1	278	110	21.38	1	1	3	-	779	456	17	26.82	3-11	-	
B & H	34	28	3	533	65	21.32	-	3	7	-	1878	1248	43	29.02	4-37	-	
Sunday	122	105	18	2501	148	28.74	1	14	31	-	4503	3345	123	27.19	4-26	-	

ROSEBERRY, A. Glamorgan

Name: Andrew Roseberry
Role: Right-hand bat, right-arm medium bowler
Born: 2 April 1971, Houghton-le-Spring, Sunderland
Height: 6ft **Weight:** 13st 7lbs
Nickname: Bud, Rosie, Deviant, Bobby Shaftoe
County debut: 1992 (Leicestershire), 1994 (Glamorgan)
1st-Class 50s: 2
1st-Class catches: 3
Place in batting averages: 88th av. 35.57
Parents: Matthew and Jean

Marital status: Single
Family links with cricket: Uncle, Peter Wyness, played for Royal Navy; brother Mike played for Middlesex, will captain Durham in 1995 and has represented England A, father is a director of DurhamCCC
Education: Tonstall Preparatory School, Sunderland; Durham School
Career outside cricket: Director of Roseberry Leisure. Coaching cricket
Off-season: 'Hoping to go to Perth, Western Australia'
Overseas tours: Les Taylor's benefit to Holland 1989; Glamorgan to Portugal 1994
Overseas teams played for: Melville, Perth 1990-92
Cricketers particularly admired: Robin Smith, Gareth Rees, Paul Nixon, Ottis Gibson
Other sports followed: Football (Sunderland FC), rugby, ice hockey (Durham Wasps)

Relaxations: All sports apart from horse racing. Shark fishing, deep sea diving. Eating out and socialising
Extras: Played for Leicestershire 1989-92 and made his first-class debut against Pakistan 1992. Played rugby for Durham School, also representing Durham and North of England
Opinions on cricket: 'I think four-day cricket is much better. All 2nd XI games should be played on first-class grounds.'
Best batting: 94 Glamorgan v Cambridge University, Fenner's 1994

1994 Season

	M	Inns	NO	Runs	HS	Avge	100s	50s	Ct	St	O	M	Runs	Wkts	Avge	Best	5wI	10wM
Test																		
All First	6	8	1	249	94	35.57	-	2	3	-								
1-day Int																		
NatWest																		
B & H																		
Sunday																		

Career Performances

	M	Inns	NO	Runs	HS	Avge	100s	50s	Ct	St	Balls	Runs	Wkts	Avge	Best	5wI	10wM
Test																	
All First	7	10	1	263	94	29.22	-	2	3	-							
1-day Int																	
NatWest																	
B & H																	
Sunday																	

ROSEBERRY, M. A.   Durham

Name: Michael Anthony Roseberry
Role: Right-hand bat, right-arm
medium fast bowler, county captain
Born: 28 November 1966,
Houghton-le-Spring, Sunderland
Height: 6ft 2in **Weight:** 14st 7lbs
Nickname: Zorro
County debut: 1985 (Middlesex)
County cap: 1990 (Middlesex)
1000 runs in a season: 4
1st-Class 50s: 44
1st-Class 100s: 18
1st-Class catches: 118
One-Day 100s: 4
Place in batting averages: 78th av. 36.56
(1993 106th av. 31.13)
Parents: Matthew and Jean
Wife and date of marriage:
Helen Louise, 22 February 1991
Children: Jordan Louise, 29 May 1992
Family links with cricket: Uncle, Peter Wyness, played for Royal Navy; brother Andrew
plays for Glamorgan; father is a director of Durham
Education: Tonstall Preparatory School, Sunderland; Durham School
Qualifications: 5 O-levels, 1 A-level, advanced cricket coach
Career outside cricket: 'Coaching cricket. Getting involved with father's business'
Overseas tours: England YC to West Indies 1984-85; England A to Australia 1992-93;
England XI and Lord's Taverners to Hong Kong 'on numerous occasions'; MCC to West
Africa 1993-94
Overseas teams played for: Fremantle, Western Australia 1986; Melville, Perth 1988
Cricketers particularly admired: 'Desmond Haynes for his help at cricket and handing
over money on the golf course'
Other sports followed: Football, rugby, etc.
Relaxations: All sports. 'Spending time with my wife Helen and daughter Jordan Louise.
Going for a pint and eating out'
Extras: Won Lord's Taverners/MCC Cricketer of the Year 1983, Cricket Society award for
Best Young Cricketer of the Year 1984 and twice won Cricket Society award for best all-
rounder in schools cricket. Played in Durham League as a professional while still at school.
At age 16, playing for Durham School v St Bees, he hit 216 in 160 minutes. In 1992 scored
2044 runs in 1992 – joint highest in first-class cricket with Peter Bowler and was named
Middlesex Player of the Year and Lucozade Player of the Year. Left Middlesex at end of
1994 to return to his native Durham as captain for the 1995 season
Opinions on cricket: 'Glad to see four-day cricket. Not convinced about the Sunday

League. Otherwise happy with Middlesex's achievements.'
Best batting: 185 Middlesex v Leicestershire, Lord's 1993
Best bowling: 1-1 Middlesex v Sussex, Hove 1988

1994 Season

	M	Inns	NO	Runs	HS	Avge	100s	50s	Ct	St	O	M	Runs	Wkts	Avge	Best	5wI	10wM
Test																		
All First	20	32	2	1097	152	36.56	2	6	21	-	1	0	5	0	-	-	-	-
1-day Int																		
NatWest	2	2	0	103	67	51.50	-	1	-	-								
B & H	2	2	0	21	17	10.50	-	-	2	-								
Sunday	14	13	1	424	119 *	35.33	2	1	7	-	0.4	0	7	0	-	-	-	-

Career Performances

	M	Inns	NO	Runs	HS	Avge	100s	50s	Ct	St	Balls	Runs	Wkts	Avge	Best	5wI	10wM
Test																	
All First	159	265	32	8693	185	37.30	18	44	118	-	489	387	4	96.75	1-1	-	-
1-day Int																	
NatWest	13	13	0	458	112	35.23	1	1	4	-	36	42	1	42.00	1-22	-	
B & H	17	15	1	447	84	31.92	-	4	5	-	6	2	0	-	-	-	
Sunday	91	87	7	2515	119 *	31.43	3	17	34	-	4	7	0	-	-	-	

RUSSELL, R. C.   Gloucestershire

Name: Robert Charles Russell
Role: Left-hand bat, wicket-keeper, county captain
Born: 15 August 1963, Stroud
Height: 5ft 8$^{1}/_{2}$in **Weight:** 9st 7lbs
Nickname: Jack
County debut: 1981
County cap: 1985
Benefit: 1994
Test debut: 1988
Tests: 36
One-Day Internationals: 26
1st-Class 50s: 43
1st-Class 100s: 4
1st-Class catches: 701
1st-Class stumpings: 94
One-Day 100s: 1
Place in batting averages: 93rd av. 34.65

(1993 94th av. 33.19)
Parents: John and Jennifer
Wife and date of marriage: Aileen Ann, 6 March 1985
Children: Stepson, Marcus Anthony; Elizabeth Ann, March 1988; Victoria, 1989; Charles David 1991
Education: Uplands County Primary School; Archway Comprehensive School
Qualifications: 7 O-levels, 2 A-levels
Career outside cricket: Professional artist
Overseas tours: England to Pakistan 1987-88, to India and West Indies 1989-90, to Australia 1990-91, to New Zealand 1991-92, to West Indies 1993-94, to Australia 1994-95; England A to Australia 1992-93
Cricketers particularly admired: Alan Knott, Bob Taylor
Other sports followed: Football ('a Spurs supporter, but only on television'), snooker
Relaxations: Drawing, sketching, painting (oil and watercolour), watching comedy, Rory Bremner and Phil Cool especially
Extras: Spotted at age nine by Gloucestershire coach, Graham Wiltshire. Youngest Gloucestershire wicket-keeper (17 years 307 days) and set record for most dismissals in a match on first-class debut: 8 (7 caught, 1 stumped) for Gloucestershire v Sri Lankans at Bristol, 1981. Hat-trick of catches v Surrey at The Oval 1986. Represented England YC v West Indies YC in 1982. Was chosen as England's Man of the Test Series, England v Australia 1989 and was one of *Wisden*'s Five Cricketers of the Year 1990. Appointed vice-captain to Martyn Moxon on the England A tour to Australia 1992-93. Called up as stand-by wicket-keeper for the England tour to Australia 1994-95 when Alec Stewart broke his finger for the second time on the tour. Had a three-week exhibition of his drawings in Bristol 1988 and published a book of his work entitled *A Cricketer's Artt* Co-author with Christopher Martin-Jenkins of *Sketches of a Season*, published in 1989. Commissioned by Dean of Gloucester to do a drawing of Gloucester Cathedral to raise funds for 900th Anniversary. Still turns out for his original club, Stroud CC, whenever he can. Runs six miles a day to keep fit and drinks up to 20 cups of tea a day.
Best batting: 128* England v Australia, Old Trafford 1989
Best bowling: 1-4 Gloucestershire v West Indians, Bristol 1991

1994 Season

	M	Inns	NO	Runs	HS	Avge	100s	50s	Ct	St	O	M	Runs	Wkts	Avge	Best	5wl	10wM
Test																		
All First	19	34	8	901	85 *	34.65	-	4	58	1								
1-day Int																		
NatWest	1	1	0	10	10	10.00	-	-	1	-								
B & H	1	1	0	31	31	31.00	-	-	2	-								
Sunday	14	13	0	196	70	15.07	-	1	10	1								

71. How many Test wickets did Shane Warne claim in the calendar year 1993?

	M	Inns	NO	Runs	HS	Avge	100s	50s	Ct	St	Balls	Runs	Wkts	Avge	Best	5wI	10wM
Test	36	58	11	1255	128 *	26.70	1	4	90	8							
All First	301	436	98	9469	128 *	28.01	4	43	701	94	38	53	1	53.00	1-4	-	-
1-day Int	26	19	6	261	50	20.07	-	1	26	5							
NatWest	31	20	5	304	42 *	20.26	-	-	37	7							
B & H	45	32	10	454	51	20.63	-	1	43	8							
Sunday	159	117	27	2005	108	22.27	1	6	131	25							

SALES, D. J. Northamptonshire

Name: David John Sales
Role: Right-hand bat, right-arm medium bowler
Born: 3 December 1977, Carshalton, Surrey
Height: 6ft **Weight:** 12st 4lbs
Nickname: Jumble
County debut: 1994 (one-day)
Parents: John and Daphne
Marital status: Single
Family links with cricket:
Father played club cricket
Education: Cumnor House Prep School,
Croydon; Caterham Boys' School
Qualifications: 7 GCSEs, cricket coach
Off-season: Helping with sport at Cumnor
House Prep School and touring with England
U19
Overseas tours. England U15 to South Africa
1993; England U19 to West Indies 1994-95
Cricketers particularly admired:
Graham Gooch, Brian Lara
Other sports followed: Football, rugby, hockey, golf
Relaxations: Golf and fishing
Extras: Youngest batsman to score a 50 in the Sunday League. Played for England U17
against India in 1994

72. Which off-break bowler, and South Africa's leading Test
wicket-taker with 150 victims, died on 25 February 1994?

1994 Season

	M	Inns	NO	Runs	HS	Avge	100s	50s	Ct	St	O	M	Runs	Wkts	Avge	Best	5wl	10wM
Test																		
All First																		
1-day Int																		
NatWest																		
B & H																		
Sunday	1	1	1	70	70 *	-		-	1	-	-							

Career Performances

	M	Inns	NO	Runs	HS	Avge	100s	50s	Ct	St	Balls	Runs	Wkts	Avge	Best	5wl	10wM
Test																	
All First																	
1-day Int																	
NatWest																	
B & H																	
Sunday	1	1	1	70	70 *	-		-	1	-	-						

SALISBURY, I. D. K.   Sussex

Name: Ian David Kenneth Salisbury
Role: Right-hand bat, leg-break
Born: 21 January 1970, Northampton
Height: 5ft 11in **Weight:** 12st
Nickname: Budgie, Sals
County debut: 1989
County cap: 1991
Test debut: 1992
Tests: 7
One-Day Internationals: 4
50 wickets in a season: 2
1st-Class 50s: 4
1st-Class 5 w. in innings: 14
1st-Class 10 w. in match: 2
1st-Class catches: 89
One-Day 5 w. in innings: 1
Place in batting averages: 222nd av. 17.42
(1993 183rd av. 21.66)
Place in bowling averages: 45th av. 27.83
(1993 108th av. 37.16)
Strike rate: 58.04 (career 68.23)
Parents: Dave and Margaret

Wife and date of marriage: Emma Louise, 25 September 1993
Family links with cricket: 'Dad is vice-president of my first club, Brixworth'
Education: Moulton Comprehensive, Northampton
Qualifications: 7 O-levels, NCA coaching certificate
Off-season: Touring with England A
Overseas tours: England A to Pakistan 1990-91, to Bermuda and West Indies 1991-92, to India 1994-95; England to India and Sri Lanka 1992-93, to West Indies 1993-94
Cricketers particularly admired: 'Any that keep performing day in, day out, for both country and county'
Other sports followed: Most sports
Relaxations: 'Spending time with wife, Emma, meeting friends and relaxing with them and eating out – with good wine'
Extras: Picked to play two Tests for England against Pakistan in 1992, 'proudest moments of my career.' Originally selected for England A tour to Australia 1992-93 but was asked to stay on in India and played in the first two Tests of the series. In 1992 was named Young Player of the Year by both the Wombwell Cricket Lovers and the Cricket Writers. One of *Wisden*'s Five Cricketers of the Year 1993
Opinions on cricket: 'Players should be asked for their opinion on changes in the game, before authorities make the changes themselves.'
Best batting: 68 Sussex v Derbyshire, Hove 1990
Best bowling: 7-54 Sussex v Yorkshire, Hove 1992

1994 Season

	M	Inns	NO	Runs	HS	Avge	100s	50s	Ct	St	O	M	Runs	Wkts	Avge	Best	5wI	10wM
Test	1	2	1	6	6 *	6.00	-	-	-	-	44	6	121	1	121.00	1-53	-	-
All First	16	25	6	331	49	17.42	-	-	19	-	474	143	1336	48	27.83	6-55	3	-
1-day Int																		
NatWest	1	1	0	0	0	0.00	-	-	-	-	12	1	44	1	44.00	1-44	-	
B & H	1	0	0	0	0	-	-	-	-	-	9	0	41	1	41.00	1-41	-	
Sunday	8	7	5	49	13 *	24.50	-	-	1	-	52	0	300	5	60.00	2-24	-	

Career Performances

	M	Inns	NO	Runs	HS	Avge	100s	50s	Ct	St	Balls	Runs	Wkts	Avge	Best	5wI	10wM
Test	7	13	1	205	50	17.08	-	1	3	-	1405	933	16	58.31	4-163	-	-
All First	120	145	41	1801	68	17.31	-	4	89	-	23063	12335	338	36.49	7-54	14	2
1-day Int	4	2	1	7	5	7.00	-	-	1	-	186	177	5	35.40	3-41	-	
NatWest	12	8	3	29	14 *	5.80	-	-	3	-	750	446	14	31.85	3-28	-	
B & H	11	7	4	54	17 *	18.00	-	-	3	-	633	420	13	32.30	3-40	-	
Sunday	63	38	13	291	27 *	11.64	-	-	18	-	2418	1968	56	35.14	5-30	1	

SARGEANT, N. F.   Surrey

Name: Neil Fredrick Sargeant
Role: Right-hand bat, wicket-keeper,
off-spin bowler
Born: 8 November 1965, Hammersmith
Height: 5ft 8in **Weight:** 11st 2lbs
Nickname: Sarge, Bilko, Grubby
County debut: 1989
1st-Class catches: 109
1st-Class stumpings: 16
Place in batting averages: 241st av. 15.09
Parents: Barry and Christine
Marital status: Single
Family links with cricket: Brother Lee
plays for the same club side,
Harrow Town CC
Education: Grange Primary School;
Whitmore High School
Qualifications: 2 O-levels, SAC cricket
coaching award, 'professional handyman'

Career outside cricket: Whatever pays the most
Overseas teams played for: Green Point, South Africa 1987-89; United, South Africa 1991
Cricketers particularly admired: Alan Knott, Bob Taylor, Richie Ryall, Alec Stewart,
Jack Russell, Danny Taylor
Other sports followed: Football, golf, horse racing
Relaxations: Horse racing, music
Extras: Played football for Tottenham Hotspur Youth Team
Opinions on cricket: 'I think we are heading the right way with all four-day matches. I
would also like to see 12-month contracts.'
Best batting: 49 Surrey v Lancashire, Old Trafford 1991
Best bowling: 1-88 Surrey v Gloucestershire, Guildford 1991

1994 Season

	M	Inns	NO	Runs	HS	Avge	100s	50s	Ct	St	O	M	Runs	Wkts	Avge	Best	5wI	10wM
Test																		
All First	9	13	2	166	46	15.09	-	-	18	-								
1-day Int																		
NatWest																		
B & H																		
Sunday	4	2	1	14	11 *	14.00	-	-	1	-								

	M	Inns	NO	Runs	HS	Avge	100s	50s	Ct	St	Balls	Runs	Wkts	Avge	Best	5wl	10wM
Test																	
All First	50	65	11	778	49	14.40	-	-	109	16	30	88	1	88.00	1-88	-	-
1-day Int																	
NatWest																	
B & H																	
Sunday	10	5	2	50	22	16.66	-	-	6	-							

SAXELBY, M.   Durham

Name: Mark Saxelby
Role: Left-hand bat, right-arm medium bowler
Born: 4 January 1969, Newark
Height: 6ft 4in **Weight:** 16st 7lbs
Nickname: Sax
County debut: 1989 (Nottinghamshire), 1994 (Durham)
1000 runs in a season: 1
1st-Class 100s: 2
1st-Class 50s: 16
1st-Class catches: 13
One-day 100s: 1
Place in batting averages: 94th av. 34.43 (1993 109th av. 31.00)
Parents: Ken and Margaret
Marital status: Single

Family links with cricket: Brother Kevin played for Notts; father played local cricket
Education: Nottingham High School; Nottingham University
Qualifications: 7 O-levels, 2 A-levels
Career outside cricket: Student
Off-season: Studying at university
Overseas teams played for: Hutt CC, New Zealand 1989-91
Cricketers particularly admired: Derek Randall
Other sports followed: Most sports, especially rugby
Injuries: Back injury, missed one month
Relaxations: Cinema, pubs, walking
Opinions on cricket: 'There should be 100 overs in four-day cricket, not 110. Cricketers should be paid better wages. A course should be set up so that cricketers can train as qualified PE teachers during the winter.'

Best batting: 181 Durham v Derbyshire, Chesterfield 1994
Best bowling: 3-41 Nottinghamshire v Derbyshire, Derby 1991

1994 Season

	M	Inns	NO	Runs	HS	Avge	100s	50s	Ct	St	O	M	Runs	Wkts	Avge	Best	5wl	10wM
Test																		
All First	17	32	0	1102	181	34.43	2	4	4	-								
1-day Int																		
NatWest	2	2	0	13	13	6.50	-	-	-	-								
B & H	1	1	0	12	12	12.00	-	-	-	-								
Sunday	11	10	1	329	79 *	36.55	-	4	3	-								

Career Performances

	M	Inns	NO	Runs	HS	Avge	100s	50s	Ct	St	Balls	Runs	Wkts	Avge	Best	5wl	10wM
Test																	
All First	53	90	7	2642	181	31.83	2	16	13	-	1086	765	9	85.00	3-41	-	-
1-day Int																	
NatWest	6	6	1	113	41	22.60	-	-	2	-	166	132	4	33.00	2-42	-	
B & H	5	4	0	49	32	12.25	-	-	-	-	156	118	1	118.00	1-36	-	
Sunday	54	44	7	1074	100 *	29.02	1	5	11	-	936	817	22	37.13	4-29	-	

SCHOFIELD, C. J.   Yorkshire

Name: Christopher John Schofield
Role: Right-hand bat
Born: 21 March 1976, Barnsley
Height: 5ft 7in **Weight:** 11st
Nickname: Scof, Linford
County debut: No first-team appearance
Parents: John and Pat
Marital status: Single
Family links with cricket:
Father played local league cricket
Education: Kingstone School
Qualifications: 6 GCSEs
Off-season: Touring with England U19 and
taking senior coaching course
Overseas tours: England U19 to Sri Lanka
1993-94, to West Indies 1994-95
Cricketers particularly admired:
Carlisle Best, Desmond Haynes
Other sports followed: Football, rugby league

Injuries: Back problem, missed two weeks. Bruised ribs and lung, missed two-three weeks
Extras: Played for England U19 in home series against India 1994
Opinions on cricket: 'Cricket needs to be made more attractive to public, e.g. televised county cricket leading to more sponsorship.'

SCOTT, C. W. Durham

Name: Christopher Wilmot Scott
Role: Right-hand bat, wicket-keeper
Born: 23 January 1964, Lincoln
Height: 5ft 8in **Weight:** 11st
Nickname: George
County debut: 1981 (Nottinghamshire), 1992 (Durham)
County cap: 1988 (Nottinghamshire)
1st-Class 50s: 12
1st-Class 100s: 2
1st-Class catches: 245
1st-Class stumpings: 17
Place in batting averages: 183rd av. 22.33 (1993 218th av. 16.33)
Parents: Kenneth and Kathleen
Wife and date of marriage: Jacqui, 18 March 1989
Family links with cricket: Fathers and brothers all play for Collingham, Lincoln

Education: Robert Pattinson Comprehensive, North Hykeham, Lincoln
Qualifications: 4 O-levels, intermediate and advanced cricket coach
Career outside cricket: Farming
Overseas tours: Durham to Zimbabwe 1991-92
Overseas teams played for: Poverty Bay, New Zealand 1983-84; Queensland University 1985-86, 1987-88; Rotorua, New Zealand 1989-90
Cricketers particularly admired: Ian Botham, Alan Knott, Bruce French
Other sports followed: Rugby union, football (Lincoln City), golf
Relaxations: Rugby, football, skiing, golf (occasionally), Chinese food, travel, current affairs
Extras: One of the youngest players to make Championship debut for Nottinghamshire – 17 years 157 days. Equalled the Nottinghamshire record for most catches in a match with ten against Derbyshire in 1988. Left Nottinghamshire at end of 1991 season to join Durham
Opinions on cricket: '100 overs in a day is plenty.'
Best batting: 108 Durham v Surrey, Darlington 1994

1994 Season

	M	Inns	NO	Runs	HS	Avge	100s	50s	Ct	St	O	M	Runs	Wkts	Avge	Best	5wI	10wM
Test																		
All First	20	33	3	670	108	22.33	2	3	56	2								
1-day Int																		
NatWest	2	1	0	2	2	2.00	-	-	2	-								
B & H	1	1	0	11	11	11.00	-	-	1	-								
Sunday	15	11	3	147	45	18.37	-	-	15	5								

Career Performances

	M	Inns	NO	Runs	HS	Avge	100s	50s	Ct	St	Balls	Runs	Wkts	Avge	Best	5wI	10wM
Test																	
All First	115	153	29	2709	108	21.84	2	12	245	17	6	10	0	-	-	-	-
1-day Int																	
NatWest	7	1	0	2	2	2.00	-	-	7	-							
B & H	6	5	1	42	18	10.50	-	-	2	-							
Sunday	45	27	9	307	45	17.05	-	-	43	7							

SEAL, P. J.   Lancashire

Name: Peter John Seal
Role: Right-hand bat, right-arm medium-fast bowler
Born: 16 April 1976, Rossendale
Height: 6ft **Weight:** 12st 9lbs
Nickname: Les, Sealo, Sealy
County debut: No first-team appearance
Parents: John and Kathleen
Marital status: Single
Family links with cricket: Father played 1st XI cricket for Rawtenstall in the Lancashire League
Education: Haslingden High School, Rossendale
Qualifications: 7 GCSEs, BTEC Business Studies
Cricketers particularly admired: Ian Botham, Michael Bevan, Merv Hughes
Other sports followed: Football (Blackburn Rovers)
Injuries: Missed most of the season
Relaxations: Listening to music, reading sports books

Extras: Represented England U17 against South Africa in 1993
Opinions on cricket: 'The game is becoming far too easy for batsmen – protection, no more than a certain amount of short balls per over, etc.'

SEARLE, J. P.   Durham

Name: Jason Paul Searle
Role: Right-hand bat, off-spin bowler
Born: 16 May 1976, Bath
Height: 5ft 10in **Weight:** 11st 7lbs
Nickname: Shaggy
County debut: 1994
Parents: Paul and Chris
Marital status: Single
Family links with cricket: Father played
for Chippenham and Wiltshire
Education: John Bentley School, Calne;
Wiltshire and Swindon Building College
Qualifications: 6 GCSEs, bricklayer
Career outside cricket: Bricklayer and
footballer
Off-season: Touring with England U19
Overseas tours: England U19 to West Indies
1994-95
Cricketers particularly admired:
Ian Botham, Robin Smith
Other sports followed: Football
Injuries: Bruised hand, missed one week
Relaxations: Fishing and watching television
Opinions on cricket: 'The game should be win or lose, so there is a result after every game.'
Best batting: 5* Durham v Lancashire, Stockton 1994

1994 Season

	M	Inns	NO	Runs	HS	Avge	100s	50s	Ct	St	O	M	Runs	Wkts	Avge	Best	5wI	10wM
Test																		
All First	1	2	2	5	5*	-	-	-	-	-	1	0	7	0	-	-	-	-
1-day Int																		
NatWest																		
B & H																		
Sunday																		

	M	Inns	NO	Runs	HS	Avge	100s	50s	Ct	St	Balls	Runs	Wkts	Avge	Best	5wl	10wM
Test																	
All First	1	2	2	5	5*	-	-	-	-	-	6	7	0	-	-	-	-
1-day Int																	
NatWest																		
B & H																		
Sunday																		

SEYMOUR, A. C. H. Worcestershire

Name: Adam Charles Hilton Seymour
Role: Left-hand bat, right-arm medium bowler
Born: 7 December 1967, Royston, Cambridgeshire
Height: 6ft 3in **Weight:** 13st 7lbs
Nickname: Zog, Zoggy
County debut: 1988 (Essex), 1992 (Worcestershire)
1st-Class 50s: 7
1st-Class 100s: 2
1st-Class catches: 17
Place in batting averages: (1993 160th av. 23.70)
Parents: Roger and Julie
Wife and date of marriage: Aundrea, 25 September 1993
Family links with cricket: Father captained his school side
Education: Millfield School
Qualifications: Coaching award
Career outside cricket: 'Work for father in his pub'
Off-season: Playing and coaching cricket in New Zealand
Overseas tours: Millfield School to Barbados 1987; Worcestershire to South Africa 1992
Overseas teams played for: Willetton District, Perth 1992-93
Cricketers particularly admired: Graham Gooch, Keith Fletcher
Other sports followed: Football, rugby and most sports
Relaxations: 'Eating out with my wife, music, golf, etc.'
Extras: First played for Essex 2nd XI in 1984, aged 16, scoring 100 on debut. In 1989 was the county's leading batsman in second-team cricket. Left Essex at end of 1991 season to join Worcestershire. Released by Worcestershire at end of 1994 season
Best batting: 157 Essex v Glamorgan, Cardiff 1991

1994 Season

	M	Inns	NO	Runs	HS	Avge	100s	50s	Ct	St	O	M	Runs	Wkts	Avge	Best	5wl	10wM
Test																		
All First	3	5	0	179	87	35.80	-	1	-	-								
1-day Int																		
NatWest	3	3	0	55	25	18.33	-	-	-	-	2	0	5	1	5.00	1-5	-	
B & H	1	1	0	3	3	3.00	-	-	-	-								
Sunday	5	5	0	111	57	22.20	-	1	3	-								

Career Performances

	M	Inns	NO	Runs	HS	Avge	100s	50s	Ct	St	Balls	Runs	Wkts	Avge	Best	5wl	10wM
Test																	
All First	36	62	5	1699	157	29.80	2	7	17	-	24	27	0	-	-	-	-
1-day Int																	
NatWest	4	4	0	55	25	13.75	-	-	1	-	12	5	1	5.00	1-5	-
B & H	6	5	0	55	23	11.00	-	-	-	-							
Sunday	16	14	0	189	57	13.50	-	1	6	-							

SHADFORD, D. J.   Lancashire

Name: Darren James Shadford
Role: Right-hand bat, right-arm medium fast bowler
Born: 4 March 1975, Oldham, Lancashire
Height: 6ft 3in **Weight:** 14st
Nickname: Dead Beat, Shed Head, Amoeba
Parents: Ken and Sue
County debut: 1994 (one-day)
Marital status: Single
Family links with cricket: Father and brother play club cricket
Education: Breeze Hill High School; Oldham College of Technology
Qualifications: Information Technology, BTEC in Business and Finance. 'No O's, no A's, no degrees, but have got First Star in canoe training and teaching'
Off-season: Playing club cricket in Australia
Overseas teams played for: Gold Coast Cricket and District Club 1994-95
Cricketers particularly admired: Paul Thompson, Peter Sleep, Peter Seal
Other sports followed: Any

Relaxations: Listening to music. Socialising and playing other sports
Extras: Represented Oldham at cricket, football and athletics
Opinions on cricket: 'Make the balls bigger and the bats wider.'

1994 Season

	M	Inns	NO	Runs	HS	Avge	100s	50s	Ct	St	O	M	Runs	Wkts	Avge	Best	5wI	10wM
Test																		
All First																		
1-day Int																		
NatWest																		
B & H																		
Sunday	3	0	0	0	0	-	-	-	1	-	8	0	42	0	-		-	-

Career Performances

	M	Inns	NO	Runs	HS	Avge	100s	50s	Ct	St	Balls		Runs	Wkts	Avge	Best	5wI	10wM
Test																		
All First																		
1-day Int																		
NatWest																		
B & H																		
Sunday	3	0	0	0	0	-	-	-	1	-	48		42	0	-		-	-

SHAH, O. A. Middlesex

Name: Owais Alam Shah
Role: Right-hand bat, off-spin bowler
Born: 22 October 1978, Karachi, Pakistan
Height: 6ft **Weight:** 12st
Nickname: Chetoo
County debut: No first-team appearance
Parents: Jamshed and Mahjabeen
Marital status: Single
Family links with cricket:
Father played up to college level
Education: Berkley's Junior School; Isleworth
and Syon School
Qualifications: Taking GCSEs in 1995
Off-season: Indoor nets and training at Finchley
Cricketers particularly admired: Robin
Smith, Viv Richards, Shane Warne, Mike
Atherton, Waqar Younis
Other sports followed: Table tennis, basketball

Relaxations: Swimming and listening to music
Extras: Middlesex Sports Federation Award winner. Man of the Series in U17 Test series against India 1994. Played for Middlesex U13, Ken Barrington Trophy (National Champions) and Middlesex U15, county competition winners, as captain. Scored record 232 for England U15 against England U16
Opinions on cricket: 'I am in favour of the third umpire at first-class level. I also approve of overseas players playing in the counties because it gives fellow players a different experience in the game.'

SHAHID, N.   Surrey

Name: Nadeem Shahid
Role: Right-hand bat, leg-spin/googly/flipper bowler
Born: 23 April 1969, Karachi
Height: 6ft **Weight:** 11st 9lbs
Nickname: Prince of Darkness, Nad, Jo
County debut: 1989 (Essex)
1000 runs in a season: 1
1st-Class 50s: 14
1st-Class 100s: 2
1st-Class catches: 64
Place in batting averages: 178th av.23.28 (1993 178th av. 22.50)
Strike rate: (career 61.22)
Parents: Ahmed and Salma
Marital status: Engaged
Family links with cricket:
Brother plays in the local Two Counties League for Felixstowe

Education: Stoke High; Northgate High; Ipswich School; Plymouth Polytechnic
Qualifications: 6 O-levels, 1 A-level, coaching certificate
Career outside cricket: 'Playing golf and taking money off Darren Robinson'
Off-season: Playing and coaching for Fairfield CC, Sydney
Overseas tours: Ipswich School to Barbados (Sir Garfield Sobers Trophy) 1987; England (South) to N Ireland (Youth World Tournament) 1988
Overseas teams played for: Gosnells, Perth, Western Australia 1989-91; Faifield, Sydney 1992-93
Cricketers particularly admired: Ian Botham, Abdul Qadir and Mark Waugh, Nasser Hussain
Other sports followed: Golf, tennis, badminton, squash, most ball sports
Relaxations: 'Playing golf, eating out, going to cinema, spending time with my fiancée, Sarah'

Extras: Youngest Suffolk player aged 17. Played for HMC, MCC Schools, ESCA U19, NCA Young Cricketers (Lord's and International Youth tournament in Belfast), England U25 and at every level for Suffolk. TSB Young Player of the Year 1987, winner of the *Daily Telegraph* Bowling Award 1987 and 1988, Cricket Society's All-rounder of the Year 1988 and Laidlaw Young Player of the Year for Essex 1993. Essex Society Player of the Year 1993. Released by Essex at end of 1994 season and signed for Surrey

Opinions on cricket: 'The pitches in the 2nd XI competition should be greatly improved, which is essential for producing good cricketers. All players should be treated equally.'

Best batting: 132 Essex v Kent, Chelmsford 1992
Best bowling: 3-91 Essex v Surrey, The Oval 1990

1994 Season

	M	Inns	NO	Runs	HS	Avge	100s	50s	Ct	St	O	M	Runs	Wkts	Avge	Best	5wI	10wM
Test																		
All First	10	18	4	326	91	23.28	-	1	13	-	30	6	106	3	35.33	2-20	-	-
1-day Int																		
NatWest	1	1	1	85	85 *	-	-	1	1	-								
B & H	2	0	0	0	0	-	-	-	-	-								
Sunday	7	7	0	113	41	16.14	-	-	2	-	3	0	11	0	-		-	-

Career Performances

	M	Inns	NO	Runs	HS	Avge	100s	50s	Ct	St	Balls	Runs	Wkts	Avge	Best	5wI	10wM
Test																	
All First	66	99	16	2562	132	30.86	2	14	64	-	1653	1081	27	40.03	3-91	-	-
1-day Int																	
NatWest	4	3	1	115	85 *	57.50	-	1	3	-	18	0	1	0.00	1-0	-	
B & H	8	4	0	51	42	12.75	-	-	1	-							
Sunday	43	34	3	561	64	18.09	-	1	14	-	18	11	0	-		-	-

SHAW, A. D.   Glamorgan

Name: Adrian David Shaw
Role: Right-hand bat, wicket-keeper
Born: 17 February 1972, Neath
Height: 5ft 11in **Weight:** 12st 7lbs
Nickname: Shawsy, Teflon, Iron Gloves, Cymbals, Clangers, Gloves
County debut: 1992 (one-day), 1994 (first-class)
1st-Class catches: 6
Parents: David Colin and Christina
Marital status: Single
Family links with cricket: 'Dad's been known to have the odd bottle of Holsten Pils up the local cricket club.'

Education: Llangatwe Comprehensive; Neath Tertiary College, 'the Market Tavern, Talk of the Abbey and the Pink Coconut – once!'

Qualifications: 9 O-levels, 3 A-levels, cricket coaching awards

Career outside cricket: Sales rep. for Pickering Safety Products and Leigh's Paints

Off-season: 'Working for former Welsh rugby captain David Pickering as above. Avoiding going for the evening with James Williams and Mike Morgan. Playing for Neath RFC in the Welsh Heineken League'

Overseas tours: Welsh Schools to Barbados 1988; England YC to New Zealand 1990-91

Cricketers particularly admired: Wayne Larkins, Richard Ellison, David Ripley, Steve Marsh, Damian D'Oliveira

Other sports followed: 'Rugby, rugby, and the odd game of rugby as well'

Injuries: Broke collar-bone playing rugby, did not miss any cricket

Relaxations: 'I spend a lot of spare time teaching my colleague, Stuart Phelps, the fundamentals of social intercourse, without a great deal of success, to be perfectly frank.'

Extras: One of youngest players (18 years 7 days) to play first-class rugby for Neath. Only current county cricketer playing first-class rugby. Played for Neath against Swansea six days after playing against Zimbabwe for Glamorgan, and had the 'pleasure' of marking Scott Gibbs. Neath RFC Back of the Year 1993-94. Hopes to become the first player for a number of years to play against South Africa in two sports when Neath play them.

Opinions on cricket: 'Greatest game in the world, apart from rugby, football, golf, tennis, etc. According to James Williams, because I was educated in a state school, this question cannot be applied to me! However, I would like to see more backdrops and bouncing cobras around the county circuit.'

Best batting: 14 Glamorgan v Middlesex, Lord's 1994

1994 Season

	M	Inns	NO	Runs	HS	Avge	100s	50s	Ct	St	O	M	Runs	Wkts	Avge	Best	5wI	10wM
Test																		
All First	3	3	1	18	14	9.00	-	-	6	-								
1-day Int																		
NatWest																		
B & H																		
Sunday	1	0	0	0	0	-	-	-	-	-								

Career Performances

	M	Inns	NO	Runs	HS	Avge	100s	50s	Ct	St	Balls	Runs	Wkts	Avge	Best	5wl	10wM
Test																	
All First	3	3	1	18	14	9.00	-	-	6	-							
1-day Int																	
NatWest																	
B & H																	
Sunday	2	0	0	0	0	-	-	-	-	-							

SHEERAZ, K. P.   Gloucestershire

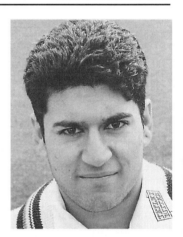

Name: Kamran Pashah Sheeraz
Role: Right-hand bat, right-arm
medium-fast bowler
Born: 28 December 1973, Wellington,
Shropshire
Height: 6ft **Weight:** 12st
County debut: 1994
Parents: Mohammed and Shamim
Marital status: Single
Family links with cricket:
Brother, Humeran, a county youth player.
Cousin, Ali, plays for Berkshire Colts
Education: Licensed Victuallers School,
Ascot; East Berks College of Further
Education; East London University
Qualifications: GCSE and BTEC National
Diploma (Business and Finance)
Off-season: Playing and coaching in Pakistan
Cricketers particularly admired:
Johnny Wardle, Imran Khan, Frank Tyson, Dennis Lillee, Ray Lindwall, Richard Hadlee
Other sports followed: Boxing and football
Injuries: Damaged left shoulder, missed two weeks
Relaxations: Reading, music and weight-lifting
Extras: Toured Australia 1991-92 with Berkshire Youth XI and attended Bull Development
of Excellence at Lilleshall 1992. Received Texaco (U16) outstanding bowling award (seven
wickets in innings) from Ted Dexter. Represented Bedfordshire in Minor Counties
Championship. Senior NABC 67kg Boxing Champion. England Amateur Boxing International
Opinions on cricket: 'Any measures designed to redress the balance of bat over ball would
be welcomed. Cricket should be played in primary and secondary/comprehensive schools
to enable the game to survive and to provide a stronger base for the future for first-class
players.'

486

Best batting: 1* Gloucestershire v Northamptonshire, Bristol 1994
Best bowling: 2-34 Gloucestershire v Northamptonshire, Bristol 1994

1994 Season

	M	Inns	NO	Runs	HS	Avge	100s	50s	Ct	St	O	M	Runs	Wkts	Avge	Best	5wI	10wM
Test																		
All First	1	2	2	1	1*	-	-	-	-	-	15	2	34	2	17.00	2-34	-	-
1-day Int																		
NatWest																		
B & H																		
Sunday	1	0	0	0	0	-	-	-	1	-	6	1	30	0	-		-	-

Career Performances

	M	Inns	NO	Runs	HS	Avge	100s	50s	Ct	St	Balls		Runs	Wkts	Avge	Best	5wI	10wM
Test																		
All First	1	2	2	1	1*	-	-	-	-	-	90		34	2	17.00	2-34	-	-
1-day Int																		
NatWest																		
B & H																		
Sunday	1	0	0	0	0	-	-	-	1	-	36		30	0	-		-	-

SHERIYAR, A.   Leicestershire

Name: Alamgir Sheriyar
Role: Right-hand bat, left-arm fast bowler
Born: 15 November 1973, Birmingham
Height: 6ft 1in **Weight:** 13st
County debut: 1993 (one-day),
1994 (first-class)
Place in bowling averages: 103rd av. 36.36
Parents: Mohammed Zaman and
Safia Sultana
Marital status: Single
Education: George Dixon Secondary School,
Birmingham; Joseph Chamberlain Sixth
Form College, Birmingham; Oxford Brookes
University
Qualifications: 6 O-levels, studying for
BEng (Hons) Combined Engineering
Off-season: Playing overseas
Cricketers particularly admired:
Wasim Akram, Imran Khan

Other sports followed: Football, basketball

Relaxations: Computing, listening to different types of music and spending time with loved ones

Extras: Played for English Schools U17 and has also played in the Indoor National League. Became only the second player to take a hat-trick on his first-class debut

Opinions on cricket: 'The rules favour the batsman too much – the bouncer rule especially. This removes one of the fast bowler's weapons.'

Best batting: 16* Leicestershire v South Africans, Leicester 1994

Best bowling: 4-44 Leicestershire v Durham, Durham University 1994

1994 Season

	M	Inns	NO	Runs	HS	Avge	100s	50s	Ct	St	O	M	Runs	Wkts	Avge	Best	5wl	10wM
Test																		
All First	4	3	2	28	16 *	28.00	-	-	-	-	98	14	400	11	36.36	4-44	-	-
1-day Int																		
NatWest																			
B & H																			
Sunday	2	1	1	0	0 *	-	-	-	-	-	8	1	44	0	-		-	-

Career Performances

	M	Inns	NO	Runs	HS	Avge	100s	50s	Ct	St	Balls	Runs	Wkts	Avge	Best	5wl	10wM
Test																	
All First	4	3	2	28	16 *	28.00	-	-	-	-	588	400	11	36.36	4-44	-	-
1-day Int																	
NatWest																		
B & H																		
Sunday	3	1	1	0	0 *	-	-	-	-	-	78	73	0	-		-	-

SHINE, K. J.   Middlesex

Name: Kevin James Shine

Role: Right-hand bat, right-arm fast bowler

Born: 22 February 1969, Bracknell, Berks

Height: 6ft 3in **Weight:** 15st

Nickname: Shiney, Shoey, Ealham, The Slippery One

County debut: 1989 (Hampshire), 1994 (Middlesex)

1st-Class 5 w. in innings: 7

1st-Class 10 w. in match: 1

1st-Class catches: 11

Place in bowling averages: 119th av. 39.86 (1993 136th av. 48.83)

Strike rate: 68.82 (career 60.62)

Parents: Joe and Clair

Marital status: Single

Education: Winnersh County Primary; Maiden Erlegh Comprehensive
Qualifications: 5 O-levels, gave up A-levels to pursue a cricket career, NCA Advanced Coach
Career outside cricket: Hardware engineer for Orico Systems (computers)
Off-season: Coaching for the Middlesex Centenary Youth Trust. Keeping fit and buying a house
Overseas teams played for: Merewether, Newcastle, NSW 1990
Cricketers particularly admired: Malcolm Marshall, Cardigan Connor, Waqar Younis, Allan Donald, Api Aymes
Other sports followed: Football, basketball, motor racing
Relaxations: Eating out, mountain biking, spending time with Nicki

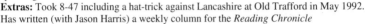

Extras: Took 8-47 including a hat-trick against Lancashire at Old Trafford in May 1992. Has written (with Jason Harris) a weekly column for the *Reading Chronicle*
Opinions on cricket: 'The difference between the Middlesex and Hampshire dressing rooms is unbelievable. Middlesex lads love a good ruck, Angus Fraser especially, even when he gets a wicket he has a ruck with someone, either on the pitch or in the crowd. The game is still 100 per cent in batsmen's favour – they've got it so easy!'
Best batting: 26* Hampshire v Middlesex, Lord's 1989
Best bowling: 8-47 Hampshire v Lancashire, Old Trafford 1992

1994 Season

	M	Inns	NO	Runs	HS	Avge	100s	50s	Ct	St	O	M	Runs	Wkts	Avge	Best	5wI	10wM
Test																		
All First	13	8	5	39	14 *	13.00	-	-	4	-	332.4	76	1156	29	39.86	4-79	-	-
1-day Int																		
NatWest	1	0	0	0	0	-	-	-	-	-	12	3	31	3	10.33	3-31	-	
B & H																			
Sunday	8	1	1	1	1 *	-	-	-	1	-	50.5	2	303	7	43.28	2-23	-	

Career Performances

	M	Inns	NO	Runs	HS	Avge	100s	50s	Ct	St	Balls	Runs	Wkts	Avge	Best	5wI	10wM
Test																	
All First	67	55	26	297	26 *	10.24	-	-	11	-	8973	5712	148	38.59	8-47	7	1
1-day Int																	
NatWest	2	0	0	0	0	-	-	-	-	-	129	92	3	30.66	3-31	-	
B & H	4	1	0	0	0	0.00	-	-	-	-	194	167	4	41.75	4-68	-	
Sunday	15	3	3	4	2 *	-	-	-	1	-	617	561	15	37.40	2-15	-	

SILVERWOOD, C. E. W. — Yorkshire

Name: Christopher Eric Wilfred Silverwood
Role: Right-hand bat, right-arm
fast-medium bowler
Born: 5 March 1975, Pontefract
Height: 6ft **Weight:** 13st 4lbs
Nickname: Spoon, Silvers
County debut: 1993
1st-Class catches: 3
Place in batting averages: 265th av. 10.58
Place in bowling averages: 82nd av. 32.70
Strike rate: 55.33 (career 57.64)
Parents: Brenda Millicent
Marital status: Single
Education: Gibson Lane School, Kippax;
Garforth Comprehensive
Qualifications: 8 GCSEs, City and Guilds in
Leisure and Recreation
Off-season: Keeping fit and coaching
Overseas teams played for: Wellington, Cape
Town 1993-94
Cricketers particularly admired: Ian Botham
Other sports followed: Rugby league (Castleford), karate
Extras: Black belt in karate. Attended the Yorkshire Cricket Academy. Represented
Yorkshire at athletics. Played for England U19 in the home series against India in 1994
Best batting: 26 Yorkshire v Essex, Headingley 1994
Best bowling: 4-67 Yorkshire v Durham, Durham University 1994

1994 Season

	M	Inns	NO	Runs	HS	Avge	100s	50s	Ct	St	O	M	Runs	Wkts	Avge	Best	5wI	10wM
Test																		
All First	9	15	3	127	26	10.58	-	-	2	-	249	46	883	27	32.70	4-67	-	-
1-day Int																		
NatWest	1	1	1	8	8 *	-	-	-	-	-	11	2	38	1	38.00	1-38	-	
B & H																		
Sunday	8	3	2	16	9	16.00	-	-	1	-	58.3	3	260	15	17.33	3-29	-	

> 73. Which former Pakistani batsman and captain retired from
> international cricket with an average of 52.57 after 124 Tests?

	M	Inns	NO	Runs	HS	Avge	100s	50s	Ct	St	Balls	Runs	Wkts	Avge	Best	5wI	10wM
Test																	
All First	10	16	3	127	26	9.76	-	-	3	-	1614	958	28	34.21	4-67	-	-
1-day Int																	
NatWest	1	1	1	8	8 *	-	-	-	-	-	66	38	1	38.00	1-38	-	
B & H	1	1	0	2	2	2.00	-	-	-	-	42	19	1	19.00	1-19	-	
Sunday	11	4	2	16	9	8.00	-	-	2	-	447	330	16	20.62	3-29	-	

SIMMONS, P. V. Leicestershire

Name: Philip Verant Simmons
Role: Right-hand bat, right-arm medium bowler
Born: 18 April 1963, Port-of-Spain, Trinidad
County debut: 1994
Test debut: 1988
Tests: 19
One-Day Internationals: 83
1st-Class 50s: 35
1st-Class 100s: 13
1st-Class 200s: 2
1st-Class 5w. in innings: 1
1st-Class catches: 124
One-Day 100s: 5
Place in batting averages: 117th av. 31.76
Place in bowling averages: 27th av. 25.63
Strike rate: 60.61 (career 75.24)
Off-season: Playing for West Indies
Overseas tours: West Indies YC to England 1982; West Indies B to Zimbabwe 1983 and 1986; West Indies to India and Pakistan (World Cup) 1987-88, to England 1988, to Sharjah and India (Nehru Cup) 1989-90, to Sharjah 1991-92, to Australia and South Africa 1992-93, to Sharjah, India (Hero Cup) and Sri Lanka 1993-94, to India 1994-95
Overseas teams played for: Crompton, Trinidad; Trinidad and Tobago 1983-95
Extras: Suffered a bad head injury on West Indies tour to England in 1988. Appointed captain of Trinidad in 1989. Scored record 261 on his debut for Leicestershire in 1994
Best batting: 261 Leicestershire v Northamptonshire, Leicester 1994
Best bowling: 5-24 Trinidad v Windward Islands, Pointe-a-Pierre 1990-91

1994 Season

	M	Inns	NO	Runs	HS	Avge	100s	50s	Ct	St	O	M	Runs	Wkts	Avge	Best	5wI	10wM
Test																		
All First	17	30	0	953	261	31.76	1	3	23	-	300.5	81	769	30	25.63	4-68	-	-
1-day Int																		
NatWest	2	2	0	37	19	18.50	-	-	2	-	23	2	118	4	29.50	3-31	-	
B & H	2	2	0	121	64	60.50	-	2	1	-	15	2	71	1	71.00	1-29	-	
Sunday	17	17	0	660	140	38.82	1	5	7	-	89.4	2	444	17	26.11	4-19	-	

Career Performances

	M	Inns	NO	Runs	HS	Avge	100s	50s	Ct	St	Balls	Runs	Wkts	Avge	Best	5wI	10wM
Test	19	35	2	807	110	24.45	1	2	15	-	396	158	2	79.00	2-34	-	-
All First	122	215	8	7030	261	33.96	13	35	124	-	5869	2720	78	34.87	5-24	1	-
1-day Int	83	81	6	2304	122	30.72	4	12	28	-	1745	1194	40	29.85	4-3	-	
NatWest	4	4	0	84	33	21.00	-	-	2	-	234	189	5	37.80	3-31	-	
B & H	2	2	0	121	64	60.50	-	2	1	-	90	71	1	71.00	1-29	-	
Sunday	17	17	0	660	140	38.82	1	5	7	-	538	444	17	26.11	4-19	-	

SINGH, A.   Warwickshire

Name: Anurag Singh
Role: Right-hand bat, off-spin bowler
Born: 9 September 1975, Kanpur, India
Height: 5ft 10in **Weight:** 11st
Nickname: Raggy, Rag, Ragga
County debut: No first-team appearance
Parents: Bijay Kumar and Rajul
Marital status: Single
Education: King Edward's School, Birmingham
Qualifications: 12 GCSEs, 4 A-levels
Career outside cricket: 'Want to be a lawyer'
Off-season: Touring with England U19
Overseas tours: England U19 to West Indies 1994-95
Overseas teams played for: Parnell, Auckland 1988-89; Avendale, Cape Town, 1992-93; North Sydney, Sydney 1993-94
Cricketers particularly admired: Brian Lara, David Gower, Dermot Reeve
Other sports followed: Football
Relaxations: Listening to music, watching sport on television, reading, going out with family and friends

Extras: Broke school record for number of runs in a season (1102). *Daily Telegraph* regional award for batting (twice) and bowling (once). Tiger Smith Memorial Award for Warwickshire Most Promising Young Cricketer 1994, Coney Edmonds Trophy for Warwickshire Best U19 Cricketer 1994, Lord's Taverners Trophy for Best Young Cricketer 1994, Gray-Nicolls Len Newberry Award for ESCA U19 Best Player 1994. Scored two centuries for England U19 against India U19 in 1994. Scored one century against West Indies U20 and was Man of the Series 1994-95. Scored 128 for Warwickshire 2nd XI v Gloucestershire 2nd XI in 1994

Opinions on cricket: 'Should have two divisions in the County Championship to make games near the end of the season more competitive.'

SLADDIN, R. W. — Derbyshire

Name: Richard William Sladdin
Role: Right-hand bat, slow left-arm bowler
Born: 8 January 1969, Halifax
Height: 5ft 11in **Weight:** 12st 4lbs
Nickname: Slads, Boris
County debut: 1991
1st-Class 50s: 1
1st-Class 5 w. in innings: 2
1st-Class catches: 14
Place in batting averages:
(1993 217th av. 16.37)
Place in bowling averages:
(1993 128th av. 44.21)
Strike rate: (career 84.53)
Parents: Raymond and Elsie
Marital status: Single
Family links with cricket: Father watches club cricket, eldest brother Nigel plays
Education: Sowerby Bridge High School
Qualification: 5 O-levels, 1 A-level
Career outside cricket: Trainee accountant
Overseas tours: Derbyshire to Bermuda 1993
Cricketers particularly admired: Richard Hadlee, Derek Underwood, Abdul Qadir
Other sports followed: Football (Leeds United) and most other sports
Relaxations: Music, travelling, fishing, eating and drinking, clubs
Extras: Played for English Schools U19 in 1988 and 1989. Topped Derbyshire's 1993 pre-season bowling averages – four matches, 16 wickets at 5 runs each. Released by Derbyshire at end of 1994 season
Best batting: 51* Derbyshire v Durham, Durham University 1993
Best bowling: 6-58 Derbyshire v Cambridge University, Fenner's 1992

1994 Season

	M	Inns	NO	Runs	HS	Avge	100s	50s	Ct	St	O	M	Runs	Wkts	Avge	Best	5wI	10wM
Test																		
All First	3	6	0	42	20	7.00	-	-	-	-	115.1	20	427	4	106.75	2-155	-	-
1-day Int																		
NatWest																		
B & H																		
Sunday	1	0	0	0	0	-	-	-	-	-	4	0	24	0	-		-	-

Career Performances

	M	Inns	NO	Runs	HS	Avge	100s	50s	Ct	St	Balls	Runs	Wkts	Avge	Best	5wI	10wM
Test																	
All First	33	42	9	372	51 *	11.27	-	1	14	-	7862	3805	93	40.91	6-58	2	-
1-day Int																	
NatWest																	
B & H																	
Sunday	11	3	2	24	16	24.00	-	-	3	-	456	378	8	47.25	2-26	-	

SMALL, G. C.   Warwickshire

Name: Gladstone Cleophas Small
Role: Right-hand bat, right-arm
fast-medium bowler
Born: 18 October 1961, St George, Barbados
Height: 5ft 11in **Weight:** 12st
Nickname: Gladys
County debut: 1980
County cap: 1982
Benefit: 1992 (£129,500)
Test debut: 1986
Tests: 17
One-Day Internationals: 53
50 wickets in a season: 6
1st-Class 50s: 7
1st-Class 5 w. in innings: 28
1st-Class 10 w. in match: 2
1st-Class catches: 92
One-Day 5 w. in innings: 2
Place in bowling averages: 32nd av. 26.27
(1993 67th av. 29.95)
Strike rate: 56.50 (career 58.09)
Parents: Chelston and Gladys

Wife: Lois
Children: Zak
Family links with cricket: Cousin Milton Small toured England with West Indies in 1984
Education: Moseley School; Hall Green Technical College, Birmingham
Qualifications: 2 O-levels
Career outside cricket: Sports promotion company
Overseas tours: England YC to New Zealand 1979-80; England to Australia 1986-87, to India and Pakistan (World Cup) 1987-88, to India and West Indies 1989-90, to Australia 1990-91, to Australia and New Zealand (World Cup) 1991-92
Overseas teams played for: South Australia 1985-86
Cricketers particularly admired: Dennis Lillee, Malcolm Marshall, Richard Hadlee, Bob Willis
Other sports followed: Athletics, golf, tennis, soccer
Relaxations: 'Playing a round of golf; listening to music and relaxing with my wife'
Extras: Was called up for England Test squad v Pakistan at Edgbaston, July 1982, but did not play. Bowled 18-ball over v Middlesex in August 1982, with 11 no-balls. Grandfather watched him take eight wickets in the Barbados Test v West Indies in 1989-90 on his return to the land of his birth. Was Andy Lloyd's best man
Opinions on cricket: 'Four-day Championship cricket should improve the first-class game; teams have to bowl out the opposition twice instead of relying on contrived results. We should play on hard, fast and true wickets that would be beneficial to both batsmen and bowlers.'
Best batting: 70 Warwickshire v Lancashire, Old Trafford 1988
Best bowling: 7-15 Warwickshire v Nottinghamshire, Edgbaston 1988

1994 Season

	M	Inns	NO	Runs	HS	Avge	100s	50s	Ct	St	O	M	Runs	Wkts	Avge	Best	5wI	10wM
Test																		
All First	11	10	1	78	23	8.66	-	-	2	-	339	79	946	36	26.27	5-46	1	-
1-day Int																		
NatWest	3	2	0	6	5	3.00	-	-	1	-	31	7	86	2	43.00	2-14	-	
B & H	3	1	1	5	5 *	-	-	-	-	-	33	9	86	2	43.00	1-22	-	
Sunday	14	3	2	15	7 *	15.00	-	-	2	-	86.2	7	397	14	28.35	3-25	-	

Career Performances

	M	Inns	NO	Runs	HS	Avge	100s	50s	Ct	St	Balls	Runs	Wkts	Avge	Best	5wI	10wM
Test	17	24	7	263	59	15.47	-	1	9	-	3927	1871	55	34.01	5-48	2	-
All First	298	381	87	4269	70	14.52	-	7	92	-	47114	23153	811	28.54	7-15	28	2
1-day Int	53	24	9	98	18 *	6.53	-	-	7	-	2793	1942	58	33.48	4-31	-	
NatWest	41	26	7	206	33	10.84	-	-	6	-	2479	1283	44	29.15	3-22	-	
B & H	52	32	8	165	22	6.87	-	-	10	-	3002	1776	59	30.10	4-22	-	
Sunday	160	73	24	364	40 *	7.42	-	-	34	-	6771	5024	200	25.12	5-29	2	

SMITH, A. M.   Gloucestershire

Name: Andrew Michael Smith
Role: Right-hand bat, left-arm medium bowler
Born: 1 October 1967, Dewsbury, West Yorks
Height: 5ft 9in **Weight:** 11st 8lbs
Nickname: Smudge
County debut: 1991
1st-Class 50s: 1
1st-Class 5 w. in innings: 1
1st-Class catches: 4
Place in batting averages: 251st av. 13.50
Place in bowling averages: 75th av. 31.37 (1993 143rd av. 56.00)
Strike rate: 55.96 (career 65.78)
Parents: Hugh and Margaret
Wife and date of marriage: Sarah, 2 October 1993
Family links with cricket: Father and uncle both played club cricket in Yorkshire; brother plays for Ossett in the Central Yorkshire League
Education: Queen Elizabeth Grammar School, Wakefield; Exeter University
Qualification: 10 O-levels, 4 A-levels, BA (Hons) French and German
Off-season: Coaching at Gloucestershire, bringing up baby and keeping fit
Overseas tours: Queen Elizabeth Grammar School to Holland 1985; Bradford Junior Cricket League to Barbados 1986; Exeter University to Barbados 1987; Gloucestershire to Kenya 1990, to Sri Lanka 1992-93
Overseas teams played for: Waimea, New Zealand 1990; WTTU, New Zealand 1991
Cricketers particularly admired: Richard Hadlee, Graham Gooch
Other sports followed: Football (Leeds United), golf, rugby
Injuries: Broken thumb, missed five weeks
Relaxations: Crosswords, playing golf, reading
Extras: Played for English Schools U19, NAYC and represented Combined Universities in the B&H Cup in 1988 and 1990
Opinions on cricket: 'With more money coming into the game from television, I think it's high time players' salaries were raised to an acceptable level.'
Best batting: 51* Gloucestershire v Warwickshire, Bristol 1992
Best bowling: 5-40 Gloucestershire v Durham, Gateshead Fell 1994

---

74. Which Sussex, Durham and England player retired from first-class cricket in Spring 1994?

1994 Season

	M	Inns	NO	Runs	HS	Avge	100s	50s	Ct	St	O	M	Runs	Wkts	Avge	Best	5wI	10wM
Test																		
All First	12	14	2	162	29	13.50	-	-	3	-	298.3	59	1004	32	31.37	5-40	1	-
1-day Int																		
NatWest	1	1	1	1	1 *	-	-	-	-	-	12	1	41	1	41.00	1-41	-	
B & H	1	1	0	8	8	8.00	-	-	-	-	11	0	40	2	20.00	2-40	-	
Sunday	10	7	4	24	7	8.00	-	-	3	-	69	5	354	9	39.33	2-24	-	

Career Performances

	M	Inns	NO	Runs	HS	Avge	100s	50s	Ct	St	Balls	Runs	Wkts	Avge	Best	5wI	10wM
Test																	
All First	45	52	10	478	51 *	11.38	-	1	7	-	6381	3494	97	36.02	5-40	1	-
1-day Int																	
NatWest	8	3	2	15	8 *	15.00	-	-	3	-	445	269	8	33.62	3-45	-	
B & H	16	14	3	68	15 *	6.18	-	-	4	-	871	621	13	47.76	4-49	-	
Sunday	56	29	17	124	15 *	10.33	-	-	10	-	2087	1735	58	29.91	4-38	-	

SMITH, A. W. Surrey

Name: Andrew William Smith
Role: Right-hand bat, right-arm off-spin bowler
Born: 30 May 1969, Sutton, Surrey
Height: 5ft 10in **Weight:** 11st
Nickname: Martini, Snickers, Tiny
County debut: 1992 (one-day), 1993 (first-class)
1st-Class 50s: 4
1st-Class 100s: 1
1st-Class 200s: 1
1st-Class 5 w. in innings: 1
1st-Class catches: 10
Place in batting averages: 108th av. 32.75 (1993 139th av. 26.66)
Place in bowling averages: 139th av. 47.85
Strike rate: 80.14 (career 84.90)
Parents: William and Gwen
Marital status: Single
Family links with cricket: Father played for Surrey 1960-69, 'mother collects a scrap book, sister hates the game'
Education: Cheam Boys Church of England School; Sutton Manor High School

Qualifications: 7 O-levels, City & Guilds in Interior Design, NCA qualified coach
Off-season: Coaching and playing in Sydney
Overseas teams played for: Richmond, Adelaide 1989-91
Cricketers particularly admired: Graham Thorpe, Adam Hollioke, Tim May, John Emburey, Michael Bevan, Tony Pigott and all Surrey team-mates
Other sports followed: 'None! I love cricket. Cricket is life.'
Injuries: Broken toe, tendonitis in fingers. Did not miss any cricket
Relaxations: 'Sleep, spending time socialising with Graham Kersey. Letting Jason de la Pena buy me a house.'
Extras: In 1992 took catch with first touch on first-team debut in Seeboard Trophy 1992 and was named 2nd XI Bowler of the Year. In 1993 received Man of the Match award in his first NatWest game against Leicestershire and was Surrey Fielder of the Year. Mark Ramprakash hit him for the biggest six of his career at The Oval, 1994
Opinions on cricket: 'Alec Stewart and Graham Thorpe should not get better bats than me. Poorly paid profession compared to other top sports. Four-day cricket slowly producing the results. We need harder cricket and less of it.'
Best batting: 202* Surrey v Oxford University, The Oval 1994
Best bowling: 5-103 Surrey v Somerset, Bath 1994

1994 Season

	M	Inns	NO	Runs	HS	Avge	100s	50s	Ct	St	O	M	Runs	Wkts	Avge	Best	5wI	10wM
Test																		
All First	14	21	5	524	202 *	32.75	1	1	3	-	374	67	1340	28	47.85	5-103	1	-
1-day Int																		
NatWest	1	0	0	0	0	-	-	-	-	-	8	1	31	0	-	-	-	-
B & H	2	1	1	15	15 *	-	-	-	1	-	14	2	61	3	20.33	2-38	-	
Sunday	13	10	4	203	50 *	33.83	-	1	5	-	25	0	175	2	87.50	2-28	-	

Career Performances

	M	Inns	NO	Runs	HS	Avge	100s	50s	Ct	St	Balls	Runs	Wkts	Avge	Best	5wI	10wM
Test																	
All First	28	44	7	1084	202 *	29.29	1	4	10	-	2802	1727	33	52.33	5-103	1	-
1-day Int																	
NatWest	2	0	0	0	0	-	-	-	-	-	120	56	3	18.66	3-25	-	
B & H	2	1	1	15	15 *	-	-	-	1	-	84	61	3	20.33	2-38	-	
Sunday	22	17	5	367	58	30.58	-	2	12	-	150	175	2	87.50	2-28	-	

SMITH, B. F.   Leicestershire

Name: Benjamin Francis Smith
Role: Right-hand bat, right-arm
medium bowler
Born: 3 April 1972, Corby
Height: 5ft 10in **Weight:** 10st
Nickname: Smudge
County debut: 1990
1st-Class 50s: 11
1st-Class 100s: 1
1st-Class catches: 55
Place in batting averages: 118th av. 31.40
(1993 231st av. 14.61)
Parents: Janet and Keith
Marital status: Single
Family links with cricket: Both uncles
played for English Schools and
Leicestershire Young Amateurs. Father
and grandfather played local league cricket
Education: Tugby Primary; Kibworth High;
Robert Smyth, Market Harborough
Qualifications: 5 O-levels, 3 CSEs, ESB distinction
Off-season: Playing in Australia
Overseas tours: England YC to New Zealand 1990-91; Rutland Tourists to South
Africa 1992
Overseas teams played for: Alexandria, Zimbabwe 1990; Bankstown Canterbury, Sydney
1993-94
Cricketers particularly admired: Viv Richards, David Gower
Other sports followed: Most sports; plays tennis, golf and football
Relaxations: Eating out, going to cinema, playing golf, listening to good music
Extras: Played tennis for Leicestershire aged 12. Young Cricketer of the Year 1991
Best batting: 100* Leicestershire v Durham, Durham University 1992
Best bowling: 1-5 Leicestershire v Essex, Ilford 1991

1994 Season

	M	Inns	NO	Runs	HS	Avge	100s	50s	Ct	St	O	M	Runs	Wkts	Avge	Best	5wI	10wM
Test																		
All First	14	23	3	628	95	31.40	-	4	10	-								
1-day Int																		
NatWest	2	2	1	69	63 *	69.00	-	1	1	-								
B & H	2	1	0	22	22	22.00	-	-	-	-								
Sunday	16	16	1	298	56	19.86	-	1	5	-								

Career Performances

	M	Inns	NO	Runs	HS	Avge	100s	50s	Ct	St	Balls	Runs	Wkts	Avge	Best	5wI	10wM
Test																	
All First	57	86	12	2025	100 *	27.36	1	11	25	-	156	121	1	121.00	1-5	-	-
1-day Int																	
NatWest	6	5	1	134	63 *	33.50	-	1	2	-							
B & H	7	5	0	108	43	21.60	-	-	3	-							
Sunday	55	54	7	1123	97 *	23.89	-	4	9	-	18	15	0	-		-	-

SMITH, D. M. Sussex

Name: David Mark Smith
Role: Left-hand bat, right-arm medium bowler
Born: 9 January 1956, Balham
Height: 6ft 4in **Weight:** 16st
County debut: 1973 (Surrey), 1984 (Worcestershire), 1989 (Sussex)
County cap: 1980 (Surrey), 1984 (Worcestershire), 1989 (Sussex)
Testimonial: 1994
Test debut: 1985-86
Tests: 2
One-Day Internationals: 2
1000 runs in a season: 7
1st-Class 50s: 76
1st-Class 100s: 28
1st-Class 200s: 1
1st-Class catches: 204
One-Day 100s: 7

Place in batting averages: 132nd av. 29.63 (1993 70th av. 36.45)
Parents: Dennis and Tina
Wife and date of marriage: Jacqui, 7 January 1977
Children: Sarah-Jane Louise, 4 April 1982
Family links with cricket: Father played cricket for the BBC
Education: Battersea Grammar School
Qualifications: 3 O-levels
Overseas tours: England to West Indies 1985-86, to West Indies 1989-90
Overseas teams played for: Universals, Harare, Zimbabwe
Cricketers particularly admired: John Edrich, Clive Lloyd, Graham Gooch
Other sports followed: Football (Charlton Athletic), golf
Relaxations: Motor racing – 'keen to race at Le Mans and any other world sports car event'

Extras: Played for Surrey 2nd XI in 1972. Was not retained by Surrey after 1977, but was reinstated in 1978, sacked by Surrey during 1983 season and joined Worcestershire in 1984. Rejoined Surrey in 1987, but released at end of 1988 season and joined Sussex for 1989. Called up as a replacement for Graham Gooch on England's tour of West Indies in 1989-90 – played in one match before breaking his thumb. Joined the Sussex coaching staff at the end of the 1994 season

Opinions on cricket: 'There is too much cricket played. Flat wickets and seamless balls do not make for good cricket. I dislike listening to ex-cricketers rubbishing today's players.'

Best batting: 213 Sussex v Essex, Southend 1992

Best bowling: 3-40 Surrey v Sussex, The Oval 1976

1994 Season

	M	Inns	NO	Runs	HS	Avge	100s	50s	Ct	St	O	M	Runs	Wkts	Avge	Best	5wI	10wM
Test																		
All First	7	14	3	326	74	29.63	-	3	6	-								
1-day Int																		
NatWest	1	1	0	64	64	64.00	-	1	-	-								
B & H	2	2	1	85	65 *	85.00	-	1	-	-								
Sunday	7	7	1	211	55 *	35.16	-	1	1	-								

Career Performances

	M	Inns	NO	Runs	HS	Avge	100s	50s	Ct	St	Balls	Runs	Wkts	Avge	Best	5wI	10wM
Test	2	4	0	80	47	20.00	-	-	-	-							
All First	319	513	91	15265	213	36.17	28	76	204	-	2797	1574	30	52.46	3-40	-	-
1-day Int	2	2	1	15	10 *	15.00	-	-	-	-							
NatWest	40	39	6	1754	124	53.15	4	12	13	-	186	118	4	29.50	3-39	-	-
B & H	69	65	10	2049	126	37.25	3	11	37	-	336	266	8	33.25	4-29	-	
Sunday	178	164	28	3856	87 *	28.35	-	19	51	-	749	606	12	50.50	2-21	-	

75. Which England player, fielding at short leg to Ian Salisbury, got hit on the arm enabling Jack Russell to catch which West Indian batsman on the rebound in the third Test at Port of Spain in 1993-94?

SMITH, N. M. K.   Warwickshire

Name: Neil Michael Knight Smith
Role: Right-hand bat, off-spin bowler,
specialist mid-on
Born: 27 July 1967, Solihull
Height: 6ft **Weight:** 14st
Nickname: Sas, Gurt
County debut: 1987
County cap: 1993
1st-Class 50s: 8
1st-Class 100s: 1
1st-Class 5 w. in innings: 8
1st-Class catches: 20
One-Day 5 w. in innings: 2
Place in batting averages: 158th av. 25.58
(1993 211th av. 17.50)
Place in bowling averages: 93rd av. 34.55
(1993 94th av. 33.18)
Strike rate: 71.26 (career 79.09)
Parents: Mike (M.J.K.) and Diana
Wife and date of marriage: Rachel, 4 December 1993
Family links with cricket: Father captained Warwickshire and England
Education: Warwick School
Qualifications: 3 O-levels (Maths, English, French), cricket coach Grade 1
Career outside cricket: Teaching
Off-season: Looking for another job
Overseas teams played for: Phoenix, Perth, Western Australia 1988-89
Cricketers particularly admired: Tim Munton, David Gower, Brian Lara
Other sports followed: Golf, rugby and football
Relaxations: Sport, family and music
Opinions on cricket: 'NatWest should be played earlier in the season for a better wicket.
Finals should not be decided by the toss of a coin. If less overs were to be bowled in a day,
the standard of cricket would be better.'
Best batting: 161 Warwickshire v Yorkshire, Headingley 1989
Best bowling: 7-42 Warwickshire v Lancashire, Edgbaston 1994

---

76. Who were the only two West Indian bowlers used in England's
second innings total of 46 in the Third Test at Port of Spain in 1993-94?

1994 Season

	M	Inns	NO	Runs	HS	Avge	100s	50s	Ct	St	O	M	Runs	Wkts	Avge	Best	5wI	10wM
Test																		
All First	18	21	4	435	65	25.58	-	2	3	-	582	141	1693	49	34.55	7-42	4	-
1-day Int																		
NatWest	5	4	1	53	20	17.66	-	-	2	-	48.5	5	181	10	18.10	4-26	-	
B & H	3	1	0	4	4	4.00	-	-	2	-	23.3	0	99	7	14.14	3-29	-	
Sunday	17	14	2	211	56	17.58	-	1	6	-	103.1	8	412	26	15.84	4-19	-	

Career Performances

	M	Inns	NO	Runs	HS	Avge	100s	50s	Ct	St	Balls	Runs	Wkts	Avge	Best	5wI	10wM
Test																	
All First	77	109	16	2299	161	24.72	1	8	20	-	12181	6138	154	39.85	7-42	8	-
1-day Int																	
NatWest	20	16	5	245	52	22.27	-	1	8	-	862	516	24	21.50	5-17	1	
B & H	12	9	1	127	32	15.87	-	-	3	-	493	336	14	24.00	3-29	-	
Sunday	90	65	16	859	56	17.53	-	2	31	-	3216	2467	95	25.96	5-26	1	

SMITH, P. A.   Warwickshire

Name: Paul Andrew Smith
Role: Right-hand bat, right-arm
fast-medium bowler
Born: 15 April 1964, Newcastle-on-Tyne
Height: 6ft 2in **Weight:** 12st 7lbs
Nickname: Smithy, Jim
County debut: 1982
County cap: 1986
Benefit: 1995
1000 runs in a season: 2
1st-Class 50s: 47
1st-Class 100s: 4
1st-Class 5 w. in innings: 7
1st-Class catches: 58
One-Day 5 w. in innings: 3
Place in batting averages: 153rd av. 25.92
(1993 214th av. 16.86)
Place in bowling averages: 84th av. 33.00
(1993 106th av. 36.07)
Strike rate: 60.66 (career 56.20)
Parents: Ken and Joy
Wife and date of marriage: Caroline, 31 July 1987

Children: Oliver James, 5 February 1988; Michael Paul 1993
Family links with cricket: Father played for Leicestershire. Both brothers played for Warwickshire
Education: Heaton Grammar School, Newcastle
Qualifications: 5 O-levels, car restoration qualifications
Overseas tours: Warwickshire to La Manga 1989, to Trinidad and Tobago 1991, to Cape Town 1992-93, to Zimbabwe 1993-94
Overseas teams played for: Florida, Johannesburg 1982-83; Belgrano, Buenos Aires 1983-84; Carlton, Melbourne 1984-85; St Augustine's, Cape Town 1992-93
Cricketers particularly admired: Ian Botham
Other sports followed: None
Relaxations: Classic cars, American cars, music, reading, family, working out in the gym at Edgbaston with Bob Woolmer
Extras: Along with Andy Moles set a new world record for most consecutive opening partnerships of over 50. In 1989 scored 140 v Worcestershire, during which scored 100 out of partnership of 123 with Dermot Reeve. Took a hat-trick against Northamptonshire in 1989 and in 1990 took another against Sussex, bowling in Tim Munton's boots – two sizes too big. Warwickshire's most successful Sunday League all-rounder and has been in the winning team in two NatWest finals
Opinions on cricket: 'Four-day cricket is better than three-day, but wickets around the country must improve. Coloured clothing has been good value. Umpires should decide Man of the Match awards.'
Best batting: 140 Warwickshire v Worcestershire, Worcester 1989
Best bowling: 6-91 Warwickshire v Derbyshire, Edgbaston 1992

1994 Season

	M	Inns	NO	Runs	HS	Avge	100s	50s	Ct	St	O	M	Runs	Wkts	Avge	Best	5wI	10wM
Test																		
All First	12	17	3	363	65	25.92	-	2	2	-	182	40	594	18	33.00	3-24	-	-
1-day Int																		
NatWest	4	4	0	98	50	24.50	-	1	-	-	27.5	2	157	4	39.25	2-13	-	
B & H	3	3	1	62	42 *	31.00	-	-	1	-	20	1	81	3	27.00	3-34	-	
Sunday	14	14	0	252	45	18.00	-	-	4	-	74.2	4	376	20	18.80	5-38	1	

Career Performances

	M	Inns	NO	Runs	HS	Avge	100s	50s	Ct	St	Balls	Runs	Wkts	Avge	Best	5wI	10wM
Test																	
All First	215	343	41	7993	140	26.46	4	47	58	-	15455	9867	275	35.88	6-91	7	-
1-day Int																	
NatWest	31	29	3	626	79	24.07	-	5	3	-	1303	914	31	29.48	4-37	-	
B & H	41	39	5	658	74	19.35	-	1	6	-	1256	903	31	29.12	3-28	-	
Sunday	158	134	25	2651	93 *	24.32	-	8	30	-	4510	3989	137	29.11	5-36	3	

SMITH, R. A.   Hampshire

Name: Robin Arnold Smith
Role: Right-hand bat, slip fielder
Born: 13 September 1963, Durban,
South Africa
Height: 6ft **Weight:** 15st
Nickname: The Judge
County debut: 1982
County cap: 1985
Test debut: 1988
Tests: 53
One-Day Internationals: 64
1000 runs in a season: 8
1st-Class 50s: 89
1st-Class 100s: 45
1st-Class 200s: 1
1st-Class catches: 174
One-Day 100s: 19
Place in batting averages: 41st av. 43.55
(1993 26th av. 46.40)
Parents: John and Joy
Wife and date of marriage: Katherine, 21 September 1988
Children: Harrison Arnold, 4 December 1991; Margaux Elizabeth, 28 July 1994
Family links with cricket: Grandfather played
for Natal in Currie Cup. Brother Chris played for
Natal, Hampshire and England
Education: Northlands Boys High, Durban
Qualifications: Matriculation, '36 England caps'
Career outside cricket: Director of Masuri Helmets and Judge Tours
Off-season: 'Hosting my first Judge Tour to Australia. Generally having a great winter and
then preparing myself for a successful 1995 season'
Overseas tours: England to India and West Indies 1989-90, to Australia 1990-91, to
Australia and New Zealand (World Cup) 1991-92, to India and Sri Lanka 1992-93, to West
Indies 1993-94
Overseas teams played for: Natal, South Africa 1980-84; Perth, Western Australia
1984-85 (grade cricket)
Cricketers particularly admired: Malcolm Marshall, Brian Lara, Graeme Hick, Graham
Gooch, Allan Lamb
Other sports followed: Soccer, athletics, rugby, golf, racing
Relaxations: 'Reading (Leslie Thomas in particular), trout fishing, assembling a good wine
cellar, keeping fit and spending as much time as possible with my lovely wife Katherine and
my children'
Extras: Played rugby for Natal Schools and for Romsey RFC as a full-back. Held 19 school

athletics records and two South African schools records in shot put and 100-metre hurdles. One of *Wisden*'s Five Cricketers of the Year 1990. First child was born while he was on tour in Australia

Opinions on cricket: 'I enjoy playing cricket for Hampshire and particularly enjoy the camaraderie of the county circuit.'

Best batting: 209* Hampshire v Essex, Southampton 1987
Best bowling: 2-11 Hampshire v Surrey, Southampton 1985

1994 Season

	M	Inns	NO	Runs	HS	Avge	100s	50s	Ct	St	O	M	Runs	Wkts	Avge	Best	5wI	10wM
Test	3	4	0	120	78	30.00	-	1	3	-								
All First	17	29	0	1263	162	43.55	5	4	6	-								
1-day Int	1	1	0	15	15	15.00	-	-	-	-								
NatWest	2	2	1	66	59 *	66.00	-	1	1	-								
B & H	3	3	1	239	108	119.50	1	2	1	-								
Sunday	15	14	2	676	110 *	56.33	1	4	5	-								

Career Performances

	M	Inns	NO	Runs	HS	Avge	100s	50s	Ct	St	Balls	Runs	Wkts	Avge	Best	5wI	10wM
Test	53	97	14	3677	175	44.30	9	24	35	-	24	6	0	-	-	-	-
All First	279	475	73	17813	209 *	44.31	45	89	174	-	924	693	12	57.75	2-11	-	-
1-day Int	64	63	8	2218	167 *	40.32	4	13	23	-							
NatWest	29	29	10	1476	125 *	77.68	4	8	19	-	17	13	2	6.50	2-13	-	
B & H	38	36	8	1645	155 *	58.75	4	7	18	-	6	2	0	-	-	-	
Sunday	118	112	14	4240	131	43.26	7	29	55	-	2	0	1	0.00	1-0	-	

SNAPE, J. N.   Northamptonshire

Name: Jeremy Nicholas Snape
Role: Right-hand bat, off-spin bowler
Born: 27 April 1973, Stoke-on-Trent, Staffordshire
Height: 5ft 9in **Weight:** 11st 5lbs
Nickname: Snapey, Coot, Jez
County debut: 1992
1st-Class catches: 4
Parents: Keith and Barbara
Marital status: Single
Family links with cricket: Brother Jonathan plays local club cricket in North Staffs and South Cheshire League
Education: Denstone College; Durham University
Qualifications: 8 GCSEs, 3 A-levels, studying for BSc (Hons) Natural Science
Off-season: Tour to Zimbabwe with Christians in Sport, then playing and coaching in

Wellington, New Zealand
Overseas tours: England U18 to Canada
1991 (captain); England U19 to Pakistan
1991-92; Durham University to South Africa
1993; Northamptonshire to Cape Town
1993; Christians in Sport to Zimbabwe
1994-95; Durham Univerity to Vienna
(Indoor European Championships) 1994
Overseas teams played for: Petone,
Wellington, New Zealand 1994-95
Cricketers particularly admired: Brian Lara,
Allan Lamb, Carl Hooper
Other sports followed: Golf, rugby union,
shove ha'penny, white-water rafting
Injuries: Broke finger and stitches, missed
three Championship matches
Relaxations: Listening to music, television,
travelling

Extras: Sir Jack Hobbs award (U15 Schoolboy
1988), Gold Award winner for Combined Universities v Worcestershire 1992 (3-34) at The
Parks. Man of the Tournament at European Indoor 6-a-side Championships
Opinions on cricket: 'Definitely in favour of four-day cricket as it induces a more
disciplined approach, although I equally enjoy the one-day matches.'
Best batting: 43* Northamptonshire v South Africans, Northampton 1994
Best bowling: 2-49 Combined Universities v Australians, The Parks 1993

1994 Season

	M	Inns	NO	Runs	HS	Avge	100s	50s	Ct	St	O	M	Runs	Wkts	Avge	Best	5wI	10wM
Test																		
All First	2	4	2	76	43 *	38.00	-	-	3	-	63	20	210	4	52.50	2-80	-	-
1-day Int																		
NatWest																		
B & H	1	1	1	41	41 *	-					11	2	37	0	-		-	-
Sunday	4	4	2	59	31 *	29.50	-	-	1	-	14	0	77	3	25.66	2-38	-	

Career Performances

	M	Inns	NO	Runs	HS	Avge	100s	50s	Ct	St	Balls	Runs	Wkts	Avge	Best	5wI	10wM
Test																	
All First	4	6	2	94	43 *	23.50	-	-	4	-	653	385	7	55.00	2-49	-	-
1-day Int																	
NatWest	1	1	1	5	5 *	-											
B & H	6	6	2	141	52	35.25	-	1	3	-	390	269	7	38.42	3-35	-	
Sunday	8	5	2	65	31 *	21.66	-	-	2	-	270	218	11	19.81	3-25	-	

SOLANKI, V. S.   Worcestershire

Name: Vikram Singh Solanki
Role: Right-hand bat, off-spin bowler, occasional wicket-keeper
Born: 1 April 1976, Udaipur, India
Height: 6ft **Weight:** 12st
Nickname: Indian
County debut: 1993 (one-day)
Parents: Vijay and Florabel
Marital status: Single
Family links with cricket: Father played to a high standard in India
Education: Regis School, Wolverhampton
Qualifications: 9 GCSEs
Off-season: Touring with England U19
Overseas tours: England U18 to South Africa 1992-93; England U19 to West Indies 1994-95
Cricketers particularly admired: Sachin Tendulkar, Wasim Akram, Viv Richards
Other sports followed: Many
Relaxations: 'Spending time with friends and family'
Opinions on cricket: 'The best game in the world.'

1994 Season (did not make any first-class or one-day appearance)

Career Performances

	M	Inns	NO	Runs	HS	Avge	100s	50s	Ct	St	Balls	Runs	Wkts	Avge	Best	5wI	10wM
Test																	
All First																	
1-day Int																	
NatWest																	
B & H																	
Sunday	1	1	0	22	22	22.00	-	-	-	-							

SPEAK, N. J.   Lancashire

Name: Nicholas Jason Speak
Role: Right-hand opening bat, off-spin bowler
Born: 21 October 1966, Manchester
Height: 6ft **Weight:** 12st
Nickname: Twenty, Vision, Pod
County debut: 1986-87 in Jamaica
County cap: 1992
1000 runs in a season: 3
1st-Class 50s: 33
1st-Class 100s: 10
1st-Class 200s: 1
1st-Class catches: 62
One-Day 100s: 1
Place in batting averages: 30th av. 46.57 (1993 74th av. 35.90)
Parents: John and Irene
Wife and date of marriage:
Michelle, 11 March 1993

Family links with cricket: Father was league professional in Lancashire and Yorkshire
Education: Parrs Wood High School and Sixth Form College
Qualifications: 5 O-levels, NCA coaching certificate
Overseas tours: Lancashire to Jamaica 1987-88, to Zimbabwe 1989, to Perth 1990-91, to Johannesburg 1992
Overseas teams played for: South Canberra 1988-89; North Canberra 1991-93
Cricketers particularly admired: Martin Crowe, Dexter Fitton, Neil Fairbrother
Other sports followed: Most sports – Manchester City FC
Extras: Scored century for Australian Capital Territories v England A at Canberra 1992-93
Opinions on cricket: 'Tea should be ten minutes longer.'
Best batting: 232 Lancashire v Leicestershire, Leicester 1992
Best bowling: 1-0 Lancashire v Warwickshire, Old Trafford 1991

1994 Season

	M	Inns	NO	Runs	HS	Avge	100s	50s	Ct	St	O	M	Runs	Wkts	Avge	Best	5wI	10wM
Test																		
All First	19	34	6	1304	143	46.57	3	7	16	-	1	0	12	0	-		-	-	-
1-day Int																		
NatWest	2	2	0	21	11	10.50	-	-	1	-								
B & H	2	2	0	32	17	16.00	-	-	-	-								
Sunday	13	12	1	251	39	22.81	-	-	1	-								

Career Performances

	M	Inns	NO	Runs	HS	Avge	100s	50s	Ct	St	Balls	Runs	Wkts	Avge	Best	5wI	10wM
Test																	
All First	93	161	15	5869	232	40.19	10	33	62	-	73	104	2	52.00	1-0	-	-
1-day Int																	
NatWest	5	5	0	116	60	23.20	-	1	2	-							
B & H	12	11	1	279	82	27.90	-	2	-	-							
Sunday	51	47	6	1166	102 *	28.43	1	6	9	-							

SPEIGHT, M. P. Sussex

Name: Martin Peter Speight
Role: Right-hand bat, reserve wicket-keeper
Born: 24 October 1967, Walsall
Height: 5ft 10in **Weight:** 12st
Nickname: Sprog, Hoover, Ginger,
Pebbles, Vincent
County debut: 1986
County cap: 1991
1000 runs in a season: 2
1st-Class 50s: 32
1st-Class 100s: 12
1st-Class catches: 91
One-Day 100s: 2
Place in batting averages: 98th av. 34.17
(1993 21st av. 48.04)
Parents: Peter John and Valerie
Marital status: Single
Education: Hassocks Infants School;
The Windmills School, Hassocks;
Hurstpierpoint College Junior and Senior Schools; Durham University (St Chad's College)
Qualifications: 13 O-levels, 3 A-levels, BA (Hons) Archaeology/Ancient History
Career outside cricket: Artist
Off-season: Painting pictures and coaching
Overseas tours: NCA U19 to Bermuda 1986; England YC to Sri Lanka 1986-87
Overseas teams played for: Karori, Wellington, New Zealand 1989-90; Wellington CC,
1990 and 1993; Victoria University of Wellington 1990-92
Cricketers particularly admired: Viv Richards, David Gower
Other sports followed: Golf, rugby, hockey, football, athletics
Injuries: Hamstring injury, missed two weeks
Relaxations: Most music, sports on television, painting and drawing
Extras: Member of Durham University UAU winning side 1987; played for Combined

Universities in B&H Cup 1987 and 1988; Sussex Most Promising Player 1989. Fastest first-class 100 in 1992 and fastest 50-overs 100 v Somerset at Taunton 1993. Painted an oil painting of the maiden first-class game at Arundel Castle between Sussex and Hampshire which was later auctioned to raise £1200 for the Sussex YC tour to India 1990-91, and of which a limited edition has also been printed and sold. Has done paintings of Hove, Southampton and The Oval for the benefits of Messrs Pigott, Parks and Greig. Member of Durham University's men's hockey team to Barbados 1988. Book of his paintings *A Cricketer's View from the Boundary* is to be published in 1995

Opinions on cricket: 'Cricket should be pleasing to watch! Within reason (i.e. leaving it to the umpire's discretion), the bowler should be able to bowl as many short-pitched balls as he wants.'

Best batting: 184 Sussex v Nottinghamshire, Eastbourne 1993
Best bowling: 1-2 Sussex v Middlesex, Hove 1988

1994 Season

	M	Inns	NO	Runs	HS	Avge	100s	50s	Ct	St	O	M	Runs	Wkts	Avge	Best	5wI	10wM
Test																		
All First	17	29	0	991	126	34.17	1	4	20	-								
1-day Int																		
NatWest	1	1	0	29	29	29.00	-	-	-	-								
B & H	2	2	0	17	16	8.50	-	-	-	-								
Sunday	14	14	0	299	66	21.35	-	3	3	-								

Career Performances

	M	Inns	NO	Runs	HS	Avge	100s	50s	Ct	St	Balls	Runs	Wkts	Avge	Best	5wI	10wM
Test																	
All First	112	185	13	6300	184	36.62	12	32	91	-	21	32	2	16.00	1-2	-	-
1-day Int																	
NatWest	13	12	1	273	50	24.81	-	1	3	-							
B & H	17	15	0	568	83	22.72	-	2	20	1							
Sunday	86	78	5	2166	126	29.67	2	11	25	1							

77. Which former England opening batsman was not re-elected as an England selector in March 1995?

SPENCER, D. J.   Kent

Name: Duncan John Spencer
Role: Right-hand bat, right-arm fast bowler
Born: 5 April 1972, Nelson, Lancashire
Height: 5ft 8in
County debut: 1993
1st-Class catches: 9
Place in bowling averages: 95th av. 34.70
Strike rate: 51.50 (career 54.88)
Marital status: Single
Education: Gosnells High School,
Western Australia
Off-season: Playing in Australia
Overseas teams played for:
Western Australia 1993-94
Best batting: 75 Kent v Zimbabwe,
Canterbury 1993
Best bowling: 4-31 Kent v Leicestershire,
Leicester 1994

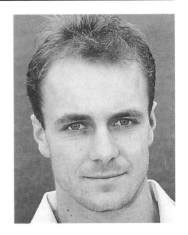

1994 Season

	M	Inns	NO	Runs	HS	Avge	100s	50s	Ct	St	O	M	Runs	Wkts	Avge	Best	5wI	10wM
Test																		
All First	4	6	1	46	13	9.20	-	-	1	-	85.5	12	347	10	34.70	4-31	-	-
1-day Int																		
NatWest																		
B & H																		
Sunday	5	2	0	18	12	9.00	-	-	-	-	33	2	130	4	32.50	2-16	-	

Career Performances

	M	Inns	NO	Runs	HS	Avge	100s	50s	Ct	St	Balls	Runs	Wkts	Avge	Best	5wI	10wM
Test																	
All First	14	16	2	200	75	14.28	-	1	9	-	1866	1257	34	36.97	4-31	-	-
1-day Int																	
NatWest																	
B & H																	
Sunday	10	6	2	60	17 *	15.00	-	-	2	-	388	268	8	33.50	2-16	-	

SPIRING, K. R.   Worcestershire

Name: Karl Reuben Spiring
Role: Right-hand opening bat
Born: 13 November 1974, Southport
Height: 5ft 11in **Weight:** 12st
County debut: 1993 (one-day),
1994 (first-class)
1st-Class 50s: 2
1st-Class catches: 2
Parents: Peter and June
Marital status: Single
Education: Monmouth School;
Durham University
Qualifications: 9 GCSEs, 3 A-levels,
NCA Senior Coach
Career outside cricket: Student
Off-season: Studying at university
Cricketers particularly admired:
Ian Botham, Alistair Brown, Martin Speight
Other sports followed: Rugby, football, golf
Injuries: Tendonitis in right shoulder
Relaxations: 'A few pints and a game of table footy with Tommy Moore in the Barrels.'
Extras: Father was a professional footballer. Rapid Cricketline 2nd XI Player of the Month
June 1994. Worcestershire Uncapped Player of the Year 1994
Opinions on cricket: 'Lunch and tea interval should be longer. I'd prefer to see a 40-over
one-day competition for the 2nd XI rather than what it is now. Too much cricket is played,
which leaves players tired and rather reluctant to play. More days should be set aside to
relax, practise and create a more positive mental attitude and appetite for the game.'
Best batting: 56 Worcestershire v Oxford University, Worcester 1994

1994 Season

	M	Inns	NO	Runs	HS	Avge	100s	50s	Ct	St	O	M	Runs	Wkts	Avge	Best	5wI	10wM
Test																		
All First	1	2	0	108	56	54.00	-	2	2	-								
1-day Int																		
NatWest																		
B & H																		
Sunday																		

> 78. Which team will compete in the NatWest Trophy for the first time
> in 1995?

	M	Inns	NO	Runs	HS	Avge	100s	50s	Ct	St	Balls	Runs	Wkts	Avge	Best	5wI	10wM
Test																	
All First	1	2	0	108	56	54.00	-	2	2	-							
1-day Int																	
NatWest																	
B & H																	
Sunday	1	1	0	7	7	7.00	-	-	-	-							

SRINATH, J.   Gloucestershire

Name: Javagal Srinath
Role: Right-hand bat, right-arm fast-medium
bowler
Born: 31 August 1969, Mysore
County debut: No first-team appearance
Test debut: 1990-91
Tests: 12
1st-Class 50s: 2
1st-Class 5 w. in innings: 4
1st-Class catches: 20
One-Day 5 w. in innings: 2
Strike rate: (career 64.23)
Off-season: Playing for India
Overseas tours:
India to Australia and New Zealand (inc World
Cup) 1991-92, to South Africa and Zimbabwe
1992-93, to New Zealand 1993-94, to New
Zealand (Centenary Tournament) 1994-95

Overseas teams played for: Karnataka
Extras: Studied fast bowling under Dennis Lillee's guidance at Madras. Signed by
Gloucestershire when David Boon decided against playing for the county in 1995
Best batting: 59 Karnataka v Maharastra, Pune 1990-91
Best bowling: 7-93 Karnataka v Maharastra, Pune 1990-91

1994 Season (did not make any first-class or one-day appearance)

> 79. Which Test cricketer took the first hat-trick of his career in a
> County Championship match for Derbyshire in May 1994?

Career Performances

	M	Inns	NO	Runs	HS	Avge	100s	50s	Ct	St	Balls	Runs	Wkts	Avge	Best	5wI	10wM
Test	12	15	8	91	21	13.00	-	-	5	-	2886	1212	33	36.72	4-33	-	-
All First	44	52	11	633	59	15.43	-	2	20	-	8415	3914	131	29.87	7-93	4	-
1-day Int	59	27	12	100	14	6.66	-	-	5	-	3045	2186	89	24.56	5-24	2	
NatWest																	
B & H																	
Sunday																	

STANFORD, E. J.   Kent

Name: Edward John Stanford
Role: Left-hand bat, left-arm spinner
Born: 21 January 1971, Dartford
Height: 5ft 10in **Weight:** 12st
Nickname: Oist
County debut: No first-team appearance
Parents: Paul and Pam
Family links with cricket:
Father plays for Dartford
Education: Downs Secondary School,
Dartford
Qualifications: Various GCSEs
Career outside cricket: 'Ex-groundsman'
Overseas tours: Kent Schools U17 to
Singapore and New Zealand 1988
Overseas teams played for: Petersham,
Sydney 1991
Cricketers particularly admired: David
Gower, Matt Walker – 'great left-handers'
Other sports followed: Charlton FC
Relaxations: All sports and music
Extras: Headed a ball for six in debut against Essex in the Bain Clarkson Championship
1993 ('Totally misjudged a top edge whilst fielding at fine leg, the ball struck me on the
forehead and carried a further 20 yards to go for six!')
Opinions on cricket: 'We come across some average wickets on club grounds in 2nd XI
cricket.'

STANGER, I. M. Leicestershire

Name: Ian Michael Stanger
Role: Right-hand bat, right-arm
fast-medium bowler
Born: 5 October 1971, Glasgow
Height: 6ft **Weight:** 12st
County debut: 1994 (one-day)
Parents: Mike and Hilary
Marital status: Single
Family links with cricket: Father is coaching
convener of the Western Cricket Association
(representative body for the West District of
Scotland) and ground convener for Clydesdale
CC (Scotland's main international venue)
Education: Hutchesons' Grammar School,
Glasgow; Dundee University
Qualifications: BA (Town Planning)
Career outside cricket: Town planner
Off-season: Assistant coach to Omar Henry,
head of cricket at Stellenbosch University,
South Africa
Overseas tours: Scottish Thistle Select tour to Pakistan 1989
Cricketers particularly admired: Tom Moody, Phil Simmons
Other sports followed: Football, rugby
Injuries: Broken finger, out for ten days
Relaxations: Music, fashion
Extras: Scottish Young Cricketer of the Year 1992 and 1993. Released by Leicestershire
at end of 1994 season

1994 Season

	M	Inns	NO	Runs	HS	Avge	100s	50s	Ct	St	O	M	Runs	Wkts	Avge	Best	5wI	10wM
Test																		
All First-Class																		
1-day Int																		
NatWest																		
B & H																		
Sunday	9	6	3	10	6	3.33	-	-	4	-	54	0	294	8	36.75	3-34	-	

> 80. How did Andy Moles break his arm on a pre-season tour to
> Zimbabwe with Warwickshire in 1994?

	M	Inns	NO	Runs	HS	Avge	100s	50s	Ct	St	Balls	Runs	Wkts	Avge	Best	5wI	10wM
Test																	
All First-Class																	
1-day Int																	
NatWest	2	0	0	0	0	-	-	-	-	-	120	77	1	77.00	1-35	-	
B & H	1	1	1	2	2*	-	-	-	1	-	30	12	0	-	-	-	-
Sunday	9	6	3	10	6	3.33	-	-	4	-	324	294	8	36.75	3-34	-	

STEELE, M. V.   Northamptonshire

Name: Mark Vincent Steele
Role: Left-hand bat, right-arm fast-medium bowler
Born: 13 November 1976, Corby
Height: 5ft 11in **Weight:** 12st 7lbs
County debut: No first-team appearance
Parents: David and Carol
Marital status: Single
Family links with cricket: Father played for Northamptonshire, Derbyshire and England, uncle John played for Leicestershire
Education: Wellingborough School; Tresham Institute, Kettering
Qualifications: 6 GCSEs
Off-season: Studying
Other sports followed: Football, table tennis
Relaxations: Playing football for Old Wellingburians
Extras: MCC U13 Young Cricketer of the Year 1984. Played for Midlands Schools from U15 upwards and played for England U16 in 1993

81. Who replaced Waqar Younis as Surrey's overseas player in 1994?

STEER, I. G. S.   Derbyshire

Name: Ian Gary Samuel Steer
Role: Right-hand opening bat, right-arm medium bowler
Born: 17 August 1970, Aston, Birmingham
Height: 5ft 7in **Weight:** 11st 9lbs
Nickname: Steery, Steersby, Barry Beer, Jib-Job
County debut: 1992 (one-day), 1993 (first-class)
1st-Class 50s: 2
1st-Class catches: 4
Parents: Derrick and Vashtee
Marital status: Single
Family links with cricket: Father played amateur cricket
Education: St Edmund Campion RC School; Sutton Coldfield College; Cheltenham and Gloucester College of Higher Education
Qualifications: 7 O-levels, City & Guilds in Recreation and Leisure, NCA coaching certificate, FA Prelim
Career outside cricket: Student
Off-season: Studying for PE Degree at Cheltenham and Gloucester College
Overseas tours: Stan Mortensen benefit tour to Denmark
Cricketers particularly admired: Brian Lara, Ian Botham, Paul Smith, Viv Richards, Simon Base, Allan Donald
Other sports followed: All ball sports, especially football (Aston Villa)
Injuries: 'Trouble with a small heart!'
Relaxations: 'Drinking at Cassidy's with college friends. Trying to drink half of what Karl Krikken consumes. Playing football, cinema and sleeping.'
Extras: Signed by Derbyshire from Warwickshire for 1992 season. Only Derby player to score 1000 runs in a season for the second team. Holds Derbyshire 2nd XI record for runs scored in a season – 1492 in all cricket 1992
Opinions on cricket: 'All new staff players, particularly under 21s should be given at least a two-year contract. This will give them more confidence and allow them to get on with their cricket. A longer tea break wold be nice.'
Best batting: 67 Derbyshire v Leicestershire, Leicester 1993
Best bowling: 3-23 Derbyshire v Surrey, Ilkeston 1993

---

82. Which overseas player missed the beginning of the 1994 county season after not appearing on the specified plane from the West Indies?

1994 Season

	M	Inns	NO	Runs	HS	Avge	100s	50s	Ct	St	O	M	Runs	Wkts	Avge	Best	5wI	10wM
Test																		
All First	3	3	1	142	67	71.00	-	1	4	-	2	0	12	0	-		-	-	-
1-day Int																		
NatWest																		
B & H	1	1	0	43	43	43.00	-	-	-	-								
Sunday	2	1	0	1	1	1.00	-	-	1	-								

Career Performances

	M	Inns	NO	Runs	HS	Avge	100s	50s	Ct	St	Balls	Runs	Wkts	Avge	Best	5wI	10wM
Test																	
All First	7	10	3	299	67	42.71	-	2	4	-	66	46	3	15.33	3-23	-	-
1-day Int																	
NatWest																	
B & H	1	1	0	43	43	43.00	-	-	-	-							
Sunday	7	4	0	27	19	6.75	-	-	1	-	66	54	1	54.00	1-33	-	

STEMP, R. D. Yorkshire

Name: Richard David Stemp
Role: Right-hand bat, slow left-arm bowler
Born: 11 December 1967, Erdington, Birmingham
Height: 6ft **Weight:** 12st 4lbs
Nickname: Stempy, Sherriff, Badger
County debut: 1990 (Worcestershire), 1993 (Yorkshire)
1st-Class 5 w. in innings: 7
1st-Class 10 w. in match: 1
1st-Class catches: 25
Place in batting averages: 269th av. 10.11 (1993 224th av. 15.58)
Place in bowling averages: 62nd av. 30.46 (1993 72nd av. 30.17)
Strike rate: 81.93 (career 78.00)
Parents: Arnold and Rita Homer
Marital status: Single
Family links with cricket: Father played Birmingham League cricket for Old Hill
Education: Britannia High School, Rowley Regis
Qualifications: NCA coaching award

Off-season: 'Going to India with England A and playing on turning wickets.'
Overseas tours: England A to India 1994-95
Overseas teams played for: Pretoria Technikon 1988-89
Cricketers particularly admired: Ian Botham, Phil Tufnell
Other sports followed: Indoor cricket, American football
Relaxations: Ornithology, music, driving
Extras: Played for England indoor cricket team v Australia in ManuLife 'Test' series 1990. Moved to Yorkshire at end of 1992 season (first English non-Yorkshireman to be signed for the county). Included in England Test squad against New Zealand in 1994
Opinions on cricket: 'Groundsmen should prepare cricket wickets, not wickets made for corporate hospitality. Is not being given run out as much human judgement as LBW or caught behind? If we are using television to check and decide on run out, why not all decisions?'
Best batting: 37 Yorkshire v Essex, Chelmsford 1993
Best bowling: 6-37 Yorkshire v Durham, Durham University 1994

1994 Season

	M	Inns	NO	Runs	HS	Avge	100s	50s	Ct	St	O	M	Runs	Wkts	Avge	Best	5wI	10wM
Test																		
All First	20	28	2	263	28	10.11	-	-	9	-	669.1	252	1493	49	30.46	6-37	2	-
1-day Int																		
NatWest	1	0	0	0	0	-	-	-	1	-	12	1	31	1	31.00	1-31	-	
B & H	1	0	0	0	0	-	-	-	-	-	11	2	47	0	-	-	-	
Sunday	9	3	1	17	14 *	8.50	-	-	1	-	58	2	321	11	29.18	3-31	-	

Career Performances

	M	Inns	NO	Runs	HS	Avge	100s	50s	Ct	St	Balls	Runs	Wkts	Avge	Best	5wI	10wM
Test																	
All First	59	68	20	652	37	13.58	-	-	25	-	10765	4408	138	31.94	6-37	7	1
1-day Int																	
NatWest	2	1	1	1	1 *	-	-	-	1	-	132	73	1	73.00	1-31	-	
B & H	3	0	0	0	0	-	-	-	-	-	180	114	0	-	-	-	
Sunday	23	7	4	56	23 *	18.66	-	-	4	-	816	693	21	33.00	3-18	-	

STEPHENSON, F. D. Sussex

Name: Franklyn Dacosta Stephenson
Role: Right-hand bat, right-arm fast bowler
Born: 8 April 1959, St James, Barbados
Height: 6ft 3in **Weight:** 13st 7lbs
Nickname: Cookie
County debut: 1982 (Gloucestershire), 1988
(Nottinghamshire), 1992 (Sussex)
County cap: 1988 (Notts), 1992 (Sussex)
1000 runs in a season: 1
50 wickets in a season: 5
1st-Class 50s: 38
1st-Class 100s: 9
1st-Class 5 w. in innings: 41
1st-Class 10 w. in match: 10
1st-Class catches: 81
One-Day 100s: 1
One-Day 5 w. in innings: 3
Place in batting averages: 143rd av. 27.85
(1993 123rd av. 28.31)
Place in bowling averages: 6th av. 20.07 (1993 55th av. 28.17)
Strike rate: 42.98 (career 50.66)
Parents: Leonard Young and Violet Stevenson
Wife and date of marriage: Julia, 2 April 1981
Children: Amanda, 20 October 1981; Orissa, 6 September 1983; Tammy, 1 November 1990
Education: St John Baptist Mixed School; Samuel Jackson Prescod Polytechnic
Qualifications: School leaving certificate
Career outside cricket: Part-time professional golfer
Off-season: Playing for Orange Free State, Bloemfontein, South Africa
Overseas tours: West Indies U19 to England 1978; unofficial West Indies XI to South
Africa 1982-83 and 1983-84
Overseas teams played for: Tasmania 1981-82; Barbados 1981-82 and 1989-90; Orange
Free State 1991-95
Cricketers particularly admired: Gary Sobers, Sylvester Clarke, Collis King, Richard Hadlee
Other sports followed: All
Relaxations: Playing golf, guitar and spending time with family
Extras: Played League cricket for Littleborough in the Central Lancashire League in 1979,
Royton in 1980 (100 wickets and 621 runs), Rawtenstall in 1981 and 1982 (100+ wickets
and 500+ runs both years). Hit 165 for Barbados in 1982, having been sent in as night-
watchman. Took ten wickets in match on debut for Tasmania. In 1988 did the double when
he scored 1018 runs and took 125 wickets in first-class cricket, being named Britannic
Assurance Player of the Year, 1988 and one of *Wisden*'s Five Cricketers of the Year. Left
Nottinghamshire at end of 1991 season and signed to play for Sussex in 1992 when he was

voted their Players' Player of the Year. Banned from Test cricket for joining rebel West Indies tour to South Africa: ban now ended
Best batting: 165 Barbados v Leeward Islands, Basseterre 1981-82
Best bowling: 8-47 Nottinghamshire v Essex, Trent Bridge 1989

1994 Season

	M	Inns	NO	Runs	HS	Avge	100s	50s	Ct	St	O	M	Runs	Wkts	Avge	Best	5wI	10wM
Test																		
All First	17	28	1	752	107	27.85	1	5	9	-	480.5	108	1345	67	20.07	6-50	6	2
1-day Int																		
NatWest	1	1	0	8	8	8.00	-	-	-	-	12	0	57	2	28.50	2-57	-	
B & H	2	1	0	4	4	4.00	-	-	-	-	22	3	65	3	21.66	2-24	-	
Sunday	14	13	0	237	46	18.23	-	-	6	-	109.2	6	463	14	33.07	4-24	-	

Career Performances

	M	Inns	NO	Runs	HS	Avge	100s	50s	Ct	St	Balls	Runs	Wkts	Avge	Best	5wI	10wM
Test		1															
All First	187	289	32	7243	165	28.18	9	38	81	-	34806	16434	687	23.92	8-47	41	10
1-day Int																	
NatWest	19	14	1	190	40	14.61	-	-	2	-	1194	592	27	21.92	3-8	-	
B & H	30	26	6	455	98 *	22.75	-	2	4	-	1790	1019	48	21.22	5-30	1	
Sunday	111	92	14	1657	103	21.24	1	4	24	-	5109	3536	172	20.55	5-23	2	

STEPHENSON, J. P.   Hampshire

Name: John Patrick Stephenson
Role: Right-hand opening bat,
right-arm fast-medium bowler
Born: 14 March 1965, Stebbing, Essex
Height: 6ft 1in **Weight:** 12st 7lbs
Nickname: Stan
County debut: 1985 (Essex)
County cap: 1989 (Essex)
Test debut: 1989
Tests: 1
1000 runs in a season: 5
1st-Class 50s: 54
1st-Class 100s: 18
1st-Class 200s: 1
1st-Class 5 w. in innings: 4
1st-Class catches: 113
One-Day 100s: 4

One-Day 5 w. in innings: 1
Place in batting averages: 197th av. 20.57 (1993 89th av. 33.70)
Place in bowling averages: 121st av. 41.00 (1993 73rd av. 30.26)
Strike rate: 76.61 (career 61.66)
Parents: Pat and Eve
Wife and date of marriage: Fiona Maria, 24 September 1994
Family links with cricket: Father was member of Rugby Meteors Cricketer Cup-winning side in 1973. Three brothers played in Felsted 1st XI; Guy played for Essex 2nd XI and now plays for Teddington
Education: Felsted Prep School; Felsted Senior School; Durham University
Qualifications: 7 O-levels, 3 A-levels, BA General Arts (Dunelm)
Off-season: Playing in Argentina
Overseas tours: English Schools U19 to Zimbabwe 1982-83; England A to Kenya and Zimbabwe 1989-90, to Bermuda and West Indies 1991-92
Overseas teams played for: Fitzroy, Melbourne 1982-83, 1987-88; Boland, South Africa 1988-89; Gold Coast Dolphins and Bond University, Australia 1990-91
Cricketers particularly admired: Brian Hardie
Injuries: Broken thumb, missed one month
Relaxations: 'Collecting vinyl, e.g. Nirvana, Slint, The Bags, Codiene, Polvo Eitzel (American music club), reading (same as music taste), baking'
Extras: Awarded 2nd XI cap in 1984 when leading run-scorer with Essex 2nd XI. Essex Young Player of the Year, 1985. Captained Durham University to victory in UAU Championship 1986 and captain of Combined Universities team 1987 in the first year that it was drawn from all universities. Called up to replace the injured Michael Atherton on England A tour to Bermuda and West Indies 1991-92 and was leading wicket-taker. Scored two not out centuries v Somerset at Taunton in 1992 and was on the field for the whole game (the first Essex player to achieve this). First Essex player to achieve 500 runs and 20 wickets in Sunday League season 1993
Best batting: 202* Essex v Somerset, Bath 1990
Best bowling: 6-54 Essex v Nottinghamshire, Colchester 1992

1994 Season

	M	Inns	NO	Runs	HS	Avge	100s	50s	Ct	St	O	M	Runs	Wkts	Avge	Best	5wI	10wM
Test																		
All First	16	27	1	535	144	20.57	1	2	9	-	332	75	1066	26	41.00	4-74	-	-
1-day Int																		
NatWest	2	2	0	74	55	37.00	-	1	1	-	19	1	118	2	59.00	2-43	-	
B & H	1	1	0	47	47	47.00	-	-	-	-	2.2	0	27	0	-	-	-	
Sunday	15	15	2	391	73	30.07	-	3	5	-	104.4	3	476	18	26.44	2-21	-	

83. Who topped England's Test match bowling averages in the West Indies in 1993-94 and took 8-75 in the Fourth Test?

Career Performances

	M	Inns	NO	Runs	HS	Avge	100s	50s	Ct	St	Balls	Runs	Wkts	Avge	Best	5wl	10wM
Test	1	2	0	36	25	18.00	-	-	-	-							
All First	188	324	32	10230	202 *	35.03	18	54	113	-	8941	4877	145	33.63	6-54	4	-
1-day Int																	
NatWest	17	16	1	593	90	39.53	-	7	6	-	491	441	8	55.12	3-78	-	
B & H	29	24	3	843	142	40.14	1	6	6	-	753	513	20	25.65	3-22	-	
Sunday	110	96	13	2548	109	30.69	3	13	42	-	2832	2098	85	24.68	5-58	1	

STEWART, A. J. Surrey

Name: Alec James Stewart
Role: Right-hand bat, 'very average'
bowler, wicket-keeper, county captain
Born: 8 April 1963, Merton
Nickname: Stewie, Ming
Height: 5ft 11in **Weight:** 12st 7lbs
County debut: 1981
County cap: 1985
Benefit: 1994
Test debut: 1989-90
Tests: 43
One-Day Internationals: 59
1000 runs in a season: 8
1st-Class 50s: 91
1st-Class 100s: 30
1st-Class 200s: 1
1st-Class catches: 341
1st-Class stumpings: 13
One-Day 100s: 10
Place in batting averages: 28th av. 46.80 (1993 45th av. 40.51)
Parents: Michael and Sheila
Wife and date of marriage: Lynn, 28 September 1991
Children: Andrew James, 21 May 1993
Family links with cricket: Father played for England (1962-64), Surrey (1954 -72) and
Malden Wanderers. Brother Neil captains Malden Wanderers
Education: Tiffin Boys School
Qualifications: 4 O-levels
Off-season: Ashes tour
Overseas tours: England to India (Nehru Cup) 1989-90, to West Indies 1989-90, to
Australia 1990-91, to Australia and New Zealand (World Cup) 1991-92, to India and Sri
Lanka 1992-93, to West Indies 1993-94, to Australia 1994-95

Overseas teams played for: Midland Guildford 1981-89

Cricketers particularly admired: Graham Monkhouse, Geoff Boycott, Graham Gooch, K. Gartrell

Other sports followed: Football (Chelsea)

Injuries: Broke finger twice on England tour to Australia 1994-95

Relaxations: 'Spending as much time with my family as possible'

Extras: Captained England in a Test match for the first time v India at Madras 1992-93 and has acted as vice-captain to both Graham Gooch and Mike Atherton. First Englishman to score a century in each innings against West Indies, at Barbados 1994

Best batting: 206* Surrey v Essex, The Oval 1989

Best bowling: 1-7 Surrey v Lancashire, Old Trafford 1989

1994 Season

	M	Inns	NO	Runs	HS	Avge	100s	50s	Ct	St	O	M	Runs	Wkts	Avge	Best	5wI	10wM
Test	6	9	1	422	119	52.75	1	2	5	-								
All First	16	23	3	936	142	46.80	3	4	20	1	2	0	10	0	-	-	-	-
1-day Int	3	3	0	67	32	22.33	-	-	2	-								
NatWest	4	4	0	66	24	16.50	-	-	10	-								
B & H	4	4	1	204	167 *	68.00	1	-	2	-								
Sunday	10	8	0	273	92	34.12	-	1	7	1								

Career Performances

	M	Inns	NO	Runs	HS	Avge	100s	50s	Ct	St	Balls	Runs	Wkts	Avge	Best	5wI	10wM
Test	43	78	5	2982	190	40.84	7	15	53	4	20	13	0	-	-	-	
All First	269	444	50	15524	206 *	39.40	30	91	341	13	439	375	3	125.00	1-7	-	-
1-day Int	59	54	4	1490	103	29.80	1	10	43	4							
NatWest	29	27	4	1055	107 *	45.86	2	7	25	-							
B & H	41	41	6	1488	167 *	42.51	2	10	23	3							
Sunday	140	126	12	3542	125	31.07	5	22	101	8	4	8	0	-	-	-	

84. Who scored most runs for England in the five-match Test series in the West Indies in 1993-94?

SUCH, P. M.   Essex

Name: Peter Mark Such
Role: Right-hand bat, off-spin bowler
Born: 12 June 1964, Helensburgh, Scotland
Height: 6ft **Weight:** 11st 7lbs
Nickname: Suchy
County debut: 1982 (Nottinghamshire),
1987 (Leicestershire), 1990 (Essex)
County cap: 1991
Test debut: 1993
Tests: 8
50 wickets in a season: 2
1st-Class 50s: 1
1st-Class 5 w. in innings: 21
1st-Class 10 w. in innings: 3
1st-Class catches: 70
One-Day 5 w. in innings: 2
Place in batting averages:

(1993 262nd av. 10.36)
Place in bowling averages: 67th av. 30.82 (1993 56th av. 28.26)
Strike rate: 70.52 (career 68.51)
Parents: John and Margaret
Marital status: Engaged
Family links with cricket: Father and brother both village cricketers
Education: Lantern Lane Primary; Harry Carlton Comprehensive, East Leake, Notts
Qualifications: 9 O-levels, 3 A-levels, advanced cricket coach
Off-season: On standby for England tours. 'Probably working for Save and Prosper'
Overseas tours: England A to Australia 1992-93, to South Africa 1993-94
Overseas teams played for: Kempton Park, South Africa 1982-83; Bathurst, Australia
1985-86; Matabeleland, Zimbabwe 1989-90
Cricketers particularly admired: Bob White, Eddie Hemmings, Graham Gooch, John Childs
Other sports followed: American football
Relaxations: Playing golf, spending time with fiancée, Kate, listening to music, watching movies
Extras: Played for England YC v Australian YC 1983 and for TCCB XI v New Zealand,
1985. Left Nottinghamshire at end of 1986 season; joined Leicestershire in 1987 and
released at end of 1989; signed by Essex for 1990. Played in one-day games for England
A v Sri Lanka 1991. Joint holder with J.H. Childs of the Essex Player of the Year Award
1992 and shared the award again in 1993. Took 6-67 on Test debut v Australia 1993 – best
figures by England Test debutant since John Lever in India 1976-77
Opinions on cricket: 'If four-day cricket is going to work, we need to play on better wickets.
At present we have a win at all costs mentality which filters down to pitch preparation. "Result
wickets" don't produce good players. I would also like to see more of the £60 million which
is being pumped into cricket finding its way into players' wages across the board.'

Best batting: 54 Essex v Worcestershire, Chelmsford 1993
Best bowling: 7-66 Essex v Hampshire, Southampton 1994

1994 Season

	M	Inns	NO	Runs	HS	Avge	100s	50s	Ct	St	O	M	Runs	Wkts	Avge	Best	5wI	10wM
Test	3	2	1	9	5 *	9.00	-	-	-	-	123	36	264	6	44.00	2-50	-	-
All First	20	23	2	167	29	7.95	-	-	9	-	670	183	1757	57	30.82	7-66	5	-
1-day Int																		
NatWest	2	1	0	6	6	6.00	-	-	1	-	19	1	72	1	72.00	1-39	-	
B & H	2	0	0	0	0	-	-	-	1	-	15	1	68	2	34.00	1-29	-	
Sunday	13	8	2	29	19 *	4.83	-	-	2	-	100	4	372	10	37.20	2-27	-	

Career Performances

	M	Inns	NO	Runs	HS	Avge	100s	50s	Ct	St	Balls	Runs	Wkts	Avge	Best	5wI	10wM
Test	8	11	4	65	14 *	9.28	-	-	2	-	2177	805	22	36.59	6-67	1	-
All First	181	166	51	753	54	6.54	-	1	70	-	31449	13833	459	30.13	7-66	21	3
1-day Int																	
NatWest	10	3	2	6	6	6.00	-	-	1	-	588	317	9	35.22	2-29	-	
B & H	17	6	2	12	4	3.00	-	-	2	-	900	590	17	34.70	4-43	-	
Sunday	66	25	13	105	19 *	8.75	-	-	16	-	2732	2078	64	32.46	5-32	2	

SUTCLIFFE, I. J.   Leicestershire

Name: Iain John Sutcliffe
Role: Left-hand bat, leg-spin bowler
Born: 20 December 1974, Leeds
Height: 6ft 1in **Weight:** 12st
Nickname: Sooty, Bertie, Ripper
County debut: No first-team appearance
1st-Class catches: 2
Parents: John and Valerie
Marital status: Single
Education: Leeds Grammar School;
Oxford University (Queens College)
Qualifications: 10 GCSEs, 4 A-levels
Off-season: Studying, boxing
Overseas tours: Leeds GS to Kenya
Cricketers particularly admired:
Paul Nixon, Brian Lara, Michael Slater,
Sachin Tendulkar
Other sports followed: Boxing, football
Relaxations: Music, boxing

Extras: Played NCA England U14 and NCA Development Team U18/U19. Oxford boxing blue 1994/95, British Universities Light-middleweight Champion 1994
Opinions on cricket: 'Sunday League should be abolished and the Championship should be divided into two leagues. Oxford and Cambridge Universities should maintain their first-class status to develop student opportunities.'
Best batting: 8* Oxford University v Nottinghamshire, The Parks 1994

1994 Season

	M	Inns	NO	Runs	HS	Avge	100s	50s	Ct	St	O	M	Runs	Wkts	Avge	Best	5wI	10wM
Test																		
All First	5	4	1	18	8*	6.00	-	-	2	-								
1-day Int																		
NatWest																		
B & H																		
Sunday																		

Career Performances

	M	Inns	NO	Runs	HS	Avge	100s	50s	Ct	St	Balls	Runs	Wkts	Avge	Best	5wI	10wM
Test																	
All First	5	4	1	18	8*	6.00	-	-	2	-							
1-day Int																	
NatWest																	
B & H																	
Sunday																	

SWANN, A. J.   Northamptonshire

Name: Alec James Swann
Role: Right-hand opening bat
Born: 26 October 1976, Northampton
Height: 6ft 1in **Weight:** 11st
Nickname: Swanny
County debut: No first-team appearance
Parents: Raymond and Mavis
Marital status: Single
Family links with cricket: Father has played for Northumberland, Bedfordshire, Northamptonshire 2nd XI and England Amateurs. Brother Graeme has played for England U14 and U15
Education: Sponne Comprehensive, Towcester
Qualifications: 9 GCSEs
Off-season: Studying for A-levels
Cricketers particularly admired: Mark and Steve Waugh, Robin Smith

Other sports followed: Football (Newcastle and Liverpool) and most other sports except athletics

Relaxations: Listening to music, especially Pink Floyd, Simple Minds and INXS, reading political thrillers, watching sports, videos and films

Extras: Played for England Schools U15 and U19. Opened batting for Bedfordshire (with father in Minor Counties game). *Daily Telegraph* U15 Young Cricketer of the Year 1992. Midlands Club Cricket Conference Young Cricketer of the Year 1992

Opinions on cricket: '2nd XI cricket should be played over four days, club cricket could also be played over more than one afternoon. Tea interval should be half an hour and there should be 15 minutes between innings.'

SYLVESTER, S. A.   Nottinghamshire

Name: Steven Antony Sylvester
Role: Right-hand bat, left-arm fast-medium bowler
Born: 26 September 1968, Chalfont St Giles, Bucks
Height: 5ft 11in **Weight:** 12st 7lbs
Nickname: Silvers
County debut: 1991 (Middlesex), 1993 (Nottinghamshire – one-day), 1994 (Nottinghamshire – first-class)
1st-Class catches: 2
Parents: Ormond Alexander and Jennifer Irene
Marital status: Single
Family links with cricket: Father has played cricket all his life, both in St Vincent, West Indies and in England for Marlow Park and Maidenhead & Bray
Education: Wellesbourne School;
The Buckinghamshire College; University of London (Goldsmith's College)
Qualifications: 7 O-levels, 3 A-levels, BSc (Hons) in Psychology
Career outside cricket: 'Yet to be discovered ...'

Off-season: Training hard at both fitness and technique

Overseas tours: Buckinghamshire to Zimbabwe 1992

Cricketers particularly admired: Angus Fraser, Curtly Ambrose, Gordon Greenidge

Other sports followed: Football, judo

Relaxations: Work-outs at local fitness studio, reading anything to do with sport, especially sports psychology

Extras: Played cricket and football for Buckinghamshire. Released by Middlesex at end of 1992 season

Opinions on cricket: 'I believe the ruling on one bouncer per over gives the batsman a slight advantage. While something has to be done about intimidatory bowling, I am not sure that restricting the bowler's use of the bouncer is the right way to do it. I feel batsmen will remain untested by the short-pitched delivery.'

Best batting: 6* Nottinghamshire v Oxford University, The Parks 1994

Best bowling: 2-34 Middlesex v Cambridge University, Fenner's 1992

1994 Season

	M	Inns	NO	Runs	HS	Avge	100s	50s	Ct	St	O	M	Runs	Wkts	Avge	Best	5wI	10wM
Test																		
All First	1	1	1	6	6 *	-	-	-	-	-	22	3	57	1	57.00	1-38	-	-
1-day Int																		
NatWest																		
B & H																		
Sunday																		

Career Performances

	M	Inns	NO	Runs	HS	Avge	100s	50s	Ct	St	Balls	Runs	Wkts	Avge	Best	5wI	10wM
Test																	
All First	6	3	2	6	6 *	6.00	-	-	2	-	756	377	5	75.40	2-34	-	-
1-day Int																	
NatWest																	
B & H	2	1	0	0	0	0.00	-	-	-	-	102	83	1	83.00	1-31	-	
Sunday	1	1	1	1	1 *	-	-	-	1	-	12	19	0	-	-	-	

SYMONDS, A.   Gloucestershire

Name: Andrew Symonds
Role: Right-hand bat, off-spin bowler
Born: 9 June 1975, Birmingham
County debut: No first-team appearance
Marital status: Single
Off-season: Playing in Australia
Overseas teams played for:
Australian Cricket Academy 1993-94;
Queensland Colts 1993-94;
Queensland 1994-95
Extras: In his first season of first-class cricket he scored a century for Queensland against England on their 1994-95 tour of Australia. Born in England, he has been brought up in Australia and is a product of the Australian Cricket Academy.

TAYLOR, C. W.   Middlesex

Name: Charles William Taylor
Role: Left-hand bat, left-arm fast-medium bowler
Born: 12 August 1966, Banbury, Oxfordshire
Height: 6ft 5in **Weight:** 14st
Nickname: Farmer
County debut: 1990
1st-Class 5 w. in innings: 1
1st-Class catches: 6
Strike rate: (career 64.51)
Parents: Richard and Ann
Marital status: Single
Family links with cricket: Brother plays for Banbury, father played village cricket for Sandford St Martin
Education: Spendlove Comprehensive School, Charlbury; North Oxon Technical College
Qualifications: 1 O-level, City & Guilds Certificate in Agriculture

Career outside cricket: Farmer
Off-season: Working on the family farm
Overseas teams played for: Cricketers Club, New South Wales 1988-89
Cricketers particularly admired: Ian Bishop, Mark Waugh, Paul Tew ('my first club captain')
Injuries: Knee injury, missed most of the season
Other sports followed: National Hunt racing, golf
Relaxations: Most kinds of sports
Extras: Returned figures of 5 for 33 in second first-class match as Middlesex gained an important win on the way to the 1990 Championship title
Best batting: 28* Middlesex v Oxford University, The Parks 1993
Best bowling: 5-33 Middlesex v Yorkshire, Headingley 1990

1994 Season

	M	Inns	NO	Runs	HS	Avge	100s	50s	Ct	St	O	M	Runs	Wkts	Avge	Best	5wI	10wM
Test																		
All First	3	1	0	0	0	0.00	-	-	1	-	79	22	217	7	31.00	2-19	-	-
1-day Int																		
NatWest																		
B & H																		
Sunday	1	1	1	2	2*	-	-	-	-	-	3	0	21	0	-		-	-

Career Performances

	M	Inns	NO	Runs	HS	Avge	100s	50s	Ct	St	Balls	Runs	Wkts	Avge	Best	5wI	10wM
Test																	
All First	32	25	9	175	28*	10.93	-	-	6	-	4387	2395	68	35.22	5-33	1	-
1-day Int																	
NatWest	1	0	0	0	0	-	-	-	-	-	66	54	1	54.00	1-54	-	
B & H																	
Sunday	11	3	2	8	3*	8.00	-	-	5	-	359	297	7	42.42	2-33	-	

TAYLOR, J. P.   Northamptonshire

Name: Jonathan Paul Taylor
Role: Left-hand bat, left-arm fast-medium bowler
Born: 8 August 1964, Ashby-de-la-Zouch, Leicestershire
Height: 6ft 2in **Weight:** 13st 8lbs
Nickname: Roadie ('as in roadrunner'), PT
County debut: 1988 (Derbyshire), 1991 (Northamptonshire)
County cap: 1992
Test debut: 1992-93
Tests: 2

One-Day Internationals: 1
50 wickets in a season: 2
1st-Class 50s: 1
1st-Class 5 w. in innings: 8
1st-Class 10 w. in match: 1
1st-Class catches: 28
Place in bowling averages: 79th av. 31.69
(1993 35th av. 25.92)
Strike rate: 55.61 (career 59.13)
Parents: Derek and Janet
Wife and date of marriage: Elaine Mary, 30
July 1993
Children: Christopher Paul, 8 July 1994
Family links with cricket: Father and brother
played local league cricket
Education: Pingle School, Swadlincote,
Derbyshire
Qualifications: 6 O-levels, NCA coaching
certificate
Career outside cricket: Management apprentice with the National Coal Board, electrical
retail management
Off-season: Playing national indoor cricket
Overseas tours: Midland Club Cricket Conference to Australia 1990-91; England to India
and Sri Lanka 1992-93; England A to South Africa 1993-94; Northamptonshire to Natal 1993
Overseas teams played for: Papakura, New Zealand 1984-85; Napier High School Old
Boys, New Zealand 1985-86; North Kalgoorlie, Western Australia 1990-91; Great Boulder,
Western Australia 1991-92
Cricketers particularly admired: Ian Botham, Dennis Lillee
Other sports followed: Soccer, rugby
Injuries: Thigh strain and hamstring strain, missed about three weeks
Relaxations: 'Watching videos, eating out, DIY'
Extras: Spent four seasons on the staff at Derbyshire 1984-87 and played Minor Counties
cricket for Staffordshire 1989-90. Won Man of the Match in the Bain Clarkson Final in 1987
for Derbyshire, after being released. Played first game at Lord's in NatWest Trophy final
1992. Called up as replacement during England A tour to South Africa 1993-94
Opinions on cricket: 'The Sunday League should revert back to limited run-ups, but the
coloured clothing and white ball should remain. More should be done by the counties to find
winter employment for players staying at home.'
Best batting: 74* Northamptonshire v Nottinghamshire, Northampton 1992
Best bowling: 7-23 Northamptonshire v Hampshire, Bournemouth 1992

---

85. Who won the Minor Counties Championship in 1994?

1994 Season

	M	Inns	NO	Runs	HS	Avge	100s	50s	Ct	St	O	M	Runs	Wkts	Avge	Best	5wI	10wM
Test	1	2	1	0	0 *	0.00	-	-	-	-	26	6	82	2	41.00	1-18	-	-
All First	13	14	7	68	26	9.71	-	-	5	-	333.4	56	1141	36	31.69	5-62	1	-
1-day Int																		
NatWest	3	1	1	3	3 *	-	-	-	-	-	30	1	130	4	32.50	2-45	-	
B & H	1	0	0	0	0	-	-	-	-	-	10	3	28	1	28.00	1-28	-	
Sunday	12	6	4	17	11 *	8.50	-	-	-	-	80	3	470	10	47.00	3-30	-	

Career Performances

	M	Inns	NO	Runs	HS	Avge	100s	50s	Ct	St	Balls	Runs	Wkts	Avge	Best	5wI	10wM
Test	2	4	2	34	17 *	17.00	-	-	-	-	288	156	3	52.00	1-18	-	-
All First	80	79	34	455	74 *	10.11	-	1	28	-	13129	6831	222	30.77	7-23	8	1
1-day Int	1	1	0	1	1	1.00	-	-	-	-	18	20	0	-	-	-	
NatWest	17	5	2	21	9	7.00	-	-	6	-	1050	665	23	28.91	3-41	-	
B & H	12	5	3	11	6 *	5.50	-	-	3	-	723	350	14	25.00	3-38	-	
Sunday	58	22	8	98	24	7.00	-	-	7	-	2604	1998	69	28.95	3-14	-	

TAYLOR, M. Derbyshire

Name: Matthew Taylor
Role: Right-hand bat, slow left-arm bowler
Born: 13 November 1973
Height: 6ft 1in **Weight:** 11st 7lbs
Nickname: Taff
County debut: 1994
Parents: Edmund and Lynn
Marital status: Single
Family links with cricket: Last three generations have played club cricket in the Bolton area
Education: Rivington & Blackrod High School; North Bolton Smithills Sixth Form College
Qualifications: 7 O-levels, 3 A-levels
Off-season: Playing in South Africa
Overseas tours: Ole Mortensen's tour to Copenhagen 1994
Overseas teams played for: Runaway Bay, Queensland 1993-94; Pirates/Kismet CC, Durban, South Africa 1994-95
Cricketers particularly admired: Derek Underwood, Phil Tufnell, Steve Waugh, David Gower, Chris Brown

Other sports followed: 'Anything and everything except synchronised swimming'
Relaxations: Drinking good beer with friends, reading, socialising, films
Extras: Played for English Schools U19 and NCA U19 in 1993, for Lancashire 2nd XI in 1991 and 1992, and for Derbyshire 2nd XI in 1993. Man of the Match in final of U19 County Festival, for Lancashire against Durham
Opinions on cricket: 'Thoroughly enjoy the Sunday League and all one-day games. However, I find that too many rules are in favour of batsmen, especially at the highest levels.'
Best batting: 14* Derbyshire v Lancashire, Blackpool 1994
Best bowling: 3-25 Derbyshire v New Zealanders, Derby 1994

1994 Season

	M	Inns	NO	Runs	HS	Avge	100s	50s	Ct	St	O	M	Runs	Wkts	Avge	Best	5wl	10wM
Test																		
All First	4	5	2	25	14 *	8.33	-	-	-	-	82.1	24	205	7	29.28	3-25	-	-
1-day Int																		
NatWest																		
B & H																		
Sunday																		

Career Performances

	M	Inns	NO	Runs	HS	Avge	100s	50s	Ct	St	Balls	Runs	Wkts	Avge	Best	5wl	10wM
Test																	
All First	4	5	2	25	14 *	8.33	-	-	-	-	493	205	7	29.28	3-25	-	-
1-day Int																	
NatWest																	
B & H																	
Sunday																	

86. Who resigned from the ICC committee after admitting to having tampered with the ball during his playing career?

TAYLOR, N. R. Kent

Name: Neil Royston Taylor
Role: Right-hand bat, occasional off-spin bowler
Born: 21 July 1959, Farnborough, Kent
Height: 6ft 1in **Weight:** 15st
Nickname: Map
County debut: 1979
County cap: 1982
Benefit: 1992 (£131,000)
1000 runs in a season: 10
1st-Class 50s: 82
1st-Class 100s: 41
1st-Class 200s: 2
1st-Class catches: 151
One-Day 100s: 5
Place in batting averages: 38th av. 43.70 (1993 124th av. 28.29)
Strike rate: (career 98.43)
Parents: Leonard and Audrey
Wife and date of marriage: Jane Claire, 25 September 1982
Children: Amy Louise, 7 November 1985; Lauren, 21 July 1988
Family links with cricket: Brother Colin played for Kent U19. Father played club cricket
Education: Cray Valley Technical High School
Qualifications: 8 O-levels, 2 A-levels, NCA coaching certificate
Off-season: 'Coaching, playing golf and watching my rugby club, Westcombe Park.'
Overseas tours: English Schools to India 1977-78; Kent to Canada 1978, to Zimbabwe 1992-93; Fred Rumsey XI to West Indies 1988
Overseas teams played for: Randburg, Johannesburg 1979-85; St Stithian's College, Johannesburg (as coach) 1980-85
Cricketers particularly admired: Chris Tavaré, Mark Benson, Mike Gatting, Robin Smith
Other sports followed: Rugby union, golf
Relaxations: Music and reading (mainly biographies)
Extras: Made 110 on debut for Kent v Sri Lankans, 1979. Won four Man of the Match awards in his first five matches and scored three successive centuries in the B&H. Played for England B v Pakistan, 1982 and twice fielded as 12th man for England – v India in 1982 and v West Indies in 1988, both matches at The Oval. Holds Kent first and second wicket record partnerships with Mark Benson (300 v Derbyshire) and Simon Hinks (366 v Middlesex). Only Kent player to score 200 and 100 in a match twice (204 and 142 v Surrey, 111 and 203* v Sussex). 13 centuries at Canterbury, beating Frank Woolley and Colin Cowdrey. Provides a weekly contribution to Radio Kent through the summer
Best batting: 204 Kent v Surrey, Canterbury 1990
Best bowling: 2-20 Kent v Somerset, Canterbury 1985

1994 Season

	M	Inns	NO	Runs	HS	Avge	100s	50s	Ct	St	O	M	Runs	Wkts	Avge	Best	5wI	10wM
Test																		
All First	16	27	3	1049	139	43.70	3	4	4	-								
1-day Int																		
NatWest	4	4	0	119	64	29.75	-	1	1	-	8	0	38	3	12.66	3-38	-	
B & H	1	1	0	30	30	30.00	-	-	1	-								
Sunday	8	8	2	143	36	23.83	-	-	3	-								

Career Performances

	M	Inns	NO	Runs	HS	Avge	100s	50s	Ct	St	Balls	Runs	Wkts	Avge	Best	5wI	10wM
Test																	
All First	296	503	66	17351	204	39.70	41	82	151	-	1575	891	16	55.68	2-20	-	-
1-day Int																	
NatWest	29	29	1	714	85	25.50	-	4	6	-	143	86	6	14.33	3-29	-	
B & H	50	47	2	1858	137	41.28	5	7	10	-	12	5	0	-	-	-	-
Sunday	145	139	14	3840	95	30.72	-	24	37	-							

TERRY, V. P.   Hampshire

Name: Vivian Paul Terry
Role: Right-hand bat,
right-arm medium bowler, slip and outfielder
Born: 14 January 1959, Osnabruck,
West Germany
Height: 6ft **Weight:** 13st 10lbs
County debut: 1978
County cap: 1983
Benefit: 1994
Test debut: 1984
Tests: 2
1000 runs in a season: 10
1st-Class 50s: 76
1st-Class 100s: 36
1st-Class catches: 290
One-Day 100s: 12
Place in batting averages: 60th av. 38.96
(1993 24th av. 47.38)
Parents: Charles Michael and Patricia Mary
Wife and date of marriage: Bernadette Mary, 4 June 1986
Children: Siobhan Catherine, 13 September 1987; Sean Paul, 1 August 1991
Education: Durlston Court, Hampshire; Millfield School

Qualifications: 8 O-levels, 1 A-level, advanced cricket coach, squash coach
Off-season: Working for Meachers Transport, some coaching
Overseas tours: English Schools to India 1977-78; English Counties XI to Zimbabwe 1984-85; Bournemouth Sports to Kenya 1986
Overseas teams played for: Northern Districts, Sydney 1979-80; Wakatu, Nelson 1980-81; Durban Collegians 1982-84; Perth 1986-88, 1991-92
Cricketers particularly admired: Gordon Greenidge, Chris Smith, Viv Richards, Malcolm Marshall
Other sports followed: Most sports – golf, rugby, football
Relaxations: Sport – playing or watching, messing around with the kids
Opinions on cricket: 'Not enough done to ease pressures on cricketers during the winter. We are expected to reach April at a level of fitness and skill but always in our own time.'
Best batting: 190 Hampshire v Sri Lankans, Southampton 1988

1994 Season

	M	Inns	NO	Runs	HS	Avge	100s	50s	Ct	St	O	M	Runs	Wkts	Avge	Best	5wI	10wM
Test																		
All First	19	34	1	1286	164	38.96	5	2	25	-								
1-day Int																		
NatWest	2	2	0	12	11	6.00	-	-	1	-								
B & H	3	3	0	18	10	6.00	-	-	1	-								
Sunday	16	16	3	428	95	32.92	-	4	7	-								

Career Performances

	M	Inns	NO	Runs	HS	Avge	100s	50s	Ct	St	Balls	Runs	Wkts	Avge	Best	5wI	10wM
Test	2	3	0	16	8	5.33	-	-	2	-							
All First	265	446	41	15036	190	37.12	36	76	290	-	95	58	0	-	-	-	-
1-day Int																	
NatWest	38	36	4	1447	165 *	45.21	4	9	15	-							
B & H	52	52	5	1733	134	36.87	2	12	21	-							
Sunday	193	179	25	5106	142	33.15	6	27	100	-							

THOMAS, S. D.   Glamorgan

Name: Stuart Darren Thomas
Role: Left-hand bat, right-arm
medium-fast bowler
Born: 25 January 1975, Morriston
Height: 5ft 11in **Weight:** 13st 3lbs
Nickname: Tomo, Boom Boom, Dough Boy, Eric Cantona
County debut: 1992
1st-Class 5 w. in innings: 3

1st-Class catches: 3
Place in bowling averages:
(1993 52nd av. 27.80)
Strike rate: (career 41.68)
Parents: Stuart and Anne
Marital status: Single
Family links with cricket: Dad played for local 1st XI
Education: Craig Comprehensive; Neath Tertiary College
Qualifications: 4 GCSEs, BTEC National Diploma in Sports Science, NCA coaching certificate
Off-season: 'Going to Greece on holiday with girlfriend for a month. Playing some rugby and training in a local gym.'
Overseas tours: England U18 to South Africa 1992-93; Glamorgan to South Africa 1992-93, to Portugal 1994; England U19 to Sri Lanka 1993-94

Cricketers particularly admired: Steve Barwick, Matthew Maynard, Hugh Morris, Ian Botham
Other sports followed: Rugby union and league
Injuries: Rib cartilage, missed six weeks
Relaxations: 'Odd pint of lager, listening to music and watching Sky Television.'
Extras: Youngest player to take five wickets on debut v Derbyshire in 1992 and finished eighth in national bowling averages. BBC Welsh Young Sports Personality 1992. Played last U19 Test against India at Edgbaston 1994
Opinions on cricket: 'Enjoy coloured clothing in Sunday League. I think that third umpires should be used in all one-day games as there are so many close decisions made. Happy to see the four-day game. This has showed a bigger advance of young cricketers and gives more opportunities for the players as there is more time to play cricket.'
Best batting: 16* Glamorgan v Hampshire, Swansea 1993
Best bowling: 5-76 Glamorgan v Worcestershire, Worcester 1993

1994 Season

	M	Inns	NO	Runs	HS	Avge	100s	50s	Ct	St	O	M	Runs	Wkts	Avge	Best	5wI	10wM
Test																		
All First	1	1	1	15	15 *	-	-	-	-	-	30	3	108	3	36.00	2-80	-	-
1-day Int																		
NatWest																		
B & H																		
Sunday																		

Career Performances

	M	Inns	NO	Runs	HS	Avge	100s	50s	Ct	St	Balls	Runs	Wkts	Avge	Best	5wI	10wM
Test																	
All First	11	15	7	86	16 *	10.75	-	-	3	-	1709	1068	41	26.04	5-76	3	-
1-day Int																	
NatWest																	
B & H																	
Sunday	3	0	0	0	0	-	-	-	1	-	70	48	1	48.00	1-34	-	

THOMPSON, D. J.   Surrey

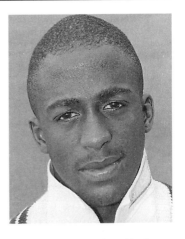

Name: David James Thompson
Role: Right-hand bat, right-arm fast bowler
Born: 11 March 1976
Height: 6ft 3in
Nickname: Thommo
County debut: 1994
Marital status: Single
Education: Ernest Bevin School;
Westminster College
Qualifications: 8 GCSEs
Off-season: Touring with England U19
Overseas tours: England U19 to
West Indies 1994-95
Cricketers particularly admired:
Michael Holding 'because of his sheer pace'
Other sports followed: Football, baseball
Relaxations: 'Listening to reggae music,
spending time with little cousins and family'
Extras: Played for Charlton FC and was
offered YTS terms, but chose cricket 'because I enjoy it much more'. Released by Surrey
at end of 1994 season
Opinions on cricket: 'I think that the rule for one bouncer is silly, because a proper
bouncer is never over head height and you can therefore bowl more than one in an over.'
Best batting: 22 Surrey v Oxford University, The Oval 1994
Best bowling: 2-37 Surrey v Oxford University, The Oval 1994

> 87. Which player took the wicket of Martin Crowe in his first over in
> international cricket for England in 1994?

1994 Season

	M	Inns	NO	Runs	HS	Avge	100s	50s	Ct	St	O	M	Runs	Wkts	Avge	Best	5wI	10wM
Test																		
All First	1	2	0	39	22	19.50	-	-	-	-	27	4	123	3	41.00	2-37	-	-
1-day Int																		
NatWest																		
B & H																		
Sunday																		

Career Performances

	M	Inns	NO	Runs	HS	Avge	100s	50s	Ct	St	Balls	Runs	Wkts	Avge	Best	5wI	10wM
Test																		
All First	1	2	0	39	22	19.50	-	-	-	-	162	123	3	41.00	2-37	-	-
1-day Int																		
NatWest																		
B & H																		
Sunday																		

THOMPSON, J. B.   Kent

Name: Julian Barton Thompson
Role: Right-hand bat, right-arm
fast-medium bowler
Born: 28 October 1968, Cape Town,
South Africa
Height: 6ft 4in **Weight:** 13st 7lbs
Nickname: Thommo, Doc
County debut: 1994
Parents: John and Joyce
Marital status: Single
Family links with cricket:
Father played club cricket
Education: The Judd School, Tonbridge, Kent;
Guy's Hospital Medical School, London
Qualifications: MB BS
Career outside cricket: Doctor
Off-season: House surgeon, Royal Berkshire
Hospital, Reading
Overseas tours:
University of London to India 1991
Overseas teams played for: Northern Districts, Sydney 1987-88
Cricketers particularly admired: Carl Hooper

Other sports followed: Golf, football
Injuries: Stress fracture of right fibula, missed two months
Relaxations: Golf, squash, P.G. Wodehouse, eating
Best batting: 2 Kent v Warwickshire, Edgbaston 1994
Best bowling: 1-89 Kent v Warwickshire, Edgbaston 1994

1994 Season

	M	Inns	NO	Runs	HS	Avge	100s	50s	Ct	St	O	M	Runs	Wkts	Avge	Best	5wI	10wM
Test																		
All First	1	2	1	3	2	3.00	-	-	-	-	33	6	120	1	120.00	1-89	-	-
1-day Int																		
NatWest																		
B & H																			
Sunday	2	1	1	3	3*	-	-	-	-	-	10	1	45	0	-		-	-

Career Performances

	M	Inns	NO	Runs	HS	Avge	100s	50s	Ct	St	Balls	Runs	Wkts	Avge	Best	5wI	10wM
Test																	
All First	1	2	1	3	2	3.00	-	-	-	-	198	120	1	120.00	1-89	-	-
1-day Int																	
NatWest																	
B & H																	
Sunday	2	1	1	3	3*	-	-	-	-	-	60	45	0	-		-	-

THORPE, G. P. Surrey

Name: Graham Paul Thorpe
Role: Left-hand bat, occasional right-arm medium bowler
Born: 1 August 1969, Farnham
Height: 5ft 10in **Weight:** 11st 7lbs
Nickname: Chalky
County debut: 1988
County cap: 1991
Test debut: 1993
Tests: 10
One-Day Internationals: 6
1000 runs in a season: 5
1st-Class 50s: 50
1st-Class 100s: 15
1st-Class 200s: 1
1st-Class catches: 99
One-Day 100s: 4

Place in batting averages: 12th av. 54.09 (1993 73rd av. 35.96)
Strike rate: (career 87.95)
Parents: Geoff and Toni
Marital status: Single
Family links with cricket: Both brothers play for Farnham, father also plays cricket and mother is 'professional scorer'
Education: Weydon Comprehensive; Farnham Sixth Form College
Qualifications: 7 O-levels, PE Diploma
Off-season: Touring with England
Overseas tours: England A to Zimbabwe and Kenya 1989-90, to Pakistan 1990-91, to Bermuda and West Indies 1991-92, to Australia 1992-93; England to West Indies 1993-94, to Australia 1994-95
Cricketers particularly admired: Viv Richards, Grahame Clinton, David Gower
Other sports followed: Football, tennis
Extras: Played for English Schools cricket U15 and U19 and England Schools football U18. Scored a century against Australia on his Test debut at Trent Bridge 1993
Best batting: 216 Surrey v Somerset, The Oval 1992
Best bowling: 4-40 Surrey v Australians, The Oval 1993

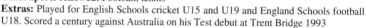

1994 Season

	M	Inns	NO	Runs	HS	Avge	100s	50s	Ct	St	O	M	Runs	Wkts	Avge	Best	5wl	10wM
Test	2	4	1	239	79	79.66	-	3	2	-								
All First	16	25	4	1136	190	54.09	2	7	11	-	5	0	23	0	-	-	-	-
1-day Int	2	2	0	81	55	40.50	-	1	1	-								
NatWest	4	4	2	335	145 *	167.50	1	2	2	-								
B & H	4	4	0	196	87	49.00	-	2	5	-								
Sunday	13	11	2	331	102 *	36.77	1	2	6	-								

Career Performances

	M	Inns	NO	Runs	HS	Avge	100s	50s	Ct	St	Balls	Runs	Wkts	Avge	Best	5wl	10wM
Test	10	19	2	708	114 *	41.64	1	6	14	-	48	15	0	-	-	-	-
All First	141	232	33	8414	216	42.28	15	50	99	-	1759	1043	20	52.15	4-40	-	-
1-day Int	6	6	0	174	55	29.00	-	1	5	-							
NatWest	17	16	4	658	145 *	54.83	1	5	8	-	13	12	0	-	-	-	
B & H	22	22	2	752	103	37.60	1	5	9	-	168	131	4	32.75	3-35	-	
Sunday	85	78	12	2399	115 *	36.34	2	18	30	-	312	293	8	36.62	3-21	-	

THURSFIELD, M. J.　　　　　　Hampshire

Name: Martin John Thursfield
Role: Right-hand bat, right-arm
medium-fast bowler
Born: 14 December 1971, South Shields
Height: 6ft 4in **Weight:** 14st
Nickname: Thursy
County debut: 1990
1st-Class 5 w. in innings: 1
1st-Class catches: 1
Place in bowling averages: 65th av. 330.82
Strike rate: 57.52 (career 60.92)
Parents: Anthony John and Maureen
Marital status: Single
Family links with cricket:
Great-grandfather played for Yorkshire, and
father is a keen club cricketer
Education: Boldon Comprehensive
Qualifications: GCSEs, NCA coaching
certificate

Off-season: 'In a gym under the guidance of Paul Terry'
Overseas tours: England YC to New Zealand 1990-91
Cricketers particularly admired: Robin Smith, Malcolm Marshall, Allan Donald
Other sports followed: Football, golf
Injuries: Ruptured ankle ligaments, missed eight weeks
Relaxations: Playing golf, watching football and sleeping
Extras: Bowled two balls with broken leg in first England YC one-day International v New
Zealand 1990-91. One of the youngest golfers in the country to achieve a hole in one, aged 10
Best batting: 47 Hampshire v Glamorgan, Southampton 1994
Best bowling: 6-130 Hampshire v Middlesex, Southampton 1994

1994 Season

	M	Inns	NO	Runs	HS	Avge	100s	50s	Ct	St	O	M	Runs	Wkts	Avge	Best	5wI	10wM
Test																		
All First	9	12	1	106	47	9.63	-	-	1	-	163	39	524	17	30.82	6-130	1	-
1-day Int																		
NatWest																			
B & H																			
Sunday	6	3	2	2	1*	2.00	-	-	1	-	41	0	187	6	31.16	3-31	-	

Career Performances

	M	Inns	NO	Runs	HS	Avge	100s	50s	Ct	St	Balls	Runs	Wkts	Avge	Best	5wI	10wM
Test																	
All First	14	16	3	142	47	10.92	-	-	1	-	1584	832	26	32.00	6-130	1	-
1-day Int																	
NatWest																	
B & H																	
Sunday	12	6	2	19	9	4.75	-	-	2	-	522	407	12	33.91	3-31	-	

TITCHARD, S. P. Lancashire

Name: Stephen Paul Titchard
Role: Right-hand bat, right-arm
medium bowler
Born: 17 December 1967, Warrington,
Cheshire
Height: 6ft 3in **Weight:** 15st
Nickname: Titch, Stainy, Tyrone
County debut: 1990
1st-Class 50s: 14
1st-Class 100s: 1
1st-Class catches: 33
Place in batting averages: 151st av. 26.14
(1993 161st av. 23.70)
Parents: Alan and Margaret
Marital status: Single
Family links with cricket: Father, uncle
and two brothers have played for
Grappenhall 1st XI in the Manchester
Association League. Father also represented
the Army
Education: Lymm County High School; Priestley College
Qualifications: 3 O-levels, NCA Senior Coaching Award
Career outside cricket: Coach
Off-season: Coaching
Overseas tours: Lancashire to Tasmania and Western Australia 1990, to Western Australia
1991, to Johannesburg 1992
Overseas teams played for: South Canberra, Australia 1991-92
Cricketers particularly admired: Graham Gooch, Malcolm Marshall
Other sports followed: Football (Manchester City) and rugby league (Warrington)
Relaxations: Snooker, golf, 'most sports'
Extras: Played for England U19. Made record scores for Manchester Association U18

(200*) and Cheshire Schools U19 (203*)
Opinions on cricket: 'In Championship games, the day should comprise of three two-hour sessions, with an extended tea break of at least ten minutes!'
Best batting: 135 Lancashire v Nottinghamshire, Old Trafford 1991

1994 Season

	M	Inns	NO	Runs	HS	Avge	100s	50s	Ct	St	O	M	Runs	Wkts	Avge	Best	5wI	10wM
Test																		
All First	13	21	0	549	99	26.14	-	3	16	-								
1-day Int																		
NatWest																		
B & H																		
Sunday	5	5	1	189	96	47.25	-	1	1	-								

Career Performances

	M	Inns	NO	Runs	HS	Avge	100s	50s	Ct	St	Balls	Runs	Wkts	Avge	Best	5wI	10wM
Test																	
All First	43	75	4	2129	135	29.98	1	14	33	-							
1-day Int																	
NatWest	2	2	0	24	20	12.00	-	-	-	-							
B & H	3	3	0	101	82	33.66	-	1	1	-							
Sunday	21	21	3	496	96	27.55	-	2	4	-							

TOLLEY, C. M.   Worcestershire

Name: Christopher Mark Tolley
Role: Right-hand bat, left-arm medium bowler
Born: 30 December 1967, Kidderminster
Height: 5ft 9in **Weight:** 11st 8lbs
Nickname: Treefrog, Red Dog
County debut: 1989
County cap: 1993
1st-Class 50s: 3
1st-Class 5 w. in innings: 1
1st-Class catches: 26
Place in batting averages: 182nd av. 22.50 (1993 179th av. 22.41)
Place in bowling averages: (1993 58th av. 28.42)
Strike rate: (career 73.03)
Parents: Ray and Liz
Marital status: Single
Family links with cricket: Father played local league; brother Richard plays in the Birmingham League

Education: Oldswinford Primary School; Redhill Comprehensive School; King Edward VI College, Stourbridge; Loughborough University
Qualifications: 9 O-levels, 3 A-levels, BSc (Hons) PE Sports Science & Recreation Management. Qualified teacher status
Career outside cricket: Teaching
Off-season: Teaching PE at Malvern Chase
Overseas tours: British Universities Sports Federation tour to Barbados October 1989; Worcestershire to Zimbabwe and South Africa
Cricketers particularly admired: Ian Botham, Richard Hadlee, Graeme Hick
Other sports followed: Football, athletics, hockey
Injuries: Shoulder problem (biceps tendon and a/c joint)
Relaxations: Food, music
Extras: Played for English Schools U19 in 1986 and for the Combined Universities in B&H Cup
Best batting: 84 Worcestershire v Derbyshire, Derby 1994
Best bowling: 5-55 Worcestershire v Kent, Worcester 1993

1994 Season

	M	Inns	NO	Runs	HS	Avge	100s	50s	Ct	St	O	M	Runs	Wkts	Avge	Best	5wI	10wM
Test																		
All First	7	11	3	180	84	22.50	-	1	3	-	148	36	486	8	60.75	3-52	-	-
1-day Int																		
NatWest	1	0	0	0	0	-	-	-	-	-	-	7	0	36	2	18.00	2-36	-	
B & H	1	0	0	0	0	-	-	-	-	-	-							
Sunday	4	1	0	1	1	1.00	-	-	1	-	8	1	24	1	24.00	1-24	-	

Career Performances

	M	Inns	NO	Runs	HS	Avge	100s	50s	Ct	St	Balls	Runs	Wkts	Avge	Best	5wI	10wM
Test																	
All First	60	69	21	1043	84	21.72	-	3	26	-	7205	3440	96	35.83	5-55	1	-
1-day Int																	
NatWest	5	2	2	21	12 *	-	-	-	-	-	252	148	6	24.66	3-25	-	
B & H	12	9	1	203	77	25.37	-	2	3	-	654	397	6	66.16	1-12	-	
Sunday	32	14	5	16	5 *	1.77	-	-	7	-	1024	812	28	29.00	4-50	-	

TOPLEY, T. D.   Essex

Name: Thomas Donald Topley
Role: Right-hand bat, right-arm
fast-medium bowler
Born: 25 February 1964, Canterbury
Height: 6ft 3in **Weight:** 15st 4lbs
Nickname: Toppers, Wimble, Jack
County debut: 1985 (Surrey), 1985 (Essex)
County cap: 1988 (Essex)
50 wickets in a season: 3
1st-Class 50s: 4
1st-Class 5 w. in innings: 15
1st-Class 10 w. in match: 2
1st-Class catches: 70
One-Day 5 w. in innings: 2
Place in batting averages:
(1993 235th av. 14.09)
Place in bowling averages:
(1993 122nd av. 41.80)

Strike rate: (career 53.00)
Parents: Tom (deceased) and Rhoda
Marital status: Engaged to Julia
Children: Reece James William, 21 February 1994
Family links with cricket: Brother Peter played for Kent (1972-76); father played for
Combined Services
Education: Royal Hospital School, Holbrook, Suffolk
Qualifications: 6 O-levels, NCA Advanced Coach, Screen Actors Guild (in America)
Career outside cricket: PE teacher, cricket coach
Overseas tours: Benefit tour to Barbados 1986
Overseas teams played for: Noodsburg and Midlands, Natal 1985-86; Roodeburg, Transvaal
1986-87; Griqualand West, South Africa 1987-88; Harare Sports Club, Zimbabwe 1990-92
Cricketers particularly admired: 'All the great bowlers' and John Lever, David Gower,
Ian Botham and Viv Richards
Other sports followed: Rugby, soccer and all other ball sports
Injuries: Continual left leg problem
Relaxations: 'Playing most other ball sports, even watching Colchester United playing
football. Travelling, especially through Africa, eating out and photography'
Extras: Spent three years on the MCC Young Professionals at Lord's. As 12th man held
famous one-handed 'catch' for England v West Indies at Lord's in 1984, stepping over the
boundary in taking it. Also played for Norfolk (1982-84) and Surrey (1985). Zimbabwe
coach during 1991-92 World Cup, where they beat England. Has received two B&H Gold
Awards and two NatWest Trophy awards. Appeared in a commercial for television, shot in
Hollywood, involving cricket and baseball. Released by Essex at end of 1994 season

Best batting: 66 Essex v Yorkshire, Headingley 1987
Best bowling: 7-75 Essex v Derbyshire, Chesterfield 1988

1994 Season

	M	Inns	NO	Runs	HS	Avge	100s	50s	Ct	St	O	M	Runs	Wkts	Avge	Best	5wI	10wM
Test																		
All First	1	1	0	2	2	2.00	-	-	-	-	16	3	47	1	47.00	1-22	-	-
1-day Int																		
NatWest																		
B & H	1	0	0	0	0	-	-	-	-	-	11	0	46	1	46.00	1-46	-	
Sunday	5	4	1	23	14	7.66	-	-	3	-	17.1	0	129	3	43.00	2-45	-	

Career Performances

	M	Inns	NO	Runs	HS	Avge	100s	50s	Ct	St	Balls	Runs	Wkts	Avge	Best	5wI	10wM
Test																	
All First	120	138	29	1693	66	15.53	-	4	70	-	19453	10147	367	27.64	7-75	15	2
1-day Int																	
NatWest	17	8	2	75	19 *	12.50	-	-	3	-	1070	663	30	22.10	4-21	-	
B & H	26	7	4	35	10 *	11.66	-	-	7	-	1488	835	36	23.19	4-22	-	
Sunday	111	58	19	309	38 *	7.92	-	-	22	-	4649	3536	126	28.06	6-33	2	

TRESCOTHICK, M. E.   Somerset

Name: Marcus Edward Trescothick
Role: Left-hand bat, right-arm swing bowler,
reserve wicket-keeper
Born: 25 December 1975, Keynsham, Bristol
Height: 6ft 3in **Weight:** 14st 7lbs
Nickname: Banger
County debut: 1993
1st-Class 50s scord: 8
1st-Class 100s: 2
1st-Class catches: 17
One-Day 100s: 1
Place in batting averages: 24th av. 48.63
Parents: Martyn and Lin
Marital status: Single
Family links with cricket: Father played
for Somerset 2nd XI; uncle played
club cricket
Education: Sir Bernard Lovell School
Qualifications: 7 GCSEs

Off-season: Touring with England U19
Overseas tours:
England U18 to South Africa 1992-93;
England U19 to Sri Lanka 1993-94, to West Indies (captain) 1994-95
Cricketers particularly admired:
Neil Fairbrother, Jack Russell, Mark Lathwell
Other sports followed: Golf, football
Relaxations: Playing golf, repairing and
renovating cricket bats and listening
to music
Extras: Member of England U19 squad for home series against West Indies 1993. Man of
the Series against India U19 in 1994, scoring most runs in the series. Whittingdale Young
Player of the Month, August 1994
Opinions on cricket: '2nd XI games should be on county grounds, instead of on bad school
and club grounds.'
Best batting: 121 Somerset v Surrey, Bath 1994

1994 Season

	M	Inns	NO	Runs	HS	Avge	100s	50s	Ct	St	O	M	Runs	Wkts	Avge	Best	5wI	10wM
Test																		
All First	11	20	1	924	121	48.63	2	8	13	-								
1-day Int																		
NatWest	3	3	0	174	116	58.00	1	-	1	-								
B & H																		
Sunday	12	12	0	370	74	30.83	-	2	4	-								

Career Performances

	M	Inns	NO	Runs	HS	Avge	100s	50s	Ct	St	Balls	Runs	Wkts	Avge	Best	5wI	10wM
Test																	
All First	14	26	1	938	121	37.52	2	8	17	-							
1-day Int																	
NatWest	3	3	0	174	116	58.00	1	-	1	-							
B & H																	
Sunday	15	15	0	402	74	26.80	-	2	5	-							

TRUMP, H. R. J.   Somerset

Name: Harvey Russell John Trump
Role: Right-hand bat, off-spin bowler,
gully/slip fielder
Born: 11 October 1968, Taunton
Height: 6ft 1in **Weight:** 14st
Nickname: Trumpy, Club Foot
County debut: 1988
County cap: 1994
50 wickets in a season: 1
1st-Class 5 w. in innings: 8
1st-Class 10 w. in match: 2
1st-Class catches: 61
Place in batting averages: 223rd av. 17.25
Place in bowling averages: 87th av. 33.57
(1993 116th av. 39.26)
Strike rate: 62.00 (career 76.93)
Parents: Gerald and Jackie
Marital status: Single
Family links with cricket: Father played
for Somerset 2nd XI and captained Devon

Education: Millfield School; Chester College of Higher Education
Qualifications: 7 O-levels, 2 A-levels, BA (Hons)
Career outside cricket: Teaching at Stamford School, Lincolnshire
Off-season: Coaching and teaching at Stamford School
Overseas tours: England YC to Sri Lanka 1986-87, to Australia (Youth World Cup) 1987-88
Cricketers particularly admired: David Graveney, John Emburey, Viv Richards
Other sports followed: Hockey, rugby and most other sports
Relaxations: Theatre, cinema, crosswords, reading
Extras: Played county hockey for Somerset U19. Qualified lifeguard, attaining bronze
medallion life-saving award, and is preliminary teacher of disabled swimming certificate.
'He's the best fielder off his own bowling I've ever seen' – David Graveney 1991
Opinions on cricket: 'Something has got to be done about the seam on the ball. Over-rates
need to be looked at and adjusted appropriately. It is vitally important for youngsters to have
a good grounding at junior levels in two and three-day cricket, not just one-day.'
Best batting: 48 Somerset v Hampshire, Taunton 1988
Best bowling: 7-52 Somerset v Gloucestershire, Gloucester 1992

---

88. Who played the longest-ever County Championship innings in
1994, how long did it last and and what was his final score?

1994 Season

	M	Inns	NO	Runs	HS	Avge	100s	50s	Ct	St	O	M	Runs	Wkts	Avge	Best	5wI	10wM
Test																		
All First	14	20	4	276	45 *	17.25	-	-	14	-	268.4	76	873	26	33.57	6-68	2	1
1-day Int																		
NatWest	1	1	0	4	4	4.00	-	-	-	-	6.1	2	41	1	41.00	1-41	-	
B & H																		
Sunday	15	4	1	8	6	2.66	-	-	8	-	96.2	4	393	9	43.66	3-19	-	

Career Performances

	M	Inns	NO	Runs	HS	Avge	100s	50s	Ct	St	Balls	Runs	Wkts	Avge	Best	5wI	10wM
Test																	
All First	88	97	30	784	48	11.70	-	-	61	-	15310	7500	199	37.68	7-52	8	2
1-day Int																	
NatWest	6	4	1	6	4	2.00	-	-	2	-	277	194	3	64.66	2-44	-	
B & H	7	4	1	3	1	1.00	-	-	2	-	318	197	4	49.25	2-23	-	
Sunday	57	17	7	80	19	8.00	-	-	21	-	2198	1622	38	42.68	3-19	-	

TUDOR, A. J. — Surrey

Name: Alexander Jeremy Tudor
Role: Right-hand bat, right-arm fast bowler
Born: 23 October 1977,
West Brompton, London
Height: 6ft 4in **Weight:** 13st 7lbs
Nickname: Big Al, Bambi, Tudes
County debut: No first-team appearance
Parents: Daryll and Jennifer
Marital status: Single
Family links with cricket: Brother was on the staff at The Oval
Education: Wandle Primary, Earlsfield; St Mark's C of E, Fulham; City of Westminster College
Off-season: Studying for GNVQ in Sport and Tourism
Overseas tours: England U15 to South Africa 1992-93
Cricketers particularly admired: Curtly Ambrose, Brian Lara
Other sports followed: Basketball, football (QPR)
Relaxations: Listening to music

Extras: Played for London Schools at all ages from U8. Played for England U17 against India in 1994. MCC Young Cricketer

TUFNELL, P. C. R.   Middlesex

Name: Philip Clive Roderick Tufnell
Role: Right-hand bat, slow left-arm spinner
Born: 29 April 1966, Hadley Wood, Hertfordshire
Height: 6ft **Weight:** 12st 7lbs
Nickname: The Cat
County debut: 1986
County cap: 1990
Test debut: 1990-91
Tests: 18
One-Day Internationals: 18
50 wickets in a season: 4
1st-Class 5 w. in innings: 23
1st-Class 10 w. in match: 2
1st-Class catches: 65
One-Day 5 w. in innings: 1
Place in batting averages:
(1993 259th av. 10.66)
Place in bowling averages: 49th av. 28.38
(1993 20th av. 23.89)
Strike rate: 71.35 (career 74.47)
Parents: Sylvia and Alan
Marital status: Divorced
Education: Highgate School, Southgate School
Qualifications: O-level in Art; City & Guilds Silversmithing
Off-season: Touring with England
Overseas tours: England YC to West Indies 1984-85; England to Australia 1990-91, to New Zealand and Australia (World Cup) 1991-92, to India and Sri Lanka 1992-93, to West Indies 1993-94, to Australia 1994-95
Overseas teams played for: Queensland University, Australia
Cricketers particularly admired: Jason Pooley
Other sports followed: American football
Relaxations: Sleeping
Extras: MCC Young Cricketer of the Year 1984 and Middlesex Uncapped Bowler of the Year 1987. Was originally a seam bowler and gave up cricket for three years in his mid-teens
Best batting: 37 Middlesex v Yorkshire, Headingley 1990
Best bowling: 8-29 Middlesex v Glamorgan, Cardiff 1993

1994 Season

	M	Inns	NO	Runs	HS	Avge	100s	50s	Ct	St	O	M	Runs	Wkts	Avge	Best	5wI	10wM
Test	1	0	0	0	0	-	-	-	1	-	55	21	112	4	28.00	2-31	-	-
All First	9	6	1	14	5	2.80	-	-	5	-	463.5	128	1107	39	28.38	6-35	1	-
1-day Int																		
NatWest	1	0	0	0	0	-	-	-	1	-	11	0	71	1	71.00	1-71	-	-
B & H	1	0	0	0	0	-	-	-	-	-	11	1	32	3	10.66	3-32	-	
Sunday	10	2	0	2	1	1.00	-	-	2	-	71	0	319	12	26.58	3-28	-	

Career Performances

	M	Inns	NO	Runs	HS	Avge	100s	50s	Ct	St	Balls	Runs	Wkts	Avge	Best	5wI	10wM
Test	18	25	14	56	22 *	5.09	-	-	8	-	5132	2229	58	38.43	7-47	4	1
All First	152	150	60	908	37	10.08	-	-	65	-	37536	15911	504	31.56	8-29	23	2
1-day Int	18	8	8	15	5 *	-	-	-	3	-	900	634	15	42.26	3-40	-	
NatWest	5	1	0	8	8	8.00	-	-	3	-	354	201	8	25.12	3-29	-	
B & H	8	5	3	41	18	20.50	-	-	1	-	468	362	8	45.25	3-32	-	
Sunday	24	5	3	16	13 *	8.00	-	-	3	-	1008	741	33	22.45	5-28	1	

TURNER, R. J.   Somerset

Name: Robert Julian Turner
Role: Right-hand bat, wicket-keeper
Born: 25 November 1967, Worcestershire
Height: 6ft 2in **Weight:** 13st 8lbs
Nickname: Noddy, Sniper, Teffers, Scissors
County debut: 1991
County cap: 1994
1st-Class 50s: 7
1st-Class 100s: 2
1st-Class catches: 103
1st-Class stumpings: 21
Place in batting averages: 168th av. 24.40
(1993 184th av. 21.66)
Parents: Derek Edward and Doris Lilian
Marital status: Single
Family links with cricket: Brother Simon played for Somerset (1984-85) as a wicket-keeper and is now captain of Weston-super-Mare. Other brother Richard also plays for Weston-super-Mare first team and father is chairman of the club
Education: Uphill Primary School; Broadoak School, Weston-super-Mare; Millfield School; Cambridge University

Qualifications: Honours Degree in Engineering, Diploma in Computer Science
Career outside cricket: Maths teacher at Stanbridge Earls School, Hampshire
Off-season: Teaching
Overseas tours: Millfield School to Barbados, 1985; Combined Universities to Barbados 1989, to Kuala Lumpur, Malaysia 1992, to Qantas, Western Australia 1993
Overseas teams played for: Claremont-Nedlands, Perth, Western Australia 1991-93
Cricketers particularly admired: Andy Brassington, Peter Roebuck, Stuart Turner 'for his never-ending determination', Mushtaq Ahmed 'for his support and advice'
Other sports followed: Nearly all sports; 'enjoy playing hockey, golf and swimming'
Relaxations: Photography, playing the piano and guitar, reading, sleeping, eating curries, golf and drinking beer
Extras: Captain of Cambridge University (Blue 1988-91) and Combined Universities 1991. Capped at end of 1994 season
Opinions on cricket: 'Owing to the effect that our overseas player has had on my career, I would be very hesitant in agreeing to no overseas players in the County Championship.'
Best batting: 104* Somerset v New Zealanders, Taunton 1994

1994 Season

	M	Inns	NO	Runs	HS	Avge	100s	50s	Ct	St	O	M	Runs	Wkts	Avge	Best	5wI	10wM
Test																		
All First	18	27	5	537	104 *	24.40	1	2	46	6								
1-day Int																		
NatWest	3	2	0	21	15	10.50	-	-	7	-								
B & H	1	1	0	6	6	6.00	-	-	2	-								
Sunday	15	13	8	179	37 *	35.80	-	-	16	-								

Career Performances

	M	Inns	NO	Runs	HS	Avge	100s	50s	Ct	St	Balls	Runs	Wkts	Avge	Best	5wI	10wM
Test																	
All First	66	101	10	1977	104 *	24.40	2	7	103	21	13	26	0	-	-	-
1-day Int																	
NatWest	3	2	0	21	15	10.50	-	-	7	-							
B & H	5	5	3	55	25 *	27.50	-	-	4	1							
Sunday	21	19	10	250	37 *	27.77	-	-	21	2							

TWEATS, T. A.   Derbyshire

Name: Timothy Andrew Tweats
Role: Right-hand bat, off-spin bowler
Born: 18 April 1974, Stoke-on-Trent
Height: 6ft 3in **Weight:** 13st
County debut: 1992
1st-Class catches: 1
Parents: Malcolm and Linda
Marital status: Single
Family links with cricket:
Father and two brothers, Jon and Simon,
play for the local club, Leek, for whom he
played before joining Derbyshire
Education: Endon High School;
Stoke-on-Trent Sixth Form College;
Staffordshire University
Qualifications: 5 GCSEs, 2 A-levels
Career outside cricket: Student
Overseas tours: Kidsgrove and District
Junior Cricket League to Australia 1991

Cricketers particularly admired: Robin Smith, Phil Tufnell
Other sports followed: Football
Best batting: 24 Derbyshire v Glamorgan, Cardiff 1992

1994 Season (did not make any first-class or one-day appearance)

Career Performances

	M	Inns	NO	Runs	HS	Avge	100s	50s	Ct	St	Balls	Runs	Wkts	Avge	Best	5wl	10wM
Test																	
All First	1	1	0	24	24	24.00	-	-	1	-							
1-day Int																	
NatWest																	
B & H																	
Sunday																	

TWOSE, R. G.   Warwickshire

Name: Roger Graham Twose
Role: Left-hand bat, right-arm medium bowler
Born: 17 April 1968, Torquay ('in a car!')
Height: 6ft **Weight:** 14st 7lbs
Nickname: Twosey, Buff, Tom Cruise
County debut: 1989
County cap: 1992
1000 runs in a season: 2
1st-Class 50s: 30
1st-Class 100s: 8
1st-Class 200s: 2
1st-Class 5 w. in innings: 2
1st-Class catches: 57
One-Day 100s: 3
Place in batting averages: 11th av. 54.26
(1993 248th av. 12.44)
Place in bowling averages: 102nd av. 36.26
(1993 49th av. 27.45)
Strike rate: 76.33 (career 68.80)
Parents: Paul and Patricia
Marital status: Single
Family links with cricket: Brother Richard plays for Devon, for whom their father played. Uncles are Roger Tolchard of Leicestershire and England and Jeff Tolchard of Leicestershire
Education: Wolborough Hill, Newton Abbot, Devon; King's College, Taunton
Qualifications: 7 O-levels, 2 A-levels, NCA coaching certificate. Currently studying for Business Management Diploma
Off season: Playing first-class cricket in New Zealand
Overseas teams played for: Northern Districts, New Zealand 1989-90; Central Districts, New Zealand 1991-94
Cricketers particularly admired: Dermot Reeve, Mark Greatbatch
Other sports followed: Rugby, hockey, etc.
Relaxations: 'Working out with my girlfriend.'
Extras: 'Once took all ten wickets in an innings whilst playing in New Zealand: a feat I plan to reproduce in first-class cricket!' Warwickshire Player of the Year 1992. Parents live in New Zealand, where he has played for the past seven winters and is considering emigrating to make himself available for New Zealand Test side. Played the first innings in the County Championship to last over 10 hours (277 v Glamorgan, 1994)
Best batting: 277 Warwickshire v Glamorgan, Edgbaston 1994
Best bowling: 6-28 Warwickshire v Surrey, Guildford 1994

1994 Season

	M	Inns	NO	Runs	HS	Avge	100s	50s	Ct	St	O	M	Runs	Wkts	Avge	Best	5wI	10wM
Test																		
All First	18	31	5	1411	277 *	54.26	3	6	8	-	190.5	41	544	15	36.26	6-28	1	-
1-day Int																		
NatWest	5	4	0	221	110	55.25	1	-	1	-	25	1	111	3	37.00	2-30	-	
B & H	3	3	0	83	46	27.66	-	-	1	-	13	1	58	2	29.00	1-25	-	
Sunday	17	16	3	397	96 *	30.53	-	2	7	-	35.4	0	199	7	28.42	3-36	-	

Career Performances

	M	Inns	NO	Runs	HS	Avge	100s	50s	Ct	St	Balls	Runs	Wkts	Avge	Best	5wI	10wM
Test																	
All First	101	172	21	5518	277 *	36.54	8	30	57	-	6949	3324	101	32.91	6-28	2	-
1-day Int																	
NatWest	16	15	2	571	110	43.92	2	1	5	-	675	441	17	25.94	3-39	-	
B & H	12	11	0	259	62	23.54	-	1	6	-	192	133	2	66.50	1-25	-	
Sunday	77	64	9	1444	100	26.25	1	7	23	-	1417	1191	35	34.02	3-31	-	

UDAL, S. D.   Hampshire

Name: Shaun David Udal
Role: Right-hand bat, off-spin bowler, fields in the deep
Born: 18 March 1969, Farnborough
Height: 6ft 2in **Weight:** 13st
Nickname: Shaggy
County debut: 1989
County cap: 1992
One-Day Internationals: 3
50 wickets in a season: 3
1st-Class 50s: 6
1st-Class 5 w. in innings: 14
1st-Class 10 w. in match: 3
1st-Class catches: 30
Place in batting averages: 147th av. 26.30 (1993 191th av. 20.36)
Place in bowling averages: 39th av. 27.13 (1993 71st av. 30.16)
Strike rate: 58.95 (career 64.13)
Parents: Robin and Mary
Wife and date of marriage: Emma Jane, 5 October 1991
Children: Katherine Mary, 26 August 1992

Family links with cricket: Father played for Surrey Colts and Camberley for 42 years; brother plays for Camberley 1st XI. Grandfather played for Leicestershire and Middlesex
Education: Tower Hill Infant and Junior Schools; Cove Comprehensive School
Qualifications: 8 CSEs, qualified print finisher
Career outside cricket: Director of a print finishing company
Off-season: Touring Australia with England
Overseas tours: England to Australia 1994-95
Overseas teams played for: Hamilton Wickham, Newcastle, NSW 1990
Cricketers particularly admired: Ian Botham, John Emburey, Robin Smith
Other sports followed: Football (Aldershot Town), golf
Relaxations: 'Camberley CC. Good food, beer and wine, and spending time with my daughter and wife.'
Injuries: Injured finger on England tour to Australia 1994-95
Extras: Has taken two hat-tricks in club cricket, scored a double hundred in a 40-over club game and took 8-50 v Sussex in the first game of 1992 season, his seventh Championship match. Man of the Match on NatWest debut against Berkshire 1991 and named Hampshire Cricket Association Player of the Year 1993
Opinions on cricket: 'Four-day cricket only good for the game as long as the pitches are good, and last four days instead of two or three. Format is better now Sunday League is back to 40 overs.'
Best batting: 94 Hampshire v Glamorgan, Southampton 1994
Best bowling: 8-50 Hampshire v Sussex, Southampton 1992

1994 Season

	M	Inns	NO	Runs	HS	Avge	100s	50s	Ct	St	O	M	Runs	Wkts	Avge	Best	5wI	10wM
Test																		
All First	17	30	4	684	94	26.30	-	4	16	-	678	174	1872	69	27.13	6-79	7	1
1-day Int	3	1	1	3	3 *	-	-	-	-	-	33	2	90	3	30.00	2-39	-	
NatWest	2	1	0	14	14	14.00	-	-	1	-	22	2	60	3	20.00	2-20	-	
B & H	3	0	0	0	0	-	-	-	-	-	25	1	99	3	33.00	2-17	-	
Sunday	16	10	2	83	35	10.37	-	-	5	-	111.3	5	571	13	43.92	2-28	-	

Career Performances

	M	Inns	NO	Runs	HS	Avge	100s	50s	Ct	St	Balls	Runs	Wkts	Avge	Best	5wI	10wM
Test																	
All First	68	93	18	1672	94	22.29	-	6	30	-	14431	7154	225	31.79	8-50	14	3
1-day Int	3	1	1	3	3 *	-	-	-	-	-	198	90	3	30.00	2-39	-	
NatWest	11	2	0	16	14	8.00	-	-	4	-	720	400	14	28.57	3-39	-	
B & H	18	5	3	26	9 *	13.00	-	-	4	-	1116	695	31	22.41	4-40	-	
Sunday	66	35	11	296	44	12.33	-	-	23	-	2946	2414	80	30.17	4-51	-	

VANDRAU, M. J. Derbyshire

Name: Matthew James Vandrau
Role: Right-hand bat, off-spin bowler
Born: 22 July 1969, Epsom
Height: 6ft 3in **Weight:** 13st
Nickname: Cat, Luther
County debut: 1993
1st-Class 50s: 3
1st-Class 5 w. in innings: 2
1st-Class catches: 17
Place in batting averages: 171st av. 24.16
(1993 198th av. 19.23)
Place in bowling averages: 109th av. 37.11
(1993 144th av. 58.56)
Strike rate: 67.11 (career 70.55)
Parents: Bruce and Maureen
Marital status: Single
Family links with cricket: Father played
for Transvaal in 1963, was Transvaal
director of cricket 1976-91 and is
now vice-president
Education: St Stithian's College, Johannesburg; St John's College, Johannesburg; University
of Witwatersrand
Qualifications: BComm
Off-season: Playing in South Africa
Overseas tours: Transvaal to England 1992
Overseas teams played for: South African Schools 1986; South African Universities
1990; Transvaal 1991-94
Cricketers particularly admired: Clive Rice
Other sports followed: Rugby, golf
Relaxations: Golf, red wine and getting away to the game parks
Best batting: 66 Derbyshire v Kent, Derby 1994
Best bowling: 5-42 Transvaal v Border, Johannesburg 1993-94

1994 Season

	M	Inns	NO	Runs	HS	Avge	100s	50s	Ct	St	O	M	Runs	Wkts	Avge	Best	5wI	10wM
Test																		
All First	13	23	5	435	66	24.16	-	1	9	-	290.5	63	965	26	37.11	4-53	-	-
1-day Int																		
NatWest	3	2	1	27	27	27.00	-	-	-	-	21	1	81	4	20.25	2-36	-	
B & H																		
Sunday	8	3	0	19	10	6.33	-	-	6	-	38	2	226	4	56.50	3-25	-	

Career Performances

	M	Inns	NO	Runs	HS	Avge	100s	50s	Ct	St	Balls	Runs	Wkts	Avge	Best	5wI	10wM
Test																	
All First	33	54	8	943	66	20.50	-	3	17	-	4798	2401	68	35.30	5-42	2	-
1-day Int																	
NatWest	4	3	1	48	27	24.00	-	-	-	-	168	90	5	18.00	2-36	-	
B & H	1	0	0	0	0	-	-	-	-	-	66	46	1	46.00	1-46	-	
Sunday	16	9	3	138	32 *	23.00	-	-	7	-	555	512	10	51.20	3-25	-	

VAN TROOST, A. P. Somerset

Name: André Pelrus van Troost
Role: Right-hand bat 'specialist no 11 batsman',
right-arm fast bowler
Born: 2 October 1972, Schiedam, Holland
Height: 6ft 7in **Weight:** 15st
Nickname: Flappie, Rooster
County debut: 1991
1st-Class 5 w. in innings: 3
1st-Class catches: 9
One-Day 5 w. in innings: 1
Place in bowling averages: 114th av. 37.97
(1993 97th av. 33.41)
Strike rate: 59.28 (career 57.43)
Parents: Aad and Anneke
Marital status: Single
Family links with cricket: Father plays for
Excelsior in Holland; brother plays for Excelsior
and Holland U23; grandfather played for
Excelsior and Holland

Education: Spieringshoek College, Schiedam
Qualifications: Finished Havo schooling – specialised in languages
Career outside cricket: Works in a bank
Off-season: Playing cricket in South Africa
Overseas tours: Holland to Zimbabwe 1989, to Namibia 1990, to Dubai 1991, to Canada,
New Zealand and South Africa 1992
Overseas teams played for: Excelsior, Holland 1979-91; Alma Marist, Cape Town 1992-
93; Griqualand West, South Africa 1994-95
Cricketers particularly admired: Richard Hadlee, Peter Roebuck, Roland Lefebvre, Eric
Van't Zelfde, Paul Van de Bosch
Other sports followed: Football, tennis and most other sports
Injuries: Shin splints, missed two matches

Relaxations: Playing football and travelling
Extras: Played for Holland at age 15 and became third Dutch national to play professional cricket. Took 6-3 v Durham 2nd XI in 1992 season
Opinions on cricket: 'When there is grass on the wicket, it's time to play cricket.'
Best batting: 35 Somerset v Lancashire, Taunton 1993
Best bowling: 6-48 Somerset v Essex, Taunton 1992

1994 Season

	M	Inns	NO	Runs	HS	Avge	100s	50s	Ct	St	O	M	Runs	Wkts	Avge	Best	5wI	10wM
Test																		
All First	14	18	6	108	33	9.00	-	-	3	-	345.5	60	1329	35	37.97	4-50	-	-
1-day Int																		
NatWest	3	1	0	7	7	7.00	-	-	-	-	22	1	111	6	18.50	5-22	1	
B & H	1	1	0	5	5	5.00	-	-	-	-	9	0	64	1	64.00	1-64	-	
Sunday	8	3	3	12	9 *	-	-	-	-	-	52.1	1	258	9	28.66	4-23	-	

Career Performances

	M	Inns	NO	Runs	HS	Avge	100s	50s	Ct	St	Balls	Runs	Wkts	Avge	Best	5wI	10wM
Test																	
All First	43	45	18	258	35	9.55	-	-	9	-	5341	3398	93	36.53	6-48	3	-
1-day Int																	
NatWest	7	3	1	27	17 *	13.50	-	-	-	-	366	274	12	22.83	5-22	1	
B & H	2	2	1	14	9 *	14.00	-	-	-	-	118	102	3	34.00	2-38	-	
Sunday	15	5	3	20	9 *	10.00	-	-	1	-	573	452	16	28.25	4-23	-	

VAUGHAN, M. P.   Yorkshire

Name: Michael Paul Vaughan
Role: Right-hand bat, off-spin bowler
Born: 29 October 1974, Eccles, Manchester
Height: 6ft 2in **Weight:** 11st 7lbs
Nickname: Virgil, Frankie, Nigel Bond
County debut: 1993
1000 runs in a season: 1
1st-Class 50s: 4
1st-Class 100s: 3
1st-Class catches: 8
Place in batting averages: 76th av. 36.75
Place in bowling averages: 140th av. 48.42
Strike rate: 97.92 (career 96.60)
Parents: Graham John and Dee
Marital status: Single

Family links with cricket: Dad played for Worsley CC and mother is related to the famous Tyldesley family (Lancashire and England)
Education: St Marks, Worsey; Dore Juniors, Sheffield; Silverdale Comprehensive, Sheffield
Qualifications: 4 GCSEs
Off-season: Touring with England A. Pre-season tour with Yorkshire to South Africa
Overseas tours: England U19 to India 1992-93, to Sri Lanka 1993-94; Yorkshire to West Indies 1994; England A to India 1994-95
Cricketers particularly admired:
Peter Hartley, Richard Blakey, Carl Hooper
Other sports followed:
Football (Sheffield Wednesday)
Injuries: Calf strain, missed last game of the season
Relaxations: Playing golf, skiing, shopping, going out with friends, following Wednesday

Extras: Played club cricket for Sheffield Collegiate in the Yorkshire League. *Daily Telegraph* U15 Batsman of the Year, 1990. Maurice Leyland Batting Award 1990. Rapid Cricketline Player of the Month, June 1993. The Cricket Society Most Promising Young Cricketer 1993. AA Thompson Memorial Trophy – The Roses Cricketer of the Year 1993. Whittingdale Cricketer of the Month, July 1994. 1066 runs in first full season of first-class cricket in 1994. Captained England U19 in home series against India 1994
Best batting: 117 Yorkshire v Northamptonshire, Luton 1994
Best bowling: 4-39 Yorkshire v Oxford University, The Parks 1994

1994 Season

	M	Inns	NO	Runs	HS	Avge	100s	50s	Ct	St	O	M	Runs	Wkts	Avge	Best	5wI	10wM
Test																		
All First	16	30	1	1066	117	36.75	3	3	8	-	228.3	53	678	14	48.42	4-39	-	-
1-day Int																		
NatWest	2	2	0	19	10	9.50	-	-	-	-								
B & H	1	1	0	0	0	0.00	-	-	-	-	3	0	13	0	-		-	-
Sunday	3	3	0	19	12	6.33	-	-	-	-								

Career Performances

	M	Inns	NO	Runs	HS	Avge	100s	50s	Ct	St	Balls	Runs	Wkts	Avge	Best	5wI	10wM
Test																	
All First	18	34	1	1184	117	35.87	3	4	8	-	1449	720	15	48.00	4-39	-	-
1-day Int																	
NatWest	2	2	0	19	10	9.50	-	-	-	-							
B & H	1	1	0	0	0	0.00	-	-	-	-	18	13	0	-		-	-
Sunday	5	5	0	36	12	7.20	-	-	-	-							

WALKER, A. Durham

Name: Alan Walker
Role: Left-hand bat, right-arm medium-fast bowler
Born: 7 July 1962, Emley, near Huddersfield
Height: 5ft 11in **Weight:** 13st
Nickname: Wacky, Walks
County debut: 1983 (Northants), 1994 (Durham)
County cap: 1987 (Northants)
1st-Class 5 w. in innings: 2
1st-Class catches: 39
Strike rate: (career 61.68)
Parents: Malcolm and Enid
Wife and date of marriage: Nicky, 2 October 1994
Children: Jessica, 3 March 1988
Family links with cricket: Grandfather played in local league
Education: Emley Junior School; Kirkburton Middle School; Shelley High School
Qualifications: 2 O-levels, 4 CSEs, qualified coal-face worker
Career outside cricket: Mining, building, coaching
Off-season: Playing in Australia
Overseas tours: NCA North U19 to Denmark; Northamptonshire to Durban
Overseas teams played for: Uitenhage, South Africa 1984-85 and 1987-88
Cricketers particularly admired: Dennis Lillee, Richard Hadlee, Jeremy Snape 'for his ability to see the funny side of things when things are not going well'
Other sports followed: Football (Huddersfield Town and Emley), rugby league (Wakefield Trinity)
Relaxations: DIY, drinking, gardening
Best batting: 41* Northamptonshire v Warwickshire, Edgbaston 1987
Best bowling: 6-50 Northamptonshire v Lancashire, Northampton 1986

1994 Season

	M	Inns	NO	Runs	HS	Avge	100s	50s	Ct	St	O	M	Runs	Wkts	Avge	Best	5wI	10wM
Test																		
All First	4	7	2	34	13	6.80	-	-	1	-	116	23	369	8	46.12	4-59	-	-
1-day Int																		
NatWest	1	1	0	13	13	13.00	-	-	-	-	12	1	61	0	-		-	-
B & H	1	1	1	9	9*	-	-	-	-	-	6	0	20	1	20.00	1-20	-	
Sunday	15	9	3	75	15	12.50	-	-	4	-	111.5	5	658	25	26.32	4-43	-	

564

Career Performances

	M	Inns	NO	Runs	HS	Avge	100s	50s	Ct	St	Balls	Runs	Wkts	Avge	Best	5wl	10wM
Test																	
All First	101	98	47	698	41 *	13.68	-	-	39	-	14310	7318	232	31.54	6-50	2	-
1-day Int																	
NatWest	18	5	1	35	13	8.75	-	-	3	-	1060	618	19	32.52	4-7	-	
B & H	28	11	8	47	15 *	15.66	-	-	6	-	1489	1091	31	35.19	4-46	-	
Sunday	115	32	14	201	30	11.16	-	-	28	-	4716	3644	136	26.79	4-21	-	

WALKER, M. J. Kent

Name: Matthew Jonathan Walker
Role: Left-hand bat, right-arm medium-fast bowler
Born: 2 January 1974, Gravesend, Kent
Height: 5ft 7in **Weight:** 12st 7lbs
Nickname: Walks
County debut: 1992-93
1st-Class 100s: 1
1st-Class catches: 3
Place in batting averages: 99th av. 34.14
Parents: Richard and June
Marital status: Single
Family links with cricket: Grandfather played for Kent and father was on Lord's groundstaff, having played for Middlesex and Kent 2nd XI
Education: Shorne Primary School; King's School, Rochester
Qualifications: 9 GCSEs, 2 A-levels, coaching certificates
Career outside cricket: 'Yet to be decided'
Off-season: Coaching cricket in north Kent
Overseas tours: Kent U17 to New Zealand 1991; England U19 to Pakistan 1991-92, to India 1992-93; Kent to Zimbabwe 1992-93
Cricketers particularly admired: Carl Hooper
Other sports followed: Rugby, hockey, skiing, football – 'most really'
Relaxations: Music, watching films; likes old pubs
Extras: Captained England U15, U16 and U17 at hockey; represented Kent U18 at rugby; had football trials with Chelsea and Gillingham. Captained England U19 tour to India 1992-93 and v West Indies in 1993 home series which England U19 won 2-0 in one-day matches and 1-0 in 'Test' series. Received Sir Jack Hobbs award for best young cricketer 1989, and *Daily Telegraph* U15 batting award 1989. Selected for Kent U21 hockey team in 1993 and

1994. Woolwich Kent League's Young Cricketer of the Year 1994
Opinions on cricket: 'Not enough interest in youth cricket. Cricket in schools is gradually becoming non-existent and talent is just being lost because of this.'
Best batting: 107 Kent v Surrey, The Oval 1994

1994 Season

	M	Inns	NO	Runs	HS	Avge	100s	50s	Ct	St	O	M	Runs	Wkts	Avge	Best	5wI	10wM
Test																		
All First	5	7	0	239	107	34.14	1	-	2	-								
1-day Int																		
NatWest																		
B & H																		
Sunday	9	9	1	187	69 *	23.37	-	1	4	-								

Career Performances

	M	Inns	NO	Runs	HS	Avge	100s	50s	Ct	St	Balls	Runs	Wkts	Avge	Best	5wI	10wM
Test																	
All First	6	9	1	278	107	34.75	1	-	3	-							
1-day Int																	
NatWest																	
B & H																	
Sunday	9	9	1	187	69 *	23.37	-	1	4	-							

WALSH, C. A.　　　　　Gloucestershire

Name: Courtney Andrew Walsh
Role: Right-hand bat, right-arm fast bowler
Born: 30 October 1962, Kingston, Jamaica
Height: 6ft 5^1/2in **Weight:** 14st 7lbs
Nickname: Mark, Walshy, Cuddy, RP
County debut: 1984
County cap: 1985
Test debut: 1984-85
Tests: 65
One-Day Internationals: 124
50 wickets in a season: 8
100 wickets in a season: 1
1st-Class 50s: 8
1st-Class 5 w. in innings: 70
1st-Class 10 w. in match: 14
1st-Class catches: 77
One-Day 5 w. in innings: 3

Place in batting averages: 238th av. 15.22 (1993 229th av. 14.77)
Place in bowling averages: 3rd av. 17.24 (1993 19th av. 23.68)
Strike rate: 34.12 (career 46.87)
Parents: Eric and Joan
Marital status: Single
Education: Excelsior High School
Qualifications: GCE and CXL
Overseas tours: West Indies YC to England 1982; West Indies B to Zimbabwe 1983-84; West Indies to England 1984, to Australia 1984-85, to Pakistan, Australia and New Zealand 1986-87, to India and Pakistan (World Cup) 1987-88, to England 1988, to Australia 1988-89, to Pakistan 1990-91, to England 1991, to Australia and South Africa 1992-93, to Sharjah, India (Hero Cup) and Sri Lanka 1993-94, to India and New Zealand 1994-95
Overseas teams played for: Jamaica 1981-95
Other sports followed: All
Injuries: Neck and lower back in a car crash, missed two-three weeks
Relaxations: Swimming, reading and listening to music
Extras: Took record 10-43 in Jamaican school cricket in 1979. On tour, he has the reputation as an insatiable collector of souvenirs. David Graveney, when captaining Gloucestershire, reckoned Walsh was the 'best old-ball bowler in the world'. One of *Wisden*'s Five Cricketers of the Year 1986. Took hat-trick for West Indies v Australia in 1988-89. Captain of Jamaica 1991-92 and 1993-94. Cricketers' Association Player of the Year and Wombwell Cricket Lovers' Cricketer of the Year 1993. Took over captaincy of West Indies from Richie Richardson
Opinions on cricket: 'Watch the changes.'
Best batting: 66 Gloucestershire v Kent, Cheltenham 1994
Best bowling: 9-72 Gloucestershire v Somerset, Bristol 1986

1994 Season

	M	Inns	NO	Runs	HS	Avge	100s	50s	Ct	St	O	M	Runs	Wkts	Avge	Best	5wI	10wM
Test																		
All First	15	24	6	274	66	15.22	-	1	2	-	506.1	119	1535	89	17.24	7-42	9	3
1-day Int																		
NatWest	1	1	0	9	9	9.00	-	-	-	-	12	1	32	2	16.00	2-32	-	
B & H	1	1	0	0	0	0.00	-	-	-	-	10	1	33	1	33.00	1-33	-	
Sunday	12	12	2	121	30	12.10	-	-	3	-	83.1	10	352	18	19.55	4-20	-	

Career Performances

	M	Inns	NO	Runs	HS	Avge	100s	50s	Ct	St	Balls	Runs	Wkts	Avge	Best	5wI	10wM
Test	65	88	27	560	30 *	9.18	-	-	9	-	13190	5824	222	26.23	6-62	6	1
All First	300	378	87	3664	66	12.59	-	8	77	-	56864	27152	1213	22.38	9-72	70	14
1-day Int	124	41	17	204	29 *	8.50	-	-	15	-	6622	4241	134	31.64	5-1	1	
NatWest	19	12	3	136	37	15.11	-	-	2	-	1218	648	41	15.80	6-21	2	
B & H	21	13	4	87	28	9.66	-	-	-	-	1255	745	24	31.04	2-19	-	
Sunday	100	64	10	493	35	9.12	-	-	20	-	4090	2725	135	20.18	4-19	-	

Name: Timothy Charles Walton
Role: Right-hand bat, right-arm medium bowler
Born: 8 November 1972, Low Lead
Height: 6ft **Weight:** 12st 10lbs
Nickname: TC, Eric Spadge
County debut: 1992 (one-day), 1994 (first-class)
1st-Class catches: 2
Parents: Alan Michael and Sally Ann
Marital status: single
Family links with cricket: Father and two brothers, Jamie and Adam, play for local village
Education: Leeds Grammar School; University of Northumbria, Newcastle
Qualifications: 7 GCSEs, 3 A-levels, studying for Sports degree
Career outside cricket: Student
Overseas tours: England U19 to Pakistan 1991-92
Cricketers particularly admired: Phillip DeFreitas
Other sports followed: Rugby union and league
Relaxations: Running, raving and listening to music
Opinions on cricket: 'Appearance should be irrelevant if the cricketer is good enough, i.e. long hair should be of no consequence. More commerciality and one-day games.'
Best batting: 11 Northamptonshire v Somerset, Taunton 1994
Best bowling: 1-46 Northamptonshire v Somerset, Taunton 1994

1994 Season

	M	Inns	NO	Runs	HS	Avge	100s	50s	Ct	St	O	M	Runs	Wkts	Avge	Best	5wI	10wM
Test																		
All First	2	2	0	16	11	8.00	-	-	2	-	20	1	98	2	49.00	1-46	-	-
1-day Int																		
NatWest																		
B & H																		
Sunday	9	9	2	267	72	38.14	-	3	6	-	22	0	108	3	36.00	1-18	-	

89. Who scored a double-century for England in the first Test against New Zealand in 1994?

Career Performances

	M	Inns	NO	Runs	HS	Avge	100s	50s	Ct	St	Balls	Runs	Wkts	Avge	Best	5wl	10wM
Test																	
All First	2	2	0	16	11	8.00	-	-	2	-	120	98	2	49.00	1-46	-	-
1-day Int																	
NatWest																	
B & H																	
Sunday	11	9	2	267	72	38.14	-	3	6	-	222	171	6	28.50	2-27	-	

WAQAR YOUNIS Surrey

Name: Waqar Younis
Role: Right-hand bat, right-arm fast bowler
Born: 16 November 1971, Vehari, Pakistan
Height: 5ft 11in **Weight:** 12st
Nickname: Wicky
County debut: 1990
County cap: 1990
Test debut: 1989-90
Tests: 29
One-Day Internationals: 83
50 wickets in a season: 3
1st-Class 50s: 1
1st-Class 5 w. in innings: 48
1st-Class 10 w. in match: 11
1st-Class catches: 29
One-Day 5 w. in innings: 9
Place in batting averages:
(1993 246th av. 12.58)
Place in bowling averages:
(1993 14th av. 22.69)
Strike rate: (career 37.22)
Marital status: Single
Education: Pakistani College, Sharjah; Government College, Vehari
Off-season: Playing for Pakistan
Overseas tours: Pakistan to India, Australia and Sharjah 1989-90, to England 1992, to New Zealand, Australia, South Africa and West Indies 1992-93, to Sharjah 1993-94, to New Zealand 1993-94, to South Africa 1994-95
Overseas teams played for: United Bank, Pakistan
Cricketers particularly admired: Imran Khan, Wasim Akram, Geoff Arnold, Alec Stewart
Other sports followed: Football, badminton, squash
Relaxations: 'Sleeping and family get-togethers'

Extras: Made Test debut for Pakistan v India aged 17, taking 4 for 80 at Karachi. Signed by Surrey during 1990 season on recommendation of Imran Khan, who had first seen him bowling on television, and made county debut in B&H quarter-final v Lancashire. Martin Crowe described his bowling during Pakistan's series with New Zealand as the best display of fast bowling he had ever seen. Named Cricketers' Association Cricketer of the Year 1991 and one of *Wisden*'s Cricketers of the Year 1992. Appointed vice-captain of Pakistan 1992-93
Opinions on cricket: 'There should be no over-rate fines.'
Best batting: 51 United Bank v PIA, Lahore 1989-90
Best bowling: 7-64 United Bank v ADBP, Lahore 1990-91

1994 Season (did not make any first-class or one-day appearance)

Career Performances

	M	Inns	NO	Runs	HS	Avge	100s	50s	Ct	St	Balls	Runs	Wkts	Avge	Best	5wI	10wM
Test	29	35	6	254	29	8.75	-	-	3	-	6082	3152	166	18.98	7-76	17	3
All First	110	119	34	1086	51	12.77	-	1	29	-	19843	10665	533	20.01	7-64	48	11
1-day Int	83	36	14	264	37	12.00	-	-	9	-	4057	2875	141	20.39	6-26	7	
NatWest	9	3	0	33	26	11.00	-	-	1	-	601	354	25	14.16	5-40	1	
B & H	6	5	2	15	5 *	5.00	-	-	1	-	341	222	8	27.75	3-29	-	
Sunday	40	16	4	104	39	8.66	-	-	7	-	1854	1298	78	16.64	5-26	1	

WARD, D. M.   Surrey

Name: David Mark Ward
Role: Right-hand bat, right-arm off-spin bowler, occasional wicket-keeper
Born: 10 February 1961, Croydon
Height: 6ft 1in **Weight:** 14st
Nickname: Cocker, Wardy, Jaws, Gnasher, Fat Boy, Piano Man
County debut: 1985
County cap: 1990
1000 runs in a season: 2
1st-Class 50s: 30
1st-Class 100s: 16
1st-Class 200s: 3
1st-Class catches: 116
1st-Class stumpings: 3
One-Day 100s: 3
Place in batting averages: 37th av. 43.85
(1993 129th av. 27.61)
Parents: Tom and Dora

Wife and date of marriage: Ruth, 2 October 1993

Family links with cricket: 'Uncle (John Goodey) local legend with Banstead and Temple Bar CC'

Education: Haling Manor High School; Croydon Technical College

Qualifications: 2 O-levels, Advanced City & Guilds in Carpentry and Joinery

Career outside cricket: Mortgage expert (Home Owners Advisory Service) and carpenter

Overseas tours: Surrey to Barbados 1984, 1989, 1991; Lancashire to Mombasa 1990; MCC to Bahrain 1994-95

Overseas teams played for: Caulfield, Melbourne 1984-87; Sunshine, Melbourne 1988-89; Perth, Western Australia 1990-91; St Augustine, Cape Town 1992-93

Cricketers particularly admired: Robert Thompson (brother of 'Candles' Thompson) of Sturt CC, Adelaide, Geoff Howarth, Grahame Clinton

Other sports followed: Greyhound racing

Extras: In 1990 became first Surrey batsman since John Edrich to score 2000 runs in a season and shared county record stand of 413 for third wicket with Darren Bicknell v Kent at Canterbury. Hit century in 70 minutes for Surrey v Northamptonshire 1992

Best batting: 294* Surrey v Derbyshire, The Oval 1994

Best bowling: 2-66 Surrey v Gloucestershire, Guildford 1991

1994 Season

	M	Inns	NO	Runs	HS	Avge	100s	50s	Ct	St	O	M	Runs	Wkts	Avge	Best	5wI	10wM
Test																		
All First	16	22	1	921	294 *	43.85	1	5	10	-								
1-day Int																		
NatWest	4	3	0	106	87	35.33	-	1	-	-								
B & H	4	4	0	197	73	49.25	-	3	2	-								
Sunday	17	15	1	582	91	41.57	-	5	10	-								

Career Performances

	M	Inns	NO	Runs	HS	Avge	100s	50s	Ct	St	Balls	Runs	Wkts	Avge	Best	5wI	10wM
Test																	
All First	150	236	33	7931	294 *	39.06	16	30	116	3	107	113	2	56.50	2-66	-	-
1-day Int																	
NatWest	21	17	1	616	101 *	38.50	1	5	8	-							
B & H	30	27	4	585	73	25.43	-	3	11	2							
Sunday	140	123	21	3109	102 *	30.48	2	21	67	1							

WARD, T. R. Kent

Name: Trevor Robert Ward
Role: Right-hand bat, occasional off-spin bowler
Born: 18 January 1968, Farningham, Kent
Height: 5ft 11in **Weight:** 13st
Nickname: Wardy, Chikka
County debut: 1986
County cap: 1989
1000 runs in a season: 4
1st-Class 50s: 46
1st-Class 100s: 18
1st-Class 200s: 1
1st-Class catches: 115
One-Day 100s: 3
Place in batting averages: 47th av. 42.75 (1993 105th av. 31.13)
Parents: Robert Henry and Hazel Ann
Wife and date of marriage: Sarah Ann, 29 September 1990
Family links with cricket: Father played club cricket
Education: Anthony Roper County Primary; Hextable Comprehensive
Qualifications: 7 O-levels, NCA coaching award
Off-season: Coaching in Kent
Overseas tours: NCA to Bermuda 1985; England YC to Sri Lanka 1986-87, to Australia (Youth World Cup) 1987-88
Overseas teams played for: Scarborough, Perth, Western Australia 1985; Gosnalls, Perth 1993
Cricketers particularly admired: Ian Botham, Graham Gooch, Robin Smith, Viv Richards
Other sports followed: Most sports
Relaxations: Fishing, watching television, golf
Opinions on cricket: 'Again, in 1994, four day wickets have not come up to standard.'
Best batting: 235* Kent v Middlesex, Canterbury 1991
Best bowling: 2-48 Kent v Worcestershire, Canterbury 1990

1994 Season

	M	Inns	NO	Runs	HS	Avge	100s	50s	Ct	St	O	M	Runs	Wkts	Avge	Best	5wI	10wM
Test																		
All First	19	33	1	1368	125	42.75	3	10	29	-								
1-day Int																		
NatWest	4	4	0	242	120	60.50	1	1	-	-	6	0	29	0	-		-	-
B & H	1	1	0	14	14	14.00	-	-	-	-								
Sunday	17	17	0	435	63	25.58	-	3	6	-								

Career Performances

	M	Inns	NO	Runs	HS	Avge	100s	50s	Ct	St	Balls	Runs	Wkts	Avge	Best	5wl	10wM
Test																	
All First	132	225	15	8039	235 *	38.28	18	46	115	-	964	537	6	89.50	2-48	-	-
1-day Int																	
NatWest	15	15	0	680	120	45.33	1	5	1	-	108	87	1	87.00	1-58	-	
B & H	24	24	2	571	94	25.95	-	3	5	-	12	10	0	-	-	-	
Sunday	94	93	3	2677	131	29.74	2	16	20	-	228	187	6	31.16	3-20	-	

WARNER, A. E. Derbyshire

Name: Allan Esmond Warner
Role: Right-hand bat, right-arm fast bowler, outfielder
Born: 12 May 1959, Birmingham
Height: 5ft 8in **Weight:** 10st
Nickname: Esis
County debut: 1982 (Worcestershire), 1985 (Derbyshire)
County cap: 1987 (Derbyshire)
Benefit: 1995
1st-Class 50s: 15
1st-Class 5 w. in innings: 5
1st-Class 10 w. in match: 1
1st-Class catches: 44
One-Day 5 w. in innings: 1
Place in batting averages:
(1993 205th av. 18.30)
Place in bowling averages: 129th av. 43.00
(1993 12th av. 21.95)
Strike rate: 80.84 (career 63.84)
Parents: Edgar and Sarah
Children: Alvin, 6 September 1980
Education: Tabernacle School, St Kitts, West Indies
Qualifications: CSE Maths
Cricketers particularly admired: Malcolm Marshall, Michael Holding
Other sports followed: Football, boxing and athletics
Relaxations: Watching movies, music (soul, reggae and calypso)
Extras: Derbyshire Player of the Year 1993
Best batting: 95* Derbyshire v Kent, Canterbury 1993
Best bowling: 5-27 Worcestershire v Glamorgan, Worcester 1984
5-27 Derbyshire v Gloucestershire, Cheltenham 1993

1994 Season

	M	Inns	NO	Runs	HS	Avge	100s	50s	Ct	St	O	M	Runs	Wkts	Avge	Best	5wI	10wM
Test																		
All First	10	15	3	96	24 *	8.00	-	-	1	-	256	53	817	19	43.00	4-39	-	-
1-day Int																		
NatWest	1	1	0	0	0	0.00	-	-	-	-	12	2	57	1	57.00	1-57	-	
B & H	2	1	1	1	1 *	-	-	-	-	-	16	0	81	2	40.50	2-57	-	
Sunday	11	2	1	27	27 *	27.00	-	-	-	-	78.5	3	410	16	25.62	4-33	-	

Career Performances

	M	Inns	NO	Runs	HS	Avge	100s	50s	Ct	St	Balls	Runs	Wkts	Avge	Best	5wI	10wM
Test																	
All First	185	250	44	3498	95 *	16.98	-	15	44	-	24643	12308	386	31.88	5-27	5	-
1-day Int																	
NatWest	15	11	2	90	32	10.00	-	-	1	-	939	593	17	34.88	4-39	-	
B & H	47	28	11	211	35 *	12.41	-	-	5	-	2581	1657	65	25.49	4-36	-	
Sunday	141	98	24	992	68	13.40	-	2	21	-	5695	4800	163	29.44	5-39	1	

WARREN, R. J.   Northamptonshire

Name: Russell John Warren
Role: Right-hand bat, occasional off-spin bowler
Born: 10 September 1971, Northampton
Height: 6ft 2in **Weight:** 12st 4lbs
Nickname: Rabbit
County debut: 1992
1st-Class 50s: 5
1st-Class catches: 17
One-Day 100s: 1
Place in batting averages: 130th av. 29.78
Parents: John and Sally
Marital status: Single
Education: Whitehills Lower School; Kingsthorpe Middle and Upper Schools
Qualifications: 8 O-levels, 2 A-levels
Overseas tours: England YC to New Zealand 1990-91
Overseas teams played for:
Lancaster Park, Christchurch, and Canterbury B, New Zealand 1991-92
Cricketers particularly admired: Viv Richards, Wayne Larkins, Graham Gooch
Other sports followed: Most sports, especially golf, football, snooker

Relaxations: 'Playing snooker at local club and having a relaxing nine holes of golf at Kingsthorpe GC; keen supporter of the Cobblers and Manchester United'
Opinions on cricket: 'Uncovered pitches should return. This will encourage more spin bowling and require batsmen and bowlers to be more flexible.'
Best batting: 94* Northamptonshire v Warwickshire, Northampton 1994

1994 Season

	M	Inns	NO	Runs	HS	Avge	100s	50s	Ct	St	O	M	Runs	Wkts	Avge	Best	5wI	10wM
Test																		
All First	12	21	2	566	94 *	29.78	-	5	14	-								
1-day Int																		
NatWest	3	3	1	138	100 *	69.00	1	-	1	-								
B & H																		
Sunday	11	9	0	98	55	10.88	-	1	7	1								

Career Performances

	M	Inns	NO	Runs	HS	Avge	100s	50s	Ct	St	Balls	Runs	Wkts	Avge	Best	5wI	10wM
Test																	
All First	19	30	4	649	94 *	24.96	-	5	17	-							
1-day Int																	
NatWest	3	3	1	138	100 *	69.00	1	-	1	-							
B & H																	
Sunday	18	15	2	307	71 *	23.61	-	3	9	1							

90. Which countries will tour England in 1996?

WASIM AKRAM   Lancashire

Name: Wasim Akram
Role: Left-hand bat, left-arm
fast-medium bowler
Born: 3 June 1966, Lahore, Pakistan
Height: 6ft 3in **Weight:** 12st 7lbs
County debut: 1988
County cap: 1989
Test debut: 1984-85
Tests: 53
One-Day Internationals: 169
50 wickets in a season: 4
1st-Class 50s: 13
1st-Class 100s: 4
1st-Class 5 w. in innings: 48
1st-Class 10 w. in match: 9
1st-Class catches: 50
One-Day 5 w. in innings: 8
Place in batting averages: 169th av. 24.40

(1993 159th av. 24.57)
Place in bowling averages: 16th av. 23.92 (1993 2nd av. 19.27)
Strike rate: 49.40 (career 49.35)
Education: Islamia College, Pakistan
Off-season: Playing for Pakistan
Overseas tours: Pakistan U23 to Sri Lanka 1984-85; Pakistan to New Zealand 1984-85, to Sri Lanka 1985-86, to India 1986-87, to England 1987, to West Indies 1987-88, to Australia 1989-90, to Australia and New Zealand (World Cup) 1991-92, to England 1992, to New Zealand, Australia, South Africa and West Indies 1992-93, to New Zealand 1993-94, to South Africa 1994-95
Overseas teams played for: PACO 1984-86; Lahore Whites 1985-86
Extras: His second first-class match was playing for Pakistan on tour in New Zealand. Imran Khan wrote of him: 'I have great faith in Wasim Akram. I think he will become a great all-rounder, as long as he realises how much hard work is required. As a bowler he is extremely gifted, and has it in him to be the best left-armer since Alan Davidson.' Hit maiden Test 100 v Australia 1989-90 during stand of 191 with Imran Khan. Signed a new four-year contract with Lancashire in 1992. Appointed captain of Pakistan 1992-93 and replaced by Salim Malik on tour to New Zealand 1993-94
Best batting: 123 Pakistan v Australia, Adelaide 1989-90
Best bowling: 8-30 Lancashire v Somerset, Southport 1994

1994 Season

	M	Inns	NO	Runs	HS	Avge	100s	50s	Ct	St	O	M	Runs	Wkts	Avge	Best	5wI	10wM
Test																		
All First	6	10	0	244	98	24.40	-	2	-	-	213.2	44	646	27	23.92	8-30	2	1
1-day Int																		
NatWest	1	1	0	50	50	50.00	-	1	-	-	12	1	70	0	-	-	-	-
B & H	1	0	0	0	0	-	-	-	-	-	10	0	30	0	-	-	-	-
Sunday	8	6	1	57	33	11.40	-	-	2	-	54.5	2	273	17	16.05	5-41	1	

Career Performances

	M	Inns	NO	Runs	HS	Avge	100s	50s	Ct	St	Balls	Runs	Wkts	Avge	Best	5wI	10wM
Test	53	69	10	1153	123	19.54	1	4	17	-	12014	5203	222	23.43	7-119	15	3
All First	155	208	25	3982	123	21.75	4	13	50	-	30442	13472	616	21.87	8-30	48	11
1-day Int	169	130	26	1467	86	14.10	-	1	32	-	8648	5487	246	22.30	5-15	5	
NatWest	14	12	2	179	50	17.90	-	1	3	-	874	552	20	27.60	4-27	-	
B & H	22	18	4	378	52	27.00	-	1	1	-	1366	849	43	19.74	5-10	2	
Sunday	76	61	17	1062	51 *	24.13	-	2	15	-	3245	2410	116	20.77	5-41	1	

WATKIN, S. L. Glamorgan

Name: Steven Llewellyn Watkin
Role: Right-hand bat, right-arm
fast-medium bowler
Born: 15 September 1964, Maesteg
Height: 6ft 3in **Weight:** 12st 8lbs
Nickname: Watty, Banger
County debut: 1986
County cap: 1989
Test debut: 1991
Tests: 3
One-Day Internationals: 4
50 wickets in a season: 6
1st-Class 5 w. in innings: 20
1st-Class 10 w. in match: 3
1st-Class catches: 33
One-Day 5 w. in innings: 1
Place in batting averages:
(1993 245th av. 12.75)
Place in bowling averages: 70th av. 31.03
(1993 16th av. 22.80)
Strike rate: 66.94 (career 59.75)
Parents: John and Sandra

Marital status: Single
Family links with cricket: One brother plays local cricket; 'older brother a good watcher'
Education: Cymer Afan Comprehensive; Swansea College of Further Education; South Glamorgan Institute of Higher Education
Qualifications: 8 O-levels, 2 A-levels, BA (Hons) in Human Movement Studies
Off-season: 'Learning Welsh'
Overseas tours: British Colleges to West Indies 1987; England A to Kenya and Zimbabwe 1989-90, to Pakistan and Sri Lanka 1990-91, to Bermuda and West Indies 1991-92; England to West Indies 1993-94
Overseas teams played for: Potchefstroom University, South Africa 1987-88; Aurora, Durban, South Africa 1991-92
Cricketers particularly admired: Richard Hadlee, Dennis Lillee, Ian Botham
Other sports followed: All sports except horse racing
Injuries: Back ligament tear, missed two weeks
Relaxations: Watching television, music, DIY, motor mechanics, 'a quiet pint'
Extras: Joint highest wicket-taker in 1989 with 94 wickets and took most (92) in 1993. Sister Lynda has played for Great Britain at hockey. Players' Player of the Year and Glamorgan Player of the Year 1993
Opinions on cricket: 'Four-day should start on Wednesday and finish Saturday, with Sunday game the same except bowling off 15 yards again.'
Best batting: 41 Glamorgan v Worcestershire, Worcester 1992
Best bowling: 8-59 Glamorgan v Warwickshire, Edgbaston 1988

1994 Season

	M	Inns	NO	Runs	HS	Avge	100s	50s	Ct	St	O	M	Runs	Wkts	Avge	Best	5wI	10wM
Test																		
All First	18	21	11	92	14	9.20	-	-	2	-	613.4	147	1708	55	31.05	6-143	2	-
1-day Int																		
NatWest	3	1	0	9	9	9.00	-	-	-	-	29	4	92	2	46.00	1-19	-	
B & H	1	0	0	0	0	-	-	-	-	-	10	2	45	1	45.00	1-45	-	
Sunday	14	7	1	17	6	2.83	-	-	-	-	101	7	379	11	34.45	3-19	-	

Career Performances

	M	Inns	NO	Runs	HS	Avge	100s	50s	Ct	St	Balls	Runs	Wkts	Avge	Best	5wI	10wM
Test	3	5	0	25	13	5.00	-	-	1	-	534	305	11	27.72	4-65	-	-
All First	157	170	53	1058	41	9.04	-	-	33	-	31430	15573	526	29.60	8-59	20	3
1-day Int	4	2	0	4	4	2.00	-	-	-	-	221	193	7	27.57	4-49	-	
NatWest	18	8	4	37	9	9.25	-	-	2	-	1146	568	22	25.81	3-18	-	
B & H	18	13	6	48	15	6.85	-	-	2	-	1071	695	19	36.57	3-28	-	
Sunday	82	33	11	175	31 *	7.95	-	-	13	-	3559	2626	93	28.23	5-23	1	

WATKINSON, M.   Lancashire

Name: Michael Watkinson
Role: Right-hand bat, right-arm medium or off-spin bowler, county captain
Born: 1 August 1961, Westhoughton
Height: 6ft 1 1/2in **Weight:** 13st
Nickname: Winker
County debut: 1982
County cap: 1987
1000 runs in a season: 1
50 wickets in a season: 6
1st-Class 50s: 40
1st-Class 100s: 7
1st-Class 5 w. in innings: 23
1st-Class 10 w. in match: 2
1st-Class catches: 118
One-Day 5 w. in innings: 2
Place in batting averages: 97th av. 34.19
(1993 56th av. 39.07)
Place in bowling averages: 52nd av. 28.93
(1993 111th av. 38.23)
Strike rate: 60.11 (career 64.83)
Parents: Albert and Marian
Wife and date of marriage: Susan, 12 April 1986
Children: Charlotte, 24 February 1989; Liam, 27 July 1991
Education: Rivington and Blackrod High School, Horwich
Qualifications: 8 O-levels, HTC Civil Engineering
Career outside cricket: Draughtsman
Off-season: Working as an estimator with William Hare Ltd, Bolton
Cricketers particularly admired: Clive Lloyd, Imran Khan
Other sports followed: Football
Relaxations: Watching Bolton Wanderers
Extras: Played for Cheshire in Minor Counties Championship and in NatWest Trophy (v Middlesex) 1982. Man of the Match in the first Refuge Assurance Cup final 1988 and in B&H Cup final 1990. Appointed county captain for 1994 season
Best batting: 155 Lancashire v Glamorgan, Colwyn Bay 1994
Best bowling: 8-30 Lancashire v Hampshire, Old Trafford 1994

91. Who was England's Player of the Series against New Zealand in 1994?

1994 Season

	M	Inns	NO	Runs	HS	Avge	100s	50s	Ct	St	O	M	Runs	Wkts	Avge	Best	5wI	10wM
Test																		
All First	18	28	2	889	155	34.19	2	3	10	-	631.1	173	1823	63	28.93	8-30	1	1
1-day Int																		
NatWest	2	2	1	40	25 *	40.00	-	-	1	-	18	2	91	2	45.50	2-45	-	
B & H	2	1	1	7	7 *	-	-	-	-	-	16.5	1	79	1	79.00	1-21	-	
Sunday	16	13	4	231	35 *	25.66	-	-	4	-	93.4	2	440	12	36.66	4-34	-	

Career Performances

	M	Inns	NO	Runs	HS	Avge	100s	50s	Ct	St	Balls	Runs	Wkts	Avge	Best	5wI	10wM
Test																	
All First	237	350	42	8097	155	26.28	7	40	118	-	37213	19259	574	33.55	8-30	23	2
1-day Int																	
NatWest	31	26	7	641	90	33.73	-	5	8	-	1871	1215	32	37.96	3-14	-	
B & H	55	39	10	623	76	21.48	-	3	11	-	2816	1954	62	31.51	5-49	1	
Sunday	173	134	36	2072	83	21.14	-	5	36	-	6787	5479	167	32.80	5-46	1	

WAUGH, M. E.　　　　　Essex

Name: Mark Edward Waugh
Role: Right-hand bat, right-arm medium pace bowler
Born: 2 June 1965, Canterbury, New South Wales
Height: 6ft **Weight:** 13st 7lbs
County debut: 1988
County cap: 1989
Test debut: 1990-91
Tests: 36
One-Day Internationals: 75
1000 runs in a season: 3
1st-Class 50s: 65
1st-Class 100s: 48
1st-Class 200s: 4
1st-Class 5 w. in innings: 1
1st-Class catches: 221
One-Day 100s: 8
One-Day 5 w. in innings: 1
Strike rate: (career 69.92)
Parents: Rodger and Beverley
Marital status: Single

Family links with cricket: Uncle a First Grade cricketer in Sydney for Bankstown/ Canterbury. Twin brother Steve plays for Australia and played for Somerset in 1988. Younger brother Dean played in Bolton League with Astley Bridge in 1989 and made debut for NSW in 1990-91

Education: East Hills Boys High School

Qualifications: Higher School Certificate, cricket coach

Off-season: Playing cricket for New South Wales

Overseas tours: Young Australia to Zimbabwe 1985-86; New South Wales to Zimbabwe 1987-88; Australia to West Indies 1990-91, to Sri Lanka and New Zealand 1992-93, to England 1993, to South Africa 1993-94, to New Zealand 1994-95, to West Indies 1994-95

Overseas teams played for: New South Wales 1985-95

Cricketers particularly admired: 'Allan Border for his guts and determination, Doug Walters for his ability and sportsmanship, Greg Chappell – pure class'

Other sports followed: 'Any – but mainly golf, football and horse racing'

Relaxations: 'Sleeping, eating and gambling.'

Extras: Steve and Mark are only twins to score centuries in the same innings of a first-class match and both to play international cricket. Chosen as New South Wales Cricketer of the Year, 1988 and Sheffield Shield Cricketer of the Year, jointly with D.Tazelaar of Queensland. First batsman to score a century on his Sunday League debut. Took English summer off in 1991 but returned to Essex for 1992 season. Returns to Essex for 1995 season after two-year absence.

Opinions on cricket: 'Too much cricket is played.'

Best batting: 229 New South Wales v Western Australia, Perth 1990-91

Best bowling: 5-37 Essex v Northamptonshire, Northampton 1990

1994 Season (did not make any first-class or one-day appearance)

Career Performances

	M	Inns	NO	Runs	HO	Avge	100s	50s	Ct	St	Balls	Runs	Wkts	Avge	Best	5wI	10wM
Test	36	57	4	2177	139 *	41.07	6	12	40	-	1920	874	23	38.00	4-80	-	-
All First	188	296	43	14346	229 *	56.70	48	65	221	-	9090	4970	130	38.23	5-37	1	-
1-day Int	75	71	6	2169	113	33.36	3	16	35	-	1302	1048	40	26.20	5-24	1	
NatWest	6	5	0	105	47	21.00	-	-	1	-	114	81	1	81.00	1-51	-	
B & H	16	14	1	438	100	33.69	1	2	5	-	95	76	4	19.00	3-31	-	
Sunday	47	45	11	1738	112 *	51.11	4	10	16	-	814	772	25	30.88	3-26	-	

WEEKES, P. N.   Middlesex

Name: Paul Nicholas Weekes
Role: Left-hand bat, off-spin bowler
Born: 8 July 1969, Hackney, London
Height: 5ft 11in **Weight:** 13st
Nickname: Weekesy, Twiddles
County debut: 1990
County cap: 1993
1st-Class 50s: 8
1st-Class 100s: 1
1st-Class 5 w. in innings: 1
1st-Class catches: 35
Place in batting averages: 100th av. 34.10
Place in bowling averages: 89th av. 53.73
Strike rate: 70.92 (career 80.44)
Parents: Robert and Carol
Marital status: 'Partner Christine'
Children: Cheri, 4 September 1993
Family links with cricket: Father played
club cricket
Education: Homerton House Secondary School, Hackney; Hackney College
Qualifications: NCA cricket coach
Career outside cricket: Coaching for Middlesex CYT
Off-season: Touring with England A
Overseas tours: England A to India 1994-95
Overseas teams played for: Newcastle University, NSW, 1989; Sunrise, Zimbabwe 1990
Cricketers particularly admired: David Gower, Richie Richardson
Other sports followed: Boxing – 'middle and heavyweight especially'
Relaxations: 'Listening to music – ragga, soca. Chilling with the family'
Extras: Scored 50 in first innings for both 2nd and 1st teams
Opinions on cricket: 'Lunch and tea intervals should be longer.'
Best batting: 117 Middlesex v Somerset, Lord's 1994
Best bowling: 5-12 Middlesex v Cambridge University, Fenner's 1994

1994 Season

	M	Inns	NO	Runs	HS	Avge	100s	50s	Ct	St	O	M	Runs	Wkts	Avge	Best	5wI	10wM
Test																		
All First	16	21	2	648	117	34.10	1	2	10	-	484.4	91	1383	41	33.73	5-12	1	-
1-day Int																		
NatWest																		
B & H	2	2	0	44	33	22.00	-	-	1	-	17	2	83	3	27.66	3-32	-	
Sunday	15	12	2	209	50	20.90	-	1	4	-	100.4	2	553	15	36.86	3-37	-	

Career Performances

	M	Inns	NO	Runs	HS	Avge	100s	50s	Ct	St	Balls	Runs	Wkts	Avge	Best	5wI	10wM
Test																	
All First	46	61	11	1659	117	33.18	1	8	35	-	5390	2581	67	38.52	5-12	1	-
1-day Int																	
NatWest	4	4	0	11	7	2.75	-	-	2	-	246	136	4	34.00	2-36	-	
B & H	11	8	2	109	44 *	18.16	-	-	3	-	414	282	8	35.25	3-32	-	
Sunday	61	41	9	758	66 *	23.68	-	2	24	-	2304	2009	71	28.29	4-37	-	

WELCH, G. Warwickshire

Name: Graeme Welch
Role: Right-hand bat, right-arm medium-fast bowler
Born: 21 March 1972, Tyne and Wear
Height: 6ft **Weight:** 13st
Nickname: Pop, Red Beard, Lalas
County debut: 1992 (one-day), 1994 (first-class)
1st-Class 50s: 4
1st-Class catches: 5
Place in batting averages 73rd av. 37.16
Place in bowling averages: 132nd av. 44.09
Strike rate: 72.81 (career 72.81)
Parents: Robert and Jean
Marital status: Girlfriend Emma
Family links with cricket:
Brother Barry and father play club cricket in Durham
Education: Hetton Lyons Junior School; Hetton Comprehensive
Qualifications: 9 GCSEs, City & Guilds in Leisure Management
Career outside cricket: 'Everything from factory work to working in an office'
Off-season: 'Playing indoor cricket and trying to get fitter than last year.'
Overseas tours: Warwickshire to Cape Town 1992 and 1993
Overseas teams played for: Avendale, Cape Town 1991-93
Cricketers particularly admired: Steve Waugh, Gladstone Small, Tim Munton, Andy Moles, Brian Lara
Other sports followed: Football (Newcastle United)
Relaxations: 'Spending time with Emma, going to the Dome with friends, watching videos, listening to music, one or two pints with friends.'
Extras: Played for England YC v Australian YC 1991. Took first ever hat-trick in 2nd XI

583

Championship v Durham 1992. Axa Equity and Law Winners Medal 1994. Britannic Assurance Winners Medal 1994

Opinions on cricket: '110 overs in a day is too many. 100 overs would be more appropriate. I would also like to see half an hour for tea instead of 20 minutes. Two runs for a no-ball is too many, and should revert back to it going on the extras (only because I bowl too many).'

Best batting: 84* Warwickshire v Nottinghamshire, Edgbaston 1994
Best bowling: 4-74 Warwickshire v Yorkshire, Scarborough 1994

1994 Season

	M	Inns	NO	Runs	HS	Avge	100s	50s	Ct	St	O	M	Runs	Wkts	Avge	Best	5wI	10wM
Test																		
All First	12	15	3	446	84 *	37.16	-	4	5	-	267	63	970	22	44.09	4-74	-	-
1-day Int																		
NatWest	2	1	1	0	0 *	-	-	-	-	-	16	4	41	0	-	-	-	-
B & H																		
Sunday	6	4	0	57	26	14.25	-	-	3	-	37	1	163	7	23.28	2-30	-	

Career Performances

	M	Inns	NO	Runs	HS	Avge	100s	50s	Ct	St	Balls	Runs	Wkts	Avge	Best	5wI	10wM
Test																	
All First	12	15	3	446	84 *	37.16	-	4	5	-	1602	970	22	44.09	4-74	-	-
1-day Int																	
NatWest	2	1	1	0	0 *	-	-	-	-	-	96	41	0	-	-	-	-
B & H																	
Sunday	11	8	3	86	26	17.20	-	-	3	-	401	299	10	29.90	2-30	-	

92. Who took 11 wickets in the match, scored his maiden first-class 50 and won the Man of the Match award in the second Test between England and New Zealand at Lord's in June 1994?

WELLS, A. P.   Sussex

Name: Alan Peter Wells
Role: Right-hand bat, right-arm medium
bowler, county captain
Born: 2 October 1961, Newhaven
Height: 6ft **Weight:** 12st 4lbs
Nickname: Morph, Bomber
County debut: 1981
County cap: 1986
Benefit: 1995
1000 runs in a season: 8
1st-Class 50s: 72
1st-Class 100s: 34
1st-Class 200s: 1
1st-Class catches: 175
One-Day 100s: 5
Place in batting averages: 134th av. 29.32
(1993 10th av. 57.28)
Parents: Ernest William Charles and
Eunice Mae

Wife and date of marriage: Melanie Elizabeth, 26 September 1987
Children: Luke William Peter, 29 December 1990
Family links with cricket: Father, Billy, played for many years for local club and had trial
for Sussex. Eldest brother Ray plays club cricket; brother Colin played for Sussex and then
joined Derbyshire
Education: Tideway Comprehensive, Newhaven
Qualifications: 3 O-levels, NCA coaching certificate
Career outside cricket: Family packaging business
Overseas tours: Unofficial England XI to South Africa 1989-90; England A to South
Africa 1993-94, to India (captain) 1994-95
Overseas teams played for: Border, South Africa 1981-82
Cricketers particularly admired: Graham Gooch
Relaxations: Good wine, cooking, spending time with family, reading books and articles
on wine
Extras: Played for England YC v India 1981. Banned from Test cricket for five years in
1990 for joining tour of South Africa, suspension remitted in 1992. Scored a century in each
of his first two matches as acting-captain of Sussex and won both matches. Won top batting
award for Sussex 1989-93, 'much to David Smith's annoyance'. Vice-captain on England
A tour to South Africa 1993-94 and captain for the highly successful tour to India 1994-95
Best batting: 253* Sussex v Yorkshire, Middlesbrough 1991
Best bowling: 3-67 Sussex v Worcestershire, Worcester 1987

1994 Season

	M	Inns	NO	Runs	HS	Avge	100s	50s	Ct	St	O	M	Runs	Wkts	Avge	Best	5wl	10wM
Test																		
All First	19	35	4	909	84	29.32	-	7	15	-	14	2	75	1	75.00	1-48	-	-
1-day Int																		
NatWest	1	1	0	1	1	1.00	-	-	-	-								
B & H	2	2	1	102	51 *	102.00	-	2	-	-								
Sunday	15	14	1	618	103	47.53	1	5	5	-								

Career Performances

	M	Inns	NO	Runs	HS	Avge	100s	50s	Ct	St	Balls	Runs	Wkts	Avge	Best	5wl	10wM
Test																	
All First	279	462	73	15415	253 *	39.62	34	72	175	-	1045	765	10	76.50	3-67	-	1
1-day Int																	
NatWest	29	26	6	791	119	39.55	2	4	12	-	6	1	0	-		-	-
B & H	46	43	5	1230	74	32.36	-	12	9	-	60	72	3	24.00	1-17	-
Sunday	188	172	21	4754	127	31.48	3	30	55	-	62	69	4	17.25	1-0	-

WELLS, C. M. Derbyshire

Name: Colin Mark Wells
Role: Right-hand bat, right-arm medium bowler
Born: 3 March 1960, Newhaven
Height: 6ft **Weight:** 13st
Nickname: Bomber, Dougie
County debut: 1979 (Sussex),
1994 (Derbyshire)
County cap: 1982 (Sussex)
Benefit: 1993 (£50,353)
One-Day Internationals: 2
1000 runs in a season: 6
50 wickets in a season: 2
1st-Class 50s: 58
1st-Class 100s: 21
1st-Class 200s: 1
1st-Class 5 w. in innings: 7
1st-Class catches: 90
One-Day 100s: 4
Place in batting averages: 227th av. 16.83
Place in bowling averages: 99th av. 36.09
Strike rate: 70.84 (career 72.40)
Parents: Ernest William Charles and Eunice Mae

Wife and date of marriage: Celia, 25 September 1982
Children: Jessica Louise, 2 October 1987
Family links with cricket: Father, Billy, had trials for Sussex and played for Sussex Cricket Association. Elder brother Ray plays club cricket and younger brother Alan is captain of Sussex
Education: Tideway Comprehensive School, Newhaven
Qualifications: 9 O-levels, 2 CSEs, 1 A-level, intermediate coaching certificate
Off-season: Running family blister-packaging company in Newhaven
Overseas tours: England to Sharjah 1984-85
Overseas teams played for: Border, South Africa 1980-81; Western Province, South Africa 1984-85
Other sports followed: Football, rugby, hockey, basketball, tennis, table tennis
Relaxations: Sea-angling, philately, listening to music
Extras: Played in three John Player League matches in 1978. Was recommended to Sussex by former Sussex player, Ian Thomson. Appointed vice-captain of Sussex in 1988 and captain in 1992. Released by Sussex at end of 1993 season and signed for Derbyshire
Opinions on cricket: 'Pleased four-day cricket has been introduced and resent clubs who have opposed it for purely financial reasons.'
Best batting: 203 Sussex v Hampshire, Hove 1984
Best bowling: 7-42 Sussex v Derbyshire, Derby 1991

1994 Season

	M	Inns	NO	Runs	HS	Avge	100s	50s	Ct	St	O	M	Runs	Wkts	Avge	Best	5wI	10wM
Test																		
All First	11	20	2	303	42	16.83	-	-	3	-	153.3	31	469	13	36.07	4-52	-	-
1-day Int																		
NatWest	1	1	0	0	0	0.00	-	-	1	-	8.3	2	22	0	-		-	-
B & H	2	2	1	73	48 *	73.00	-	-	-	-	11	0	57	1	57.00	1-57	-	
Sunday	12	5	3	49	26 *	24.50	-	1	-	-	85.5	5	431	14	30.78	3-55	-	

Career Performances

	M	Inns	NO	Runs	HS	Avge	100s	50s	Ct	St	Balls	Runs	Wkts	Avge	Best	5wI	10wM
Test																	
All First	290	461	72	12704	203	32.65	21	58	90	-	29613	13982	409	34.18	7-42	7	-
1-day Int	2	2	0	22	17	11.00	-	-	-	-							
NatWest	32	26	3	433	76	18.82	-	1	8	-	1477	713	17	41.94	3-16	-	
B & H	53	52	6	1377	117	29.93	3	4	13	-	1938	1257	37	33.97	4-21	-	
Sunday	194	169	28	3713	104 *	26.33	1	18	42	-	6678	4317	138	31.28	4-15	-	

WELLS, V. J.   Leicestershire

Name: Vincent John Wells
Role: Right-hand bat, right-arm medium
bowler, occasional wicket-keeper
Born: 6 August 1965, Dartford
Height: 6ft **Weight:** 13st 3lbs
Nickname: Wellsy, Vinny, Both, Clarke Kent
County debut: 1987 (Kent),
1992 (Leicestershire)
1st-Class 50s: 14
1st-Class 100s: 1
1st-Class 5 w. in innings: 2
1st-Class catches: 37
One-Day 100s: 3
Place in batting averages: 80th av. 36.29
(1993 117th av. 28.66)
Place in bowling averages: 25th av. 25.07
(1993 115th av. 39.16)
Strike rate: 43.11 (career 52.98)
Parents: Pat and Jack

Wife and date of marriage: Deborah Louise, 14 October 1989
Family links with cricket: Brother plays league cricket in Kent
Education: Downs School, Dartford; Sir William Nottidge School, Whitstable
Qualifications: 1 O-level, 8 CSEs, coaching certificate
Off-season: Having an ankle operation, then coaching at Leicestershire
Overseas tours: Leicestershire to Jamaica 1993, to Bloemfontein, 1994
Overseas teams played for: Parnell, Auckland 1986; Avendale, Cape Town 1986-89,
1990-91
Cricketers particularly admired: David Gower, Ian Botham
Other sports followed: Most sports especially football
Injuries: Broken toe and twisted ankle, missed two matches
Relaxations: Eating out
Extras: Was a schoolboy footballer with Leyton Orient. Scored 100* on NatWest debut v
Oxfordshire. Left Kent at the end of 1991 season to join Leicestershire. Missed 1992
NatWest final owing to viral infection. Hat-trick against Durham, 1994
Opinions on cricket: 'Four-day cricket is a great idea, but the standard of pitches should
be improved. NatWest Final should be played earlier in the season to cancel out the
importance of the toss.'
Best batting: 167 Leicestershire v Glamorgan, Leicester 1993
Best bowling: 5-43 Kent v Leicestershire, Leicester 1990

1994 Season

	M	Inns	NO	Runs	HS	Avge	100s	50s	Ct	St	O	M	Runs	Wkts	Avge	Best	5wI	10wM
Test																		
All First	16	28	4	871	87 *	36.29	-	6	13	-	301.5	78	1053	42	25.07	5-50	1	-
1-day Int																		
NatWest	2	2	0	50	31	25.00	-	-	-	-	24	3	104	1	104.00	1-35	-	
B & H	2	1	0	0	0	0.00	-	-	-	-	9	0	48	0	-	-	-	
Sunday	15	15	1	422	101	30.14	2	1	1	-	95	7	435	25	17.40	5-10	1	

Career Performances

	M	Inns	NO	Runs	HS	Avge	100s	50s	Ct	St	Balls	Runs	Wkts	Avge	Best	5wI	10wM
Test																	
All First	62	99	13	2481	167	28.84	1	14	37	-	5881	2923	111	26.33	5-43	2	-
1-day Int																	
NatWest	8	8	3	203	100 *	40.60	1	-	-	-	353	222	8	27.75	3-38	-	
B & H	14	11	3	143	25	17.87	-	-	3	-	516	384	13	29.53	4-37	-	
Sunday	50	44	11	870	101	26.36	2	2	15	-	1826	1358	57	23.82	5-10	1	

WESTON, R. M. S.   Durham

Name: Robin Michael Swann Weston
Role: Right-hand bat, leg-break bowler
Born: 7 June 1975, Durham
Height: 6ft **Weight:** 13st
County debut: No first-team appearance
Parents: Michael Philip and Kathleen Mary
Marital status: Single
Family links with cricket: Father played
for Durham; brother Philip plays
for Worcestershire
Education: Bow School; Durham School;
Loughborough University
Qualifications: 10 GCSEs, 4 A-levels,
basic cricket coaching certificate
Career outside cricket:
Student at Loughborough
Off-season: Loughborough University
Overseas tours: England U18 to
South Africa 1992-93, to Denmark 1993;
England U19 to Sri Lanka 1993-94
Cricketers particularly admired: Graeme Hick and Wayne Larkins
Other sports followed: Rugby and most other sports

Injuries: Broken finger, did not miss any cricket
Relaxations: Most sports, listening to music and socialising with friends
Extras: Youngest to play for Durham 1st XI, in Minor Counties competition, aged 15 in 1991. Played rugby for England U18
Opinions on cricket: 'Second XI cricket should be played on first-class pitches or those of similar standard.'

WESTON, W. P. C. Worcestershire

Name: William Philip Christopher Weston
Role: Left-hand bat, left-arm medium bowler
Born: 16 June 1973, Durham
Height: 6ft 4in **Weight:** 14st
Nickname: Junior, Sven, K.O.S.
County debut: 1991
1st-Class 50s: 12
1st-Class 100s: 2
1st-Class catches: 17
Place in batting averages: 125th av. 30.29 (1993 101st av. 32.10)
Parents: Michael Philip and Kathleen Mary
Marital status: Single
Family links with cricket: Father played Minor Counties cricket for Durham and rugby for England, brother plays for Durham CCC
Education: Bow School, Durham; Durham School
Qualifications: 9 GCSEs, 4 A-Levels, NCA Senior Coach
Off-season: Playing cricket in Perth, Western Australia
Overseas tours: England U18 to Canada; England YC to New Zealand 1990-91, to Pakistan 1991-92 (captain)
Overseas teams played for: Melville, Perth 1992-95
Cricketers particularly admired: Steve Rhodes, Graeme Hick, Phil Newport, Justin Langer
Other sports followed: Rugby union and football (Sunderland AFC)
Injuries: Bruised retina in left eye, broken bone in right hand. Missed four weeks in total
Relaxations: Spending time with friends and family, sleeping and lying on a beach
Extras: Scored century for England YC v Australian YC 1991. Was appointed captain of England U19 for their tour to Pakistan 1991-92 and told by Keble College, Oxford, that he would not be accepted if he decided to tour, he chose to sacrifice his place at Oxford. Downing Collge, Cambridge, offered him a place the following year, but by then he was so disillusioned with universities that he turned down the offer and decided to concentrate on

590

his cricket. Played for Northamptonshire 2nd XI and Worcestershire 2nd XI in 1989. Cricket Society's Most Promising Young Cricketer 1992. Worcestershire Uncapped Player of the Year, 1992. Member of Whittingdale Fringe Squad 1993

Opinions on cricket: 'Too many to mention!'

Best batting: 113 Worcestershire v Oxford University, Worcester 1993

Best bowling: 2-39 Worcestershire v Pakistanis, Worcester 1992

1994 Season

	M	Inns	NO	Runs	HS	Avge	100s	50s	Ct	St	O	M	Runs	Wkts	Avge	Best	5wI	10wM
Test																		
All First	17	28	1	818	94	30.29	-	6	6	-	21	6	85	0	-		-	-	-
1-day Int																		
NatWest	1	1	0	7	7	7.00	-	-	1	-								
B & H																		
Sunday																		

Career Performances

	M	Inns	NO	Runs	HS	Avge	100s	50s	Ct	St	Balls	Runs	Wkts	Avge	Best	5wI	10wM
Test																	
All First	48	79	9	2236	113	31.94	2	12	17	-	681	390	4	97.50	2-39	-	-
1-day Int																	
NatWest	4	4	0	90	31	22.50	-	-	1	-							
B & H	2	2	1	33	32*	33.00	-	-	1	-							
Sunday	8	7	1	84	26	14.00	-	-	-	-	6	2	1	2.00	1-2	-	

94. Which visiting player, while practising in the nets, smashed a ball through the back window of a committee member's Porsche at Northampton?

WHARF, A. G. Yorkshire

Name: Alexander George Wharf
Role: Right-hand bat, right-arm fast-medium bowler
Born: Bradford
Height: 6ft 5in **Weight:** 14st 8lbs
Nickname: Gangster, Frank, River, Big'un
County debut: 1994
Parents: Derek and Jane
Marital status: Single
Family links with cricket: Father used to play in local league cricket
Education: Buttershaw Upper School
Qualifications: 6 GCSEs, City and Guilds in Sports Management
Off-season: Training and getting fit for 1995 season
Overseas teams played for: Somerset West, Cape Town 1993-94
Cricketers particularly admired: Wasim Akram, Curtly Ambrose, Bradley Parker
Other sports followed: Football (Manchester United)
Injuries: Knee (left), missed last month of season
Relaxations: Watching movies, eating out, sleeping. Spending time with friends outside cricket
Opinions on cricket: 'It's too much of a batter's game – a pitch should be 20 yards.'
Best batting: 46 Yorkshire v Warwickshire, Scarborough 1994
Best bowling: 1-78 Yorkshire v Warwickshire, Scarborough 1994

1994 Season

	M	Inns	NO	Runs	HS	Avge	100s	50s	Ct	St	O	M	Runs	Wkts	Avge	Best	5wI	10wM
Test																		
All First	1	2	0	46	46	23.00	-	-	-	-	23	4	78	1	78.00	1-78	-	-
1-day Int																		
NatWest																		
B & H																		
Sunday	1	0	0	0	0	-	-	-	1	-	8	2	39	3	13.00	3-39	-	

95. Who was Man of the Match in the first Test of the series against South Africa at Lord's in 1994?

Career Performances

	M	Inns	NO	Runs	HS	Avge	100s	50s	Ct	St	Balls	Runs	Wkts	Avge	Best	5wI	10wM
Test																	
All First	1	2	0	46	46	23.00	-	-	-	-	138	78	1	78.00	1-78	-	-
1-day Int																	
NatWest																	
B & H																	
Sunday	1	0	0	0	0	-	-	-	-	1	-	48	39	3	13.00	3-39	-

WHITAKER, J. J. — Leicestershire

Name: John James Whitaker
Role: Right-hand bat, off-spin bowler
Born: 5 May 1962, Skipton, Yorkshire
Height: 6ft **Weight:** 13st 7lbs
Nickname: Jimmy
County debut: 1983
County cap: 1986
Benefit: 1993
Test debut: 1986-87
Tests: 1
One-Day Internationals: 2
1000 runs in a season: 8
1st-Class 50s: 69
1st-Class 100s: 27
1st-Class 200s: 1
1st-Class catches: 160
One-Day 100s: 6
Place in batting averages: 114th av. 31.93
(85th av. 34.25)
Parents: John and Ann
Family links with cricket: Father plays club cricket for Skipton
Education: Malsis Hall Prep School; Uppingham School
Qualifications: 7 O-levels
Overseas tours: Uppingham to Australia 1980-81; England to Australia 1986-87; England A to Zimbabwe and Kenya 1990-91; Hong Kong Sixes 1991, 1992
Overseas teams played for: Glenelg, Australia 1982-83; Old Scotch, Tasmania 1983-84; Somerset West, Cape Town 1984-85
Cricketers particularly admired: Geoff Boycott, Dennis Amiss, Brian Davison
Other sports followed: Football, golf, rugby
Relaxations: Watching movies, reading, eating out
Extras: One of *Wisden*'s Five Cricketers of the Year 1986

Opinions on cricket: 'There is too much first-class cricket.'
Best batting: 200* Leicestershire v Nottinghamshire, Leicester 1986
Best bowling: 1-29 Leicestershire v Somerset, Leicester 1992

1994 Season

	M	Inns	NO	Runs	HS	Avge	100s	50s	Ct	St	O	M	Runs	Wkts	Avge	Best	5wl	10wM
Test																		
All First	18	32	2	958	148	31.93	2	6	9	-								
1-day Int																		
NatWest	2	2	1	78	73 *	78.00	-	1	-	-								
B & H	2	1	0	53	53	53.00	-	1	-	-								
Sunday	8	8	1	133	44 *	19.00	-	-	-	-								

Career Performances

	M	Inns	NO	Runs	HS	Avge	100s	50s	Ct	St	Balls	Runs	Wkts	Avge	Best	5wl	10wM
Test	1	1	0	11	11	11.00	-	-	1	-							
All First	261	417	46	13886	200 *	37.42	27	69	160	-	176	268	2	134.00	1-29	-	-
1-day Int	2	2	1	48	44 *	48.00	-	-	1	-							
NatWest	25	25	2	1006	155	43.73	1	5	1	-	24	9	0	-		-	-
B & H	43	38	2	1018	100	28.27	1	4	7	-							
Sunday	148	138	15	4212	132	34.24	4	25	35	-	2	4	0	-		-	-

WHITAKER, P. R. Hampshire

Name: Paul Robert Whitaker
Role: Left-hand opening bat,
right-arm off spin
Born: 28 June 1973, Keighley, West Yorkshire
Height: 5ft 10in **Weight:** 11st 7lbs
Nickname: Ticket, Chicken Tikka,
Finger-lickin'
County debut: 1994
1st-Class 50s: 1
Parents: Robert and Maureen
Marital status: Single
Family links with cricket: Father played for
Bingley in Bradford League, and now coaches
Yorkshire U15
Education: 8 GCSEs, 2 A-levels
Career outside cricket: PE teacher
Off-season: Playing and coaching in Hawkes
Bay, New Zealand

Overseas tours: Represented England U17, U18 and U19
Overseas teams played for: Bedford, Perth, Australia 1992-93; Southern Hawkes Bay, New Zealand 1993-94
Cricketers particularly admired: Ian Botham, Tim Tweats, Gary Streer
Other sports followed: Rugby league, football, horse racing
Injuries: Side strain, did not miss any cricket
Relaxations: 'A quiet meal in a restaurant drinking a bottle of Liebfraumilch 1982 wine.'
Opinions on cricket: 'Players should concentrate as hard at their fielding as they do with their batting and bowling. Also no matter what situation the game is in, always give 100 per cent.'
Best batting: 94 Hampshire v Leicestershire, Leicester 1994

1994 Season

	M	Inns	NO	Runs	HS	Avge	100s	50s	Ct	St	O	M	Runs	Wkts	Avge	Best	5wI	10wM
Test																		
All First	2	3	0	134	94	44.66	-	1	-	-	0.1	0	4	0	-		-	-
1-day Int																		
NatWest																		
B & H																		
Sunday	2	2	0	12	7	6.00	-	-	3	-	2	0	8	0	-		-	-

Career Performances

	M	Inns	NO	Runs	HS	Avge	100s	50s	Ct	St	Balls	Runs	Wkts	Avge	Best	5wI	10wM
Test																	
All First	2	3	0	134	94	44.66	-	1	-	-	1	4	0	-		-	-
1-day Int																	
NatWest																	
B & H																	
Sunday	2	2	0	12	7	6.00	-	-	3	-	12	8	0	-		-	-

WHITE, C. Yorkshire

Name: Craig White
Role: Right-hand bat, off-spin bowler, cover fielder
Born: 16 December 1969, Morley, Yorkshire
Height: 6ft 1in **Weight:** 11st 11lbs
Nickname: Chalky, Leather
County debut: 1990
County cap: 1993
Test debut: 1994
Tests: 4
1st-Class 50s: 16
1st-Class 100s: 2
1st-Class 5 w. in innings: 3
1st-Class catches: 42
Place in batting averages: 75th av. 36.83
(1993 82nd av. 34.46)
Place in bowling averages: 10th av. 23.06
(1993 8th av. 20.66)

Strike rate: 42.78 (career 52.88)
Parents: Fred Emsley and Cynthia Anne
Wife and date of marriage: Elizabeth Anne, 19 September 1992
Family links with cricket: Father played for Pudsey St Lawrence
Education: Kennington Primary; Flora Hill High School; Bendigo Senior High School (all Victoria, Australia)
Off-season: Ashes tour with England
Overseas tours: Australian YC to West Indies 1989-90; England to Australia 1994-95
Overseas teams played for: Victoria, Australia 1990-94
Cricketers particularly admired: Allan Border, Dean Jones, David Gower, Martyn Moxon, Sachin Tendulkar
Other sports followed: Australian rules football
Injuries: Shin splints. Injury forced him to come home early from the England tour to Australia 1994-95
Relaxations: Holidaying at Surfers Paradise in Queensland, mountain bike riding
Extras: Recommended to Yorkshire by Victorian Cricket Academy, being eligible to play for Yorkshire as he was born in the county. 'Fred Trueman and I are the only Yorkshire players to debut in the 1st XI before the 2nd XI'
Best batting: 146 Yorkshire v Durham, Headingley 1993
Best bowling: 5-40 Yorkshire v Essex, Headingley 1994

1994 Season

	M	Inns	NO	Runs	HS	Avge	100s	50s	Ct	St	O	M	Runs	Wkts	Avge	Best	5wI	10wM
Test	4	6	0	131	51	21.83	-	1	3	-	78.1	17	258	8	32.25	3-18	-	-
All First	13	20	2	663	108 *	36.83	1	5	8	-	235.2	53	761	33	23.06	5-40	2	-
1-day Int																		
NatWest	2	2	1	70	65 *	70.00	-	1	1	-	10.5	0	57	1	57.00	1-25	-	
B & H	1	1	0	12	12	12.00	-	-	-	-	3	0	10	0	-	-	-	
Sunday	6	5	1	162	54 *	40.50	-	1	-	-	38	2	176	7	25.14	3-25	-	

Career Performances

	M	Inns	NO	Runs	HS	Avge	100s	50s	Ct	St	Balls	Runs	Wkts	Avge	Best	5wI	10wM
Test	4	6	0	131	51	21.83	-	1	3	-	469	258	8	32.25	3-18	-	-
All First	65	95	18	2617	146	33.98	2	16	42	-	3332	1771	63	28.11	5-40	3	-
1-day Int																	
NatWest	7	5	1	185	65 *	46.25	-	1	3	-	227	151	4	37.75	2-41	-	
B & H	6	5	1	72	26	18.00	-	-	1	-	138	71	3	23.66	2-30	-	
Sunday	46	38	12	866	63	33.30	-	3	17	-	967	745	24	31.04	3-25	-	

WHITE, G. W.   Hampshire

Name: Giles William White
Role: Right-hand bat, leg-break bowler
Born: 23 March 1972, Barnstaple
Height: 5ft 11in **Weight:** 12st 7lbs
Nickname: Chalky
County debut: 1991 (Somerset),
1994 (Hampshire)
1st-Class 50s: 2
1st-Class 100s: 1
1st-Class catches: 13
Place in batting averages: 166th av. 24.57
Parents: John and Tina
Marital status: Single
Family links with cricket: Father played
club cricket in Devon
Education: Millfield School;
Loughborough University
Qualifications: GCSEs, A-levels, BA (Hons),
coaching certificate
Off-season: Playing for Tigers Parrow, Cape Town
Overseas tours: Millfield School to Australia 1989
Overseas teams played for: Waverley, Sydney 1990-91

Cricketers particularly admired:
Wayne Larkins, Brian Lara, Robin Smith, Mark Lathwell
Other sports followed: Rugby, football, tennis, golf
Relaxations: Painting, reading, sleeping, eating and the odd drink
Opinions on cricket: 'Devon have the finances, the players and the leadership to become a first-class county. Tea should be 30 minutes and lunch an hour.'
Best batting: 104 Combined Universities v New Zealanders, Fenner's 1994
Best bowling: 1-30 Somerset v Sri Lanka, Taunton 1991

1994 Season

	M	Inns	NO	Runs	HS	Avge	100s	50s	Ct	St	O	M	Runs	Wkts	Avge	Best	5wI	10wM
Test																		
All First	11	20	1	467	104	24.57	1	2	13	-	5	1	13	0	-	-	-	-
1-day Int																		
NatWest	1	1	0	1	1	1.00	-	-	-	-								
B & H																		
Sunday	5	5	1	130	49 *	32.50	-	-	-	-								

Career Performances

	M	Inns	NO	Runs	HS	Avge	100s	50s	Ct	St	Balls	Runs	Wkts	Avge	Best	5wl	10wM
Test																	
All First	12	21	1	509	104	25.45	1	2	13	-	66	43	1	43.00	1-30	-	-
1-day Int																	
NatWest	3	3	0	12	11	4.00	-	-	2	-	72	45	1	45.00	1-45	-	
B & H																	
Sunday	8	8	1	171	49 *	24.42	-	-	1	-							

WHITTICASE, P.   Leicestershire

Name: Philip Whitticase
Role: Right-hand bat, wicket-keeper
Born: 15 March 1965, Wythall, Birmingham
Height: 5ft 8in **Weight:** 11st
Nickname: Jasper, Tracy, Boggy, Rat
County debut: 1984
County cap: 1987
1st-Class 50s: 15
1st-Class 100s: 1
1st-Class catches: 302
1st-Class stumpings: 13
Parents: Larry Gordon and Ann
Marital status: Single

Family links with cricket: Grandfather and father played local club cricket (both were wicket-keepers)
Education: Belle Vue Junior and Middle School; Buckpool Secondary; Crestwood Comprehensive
Qualifications: 5 O-levels, 4 CSEs, senior coaching certificate
Overseas teams played for: South Bunbury, Western Australia 1983-85
Cricketers particularly admired: Bob Taylor, Alan Knott, Dennis Amiss
Other sports followed: Football, rugby
Relaxations: Playing soccer, watching rugby and 'a good night out'
Extras: Played schoolboy football for Birmingham City. Was Derek Underwood's last first-class victim

Best batting: 114* Leicestershire v Hampshire, Bournemouth 1991

1994 Season (did not make any first-class or one-day appearance)

Career Performances

	M	Inns	NO	Runs	HS	Avge	100s	50s	Ct	St	Balls	Runs	Wkts	Avge	Best	5wI	10wM
Test																	
All First	129	169	39	2963	114 *	22.79	1	15	302	13	5	7	0	-	-	-	-
1-day Int																	
NatWest	13	6	1	67	02	12.40	-	-	14	-							
B & H	26	17	6	313	45	28.45	-	-	28	4							
Sunday	68	45	9	413	38	11.47	-	-	56	4							

96. Which England batsman scored his first Test century on home soil in the series between England and South Africa in 1994?

WIGHT, R. M.   Gloucestershire

Name: Robert Marcus Wight
Role: Right-hand bat, off-spin bowler
Born: 12 September 1969, London
Height: 6ft 2in **Weight:** 13st 8lbs
Nickname: Chalky
County debut: 1993
1st-Class 50s: 3
1st-Class catches: 10
Place in batting averages:
(1993 226th av. 15.20)
Strike rate: (career 85.00)
Parents: Philip and Penny
Marital status: Single
Family links with cricket: Cousin of
Peter Wight (ex Somerset) and related to
Leslie and Vibart Wight who both played
for the West Indies
Education: KCS Wimbledon;
Exeter University; Cambridge University

Qualifications: 11 O-levels, 3 A-levels, BA (Hons) History, PGCE History
Career outside cricket: Financial adviser
Off-season: Working for Sun Life of Canada (UK)
Overseas tours: Surrey U21 to Australia 1989-90; MCC to Kenya 1993
Overseas teams played for: Manly, Sydney 1988
Cricketers particularly admired: Gary Sobers, Geoff Boycott
Other sports followed: Hockey, rugby, baseball, football, most sports
Relaxations: Journalism, playing hockey for Wimbledon, drinking and travelling
Extras: Captained Surrey U21 and made first-class debut for Cambridge University in the 1992 season. Released by Gloucestershire at end of 1994 season
Opinions on cricket: 'Four-day cricket is an excellent idea but matches should finish on a Saturday. This would force counties to prepare suitable wickets to avoid the financial loss of no play on this day, and would allow counties to put greater emphasis on the Sunday competition. A regional competition, comprising six sides coming from the three local county teams, would provide another effective method of judging international players. Such a competition would replace one of the one-day tournaments with the revenue being split amongst all the counties.'
Best batting: 62* Cambridge University v Oxford University, Lord's 1992
Best bowling: 3-65 Cambridge University v Kent, Fenner's 1992

1994 Season

	M	Inns	NO	Runs	HS	Avge	100s	50s	Ct	St	O	M	Runs	Wkts	Avge	Best	5wI	10wM
Test																		
All First	2	3	1	53	22	26.50	-	-	-	-	55	9	230	5	46.00	3-76	-	-
1-day Int																		
NatWest	1	1	1	2	2 *	-	-	-	-	-	7	0	32	0	-	-	-	-
B & H																		
Sunday	4	3	0	14	10	4.66	-	-	3	-	23	0	97	5	19.40	2-28	-	

Career Performances

	M	Inns	NO	Runs	HS	Avge	100s	50s	Ct	St	Balls	Runs	Wkts	Avge	Best	5wI	10wM
Test																	
All First	19	31	5	593	62 *	22.80	-	3	10	-	2807	1456	33	44.12	3-65	-	-
1-day Int																	
NatWest	3	2	1	20	18	20.00	-	-	2	-	162	90	2	45.00	1-24	-	
B & H																	
Sunday	9	7	1	31	11 *	5.16	-	-	3	-	264	189	7	27.00	2-28	-	

WILCOCK, P. J.   Durham

Name: Peter James Wilcock
Role: Right-hand bat,
right-arm medium bowler
Born: 6 August 1974, Rochdale, Lancashire
Height: 6ft 3in **Weight:** 14st 7lbs
Nickname: Noddy
County debut: No first-team appearance
Parents: John and June
Marital status: Single
Family links with cricket: Father played
local league cricket for approx 15 years
Education: Balderstone Community School;
Hopwood Hall Sixth Form College
Qualifications: 8 GCSEs
Career outside cricket: Butcher
Off-season: Working and keeping fit
Overseas tours:
England U19 to India 1992-93
Cricketers particularly admired:
Dave Callaghan, Graeme Hick, Paul Gill (Rochdale CC)
Other sports followed: Rugby league (Leeds), football (Manchester United)
Relaxations: 'Spending time with best "mate" Linda. Socialising, eating and sleeping.'

Extras: Holds rugby league level 1 coaching certificate. Man of the Match in Lancashire Cup Final (1994), Rochdale against Darwin
Opinions on cricket: 'Teams should be more willing to give youth a chance at a higher level.'

WILEMAN, J. R.   Nottinghamshire

Name: Jonathan Ritchie Wileman
Role: Right-hand bat
Born: 19 August 1970, Sheffield
Height: 6ft 1in **Weight:** 12st 12lbs
County debut: 1992
1st-Class 100s: 1
1st-Class catches: 6
Parents: Peter and Joan
Marital status: Single
Education: Malvern College;
Salford University
Qualifications: 12 0-levels, 3 A-levels,
BA in Modern Languages
Cricketers particularly admired:
Ian Botham, Geoff Boycott
Other sports followed: Football, skiing, tennis
Relaxations: Listening to music, watching
films, doing crosswords
Extras: Scored 109 on first-class debut for
Nottinghamshire against Cambridge University. Played for Lincolnshire and Minor Counties in 1994, did not play any first-team games for Nottinghamshire
Opinions on cricket: 'A fascinating game that is underestimated by much of the general public. It is a pity it is not played at a higher level in Europe.'
Best batting: 109 Nottinghamshire v Cambridge University, Trent Bridge 1992

1994 Season

	M	Inns	NO	Runs	HS	Avge	100s	50s	Ct	St	O	M	Runs	Wkts	Avge	Best	5wl	10wM
Test																		
All First	1	2	1	50	42 *	50.00	-	-	3	-								
1-day Int																		
NatWest	1	1	0	14	14	14.00	-	-	2	-								
B & H																		
Sunday																		

	M	Inns	NO	Runs	HS	Avge	100s	50s	Ct	St	Balls	Runs	Wkts	Avge	Best	5wl	10wM
Test																	
All First	3	5	2	217	109	72.33	1	-	6	-							
1-day Int																	
NatWest	1	1	0	14	14	14.00	-	-	2	-							
B & H																	
Sunday																	

WILLIAMS, J. R. A.   Glamorgan

Name: James Robert Alexander Williams
Role: Right-hand opening bat,
off-spin bowler
Born: 20 July 1973, Neath
Height: 5ft 11in **Weight:** 11st 7lbs
County debut: 1993
Parents: John and Beverly
Marital status: Single
Family links with cricket: Father and
grandfather 'very competent' league
cricketers
Education: Clifton College Prep School;
Clifton College; Durham University
Qualifications: 9 GCSEs, 3 A-levels,
NCA coaching award
Career outside cricket: Student
Off-season: 'Relaxing in the north-east'
Overseas tours: Clifton College to
Barbados 1987 and 1991; WCA U16 to Jersey
1989; Scorpions to The Gambia 1991; Durham University to South Africa 1992
Cricketers particularly admired: Michael Atherton, Courtney Walsh, Carl Hooper
Other sports followed: Rugby union, soccer
Relaxations: 'Reading, travelling and arguing with "Gloves"!'
Extras: Represented Welsh Schools and England U19. ASW Young Player of the Month,
June 1993; Glamorgan Supporters 2nd XI Player of the Season 1993
Opinions on cricket: 'Wickets at club grounds for 2nd XI matches are generally sub-
standard. I would like to see the development of cricketers as individual players monitored
more closely, i.e. more attention to individual aims and objectives.'
Best batting: 6 Glamorgan v Australians, Neath 1993

1994 Season (did not make any first-team or one-day appearance)

Career Performances

	M	Inns	NO	Runs	HS	Avge	100s	50s	Ct	St	Balls	Runs	Wkts	Avge	Best	5wI	10wM
Test																	
All First	1	2	0	6	6	3.00	-	-	-	-							
1-day Int																	
NatWest																	
B & H																	
Sunday																	

WILLIAMS, N. F. Essex

Name: Neil FitzGerald Williams
Role: Right-hand bat, right-arm
fast-medium bowler
Born: 2 July 1962, Hope Well, St Vincent,
West Indies
Height: 5ft 10in **Weight:** 11st 7lbs
Nickname: Joe
County debut: 1982 (Middlesex)
County cap: 1984 (Middlesex)
Benefit: 1994
Test debut: 1990
Tests: 1
50 wickets in a season: 3
1st-Class 50s: 13
1st-Class 5 w. in innings: 18
1st-Class 10 w. in match: 2
1st-Class catches: 59
Place in batting averages:
(1993 243rd av. 13.27)
Place in bowling averages: 124th av. 41.84 (1993 61st av. 29.00)
Strike rate: 75.23 (career 55.64)
Parents: Alexander and Aldreta
Marital status: Single
Family links with cricket: 'Uncle Joe plays first division cricket in St Vincent and the Grenadines'
Education: Cane End Primary School, St Vincent; Acland Burghley School, Tufnell Park
Qualifications: School Leaver's Certificate, 6 O-levels, 1 A-level
Overseas tours: English Counties to Zimbabwe 1984-85; MCC to Leeward Islands 1992
Overseas teams played for: St Vincent 1982-92; Windward Islands 1982-92; Tasmania 1983-84

Cricketers particularly admired: Viv Richards, Desmond Haynes, David Gower
Other sports followed: Athletics
Relaxations: Music, 'useful DJ', cinema
Extras: Was on stand-by for England in New Zealand and Pakistan 1983-84. Joined Essex for the 1995 season
Opinions on cricket: 'Happy with four-day cricket.'
Best batting: 77 Middlesex v Warwickshire, Edgbaston 1991
Best bowling: 8-75 Middlesex v Gloucestershire, Lord's 1992

1994 Season

	M	Inns	NO	Runs	HS	Avge	100s	50s	Ct	St	O	M	Runs	Wkts	Avge	Best	5wI	10wM
Test																		
All First	10	9	4	134	63	26.80	-	1	2	-	326	71	1088	26	41.84	6-49	1	-
1-day Int																		
NatWest																		
B & H	2	1	0	5	5	5.00	-	-	-	-	16.2	1	71	1	71.00	1-47	-	
Sunday	6	3	1	2	2 *	1.00	-	-	2	-	42.2	8	123	5	24.60	2-17	-	

Career Performances

	M	Inns	NO	Runs	HS	Avge	100s	50s	Ct	St	Balls	Runs	Wkts	Avge	Best	5wI	10wM
Test	1	1	0	38	38	38.00	-	-	-	-	246	148	2	74.00	2-148	-	-
All First	222	253	51	3909	77	19.35	-	13	59	-	32276	17360	580	29.93	8-75	18	2
1-day Int																	
NatWest	19	10	3	49	10	7.00	-	-	4	-	913	618	15	41.20	4-36	-	
B & H	52	29	7	256	29 *	11.63	-	-	6	-	2769	1705	55	31.00	3-16	-	
Sunday	122	53	20	443	43	13.42	-	-	31	-	5069	3764	135	27.88	4-39	-	

97. Which Leicestershire player took a hat-trick on his first-class debut in 1994 and who else took a hat-trick in the same match?

WILLIAMS, R. C. — Gloucestershire

Name: Ricardo Cecil Williams
Role: Right-hand bat,
right-arm fast-medium bowler
Born: 7 February 1968, Camberwell, London
Height: 5ft 10in **Weight:** 11st
Nickname: Raw Deal, Tricky Ricky, Gus
County debut: 1991
1st-Class catches: 6
Place in batting averages: 246th av. 14.25
Place in bowling averages: 83rd av. 32.92
Strike rate: 56.73 (career 69.36)
Parents: Wilfred Harry Williams and
Cecile Yvonne Jordan
Marital status: Single
Education: Haringey College; Ellerslie
Secondary School, Barbados; Haringey
Cricket College
Qualifications: 3 O-levels,
NCA coaching award

Overseas tours: Haringey Cricket College to Jamaica 1988, 1989, 1990
Overseas teams played for: Geelong City, Victoria, Australia 1991-92
Cricketers particularly admired: Malcolm Marshall, Viv Richards, Richie Richardson,
Jimmy Cook, Gordon Greenidge, Jack Russell, David Lawrence
Other sports followed: Football, tennis, volleyball, basketball, athletics, baseball
Relaxations: Listening to music, buying clothes, relaxing with friends, watching videos
Extras: Rapid Cricketline Player of the Year 1992
Opinions on cricket: 'Prepare faster wickets for batsmen and bowlers to compete on in
both 1st and 2nd XIs.'
Best batting: 44 Gloucestershire v Nottinghamshire, Worksop 1992
Best bowling: 4-28 Gloucestershire v Cambridge University, Bristol 1994

1994 Season

	M	Inns	NO	Runs	HS	Avge	100s	50s	Ct	St	O	M	Runs	Wkts	Avge	Best	5wI	10wM
Test																		
All First	10	14	2	171	38	14.25	-	-	5	-	245.5	46	856	26	32.92	4-28	-	-
1-day Int																		
NatWest																			
B & H																			
Sunday	15	14	5	139	31	15.44	-	-	1	-	106	7	548	19	28.84	3-33	-	

Career Performances

	M	Inns	NO	Runs	HS	Avge	100s	50s	Ct	St	Balls	Runs	Wkts	Avge	Best	5wI	10wM
Test																	
All First	22	34	6	393	44	14.03	-	-	6	-	2636	1599	38	42.07	4-28	-	-
1-day Int																	
NatWest																	
B & H																	
Sunday	24	19	5	148	31	10.57	-	-	2	-	966	790	27	29.25	3-33	-	

WILLIAMS, R. C. J.   Gloucestershire

Name: Richard Charles James Williams
Role: Left-hand bat, wicket-keeper
Born: 8 August 1969, Bristol
Height: 5ft 10in **Weight:** 10st 5lbs
Nickname: Reggie
County debut: 1990
1st-Class 50s: 2
1st-Class catches: 57
1st-Class stumpings: 13
Parents: Michael (deceased 1991)
and Angela
Marital status: Single
Family links with cricket: Father played
local club cricket
Education: Clifton College
Preparatory School; Millfield School
Qualifications: PE Diploma
Overseas tours: Gloucestershire to Namibia
1990, to Kenya 1991, to Sri Lanka 1992-93;
Romany CC to Durban & Cape Town 1993
Overseas teams played for: Manicaland, Zimbabwe 1990-91
Cricketers particularly admired: Andy Brassington, Jack Russell, Alan Knott, David
Gower
Other sports followed: Football, hockey, squash, windsurfing
Relaxations: Listening to music, watching and playing sport
Best batting: 55* Gloucestershire v Derbyshire, Gloucester 1991

> 98. Who was England's Player of the Series against South Africa in
> 1994, despite playing in only one Test?

1994 Season

	M	Inns	NO	Runs	HS	Avge	100s	50s	Ct	St	O	M	Runs	Wkts	Avge	Best	5wI	10wM
Test																		
All First	1	0	0	0	0	-	-	-	3	1								
1-day Int																		
NatWest																		
B & H																		
Sunday	2	1	1	13	13 *	-	-	-	2	-								

Career Performances

	M	Inns	NO	Runs	HS	Avge	100s	50s	Ct	St	Balls	Runs	Wkts	Avge	Best	5wI	10wM
Test																	
All First	25	27	8	284	55 *	14.94	-	2	57	13							
1-day Int																	
NatWest																	
B & H																	
Sunday	11	2	1	30	17	30.00	-	-	10	-							

WILLIS, S. C.   Kent

Name: Simon Charles Willis
Role: Right-hand bat, wicket-keeper
Born: 19 March 1974, Greenwich, London
Height: 5ft 8in **Weight:** 12st
Nickname: Wilco, Bruce
County debut: 1993
1st-Class catches: 2
Parents: Ray and Janet
Marital status: Single
Family links with cricket: Father plays
for Gravesend in Kent League
Education: Wilmington Grammar School
Qualifications: 9 GCSEs,
NCA Junior Coaching Certificate
Off-season: Coaching youngsters around Kent,
and training for the forthcoming season
Overseas tours: Kent U17 to New Zealand
1990-91; Kent to Zimbabwe 1993

Overseas teams played for: Scarborough, Western Australia 1992-93
Cricketers particularly admired: Alan Knott, Viv Richards, Robin Smith, Eddie Stanford
Other sports followed: Golf and soccer
Relaxations: Listening to music, playing golf and going out for meals

Opinions on cricket: 'Pitches overall are going downhill. Maybe groundsmen should be employed by the TCCB, so wickets are not prepared to what each individual county wants.'
Best batting: 0* Kent v Zimbabweans, Canterbury 1993

1994 Season

	M	Inns	NO	Runs	HS	Avge	100s	50s	Ct	St	O	M	Runs	Wkts	Avge	Best	5wI	10wM
Test																		
All First																		
1-day Int																		
NatWest																		
B & H																		
Sunday	1	0	0	0	0	-	-	-	3	-								

Career Performances

	M	Inns	NO	Runs	HS	Avge	100s	50s	Ct	St	Balls	Runs	Wkts	Avge	Best	5wI	10wM
Test																	
All First	1	1	1	0	0*	-	-	-	2	-							
1-day Int																	
NatWest																	
B & H																	
Sunday	1	0	0	0	0	-	-	-	3	-							

WINDOWS, M. G. N.   Gloucestershire

Name: Matthew Guy Newman Windows
Role: Right-hand bat, left-arm bowler
Born: 5 April 1973, Clifton, Bristol
Height: 5ft 7in   **Weight:** 11st 7lbs
Nickname: Steamy, Nic-Nac
County debut: 1992
1st-Class 50s: 6
1st-Class 100s: 1
1st-Class catches: 13
Place in batting averages: 92nd av. 34.76
Parents: Tony and Carolyn
Marital status: Single
Family links with cricket: Father (A.R.)
played for Gloucestershire (1960-69) and
Cambridge University; brother plays for
Clifton Flax Bourton
Education: Clifton College;
Durham University

Qualifications: 8 GCSEs, 3 A-levels
Career outside cricket: Student
Off-season: At university
Overseas tours: England U19 to Pakistan 1991-92; Durham University to South Africa 1992
Cricketers particularly admired: Mike Procter, Graham Gooch
Other sports followed: Rugby
Relaxations: Listening to music, playing other sports
Extras: Played for Lincolnshire and in England U19 home series v Sri Lanka 1992. Public schools rackets and fives champion
Opinions on cricket: 'Leg-byes should be abolished and lunch time should be extended to an hour.'
Best batting: 106 Gloucestershire v New Zealanders, Bristol 1994

1994 Season

	M	Inns	NO	Runs	HS	Avge	100s	50s	Ct	St	O	M	Runs	Wkts	Avge	Best	5wI	10wM
Test																		
All First	11	21	0	730	106	34.76	1	5	11	-								
1-day Int																		
NatWest	1	1	0	33	33	33.00	-	-	-	-								
B & H	1	1	1	16	16*	-	-	-	-	-								
Sunday	12	12	0	347	72	28.91	-	2	1	-								

Career Performances

	M	Inns	NO	Runs	HS	Avge	100s	50s	Ct	St	Balls	Runs	Wkts	Avge	Best	5wI	10wM
Test																	
All First	14	26	0	939	106	36.11	1	6	13	-	6	3	0	-	-	-	-
1-day Int																	
NatWest	1	1	0	33	33	33.00	-	-	-	-							
B & H	1	1	1	16	16*	-	-	-	-	-							
Sunday	16	16	1	392	72	26.13	-	2	2	-							

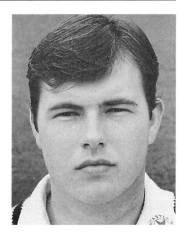

Name: John Wood
Role: Right-hand bat, right-arm fast-medium bowler
Born: 22 July 1970, Wakefield
Height: 6ft 3in **Weight:** 16st
Nickname: Woody
County debut: 1992
1st-Class 50s: 2
1st-Class 5 w. in innings: 4
1st-Class catches: 6
Place in batting averages: 267th av. 10.21 (1993 210th av. 17.85)
Place in bowling averages: 85th av. 33.35 (1993 129th av. 45.93)
Strike rate: 46.08 (career 51.69)
Parents: Brian and Anne
Wife and date of marriage: Emma Louise, 30 October 1994
Family links with cricket: Father played village cricket for over 20 years
Education: Crofton High School; Wakefield District College; Leeds Polytechnic
Qualifications: HND in Electrical and Electronic Engineering
Off-season: Going to New Zealand for six months for a honeymoon and a bit of club cricket
Overseas teams played for: Griqualand West Cricket Union, South Africa 1990-91; Wellington, New Zealand, 1993
Cricketers particularly admired: Ian Botham, Wayne Larkins
Injuries: Hip flexer injury, missed two weeks
Relaxations: Television, going to the pub with friends, snooker, all sports and holidays
Extras: Played in the Bradford League. Made his debut for Durham (Minor Counties) in 1991
Opinions on cricket: 'The idea that cricketers should be happy with low pay because they have a great job is the most stupid thing I have ever heard. Salaries should be much higher, after all, we are professional sportsmen. Also two runs for a no-ball is a crazy idea – let's get back to normal.'
Best batting: 63* Durham v Nottinghamshire, Chester-le-Street 1993
Best bowling: 6-110 Durham v Essex, Stockton 1994

---

99. Who scored 180* and took part in a record partnership in a semi-final of the NatWest Trophy in 1994?

1994 Season

	M	Inns	NO	Runs	HS	Avge	100s	50s	Ct	St	O	M	Runs	Wkts	Avge	Best	5wl	10wM
Test																		
All First	15	22	3	194	51	10.21	-	1	3	-	345.4	38	1501	45	33.35	6-110	3	-
1-day Int																		
NatWest	1	0	0	0	0	-	-	-	-	-	9	2	29	1	29.00	1-29	-	
B & H																		
Sunday	9	6	1	44	28	8.80	-	-	-	-	66.3	5	340	8	42.50	2-26	-	

Career Performances

	M	Inns	NO	Runs	HS	Avge	100s	50s	Ct	St	Balls	Runs	Wkts	Avge	Best	5wl	10wM
Test																	
All First	32	45	7	524	63 *	13.78	-	2	6	-	4032	2770	78	35.51	6-110	4	-
1-day Int																	
NatWest	5	1	0	1	1	1.00	-	-	-	-	228	168	4	42.00	2-22	-	
B & H	2	0	0	0	0	-	-	-	-	-	84	42	1	42.00	1-19	-	
Sunday	18	12	3	77	28	8.55	-	-	2	-	720	619	15	41.26	2-26	-	

WOOD, N. T. — Lancashire

Name: Nathan Theodore Wood
Role: Left-hand opening bat,
right-arm off-spin bowler
Born: 4 October 1974, Thornhill Edge,
Yorkshire
Height: 5ft 8in **Weight:** 10st 7lbs
Nickname: Hot Rod, Proff, Crickle
County debut: No first-team appearance
Parents: Barry and Janet
Marital status: Single
Family links with cricket: Father played for
Lancashire, Derbyshire and England; uncle
(Ron) played for Yorkshire
Education: Altrincham Prep School;
William Hulme's Grammar School
Qualifications: 8 GCSEs, coaching awards
Career outside cricket: 'Various courses and
just chilling'
Off-season: Taking a coaching course,
touring with England U19
Overseas tours: England U18 to South Africa 1992-93, to Denmark 1993; England U19
to Sri Lanka 1993-94

Cricketers particularly admired: 'My father', David Gower, Michael Holding, Viv Richards, Les 'The Whirlwind' Seal
Other sports followed: Rugby, tennis, football (Manchester United)
Relaxations: 'Music (house and soul), cinema, socialising, reading, buying clothes. Heated debate with sister, Fiona, and educating niece, Georgina.'
Extras: Represented England at all levels U14 to U19 and made U19 debut in final 'Test' against West Indies in summer 1993

WREN, T. N. Kent

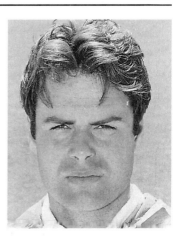

Name: Timothy Neil Wren
Role: Right-hand bat, left-arm medium bowler
Born: 26 March 1970, Folkestone
Height: 6ft 3in **Weight:** 14st 7lbs
Nickname: Bear, Balou
County debut: 1989 (one-day), 1990 (first-class)
1st-Class 5 w. in innings: 1
1st-Class catches: 7
Place in bowling averages: 74th av. 31.35
Strike rate: 58.17 (career 64.56)
Parents: James and Gillian
Marital status: Single
Family links with cricket: 'Brother disillusioned with comeback, but is receiving some very fine coaching!'
Education: Lyminge Primary; Harvey Grammar School, Folkestone
Qualifications: 6 O-levels, NCA coaching certificate
Career outside cricket: Plumber
Off-season: Working, playing rugby, staying fit
Overseas teams played for: Universals, Zimbabwe 1989-90
Cricketers particularly admired: Ian Botham, David Gower, Graeme Hick, Carl Hooper
Other sports followed: All sports, particularly rugby, golf, mountain biking
Relaxations: Mountain biking, watching any sport and reading
Extras: First played for Kent 2nd XI in 1987, aged 17
Opinions on cricket: 'The standard of wickets has got to improve, not only in first-class cricket, but also second team cricket should be played on first-class pitches and under first-class conditions. Cricketers are poorly paid in relation to other sports. If the third umpire is to be used in semi-finals and finals, then it should be used in all rounds of the competition.'
Best batting: 18* Kent v Worcestershire, Canterbury 1994
Best bowling: 6-48 Kent v Somerset, Canterbury 1994

1994 Season

	M	Inns	NO	Runs	HS	Avge	100s	50s	Ct	St	O	M	Runs	Wkts	Avge	Best	5wI	10wM
Test																		
All First	7	11	4	31	18 *	4.42	-	-	2	-	164.5	30	533	17	31.35	6-48	1	-
1-day Int																		
NatWest	1	1	0	0	0	0.00	-	-	-	-	10	0	41	0	-		-	-
B & H																		
Sunday	10	2	2	5	5 *	-	-	-	4	-	65	5	272	8	34.00	3-29	-	

Career Performances

	M	Inns	NO	Runs	HS	Avge	100s	50s	Ct	St	Balls	Runs	Wkts	Avge	Best	5wI	10wM
Test																	
All First	15	17	6	55	18 *	5.00	-	-	7	-	2066	1200	32	37.50	6-48	1	-
1-day Int																	
NatWest	1	1	0	0	0	0.00	-	-	-	-	60	41	0	-		-	-
B & H																	
Sunday	13	3	3	5	5 *	-	-	-	4	-	501	377	11	34.27	3-29	-	

WRIGHT, A. J.   Gloucestershire

Name: Anthony John Wright
Role: Right-hand bat, off-spin bowler
Born: 27 July 1962, Stevenage,
Hertfordshire
Height: 6ft **Weight:** 14st
Nickname: Billy, Horace
County debut: 1982
County cap: 1987
1000 runs in a season: 5
1st-Class 50s: 57
1st-Class 100s: 13
1st-Class catches: 183
One-Day 100s: 1
Place in batting averages: 79th av. 36.42
(1993 213th av. 16.94)
Parents: Michael and Patricia
Wife and date of marriage:
Rachel, 21 December 1986
Children: Hannah, 3 April 1988
Education: Alleyn's School, Stevenage
Qualifications: 6 O-levels
Cricketers particularly admired: Viv Richards, Ian Botham, Malcolm Marshall, Jack Russell

Other sports followed: All sports except motor racing
Relaxations: Eating out, reading, playing golf
Extras: Captain of Gloucestershire for 1990-93
Best batting: 184* Gloucestershire v Leicestershire, Bristol 1994
Best bowling: 1-16 Gloucestershire v Yorkshire, Harrogate 1989

1994 Season

	M	Inns	NO	Runs	HS	Avge	100s	50s	Ct	St	O	M	Runs	Wkts	Avge	Best	5wI	10wM
Test																		
All First	19	36	3	1202	184 *	36.42	1	7	32	-								
1-day Int																		
NatWest	1	1	0	0	0	0.00	-	-	-	-								
B & H	1	1	0	55	55	55.00	-	1	-	-								
Sunday	16	16	1	394	69	26.26	-	3	7	-								

Career Performances

	M	Inns	NO	Runs	HS	Avge	100s	50s	Ct	St	Balls		Runs	Wkts	Avge	Best	5wI	10wM
Test																			
All First	236	411	31	10863	184 *	28.58	13	57	183	-	74		68	1	68.00	1-16	-	-
1-day Int																		
NatWest	23	22	1	808	107 *	38.47	1	8	5	-								
B & H	33	30	0	848	97	28.26	-	6	6	-								
Sunday	146	135	16	3078	93	25.86	-	22	56	-	26		22	0	-	-	-	

100. Who was South Africa's Player of the Series against England in 1994, averaging 58 with the bat and 34.84 with the ball?

Name: Alex Wylie
Role: Left-hand bat, right-arm fast bowler
Born: 20 February 1973, Tamworth
Height: 6ft 2in
County debut: 1993
Education: Bromsgrove School,
Warwick College of Agriculture
Best bowling: 1-50 Worcestershire v
Nottinghamshire, Trent Bridge 1993

1994 Season (did not make any first-class or one-day appearance)

Career Performances

	M	Inns	NO	Runs	HS	Avge	100s	50s	Ct	St	Balls	Runs	Wkts	Avge	Best	5wl	10wM
Test																	
All First	1	1	0	0	0	0.00	-	-	-	-	132	73	1	73.00	1-50	-	-
1-day Int																	
NatWest																		
B & H																		
Sunday																		

YATES, G.   Lancashire

Name: Gary Yates
Role: Right-hand bat, off-spin bowler
Born: 20 September 1967,
Ashton-under-Lyne
Height: 6ft 1in **Weight:** 12st 10lbs
Nickname: Yugo, Pearly, Backyard, Zippy
County debut: 1990
County cap: 1994
1st-Class 50s: 3
1st-Class 100s: 3
1st-Class 5 w. in innings: 2
1st-Class catches: 16
Place in batting averages: 195th av. 20.92
Place in bowling averages: 41st av. 27.37
(1993 127th av. 43.25)
Strike rate: 52.02 (career 85.55)
Parents: Alan and Patricia
Marital status: Single
Family links with cricket: Father played
in Lancashire Leagues
Education: Manchester Grammar School
Qualifications: 6 O-levels, Australian Coaching Council coach
Career outside cricket: 'Getting more involved in family business (Digical Ltd), selling diaries, calendars and business gifts.'
Off-season: Playing and coaching for Hermanus, Boland, South Africa
Overseas tours: Lancashire to Tasmania and Western Australia 1990, to Western Australia 1991, to Johannesburg 1992, to Barbados and St Lucia 1992
Overseas teams played for: South Barwon, Geelong, Australia 1987-88; Johnsonville, Wellington, New Zealand 1989-90; Western Suburbs, Brisbane 1991-92; Old Selbornian, East London, South Africa 1992-93
Cricketers particularly admired: Michael Atherton, Ian Botham, John Emburey
Other sports followed: All sports, especially football (Manchester City), golf, motor rallying
Relaxations: Playing golf, watching football and good films, eating
Extras: Played for Worcestershire 2nd XI in 1987; made debut for Lancashire 2nd XI in 1988 and taken on to county staff in 1990; scored century on Championship debut v Nottinghamshire at Trent Bridge. Rapid Cricketline Player of the Month April/May 1992
Opinions on cricket: 'Would like to see more points awarded for rained-off games or draws. This would hopefully help to abolish contrived matches. Hope four-day cricket is here to stay.'
Best batting: 134* Lancashire v Northamptonshire, Old Trafford 1993
Best bowling: 5-34 Lancashire v Hampshire, Old Trafford 1994

1994 Season

	M	Inns	NO	Runs	HS	Avge	100s	50s	Ct	St	O	M	Runs	Wkts	Avge	Best	5wI	10wM
Test																		
All First	13	20	7	272	54 *	20.92	-	2	3	-	320.5	70	1013	37	27.37	5-34	1	-
1-day Int																		
NatWest	2	1	1	7	7 *	-	-	-	-	-	24	2	89	3	29.66	2-61	-	
B & H	2	0	0	0	0	-	-	-	1	-	21	1	77	3	25.66	2-49	-	
Sunday	17	4	2	26	14	13.00	-	-	6	-	91.4	1	491	19	25.84	4-34	-	

Career Performances

	M	Inns	NO	Runs	HS	Avge	100s	50s	Ct	St	Balls	Runs	Wkts	Avge	Best	5wI	10wM
Test																	
All First	45	60	28	1119	134 *	34.96	3	3	16	-	7871	4039	92	43.90	5-34	2	-
1-day Int																	
NatWest	2	1	1	7	7 *	-	-	-	-	-	144	89	3	29.66	2-61	-	
B & H	5	0	0	0	0	-	-	-	2	-	258	162	5	32.40	2-49	-	
Sunday	28	6	3	35	14	11.66	-	-	8	-	1018	853	28	30.46	4-34	-	

YEABSLEY, R. S.   Middlesex

Name: Richard Stuart Yeabsley
Role: Right-hand bat,
right-arm medium bowler
Born: 2 November 1973, St Albans
Height: 6ft 5in **Weight:** 15st 6lbs
Nickname: Yeabo
County debut: 1994 (one-day)
1st-Class 50s: 1
1st-Class 5 w. in innings: 1
1st-Class catches: 10
Place in batting averages:
(1993 225th av. 15.33)
Place in bowling averages: 38th av. 27.00
(1993 109th av. 38.10)
Strike rate: 49.90 (career 60.26)
Parents: Douglas and Jacqueline
Marital status: Single
Family links with cricket:
Father played for Devon for 30 years and
for Minor Counties; brother played for Hertfordshire U19
Education: Haberdashers' Aske's School, Elstree, Hertfordshire; Keble College, Oxford
Qualifications: O-levels and A-levels

Career outside cricket: 'Lion tamer'
Off-season: Studying at Oxford University
Overseas tours: Haberdashers' Aske's to Far East 1991-92
Cricketers particularly admired: 'A.N.S. Bryce, R. Kid, G. Hick'
Other sports followed: Baseball, American football, rugby
Injuries: Broken finger, missed three months
Relaxations: 'Diving, white-water rafting, banter'
Extras: Made NatWest debut for Devon against Somerset in 1990, aged 16, and his first-class debut for Oxford University in 1993. Oxford Blue 1993 and 1994. Secretary of OUCC 1994. Played rugby for Oxford in U21 Varsity match 1992 and 1993 and toured Ireland with the full Oxford University Blues squad in 1993. Rugby Blue against Cambridge at Twickenham 1994.
Opinions on cricket: 'Cambridge University to lose first-class status!'
Best batting: 52* Oxford University v Yorkshire, The Parks 1994
Best bowling: 6-54 Oxford University v Cambridge University, Lord's 1994

1994 Season

	M	Inns	NO	Runs	HS	Avge	100s	50s	Ct	St	O	M	Runs	Wkts	Avge	Best	5wl	10wM
Test																		
All First	6	3	1	53	52*	26.50	-	1	5	-	174.4	27	567	21	27.00	6-54	1	-
1-day Int																		
NatWest																		
B & H																		
Sunday	3	0	0	0	0	-	-	-	-	-	17	1	76	5	15.20	5-32	1	

Career Performances

	M	Inns	NO	Runs	HS	Avge	100s	50s	Ct	St	Balls	Runs	Wkts	Avge	Best	5wl	10wM
Test																	
All First	16	16	5	191	52*	17.36	-	1	10	-	2471	1329	41	32.41	6-54	1	
1-day Int																	
NatWest	1	1	0	2	2	2.00	-	-	-	-	72	77	0	-	-	-	-
B & H																	
Sunday	3	0	0	0	0	-	-	-	-	-	102	76	5	15.20	5-32	1	

THE UMPIRES

BALDERSTONE, J. C.

Name: John Christopher Balderstone
Role: Right-hand opening bat, slow
left-arm bowler
Born: 16 November 1940, Huddersfield
Height: 6ft 1in **Weight:** 12st 10lbs
Nickname: Baldy
Appointed to 1st-class list: 1988
Appointed to Test panel: Stand-by
umpire in 1991
One-Day Internationals: 1
Counties: Yorkshire, Leicestershire
County debut: 1961 (Yorkshire),
1971 (Leicestershire)
County cap: 1973 (Leicestershire)
Test debut: 1976
Tests: 2
1000 runs in a season: 11
1st-Class 50s: 102
1st-Class 100s: 32
1st-Class 5 w. in innings: 5
One-Day 100s: 5
1st-Class catches: 210
Parents: Frank and Jenny (deceased)
Wife and date of marriage: Angela, January 1991
Children: Sally, 15 September 1970; Michael, 3 January 1973
Education: Paddock County School, Huddersfield
Qualifications: Advanced cricket coach, soccer coach
Career outside cricket: Professional footballer 1958-78
Off-season: Coaching cricket
Overseas tours: Leicestershire to Zimbabwe 1981, to Oman 1984
Cricketers particularly admired: Willie Watson, Brian Close, Fred Trueman, David
Gower, Ray Illingworth
Other sports followed: All sports
Relaxations: Golf
Extras: 14 One-Day Man of the Match Awards. Played a first-class cricket match and
football league game on the same day in 1975 (Leicestershire v Derbyshire, Doncaster v
Brentford). Was the first man to act as 'third umpire' in Test in England, in the second Test
against Australia at Lord's in 1993. Umpired first one-day International, England v South
Africa 1994
Best batting: 181* Leicestershire v Gloucestershire, Leicester 1984
Best bowling: 6-25 Leicestershire v Hampshire, Southampton 1978

First-Class Career Performances

	M	Inns	NO	Runs	HS	Avge	100s	Ct	St	Runs	Wkts	Avge	Best	5wl	10wM
Test	2	4	0	39	35	9.75	-	-	1	80	1	80.00	1-80	-	-
All First	390	619	61	19034	181 *	34.11	32	210	-	8160	310	26.32	6-25	5	-

BIRD, H. D.

Name: Harold Dennis Bird, MBE
Role: Right-hand opening bat
Born: 19 April 1933, Barnsley
Height: 5ft 10in **Weight:** 12st
Nickname: Dickie
Appointed to 1st-class list: 1969
Appointed to Test panel: 1972
Appointed to International Panel: 1994
Tests umpired: 64
One-Day Internationals umpired: 91
Counties: Yorkshire, Leicestershire
County debut: 1956 (Yorkshire),
1960 (Leicestershire)
County cap: 1960 (Leicestershire)
1000 runs in a season: 1
1st-Class 50s: 14
1st-Class 100s: 2
1st-Class catches: 28
Parents: James Harold and Ethel
Marital status: Single
Education: Raley School, Barnsley
Qualifications: MCC advanced cricket coach
Career outside cricket: 'Cricket is my life'
Off-season: After-dinner speaking and umpiring overseas
Cricketing superstitions or habits: Twitch of the shoulders, wears distinctive white cap
Other sports followed: Football
Cricketers particularly admired: Gary Sobers, Dennis Lillee, Viv Richards
Cricketers particularly learnt from: Gubby Allen, Johnny Wardle
Relaxations: Listening to recordings of Barbra Streisand and Diana Ross
Extras: Has umpired 155 international matches to date, including three World Cup finals at Lord's (1975, 1979, 1983); also umpired at the World Cup in India in 1987. Umpired the Queen's Silver Jubilee Test, England v Australia 1977, the Centenary Test, England v Australia 1980 and the MCC Bicentenary Test, England v Rest of the World 1987. In 1982 he umpired the Women's World Cup final in Christchurch, New Zealand. During the mid-1980s he umpired several times in the various competitions staged at Sharjah, UAE.

To date he has umpired 34 Cup finals all over the world, as well as the finals of other cricket events such as The Best All-rounder in the World, The Best Batsman in the World and the World Double Wicket competition. In 1977 he was voted Yorkshire Personality of the Year. He is an MCC member and author of three bestselling books, *Not Out*, *That's Out* and *From the Pavilion End*. Despite lucrative offers to join the 'Packer circus' and to visit South Africa with rebel tours, he remained loyal to the TCCB and to the established game on which he had been brought up in Yorkshire and which had given him so much in life. In June 1986 he received an MBE in the Queen's Birthday Honours List. With David Shepherd and Steve Bucknor became the first ICC officially-sponsored umpires in 1992, and was appointed to stand in Zimbabwe's first Test match (against India) in Harare. Subsequently, in Zimbabwe's second Test against New Zealand (also in Harare), he became the first umpire to officiate in 50 Test matches, having passed Frank Chester's world record of 48 Tests at Bulawayo six days earlier. Umpired all three Tests in West Indies home series against Pakistan in 1993. In 1994 he umpired Tests in New Zealand, England, Pakistan and India. Made Honorary Life Member of Yorkshire CCC in March 1994

Opinions on cricket: 'The greatest game in the world. A game to be enjoyed by young and old. I have consistently advocated playing through all light unless the umpires are convinced that there is genuine physical danger to the batsman.'

Best batting: 181* Yorkshire v Glamorgan, Bradford 1959

First-Class Career Performances

	M	Inns	NO	Runs	HS	Avge	100s	Ct	St	Runs	Wkts	Avge	Best	5wI	10wM
Test															
All First	93	170	10	3314	181*	20.71	2	28	-	22	0	-	-	-	-

BOND, J. D.

Name: John David Bond
Role: Right-hand bat
Born: 6 May 1932, Kearsley, Lancashire
Nickname: Jackie
Appointed to 1st-class list: 1988
Counties: Lancashire, Nottinghamshire
County debut: 1955 (Lancashire),
1974 (Nottinghamshire)
County cap: 1961 (Lancashire)
1000 runs in a season: 2
1st-Class 50s: 54
1st-Class 100s: 14
1st-Class catches: 222
Education: Bolton School
Extras: Captain of Lancashire 1968-1972,
during which time Lancashire won
the Gillette Cup three years in succession
(1970, 1971, 1972) and the John Player
Sunday League in 1969 and 1970. He
moved to Nottinghamshire in 1974 and was a Test selector in the same year. He
appointed cricket manager at Lancashire CCC in 1980 and held the position until 1986
Best batting: 157 Lancashire v Hampshire, Old Trafford 1962

First-Class Career Performances

	M	Inns	NO	Runs	HS	Avge	100s	Ct	St	Runs	Wkts	Avge	Best	5wl	10wM
Test															
All First	362	548	80	12125	157	25.90	14	222	-	69	0	-	-	-	-

BURGESS, G. I.

Name: Graham Iefvion Burgess
Role: Right-hand bat, right-arm
medium bowler
Born: 5 May 1943,
Glastonbury, Somerset
Appointed to 1st-class list: 1991
County: Somerset
County debut: 1966
County cap: 1968
Testimonial: 1977
1st-Class 100s: 2
1st-Class 5 w. in innings: 18
1st-Class 10 w. in match: 2
1st-Class catches: 120
Education: Millfield School
Extras: Played Minor Counties cricket
for Wiltshire 1981-82 and for
Cambridgeshire 1983-84

Best batting: 129 Somerset v Gloucestershire, Taunton 1973
Best bowling: 7-43 Somerset v Oxford University, The Parks 1975

First-Class Career Performances

	M	Inns	NO	Runs	HS	Avge	100s	Ct	St	Runs	Wkts	Avge	Best	5wI	10wM
Test															
All First	252	414	37	7129	129	18.90	2	120	-	13543	474	28.57	7-43	18	2

CONSTANT, D. J.

Name: David John Constant
Role: Left-hand bat, slow left-arm bowler
Born: 9 November 1941,
Bradford-on-Avon, Wiltshire
Nickname: Connie
Appointed to 1st-class list: 1969
Appointed to Test panel: 1971
Tests umpired: 36
One-Day Internationals umpired: 29
Counties: Kent, Leicestershire
County debut: 1961 (Kent),
1965 (Leicestershire)
1st-Class 50s: 6
1st-Class catches: 33
Extras: County bowls player for
Gloucestershire 1984-86
Best batting:
80 Leicestershire v Gloucestershire,
Bristol 1966

First-Class Career Performances

	M	Inns	NO	Runs	HS	Avge	100s	Ct	St	Runs	Wkts	Avge	Best	5wI	10wM
Test															
All First	61	93	14	1517	80	19.20	-	33	-	36	1	36.00	1-28	-	-

DUDLESTON, B.

Name: Barry Dudleston
Role: Right-hand opening bat, slow
left-arm bowler, occasional wicket-keeper
Born: 16 July 1945, Bebington, Cheshire
Height: 5ft 9in **Weight:** 13st
Nickname: Danny, Dapper
Appointed to 1st-class list: 1984
Appointed to Test panel: 1991
Tests umpired: 2
One-Day Internationals umpired: 1
Counties: Leicestershire, Gloucestershire
County debut: 1966 (Leicestershire),
1981 (Gloucestershire)
County cap: 1969 (Leicestershire)
Benefit: 1980 (£25,000)
1000 runs in a season: 8
1st-Class 100s: 32
1st-Class 200s: 1
One-Day 100s: 4
1st-Class catches: 234

Parents: Percy and Dorothy Vera
Marital status: Divorced
Children: Sharon Louise, 29 October 1968; Matthew Barry, 12 September 1988
Education: Stockport School
Qualifications: O-levels, junior coaching certificate, Shell marketing exams
Career outside cricket: Managing director of Sunsport Tours
Other sports followed: Most
Cricketers particularly admired: Gary Sobers, Tom Graveney
Cricketers particularly learnt from: Vinoo Mankad
Relaxations: Television, bridge, wine, golf
Extras: Played for England U25. Suffered badly from broken fingers, breaking fingers on the same hand three times in 1978. Played for Rhodesia in the Currie Cup 1976-80. Acted as 'third umpire' in the third Test against Australia at Trent Bridge 1993
Opinions on cricket: 'It is still the greatest test of skill and character – beautiful to watch when played well. Am worried about the declining standards of behaviour.'
Best batting: 202 Leicestershire v Derbyshire, Leicester 1979
Best bowling: 4-6 Leicestershire v Surrey, Leicester 1972

First-Class Career Performances

	M	Inns	NO	Runs	HS	Avge	100s	Ct	St	Runs	Wkts	Avge	Best	5wI	10wM
Test															
All First	295	501	47	14747	202	32.48	32	234	7	1365	47	29.04	4-6	-	-

HAMPSHIRE, J. H.

Name: John Harry Hampshire
Role: Right-hand bat
Born: 10 February 1941,
Thurnscoe, Yorkshire
Height: 6ft **Weight:** 13st
Nickname: Hamp
Appointed to 1st-class list: 1985
Appointed to Test panel: 1989
Tests umpired: 11
One-Day Internationals umpired: 5
Counties: Yorkshire, Derbyshire
County debut: 1961 (Yorkshire),
1982 (Derbyshire)
County cap: 1963 (Yorkshire),
1982 (Derbyshire)
Benefit: 1976
Test debut: 1969
Tests: 8
1000 runs in a season: 15
1st-Class 50s: 142
1st-Class 100s: 43
1st-Class catches: 445
1st-Class 5 w. in innings: 2
One-Day 100s: 7
Parents: Jack and Vera
Wife and date of marriage: Judith Ann, 5 September 1964
Children: Ian Christopher, 6 January 1969; Paul Wesley, 12 February 1972
Family links with cricket: Father (J.) and brother (A.W.) both played for Yorkshire
Education: Oakwood Technical High School, Rotherham
Qualifications: City and Guilds in Printing
Off-season: Coach to Zimbabwe 1992-95
Overseas tours: MCC to Australia and New Zealand, 1970-71
Overseas teams played for: Tasmania, 1966-69, 1977-79
Cricketers particularly admired: Peter May, Gary Sobers
Other sports followed: Most sports
Relaxations: Gardening and cooking
Extras: Captained Yorkshire 1979-80. Played for Tasmania 1967-69 and 1977-79. Scored a century (107) in his first Test match, against West Indies at Lord's 1969. Appointed manager/coach of the Zimbabwe Test squad for their first Test matches against India and New Zealand. Umpired four Tests in Pakistan 1989-90
Best batting: 183* Yorkshire v Surrey, Hove 1971
Best bowling: 7-52 Yorkshire v Glamorgan, Cardiff 1963

First-Class Career Performances

	M	Inns	NO	Runs	HS	Avge	100s	Ct	St	Runs	Wkts	Avge	Best	5wl	10wM
Test	8	16	1	405	107	26.86	1	9	-						
All First	577	924	112	28059	183 *	34.55	43	445	-	1637	30	54.56	7-52	2	-

HARRIS, J. H.

Name: John Henry Harris
Role: Left-hand bat, right-arm
fast-medium bowler
Born: 13 February 1936, Taunton
Appointed to 1st-class list: 1983
County: Somerset
County debut: 1952
1st-Class catches: 6
Extras: Made his debut for Somerset
aged 16 years 99 days. Played Minor
Counties cricket for Suffolk (1960-62)
and Devon (1975). Third year as Chairman of
the First-Class Cricket Umpires Association
Best batting:
41 Somerset v Worcestershire,
Taunton 1957
Best bowling:
3-29 Somerset v Worcestershire,
Bristol 1959

First-Class Career Performances

	M	Inns	NO	Runs	HS	Avge	100s	Ct	St	Runs	Wkts	Avge	Best	5wl	10wM
Test															
All First	15	18	4	154	41	11.00	-	6	-	609	19	32.05	3.29	-	-

HOLDER, J. W.

Name: John Wakefield Holder
Role: Right-hand bat, right-arm
fast bowler
Born: 19 March 1945,
St George, Barbados
Height: 6ft **Weight:** 13st 10lbs
Nickname: Benson
Appointed to 1st-class list: 1983
Appointed to Test panel: 1988
Tests umpired: 10
One-Day Internationals umpired: 8
County: Hampshire
County debut: 1968
50 wickets in a season: 1
1st-Class 5 w. in innings: 5
1st-Class 10 w. in match: 1
1st-Class catches: 12
Parents: Charles and Carnetta
Wife: Glenda

Children: Christopher 1968; Nigel 1970
Family links with cricket: Both sons have played for Royston in the Central Lancashire
League
Education: St Giles Boys School; Combermere High School, Barbados; Rochdale College
Qualifications: 3 O-levels, MCC advanced cricket coach
Off-season: Coaching part-time
Other sports followed: Football (Manchester United)
Relaxations: Keeping fit and helping coach the Rochdale Indoor Cricket Team which
plays in the National League in the winter
Extras: Recorded best bowling figures in Rothmans International Cavaliers cricket
matches – 6-7 for Hampshire Cavaliers at Tichborne Park in 1968. Played professional
league cricket in Yorkshire and Lancashire (1974-82). Took one first-class hat-trick,
Hampshire v Kent 1972, 'but finished with 3-100!' Umpired four Tests in Pakistan 1989-90
Best batting: 33 Hampshire v Sussex, Hove 1971
Best bowling: 7-79 Hampshire v Gloucestershire, Gloucester 1972

First-Class Career Performances

	M	Inns	NO	Runs	HS	Avge	100s	Ct	St	Runs	Wkts	Avge	Best	5wI	10wM
Test															
All First	47	49	14	374	33	10.68	-	12	-	3415	139	24.56	7-79	5	1

HOLDER, V. A.

Name: Vanburn Alonza Holder
Role: Right-hand bat, right-arm
fast-medium bowler
Born: 8 October 1945,
St Michael, Barbados
Nickname: Van
Appointed to 1st-class list: 1992
County: Worcestershire
County debut: 1968
County cap: 1970
Test debut: 1969
Tests: 40
1st-Class 50s: 4
1st-Class 100s: 1
1st-Class 5 w. in innings: 38
1st-Class 10 w. in match: 3
1st-Class catches: 98
Overseas tours: West Indies to England
1969, 1973, to India, Sri Lanka and
Pakistan 1974-75, to Australia 1975-76, to England 1976, to India and Sri Lanka 1978-79
(as vice-captain)
Extras: Made his debut for Barbados in the Shell Shield competition in 1966-67
Best batting: 122 Barbados v Trinidad, Bridgetown 1973-74
Best bowling: 7-40 Worcestershire v Glamorgan, Cardiff 1974

First-Class Career Performances

	M	Inns	NO	Runs	HS	Avge	100s	Ct	St	Runs	Wkts	Avge	Best	5wI	10wM
Test	40	59	11	682	42	14.20	-	16	-	3627	109	33.27	6-28	3	-
All First	311	354	81	3559	122	13.03	1	98	-	23183	948	24.45	7-40	38	3

JESTY, T. E.

Name: Trevor Edward Jesty
Role: Right-hand bat, right-arm
medium bowler
Born: 2 June 1948, Gosport, Hampshire
Height: 5ft 9in **Weight:** 11st 9lbs
Nickname: Jets
Appointed to 1st-class list: 1994
Counties: Hampshire, Surrey, Lancashire
County debut: 1966 (Hampshire),
1985 (Surrey), 1988 (Lancashire)
County cap: 1971 (Hampshire),
1985 (Surrey)
Benefit: 1982
One-Day Internationals: 10
1000 runs in a season: 10
50 wickets in a season: 2
1st-Class 50s: 110
1st-Class 100s: 35
1st-Class 200s: 2
1st-Class 5 w. in innings: 19
1st-Class catches: 265
1st-Class stumpings: 1
One-Day 100s: 7

Parents: Aubrey Edward and Sophia
Wife and date of marriage: Jacqueline, 12 September 1970
Children: Graeme Barry, 27 September 1972; Lorna Samantha, 7 November 1976
Education: Privet County Secondary Modern, Gosport
Overseas tours: International XI to West Indies 1982; England to Australia and New Zealand 1982-83
Overseas teams played for: Border, South Africa 1973-74; Griqualand West 1974-77, 1980-81; Canterbury, New Zealand 1979-80
Cricketers particularly admired: Sir Garfield Sobers, Barry Richards
Relaxations: Watching football, gardening, golf
Extras: One of *Wisden*'s Five Cricketers of the Year 1982. Left Hampshire at end of 1984 when not appointed captain and offered the captaincy of Surrey for 1985 season.
Best batting: 248 Hampshire v Cambridge University, Fenner's 1984
Best bowling: 7-75 Hampshire v Worcestershire, Southampton 1976

First-Class Career Performances

	M	Inns	NO	Runs	HS	Avge	100s	Ct	St	Runs	Wkts	Avge	Best	5wI	10wM
Test															
All First	490	777	107	21916	248	32.71	35	265	1	16075	585	27.47	7-75	19	-

JONES, A. A.

Name: Alan Arthur Jones
Role: Right-hand bat, right-arm
fast-medium bowler
Born: 9 December 1947, Horley, Surrey
Height: 6ft 3in **Weight:** 14st
Nickname: Jonah
Appointed to 1st-class list: 1985
Counties: Sussex, Somerset,
Middlesex, Glamorgan
County debut: 1964 (Sussex),
1970 (Somerset), 1976 (Middlesex),
1980 (Glamorgan)
County cap: 1972 (Somerset),
1976 (Middlesex), 1980 (Glamorgan)
50 wickets in a season: 4
1st-Class 5 w. in innings: 23
1st-Class 10 w. in match: 3
1st-Class catches: 50
Parents: Leslie and Hazel
Wife: Marilyn
Children: Clare Michelle
Education: St John's College, Horsham
Qualifications: 5 O-levels, MCC advanced coach, NCA staff coach
Off-season: 'Pleasing myself.'
Overseas teams played for: Northern Transvaal 1972-73; Orange Free State 1976-77
Other sports followed: All sports
Cricketers particularly admired: Tom Cartwright, Brian Close
Other sports followed: Golf, rugby league
Relaxations: Golf
Extras: Acted as 'third umpire' in the sixth Test against Australia at The Oval 1993
Opinions on cricket: 'I have many opinions on the game, but my contract restricts me from revealing them.'
Best batting: 33 Middlesex v Kent, Canterbury 1978
Best bowling: 9-51 Somerset v Sussex, Hove 1976

First-Class Career Performances

	M	Inns	NO	Runs	HS	Avge	100s	Ct	St	Runs	Wkts	Avge	Best	5wl	10wM
Test															
All First	214	216	68	799	33	5-39	-	50	-	15414	549	28.07	9-51	23	3

JULIAN, R.

Name: Raymond Julian
Role: Right-hand bat, wicket-keeper
Born: 23 August 1936,
Cosby, Leicestershire
Height: 5ft 11in **Weight:** 13st 3lbs
Nickname: Julie
Appointed to 1st-class list: 1972
County: Leicestershire
County debut: 1953
County cap: 1961
1st-Class 50s: 2
1st-Class catches: 381
1st-Class stumpings: 40
Parents: George Ernest and Doris
Wife and date of marriage:
Megan, 3rd April 1993
Children:
Peter Raymond, 1 February 1958;
John Kelvin, 13 October 1960;
David Andrew, 15 October 1963; Paul Anthony, 22 September 1967
Family links with cricket: Father and two brothers all played local cricket
Education: Wigston Secondary Modern
Qualifications: Cricket coach, decorator and gardener
Career outside cricket: As above
Off-season: Watching Ashes tour and holidays
Overseas tours: MCC to West Africa, 1975
Cricketers particularly admired: Gary Sobers, Keith Andrew
Other sports followed: Football, boxing, rugby
Relaxations: Gardening, holidays, travelling
Extras: Youngest player to make debut for Leicestershire (aged 15 years). Youngest wicket-keeper to play first-class cricket in 1953. Took six catches in an innings, Leicestershire v Northants, Kettering 1965. Played for the Army 1955-57. Gave eight LBW decisions in succession, Glamorgan v Sussex at Cardiff 1986. Has umpired three B&H semi-finals and one Gillette Cup semi-final. Has been stand-by umpire for two Test matches
Opinions on cricket: 'Enjoy all cricket – a lovely way of life.'
Best batting: 51 Leicestershire v Worcestershire, Worcester 1962

First-Class Career Performances

	M	Inns	NO	Runs	HS	Avge	100s	Ct	St	Runs	Wkts	Avge	Best	5wI	10wM
Test															
All First	192	288	23	2581	51	9.73	-	381	40						

KITCHEN, M. J.

Name: Mervyn John Kitchen
Role: Left-hand bat, right-arm
medium bowler
Born: 1 August 1940,
Nailsea, Somerset
Appointed to 1st-class list: 1982
Appointed to Test panel: 1990
Tests umpired: 7
One-Day Internationals umpired: 11
County: Somerset
County debut: 1960
County cap: 1966
Testimonial: 1973
1000 runs in a season: 7
1st-Class 50s: 68
1st-Class 100s: 17
1st-Class catches: 157
One-Day 100s: 1
Education: Blackwell Secondary Modern,
Nailsea
Extras: Was third (replay) umpire for two Tests in 1994
Best batting: 189 Somerset v Pakistanis, Taunton 1967

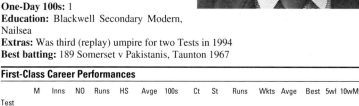

First-Class Career Performances

	M	Inns	NO	Runs	HS	Avge	100s	Ct	St	Runs	Wkts	Avge	Best	5wI	10wM
Test															
All First	354	612	32	15230	189	26.25	17	157	-	109	2	54.50	1-4	-	-

LEADBEATER, B.

Name: Barrie Leadbeater
Role: Right-hand opening bat, right-arm medium bowler, slip fielder
Born: 14 August 1943, Leeds
Height: 6ft **Weight:** 13st
Nickname: Leady
Appointed to 1st-class list: 1981
County: Yorkshire
County debut: 1966
County cap: 1969
Benefit: 1980 (joint benefit with G.A. Cope)
1st-Class 50s: 27
1st-Class 100s: 1
1st-Class catches: 82
Parents: Ronnie (deceased) and Nellie
Wife and date of marriage: Jacqueline, 18 September 1971
Children: Richard Barrie, 23 November 1972; Michael Spencer, 21 March 1976; Daniel Mark Ronnie, 19 June 1981
Education: Brownhill County Primary; Harehills Secondary Modern, Leeds
Qualifications: 2 O-levels
Career outside cricket: Coach, driver
Overseas tours: Duke of Norfolk's XI to West Indies 1970
Overseas teams played for: Johannesburg Municipals 1978-79
Other sports followed: Rugby union, most other sports
Cricketers particularly admired: Colin Cowdrey, Clive Rice, Richard Hadlee, Gary Sobers, Michael Holding
Cricketers learnt from: Brian Close, Willie Watson, Arthur Mitchell, Maurice Leyland
Relaxations: Family, car maintenance, DIY, music
Extras: Acted as 'third umpire' in the fourth Test against Australia at Headingley 1993
Opinions on cricket: 'Disappointed in players who lack self-control and professional pride and set bad examples to young players and public alike. Public should be regularly and properly informed during stoppages in play. Stoppages for bad light cause more frustration for public, players and, not least, umpires and a change in regulations may be needed soon if the game is to retain its support and credibility.'
Best batting: 140* Yorkshire v Hampshire, Portsmouth 1976

First-Class Career Performances

	M	Inns	NO	Runs	HS	Avge	100s	Ct	St	Runs	Wkts	Avge	Best	5wI	10wM
Test															
All First	147	241	29	5373	140 *	25.34	1	82	-	5	1	5.00	1-1	-	-

LYONS, K. J.

Name: Kevin James Lyons
Role: Right-hand opening bat, right-arm medium bowler
Born: 18 December 1946, Cardiff
Appointed to 1st-class list: 1985-91, re-appointed 1994
County: Glamorgan
County debut: 1967
1st-Class 50s: 8
1st-Class catches: 27
Education: Lady Mary's High School, Cardiff
Overseas tours:
Glamorgan to West Indies 1969-70
Extras: Glamorgan coach 1972-84, coach to Western Province, South Africa 1983-84, coach at Worcestershire 1992-93
Best batting: 92 Glamorgan v Cambridge University, Fenner's 1972

First-Class Career Performances

	M	Inns	NO	Runs	HS	Avge	100s	Ct	St	Runs	Wkts	Avge	Best	5wI	10wM
Test															
All First	62	99	14	1673	92	19.68	-	27	-	252	2	126.00	-	-	-

MEYER, B. J.

Name: Barrie John Meyer
Role: Right-hand bat, wicket-keeper
Born: 21 August 1931, Bournemouth
Height: 5ft 10^1/$_2$in **Weight:** 12st 5lbs
Nickname: BJ
Appointed to 1st-class list: 1973
Appointed to Test panel: 1978
Tests umpired: 26
One-Day Internationals umpired: 23
County: Gloucestershire
County debut: 1957
County cap: 1958
Benefit: 1971
1st-Class 50s: 11
1st-Class catches: 707
1st-Class stumpings: 118
Parents: Deceased
Wife and date of marriage: Gillian,
4 September 1965
Children: Stephen Barrie; Christopher John; Adrian Michael
Education: Boscombe Secondary School, Bournemouth
Career outside cricket: Salesman
Off-season: Coaching and umpiring in South Africa
Other sports followed: Golf (handicap 8), football (was a pro footballer for Bristol Rovers, Plymouth Argyle, Newport County and Bristol City)
Cricketers particularly learnt from: Andy Wilson and Sonny Avery (coaches for Gloucestershire)
Relaxations: Golf, music, reading
Extras: Umpired 1979 and 1983 World Cup finals
Best batting: 63 (three times) Gloucestershire v Indians, Cheltenham 1959; Gloucestershire v Oxford University, Bristol 1962; Gloucestershire v Sussex, Bristol 1964

First-Class Career Performances

	M	Inns	NO	Runs	HS	Avge	100s	Ct	St	Runs	Wkts	Avge	Best	5wI	10wM
Test															
All First	406	569	191	5367	63	14.19	-	707	118						

PALMER, K. E.

Name: Kenneth Ernest Palmer
Role: Right-hand bat, right-arm
fast-medium bowler
Born: 22 April 1937, Winchester
Height: 5ft 10in **Weight:** 13st
Nickname: Pedlar
Appointed to 1st-class list: 1972
Appointed to Test panel: 1978
Appointed to International Panel: 1994
Tests umpired: 22
One-Day Internationals umpired: 19
County: Somerset
County debut: 1955
County cap: 1958
Testimonial: 1968
Test debut: 1965
Tests: 1
1000 runs in a season: 1
50 wickets in a season: 6
1st-Class 50s: 27
1st-Class 100s: 2
1st-Class 5 w. in innings: 46
1st-Class 10 w. in match: 5
1st-Class catches: 156
Parents: Harry and Cecilia

Wife and date of marriage: Wife deceased
Children: Gary Vincent, 6 September 1961
Family links with cricket: Son played for Somerset, as did brother Roy, also a Test umpire
Education: Southbroom Secondary Modern, Devizes
Overseas tours: Commonwealth XI to Pakistan 1962; International Cavaliers to West
Indies 1963-64
Other sports followed: Football and squash
Cricketers particularly admired: Gary Sobers, Richard Hadlee, Viv Richards, David
Gower, Michael Holding, Malcolm Marshall
Cricketers particularly learnt from: Father and Maurice Tremlett
Relaxations: Car enthusiast
Extras: Called into Test side while coaching in South Africa 1964-65. Umpired two B&H
finals and two NatWest finals and was twice on World Cup panel in England. Won Carling
Single Wicket Competition 1961. Did the 'double' in 1961 (114 wickets, 1036 runs). With
Bill Alley holds the Somerset record for 6th wicket partnership.
Best batting: 125* Somerset v Northamptonshire, Northampton 1961
Best bowling: 9-57 Somerset v Nottinghamshire, Trent Bridge 1963

First-Class Career Performances

	M	Inns	NO	Runs	HS	Avge	100s	Ct	St	Runs	Wkts	Avge	Best	5wl	10wM
Test	1	1	0	10	10	10.00	-	-	-	189	1	189.00	1-113	-	-
All First	314	481	105	7771	125 *	20.66	2	156	-	18485	866	21.34	9-57	46	5

PALMER, R.

Name: Roy Palmer
Role: Right-hand bat, right-arm
fast-medium bowler
Born: 12 July 1942, Devizes, Wiltshire
Appointed to 1st-class list: 1980
Appointed to Test panel: 1992
Tests umpired: 2
One-Day Internationals umpired: 7
County: Somerset
County debut: 1965
50 wickets in a season: 1
1st-Class 50s: 1
1st-Class 5 w. in innings: 4
1st-Class catches: 25
Family links with cricket: Brother of
Ken Palmer, Test umpire and former
Somerset player; nephew Gary also
played for Somerset
Education: Southbroom Secondary
Modern, Devizes
Best batting:
84 Somerset v Leicestershire, Taunton 1967
Best bowling: 6-45 Somerset v Middlesex, Lord's 1967

First-Class Career Performances

	M	Inns	NO	Runs	HS	Avge	100s	Ct	St	Runs	Wkts	Avge	Best	5wl	10wM
Test															
All First	74	110	32	1037	84	13.29	-	25	-	5439	172	31.62	6-45	4	-

PLEWS, N. T.

Name: Nigel Trevor Plews
Role: Right-hand opening bat
Born: 5 September 1934, Nottingham
Height: 6ft 6½in **Weight:** 16st 8lbs
Appointed to 1st-class list: 1982
Appointed to Test panel: 1988
Appointed to International Panel: 1994
Tests umpired: 7
One-Day Internationals umpired: 5
Parents: Deceased
Wife and date of marriage:
Margaret, 1956
Children: Elaine, 1961; Douglas, 1964
Education: Mundella Grammar School,
Nottingham
Qualifications: School Certificate in
Commercial Subjects, RSA Advanced
Book-keeping
Career outside cricket: Nottingham City

police for 25 years (Det. Sgt in Fraud Squad)
Other sports followed: Football, rugby union
Relaxations: Hill-walking, reading, travel, cricket administration
Extras: Played local league and club cricket in Nottingham. Toured as umpire with MCC
to Namibia 1991.

Did not play first-class cricket

SHARP, G.

Name: George Sharp
Role: Right-hand bat, wicket-keeper
Born: 12 March 1950,
Hartlepool, County Durham
Height: 5ft 11in **Weight:** 15st
Nickname: Blunt, Toffee, Sharpie
Appointed to 1st-class list: 1992
County: Northamptonshire
County debut: 1967
County cap: 1972
1st-Class catches: 565
1st-Class stumpings: 90
Parents: George and Grace
Wife: Audrey, 14 September 1974
Children: Gareth James, 27 June 1984
Career outside cricket: Director of GSB
Loams Ltd, suppliers of soil and turf for sports
areas
Off-season: Producing and selling for GSB
Overseas tours: England Counties XI to West Indies 1974
Cricketers particularly admired: Alan
Knott, Bob Taylor, Keith Andrew
Other sports followed: Most ball games
Relaxations: Golf
Best batting: 98 Northamptonshire v Yorkshire, Northampton 1983

First-Class Career Performances

	M	Inns	NO	Runs	HS	Avge	100s	Ct	St	Runs	Wkts	Avge	Best	5wI	10wM
Test															
All First	306	396	81	6254	98	19.85	-	565	90	70	1	70.00	1-47	-	-

SHEPHERD, D. R.

Name: David Robert Shepherd
Role: Right-hand bat, right-arm
medium bowler
Born: 27 December 1940,
Bideford, Devon
Height: 5ft 10in **Weight:** 16st
Nickname: Shep
Appointed to 1st-class list: 1981
Appointed to Test panel: 1985
Appointed to International Panel: 1994
Tests umpired: 21
One-Day Internationals umpired: 51
County: Gloucestershire
County debut: 1965
County cap: 1969
Benefit: 1978 (joint benefit with J. Davey)
1000 runs in a season: 2
1st-Class 50s: 55
1st-Class 100s: 12
1st-Class catches: 95
One-Day 100s: 2

Parents: Herbert and Doris (both deceased)
Marital status: Single
Education: Barnstaple Grammar School; St Luke's College, Exeter
Career outside cricket: Teacher
Off-season: Assisting brother in local post office/newsagent
Other sports followed: Rugby, football, most ball sports
Cricketers particularly admired: Gary Sobers, Mike Procter
Relaxations: All sports, philately, television
Extras: Played Minor Counties cricket for Devon 1959-64. Only Gloucestershire player
to score a century on his first-class debut. Umpired the MCC Bicentenary Test, England
v Rest of the World, at Lord's in 1987. With Dickie Bird and Steve Bucknor was one of
the first umpires officially sponsored by the ICC. Known for his superstition regarding
'Nelson' score 111, and multiples – 222, 333 etc
Best batting: 153 Gloucestershire v Middlesex, Bristol 1968

First-Class Career Performances

	M	Inns	NO	Runs	HS	Avge	100s	Ct	St	Runs	Wkts	Avge	Best	5wI	10wM
Test															
All First	282	476	40	10672	153	24.47	12	95	-	106	2	53.00	1-1	-	-

WHITE, R. A.

Name: Robert Arthur White
Role: Left-hand bat, off-break bowler
Born: 6 October 1936, Fulham
Height: 5ft 9¹/₂in **Weight:** 12st 4lbs
Nickname: Knocker
Appointed to 1st-class list: 1982
Counties: Middlesex, Nottinghamshire
County debut: 1958 (Middlesex),
1966 (Nottinghamshire)
County cap: 1963 (Middlesex),
1966 (Nottinghamshire)
Benefit: 1974
1000 runs in a season: 1
50 wickets in a season: 2
1st-Class 50s: 50
1st-Class 100s: 5
1st-Class 5 w. in innings: 28
1st-Class 10 w. in match: 4
1st-Class catches: 190

Wife: Janice
Children: Robin and Vanessa
Education: Chiswick Grammar School
Qualifications: Matriculation
Career outside cricket: Self-employed salesman
Other sports followed: All sports – football, ice-hockey and horse racing in particular
Cricketers particularly admired: 'Gary Sobers more than anyone else.'
Cricketers particularly learnt from: 'I tried to learn from everyone I encountered'
Relaxations: Theatre-going
Extras: Made independent coaching trips to South Africa 1959, 1960, 1966, 1967, 1968.
Together with M.J. Smedley broke the Nottinghamshire seventh wicket record with 204
v Surrey at The Oval 1967
Opinions on cricket: 'Too controversial to go into print'
Best batting: 116* Nottinghamshire v Surrey, The Oval 1967
Best bowling: 7-41 Nottinghamshire v Derbyshire, Ilkeston 1971

First-Class Career Performances

	M	Inns	NO	Runs	HS	Avge	100s	Ct	St	Runs	Wkts	Avge	Best	5wI	10wM
Test															
All First	413	642	105	12452	116 *	23.18	5	190	-	21138	693	30.50	7-41	28	4

WHITEHEAD, A. G. T.

Name: Alan Geoffrey Thomas Whitehead
Role: Left-hand bat,
slow left-arm bowler
Born: 28 October 1940,
Butleigh, Somerset
Appointed to 1st-class list: 1970
Appointed to Test panel: 1982
Tests umpired: 5
One-Day Internationals umpired: 12
County: Somerset
County debut: 1957
1st-Class 5 w. in innings: 3
1st-Class catches: 20
Extras: Acted as third (replay) umpire in the
fifth Test against Australia at Edgbaston 1993
and in two Tests in 1994
Best batting: 15 Somerset v Hampshire,
Southampton 1959
Best bowling: 6-74 Somerset v Sussex,
Eastbourne 1959

First-Class Career Performances

	M	Inns	NO	Runs	HS	Avge	100s	Ct	St	Runs	Wkts	Avge	Best	5wl	10wM
Test															
All First	38	49	25	137	15	5.70	-	20	-	2306	67	34.41	6-74	3	-

WIGHT, P. B.

Name: Peter Bernard Wight
Role: Right-hand bat, off-break bowler
Born: 25 June 1930,
Georgetown, British Guiana
Height: 5ft 10in **Weight:** 11st
Nickname: Flipper
Appointed to 1st-class list: 1966
County: Somerset
County debut: 1953
County cap: 1954
Benefit: 1963
1000 runs in a season: 10
1st-Class 50s: 207
1st-Class 100s: 28
1st-Class 200s: 2
1st-Class 5 w. in innings: 1
1st-Class catches: 204
Parents: Henry DeLisle and Mary Matilda
Wife and date of marriage: Joyce,
26 January 1957
Children: Paul Anthony, 22 August 1965; Anne-Marie, 14 October 1967
Family links with cricket: Three brothers played for British Guiana and one, G.L., played for West Indies
Education: St Stanislaus College, Georgetown
Qualifications: MCC Intermediate and Advanced Cricket Coach
Career outside cricket: Owns his own indoor cricket school
Off-season: Coaching and running his indoor school
Overseas teams played for: Canterbury, New Zealand
Cricketers particularly admired: Alec Bedser, Gary Sobers, Tony Lock, Everton Weekes, Frank Worrell
Other sports followed: All ball games, football, squash, skittles, rugby
Relaxations: Gardening, all kinds of sport
Extras: Has coached in East Africa and New Zealand. 'Encouraged in cricket by my father and brothers – Arnold, Norman and Leslie' Was third (replay) umpire for two one-day Internationals in 1994
Opinions on cricket: 'I would like to see more youngsters given the opportunity to play better class cricket which is the aim of most clubs in our area. I am proud to be President of Somerset Wanderers Ladies Cricket Club.'
Best batting: 222* Somerset v Kent, Taunton 1959
Best bowling: 6-29 Somerset v Derbyshire, Chesterfield 1957

First-Class Career Performances

	M	Inns	NO	Runs	HS	Avge	100s	Ct	St	Runs	Wkts	Avge	Best	5wI	10wM
Test															
All First	333	590	53	17773	222 *	33.09	28	204	-	2262	68	33.26	6-29	1	-

WILLEY, P.

Name: Peter Willey
Role: Right-hand bat, off-break bowler
Born: 6 December 1949, Sedgefield, County Durham
Height: 6ft 1in **Weight:** 13st 4lbs
Nickname: Will, 'many unprintable'
Appointed to 1st-class list: 1993
Counties: Northamptonshire, Leicestershire
County debut: 1966 (Northamptonshire), 1984 (Leicestershire)
County cap: 1971 (Northamptonshire), 1984 (Leicestershire)
Benefit: 1981 (£31,400)
Test debut: 1976
Tests: 26
One-Day Internationals: 26
1000 runs in a season: 10
50 wickets in a season: 2
1st-Class 50s: 101
1st-Class 100s: 44
1st-Class 200s: 1
1st-Class 5 w. in innings: 26
1st-Class 10 w. in match: 3
1st-Class catches: 235
One-Day 100s: 9
Parents: Oswald and Maisie
Wife and date of marriage: Charmaine, 23 September 1971
Children: Heather Jane, 11 September 1985; David, 28 February 1990
Family links with cricket: Father played local club cricket in County Durham
Education: Seaham Secondary School, County Durham
Off-season: 'House husband'
Overseas tours: England to Australia and India 1979-80, to West Indies 1980-81 and 1985-86; with unofficial England XI to South Africa 1981-82
Overseas teams played for: Eastern Province, South Africa 1982-85

Cricketers particularly admired: Malcolm Marshall

Other sports followed: All sports

Relaxations: Gardening, dog walking

Extras: With Wayne Larkins, received 2016 pints of beer (seven barrels) from a brewery in Northampton as a reward for their efforts in Australia with England in 1979-80. Youngest player ever to play for Northamptonshire at 16 years 180 days v Cambridge University in 1966. Banned from Test cricket for three years for joining England rebel tour of South Africa in 1982. Left Northamptonshire at end of 1983 and moved to Leicestershire as vice-captain. Appointed Leicestershire captain for 1987, but resigned after only one season. Released by Leicestershire at end of 1991 season to play for Northumberland in 1992

Opinions on cricket: 'I think the fun has gone out of the game for many of the players. Not enough hard work and practice is done to improve playing standards throughout the first-class game. Players of average ability are being paid silly money in the modern game, by clubs, so they may not need to try and improve their standards. Why does the English game need overseas coaches? Why do we also need team managers?'

Best batting: 227 Northamptonshire v Somerset, Northampton 1976

Best bowling: 7-37 Northamptonshire v Oxford University, The Parks 1975

First-Class Career Performances

	M	Inns	NO	Runs	HS	Avge	100s	Ct	St	Runs	Wkts	Avge	Best	5wI	10wM
Test	26	50	6	1184	102 *	26.90	2	3	-	456	7	65.14	2-73	-	-
All First	559	918	121	24361	227	30.56	44	235	-	23400	756	30.95	7-37	26	3

ROLL OF HONOUR
1994

BRITANNIC ASSURANCE CHAMPIONSHIP

Final Table

		P	W	L	D	T	Bt	Bl	Pts
1	Warwickshire (16)	17	11	1	5	0	41	55	272
2	Leicestershire (9)	17	8	7	2	0	42	60	230
3	Nottinghamshire (7)	17	8	5	4	0	39	51	218
4	Middlesex (1)	17	7	3	7	0	43	57	212
5	Northamptonshire (4)	17	8	4	5	0	28	53	209
6	Essex (11)	17	7	5	5	0	32	63	207
7	Surrey (6)	17	7	7	3	0	32	57	201
8	Sussex (10)	17	7	5	5	0	28	60	200
9	Kent (8)	17	6	7	4	0	44	58	198
10	Lancashire (13)	17	8	6	3	0	32	59	194
11	Somerset (5)	17	7	7	3	0	32	47	191
12	Gloucestershire (17)	17	5	8	4	0	28	56	172
13	Yorkshire (12)	17	4	6	7	0	38	57	159
	Hampshire (13)	17	4	7	6	0	32	55	159
15	Worcestershire (2)	17	4	6	7	0	42	52	158
16	Durham (18)	17	4	10	3	0	32	57	153
17	Derbyshire (15)	17	4	9	4	0	25	54	143
18	Glamorgan (3)	17	2	8	7	0	29	50	111

1993 positions shown in brackets

BENSON & HEDGES CUP

Winners: Warwickshire
Runners-up: Worcestershire
Losing semi-finalists: Surrey and Hampshire

NATWEST TROPHY

Winners: Worcestershire
Runners-up: Warwickshire
Losing semi-finalists: Surrey and Kent

AXA EQUITY & LAW SUNDAY LEAGUE

Final Table

		P	W	L	T	NR	Pts	Run rate	Runs	Balls
1	Warwickshire (10)	17	13	3	0	1	54	83.47	3122	3740
2	Worcestershire (16)	17	12	4	0	1	50	77.78	2770	3561
3	Kent (2)	17	12	5	0	0	48	90.31	3377	3739
4	Lancashire (6)	17	11	5	0	1	46	84.66	3086	3645
5	Yorkshire (9)	17	10	6	0	1	42	78.83	2976	3775
6	Surrey (3)	17	9	5	0	3	42	97.99	3364	3433
7	Glamorgan (1)	17	9	6	1	1	40	76.60	2957	3860
8	Derbyshire (11)	17	8	7	0	2	36	86.27	2929	3395
9	Durham (7)	17	6	7	1	3	32	85.89	2734	3183
10	Leicestershire (14)	17	7	9	0	1	30	82.86	3342	4033
11	Nottinghamshire (11)	17	6	8	0	3	30	85.91	2946	3429
12	Hampshire (15)	17	7	10	0	0	28	78.14	2940	3762
13	Northamptonshire (5)	17	6	9	1	1	28	81.30	3122	3840
14	Middlesex (8)	17	6	10	0	1	26	80.81	3012	3727
15	Sussex (4)	17	5	11	0	1	22	77.78	2868	3687
16	Somerset (18)	17	5	12	0	0	20	85.09	3242	3810
17	Essex (12)	17	4	11	1	1	20	73.44	2746	3739
18	Gloucestershire (13)	17	4	12	0	1	18	78.70	2854	3626

1993 positions shown in brackets

FIRST-CLASS AVERAGES
1994

1994 AVERAGES (all first-class matches)

BATTING AVERAGES - Including fielding
Qualifying requirements : 6 completed innings

Name	Matches	Inns	NO	Runs	HS	Avge	100s	50s	Ct	St
J.D.Carr	20	27	10	1542	261 *	90.70	6	7	31	-
B.C.Lara	15	25	2	2066	501 *	89.82	9	3	11	-
M.W.Gatting	19	27	3	1671	225	69.62	6	6	28	-
G.A.Gooch	17	29	2	1747	236	64.70	6	5	15	-
C.C.Lewis	12	19	4	881	220 *	58.73	2	5	18	-
B.M.McMillan	9	11	3	467	132	58.37	1	3	10	-
M.D.Moxon	17	30	4	1458	274 *	56.07	4	6	8	-
S.J.Rhodes	18	27	11	896	100 *	56.00	1	5	59	8
G.A.Hick	17	29	1	1538	215	54.92	5	5	22	-
C.L.Hooper	16	29	0	1579	183	54.44	5	7	26	-
R.G.Twose	18	31	5	1411	277 *	54.26	3	6	8	-
G.P.Thorpe	16	25	4	1136	190	54.09	2	7	11	-
M.R.Ramprakash	18	26	2	1271	135	52.95	4	6	13	-
A.N.Hayhurst	18	30	6	1250	121	52.08	2	10	10	-
D.J.Bicknell	18	30	4	1354	235 *	52.07	3	7	4	-
C.J.Hollins	8	10	2	415	131	51.87	1	2	6	-
P.A.Cottey	19	33	6	1393	191	51.59	3	6	16	-
A.J.Moles	11	20	3	863	203 *	50.76	1	5	5	-
J.P.Crawley	20	34	3	1570	281 *	50.64	3	6	25	-
N.H.Fairbrother	12	22	2	1002	204	50.10	4	1	16	-
P.N.Kirsten	10	16	5	549	130	49.90	2	1	5	-
R.S.M.Morris	9	17	3	686	174	49.00	2	3	4	-
K.M.Curran	15	25	5	973	114	48.65	1	8	7	-
M.E.Trescothick	11	20	1	924	121	48.63	2	8	13	-
A.D.Brown	17	24	2	1049	172	47.68	2	6	16	-
N.V.Knight	12	21	1	944	157	47.20	4	3	22	-
G.Kirsten	11	19	3	751	201 *	46.93	2	5	5	-
A.J.Stewart	16	23	3	936	142	46.80	3	4	20	1
M.D.Crowe	9	16	2	654	142	46.71	3	3	6	-
N.J.Speak	19	34	6	1304	143	46.57	3	7	16	-
T.M.Moody	18	28	3	1160	159	46.40	3	6	20	-
R.J.Blakey	20	36	9	1236	94 *	45.77	-	11	65	4
M.C.J.Nicholas	19	32	6	1182	145	45.46	3	5	7	-
D.A.Leatherdale	17	25	3	987	139	44.86	2	3	17	-
M.Azharuddin	9	17	1	712	205	44.50	2	1	5	-
A.Fordham	11	20	1	844	158	44.42	3	4	7	-
D.M.Ward	16	22	1	921	294 *	43.85	1	5	10	-
N.R.Taylor	16	27	3	1049	139	43.70	3	4	4	-
J.E.R.Gallian	12	20	0	874	171	43.70	2	5	6	-
P.E.Robinson	5	7	0	305	86	43.57	-	3	8	-
R.A.Smith	17	29	0	1263	162	43.55	5	4	6	-
R.J.Bailey	18	33	5	1214	129 *	43.35	3	7	12	-
P.Johnson	17	29	2	1170	132	43.33	4	5	6	-

Name	Matches	Inns	NO	Runs	HS	Avge	100s	50s	Ct	St
A.J.Lamb	15	22	1	908	131	43.23	2	5	17	-
D.P.Ostler	18	29	2	1161	186	43.00	2	6	14	-
R.I.Dawson	16	30	4	1112	127 *	42.76	1	7	7	-
T.R.Ward	19	33	1	1368	125	42.75	3	10	29	-
D.L.Hemp	21	38	4	1452	136	42.70	4	8	16	-
R.T.Robinson	19	31	1	1276	182	42.53	2	10	7	-
K.C.Wessels	12	18	2	679	105	42.43	1	4	17	-
J.E.Morris	20	35	1	1433	204	42.14	4	6	8	-
R.C.Irani	18	29	6	965	119	41.95	2	8	6	-
R.J.Harden	18	31	5	1061	131 *	40.80	2	7	13	-
W.Larkins	16	27	3	976	158 *	40.66	1	6	11	-
K.R.Brown	20	25	9	639	102 *	39.93	1	1	55	1
M.B.Loye	15	26	3	914	132	39.73	3	5	7	-
M.N.Lathwell	18	32	1	1230	206	39.67	2	9	10	-
M.A.Lynch	4	7	1	238	60	39.66	-	1	6	-
S.P.Fleming	9	16	1	591	151	39.40	2	1	5	-
V.P.Terry	19	34	1	1286	164	38.96	5	2	25	-
D.L.Haynes	17	27	2	973	134	38.92	5	2	6	-
D.J.Cullinan	9	14	3	428	94	38.90	-	4	5	-
P.A.Nixon	19	30	3	1046	131	38.74	3	4	60	2
A.P.Grayson	19	31	4	1046	100	38.74	1	7	19	-
K.J.Barnett	15	24	2	847	148	38.50	1	7	7	-
B.A.Young	10	18	0	688	122	38.22	1	5	11	-
S.P.James	16	28	5	877	150	38.13	3	1	18	-
R.Q.Cake	10	18	1	647	107	38.05	1	3	4	-
N.E.Briers	19	35	3	1216	154	38.00	2	5	5	-
T.L.Penney	16	24	3	798	111	38.00	1	1	14	-
P.J.Prichard	11	17	2	569	119	37.93	3	2	6	-
K.R.Rutherford	9	17	1	603	129	37.68	2	2	1	-
G.Welch	12	15	3	446	84 *	37.16	-	4	5	-
D.Byas	20	36	1	1297	104	37.05	2	9	23	-
C.White	13	20	2	663	108 *	36.83	1	5	8	-
M.P.Vaughan	16	30	1	1066	117	36.75	3	3	8	-
J.N.Rhodes	12	16	3	477	77	36.69	-	3	8	-
M.A.Roseberry	20	32	2	1097	152	36.56	2	6	21	-
A.J.Wright	19	36	3	1202	184 *	36.42	1	7	32	-
V.J.Wells	16	28	4	871	87 *	36.29	-	6	13	-
W.S.Kendall	9	10	3	253	113 *	36.14	1	-	8	-
B.Parker	10	18	2	578	127	36.12	1	4	6	-
A.J.Hollioake	17	23	3	722	138	36.10	3	3	12	-
M.P.Maynard	16	28	1	974	118	36.07	2	5	18	1
C.M.Gupte	10	17	2	541	122	36.06	2	1	7	-
M.A.Butcher	12	19	2	613	134	36.05	1	3	21	-
M.A.Atherton	16	27	2	899	111	35.96	2	4	14	-
A.Roseberry	6	8	1	249	94	35.57	-	2	3	-
M.J.Greatbatch	9	18	3	528	84	35.20	-	3	4	-
J.C.Adams	18	32	5	950	144 *	35.18	3	2	17	-
W.J.Cronje	13	20	1	661	108	34.78	1	3	11	-
M.G.N.Windows	11	21	0	730	106	34.76	1	5	11	-
R.C.Russell	19	34	8	901	85 *	34.65	-	4	58	1

Name	Matches	Inns	NO	Runs	HS	Avge	100s	50s	Ct	St
M.Saxelby	17	32	0	1102	181	34.43	2	4	4	-
R.B.Richardson	9	16	0	551	76	34.43	-	5	9	-
R.R.Montgomerie	19	34	3	1062	151	34.25	2	8	12	-
M.Watkinson	18	28	2	889	155	34.19	2	3	10	-
M.P.Speight	17	29	0	991	126	34.17	1	4	20	-
M.J.Walker	5	7	0	239	107	34.14	1	-	2	-
P.N.Weekes	16	21	2	648	117	34.10	1	2	10	-
G.R.Haynes	20	32	2	1021	141	34.03	2	4	12	-
S.A.Thomson	10	19	7	408	69	34.00	-	4	5	-
G.F.Archer	16	26	0	878	168	33.76	2	4	17	-
T.J.G.O'Gorman	16	28	2	872	145	33.53	3	3	12	-
C.J.Adams	18	32	3	969	109 *	33.41	1	5	17	-
A.L.Penberthy	17	25	5	658	88 *	32.90	-	5	9	-
M.W.Alleyne	20	37	1	1184	109	32.88	2	6	16	-
A.W.Smith	14	21	5	524	202 *	32.75	1	1	3	-
A.R.Roberts	9	12	4	261	51	32.62	-	1	3	-
G.Fowler	4	7	0	227	68	32.42	-	3	2	-
S.A.Marsh	19	31	6	807	88	32.28	-	5	69	5
J.A.Daley	10	18	2	513	159 *	32.06	1	3	3	-
N.A.Folland	13	22	1	671	91	31.95	-	4	6	-
J.J.Whitaker	18	32	2	958	148	31.93	2	6	9	-
N.Hussain	19	31	2	922	115 *	31.79	2	5	34	-
D.J.Richardson	10	12	3	286	88	31.77	-	2	23	1
P.V.Simmons	17	30	0	953	261	31.76	1	3	23	-
B.F.Smith	14	23	3	628	95	31.40	-	4	10	-
G.R.Cowdrey	10	16	1	470	114	31.33	1	2	4	-
B.A.Pocock	7	14	2	374	103 *	31.16	1	2	8	-
N.J.Lenham	14	27	1	809	102	31.11	1	5	2	-
C.W.J.Athey	18	34	1	1022	169 *	30.96	2	3	14	-
T.S.Curtis	18	32	1	960	180	30.96	3	1	7	-
H.Morris	16	31	2	885	106	30.51	1	6	13	-
W.P.C.Weston	17	28	1	818	94	30.29	-	6	6	-
K.P.Evans	16	21	4	514	104	30.23	1	3	12	-
P.R.Pollard	18	31	1	905	134	30.16	2	4	11	-
S.Hutton	14	24	2	662	101	30.09	1	3	10	-
N.A.Mallender	8	12	3	270	43 *	30.00	-	-	1	-
R.J.Warren	12	21	2	566	94 *	29.78	-	5	14	-
S.R.Lampitt	17	26	5	624	122	29.71	1	2	12	-
D.M.Smith	7	14	3	326	74	29.63	-	3	6	-
R.J.Cunliffe	7	13	1	354	177 *	29.50	1	-	5	-
A.P.Wells	19	35	4	909	84	29.32	-	7	15	-
J.W.Hall	14	27	0	789	85	29.22	-	7	9	-
M.V.Fleming	16	29	1	810	73	28.92	-	6	3	-
J.J.B.Lewis	16	29	3	751	109	28.88	1	4	9	-
M.Davies	4	8	2	173	54	28.83	-	1	1	-
P.A.J.DeFreitas	14	21	2	545	108	28.68	1	3	5	-
G.D.Lloyd	16	27	3	684	112	28.50	1	5	11	-
A.C.Parore	11	18	4	399	71	28.50	-	2	21	-
G.I.MacMillan	10	17	3	395	69	28.21	-	3	20	-
F.D.Stephenson	17	28	1	752	107	27.85	1	5	9	-

Name	Matches	Inns	NO	Runs	HS	Avge	100s	50s	Ct	St
M.R.Benson	16	28	1	737	159	27.29	1	4	10	-
D.P.Fulton	10	16	0	433	109	27.06	1	1	17	-
M.A.Ealham	15	26	2	638	68 *	26.58	-	4	8	-
S.D.Udal	17	30	4	684	94	26.30	-	4	16	-
O.D.Gibson	20	31	4	710	85	26.29	-	7	7	-
A.S.Rollins	16	29	2	708	97	26.22	-	6	18	-
T.C.Middleton	13	23	3	524	102	26.20	1	1	8	-
S.P.Titchard	13	21	0	549	99	26.14	-	3	16	-
R.D.B.Croft	19	25	2	600	80	26.08	-	2	7	-
P.A.Smith	12	17	3	363	65	25.92	-	2	2	-
G.J.Parsons	16	25	6	491	70	25.84	-	2	17	-
J.I.Longley	14	25	2	594	100 *	25.82	1	5	7	-
I.D.Austin	11	16	1	386	50	25.73	-	1	5	-
W.M.Noon	18	30	6	617	75	25.70	-	3	38	5
N.M.K.Smith	18	21	4	435	65	25.58	-	2	3	-
T.H.C.Hancock	20	37	1	920	123	25.55	1	7	10	-
P.Moores	18	32	2	766	70 *	25.53	-	4	61	1
A.Dale	18	29	1	711	131	25.39	2	2	3	-
K.M.Krikken	15	27	10	426	85 *	25.05	-	2	26	2
G.D.Rose	16	24	2	548	121	24.90	1	2	16	-
B.C.Broad	10	20	0	496	128	24.80	1	2	9	-
N.A.Felton	10	19	1	445	87	24.72	-	2	5	-
G.W.White	11	20	1	467	104	24.57	1	2	13	-
G.D.Hodgson	9	16	1	367	113	24.46	1	1	3	-
R.J.Turner	18	27	5	537	104 *	24.40	1	2	46	6
Wasim Akram	6	10	0	244	98	24.40	-	2	-	-
S.G.Hinks	5	10	0	242	74	24.20	-	2	4	-
M.J.Vandrau	13	23	5	435	66	24.16	-	1	9	-
D.G.Cork	13	21	0	507	94	24.14	-	4	15	-
A.N Aymes	19	32	3	697	76	24.03	-	2	36	4
P.D.Bowler	13	23	0	546	88	23.73	-	2	11	-
A.J.Dalton	6	10	2	188	51 *	23.50	-	1	5	-
T.J.Boon	16	28	2	606	74	23.30	-	4	5	-
A.C.Cummins	17	29	2	629	65	23.29	-	3	3	-
N.Shahid	10	18	4	326	91	23.28	-	1	13	-
R.K.Illingworth	20	25	6	438	59 *	23.05	-	3	8	-
K.J.Piper	17	24	4	454	116 *	22.70	1	1	61	5
G.F.J.Liebenberg	7	11	1	226	64 *	22.60	-	2	9	3
C.M.Tolley	7	11	3	180	84	22.50	-	1	3	-
C.W.Scott	20	33	3	670	108	22.33	2	3	56	2
A.R.K.Pierson	15	20	5	334	43 *	22.26	-	-	15	-
S.C.Ecclestone	13	19	4	334	80 *	22.26	-	1	3	-
D.Gough	13	19	3	355	65	22.18	-	2	1	-
C.P.Metson	18	22	4	398	51	22.11	-	1	54	7
P.Bainbridge	18	31	1	660	68	22.00	-	5	13	-
M.J.McCague	10	16	3	285	56	21.92	-	1	5	-
R.P.Lefebvre	12	14	3	240	33	21.81	-	-	5	-
M.A.Garnham	18	30	5	542	62	21.68	-	4	33	5
A.R.Whittall	9	11	2	193	91 *	21.44	-	1	3	-
A.C.Hudson	12	19	1	382	116	21.22	1	1	8	-

Name	Matches	Inns	NO	Runs	HS	Avge	100s	50s	Ct	St
B.R.Hartland	8	16	0	337	65	21.06	-	2	6	-
G.Yates	13	20	7	272	54 *	20.92	-	2	3	-
K.D.James	13	22	2	417	53	20.85	-	2	2	-
J.P.Stephenson	16	27	1	535	144	20.57	1	2	9	-
R.L.Johnson	11	13	3	205	50 *	20.50	-	1	5	-
D.J.Millns	19	27	10	348	64 *	20.47	-	1	12	-
W.K.Hegg	19	30	4	518	66	19.92	-	2	46	3
I.Fletcher	6	10	1	179	54 *	19.88	-	2	3	-
D.A.Graveney	13	22	6	315	65 *	19.68	-	1	5	-
C.C.Remy	6	11	1	194	60	19.40	-	2	3	-
W.A.Dessaur	5	9	1	154	35	19.25	-	-	2	-
P.C.L.Holloway	4	6	0	114	50	19.00	-	1	1	-
N.J.Llong	7	11	0	209	44	19.00	-	-	3	-
R.M.F.Cox	4	7	1	114	46	19.00	-	-	3	-
J.P.Carroll	9	15	2	246	90	18.92	-	1	2	-
R.J.Maru	9	15	4	207	38 *	18.81	-	-	13	-
D.Ripley	16	23	9	263	36 *	18.78	-	-	40	6
M.C.J.Ball	17	28	3	468	45	18.72	-	-	31	-
R.P.Davis	12	9	2	131	35 *	18.71	-	-	15	-
G.R.Larsen	8	12	3	168	40 *	18.66	-	-	4	-
C.E.L.Ambrose	14	16	2	257	78	18.35	-	1	16	-
H.S.Malik	5	7	1	110	53 *	18.33	-	1	3	-
J.S.Hodgson	9	15	1	256	54	18.28	-	1	8	-
M.N.Hart	9	11	3	146	36	18.25	-	-	5	-
P.J.Newport	17	24	5	345	41	18.15	-	-	3	-
S.J.E.Brown	19	25	10	268	69	17.86	-	1	9	-
W.K.M.Benjamin	9	14	1	231	54	17.76	-	2	4	-
M.C.Ilott	14	16	5	194	45 *	17.63	-	-	3	-
I.D.K.Salisbury	16	25	6	331	49	17.42	-	-	19	-
H.R.J.Trump	14	20	4	276	45 *	17.25	-	-	14	-
P.J.Hartley	16	23	3	343	61	17.15	-	1	3	-
M.A.Feltham	13	16	1	256	71	17.06	-	1	7	-
G.W.Jones	8	13	0	220	74	16.92	-	1	-	-
C.M.Wells	11	20	2	303	42	16.83	-	-	3	-
D.W.Headley	9	13	5	134	46 *	16.75	-	-	5	-
S.A.Kellett	9	16	0	266	50	16.62	-	1	11	-
P.W.Jarvis	17	27	6	347	70 *	16.52	-	1	4	-
M.S.Kasprowicz	17	24	4	326	44	16.30	-	-	9	-
P.J.Martin	18	27	3	383	57	15.95	-	1	4	-
G.W.Mike	17	26	3	365	60 *	15.86	-	1	1	-
M.Keech	5	9	0	141	57	15.66	-	1	6	-
M.P.Bicknell	9	11	2	140	41	15.55	-	-	5	-
R.D.Mann	9	16	0	248	53	15.50	-	1	2	-
Mushtaq Ahmed	9	14	3	168	38	15.27	-	-	4	-
C.A.Walsh	15	24	6	274	66	15.22	-	1	2	-
D.E.Stanley	5	8	2	91	48	15.16	-	-	2	-
R.A.Pick	16	22	7	227	65 *	15.13	-	1	4	-
N.F.Sargeant	9	13	2	166	46	15.09	-	-	18	-
G.Chapple	15	21	11	150	26 *	15.00	-	-	11	-
S.J.Base	8	12	1	160	33	14.54	-	-	6	-

Name	Matches	Inns	NO	Runs	HS	Avge	100s	50s	Ct	St
A.C.S.Pigott	8	11	0	160	40	14.54	-	-	1	-
J.E.Emburey	15	19	5	203	78 *	14.50	-	1	11	-
R.C.Williams	10	14	2	171	38	14.25	-	-	5	-
V.Pike	9	12	4	114	27	14.25	-	-	2	-
J.Ratledge	9	16	0	227	79	14.18	-	1	1	-
G.J.Kersey	7	11	2	127	39	14.11	-	-	16	2
A.R.Caddick	12	18	2	219	58 *	13.68	-	1	5	-
A.M.Smith	12	14	2	162	29	13.50	-	-	3	-
D.L.Maddy	3	6	0	80	34	13.33	-	-	3	-
F.J.Cooke	9	10	4	80	34 *	13.33	-	-	9	1
M.A.Crawley	8	14	1	172	45	13.23	-	-	7	-
D.A.Reeve	9	10	1	116	33	12.88	-	-	18	-
N.M.Kendrick	7	11	2	112	25	12.44	-	-	6	-
K.E.Cooper	12	16	9	84	18 *	12.00	-	-	2	-
C.M.Pitcher	10	14	4	116	43	11.60	-	-	4	-
C.A.Connor	15	22	3	215	25	11.31	-	-	4	-
P.N.Hepworth	5	10	0	113	60	11.30	-	1	1	-
J.C.Hallett	4	8	1	79	52	11.28	-	1	1	-
N.J.Haste	9	12	2	112	22	11.20	-	-	2	-
C.Pringle	8	8	0	88	24	11.00	-	-	2	-
T.A.Munton	18	17	7	106	36	10.60	-	-	4	-
C.E.W.Silverwood	9	15	3	127	26	10.58	-	-	2	-
M.M.Patel	18	27	2	256	39	10.24	-	-	12	-
J.Wood	15	22	3	194	51	10.21	-	1	3	-
C.J.Townsend	10	9	3	61	22	10.16	-	-	13	4
R.D.Stemp	20	28	2	263	28	10.11	-	-	9	-
N.V.Radford	15	20	4	161	25	10.06	-	-	6	-
J.P.Taylor	13	14	7	68	26	9.71	-	-	5	-
M.J.Thursfield	9	12	1	106	47	9.63	-	-	1	-
J.E.Benjamin	16	17	1	148	33 *	9.25	-	-	5	-
S.L.Watkin	18	21	11	92	14	9.20	-	-	2	-
A.P.van Troost	14	18	6	108	33	9.00	-	-	3	-
N.G.B.Cook	11	12	1	98	43 *	8.90	-	-	3	-
G.C.Small	11	10	1	78	23	8.66	-	-	2	-
N.F.C.Martin	10	10	1	74	26	8.22	-	-	5	-
A.E.Warner	10	15	3	96	24 *	8.00	-	-	1	-
P.M.Such	20	23	2	167	29	7.95	-	-	9	-
J.G.Hughes	4	6	0	47	17	7.83	-	-	2	-
A.P.Igglesden	11	16	8	61	15 *	7.62	-	-	2	-
A.D.Mullally	14	19	4	114	23	7.60	-	-	6	-
M.T.Brimson	5	9	3	45	17 *	7.50	-	-	-	-
E.E.Hemmings	14	24	12	88	14 *	7.33	-	-	5	-
R.W.Sladdin	3	6	0	42	20	7.00	-	-	-	-
D.E.Malcolm	18	22	9	89	15 *	6.84	-	-	2	-
C.E.Cuffy	12	15	8	42	10	6.00	-	-	1	-
A.R.C.Fraser	14	15	1	80	16	5.71	-	-	3	-
N.G.Cowans	12	15	6	51	19	5.66	-	-	3	-
S.J.W.Andrew	6	8	1	37	11	5.28	-	-	-	-
E.S.H.Giddins	17	22	4	83	24	4.61	-	-	2	-
T.N.Wren	7	11	4	31	18 *	4.42	-	-	2	-

Name	Matches	Inns	NO	Runs	HS	Avge	100s	50s	Ct	St
M.A.Robinson	19	23	8	58	9	3.86	-	-	5	-
S.R.Barwick	12	16	6	35	8	3.50	-	-	3	-
J.A.Afford	15	17	6	36	10	3.27	-	-	5	-
J.E.Brinkley	10	10	2	16	5	2.00	-	-	3	-

BOWLING AVERAGES
Qualifying requirements : 10 wickets taken

Name	Overs	Mdns	Runs	Wkts	Avge	Best	5wI	10wM
K.J.Barnett	54.2	5	173	13	13.30	5-31	1	-
C.E.L.Ambrose	540	159	1113	77	14.45	7-44	6	2
C.A.Walsh	506.1	119	1535	89	17.24	7-42	9	3
M.J.McCague	341.1	67	1084	57	19.01	9-86	5	1
I.D.Austin	251.5	72	662	33	20.06	5-23	3	1
F.D.Stephenson	480.5	108	1345	67	20.07	6-50	6	2
J.E.Benjamin	591.2	130	1658	80	20.72	6-27	5	1
T.A.Munton	699.4	181	1748	81	21.58	7-52	6	2
M.M.Patel	811.2	202	2058	90	22.86	8-96	6	3
C.White	235.2	53	761	33	23.06	5-40	2	-
S.R.Lampitt	512.4	127	1484	64	23.18	5-33	2	-
A.R.Caddick	373.1	73	1186	51	23.25	6-51	3	-
C.C.Lewis	345.2	69	1082	46	23.52	5-55	2	-
G.R.Larsen	226.4	73	494	21	23.52	5-24	1	-
M.C.Ilott	497.5	115	1391	59	23.57	6-24	3	1
Wasim Akram	213.2	44	646	27	23.92	8-30	2	1
P.S.de Villiers	277.3	59	922	38	24.26	6-67	2	-
W.K.M.Benjamin	281	97	585	24	24.37	6-46	2	-
E.S.H.Giddins	450.4	89	1463	60	24.38	5-38	3	-
C.A.Connor	574.4	131	1764	72	24.50	7-47	2	2
D.Gough	479.2	100	1526	62	24.61	6-66	3	-
P.A.J.DeFreitas	530	108	1621	65	24.93	6-39	4	-
M.B.Owens	127	31	424	17	24.94	5-74	1	-
D.J.Millns	532	99	1901	76	25.01	6-44	4	-
V.J.Wells	301.5	78	1053	42	25.07	5-50	1	-
A.C.S.Pigott	268.3	73	737	29	25.41	6-46	1	-
P.V.Simmons	300.5	81	769	30	25.63	4-68	-	-
J.E.Emburey	674	204	1514	59	25.66	6-89	2	-
G.D.Rose	344.1	70	1136	44	25.81	4-40	-	-
D.M.Cousins	112	21	337	13	25.92	6-35	1	-
R.A.Pick	507.2	122	1413	54	26.16	6-62	2	-
G.C.Small	339	79	946	36	26.27	5-46	1	-
R.L.Johnson	350.4	85	1059	40	26.47	10-45	1	1
Mushtaq Ahmed	404	114	1196	45	26.57	7-94	4	1
G.Chapple	458.4	110	1474	55	26.80	6-48	4	-
A.R.C.Fraser	532.5	142	1343	50	26.86	3-16	-	-
M.W.Alleyne	351.3	68	1103	41	26.90	5-78	1	-

Name	Overs	Mdns	Runs	Wkts	Avge	Best	5wI	10wM
R.S.Yeabsley	174.4	27	567	21	27.00	6-54	1	1
S.D.Udal	678	174	1872	69	27.13	6-79	7	1
P.L.Symcox	280.5	86	761	28	27.17	5-29	2	-
G.Yates	320.5	70	1013	37	27.37	5-34	1	-
G.J.Parsons	462.2	131	1208	44	27.45	5-34	1	-
D.W.Headley	295.3	48	989	36	27.47	5-60	2	-
P.W.Trimby	243.3	48	718	26	27.61	5-84	1	-
I.D.K.Salisbury	474	143	1336	48	27.83	6-55	3	-
P.J.Hartley	562.1	116	1701	61	27.88	5-89	1	-
S.J.E.Brown	578.5	88	2108	75	28.10	6-68	6	-
M.A.Ealham	265.4	62	762	27	28.22	7-53	1	-
P.C.R.Tufnell	463.5	128	1107	39	28.38	6-35	1	-
K.E.Cooper	418.2	99	1095	38	28.81	4-38	-	-
V.Pike	199	51	578	20	28.90	6-41	1	-
M.Watkinson	631.1	173	1823	63	28.93	8-30	1	1
E.E.Hemmings	422	140	959	33	29.06	7-66	2	-
D.E.Malcolm	551.3	97	2015	69	29.20	9-57	3	1
P.J.Martin	614.4	177	1580	54	29.25	5-61	2	-
R.C.Irani	249.4	42	834	28	29.78	4-27	-	-
K.P.Evans	411.5	105	1141	38	30.02	4-46	-	-
D.G.Cork	329.1	55	1112	37	30.05	6-29	2	-
C.E.Cuffy	389.3	107	1082	36	30.05	4-70	-	-
J.N.B.Bovill	119.4	23	421	14	30.07	5-108	1	-
W.J.Cronje	159.5	45	395	13	30.38	4-47	-	-
R.D.Stemp	669.1	252	1493	49	30.46	6-37	2	-
J.G.Hughes	137.2	38	428	14	30.57	5-69	1	-
R.K.Illingworth	679	212	1499	49	30.59	4-51	-	-
D.A.Reeve	144	48	308	10	30.80	2-9	-	-
M.J.Thursfield	163	39	524	17	30.82	6-130	1	-
P.M.Such	670	183	1757	57	30.82	7-66	5	-
A.A.Donald	212.2	42	775	25	31.00	5-58	2	-
D.J.Nash	228.4	51	775	25	31.00	6-76	2	1
S.L.Watkin	613.4	147	1708	55	31.05	6-143	2	-
M.S.Kasprowicz	527.3	92	1869	60	31.15	7-83	3	-
P.J.Newport	516.2	103	1654	53	31.20	4-50	-	-
J.C.Adams	340.5	125	720	23	31.30	4-63	-	-
T.N.Wren	164.5	30	533	17	31.35	6-48	1	-
A.M.Smith	298.3	59	1004	32	31.37	5-40	1	-
S.R.Barwick	549.4	208	1131	36	31.41	5-44	1	-
A.C.Cummins	520.3	92	1768	56	31.57	6-64	4	1
G.W.Mike	405.5	92	1422	45	31.60	5-44	1	-
J.P.Taylor	333.4	56	1141	36	31.69	5-62	1	-
R.P.Davis	341	102	986	31	31.80	6-94	2	-
J.H.Childs	464.5	122	1254	39	32.15	6-71	2	-

Name	Overs	Mdns	Runs	Wkts	Avge	Best	5wI	10wM
C.E.W.Silverwood	249	46	883	27	32.70	4-67	-	-
R.C.Williams	245.5	46	856	26	32.92	4-28	-	-
P.A.Smith	182	40	594	18	33.00	3-24	-	-
J.Wood	345.4	38	1501	45	33.35	6-110	3	-
M.A.Feltham	382.3	83	1140	34	33.52	5-69	1	-
H.R.J.Trump	268.4	76	873	26	33.57	6-68	2	1
M.P.Bicknell	319.4	75	977	29	33.68	5-44	1	-
P.N.Weekes	484.4	91	1383	41	33.73	5-12	1	-
S.J.Base	199	30	782	23	34.00	5-92	1	-
A.R.K.Pierson	500.4	131	1267	37	34.24	8-42	1	-
J.A.Afford	541.3	164	1376	40	34.40	5-48	2	-
N.M.K.Smith	582	141	1693	49	34.55	7-42	4	-
K.D.James	280.1	56	900	26	34.61	4-78	-	-
D.J.Spencer	85.5	12	347	10	34.70	4-31	-	-
P.W.Jarvis	496.2	89	1773	51	34.76	7-58	1	-
B.M.McMillan	222.4	49	662	19	34.84	4-47	-	-
R.P.Lefebvre	365.2	108	896	25	35.84	4-63	-	-
C.M.Wells	153.3	31	469	13	36.07	4-52	-	-
N.V.Radford	459.1	106	1408	39	36.10	5-93	1	-
O.D.Gibson	579.4	100	2169	60	36.15	6-64	4	1
R.G.Twose	190.5	41	544	15	36.26	6-28	1	-
A.Sheriyar	98	14	400	11	36.36	4-44	-	-
C.L.Hooper	414.1	93	1055	29	36.37	5-52	1	-
J.E.R.Gallian	95	10	368	10	36.80	2-27	-	-
M.A.Robinson	619	171	1658	45	36.84	5-48	1	-
A.J.Hollioake	264.1	44	958	26	36.84	4-48	-	-
R.P.Snell	200.1	38	666	18	37.00	3-38	-	-
M.J.Vandrau	290.5	63	965	26	37.11	4-53	-	-
A.L.Penberthy	400.1	83	1374	37	37.13	5-54	1	-
S.C.Ecclestone	298.3	70	825	22	37.50	4-66	-	-
N.A.Mallender	193.3	50	602	16	37.62	3-23	-	-
N.G.Cowans	349.3	93	986	26	37.92	4-76	-	-
A.P.van Troost	345.5	60	1329	35	37.97	4-50	-	-
A.D.Mullally	448.1	121	1255	33	38.03	5-85	1	-
T.M.Moody	195	48	572	15	38.13	4-24	-	-
A.P.Igglesden	316.1	75	929	24	38.70	5-38	1	-
T.G.Shaw	312.4	90	828	21	39.42	4-29	-	-
K.J.Shine	332.4	76	1156	29	39.86	4-79	-	-
D.A.Graveney	456	121	1247	31	40.22	6-80	1	-
J.P.Stephenson	332	75	1066	26	41.00	4-74	-	-
C.Pringle	258	74	739	18	41.05	5-58	1	-
R.J.Maru	254.1	75	621	15	41.40	3-61	-	-
N.F.Williams	326	71	1088	26	41.84	6-49	1	-
M.A.Butcher	206.4	50	670	16	41.87	4-31	-	-

Name	Overs	Mdns	Runs	Wkts	Avge	Best	5wI	10wM
G.A.Hick	173.2	55	462	11	42.00	3-64	-	-
N.G.B.Cook	283.3	85	715	17	42.05	3-46	-	-
A.Dale	277	65	975	23	42.39	2-7	-	-
A.E.Warner	256	53	817	19	43.00	4-39	-	-
J.E.Brinkley	233	40	779	18	43.27	6-98	1	-
C.R.Matthews	263.3	71	749	17	44.05	3-25	-	-
G.Welch	267	63	970	22	44.09	4-74	-	-
M.G.Field-Buss	245.1	71	540	12	45.00	2-23	-	-
C.M.Pitcher	258.5	56	902	20	45.10	4-37	-	-
M.C.J.Ball	325.3	78	955	21	45.47	5-69	1	-
C.J.Hollins	236.3	32	890	19	46.84	4-64	-	-
K.M.Curran	423.5	86	1463	31	47.19	4-65	-	-
M.N.Hart	335.3	105	850	18	47.22	4-106	-	-
A.W.Smith	374	67	1340	28	47.85	5-103	1	-
M.P.Vaughan	228.3	53	678	14	48.42	4-39	-	-
J.S.Hodgson	272.3	85	732	15	48.80	4-14	-	-
A.R.Roberts	242	49	870	17	51.17	3-106	-	-
R.J.Bailey	166.1	33	568	11	51.63	5-59	1	-
R.D.B.Croft	715.3	158	2166	41	52.82	5-80	1	-
A.A.Barnett	191.4	39	627	10	62.70	2-35	-	-
N.J.Haste	233	39	910	13	70.00	4-69	-	-
P.Bainbridge	315.4	67	1082	14	77.28	4-72	-	-
A.R.Whittall	295.3	59	1060	11	96.36	2-34	-	-

INDEX OF PLAYERS BY COUNTY

*denotes not registered for 1995 season. Where a player is known to have moved in the off-season he is listed under his new county.

INDEX OF PLAYERS BY COUNTY

GLAMORGAN

BARWICK, S. R.
BASTIEN, S.*
BUTCHER, G. P.
COTTEY, P. A.
CROFT, R. D. B.
DALE, A.
DALTON, A. J.
DAVIES, A. P.
GIBSON, O. D..
HEMP, D. L.
JAMES, S. P.
JONES, P. S.
LEFEBVRE, R. P.
MAYNARD, M. P.
METSON, C. P.
MORRIS, H.
PARKIN, O. T.
PHELPS, B. S.
REES, G. H. J.
ROSEBERRY, A.
SHAW, A. D.
THOMAS, S. D.
WATKIN, S. L.
WILLIAMS, J. R. A

GLOUCESTERSHIRE

ALLEYNE, M. W.
AVERIS, J. M. M.
BABINGTON, A. M.*
BALL, M. C. J.
BODEN, D. J. P.
BROAD, B. C.
CAWDRON, M. J.
COOPER, K. E.
CUNLIFFE, R. J.
DAVIES, M.
DAWSON, R. I.
HANCOCK, T. H. C.
HEWSON, D. R.
HINKS, S. G.*
HODGSON, G. D.
LYNCH, M.
PIKE, V. J.
RUSSELL, R. C.
SHEERAZ, K. P.
SMITH, A. M.
SRINATH, J.
SYMONDS, A.
WALSH, C. A.*
WIGHT, R. M.*
WILLIAMS, R. C.
WILLIAMS, R. C. J.
WINDOWS, M. G. N.
WRIGHT, A. J.

HAMPSHIRE

AYMES, A. N.
BENJAMIN, W. K. M.*
BOTHAM, L. J.
BOVILL, J. N. B.
CONNOR, C. A.
COWANS, N. G.
COX, R. M. F.*
FLINT, D. P. J.
GARAWAY, M.
JAMES, K. D.
JEAN-JACQUES, M.*
LANEY, J. S.
KEECH, M.
KENDALL, W. S.
MARU, R. J.
MIDDLETON, T. C.
MORRIS, R. S. M.
NICHOLAS, M. C. J.
SMITH, R. A.
STEPHENSON, J. P.
TERRY, V. P.
THURSFIELD, M. J.
UDAL, S. D.
WHITAKER, P. R.
WHITE, G. W.

INDEX OF PLAYERS BY COUNTY

KENT

BENSON, M. R.
COWDREY, G. R.
DE SILVA, P. A.
EALHAM, M. A.
FLEMING, M. V.
FULTON, D. P.
HEADLEY, D. W.
HOOPER, C. L.
IGGLESDEN, A. P.
LLONG, N. J.
MARSH, S. A.
McCAGUE, M. J.
PATEL, M. M.
PENN, C.
PRESTON, N. W.
SPENCER, D. J.
STANFORD, E. J.
TAYLOR, N. R.
THOMPSON, J. B.
WALKER, M. J.
WARD, T. R.
WILLIS, S. C.
WREN, T. N.

LANCASHIRE

ATHERTON, M. A.
AUSTIN, I. D.
BARNETT, A. A.
BROWN, C.
CHAPPLE, G.
CRAWLEY, J. P.
FAIRBROTHER, N. H.
FLINTOFF, A.
GALLIAN, J. E. R.
GREEN, R. J.
HARVEY, M. E.
HARVEY, N. P.
HEGG, W. K.
KEEDY, G.
LLOYD, G. D.
MARLAND, L. J.
MARTIN, P. J.
MCKEOWN, P. C.
SEAL, P. J.
SHADFORD, D. J.
SPEAK, N. J.
TITCHARD, S. P.
WASIM AKRAM
WATKINSON, M.
WOOD, N. T.
YATES, G.

LEICESTERSHIRE

BARTLE, S.
BOON, T. J.
BRIERS, N. E.
BRIMSON, M. T.
CRONJE, W. J.
CROWE, C. D.
DAKIN, J. M.
DITTA, A. I.
DURRANT, C.
HAYE, A. F.*
HEPWORTH, P. N.*
MACMILLAN, G. I.
MADDY, D. L.
MASON, T. J.
MILLNS, D. J.
MULLALLY, A. D.
NIXON, P. A.
PARSONS, G. J.
PIERSON, A. R. K.
ROBINSON, P. E.
SHERIYAR, A.
SIMMONS, P. V.*
SMITH, B. F.
STANGER, I. M.*
SUTCLIFFE, I.
WELLS, V. J.
WHITAKER, J. J.
WHITTICASE, P.

INDEX OF PLAYERS BY COUNTY

MIDDLESEX

BROWN, K. R.
CARR, J. D.
DUTCH, K. P.
EMBUREY, J. E.
FARBRACE, P.
FELTHAM, M. A.
FOLLETT, D.
FRASER, A. R. C.
GATTING, M. W.
HABIB, A.*
HARRIS, G. A. R.
HARRISON, J. C.
HAYNES, D. L.*
JOHNSON, R. L.
MARC, K.
NASH, D. C.
NASH, D. J.
POOLEY, J. C.
RADFORD, T.
RAMPRAKASH, M. R.
SHAH, O.
SHINE, K. J.
TAYLOR, C. W.
TUFNELL, P. C. R.
WEEKES, P. N.
YEABSLEY, R. S.

NORTHAMPTONSHIRE

AMBROSE, C. E. L.*
BAILEY, R. J.
BOSWELL, S. A. J.
BOWEN, M. N.
BROWN, J. F.
CAPEL, D. J.
COOK, N. G. B.
CURRAN, K. M.
DAWOOD, I.
FELTON, N. A.*
FORDHAM, A.
FOSTER, M. J.
HUGHES, J. G.
INNES, K. J.
KUMBLE, A.
LAMB, A. J.
LOYE, M. B.
MALLENDER, N. A.
MONTGOMERIE, R. R.
PENBERTHY, A. L.
RIPLEY, D.
ROBERTS, A. R.
ROBERTS, D. J.
SALES, D. J.
SNAPE, J. N.
STEELE, M. V.
SWANN, A.
TAYLOR, J. P.
WALTON, T. C.
WARREN, R. J.

NOTTINGHAMSHIRE

ADAMS, J. C.*
AFFORD, J. A.
AFZAAL, U.
ARCHER, G. F.
BANTON, C.
BATES, R. T.
BROADHURST, M.
CAIRNS, C. L.
CHAPMAN, R. J.
CRAWLEY, M. A.*
DESSAUR, W. A.*
DOWMAN, M. P.
EVANS, K. P.
FIELD-BUSS, M. G.
FRENCH, B. N.
HINDSON, J. E.
JOHNSON, P.
LEWIS, C. C.
MIKE, G. W.
NEWELL, M.
NOON, W. M.
PENNETT, D. B.
PICK, R. A.
POLLARD, P. R.
ROBINSON, R. T.
WILEMAN, J. R.

INDEX OF PLAYERS BY COUNTY

SOMERSET

BATTY, J. D.
BIRD, P. J.
CADDICK, A. R.
CLARKE, V. P.*
DIMOND, M.
DONELAN, B. T. P.*
ECCLESTONE, S. C.
FLETCHER, I.*
FOLLAND, N. A*
HALLETT, J. C.
HARDEN, R. J.
HAYHURST, A. N.
HOLLOWAY, P. C. L.
KERR, J. I. D.
LATHWELL, M. N.
MUSHTAQ AHMED
PARSONS, K. A.
PAYNE, A.*
ROSE, G. D.
TRESCOTHICK, M. E.
TRUMP, H. R. J.
TURNER, R. J.
VAN TROOST, A. P.

SURREY

BAINBRIDGE, M. R.
BENJAMIN, J. E.
BICKNELL, D. J.
BICKNELL, M. P.
BROWN, A. D.
BUTCHER, M. A.
CUFFY, C. E.*
DE LA PENA, J.
HOLLIOAKE, A. J.
KENDRICK, N. M.*
KENLOCK, M.
KENNIS, G. J.
KERSEY, G. J.
MURPHY, A. J.*
NOWELL, R. W.
PIGOTT, A. C. S.
RATCLIFFE, J. D.
SARGEANT, N. F.
SHAHID, N.
SMITH, A. W.
STEWART, A. J.
THOMPSON, D. J.*
THORPE, G. P.
TUDOR, A. J.
WAQAR YOUNIS
WARD, D. M.

SUSSEX

ATHEY, C. W. J.
BATES, J. J.
GIDDINS, E. S. H.
GREENFIELD, K.
HALL, J. W.
HEMMINGS, E. E.
HUMPHRIES, S.
JARVIS, P.W.
KIRTLEY, R. J.
LAW, D. R.
LENHAM, N. J.
LEWRY, J. D.
MOORES, P.
NEWELL, K.
NEWELL, M.
NORTH, J. A.
PEIRCE, M. T. E.
PHILLIPS. N. C.
REMY, C. C.
SALISBURY, I. D. K.
SMITH, D. M.
SPEIGHT, M. P.
STEPHENSON, F. D.
WELLS, A. P.

INDEX OF PLAYERS BY COUNTY

WARWICKSHIRE

ALTREE, D.
ASIF DIN, M.
BELL, M. A. V.
BROWN, D. R.
BURNS, M.
DAVIS, R. P.
DONALD, A. A.
FROST, A.
GILES, A. F.
KHAN, W. G.
KNIGHT, N. V.
LARA, B. C.*
MOLES, A. J.
MUNTON, T. A.
OSTLER, D. P.
PENNEY, T. L.
PIPER, K. J.
POWELL, M. J.
REEVE, D. A.
SINGH, A.
SMALL, G. C.
SMITH, N. M. K.
SMITH, P. A.
TWOSE, R. G.
WELCH, G.

WORCESTERSHIRE

BRINKLEY, J. E.
BROOKE, M. P.*
CHURCH, M. J.
CURTIS, T. S.
D'OLIVEIRA, D. B.
EDWARDS, T.
ELLIS, S. W. K.
EYERS, C. J.
HAYNES, G. R.
HICK, G. A.
ILLINGWORTH, R. K.
LAMPITT, S. R.
LEATHERDALE, D. A.
McCORKILL, B. M.
MIRZA, P.
MOODY, T. M.
NEWPORT, P. J.
RADFORD, N. V.
RHODES, S. J.
SEYMOUR, A. C. H.*
SOLANKI, V. S.
SPIRING, K. R.
TOLLEY, C. M.
WESTON, W. P. C.
WYLIE, A.

YORKSHIRE

BEVAN, M. G.
BLAKEY, R. J.
BYAS, D.
CHAPMAN, C. A.
GOUGH, D.
GRAYSON, A. P.
HAMILTON, G. M.
HARTLEY, P. J.
KEEDY, G.
KELLETT, S. A.
KETTLEBOROUGH, R. A.
McGRATH, A.
METCALFE, A. A.
MILBURN, S. M.
MORRIS, A. C.
MOXON, M. D.
PARKER, B.
RICHARDSON, R. B.*
ROBINSON, M. A.
SCHOFIELD, C. J.
SILVERWOOD, C. E. W.
STEMP, R. D.
VAUGHAN, M. P.
WHARF, A. G.
WHITE, C.

ANSWERS TO THE QUIZ

1. Mike Edwards
2. John Crawley, 286, England A v Eastern Province
3. Keith Piper, 116*
4. Alec Stewart, 18
5. Graham Gooch
6. Robin Smith
7. Geoff Marsh
8. Sir Colin Cowdrey
9. 4 leg byes
10. c. Russell b. Caddick
11. David Graveney
12. Mike Gatting
13. Alec Stewart 118 and 143, Barbados 1993-94
14. India, Pakistan and Sri Lanka
15. Imperial Cricket Conference, International Cricket Conference, International Cricket Council
16. Bob Woolmer
17. Marcus Trescothick, Somerset
18. David Gower
19. Phil Simmons, 261 for Leicestershire against Northamptonshire
20. John Carr, Middlesex
21. Ian Thomson in 1964
22. Ted Dexter
23. Craig McDermott
24. 18
25. John Morris
26. Graeme Hick
27. James Williams and Gareth Rees
28. The National Grid
29. Trevor Jesty
30. It was accidentally rolled in to the pitch
31. Phillip DeFreitas
32. Mike Procter
33. Fanie de Villiers, 10-123
34. 23
35. Richie Benaud
36. Matthew Hayden
37. Devon Malcom
38. Hansie Cronje
39. Steve Waugh
40. John Crawley
41. Mark Ilott
42. India beat Sri Lanka
43. Paul Prichard
44. Manoj Prabhakar
45. Kapil Dev, 434
46. Mark Waugh and Mike Atherton
47. David Boon, 9
48. Highclere Castle, Earl of Carnarvon's XI
49. Zimbabwe
50. Steve Bucknor
51. Malcolm Nash (by Gary Sobers 1967) and Tilak Raj (by Ravi Shastri 1984-85)

52. Yorkshire
53. Australia, 1978, 1982, 1988
54. Kim Barnett
55. Aqib Javed, 7-37, Pakistan v West indies, 1991-92
56. Allan Border, 1979-1993
57. Jason Gallian
58. Jamie Hall, 5 hours 4 minutes, Sussex v Surrey, July 1994
59. He took all 10 wickets in an innings in 27 balls for 0 runs
60. 499 by Hanif Mohammad, Karachi v Bahawalpur, 1958-59
61. Kensington Oval, Bridgetown, Barbados
62. Surrey against Yorkshire, September 1994
63. Worcestershire
64. 57
65. Desmond Haynes
66. Amol Muzumdar
67. David Lawrence
68. UAE beat Kenya in Nairobi
69. Saeed Anwar
70. Shane Thompson
71. 72
72. Hugh Tayfield
73. Javed Miandad
74. Paul Parker
75. Robin Smith, Jimmy Adams
76. Curtly Ambrose and Courtney Walsh
77. Brian Bolus
78. Holland
79. Phillip DeFreitas
80. He was hit by a Paul Smith drive while at the non-stiker's end
81. Cameron Cuffy
82. Curtly Ambrose
83. Angus Fraser
84. Mike Atherton, 510 runs at 56.66
85. Devon
86. Imran Khan
87. Darren Gough
88. Roger Twose, 10 hours, 6 minutes, 277*, Warwickshire v Glamorgan
89. Graham Gooch
90. India and Pakistan
91. Phillip DeFreitas
92. Dion Nash
93. Hansie Cronje
94. Winston Benjamin
95. Kepler Wessels
96. Graeme Hick
97. Alamgir Sheriyar , Vince Wells
98. Devon Malcolm
99. Tom Moody
100. Brian McMillan